The Routledge Handbook of Semantics

The Routledge Handbook of Semantics provides a broad and state-of-the-art survey of this field, covering semantic research at both word and sentence level. It presents a synoptic view of the most important areas of semantic investigation, including contemporary methodologies and debates, and indicating possible future directions in the field.

Written by experts from around the world, the 29 chapters cover key issues and approaches within the following areas:

- meaning and conceptualisation
- meaning and context
- lexical semantics
- semantics of specific phenomena
- development, change and variation.

The Routledge Handbook of Semantics is essential reading for researchers and postgraduate students working in this area.

Nick Riemer is a senior lecturer in the English and Linguistics Departments at the University of Sydney, and a member of the Laboratoire d'histoire des théories linguistiques, Université Paris-Diderot. He specializes in semantics and in the history and philosophy of linguistics.

Routledge Handbooks in Linguistics

Routledge Handbooks in Linguistics provide overviews of a whole subject area or sub-discipline in linguistics, and survey the state of the discipline including emerging and cutting-edge areas. Edited by leading scholars, these volumes include contributions from key academics from around the world and are essential reading for both advanced undergraduate and postgraduate students.

The Routledge Handbook of Syntax
Edited by Andrew Carnie, Yosuke Sato and Daniel Siddiqi

The Routledge Handbook of Historical Linguistics
Edited by Claire Bowern and Bethwyn Evans

The Routledge Handbook of Language and Culture
Edited by Farzad Sharifan

The Routledge Handbook of Semantics
Edited by Nick Riemer

The Routledge Handbook of Morphology
Edited by Francis Katamba

The Routledge Handbook of Linguistics
Edited by Keith Allan

The Routledge Handbook of the English Writing System
Edited by Vivian Cook and Des Ryan

The Routledge Handbook of Language and Media
Edited by Daniel Perrin and Colleen Cotter

The Routledge Handbook of Phonological Theory
Edited by S. J. Hannahs and Anna Bosch

The Routledge Handbook of Theoretical and Experimental Sign Language Research
Edited by Annika Hermann, Roland Pfau and Josep Quer

The Routledge Handbook of Linguistic Anthropology
Edited by Nancy Bonvillain

The Routledge Handbook of Semantics

Edited by
Nick Riemer

LONDON AND NEW YORK

First published 2016
by Routledge
2 Park Square, Milton Park, Abingdon, Oxon OX14 4RN

and by Routledge
711 Third Avenue, New York, NY 10017

Routledge is an imprint of the Taylor & Francis Group, an informa business

© 2016 selection and editorial matter, Nick Riemer; individual chapters, the contributors

The right of the editor to be identified as the author of the editorial material, and of the authors for their individual chapters, has been asserted in accordance with sections 77 and 78 of the Copyright, Designs and Patents Act 1988.

All rights reserved. No part of this book may be reprinted or reproduced or utilised in any form or by any electronic, mechanical, or other means, now known or hereafter invented, including photocopying and recording, or in any information storage or retrieval system, without permission in writing from the publishers.

Trademark notice: Product or corporate names may be trademarks or registered trademarks, and are used only for identification and explanation without intent to infringe.

British Library Cataloguing-in-Publication Data
A catalogue record for this book is available from the British Library

Library of Congress Cataloging-in-Publication Data
The Routledge Handbook of Semantics/Edited by Nick Riemer.
pages cm. – (Routledge handbooks in linguistics)
Includes index.
1. Semantics–Handbooks, manuals, etc. 2. Historical semantics–Handbooks, manuals, etc. 3. Generative semantics–Handbooks, manuals, etc.
4. Lexicology. I. Riemer, Nick, 1972-
P325.R78 2015
401'.43–dc23
2015003748

ISBN: 978-0-415-66173-7 (hbk)
ISBN: 978-1-315-68553-3 (ebk)

Typeset in Times New Roman
by Swales & Willis Ltd, Exeter, Devon, UK

Printed and bound in the United States of America by Publishers Graphics, LLC on sustainably sourced paper.

i.m. Peter Koch

Contents

List of figures	x
List of tables	xi
List of contributors	xii
Acknowledgements	xvi
Introduction: Semantics – a theory in search of an object *Nick Riemer*	1

PART I
Foundational issues — 11

1	(Descriptive) Externalism in semantics *Steven Gross*	13
2	Internalist semantics: meaning, conceptualization and expression *Nick Riemer*	30
3	A history of semantics *Keith Allan*	48

PART II
Approaches — 69

4	Foundations of formal semantics *Jon Gajewski*	71
5	Cognitive semantics *Maarten Lemmens*	90
6	Corpus semantics *Michael Stubbs*	106

PART III
Meaning and conceptualization   123

7   Categories, prototypes and exemplars   125
James A. Hampton

8   Embodiment, simulation and meaning   142
Benjamin Bergen

9   Linguistic relativity   158
Daniel Casasanto

PART IV
Meaning and context   175

10   Semantics and pragmatics   177
John Saeed

11   Contextual adjustment of meaning   195
Robyn Carston

PART V
Lexical semantics   211

12   Lexical decomposition   213
Nick Riemer

13   Sense individuation   233
Dirk Geeraerts

14   Sense relations   248
Petra Storjohann

15   Semantic shift   266
John Newman

PART VI
Semantics of specific phenomena   281

16   The semantics of nominals   283
Sebastian Löbner

17   Negation and polarity   303
Doris Penka

18	Varieties of quantification *Anna Szabolcsi*	320
19	Lexical and grammatical aspect *Stephen Dickey*	338
20	Tense *Ilse Depraetere and Raphael Salkie*	354
21	Modality *Ilse Depraetere*	370
22	Event semantics *Jean-Pierre Koenig*	387
23	Participant roles *Beatrice Primus*	403
24	Compositionality *Adele E. Goldberg*	419
25	The semantics of lexical typology *Maria Koptjevskaja-Tamm, Ekaterina Rakhilina and Martine Vanhove*	434

PART VII
Extensions

455

26	Acquisition of meaning *Soonja Choi*	457
27	Expressives *Ad Foolen*	473
28	Interpretative semantics *François Rastier*	491
29	Semantic processing *Steven Frisson and Martin J. Pickering*	507
	Index	525

Figures

5.1	Semantic prototype category (radial network)	95
5.2	Extension, schematisation and instantiation in a schematic network	96
5.3	A (simplified) schematic network for *kill*	96
5.4	A (simplified) schematic network for *work one's X off*	102
7.1	A semantic network representation of the meaning of BIRD	126
7.2	A feature representation of the meaning of BIRD	127
12.1	Componential analysis of some English words for marine vessels	217
15.1	The core concepts underlying semantic shift in Cognitive Grammar	270
15.2	Core concepts applied to a semantic shift in fruit	270
15.3	Isolectal map for Russian *dux*	276
16.1	Operations of the Relation layer	291
16.2	Operations of the levels Unit and Quantity	294
16.3	Operations of determination on the seven layers	300
17.1	Hierarchy of negation and distribution of different classes of NPIs	313
25.1	Semantic maps of EMPTINESS in Mandarin and in Serbian	446
25.2	A three-dimensional plot of cutting and breaking events	447
25.3	Probabilistic semantic maps of the "go", "come" and "arrive" domain in Sora and Classical Greek in the Gospel according to Mark	448
25.4	"Cold" in Armenian, English, Palula and Kamang	449

Tables

3.1	A componential table	59
19.1	Extended typology of situation type	339
19.2	PF:IMPF in Classical Arabic (Dahl, 1985: 83)	342
19.3	Figures for four Russian aspectual pairs by tense and aspect	343
19.4	Perfective and imperfective markers in Mandarin Chinese	344
19.5	The Russian system of aspectual pairs	347
19.6	Russian viewpoint aspect and tense	347
19.7	Parallels between nouns and situation type	351
21.1	Classifications of modal meaning	373
21.2	Classification of root possibility meanings based on Depraetere and Reed (2011)	375
24.1	Georgian morphological paradigm based on Gurevich (2006: section 3.2)	423
24.2	English argument structure constructions	424
25.1	*Hand* vs. *arm*, *foot* vs. *leg*, *finger* vs. *toe* in English, Italian, Romanian, Estonian, Japanese and Khalkha Mongolian	435
25.2	Sibling terms in six languages	438

Contributors

Keith Allan MLitt, PhD (Edinburgh), FAHA, is Emeritus Professor of Linguistics at Monash University and Honorary Associate Professor at the University of Queensland. His research interests focus mainly on aspects of meaning in language, with a secondary interest in the history and philosophy of linguistics. Author of several books and many contributions to scholarly books and journals, he has also edited several books and edits the *Australian Journal of Linguistics*. Email: keith.allan@monash.edu. Homepage: http://profiles.arts.monash.edu.au/keith-allan.

Benjamin Bergen is Professor of Cognitive Science at the University of California, San Diego, where he directs the Language and Cognition Lab. His research addresses meaning-making processes in language production and comprehension, including how lexical and grammatical knowledge contribute to meaning in both literal and figurative language.

Robyn Carston is Professor of Linguistics at University College London and Research Coordinator at the Centre for the Study of Mind in Nature, Oslo. Her main research interests are in pragmatics, semantics, relevance theory, word meaning and figurative language. She has published a monograph, *Thoughts and utterances: the pragmatics of explicit communication* (Blackwell, 2002), and is currently preparing a collection of papers to be published under the title *Pragmatics and semantic content* (Oxford University Press).

Daniel Casasanto is Assistant Professor of Psychology at the University of Chicago, and a founding editor of the journal *Language and Cognition* (Cambridge University Press). His research explores how linguistic, cultural and bodily experiences shape our brains and minds.

Soonja Choi has conducted cross-linguistic studies since the mid-1980s (using both naturalistic and experimental data) comparing acquisition of Korean with other languages on negation, modality, lexicon and, more recently, spatial semantics and motion event expressions. Her primary goal is to understand the nature of interaction between language and cognition from infancy to adulthood in these semantic domains.

Ilse Depraetere is Professor of English Linguistics at the University of Lille III. Most of her publications relate to tense, aspect and modality in English. She has written a grammar of English with Chad Langford.

Stephen Dickey is Associate Professor in the Department of Slavic Languages and Literatures at the University of Kansas. His research interests are in comparative Slavic verbal aspect and the history of Slavic aspectual systems, especially with regards to prefixation, language contact and theories of language change, and cognitive grammar.

Ad Foolen taught general linguistics at Radboud University Nijmegen for 40 years (he retired in 2015). His research focused on modal particles, expressive constructions, the conceptualization of emotions and the history of twentieth-century linguistics. From 2004 to 2015, he was secretary/treasurer of ICLA, the International Cognitive Linguistics Association.

Steven Frisson is a lecturer in the School of Psychology at the University of Birmingham. His principal research interest is semantic processing, especially the interpretation of words in context. He has published widely on this and related questions. Some of the projects he is currently involved in include reading processes in people who stutter, semantic processing in people with schizophrenia, online perspective-taking and theory of mind use, and low-level eye movements in clinical populations.

Jon Gajewski received his PhD from MIT in 2005 with a dissertation titled *Neg-raising: polarity and presupposition*. Since 2005 he has worked at the University of Connecticut, where he is currently Associate Professor. He is also currently an Associate Editor for the *Journal of Semantics* and a member of the associate editorial board of *Linguistic Inquiry*.

Dirk Geeraerts is Professor of Linguistics at the University of Leuven. His main research interests are in lexical semantics, lexicology and lexicography, with a specific focus on social variation and diachronic change. He is the author, among many other works, of *Theories of lexical semantics* (Oxford University Press, 2010). Homepage: http://wwwling.arts.kuleuven.be/qlvl/dirkg.htm.

Adele E. Goldberg is Professor of Psychology at Princeton. Her research focuses on the psychology of language, including theoretical and experimental aspects of grammar and its representation, acquisition of form-function correspondences, and constructional priming. She is the author, among other works, of *Constructions at work: the nature of generalization in language* (Oxford University Press, 2006) and *Constructions: a construction grammar approach to argument structure* (University of Chicago Press, 1995).

Steven Gross is Associate Professor of Philosophy at Johns Hopkins University, with secondary appointments in Cognitive Science and Psychological and Brain Sciences. He specializes in the philosophy of language, philosophy of mind and metaphysics. Forthcoming work includes *Meaning without representation*, co-edited with Nicholas Tebben and Michael Williams for Oxford University Press.

James A. Hampton, educated at Cambridge and UCL, is currently Professor of Psychology at City University London, and is a recognized expert on how people conceptualize the world, with particular reference to prototype representations, intuitive thought and conceptual combination.

Jean-Pierre Koenig first studied at the École Normale Supérieure (rue d'Ulm) and the École des Hautes Etudes en Science Sociales in Paris and then at the University of California, Berkeley, where he received his PhD in 1994. He joined the Linguistics department at the University at Buffalo (the State University of New York) that same year and is now the chair of that department.

Contributors

Maria Koptjevskaja-Tamm is Professor in General Linguistics at the Department of Linguistics, Stockholm University. Her main research interests include semantically oriented typology, where she often combines synchronic and diachronic approaches across many languages, and in particular areal typology.

Maarten Lemmens is Professor of Linguistics and Language Teaching at the Université de Lille 3. His current research focuses on causative, posture and static location verbs, on the grammaticalization of light verbs in Odia, and on co-verbal gesture. He is President of the International Cognitive Linguistics Association and former editor-in-chief of the journal *Cognitextes*.

Sebastian Löbner is Professor for Semantics at the Institute for Language and Information at Heinrich Heine University Düsseldorf, Germany. His major research interests include nominal semantics, verb semantics, lexical semantics and frames. He is the author of *Understanding semantics* (2nd edition, Routledge, 2013).

John Newman is Professor Emeritus in the Department of Linguistics, University of Alberta. He is the author of the monograph *Give: a cognitive linguistic study*, editor of the volumes *The linguistics of giving*, *The linguistics of sitting, standing, and lying* and *The linguistics of eating and drinking*, and editor-in-chief of the journal *Cognitive Linguistics*. He has published on corpus linguistics and cognitive linguistics, with a particular focus on the syntax and semantics of verbs.

Doris Penka is a research fellow in the Zukunftskolleg of the University of Konstanz. She received her PhD in 2007 from the University of Tübingen with a dissertation on the syntax and semantics of negative indefinites, which was published by Oxford University Press in 2011.

Martin J. Pickering is Professor of the Psychology of Language and Communication at the University of Edinburgh. His research focuses on language production, language comprehension, dialogue, reading and bilingualism, with a concentration on syntax and semantics. He has published widely on all these topics.

Beatrice Primus is Professor of Linguistics at the University of Cologne. Her major areas of research include cases, semantic roles and grammatical relations. She is the author of *Cases and thematic roles – ergative, accusative and active* (1999) and *Semantische Rollen* (2012).

Ekaterina Rakhilina is Professor of Semantics at the School of Linguistics, National Research University, Higher School of Economics, Moscow. Specializing in theoretical and corpus linguistics, her main interests are lexical typology, especially comparison of coherent lexical fields, meaning structure and polysemy, and construction grammar in cross-linguistic studies of meaning.

François Rastier is Directeur de recherche (Senior Researcher) at the CNRS (Centre national de la recherche scientifique) in France, specializing in semantics. His research focuses on the study of texts from philology to hermeneutics, working on textual typology from a historical and comparative point of view. He is the author of 500 publications, including ten books, notably *Sémantique interprétative* (PUF, 1987), *Meaning and textuality* (Toronto UP, 1997),

Arts et sciences du texte (PUF, 2001), *Semantics for descriptions* (Chicago UP, 2002, with Anne Abeille and Marc Cavazza) and *La mesure et le grain. Sémantique de corpus* (Champion, 2011).

Nick Riemer is in the English and Linguistics Departments at the University of Sydney, and the Laboratoire d'histoire des théories linguistiques, Université Paris-Diderot. He specializes in semantics and in the history and philosophy of linguistics.

John Saeed is Professor of Linguistics and a Fellow of Trinity College, University of Dublin. He is the author of *Somali* (John Benjamins, 1999), *Semantics* (3rd ed., Wiley-Blackwell, 2009), and *Irish sign language: a cognitive linguistic account* (Edinburgh University Press, 2012, with Lorraine Leeson).

Raphael Salkie is Professor of Language Studies at the University of Brighton, where he teaches grammar, translation and discourse analysis. He is responsible for the INTERSECT translation corpus.

Petra Storjohann is a researcher at the Institut für Deutsche Sprache in Mannheim, where she is editor-in-chief of the Paronymwörterbuch lexicographical project. Her research focuses on the corpus analytic study of lexical-semantic relations in texts and discourse, methodological aspects of corpus linguistics and critical discourse analysis. Her publications include an edited volume, *Lexical-semantic relations. Theoretical and practical perspectives* (John Benjamins, 2010).

Michael Stubbs has been Professor of English Linguistics, University of Trier, Germany since 1990. He previously taught at the Universities of Nottingham and London, UK. He has published widely on educational linguistics, text and discourse analysis and corpus linguistics. He retired from regular teaching in 2013, but continues to write about corpus semantics and stylistics.

Anna Szabolcsi received her PhD from the Hungarian Academy of Sciences. From 1990 to 1998 she taught in the Linguistics Department of UCLA; since 1998 she has been Professor of Linguistics at New York University. Her research is in syntax and semantics.

Martine Vanhove is Director of Research at the CNRS-INALCO research unit LLACAN (France). As a field linguist, she is specialized in Cushitic and Semitic languages. Her main research interests include the syntax-prosody interface and semantic and lexical typology.

Acknowledgements

Figure 15.3 in Chapter 15 is reproduced from page 208 of Alexandre François' chapter "Semantic Maps and the typology of colexification", in Martine Vanhove (ed.) *From polysemy to semantic change: towards a typology of lexical semantic associations* (2008), by kind permission of John Benjamins Publishing Company, Amsterdam/Philadelphia.

Figure 25.2 in Chapter 25 is reproduced from page 143 of Asifa Majid, Melissa Bowerman, Miriam van Staden and James S. Boster's article "The semantic categories of cutting and breaking events: a crosslinguistic perspective", *Cognitive Linguistics* 18: 133–152, by kind permission of de Gruyter, Berlin.

Introduction

Semantics – a theory in search of an object

Nick Riemer

The French Marxist Georges Politzer – later to be executed by the Nazis at Mont Valérien – began his classic *Critique of the foundations of psychology* with the following remark:

> Even if no one considers protesting against the general claim that theories are mortal and that science can only advance over its own ruins, it is barely possible to make the proponents of an existing theory recognize its death. The majority of academics is composed of researchers who, having neither the sense of life, nor that of truth, can only work in the shelter of officially recognized theories: it is impossible to ask them to acknowledge a fact which isn't a *given*, but which has to be created . . . And so they acknowledge the mortality of all theories, even their own, but only in the abstract: it always strikes them as unlikely that, for *them*, the instant of death could already have arrived.
>
> (1974 [1928]: 1; trans NR)

The young philosopher's declaration is impressive for many reasons. But if Politzer's disdain for his contemporaries smacks of the anticlericalism of the (future) cardinal, he can also be criticized for grounding the explanation of a social phenomenon – the longevity of classical psychology, in an "experimental" or "scientific" guise, in the wake of Wundt – on personal and moral considerations, not on the concrete ones to which, as a good materialist, he ought really to have appealed.

Both Politzer's evaluation of the state of psychology in his time and the explanation for it he offers are worth considering in light of current linguistic semantics, a subfield whose object – meaning and reference – could hardly be more ambiguous or protean, and which is studied by a highly various scatter of often incompatible theoretical approaches, each of which makes truth-claims, at least implicitly, in favour of its own kind of analysis. As the different chapters of this handbook attest, these various approaches are all in rude good health, offering stimulating insights into different aspects of the phenomenon we call meaning. In such a situation of rich theoretical heterogeneity, it is no surprise that consensus is almost wholly absent about any of the key questions semantics sets out to answer: what meaning as an object of study might, in detail, amount to; how it – whatever "it" is – should be theoretically approached; how – even pretheoretically – it should be characterized on the level of individual expressions, constructions, and utterances; and what relation semantics should entertain with other fields of enquiry within and outside linguistics. Significantly differing points of view on some or all of these questions are characteristic of the different competitor theories that populate the field. Depraetere and Salkie's generalization in Chapter 20 about the study of tense – "even the basics are controversial" – applies in spades to semantics as a whole.

This heterogeneity might, of course, be no more than a consequence of the comparative youth of the modern empirical study of language, especially in so far as meaning is concerned. If this is the case, however, it's striking how little explicit theory-evaluation is undertaken by semantics researchers, and how rarely theoretical bridges between different research programmes are even sought, let alone found. Exceptions exist, of course, such as the effort made to assess the compatibility between Cognitive Semantics and Relevance Theory (e.g. Wilson (2011)) or the consistent effort by Anna Wierzbicka to compare her Natural Semantic Metalanguage (NSM) theory to alternative accounts. In general, though, the various schools of semantic research pursue largely independent programmes. No doubt as a result, the lack of consensus within the discipline is all too rarely even acknowledged. This is particularly the case for the most basic characterization of descriptive meaning in lexical semantics, on which so many subsequent theoretical explorations rest.

Before one can investigate how meanings relate to syntax or pragmatics, or to each other, or how they change, vary, or are acquired, one has to have an account of what these meanings are. This, however, is the locus of the most vexed, but also the most disavowed, questions in the field. Unless they take lexical meaning as atomic, semanticists of different schools continue to assert that the "meaning" of such and such an expression is such and such, despite the fact that many in the discipline are likely not to agree with them, and assuming that any disagreements are merely a consequence of lack of research, likely to be resolved with further work – something of a convenient fiction, given that people have been trying to write systematic definitions for many centuries at least. The disagreements are not trivial, and have substantive consequences for semantic modelling, as I have argued elsewhere (Riemer 2005). Since the methodological canons linguistics has adopted from the natural sciences make expert consensus a necessary, if not a sufficient, condition for confidence in the discipline's results, its almost complete absence in the study of meaning is the elephant in the room of any semantics that wants to associate itself with the empiricism and scientificity mostly assumed in "mainstream" linguistics, and it should, I believe, prompt some serious reconsideration of the nature of the discipline.

To say that the heterogeneity of current theoretical efforts should be the occasion for disciplinary self-reflection is not to say that there is anything intrinsically problematic in it. The theoretical balkanization in studies of meaning need only be seen as a flaw if it is taken for granted that semantics, on the model of physics, should be aiming at a unique theory of all meaning. Given the ongoing influence on linguistics of a model of enquiry rooted in how the natural sciences are, at least, imagined to be, this assumption is the one that is either typically made, or that seems tacitly presupposed by most semanticists' work. Different semantic investigations are most naturally understood as early contributions to the search for *the* authoritative, final account of natural language meaning. Investigators are likely to construe themselves as collectively engaged, at least ideally, in a convergent intellectual project, which will ultimately issue in the emergence of a single theory of meaning in natural language – itself taken to be an objective phenomenon open to techniques of observation and explanation that are certainly exacting and labour-intensive, but at least epistemically uncontroversial. Theoretical heterogeneity is therefore likely to be seen, in principle, as nothing other than a staging post on the road towards a final theory of meaning for natural language.

Current investigations into semantics characteristically form part of a project intended to illustrate and stress the pluralism and diversity of human mentality and culture. Nevertheless, the overarching tendency of semantic research I have just sketched, along with its default goal – to characterize *the* semantic *structure* of languages – arguably sits uneasily with this intention, for two reasons. First, it presupposes that linguistic expressions function in linguistic interaction by conveying fixed and invariant content, which it is the semanticist's task to characterize. This assumption is not only less self-evident than it seems (Riemer 2013), it also implies the controversial postulation of a clear boundary between linguistic and non-linguistic information, and sidelines a hermeneutic perspective that might do better justice to the contextual co-construction of significance between speaker and hearer (the ideas developed in Gadamer (2004) [1960], especially chapter 5, give some indication of the premises of such a perspective).

Second, it all too often implies the existence of a level of analysis on which cultural and cognitive diversity bottoms out into a format that can be captured in a unique analytical metalanguage – typically, given the history of linguistics, one built out of meaningful elements of English or some other first-world, Western language. English (or French, or German, or . . .), we assume, can be used to semantically analyze any other language, but not any language can be used to semantically analyze English or other first-world languages, since many languages lack the appropriate lexical and other resources. If semantic theory had succeeded in achieving a widely accepted body of confirmed results in its "Standard Average European" (SAE)-based metalanguages, it would be hard to see this asymmetry as anything more than an instance of the obvious dependence of theoretical enquiry on highly developed technical registers in the languages in which it is conducted. But in the absence of consensus in the discipline, it is reasonable to ask whether the assumption that all meanings can be represented in SAE metalanguages is justified.

In its totalizing ambition, there are many reasons to think that the project of reductively characterizing semantic structure may be undesirable in itself. As Stanley Rosen notes, "every hermeneutical program is at the same time itself a political manifesto or the corollary of a political manifesto" (2003: 141). This applies *a fortiori* to the programme of linguistic semantics, the goal of which is not, as in (applied) hermeneutics, to interpret texts, but to give an account of the very constituents of meaning that any textual interpretation presupposes. Since semantic analyses of *language* – or, to give them an older name, attempts to identify the "language of thought" – are closely related to claims about the conceptual abilities of *speakers* and the cultural resources of *communities*, we semanticists surely should be – and often are – cautious in arguing for the theoretical uniqueness for our current models of meaning. Claiming that, from the point of view of the linguistic system, such and such an expression has such and such *core* or *central* semantic properties risks reductively diminishing our picture of the complexity of languages, and hence of the linguistic practices and conceptual and cultural richness of their speakers.

Science, however, always operates through idealizing analytical procedures which carry exactly these kinds of risk. If there were strong evidence in *favour* of the correctness of one particular semantic model over another, and hence of the particular characterizations of meaning it supplied, the qualms that I am airing here could be dismissed as misguided and antiscientific Romanticism. But in the absence of consensus about meaning and its study, semanticists should surely be careful not to give the wrong impression about the status of our investigations into meaning. The down-side of doing so is starkly revealed when we consider the situation of semanticists from the first world turning their attention to mapping the underlying meaning structure of indigenous and minority languages currently threatened by the forces of global capitalism. Moody-Adams' (2014) observation, in a recent review of a book on anthropology and philosophy, about anthropologists' claim to theoretically account for culture and society also applies to linguists' claim to theoretically account for meaning:

> as a discipline, ethnography has rightly felt the need to come to terms with its origins in the context of colonialism, and the question of whether, even unwittingly, the claims of the (mostly western) "outsider" to be able to provide authoritative understandings of another's way of life might be inextricably bound up with the effort to dominate the other.

In this light, the claim of, for instance, Wierzbicka (2014) to transcend the intellectual domination of English through a rigorously established unique metalanguage for meaning description simply seems to replace one code (English) with another (NSM) as the uniquely authoritative metalanguage of semantic analysis. Wierzbicka's impetus to resist ethnocentrism in semantic analysis and its accompanying "colonialism of thought" are admirable and would be widely shared. But regardless of the particular theoretical framework adopted, it is offset by the objectivation of meaning that flows from the adoption of a unique and exclusive metalanguage for the description of semantic content, which arguably duplicates the very hegemonic move it sets out to avoid. Whether it is English, the NSM, cognitive semantics analyses, or model-theoretic formalizations that are claimed as the best representational format for characterizing semantic structure, the result is to reduce what arguably should be seen as an inherently plural, hermeneutically open-ended and fluid object – the significance of natural discourse – to a unique and unambiguous level of content, fully capturable in the theorist's own code. This theoretical move is, arguably, impoverishing, since it enforces a unitary conception of meaning, fixes interpretations, and, more often than not, presupposes the existence of a unique metalanguage in which all meaning can be represented. If semantic theory had commonly agreed-on explanatory achievements to show for this move, there would be some reason to think that the attendant impoverishment was no more than a characteristic instance of the idealization and simplification that always accompanies naturalistic enquiry. In the absence of such achievements, different questions should arise.

The fact that these kinds of scruple are not usually raised in linguistic semantics makes it all the more interesting to entertain them. While in other domains of enquiry the abstraction, reduction, and idealization of descriptive facts reflects no more than the standard objectivizing procedures of science, in a domain that, like semantics, is inherently bound up with the intentions, values, and subjective interpretations of human actors, such a methodological decision risks excluding the hermeneutic dimension arguably unique to meaningful interaction, and it should not be taken lightly. As a human "science", semantics concerns a sphere that is intrinsically bound up with the behaviour of autonomous creatures with their own pluralistic ways of being and understanding. In such a domain, it is not immediately clear that theoretical insight is best obtained by objectifying reduction, assimilating meaning to a unique object open to empirical methods deriving from the study of the objective world, instead of by pluralistic interpretation, assimilating the study of meaning to that of higher-level socio-cultural manifestations. Cultural anthropology, literary history, and sociology – all three empirical disciplines that offer explanations, and not just descriptions, of their objects of study – do not aim to produce unique and reductive analyses of their explananda; it is no more obvious that semanticists should try to uniquely characterize *the* literal meaning of an expression than it is that literary historians should try to uniquely pin down *the* single correct interpretation of a canonical text.

There is nothing antiscientific, relativist, or irrational in this suggestion. Endorsing a pluralistic conception of meaning doesn't entail somehow exempting linguistic behaviour from the scope of objectifying empirical science. There will, no doubt, one day be a science of linguistic behaviour, in the sense of a deterministic and causal account of the production and reception of utterances, and it is unjustified, at the moment, to assume otherwise. But we should recognize that any future, predictive understanding of linguistic behaviour seems unlikely to emerge from theories of the language system developed in linguistics or some other human science, but will instead arise within the neurosciences, with their entirely different explanatory regimes.

In approaching meaning in semanticists' characteristic reductive manner, there seems plenty of grounds for us to worry that we ourselves are guilty of the "refusal" that Gadamer identifies as key to the methodology of modern natural science – "namely, to exclude all that which actually eludes its own methodology and procedures" (1972: 93). We are so used to pretheoretical talk about meanings and definitions that it is easy to forget how alien such constructs are to our experience of language use. Phenomenologically, it is a commonplace observation that we do not usually even experience utterances as having meanings, if by "meaning" we mean some *extra* factor that is separable from the chain of sounds being spoken, and of which we are independently aware. Only in cases of communicative "breakdown", where the speaker's communicative intention fails to be realized and misunderstanding ensues, are linguistic actors forced to scrutinize the relation between their intention, the words spoken, and the communicative result, and hence posit meanings to clarify the way in which communicative purpose has not been adequately fulfilled (see Riemer (2015) for some discussion). At other times, language resembles other complex symbolic activities, like music or gesture, for which it would never occur to us to posit invariant contents underlying the different units of which they are composed.

A semiotic conception of language, in which words are above all signs – for propositions, things, or concepts – goes hand in hand with an instrumentalist one, in which speakers are, above all, in a relation of *use* towards their utterances, which they consciously select and put to the service of communicating their thoughts. Gadamer, once again, observes that:

> Semantics is a doctrine of signs, in particular, of linguistic signs. Signs, however, are a means to an end. They are put to use as one desires and then laid aside just as are all other means to the ends of human activity . . . . Actual speaking is more than the choice of means to achieve some purpose in communication. The language one masters is such that one lives within it, that is "knows" what one wishes to communicate in no way other than in linguistic form. "Choosing" one's words is an appearance or effect created in communication when speaking is inhibited. "Free" speaking flows forward in forgetfulness of oneself and in self-surrender to the subject-matter made present in the medium of language.
>
> (1972: 87)

The instrumentalist conception, by contrast, makes language simply a tool. Here too, we should register the phenomenological implausibility of such an approach to linguistic interaction. Against it, it can be objected that the description of people as *using* language rings just as false as a description of them "using" light to see or "using" notes to sing melodies. In all three cases, any initial appeal that the instrumental construal of these situations might have is quickly challenged by an alternative conception in which language, light, or the musical scale are seen not as tools, but as conditions of possibility of the situations involving them. Just as light is the condition of possibility of seeing and the musical scale the condition of possibility of music, so too language should be conceived of not as a simple *tool* of communication, but as a necessary condition for the enactment of subjectivity – or, to use Enfield's (2009: 74) phrase, "situated micro-politics" – a formulation that also entails intersubjectivity and all the forms of coordinated interaction that we call communication. Our agentive relationship to language mostly seems better construed not on the instrumental model of the speaker consciously selecting particular words in the same way that the carpenter, for instance, selects a particular hammer for a specific and independently defined task. Instead, a better analogy for the speaker's relation to her words is that between a sculptor and the wood or stone she is carving; just as the wood or stone plays a major role in shaping and constraining the sculptor's physical gestures, language plays a major role in constraining and shaping the speaker's linguistics ones, which are structured as much, if not more, by the contextual affordances of the medium of language as by the specific intentions of the speaker.

The lack of phenomenological warrant for talk of meaning opens semantics up to the various "situated" critiques of broader cognitive science that have come to the fore in the last several decades (see Riemer (2013) for further comments). It is just one of many reasons to be open to alternatives to the assumption that language is subtended by fixable, deterministic meanings of the kind that many linguists usually presuppose – invariant items of (conceptual) content, perhaps decomposable, and shared between participants in communicative exchanges. Just as we can explain the complex kinds of coordination that we achieve with each other in music, dance, or gesture without recourse to such factors, so an explanation of language use along similar lines would not seem to be impossible – and is, in fact, already present to a greater or lesser extent in some of the chapters of this volume.

It bears emphasizing once more that these scruples would be much less justified if semanticists had succeeded in developing comprehensive and plausible analyses of meaning that had won acceptance through the discipline as a whole. In their absence, there seems good reason to question the presuppositions that inform our work. Rather than seeing the goal of semantics as being to develop final, exhaustive analyses of the "content" putatively conveyed by every expression of a language, and an account of the way these contents combine, we might see the discipline as engaged in an inherently pluralistic and hermeneutic explanatory enterprise, where what matters is not the generation of final statements about what any expression means, but a dialectical encounter with the multifarious ways in which expressions can be significant for us and for the people who use them. As Faye has recently reminded us, "we never just explain something; we always do it from a particular perspective, focusing on some features and ignoring others. An explanation is always about something; it is never of something" (2014: xi); it is part of a "rhetorical practice of communication" (ibid, viii), not the last word on the object being studied.

Approached in this way, the different incompatible projects that constitute the field of semantics today emerge as appropriately varied responses to differing questions, not, as a positivistic critic might claim, as final proof that semantics is a pseudoscience. Abandoning the expectation that we will achieve a unique theoretical account of meaning does not entail jettisoning any of the rich and explanatory achievements of semantic theory. If meaning is neither singular nor objective, then the interest of pursuing a theoretically centripetal, converging programme diminishes, and the kaleidoscopic character of existing semantics on display in this book should no longer cause us anxiety. There are, after all, many complex symbolic behaviours which do not call for reductive analysis in terms of fixed underlying "contents". Music is only the most obvious example.

If some kind of unifying identity is wanted for contemporary semantic investigations, however, perhaps one can be suggested by the questions that motivate differing research projects' enquiry into meaning. According to the traditional conception, a meaning is attributed to an expression to account for certain aspects of its use – particularly its referential and inferential properties. Even though one might question the extent to which reference and inference are either intrinsic to meaning or exhaustive – in particular, the concentration on reference forms part of a conception of language which Austin's illocutionary perspective has not sufficiently eclipsed – both define important questions to which we do not yet have satisfying answers. What determines the range of objects, situations, or properties to which an expression can be used to refer? What governs the links of compatibility and exclusion of various strengths to which expressions are subject? What non-referential factors affect the coordination between expressions and the interpersonal, environmental, and mental contexts in which they appear? In offering answers, semantic theories can be seen as supplying, in tandem with pragmatics, explanations for those dimensions of language "use" not covered by the other linguistics subfields. When it identifies "meaning" as the hidden explanatory factor in question, semantics invokes a shorthand explanatory concept which will, no doubt, not prove to correspond to any single unitary phenomenon, but which provides an abridged way of invoking whichever explanatory factor is relevant. Meaning becomes, in other words, not the *object* of which semantic theories offer explanatory accounts, as it has usually previously been conceived, but a portmanteau name for the variety of explanatory *factors* to which semantics appeals to explain *use*. On this way of conceiving of things, meaning is not the monolithic *explanandum* of the discipline of semantics, but the name of a variety of *explanantia* that are invoked in a variety of forms to account for particular facts about the way language is used.

It follows from this way of thinking about semantics that we should not expect to uncover any unique and monolithic "meaning" that expressions convey. Meaning is a shorthand concept that ties together a variety of diverse explanatory factors. There are, no doubt, many shorthand concepts of this nature. Colour, for example, seems to be one. To describe a book as "red" is a shorthand way of expressing the fact that when observed by normal eyes in normal lighting conditions, the book has a particular hue. But it is readily apparent that redness isn't a property the book has inherently; it's a relational property that holds between our nervous system, the surface of the book, and the quality of the light. Given different conditions, the same book would be a different colour: if we were wearing coloured glasses, for instance, or observing under certain artificial lighting situations. To talk of a word's literal meaning may be a similar sort of shorthand, which provides us with a provisional starting point for the exploration of the way in which the use of expressions is underdetermined by their phonology and syntax. Like the other posits of synchronic linguistics, a description of literal meaning provides, in Vološinov's useful phrase, a "conventional scale" on which actually occurring deviation can be plotted, but which "does not correspond to any real moment in the historical process of [linguistic] becoming" (Vološinov 1973 [1930]: 66).

*

Each of the chapters of this handbook – the ambition of which is to display the state of the art of some important parts of semantics as it is currently constituted – presents a snapshot of an existing area of ongoing semantic investigation, each characterized by its own internal logic. My intention in exploring the considerations above has not been to speak for any of the contributors, none of whom should be assumed to share any of the points of view reflected in this introduction. It is, in any case, only in trying to cohere the varying research projects of the subfield as part of a single intellectual effort that the considerations mooted above arise. Nevertheless, the pluralism I have been recommending as desirable in the way we think about semantics does, perhaps, offer a perspective from which the reader can approach this book.

It is in the nature of this kind of volume that many readers will consult the chapters individually, with none of them necessarily being read in the context of the rest. For this kind of reader, the theoretical heterogeneity of these pages will not present an obstacle. More comprehensive readers, however, will hardly fail to be struck by the major contrast between approaches to meaning rooted in formal logic and those rooted in cognitive hypotheses about meaning as mental representation. The latter approaches are inherently internalistic, in the sense that meaning, for them, is individuated on the basis of differences of underlying mental structure (see Chapter 2); formal approaches, on the other hand, while they may be internalistic, are inspired by a truth-functional, externalist conception of meaning, the bases of which are outlined in Chapter 1.

Because semantics, like any other discipline, is a product of an ongoing tradition, the handbook includes a sketch of the history of investigations into meaning in the Western tradition (Chapter 3). This tradition, however, is much more diverse than is often appreciated, and is characterized by a number of different more or less "national" approaches. In my view, it is salutary for a book like this to look beyond the usual confines of what we can, without too much distortion, dub "mainstream" linguistic semantics – by which I mean the complex of theories and approaches originating with Montague for the formal side and with figures like Katz and Fodor, Goodenough, Lyons, and others on the non-formal. For this reason, I have chosen to include, in the form of Chapter 28, an introduction to the work of perhaps the most important French semanticist, François Rastier, whose achievements in the field remain largely unknown to English-language researchers. Rastier is far from the only scholar working outside the confines familiar to most proponents of the discipline in the mainstream tradition. His inclusion here is meant to suggest some of the ways in which semantics as it is mostly practised could be different. The other three chapters in this final part of the volume – on meaning acquisition, semantic processing, and the descriptive/expressive contrast – similarly suggest new directions for the discipline, either through confronting it with experimental studies of acquisition, comprehension or production, or by opening the study of meaning out to the non-cognitive domain of affect, hitherto considered almost wholly marginal to any serious semantic questions.

The other sections of the handbook address, in a self-explanatory way, some important dimensions of semantic study. Part II discusses three approaches to meaning – formal, cognitive, and corpus. Part III discusses the relationship between meaning and conceptualization; Part IV that between meaning and context. Lexical semantic topics are addressed in Part V, and Part VI contains discussions of certain central topics in semantic research, from nominals to lexical typology. A number of these make some use of formal machinery and will, as such, be less accessible to much of the general readership of a handbook like this. This should not, however, be a cause of concern: the split between formal and non-formal approaches is intrinsic to the discipline and cannot be papered over. Since, like any handbook, readers are unlikely to read the whole text, but will selectively choose only certain chapters, the most important consideration is to ensure that each chapter adopts a level of formalization appropriate for its likely readership.

Originally, a chapter on meaning change had been projected, to complement the discussion of diachronic issues in the chapters on semantic shift and on semantic typology. Peter Koch had completed most of a first draft, in German, of an extended version of this chapter at the time of his sudden death in July 2014. Peter's death has not just deprived this volume of a greater diachronic dimension; it has deprived the discipline of a highly respected figure, to whom it is an honour to dedicate this book. Peter's full chapter will be appearing in a translation by Tessa Say in Päivi Juvonen's and Maria Koptjevskaja-Tamm's forthcoming volume on *Lexico-typological approaches to semantic shifts and motivation patterns in the lexicon*, currently in preparation.

*

As Politzer noted, it is in the nature of theory-development that the ideas in any published research will mostly be superseded. The spirit of cooperation and collective enquiry, by contrast, is altogether more durable. It's therefore a great pleasure to acknowledge the numerous contributions to this volume from researchers from all over the world, whose help in various ways while the manuscript was being prepared was indispensable. It goes without saying that my greatest debt is to the authors of the various chapters. But I'm also very grateful to the numerous other people who made it easier, in different ways, to see this project through. In particular, I would like to thank Asifa Majid, Bart Geurts, Bernhard Wälchli, Beth Levin, Bill Carrasco, Brigitte Nerlich, Briony Neilson, Chris Kennedy, Derek Herforth, Elizabeth Traugott, Jacqueline Léon, James McElvenny, Jean-Michel Fortis, Lynne Murphy, Nick Enfield, Noella Budd, Paul Elbourne, Paul Portner, Peter Slezak, Phil Staines, Renaat Declerck, and Sam Jones. Participants in seminars and reading groups at the University of Sydney, the Laboratoire d'histoire des théories linguistiques (Université Paris-Diderot), and the University of New South Wales also played an invaluable role. All research is intrinsically collaborative, even when it is single-authored. Without the existence of a discipline – a collective intellectual environment, sustained over generations by thousands of people – no individual contributions would ever be possible. That general principle is even more applicable here since, without the generosity of all the people I have mentioned, it would have been simply impossible to finish this book.

References

Enfield, Nick 2009. Relationship thinking and human pragmatics. *Journal of Pragmatics* 41: 60–78.
Faye, Jan 2014. *The Nature of Scientific Thinking. On Interpretation, Explanation, and Understanding*. Houndmills: Palgrave Macmillan.
Gadamer, Hans-Georg 1972. *Philosophical Hermeneutics* (Linge, ed. and trans.). Berkeley: University of California Press.
Gadamer, Hans-Georg 2004 [1960]. *Truth and Method*. 2nd edition (Joel Weinsheimer and Donald G. Marshall, trans.). London: Continuum.
Moody-Adams, Michele M. 2014. Review of Veena Das, Michael Jackson, Arthur Kleinman, and Bhrigupati Singh (eds.), *The Ground Between: Anthropologists Engage Philosophy*. http://ndpr.nd.edu/news/53790-the-ground-between-anthropologists-engage-philosophy.
Politzer, Georges 1974 [1928]. *Critique des fondements de la psychologie*. Paris: PUF.
Riemer, N. 2005. *The Semantics of Polysemy*. Berlin: Mouton.
Riemer, N. 2013. Conceptualist semantics: explanatory power, scope and uniqueness. *Language Sciences* 35: 1–19.
Riemer, N. 2015. Word meaning. In John R. Taylor (ed.) *The Oxford Handbook of the Word*. Oxford: Oxford University Press.
Rosen, Stanley 2003. *Hermeneutics as Politics*. New Haven, London: Yale University Press.
Vološinov, V. 1973 [1930]. *Marxism and the Philosophy of Language*. Ladislav Matejka and I.R Titunik (trans.). New York: Seminar Press.

Wierzbicka, Anna 2014. *Imprisoned in English. The Hazards of English as a Default Language*. Oxford: Oxford University Press.

Wilson, Deirdre 2011. Parallels and differences in the treatment of metaphor in relevance theory and cognitive linguistics. *Intercultural Pragmatics* 8: 177–196.

Part I
Foundational issues

1
(Descriptive) Externalism in semantics

Steven Gross

1 Introduction

Semantics is the study of meaning—in some sense. In what sense? According to a common view, semantics concerns *inter alia* the relation between words and the world—in particular, their *intentional* (or *representational*, *aboutness*) relations. When a competent user utters "Schnee ist weiss" to make an assertion, she makes a claim about how the world is. What in part enables her to represent the world as being this way is that "Schnee" refers to snow, something satisfies "ist weiss" just in case it's white, and so "Schnee ist weiss" is true just in case snow is white. As David Lewis (1970: 18) famously put it: "semantics with no treatment of truth-conditions is not semantics." Similar sentiments are found in leading semantics textbooks:

> To know the meaning of a sentence is to know its truth-conditions. If I say to you ["There is a bag of potatoes in my pantry"] you may not know whether what I said is true. What you do know, however, is what the world would have to be like for it to be true . . . . A theory of meaning, then, pairs sentences with their truth-conditions.
> (Heim and Kratzer 1998: 1)

> The study of the relation of symbols to what they stand for ["refer to," "denote," "their informational content"] must indeed be a part of an account of meaning. For otherwise how could we understand the fundamental fact that configurations of symbols carry information about all the diverse aspects of our experience?
> (Chierchia and McGonnell-Ginet 1990: 53)

Characterizing these semantic properties is no easy matter. Language users understand many more expressions than they could store individually in memory. So much of the hard work involves compositionally characterizing the semantic properties of a potentially infinite number of complex expressions as a function of those of their constituents and their mode of combination. Moreover, the subtleties of these semantic properties are often masked by our own competence with the terms. "Snow" is a mass term, apparently denoting some sort of undifferentiated stuff, unlike a count noun such as "snowballs"; and "snow is white" expresses a generic claim that is not falsified by a bit of yellow snow. How best to (compositionally) characterize the semantics of mass nouns and of generics is much disputed.

Our focus, however, is not these complexities, but the underlying word-world, or *externalist*, conception of semantics. A central debate in the foundations of semantics concerns whether it's correct. *Internalist* opponents maintain that semantics rather concerns, or ought to concern, only *non*-intentional relations among linguistic items and (other) mental structures (see Chapter 2). On their view, semantics lays out what concepts or thoughts expressions directly activate or express, *without* recourse to intentional relations to things external to the mind/brain. (The qualification "directly" is meant to put to one side priming, association, and inference via world knowledge.) For example, the word "Schnee" might activate one's concept SNOW; one might utter "Schnee ist weiss" to express one's belief that snow is white. Whether these *concepts and thoughts* represent aspects of the world—and whether such representational properties have a place in empirical inquiry into the mind-brain—is another matter, not a question for *linguistic* semantics, which concerns itself only with the semantic properties of *linguistic* items (words, phrases, sentences, etc.).

In this chapter, we examine some of the prominent arguments for and against externalism, as well as the dispute's upshot for existing work in the field. Note that the question is not what the word "semantics" means, but rather what are, or would be, fruitful paths for work in semantics to take. Also, the question is not whether characterizing words' intentional relations to the world *exhausts* semantics, but rather whether it is, or should be, a *part* of semantics. This allows that semantics might concern *both* words' non-intentional relations to other mental structures *and* their intentional relations to the world, so that work championed by typical externalists and work championed by typical internalists could turn out to be compatible. As we frame things, however, the *theses* of externalism and internalism are opposed to one another, even if work championed by their proponents is not—since we include in internalism the *rejection* of intentional relations so far as the scientific study of linguistic semantics is concerned. Finally, regarding the upshot for extant work, we will need to consider whether, if internalist considerations win the day, this requires us to jettison work in truth-conditional semantics or rather just to reconstrue it in internalist terms.

2 Varieties of externalism and internalism

The "externalist vs. internalist" label is also applied to other disagreements concerning the nature of semantics. This is no accident, as the various externalisms sometimes come packaged together, likewise for the various internalisms. But the disagreements are, or seem to be, dissociable. So our first order of business is to clarify our main topic further by distinguishing it from these other externalist/internalist debates.

Let's first distinguish *descriptive* and *foundational* semantics (Stalnaker 1997; cf. Kaplan 1989 on semantics vs. metasemantics). Descriptive semantics asks what semantic properties expressions have. Foundational semantics asks *in virtue of what* they have them. A candidate *descriptive* semantic claim, in this case externalist, might be: "Hund" means *dog*. Foundational semantics assumes that this descriptive fact (granting it is one) obtains in virtue of something more basic. It assumes that a dependence relation obtains between semantic properties and more fundamental non-semantic properties (the *supervenience base*), and it inquires into that relation. A candidate foundational semantic claim, again from an externalist, might be: The descriptive semantic fact that "Hund" means *dog* obtains in virtue of a convention among Germans, involving attitudes and expectations they have towards one another (cf. Lewis 1975). Note that the foundational question is not about *causes* (though answers may invoke them), but about *constitution*. Phylogeny, glossogeny, and ontogeny might bear on how it *came to pass* that "Hund" means *dog*, but it's a further question whether elements of the causal story are also among the supervenience base for "Hund" *now having* that semantic property. (Compare: this is a water molecule in virtue of the relations among the hydrogen and oxygen atoms that constitute it, however they came to be so arranged.)

Distinct externalist/internalist debates correspond to the descriptive/foundational distinction. Our focus is the *descriptive* externalist/internalist debate: whether intentional relations to aspects of the world are among the semantic properties of linguistic items. The *foundational* externalist/internalist debate concerns what makes it the case that those properties obtain—in particular, whether the supervenience base for semantic properties includes only properties internal to language users or rather also includes relations to things external to them. It is this second debate that philosophers of language usually have in mind when they talk of semantic externalism and internalism. A typical foundational externalist allows that neurophysiological twins can have otherwise identical lexical items with different semantic properties; what makes the difference must thus reside in some relation to something external. Hilary Putnam (1975), for example, argues that what a speaker's natural kind terms refer to depends in part on the speaker's natural and social environments. A typical foundational internalist denies this.

Putnam argues for foundational externalism by arguing that a descriptively externalist semantic property—the reference of natural kind terms—does not supervene on an internalist supervenience base. His view is thus both foundationally and descriptively externalist. But it would seem that (pending substantive argument to the contrary) a descriptive externalist may be either a foundational internalist or a foundational externalist—similarly for descriptive internalists. The debates thus cross-cut. Various descriptive externalists (e.g. Segal 2000) have challenged Putnam's arguments for foundational externalism, maintaining instead that speakers' intrinsic properties fix the reference of their terms. Likewise, it's a possible position (though proponents are not readily found) to deny, with descriptive internalists, that linguistic items stand in *representational* relations to worldly items, but also hold, with foundational externalists, that the non-intentional semantic properties expressions *do* have are determined in part by (non-intentional) relations to things in the world. For example, one might hold that linguistic items are computational mental structures without representational properties, but also that computational structures are themselves individuated in part in virtue of the mind/brain's relation to its environment (cf. Bontly 1998, Ludlow 2003a).

These externalist/internalist debates—descriptive and foundational—both concern the semantic properties of *linguistic* items. It's worth noting that parallel debates arise concerning the properties of *non*-linguistic items, particularly non-linguistic mental structures: what, if any, representational properties do they have, and in virtue of what do they have them? In the introduction, we said in effect that linguistic descriptive internalism needn't address whether the concepts and thoughts that they take linguistic items to activate or express are themselves representational. Having drawn the descriptive/foundational distinction, we can now add that linguistic descriptive internalism also needn't address foundational questions concerning what makes concepts and thoughts have whatever properties they do. (For a seminal extension of Putnam's linguistic foundational externalism to mental content, see Burge 1979; cf. also Burge 2003 on Chomsky's internalism more generally.)

Though one can contrast linguistic items with concepts and thoughts, it doesn't follow that linguistic items are not mental structures (of some other kind). This brings us to yet another debate to which the label "externalist vs. internalist" gets applied—now concerning what words are, as opposed to what semantic properties they have.

Chomsky (1986) famously distinguishes two conceptions of language. An I-language—or "internalized" language—is the computational system, realized in an individual's mind/brain, that generates the structures specifically implicated in linguistic behavior. An E-language is an "externalized" language that is understood independently of the properties of the mind/brain. Chomsky introduces the notion of E-language in discussing proposed technical constructs in the scientific study of language. But it also naturally comprises pre-theoretic conceptions of languages—English, German, etc.—as existing external to and independently of any particular person.

Chomsky argues that I-languages are the proper target of scientific inquiry: E-languages, among other things, have insufficiently clear identity conditions, while a focus on I-languages opens fruitful lines of inquiry concerning acquisition, the causal basis of linguistic behavior, the interface of linguistic competence with other cognitive capacities, cross-linguistic commonalities and variation, etc. (See Wiggins (1997) for a defense of E-language, and Heck (2006) in reply; see also Stainton (2006) for an overview of Chomsky's views on these and related matters.) But debates about the proper object of linguistic inquiry—I-languages or E-languages (or both)—again seem to cross-cut our primary concern, at least pending substantive argument. Various authors (Larson and Segal 1995; Ludlow 2003b, 2011) explicitly present themselves as providing a descriptive externalist semantics (a characterization of intentional word-world relations) for the structures generated by an I-language. Others (Brandom 1994) embrace a social, E-language conception of language while eschewing representational properties in their theorizing.

Finally, the externalist/internalist debate is sometimes formulated as one concerning what kind of *thing* a meaning is: whether it is something that can be external to the mind/brain (the referent of a term) or something internal to it (a concept). But descriptive externalism need not commit one to external meaning *entities*. Some descriptive externalists—notably Donald Davidson (1984, cf. also Lepore and Ludwig 2005)—eschew meaning entities altogether as obscure and explanatorily otiose. The claim is not that the putative referents of words—tables, rocks, Donald Davidson—don't exist, but rather that there are no entities that are *meanings*; so, in particular, those entities aren't meanings. Moreover, a meaning-entity internalist can embrace descriptive externalism. Elbourne (2011), who casts the externalist/internalist debate in meaning-entity terms, favors meaning-entity internalism (meanings are concepts), but maintains that meaning-entity externalists and internalists agree that the meanings of words—whatever they are—are what enable words to "hook on" to the world. (Incidentally, instead of identifying meanings either with referents or with concepts, one might suggest that they are the combination of the two, with concepts determining reference. Cf. Frege (1918), albeit this use of "concept" aligns more with his "*Sinn*" (sense). His use of the term "*Begriff*" (concept) corresponds more closely, albeit imperfectly, to our "property." We should note also that some take concepts to be non-spatial *abstracta*, and so in that sense neither internal nor external.)

These other externalist/internalist debates deserve further discussion—as do their bearings on one another. Various ways of arguing for descriptive externalism or internalism may commit one as well concerning the other debates. But in any event it is important to distinguish the debates. They involve distinct claims, and underscoring this better places us to see clearly how one might be connected with another. That noted, we shall henceforth concentrate on the debate between descriptive externalists and internalists concerning linguistic items. Should semantics include a characterization of intentional relations between linguistic items and aspects of the world?

3 Against externalism

Internalists (e.g. Chomsky 2000; Jackendoff 2002; Pietroski 2005) have answered this question in the negative on various grounds. This section catalogs some of the considerations an internalist might put forth, as well as some lines of reply. The remarks are intended only to indicate the issues, not to settle them. In the next section, we turn to arguments in favor of externalism.

First, some internalists raise questions concerning the objects to which words putatively bear intentional relations. Some of these objects can seem in various ways suspect or at least such that they have no place in empirical inquiry—for example, because they are vague, mind-dependent, fictional, or otherwise odd (Jackendoff 2002). For example:

- rivers (which "river" putatively denotes) have unclear boundaries, for example at a confluence;
- political entities like Arizona (which "Arizona" putatively denotes) only exist in virtue of there being people with various beliefs and intentions;
- the use of some terms—such as "book" in "This book weighs 2 pounds and is a best-seller"—would seem to commit us to entities that are both abstract and concrete;
- names for fictional beings, like "Superman," seem not to refer at all;
- and various putatively referring terms—such as "sake" (as in "for my sake") and "the average American"—would seem to commit us to recognizing odd entities indeed.

There are several possible lines of reply, perhaps different ones appropriate to different cases. First, the descriptive externalist might deny that her semantics involves reference to the alleged objects. For instance, Kennedy and Stanley (2009), building on previous proposals (e.g. Higginbotham 1985), argue that "the average American," far from denoting some particular person with 2.3 children, is not a genuine singular referring expression at all. They develop a view on which "average" denotes the property of being a measure function, a domain, and degree such that the sum of the result of applying that measure function to that domain, divided by the number of items in the domain, equals that degree. So sentences such as "The average American has 2.3 children" yield truth-conditions to the effect that the number of children of Americans divided by the number of Americans is 2.3. On their analysis, the terms here refer to numbers, Americans, their children, and relations among them.

Second, the descriptive externalist might deny in some cases that the relevant referent is so odd, or otherwise objectionable, after all. The general strategy is to argue that the internalist sets the bar too high, perhaps even precluding otherwise accepted objects of scientific inquiry. For example, if purposes or interests aren't odd, why are sakes? That the word "sake" has a distinct distribution, apparently restricted to certain collocations, is interesting but arguably orthogonal to the internalist's objection. The internalist might rejoin that sakes, like purposes or interests, are not tangible things, or are mental and thus mind-dependent. But, again, why should this cause alarm? The internalist herself happily wallows in such non-tangible mental stuff as concepts and thoughts, so presumably would deny that they can be a priori debarred from scientific inquiry. Similar remarks apply to other mind-dependent things such as Arizona. Likewise, the vague boundaries of brains and other objects of scientific inquiry can be used to turn aside the worry about rivers.

The "book" example—"This book weighs 2 pounds and is a best-seller"—is one of various mismatch cases to which Chomsky (2000) has drawn attention. They involve apparent reference to objects with shifting sets of incompatible properties. The best-seller isn't any particular copy of the book: it's a best-seller because of the many copies sold. But only particular copies have weight. Yet the sentence seems to treat the book type and the book token as one, as if one and the same thing could be both abstract and concrete. Externalists might reply here as well that no particular odd object gets referred to. The cases rather bring out the complexity of speakers' understanding of relations among objects and their properties. In this case, the proper interpretation of the sentence (or at least of what the speaker says in uttering it) requires knowledge of how types and tokens relate—in particular, how a token might be said by courtesy to have a property in virtue of a property of its type (and vice versa). What it *is* for a particular copy of a book to be a best-seller, for example, is for it to be a token of a type that's a best-seller. Indeed, externalists might even allow in their ontology items, in addition to book-types and book-tokens, which are hybrids of the two—and they may suggest that much social ontology involves things with hybrid natures (consider institutions such as universities which are both located and abstractly constituted). If internalists object that items constituted of, for example, aspects that are abstract and aspects that are concrete are ontologically odd, externalists can suggest that internalists are not being psychologistic enough: their intuitions of oddness might themselves be the product of a "folk metaphysics" whose bearing is open to question.

Externalists might try adding that it's unclear that internalists have anything better to offer concerning such cases (cf. Elbourne 2011: 26). Moreover, the problem—if it is one—does not seem specific to language, since we can also entertain the *thought* that this book weighs 2 pounds and is a best-seller. Again, internalists run the risk of proving too much—though some might reply that these cases help mark the limits of scientific tractability concerning aspects of both language and thought. (Chomsky (1975) also raises various other challenges for externalist semantics. For example, he suggests that such sentences as "Poems are written by fools like Smith" and "Mountains are climbed by fools like Jones" pose problems for semantic compositionality: why does the first, but not the second, require that *all* X's be A-ed by such fools? For an externalist reply, see Forbes (2012).)

Some of the preceding remarks apply as well to the difficult topic of fictional names and other apparently non-referring terms, which introduce a variety of complications and have been addressed in various ways (see Everett and Hofweber (2000)). Here I use them to put on the table a third line of reply available to descriptive externalists. The internalist objections canvassed so far assume that externalist semantics requires that the world in fact contain that which words are about. The reference relation, for example, must relate words to things that exist. But many intentional terms are arguably ambiguous between a weaker and stronger sense, where only the latter has existential import (cf. Rey 2006). Thus, we can say that "Superman" refers to Superman, not to Lex Luther, while also acknowledging that there is no actual person to whom the name applies. To mark the difference, we might say that the weak sense concerns what the term *purports* to refer to in the stronger "success" sense. Accounts of fictional names attempt to accommodate this in various ways. One suggestion is that fictional names are used within the scope of a pretense: *suppose* things are as depicted in this story, then "Superman" refers to Superman. Or at least so it might be for the name as used in "Superman is strong." For sentences "outside" the fiction—such as "Superman appears in DC Comics"—one might say that the name refers to an *abstractum*. Particularly problematic are negative existential sentences such as "Superman does not exist" (cf. Evans 1983, Kripke 2013).

More generally, the externalist may claim that semantics should include a characterization of what words *purport* to be about. Emmon Bach (1986, 1989) thus speaks of natural language metaphysics: the semanticist, in characterizing a language's semantic properties, lays bare how things are represented in language to be, but prescinds from drawing conclusions therefrom concerning how the world in fact is. (Cf. Pelletier 2011, with reference to the mass/count distinction.) Indeed, since much of the fine-grain work ascribes semantic properties arguably not consciously available to speakers themselves—including properties concerning sets, possible worlds, and other esoterica—perhaps some of the seeming metaphysical commitments of our semantic competence should not be viewed as commitments of the speakers themselves. The idea is that the sentences of speakers' I-languages might possess truth-conditions under the supposition that certain kinds of things exist. Such suppositions might facilitate the modeling and computation of semantic properties and relations. But the speaker herself needn't be committed to such entities in virtue simply of using the language—far less the semanticist who merely describes the speaker's semantic competence (cf. Gross 2006).

Should this still count as a kind of externalism? We are allowing that the worldly correlates needn't exist, yet we are preserving the idea that words have representational content and that semantics goes beyond mere causal relations between words and other mental structures. I count this as a kind of externalism, in part given some prominent internalists' critical focus on appeals to intentionality at least so far as semantics is concerned (see the next paragraph). But one could reasonably choose to use the labels differently. (Cf. Collins' (2011: 137) characterization of internalism: "The explanations offered by successful linguistic theory neither presuppose nor entail externalia"—also Collins 2009: 53.) What matters are the possible positions, not how we label them. But to the extent that the applicability of the label is uncertain, the debate itself is unclear. It's possible that at least some of the disagreement among semanticists concerning the proper construal of extant work stems from confusion concerning the terms of the debate.

The objections so far canvassed concern the things to which words are supposed to relate. But some have also objected to intentional relations themselves. For example, Jackendoff (2002) argues that because we cannot make physical sense of intentional relations, there in fact are none. His remarks suggest that this basis for rejecting descriptive externalism depends on a foundational demand that (it's maintained) externalism can't satisfy—viz., that the intentional relation be at least in principle reducible to a physical relation. Jackendoff's claim is akin to the content eliminativism of Quine (1960) and Churchland (1981). It also calls to mind behaviorist scruples, but Jackendoff is a cognitivist who parts company with behaviorists by allowing computational mental structures a central explanatory role.

There are in fact proposals for rendering intentionality physicalistically acceptable (Loewer 1996 surveys some). But it might also be replied that the explanatory credentials of theories invoking intentionality do not require satisfying Jackendoff's foundational demand (Gross, 2005a; Burge, 2010). On this view, a notion earns its keep to the extent that it's invoked in successful, fruitful theories (cf. Chomsky 2000 on methodological naturalism). We may still aim for integration with other theories in other domains to the extent possible (this would increase explanatory scope and deepen understanding); but such integration is just one virtue among many and, in any event, should not be imposed prematurely. Still, perceived barriers to integration, whether in principle or in practice, may suggest to some that inquiry is on the wrong track. The proof of the pudding is in the eating. Note that Chomsky (2000), like Jackendoff, is skeptical of representational notions playing a role in scientific inquiry as things now stand and in the foreseeable future. But he does not go so far as to deny the phenomenon of intentionality. It's one thing to deny a phenomenon; it's another to deny merely its scientific tractability. (For some further comparison of Jackendoff and Chomsky on these matters, see Gross 2005a, 2007. Gross 2005a also discusses the implausibility of rejecting intentionality altogether.)

One needn't throw out the very phenomenon of aboutness, however, to question whether *words* bear an intentional relation to aspects of the world (even if speakers or their thoughts do). Another challenge comes from the pervasive phenomenon of content context-sensitivity (see Chapters 10 and 11). What words are about, or what speakers say in using one and the same expression, varies across conversational contexts. Obvious examples include demonstratives, indexicals, pronouns, tense markers, and the like. But virtually all expressions seem to be context-sensitive in various ways. Thus "drink" in, say, "Do you want something to drink?" can sometimes be restricted to alcoholic drinks, other times not, while in still others it might include motor oil (suppose that's the beverage favored by some visiting space aliens). When someone utters "Hand me the green book," various different parts of the book might be relevant, depending on the conversational context: the cover, the spine, the pages, the ink, etc. In particular, as these and countless other examples suggest, it can seem wellnigh impossible to keep all the complexities of speakers' interests from intruding into the study of meaning (cf., e.g. Travis 2008; Sperber and Wilson 1986; Wilson and Sperber 2012; Carston 2002; Gross 2001 and 2005b; Bach 1994; Recanati 2004). One might further tie this pervasive context-sensitivity to a broader (if perhaps amorphous) *flexibility* inherent in natural language, reflected as well in such phenomena mentioned above as vagueness, fiction, and property-mismatch. One might also include various other phenomena for which we lack space, such as some of those that motivate dynamic semantics.

The idea that, in natural languages, pragmatics intrudes into semantics has an august lineage. It was a central theme of so-called ordinary language philosophy and related work (Austin 1961, Strawson 1971, Wittgenstein 1953). It's also consonant with the thought of "ideal language" philosophers, who intended formal languages to *replace* natural languages for certain purposes (Tarski 1983; Russell 1957; Carnap 1950). It was thus a bold step when Davidson (1984) and Montague (1974) suggested that natural languages might be studied as formal languages even regarding their semantics. Current skeptics often credit the insights of ordinary language philosophers—e.g. Chomsky (2000). (Skeptics then differ as to whether these insights merely render descriptive externalist semantics implausible or further suggest the scientific intractability of pragmatics and linguistic intentionality altogether. *Contra* the latter, see, e.g. Sperber and Wilson (1986) and Wilson and Sperber (2012).)

But now how might this idea pose a challenge to externalism? A first worry is simply that the phenomenon of context-sensitivity shows that no semantics can be adequate that assigns expressions an invariant intentional relation to the world; so a two-place word-world relation is inadequate on empirical grounds. But this is too quick. First, perhaps some of the phenomena are not really semantic at all and so don't require any tinkering with the basic externalist framework. For example, they might involve lexical or structural ambiguity (that is, a multiplicity of *expressions* rather than variation in the externalist import of one expression on different occasions), or they might reflect *post*-semantic pragmatic effects, such as conversational implicature, rather than something that must be captured in the expression's standing linguistic meaning. That said, no externalist thinks all the phenomena can be so handled (though for arguments that context-sensitivity is a much more limited phenomenon than has been thought; see Cappelen and Lepore (2005) and Borg (2007, 2012)). The second, more important reply is that externalists, despite the word-world shorthand, in fact do not take the intentional relation to be two-placed. It's standard to include context as a further *relatum*—or various elements of context (for example, the speaker, the time of utterance, etc.; cf. Ludlow 2003b.) On one way of developing the idea, expressions can then still be seen as denoting aspects of the world, but now the aspects they denote—viz., functions from contexts to the world—will be more abstract than one might have thought they would generally be. On other views, only speakers (perhaps also word-tokens) strictly speaking refer and the like, but intentional notions nonetheless play a central role in characterizing the specific contributions of word types.

The fundamental issue here, then, is whether a truth-conditional semantics can adequately and plausibly accommodate the phenomena—where adequacy concerns getting the (contextualized) truth-conditions right, and plausibility concerns getting them right in a way that aligns with speakers' actual semantic competence. (Cf. Pietroski 2003 and Gross 2005b. This plausibility consideration arguably does not apply to Soames (1989) and others who sharply distinguish semantics and accounts of semantic competence. But it is central to those who take an I-language perspective.) Many internalists think not, maintaining instead that expressions are constraints on, or instructions to construct, concepts, and that these word-concept relations are not illuminated by contextualized truth-conditional semantics (Pietroski 2005, Carston 2012). Externalists, for their part, have replied that at least some internalist alternatives over-generate and that, anyway, one must posit contextual parameters in semantics to accommodate other phenomena, such as certain kinds of binding. (On the binding argument, see Stanley and Szabo (2000). For replies, see, e.g. Recanati (2004), Collins (2007), and others surveyed in Sennett (2008). For a more general development of the view, see Stanley (2007), which also reprints Stanley (2002) containing the over-generation charge.) Further, one might try arguing that any internalist proposal that expressions are constraints on, or instructions to construct, concepts *ipso facto* conceives of expressions semantically as functions from contexts to concepts; and insofar as *concepts* bear intentional relations to the world, there would seem no in principle bar to characterizing the truth-conditional contributions of expressions in terms of such a function. If this is right, then the internalist's case would have to rest not on the technical infeasibility of constructing a truth-conditional semantics, but on its lack of explanatory interest.

In a moment, we'll turn to just this objection: that descriptive externalist semantics lacks explanatory interest. But before passing from the context-sensitivity worry, it's worth noting that if it has force, it raises problems as well for *certain* forms of internalism. First, some internalist proposals see words and their meanings, on the one hand, and concepts, on the other, as fairly well aligned (Jackendoff 2002) and would have to replace this one-one mapping with one that's one-many if the contextualist's point is correct. Second, some have attempted to reject intentional relations in semantics, while preserving the structure of extant theories, by construing "true," "refers," and other semantic vocabulary in "deflationist," non-intentional terms (Williams 1999; cf. Gross 2015). On such views, the word "true," for example, does not denote a substantive, explanatory property, but rather has the expressive function of allowing us to indirectly endorse claims we cannot endorse directly—for example, because we don't know what was said ("What Joan said, whatever it was, is true—I trust her"), or because the relevant claims are too numerous ("Every claim of the form 'P or not P' is true"). But if pervasive context-sensitivity prevents truth-conditional semantics from illuminatingly characterizing the semantic properties of words, it does so regardless of whether truth-talk and the like is construed intentionally or in a deflationary manner. Finally, some have suggested recasting truth-conditional semantics in terms of the beliefs, or other mental states, sentences express. For example, instead of a theory that yields such theorems as "'Schnee ist weiss' is true iff snow is white," we might aim to construct theories yielding, for example, "'Schnee ist weiss' expresses the belief that snow is white." (See, e.g. Schroeder (2008), Richard (2015), and Ludlow (2003b, 2011, 2014). The approach is a generalization of familiar proposals for handling sentences that arguably do not describe objective facts in the world or at least whose terms arguably do not denote naturalistically acceptable properties—such as sentences containing moral vocabulary. Indeed, in some cases, the philosophical motivations for such proposals are not unlike some of those canvassed above concerning odd objects.) If it's allowed that the relation of expression is not intentional, then perhaps we can preserve the structure of a truth-conditional semantics without employing notions of truth, reference, and the like. There are technical problems specific to this approach. For example, because not believing something does not entail believing its negation (one might suspend judgment), the semantics of negation must be handled with care. But the point here is just that any problems posed by pervasive context-sensitivity to truth-conditional semantics would again seem to threaten this alternative just as much.

We turn now to our final argument against externalism. It suggests that intentional relations to the world play no role in linguistics' explanatory successes. For example, semantic theories are often said to account for facts about ambiguity. But what explains the fact that "Mary saw the man leaving the school" is three ways ambiguous, while "Mary saw the man from Manchester" is two ways ambiguous, are syntactic constraints on possible meanings, independent of the expressions' worldly intentional relations. Again, our knowledge that "him" in "Homer was impressed with him" is not referentially dependent on "Homer" in no way depends on whether Homer existed or whether we know to whom "Homer" refers, if anyone. The suggestion is that in these and many other cases, externalist semantic theorizing in fact does none of the explanatory work. (See, e.g. Collins (2009), from whom the examples above are adapted. A somewhat different objection is that externalist semantics—at least in its usual guises—can *obscure* phenomena in need of explanation (Yalcin 2014). Perhaps such worries are blunted by the non-exhaustive, ecumenical attitude I have assigned the externalist.) Combined with the previous objection, we arrive at Chomsky's (2000: 132) suspicion that perhaps natural language has only syntax and pragmatics. But a descriptive internalist about semantics need not go so far. Jackendoff (2002), for example, argues for an autonomous internalist semantics that explains, e.g. alternation data not explained by syntax (cf. Chomsky's (2003: 287) remark that he's not opposed to semantics; he just calls it syntax). In any event, successfully showing that externalist semantics plays no explanatory role might not by itself show that words lack intentional relations to the world. It would, however, render suspect the scientific interest of semantic theorizing that emphasizes such relations. But *has* their explanatory vacuity been shown? Showing that *some*, even *many*, explanations do not turn on such relations does not show there are *none* that do. The challenge to externalists is thus to point to such explanatory successes.

4 For externalism

Insofar as semantics can be said to have had some success in pursuing its aims, it should not be surprising if semanticists who understand their field externalistically feel that there are explanatory successes ready to hand. The trick for the internalist is thus to undermine the claim to explanatory power or to argue that the explanations don't turn on an externalist construal of semantic theorizing. We have just noted some examples of the latter sort. How might an externalist more directly advance her cause, and how might an internalist reply?

A first argument for externalist semantics is the light it has shed on a variety of lexical items and constructions—from quantifiers to conditionals to modals, etc. Take generalized quantifier theory, according to which quantifiers denote higher-order properties concerning the size of sets associated with noun phrases (Barwise and Cooper 1981). This approach, which was developed and motivated within a broadly externalist framework, enabled various interesting properties of quantifiers to be uncovered such as conservativity and (non)monotonicity, some of which illuminate other interesting linguistic phenomena that otherwise do not seem obviously tied to representational factors—e.g. that monotone decreasing quantifiers license negative polarity items (Ladusaw 1979; see Chapters 4 and 17). Descriptive internalists must argue that these insights can be absorbed and accommodated into their framework. They will also want to argue that any role of semantic externalist thinking in arriving at these insights was incidental or merely heuristic. A natural move is to suggest, first, that the relevant representational properties are possessed by the concepts to which quantifiers are related, not by the quantifiers themselves (unless one is an internalist who rejects intentionality *tout court*), and second, that the patterns of entailment judgments that the theory aims to explain can flow from constraints built into the semantic instructions to build concepts.

A second argument is that externalist semantics is necessary to explain the success of language use—our success both in communicating and in using communication to achieve further ends. We use language *inter alia* to inform others about how things are in the world. When I say, "I'll leave the keys under the mat," you know where to look and can thereby succeed in finding them. How could there have been this success unless you knew that, in uttering those words, I had said something quite specific about an aspect of the world—viz., that a particular place would have a certain set of keys there at a particular time? And how could you have known that, in uttering those words then, I had said that, unless you knew what those words mean? Finally, how could your words' meaning what they do issue in a speech act with representational content unless they too had content—that is, bore intentional relations to the world? The implied answer is that an explanation of communicative success requires an externalist conception of semantics. This argument can be viewed as an expansion of the textbook motivations for descriptive semantic externalism quoted in our introduction.

One can run this sort of line in two ways (perhaps in both). It may be offered as a partial *causal* explanation of linguistic behavior or as an account of the *rationality*, or *justification*, of linguistic action. To expand briefly on the latter, the thought is that our linguistic behavior is typically a species of intentional action, done for reasons. (This does not require that language users consciously entertain these reasons.) And among the *reasons*—not just the *causes*—that explain why speakers do what they do, and why hearers do what they do in response, are their beliefs about what the uttered words' standing meaning is. It must be noted, however, that there seems to be a mismatch between the semantic knowledge typically cited in causal accounts of linguistic behavior and the semantic knowledge in principle available to supply justification. While the latter can be to a significant extent characterized homophonically, can be warrantedly self-ascribed without reliance on third-person evidence, and is—perhaps must be—accessible to consciousness, the former is typically non-homophonic (even bracketing context-sensitivity), cannot be warrantedly self-ascribed without reliance on third-person evidence, and seems in large part *in*accessible to consciousness (Gross 2010). It's thus unclear that the justificatory version of this line of thought can vindicate scientific externalist semantics.

There are also further replies an internalist can make, even to the *causal* version of the story. The argument assumes that speech acts have intentional content and claims that the best explanation of this assigns intentional content to word types as well. But the assumption that speech acts have intentional content will presumably be denied by those who reject intentionality *tout court*, as we saw Jackendoff seems to do. Less radically, without denying that speech act content has intentional content, an internalist might question the claim that the best explanation of speech acts' having intentional content requires ascribing intentional content to word types.

Why might one think the best explanation does require this? Suppose one thinks the best explanation of speech act content includes plugging contextual values into the parameters supplied by a contextualized statement of truth-conditions (Stanley 2007). One might reasonably take such a truth-conditional account of words' contributions to the determination of speech act content to suffice for holding that word types themselves have intentional content—for example, that they denote the relevant functions from context to the world. But recall that one argument *against* externalism challenges just this picture. It's claimed that pervasive context-sensitivity renders the view at best psychologically implausible. If so, this undermines the externalists' best grounds for inferring externalist semantic properties from speech act content and its role in communicative success.

Of course, externalists might reply by arguing that they have a better take on the relation of semantic properties to speech act content. Stainton (2011: 484, fn. 2), for example, argues that intentional content is needed to explain such negative facts as what we *can't* (readily) say using certain words (cf. the over-generation worry mentioned above):

> That it is very easy to talk about puppies using the Spanish word "perrito," but very hard to refer to chainsaws thereby, is partly explained by the fact that the public word "perrito" is semantically related to puppies. That a person who says "I promise to plant two beeches in your yard tomorrow" in English cannot satisfy their commitments by planting two elms is partly explained by . . . [Stainton's elision] And so on. Thus, referential semantics explains something.

(The emphasis on the terms being part of a public language, however, is orthogonal to our focus.)

They might argue further that, on the internalist's alternative, it's left mysterious how contextually sensitive processing of word types—items *without* intentional content—leads to concepts and thoughts that *do* possess intentional content (assuming again one doesn't deny representationality altogether). Externalist explanations, because they do not have this problem, are at least in that regard better. Some internalists might embrace this mystery, however, favoring a frank admission of our ignorance over what they would consider no good explanation at all. Chomsky (2000), for example, suggests that intentionality might remain a mystery to us; correspondingly, he might not hold out much hope for our coming to understand the complex details that yield intentional content from non-intentional linguistic items. Other internalists are more sanguine that pragmatics and mental intentionality, or at least aspects thereof, may prove scientifically tractable (Sperber and Wilson 1986). In any event, we see again that at least one strand of the externalist/internalist debate is deeply entwined with questions concerning the semantics-pragmatics interface. These issues arise as well with our next argument.

The third argument is that denying words' intentional relations to the world renders mysterious why and how some of the primary data of semantics—truth-value judgments—have the bearing on semantic theorizing that they are taken to have. (Cf. Stanley (2007), who seems to suggest further that truth-value judgments provide the *only* evidence, or at least the only "viable basis" (p. 6), for semantic theorizing. But even just limiting ourselves to judgment data, there are also, for example, the entailment judgments and judgments concerning possible readings to which linguists commonly advert.) The idea might be developed as follows. Language users have intuitions concerning the truth-values of sentences judged against various circumstances, and a semantic theory explains these judgments by attributing semantic knowledge of sentences' truth-conditions—i.e. of in what circumstances sentences would have what truth-value. If semantics did not involve intentional relations, how could it explain how speakers make such judgments, and, if it doesn't, how could those judgments provide any evidence? Further, without such evidence, on what basis could semanticists develop and justify their theories?

A reply is that language users' truth-value judgments concern speech act contents, not the standing semantic properties of sentences and their parts, since it's the former that ultimately matter to communication (Bach 2002). If speakers' judgments do not concern (contextualized) sentential truth-conditions, then it should not be a requirement on semantic theorizing that it assign sentences truth-conditions that by and large match the assignments of sentential truth-conditions (allegedly) displayed by speakers' judgments. The relevant constraint on semantic theorizing, rather, is that it best explain those judgments—and any other relevant data—while meshing with the rest of our theoretical commitments. Or, better, that it *plays a role* in best explaining these judgments and any other relevant data, since the judgments in fact result from the interaction of various aspects of the mind/brain, including whatever aspects are implicated in our navigating the contextual complexities that (some) internalists invoke against externalist linguistic semantics. But if this is how language users' judgments constrain semantic theorizing, then an independent argument is required for the claim that the best explanation requires assigning representational properties to linguistic items.

As with the previous argument, externalists might here complain that internalism leaves it mysterious *how* semantic competence, in concert with whatever else, could explain the judgment data. For, again, it is unclear how *non*-intentional items cause *intentional* items to come into being. Moreover, they might claim that it is required of an inference to the best explanation that it include a sufficiently detailed causal story of how the inferred explanatory stuff causally leads to the data for it (Devitt 2006 and 2010; Fodor and Lepore 2012). However, this requirement of inference to the best explanation is controversial. For example, it's unclear whether it's required by best practices in the physical sciences (Bogen and Woodward, 1988, applied to linguistic theorizing in Gross and Culbertson 2011 and Maynes and Gross 2013).

The worry of non-intentional/intentional causal fit applies generally to forms of semantic internalism that allow mental intentionality. There are also more specific worries that externalists can raise against more specific forms of internalism. (These count as arguments for externalism insofar as supporting an inference to a best explanation involves showing that one's preferred explanation is better than the rest.) We have already encountered some: deflationism and expressivism do not of themselves address arguments from pervasive context-sensitivity, nor do forms of internalism that identify meanings with concepts; handling negation is a delicate matter for expressivism. It's beyond our scope to explore the specifics of internalist alternatives further. We note only that, like any theory, an internalist semantics has to earn its keep.

5 Concluding remark

Our intention has been to offer an overview, not to advocate a position. But we may conclude by underscoring two themes for which our discussion has made a case. First, externalism-internalism debates gain in clarity when distinct strands are separated. Indeed, it is possible that at least some writers have been at cross-purposes, even perhaps construing our more specific focus—descriptive semantic externalism—in varying ways. Second, the debate between descriptive externalists and internalists is bound up at crucial junctures with debates concerning the semantics-pragmatics border and interface.

It might be suggested that reflection on these themes points in opposite directions. Distinguishing among externalist claims creates room for a kind of externalism that preserves the results and perspective of much mainstream semantics while yet meshing with the psychologistic motivations that drive various forms of internalism. Pervasive context-sensitivity, on the other hand, if it cannot be adequately addressed within an externalist semantic framework, arguably suggests the need for semantic theorizing to head in a different direction—albeit one that would hopefully absorb the structural insights of whatever idealizations it turns out externalist semantics has made. No doubt the situation will become clearer with further first-order semantic theorizing.

Acknowledgments

Thanks to John Collins, Paul Pietroski, Kyle Rawlins, and Chris Vogel for discussion, as well as members of my lab meeting. Thanks also to the editor for his patience, encouragement, and feedback.

Further reading

Chierchia, Gennaro, and Sally McConnell-Ginet 1990. *Meaning and grammar: an introduction to semantics*. Cambridge: MIT Press. (Second edition published in 2000.)
Provides a textbook discussion of many of these issues, ultimately defending a version of our externalist thesis while attempting to accommodate internalist motivations and theorizing.
Elbourne, Paul 2011. *Meaning: a slim guide to semantics*. Oxford: Oxford University Press.
A briefer, chattier introduction, with internalist leanings.
Lewis, David 1970. "General semantics." *Synthese* 22: 18–67, and 1975 "Languages and language." In K. Gunderson (ed.), *Language, mind and knowledge. Minnesota studies in the philosophy of science*, vol. 7. Minneapolis: University of Minnesota Press, 3–35.
These papers contain a classic articulation of an externalist perspective—but see Chomsky (1986, 2000) and Jackendoff (2002) for an internalist counter-balance.
Sperber, Dan, and Deirdre Wilson 1986. *Relevance: communication and cognition*. Oxford: Blackwell. (Second revised edition, 1995.)
A central source for pragmatic intrusion into semantics; Stanley (2007) treats these matters externalistically.

References

Austin, John 1961. *Philosophical papers*. Oxford: Oxford University Press. (Third edition published in 1979.)
Bach, Emmon 1986. "Natural language metaphysics." In R. Barcan Marcus, G. Dorn, and P. Weingartner (eds), *Logic, methodology, and philosophy of science* VII. Amsterdam: North-Holland, 573–95.
Bach, Emmon 1989. *Informal lectures on formal semantics*. Albany, NY: SUNY Press.
Bach, Kent 1994. Conversational impliciture. *Mind & Language* 9: 124–62.
Bach, Kent 2002. "Seemingly semantic intuitions." In J. Keim Campbell, M. O'Rourke, and D. Shier (eds), *Meaning and truth*. New York: Seven Bridges Press, 21–33.
Barwise, Jon, and Robin Cooper 1981. Generalized quantifiers and natural language. *Linguistics and Philosophy* 4: 159–219.
Bogen, James, and James Woodward 1988. Saving the appearances. *The Philosophical Review* 97: 303–52.
Bontly, Thomas 1998. Individualism and the nature of syntactic states. *British Journal for the Philosophy of Science* 49: 557–74.
Borg, Emma 2007. *Minimal semantics*. Oxford: Oxford University Press.
Borg, Emma 2012. *Pursuing meaning*. Oxford: Oxford University Press.

Brandom, Robert 1994. *Making it explicit: reasoning, representing, and discursive commitment.* Cambridge: Harvard University Press.
Burge, Tyler 1979. Individualism and the mental. *Midwest Studies in Philosophy* 4: 73–121.
Burge, Tyler 2003. "Reply to Chomsky." In M. Hahn and B. Ramberg (eds), *Reflections and replies: essays on the philosophy of Tyler Burge.* Cambridge: MIT Press, 451–70.
Burge, Tyler 2010. *Origins of objectivity.* Oxford: Oxford University Press.
Cappelen, Herman, and Ernie Lepore 2005. *Insensitive semantics.* Oxford: Blackwell.
Carnap, Rudolf 1950. *Logical foundations of probability.* Chicago: University of Chicago Press.
Carston, Robyn 2002. *Thoughts and utterances: the pragmatics of explicit communication.* Oxford: Blackwell.
Carston, Robyn 2012. Word meaning and concept expressed. *The Linguistics Review* 29: 607–23.
Chierchia, Gennaro, and Sally McConnell-Ginet 1990. *Meaning and grammar: an introduction to semantics.* Cambridge: MIT Press. (Second edition published in 2000.)
Chomsky, Noam 1975. *Essays on form and interpretation.* New York: North-Holland.
Chomsky, Noam 1986. *Knowledge of language.* New York: Praeger.
Chomsky, Noam 2000. *New horizons in the study of language and mind.* Cambridge: Cambridge University Press.
Chomsky, Noam 2003. "Reply to Ludlow." In L. Antony and N. Hornstein (eds), *Chomsky and his critics.* Oxford: Blackwell, 287–95.
Churchland, Paul 1981. Eliminative materialism and the propositional attitudes. *Journal of Philosophy* 78: 67–90.
Collins, John 2007. Syntax, more or less. *Mind* 116: 805–50.
Collins, John 2009. Methodology, not metaphysics: against semantic externalism. *Proceedings of the Aristotelian Society Supplementary Volume* 83: 53–69.
Collins, John 2011. *The unity of linguistic meaning.* Oxford: Oxford University Press.
Davidson, Donald 1984. *Inquiries into truth and interpretation.* Oxford: Oxford University Press.
Devitt, Michael 2006. *Ignorance of language.* Oxford: Oxford University Press.
Devitt, Michael 2010. Linguistic intuitions revisited. *British Journal for the Philosophy of Science* 61: 833–65.
Elbourne, Paul 2011. *Meaning: a slim guide to semantics.* Oxford: Oxford University Press.
Everett, Anthony, and Thomas Hofweber 2000. *Empty names, fiction, and the puzzles of non-existence.* Stanford: CSLI Publications.
Evans, Gareth 1983. *The varieties of reference.* Oxford: Oxford University Press.
Fodor, Jerry, and Ernie Lepore 2012. "What sort of science is semantics?" In G. Peter and R.-M. Krauße (eds), *Selbstbeobachtung der modernen Gesellschaft und die neuen Grenzen des Sozialen.* Dordrecht: Springer, 217–26.
Forbes, Graeme 2012. "Some examples of Chomsky's." In R. Schantz (ed.), *Prospects for meaning.* Berlin: de Gruyter, 121–42.
Frege, Gottlob 1918. Der Gedanke. Eine Logische Untersuchung. *Beiträge zur Philosophie des deutschen Idealismus* I: 58–77. Translated as "Thoughts," by P. Geach and R. Stoothoff, in his *Collected papers on mathematics, logic, and philosophy* (B. McGuinness, ed.), Oxford: Blackwell, 1984, 351–72.
Gross, Steven 2001. *Essays on linguistic context-sensitivity and its philosophical significance.* London: Routledge.
Gross, Steven 2005a. The nature of semantics: on Jackendoff's arguments. *The Linguistic Review* 22: 249–70.
Gross, Steven 2005b. Context-sensitive truth-theoretic accounts of semantic competence. *Mind & Language* 20: 68–102.
Gross, Steven 2006. Can empirical theories of semantic competence really help limn the structure of reality? *Nous* 40: 43–81.
Gross, Steven 2007. Reply to Jackendoff. *The Linguistics Review* 24: 423–9.
Gross, Steven 2010. Knowledge of meaning, conscious and unconscious. In B. Armour-Garb, D. Patterson, and J. Woodbridge (eds), *Meaning, understanding, and knowledge* (Vol. 5: The Baltic International Yearbook of Cognition, Logic and Communication), 1–44.

Gross, Steven 2015. "Does true's expressive role preclude deflationary Davidsonian semantics?" In S. Gross, N. Tebben, and M. Williams (eds), *Meaning without representation*. Oxford: Oxford University Press.

Gross, Steven, and Jennifer Culbertson 2011. Revisited linguistic intuitions. *British Journal for the Philosophy of Science* 62: 639–56.

Heck, Richard 2006. "Idiolects." In J. Thomson and A. Byrne (eds), *Content and modality: themes from the philosophy of Robert Stalnaker*. Oxford: Oxford University Press, 61–92.

Heim, Irene, and Angelika Kratzer 1998. *Semantics in generative grammar*. Oxford: Blackwell.

Higginbotham, James 1985. On semantics. *Linguistic Inquiry* 16: 547–93.

Jackendoff, Ray 2002. *Foundations of language*. Oxford: Oxford University Press.

Kaplan, David 1989. "Afterthoughts." In J. Almog, J. Perry, and H. Wettstein (eds), *Themes from Kaplan*. Oxford: Oxford University Press, 565–614.

Kennedy, Christopher, and Jason Stanley 2009. On "Average." *Mind* 118: 583–646.

Kripke, Saul 2013. *Reference and existence: the John Locke lectures*. Oxford: Oxford University Press.

Ladusaw, William 1979. *Polarity sensitivity as inherent scope relations*. PhD dissertation, University of Texas, Austin.

Larson, Richard, and Gabriel Segal 1995. *Knowledge of meaning*. Cambridge: MIT Press.

Lepore, Ernie, and Kirk Ludwig 2005. *Donald Davidson: meaning, truth, language, and reality*. Oxford: Oxford University Press.

Lewis, David 1970. General semantics. *Synthese* 22: 18–67.

Lewis, David 1975. "Languages and language." In K. Gunderson (ed.), *Language, mind and knowledge. Minnesota studies in the philosophy of science*, vol. 7. Minneapolis: University of Minnesota Press, 3–35.

Loewer, Barry 1996. "A guide to naturalizing semantics." In B. Hale and C. Wright (eds), *The Blackwell companion to the philosophy of language*. Oxford: Blackwell, 108–26.

Ludlow, Peter 2003a. "Externalism, logical form, and linguistic intentions." In A. Barber (ed.), *Epistemology of language*. Oxford: Oxford University Press, 399–414.

Ludlow, Peter 2003b. "Referential semantics for I-language?" In L. Antony and N. Hornstein (eds), *Chomsky and his critics*. Oxford: Blackwell, 140–61.

Ludlow, Peter 2011. *The philosophy of generative linguistics*. Oxford: Oxford University Press.

Ludlow, Peter 2014. "Recursion, legibility, use." In T. Roeper and M. Speas (eds), *Recursion: complexity in cognition*. Dordrecht: Springer, 89–112.

Maynes, Jeffrey, and Steven Gross 2013. Linguistic intuitions. *Philosophy Compass* 8: 714–30.

Montague, Richard 1974. *Formal philosophy*. New Haven, CT: Yale University Press.

Pelletier, Francis Jeffrey 2011. Descriptive metaphysics, natural language metaphysics, Sapir-Whorf, and all that stuff: evidence from the mass-count distinction. *The Baltic International Yearbook of Cognition, Logic and Communication, Volume 6: Formal Semantics and Pragmatics: Discourse, Context, and Models*, 1–46.

Pietroski, Paul 2003. "The character of natural language semantics." In A. Barber (ed.), *Epistemology of language*. Oxford: Oxford University Press, 217–56.

Pietroski, Paul 2005. "Meaning before truth." In G. Preyer and G. Peter (eds), *Contextualism in philosophy: knowledge, meaning, and truth*. Oxford: Oxford University Press, 255–302.

Putnam, Hilary 1975. "The meaning of 'meaning'." In K. Gunderson (ed.), *Language, mind and knowledge. Minnesota studies in the philosophy of science*, vol. 7. Minneapolis: University of Minnesota Press, 131–93.

Quine, Willard van Orman 1960. *Word and object*. Cambridge: MIT Press.

Recanati, Francois 2004. *Literal meaning*. Cambridge: Cambridge University Press.

Rey, Georges 2006. "The intentional inexistence of language—but not cars." In R. Stainton (ed.), *Contemporary debates in cognitive science*. Oxford: Blackwell, 237–55.

Richard, Mark 2015. "What would an expressivist semantics be?" In S. Gross, N. Tebben, and M. Williams (eds), *Meaning without representation*. Oxford: Oxford University Press.

Russell, Bertrand 1957. Mr. Strawson on referring. *Mind* 66: 385–9.

Schroeder, Mark 2008. *Being for: evaluating the semantic program of expressivism*. Oxford: Oxford University Press.
Segal, Gabriel 2000. *A slim book about narrow content*. Cambridge: MIT Press.
Sennett, Adam 2008. The binding argument and pragmatic enrichment, or, why philosophers care even more than weathermen about "raining." *Philosophy Compass* 3: 135–57.
Soames, Scott 1989. Semantics and semantic competence. *Philosophical Perspectives* 3: 575–96.
Sperber, Dan, and Deirdre Wilson 1986. *Relevance: communication and cognition*. Oxford: Blackwell. (2nd revised edition, 1995.)
Stainton, Robert 2006. "Meaning and reference: some Chomskian themes." In E. Lepore and B. Smith (eds), *The Oxford handbook of philosophy of language*. Oxford: Oxford University Press, 913–40.
Stainton, Robert 2011. In defense of public languages. *Linguistics and Philosophy* 34: 479–88.
Stalnaker, Robert 1997. "Reference and necessity." In B. Hale and C. Wright (eds), *The Blackwell companion to the philosophy of language*. Oxford: Blackwell, 534–54.
Stanley, Jason 2002. Making it articulated. *Mind & Language* 17: 149–68.
Stanley, Jason 2007. *Language in context*. Oxford: Oxford University Press.
Stanley, Jason, and Zoltan Szabo 2000. On quantifier domain restriction. *Mind & Language* 15: 219–61.
Strawson, Peter 1971. *Logico-linguistic papers*. London: Methuen.
Tarski, Alfred 1983. *Logic, semantics, metamathematics*, second edition, ed. by J. Corcoran. Indianapolis, IN: Hackett.
Travis, Charles 2008. *Occasion-sensitivity*. Oxford: Oxford University Press.
Wiggins, David 1997. Languages as social objects. *Philosophy* 72: 499–524.
Williams, Michael 1999. Meaning and deflationary truth. *Journal of Philosophy* 96: 545–64.
Wilson, Deirdre, and Dan Sperber 2012. *Meaning and relevance*. Cambridge: Cambridge University Press.
Wittgenstein, Ludwig 1953. *Philosophical investigations*. Oxford: Blackwell.
Yalcin, Seth 2014. "Semantics and metasemantics in the context of generative grammar." In A. Burgess and B. Sherman (eds), *Metasemantics: new essays on the foundations of meaning*. Oxford: Oxford University Press.

Related topics

Chapter 2, Internalist semantics; Chapter 4, Foundations of formal semantics; Chapter 11, Contextual adjustment of meaning; Chapter 17, Negation and polarity.

2
Internalist semantics
Meaning, conceptualization and expression

Nick Riemer

1 Introduction

For externalists, semantic content – meaning – consists in the connection between language and the external environment: words' meaning, roughly speaking, *is* their reference to the world (see Chapter 1). Classic externalist arguments notwithstanding (Putnam 1975; Burge 1979; Kripke 1980), there clearly must be mechanisms internal to people that make it possible for us to use language to refer. Equally clearly, those mechanisms should be sought in the head. Beyond that point, however, consensus is lacking: not only is the internalism/externalism question the subject of ongoing debate within cognitive science and philosophy (Farkas 2008; Mendola 2008; Egan 1992, 1995), but the details of the various internalist accounts of meaning within linguistics itself are all contested.

Nevertheless, internalist linguistic semantics generally speaking assumes that mental representations called *concepts* are key parts of the mechanisms linking mind to world. This apparently innocuous assumption is foundational to lexical semantics in particular and is widely shared among researchers who agree on little else (Langacker 1997; Lakoff 1987; Bierwisch and Schreuder 1992; Allan 2001; Jackendoff 2002; Wierzbicka 1999; Sperber and Wilson 1995; Evans and Green 2006; Pietroski 2003). As we will see, however, it represents only one of the theoretical possibilities within a broadly internalist approach to meaning. There is a sense in which, construed internalistically, meaning might not have anything to do with concepts at all, despite current assumptions.

We will shortly clarify just what is involved in the claim that meaning is a matter of concepts. First, however, it is worth asking where the very idea of a concept comes from. In the case of semantics, as elsewhere, paying attention to the history of basic notions will allow us to avoid naive overconfidence in the obviousness of our starting assumptions. An earlier philosophical tradition associated with British Empiricism spoke not of concepts but of "ideas" as the relevant mental entities underlying thought and communication (Locke 1691 [1979]): "concept", indeed, comes from the Latin verb meaning "comprehend intellectually, imagine, think". The postulation of "ideas" and later of "concepts" as part of the explanation of human intelligence reflects a particular psychological folk-taxonomy which appears to not be universal by any means. This taxonomy assumes a categorical division between cognitive and affect-based internal processes – "thought" and "feeling" – with concepts, obviously, falling uniquely on the side of "thought". However, as documented by Lillard (1998), among others, even a non-exhaustive survey reveals a number of cultures in which "thought" and "feeling" are either not distinguished, or in which "thought" does not exist as a named psychological state at all. Outlandish as this strikes Western ears, the fact that a thinking–feeling contrast cannot always be found outside the bubble of our own first-world cultures reminds us that the theoretical cuts we inherit from our pretheoretical background should not be taken for granted. This is even more the case since, as Waskan (2006) emphasizes, the traditional folk-psychology familiar to speakers of "standard Average European" provides nothing like a satisfying explanation of a host of common mental phenomena, and should not therefore be the object of unconditional theoretical allegiance. (In section 3.3 below we will consider the relation of cognition and emotion in the generation of linguistic meaning.)

For the sake of clarity, two uses of the term "concept" in semantics need to be kept apart. In one sense, "concept" is used simply to refer to *whatever* psychological structures support meaning. This "weak" use entails no commitments about the nature of the structures in question. We know that whatever is discovered about the nature of human mentality, we will always be able to attribute "concepts" to language users as part of the explanation of their linguistic capacities – just as we will always be able to describe as a "disease" any disorder that compromises an organism's health, whether it is the result of an infection, hereditary condition, organ damage, psychological condition, or some new kind of physical dysfunction yet to be discovered.

This weak sense of "concept" is not the one of interest here. Because our goal is to clarify the psychological assumptions underlying specific proposals about the nature of semantic content, we have to operate with a substantive definition of "concept" that will stand or fall empirically, and that is not merely a cover-all term for "whatever it is in the head that constitutes meaning". In section 2 we will delineate the characteristics of concepts as they are mostly assumed in linguistic semantics, and illustrate the way in which concept-attribution functions as an explanation of semantic facts. Section 3 discusses criticisms of this conception. Section 4 considers alternatives to concepts and indicates possible future directions for conceptualist research in semantics.

2 Features of concepts

Word meanings are the clearest examples of concepts. However, language is just one among the many cognitive capacities that concepts are intended to explain. On the standardly assumed picture, concepts are the "units" of rational thought and so at the origin of our most elementary intellectual capacities: unless we possessed the appropriate concepts, we could not identify, sort, name, or imagine the objects of our environment, or reason, plan, or communicate about them. In this section we will explore some of the properties traditionally attributed to concepts. These properties are often not explicit in linguistic semantic theories. Nevertheless, they are presupposed by them, and they are typically the objects of direct theorization in related disciplines within the cognitive sciences.

2.1 Conceptualization and perception

In the most general terms, concepts can be thought of as mental instructions or rules for binding the representations of different properties together. The concept RAINBOW, for instance, binds together such properties as "coloured", "in the sky", "striped", "curved", and "occurs after rain" into a single representation. Only if someone possesses the concept RAINBOW can they identify actual rainbows and reason and communicate about them. In contrast, there is no mental instruction to bind together the properties "coloured", "observed last week", and "reminiscent of the art of Anish Kapoor" – even though such properties might well present themselves at the same time in the same context – since there is no unitary concept that contains those properties (although, as with any arbitrary concatenation of properties, we could always create such a concept and stipulate a name for it). In binding properties in this way, concepts establish categories which group individual diverse objects together as instances of the same kind of thing. Individual rainbows will differ in intensity, length, and other phenomenal properties but they will all belong to the category RAINBOW because they possess the necessary properties for the satisfaction of that concept.

This way of thinking about concepts immediately raises an important issue, namely the question of how perceptual signals – in the case of a rainbow, patterns of retinal stimulation – make their way into the conceptual system. What mechanisms, in other words, govern the "transduction" of perceptual information in such a way that it can interface with thought? Without a detailed answer, accounts of conceptualization have a major explanatory gap, since they fail to specify how the cognitive system "decides" when the various features that constitute a concept are sufficiently present. Consider the concept BOTTLE. The kinds of perceptual information that can trigger this concept are staggeringly diverse: the objects we call "bottles" are of an almost unlimited variety of appearances and can be apprehended from many different angles and under very different visual conditions. Two people talking about the same bottle on a table in front of them will necessarily be observing it from different perspectives and will therefore be in qualitatively different perceptual states. Yet these enormously divergent kinds of perceptual information all somehow get connected to the concept BOTTLE in a reliable enough way for people to reason and communicate about bottles in the way they do.

Just how perceptual signals are converted ("transduced") into conceptual information is poorly understood, even for simple objects (see e.g. Sudre et al. 2012; Hummel 2013; Peterson and Kimchi 2013; Di Lollo 2012; Palmer 1999). What is clear is that in the absence of a solid explanation of transduction, traditional accounts of concepts remain indeterminate in significant respects. We might imagine, for example, that one of the properties bound in the concept BOTTLE is "has a neck". But unless we can operationalize recognition of this property in a way that does not tacitly rely on the very cognitive capacities we are trying to understand, we have not achieved any explanation worthy of the name. A genuine solution of the transduction problem would give us a description of the process by which the conceptual system recognizes bottles that could be simulated computationally. Like our minds, a computer would token the concept BOTTLE if and only if it was presented with an actual, neck-possessing bottle – precisely by being able to automatically recognize the presence of the relevant BOTTLE-constituting properties. We are a very long way from being able to do this. When analysing BOTTLE as involving the property "has a neck", we are tacitly relying on our own conceptual abilities to do all the work for us by identifying what does and does not count as neck-possession. Without a formal account of this property, our "theory" is therefore entirely beholden to the very conceptual ability it purports to explain (see Chapter 8).

This explanatory deficit is particularly serious when concepts are enlisted as part of a theory of human linguistic ability. One of the tasks of a semantic theory is to explain acts of reference. Yet without an account of transduction, we are missing a crucial part of the explanation of how speakers and hearers make the link between what they see and the language they use to refer to it.

2.2 Concepts, information, and invariance

As we have already noted, concepts are traditionally seen as uniquely belonging to the intellectual, rational dimension of human subjectivity. This has a significant consequence on theories of linguistic meaning: since meanings are identified with concepts, they are always taken to be constituents of thoughts, not constituents of feelings or emotions. The validity of this assumption will only be confirmed if it turns out that concepts as traditionally conceived are able to provide a complete account of the human intellectual capacities they are intended to explain and that non-rational factors are consequently explanatorily redundant. Since we do not have anywhere near a complete account of human intellectual capacities, this demonstration has certainly not yet been made.

We cannot capture the rationality of concepts without referring to their informational or representational role. The reason that concepts represent such a key psychological resource in those organisms that possess them is arguably that they allow the *representation* of the organism's environment (Fodor 1975, 1981; Pylyshyn 1984). For the purposes of this discussion, x represents or conveys information about y if x is a *veridical indicator* of y – if, given x, one can draw many appropriate conclusions about y that one could not otherwise draw. A passport photograph represents its subject because it licenses many true inferences about it: if the photograph shows a woman's face, then we are justified in concluding that its subject is a woman. Concepts stand in a relation of accurate representation to, and thus constitute information about, their referents.

The ability to manipulate mental representations is a crucial psychological advantage for any organism fortunate enough to possess it. The correct analysis of this ability forms the essential topic of controversy between externalists and internalists in the philosophy of mind and language (see e.g. Wikforss 2008; Egan 1992, 1995), and is rich in consequences for linguistics. Externalists about concepts believe that how a concept is individuated, and what it represents, is a matter of the way it is connected to its external referents. According to one influential strain of externalist theorizing, x represents y if x is triggered by the presence of y (Fodor 1987, 1990). The full story is considerably more complicated than this, since we can of course both entertain mental representations (concepts) of things that are not immediately present, and sometimes mistakenly entertain concepts that ought not to have been triggered. For instance, the concept STRAWBERRY JAM might be triggered by raspberry jam when I mistakenly have the thought "this is strawberry jam" in the presence of raspberry jam. Nevertheless, the idea that meaning consists in an essentially causal or other law-like link between mental symbols and their referents is a key commitment of externalist semantics (see Chapter 1).

For internalists, by contrast, the meaningfulness of mental representations does not derive from any causal or other law-like connection to real-world referents, but from the representations' own intrinsic properties. For example, proponents of one species of internalism, the computational theory of mind (Pylyshyn 1984), hold that it is the *formal*, *computational* properties of the way that mental symbols are coded that underlies their ability to convey information about the world. Consider for example the concept FIRE. This concept must be of such a kind as to license the inference *if this is fire, then it is hot*. On an internalist account, this could either be done because the concept FIRE contains the concept HOT, as is assumed in most decompositional theories of conceptual content in linguistics (see Chapter 12), or because the conceptual system licenses the inference from FIRE to HOT, as in so-called inferential role theories (for both stories, see the discussion in Fodor 2008). What makes these stories internalist is that neither depends on any intrinsic connection between the concept FIRE and actual instances of fire. Certainly, speakers *use* the word *fire* to refer to actual fire and, as it happens, their concept FIRE does reflect the actual properties of fire itself. But on both the decompositional and the inferential role account, these representational properties are the result of purely formal characteristics of the underlying concept: the fact that one concept is contained in another, or the fact that a particular chain of inference is marked as valid. This is exactly analogous to the way in which the purely formal arrangement of zeros and ones in strings of software code support that code's ability to symbolize the functions visible to the user of a computer application.

Internalists and externalists therefore both place central importance on concepts' representational or informational character. For externalists, representation is constituted by concepts' causal or other law-like connection to the actual, objective aspects of the world they pick out. For internalists, representation occurs because concepts intrinsically symbolize those aspects without having any necessary causal or other relation to them. In both cases, the concept is objectively correlated with its referent – either by being caused by or otherwise nomologically linked to it, or by symbolizing it in such a way that the concept supports veridical inferences about its referent.

In both cases, the properties of concepts reflect the way things actually are: it would be unthinkable to propose that our FIRE concept functioned in such a way as to license the inference *if this is fire, then it is a solid*. Concepts are, and must be, beholden to the objective state of the actual world, because only in that case can we deploy them to successfully reason about and plan our actions. If the information that fire is hot isn't made available in my conceptual structure, then I won't be able to plan my interactions with fire accurately: I may, for instance, think that I can touch it safely, or that I cannot use it to cook food. Clearly, there must be a basic fit between the conceptual system and the environment its possessors must survive in.

An important consequence of the representational character of concepts is that they are taken to be invariant – in all essential respects – from one individual to another, and within the one individual over time. Since concepts reflect the actual way the world objectively is, they must, like the world itself, be the same for everyone. Since the body's physical structure determines a similar array of affordances (interactional possibilities), it is plausible to imagine that the psychological structures that govern action in healthy humans must be essentially similar, at least at the level of grain on which they control action. Whatever the differences in how two different agents do so, they must both represent fire as non-solid and (other things being equal) hot. The environment is the same for everyone, so the conceptualizations with which we control our interactions with it must also ultimately be identical.

What goes for non-linguistic cognition also goes for language. Speakers can only coordinate their linguistic action on the world successfully if they share a similar enough way of using words to refer to aspects of the environment, and if the factual knowledge they have of referents is, in essential respects, shared. Different individuals must not only have congruent internal knowledge of fire (the thing); they must use the *word* "fire" in highly similar patterns of reference and inference if it is to serve as a useful tool of coordinated action. The assertion *the house is on fire* will only serve its purpose if the thoughts it produces in the hearer are sufficiently similar to the thoughts that prompted it in the speaker. The possibilities of successful, coordinated action in the world require, in other words, an identity in language-world relations between individuals (and, for similar reasons, within the same individual over time).

A subsidiary question raised by our received picture of conceptualization concerns the extent to which it is possible to distinguish any distinctively linguistic information within the general stock of concepts with which we think. Words, it is standardly accepted, label (configurations of) concepts. But many investigators have thought that there is something wrong about declaring that the *meaning* of a given word – say, *rainbow* – includes *all* the conceptual information that we have stocked in long-term memory about the word's referents. Everyone has had different experiences of different rainbows, and will therefore access slightly different sets of concepts. But it seems wrong to say that we do not still share a single meaning for the *word* "rainbow". So perhaps it is possible to separate out an essential core of information which *all* speakers must share in order to count as having the *linguistic meaning* RAINBOW, as distinct from the world knowledge we have about rainbows? A now rather old-fashioned way of describing this putative purely linguistic information is as *dictionary meaning*, in contrast to the broader stock of *encyclopaedic* concepts associated with the referent. If such dictionary meaning exists, no one has yet managed to define it to the satisfaction of competent experts – either in the case of *rainbow* or in that of any other word (see the Introduction to the present volume and Chapter 12 for further remarks).

On the other hand, if it is impossible to make a principled distinction between "dictionary" and "encyclopaedic" information, then we must relax the standard definition of "communication" as the exchange of the *same* thoughts from speaker to hearer. If your and my concepts of "rainbow" are slightly different, then we can no longer claim to be sharing them perfectly when we use the word *rainbow* to communicate. This relaxation may appear innocent, but it is rich in consequences: once we admit that the conceptualizations underlying a single word may not fully coincide between members of the same speech community, we are no longer entitled to assume that apparent identities of language use reflect the same underlying conceptualizations. You and I may use *rainbow* to refer to the same kind of thing, but perhaps we do so in virtue of slightly different underlying conceptualizations – a possibility that there are other, more general reasons to take seriously.

2.3 Explanatory autonomy

The last feature of concepts we will address is not one that we know they possess: it is a *potential* feature that they may or may not turn out to have. Nevertheless, it is worth exploring since it concerns the place of meaning as a phenomenon within the science of the mind, and reveals some fundamental characteristics of semantic theorizing. The feature is *explanatory autonomy*. The postulation of concepts is justified by the hypothesis that our rational capacities are open to analysis on a distinctive, autonomous *cognitive* level of explanation – that is, a level fundamentally different from that of electrochemical brain processes on the one hand, and that of the common-sense, folk-psychological categories we use to talk about meaning and the mind informally on the other (on levels in psychological explanation, see Marr 1982).

A commitment to the explanatory autonomy of concepts involves acknowledging that the facts that we characterize in conceptual terms on the cognitive level will not prove to be reducible to (or to supervene on) facts of any other kind. As it happens, many linguists apparently assume the opposite: they believe that the language-related phenomena presently characterized using the tools of theoretical linguistics will in the future yield to an account couched in quite different terms – those of neurophysiology. Linguistics will, as a result, be entirely superseded, and therefore decidedly *not* explanatorily autonomous. However, it is not at all clear that such a reduction is possible. We will explore this issue in the following paragraphs.

It is occasionally the case in science that an existing theoretical description can be entirely superseded by one of a greater degree of detail and power on a lower level. In this case we speak of the first theory being *reduced* to the second (Hooker 1981; Churchland 1986). Many facts about the behaviour of light, such as its propagation, reflection, and refraction, can be explained by classical optics (for details see chapter 7 of Churchland 1986). However, it turns out that all these effects completely depend on facts about electromagnetic radiation. After the advent of Maxwell's theory of electromagnetism, optics need no longer be invoked, since everything we can explain using the theoretical tools of optics can also be explained electromagnetically. Furthermore – and crucially – the theory of electromagnetism relates to microstructural properties of the physical world and therefore reveals more fundamental determinants of the facts previously described in optical terms. Classical optics is therefore said to be reduced to electromagnetism. (Another example of reduction is that of thermodynamics to statistical mechanics.)

There are, however, many explanatory situations where no reduction is possible. This is regularly the case with the so-called *special sciences* (Fodor 1974); that is, those sciences that only apply to some particular aspect of nature – as opposed to physics, which applies to everything. Geology, neuroscience, and organic chemistry are all special sciences. Linguistics – if it is a science at all (see Introduction) – is clearly a special science, since it only applies to language. To appreciate why reduction isn't usually feasible for the special sciences, we need to recognize the role that generalization plays in scientific explanation. Science works by identifying certain general classes of phenomena that obey distinctive regularities, which are stated in the "laws" of the science in question. Philosophers refer to these general classes of phenomena that figure in laws as *natural kinds*. Planets are natural kinds for the purposes of Kepler's laws of planetary motion, genes are natural kinds for Mendel's laws of inheritance, and certain types of liquid are natural kinds for Poiseuille's equation (which describes Newtonian liquid-flow through pipes).

The possibility of reduction turns on the question of whether the natural kinds that figure in higher-level theories can also be identified in the lower-level theories to which they are to be reduced. Whether this is possible in science is often a matter of debate. There are, however, many cases where it is obvious that any such reduction, if attempted, would be unlikely to succeed. To illustrate this, let us consider the prospects for reducing a future theory of human behaviour to physics. We will confine ourselves to a very narrow subset of human behaviour – that manifested on tennis courts. To play tennis, participants must consciously follow the rules of the game. We can therefore say an enormous amount about what happens on tennis courts by referring to the explicit rules of tennis. These rules can be interpreted as a partial theory of tennis-court behaviour, since they allow us to state quite robust regularities: the server only has two chances to hit the ball over the net; if the ball bounces twice on the court then it is served again, and certain adjustments are made to the scores of the players; if the ball lands outside the line of the court then either the server serves again or the game is over, and so on. These rules certainly don't exhaustively describe how people behave on tennis courts – they don't, for example, have anything to say about when a player will cough, or trip, or wipe their brow, or about the myriad activities that occur on tennis courts *other* than games of tennis. They are also subject to all kinds of conditions: for instance, if the server is injured after a first serve, there won't be a second one. Nevertheless, they express something essential to the game of tennis. No explanation of what is happening on a tennis court could avoid appealing to them.

Note, however, that this aspect of a future theory of human behaviour could in no way be *reduced* to the laws of physics. There are a large number of physically different actions that constitute, for example, holding a racquet: this will differ in any number of physical parameters (the hand used, the precise configuration and force of the grip, the physical differences between different players' hands). Holding the racquet is a natural kind for the purposes of the rules of tennis – which require that the racquet be held horizontally in one hand, not vertically in both, as one holds a cricket bat – but it certainly isn't for those of physics: there is no single physical description, in terms of the fundamental constituents of matter, that we could possibly advance which would capture all and only those events that constitute holding a tennis racquet.

As argued by Fodor and others, psychological abilities, including language, are like this. It seems not to be possible, at this stage at least, to localize semantic representation to any particular brain region (Hinzen and Poeppel 2011), even though the angular gyrus of the left inferior parietal lobe appears to be particularly implicated (Binder et al. 2009).

Another way of putting this is to say that psychological states have the property of *multiple realizability* (Funkhouser 2007). This means that there are a variety of different brain states which instantiate any one of them. There may be no unique neurophysiological signature for the mental state one is in when, for instance, understanding the word *spoon*: the brain mechanisms corresponding to this psychological state differ from individual from individual, and within one individual over time. Whether psychological states are in fact multiply realizable is currently controversial (Bechtel and Mundale 1999; Aizawa and Gillett 2009). If they are, we have a strong argument for the explanatory autonomy of the conceptual level of explanation. Once we have identified a particular semantic phenomenon – say, the fact that a particular verb means "hear" – we can draw various conclusions about other aspects of its semantics – for instance, we can conclude that it may develop an extra sense meaning "touch", but not one meaning "see" (Viberg 1984) – but we cannot – at the moment, and perhaps ever – reduce it to any kind of neurophysiological fact. If this situation persists, semantic facts as characterized on the cognitive level will retain explanatory autonomy. If it does not, then semantics will eventually melt away into neurophysiology, gloriously martyring any remaining linguistic semanticists on the altar of scientific progress.

3 Critiques of internalist semantics

In this section we discuss some of the serious critiques of internalist semantics that any proponent of concepts or other psychological supports of meaning must address.

3.1 Two traditional pseudo-critiques

First, however, we can dismiss two pseudo-critiques, albeit well-known ones. First, a traditional objection to the conceptualist identification of meaning is that it makes meanings *private* mental entities which cannot be shared. Since communication is thought of as the transfer of the *same* thoughts or concepts from speaker to hearer, the hypothesis that meanings are essentially private might seem to require us to jettison our view of communication. However, as long as we assume that there is *some* overlap in the mental content expressed by words, we can retain the traditional view of communication while upholding a conceptualist theory of meaning. To identify meanings with concepts internal to each language-user does not exclude the possibility that there is a *type*-identity between concepts from one user to another, just as there is a type-identity between different individuals' kidneys. (Type-identity is the kind of identity that holds between two instances of the same category. In the previous sentence, the third word and the third last word are type-identical because they are both occurrences – "tokens" – of the word "the". Similarly, your concept RED and my concept RED are also type-identical, even though they are different tokens or instances of the concept.) Concepts can be private *and* shared because they are, by hypothesis, type-identical from one speaker to another.

Second, John Stuart Mill criticized the idea that meanings might correspond to mental entities on the grounds that speakers routinely presuppose that words refer to actual objects. "When I say that fire causes heat," he asked (1875: 98), "do I mean that my idea of fire causes my idea of heat?" "No," he answered: "I mean that the natural phenomenon, fire, causes the natural phenomenon, heat" (see Adams 2003 for a contemporary restatement of this critique directed against Jackendoff). Mill is right: speakers obviously do not take their language to refer to the world of ideas. However, this truism does not constitute any argument against internalism. Mill's critique rests on a classic error. Of course the speaker means that the natural phenomenon, fire, causes heat – but it is the meaning of the word *fire* that, for internalists, *explains* the speaker's referential behaviour; that meaning itself is not the object of any predication, as Mill mistakenly seems to think. The situation in other domains is exactly equivalent. The statement *France is beautiful* does not mean that *the six-letter word* France *is beautiful*, any more than it means that the *meaning* of the word *France* is beautiful: rather, it predicates beauty of France, the actual country. Mill's critique only works by conflating the *linguistic* viewpoint of the speaker and the *metalinguistic* viewpoint of the theorist. Clearly, these two must be kept separate, at the price of major confusion.

3.2 Explanatory inertia

Many critics have drawn attention to the minimal explanatory force of conceptualist explanations (Kamp and Reyle 1993; Givón 1995). Concepts are the internal structures we take to instantiate meaning. The attribution of a meaning to an expression allows us to capture a generalization about its linguistic behaviour by identifying the regularities of reference and inference in which it participates, but, once hypothesized, the meaning does not in itself hold any further explanatory power. To simply relabel meanings as "concepts' is not therefore an explanatory advance: as noted by Murphy (2011: 395):

> in order to have a cognitive theory of something, it is not sufficient to add the word cognitive to the name of one's theory. Empirical evidence from cognitive psychology and psycholinguistics should inform an account that is supposed to be based on psychological principles.

However, to say that *spoon* means "hand-held implement with handle and bowl for use with liquids", and to flesh out the concept SPOON in equivalent ways, is to do no more than state a generalization about the way the word *spoon* is used without bringing in any of the empirical evidence Murphy rightly requires. Generalizing about patterns of use is, of course, a necessary first step towards an explanation, but it is not yet an explanation in itself, since we have not said anything about the underlying structures in virtue of which this behaviour is manifested. All we have done is describe a generalization about the word's use, attributed it to the psychology of the language-user, and called this description a "meaning" or a "concept". There is a striking analogy here with the classic "dormitive virtue" explanation for the soporific power of opium. Before the chemical agent responsible for this effect – morphine – had been identified, a standard explanation of opium's power to induce sleep was that it possessed a "dormitive virtue" – clearly not an explanation of any kind, but simply a relabelling of the sleep-inducing property in question (see Riemer 2013 for details).

What makes this objection possible is the lack of constraints facing analysts in hypothesizing the existence of concepts. Linguists have felt entitled to engage in quite straightforward kinds of armchair, notional analysis when making hypotheses about the conceptual structures underlying meaning. The conceptual structures hypothesized by most semanticists ultimately look a lot like ordinary dictionary definitions. This is something of a worry, since the scientific study of meaning should do more than simply relabel as concepts the descriptions lexicographers give of word-meaning. Lexicography is, after all, a branch of applied, not theoretical linguistics: our suspicions should be aroused if there is a strong commonality between the two. Perhaps the conceptual structures of interest to semantics are more complex, messy, and cross-cutting than the one-to-one word-concept model that still dominates most semanticists' thinking (apart, of course, from cases of polysemy and synonymy, which are, on the traditional picture, precisely of interest since they are departures from this basic case; see Chapter 13). Cummins (2000: 131) draws a comparison with the "almost irresistible temptation in biology to believe that the morphological traits of importance and interest to us must correspond to our genes in some neat way".

3.3 Explanatory priority

Classical cognitive science, linguistics included, makes two important assumptions about concepts, each of which is open to question. First, it assumes that concepts in the strong sense introduced above are *always* involved in the mental operations underlying language, and that they are the principal mental entity of importance in the study of the mind. Let's call this the assumption of explanatory priority. It may well be, however, that a variety of other kinds of mental process underlie our intelligent abilities, language included. Take for example the conjunction "or". The natural hypothesis is that "or" corresponds to an underlying concept – that, in other words, the "language of thought" contains a concept for disjunction. However, there are other, non-conceptual ways in which the cognitive system could represent disjunction (see Waskan 2006: 152). For instance, entertaining the thought "either it will rain or it will snow" could amount to entertaining the separate thoughts "it will rain" and "it will snow", accompanied by an appropriate *modal attitude* to them – as for example when one holds two objects – different bottles of wine, say – in each hand, weighing up which to buy. This latter situation does not involve any explicit representation of an "or" operator, yet the two objects are related disjunctively, since *either* one *or* the other will be bought. This kind of attitudinal alternative to explicit conceptual representation has been explored in the context of simulation theories of conceptualization (Barsalou 1999; 2008).

Second, the received view of conceptualization presupposes that concepts are essentially static: they represent recurrent states of the cognizer which stand out as fixed islands of regularity in the surrounding flow of mental processes, themselves best understood as points of transition between distinct conceptual states. For Aristotle and Aristotelians like Augustine and Locke, nouns, for instance, are meaningful because

> the speaker *stops his process of thinking* and the mind of the hearer acquiesces.
> (Aristotle, *On interpretation* 16b III; italics added)

In this way of looking at things, it's only by "freezing" the mental process that meaning is created. As Aquinas put it in the thirteenth century, the mind of a hearer "comes to rest" when they understand the meaning of a word (*De Int.* I.5.16–17; Aquinas 1962). For this reason, the concepts involved in understanding linguistic meaning can be characterized independently of this wider mental flow, using the various analytical frameworks developed by semanticists to do so: Jackendovian or Wierzbickian primitives (Jackendoff 2002; Goddard and Wierzbicka 2002), Idealized Cognitive Models (Lakoff 1987), event-structure decompositions (see Chapter 22), and so on. In each of these formalisms, it is possible to represent the underlying conceptual content expressed by a lexeme in a static theoretical structure; these static structures recur in different combinations depending on the propositions being expressed. Various currents of research in cognitive science and the philosophy of mind have taken issue with the assumption of the static nature of conceptualization (Peirce 1868; Rumelhart et al. 1986; O'Regan and Noe 2001; Port and Van Gelder 1995; Van Gelder 1998; Barsalou 2008), on the grounds that "natural cognition happens in real time" (Van Gelder 1998: 622). For Van Gelder, cognitive processes are best thought of as "always ongoing, not starting anywhere and not finishing anywhere" (1998: 621), and the goal of the sciences of the mind "is not to map an input at one time to an output at some later time, but to constantly maintain appropriate change" (ibid.).

Correspondingly, many modern theories of linguistic behaviour (Langacker 1997) stress the extent to which meaning must be conceived of as a dynamic process. However, since all of them, even the most revisionist (Jasperson et al. 1994), still recognize a fixed, invariant core of meaning carried by expressions, there is something of a lack of fit between the machinery of their analysis and the accompanying theorizing. As discussed in Chapter 29 of this volume, studies of semantic processing (Sanford 2002) suggest that the mental representations involved in on-line language understanding are actually much *less* static than this traditional picture assumes, with the degree to which fully consolidated semantic structures are activated depending on a range of variables including, among other things, attention. Since other areas of language structure are known to display variation dependent on factors like these (Coupland 2001; Eckert 2000; Schilling-Estes 2007), there is no a priori reason why semantic structure should be different. We should expect that the kinds of meaning expressed by lexical items will vary as a function of variables like the degree of attention and planning on the part of the speaker, the mode (spoken or written), the register, and perhaps others.

A limiting case is, in fact, plausible in which *no* distinctly linguistic semantic information needs to be activated for understanding to be achieved. This is where the context itself supplies *all* the information that the conceptualizer needs to represent the intended meaning. Consider the passengers on a plane hearing the announcement *fasten your seatbelts*. On traditional models of sentence comprehension, the meaning of *seatbelt* would be processed exhaustively, with the word's full semantic representation being activated to allow the hearer to decide which aspects of the current context satisfy it. Since the seatbelts satisfy the specifications of the meaning of *seatbelt* – say, "safety restraint secured at waist" – the hearer identifies the appropriate referent by realizing that the strap in front of her is a safety restraint secured at the waist.

In that context, however, *none* of this information is relevant. The hearer does not need to specifically represent the information that the strap on her seat is a waist-secured safety restraint; all she needs to realize is that it is the *only* object capable of being fastened in the current circumstances. There is therefore *no need* for the hearer to instantiate any of the information that appears in a conceptual definition of the word *seatbelt*. The structure of the environment itself means that the word *seatbelt* need not trigger any form of consolidated representation for the hearer to respond appropriately in the context in which it is uttered. The hearer can "understand" without having to decode the meaning of the word *seatbelt*, because the context only makes available a single reasonable response to the speaker's request. For further details, see Riemer (2013).

3.4 Expressivity

The explanatory priority of conceptual explanation is also called into question by the possibility that non-cognitive factors play a more central role in cognition than has been acknowledged. In particular, emotion has traditionally been excluded from any *deep* or *essential* role in our picture of the operation of human psychology. As suggested at the start of this chapter, we can once again attribute a role to pretheoretical understandings in determining the direction of research on this point. As Schwarz-Friesel (2007: 92) notes, emotion episodes are often viewed in post-Enlightenment thinking as *temporary disruptions* of a permanent rational background – a "cold and neutral state of intellectual perception", in James' words (1884: 193) – which represents the default state of human subjectivity. This goes against the culturally widespread assumption that people are always experiencing some emotion or other (see e.g. Wierzbicka 1999: 17–18).

The secondary role attributed to emotion generally is reflected in the linguistic presupposition that the principal genus of meaning is *descriptive* – that is, conceptual or cognitive. (Indeed, it's worth recalling the fact that, according to Aquinas, Aristotle's *De Interpretatione*, arguably the founding document of European semantics, had been excluded by Andronicus from the Aristotelian canon on the grounds that it contained an assimilation of the cognitive and non-cognitive domains that, for Andronicus, confirmed its inauthenticity (see Couillaud and Couillaud 2004: 17–18).) A small class of the vocabulary is considered to be *expressive*, which means that the psychological states with which it is associated are emotions or feelings, not thoughts or concepts (Potts 2007). The clearest examples of expressive meaning are exclamations (*damn!*, *yuck!*, *shit!*, etc.), though the case has been made at different times that many other items are also expressive (Stevenson 1937; see Chapter 27). It is of course recognized that descriptive vocabulary can have emotion-related aspects, but they are taken to be accessory and accounted for as connotations without ever receiving significant study. Overall, then, expressive meaning is assumed to be numerically and theoretically marginal in the lexicon, and all existing semantic theories take descriptive, i.e. conceptual, meaning as basic.

There are at least two reasons to be suspicious about the claim that cognition is essentially concept-driven and that as a result meaning is mostly descriptive. First is the undeniable fact that emotion constitutes an intimate part of the subjective experience of language. Expressions' subjective, emotional "loading" is often just as salient phenomenologically as any propositional, informational "content". If we are sometimes aware of broadly conceptual characteristics of words as we speak (of, for instance, the fact that a *logarithm* is a particular kind of "arithmetic function"), we are just as, if not more often, aware of their personal emotional qualities (the feeling of dread inspired by the word *logarithm* in high school, perhaps). It is remarkable that this fact has been recognized for so long without being the object of serious theorizing. In the eighteenth century, Berkeley suggested that non-cognitive factors outweigh the importance of cognitive ones in the economy of speech:

> Besides, the communicating of ideas marked by words is not the chief and only end of language, as is commonly supposed. There are other ends, as the raising of some passion, the exciting to, or deterring from an action, the putting of the mind in some particular disposition; to which the former is in many cases barely subservient, and sometimes entirely omitted, when these can be obtained without it, as I think doth not infrequently happen in the familiar use of language. I entreat the reader to reflect within himself, and see if it doth not often happen either in hearing or reading a discourse, that the passions

of fear, love, hatred, admiration, disdain, and the like arise, immediately in his mind upon the perception of certain words, without any ideas coming between.
(*Principles of Human Knowledge*, Introduction §20)

For their part, Vigliocco et al. (2009: 221) suggest that "emotion . . . may play a crucial role in the representation and processing of abstract concepts". As a result, any theory in which meanings are identified with conscious or unconscious mental entities (like concepts) needs a good reason to exclude emotions from the characterization of these entities, since the emotional dimension seems to be on an equal footing with propositional/conceptual meaning in the makeup of the phenomenologically accessible states by which meaning is experienced. This is even more the case as the role of non-conceptual factors in cognition more generally is increasingly emphasized (Gunther 2003).

The second reason to doubt the soundness of the claim that cognition is wholly concept-driven is that the very basis for the distinction between concepts and emotions is itself unclear. As is frequently acknowledged, we have no good definition of what makes something cognitive or a concept (Hooijmans and Keijzer 2007; Prinz 2004). However, the very act of describing meaning in one of the recognized metalanguages of semantic analysis implies that these meanings are conceptual and therefore not emotion-based. The problem here is that *anything* can be described in conceptual terms: there is no meaning for which some kind of semantic analysis cannot be advanced. This means that the very representational medium used to characterize meaning excludes from the outset a non-conceptual definition of meaning, and thereby discounts the role of a whole dimension of human psychology. Semantic theorizing, as we have already noted, typically proceeds in something of a vacuum of independent psychological evidence of human conceptual capacities: semanticists develop semantic analyses on the basis of linguistic evidence, and then declare that these analyses correspond to stored conceptual mental representations. The latter claim is rarely argued for, and is the one that should excite scepticism.

3.5 Modality

Semantic analysis as traditionally undertaken in linguistics is predicated on the assumption of a "language of thought" – a neutral, language-like mental format or code that supports cognitive processes, like the software codes running a computer (Fodor 1975, 2008; Fortis 1996). This language of thought is often conceived of as the medium in which central mental processes unfold, neutral between the different perceptual channels that input to it. Simulation theories of cognition, however, hold that conceptual information is "couched in representational codes that are specific to our perceptual systems" (Prinz 2002: 119; see Chapter 8 of the present volume). On the basis of neurophysiological (Damasio 1994, 2000) and psychological (Barsalou 1999, 2008) research, simulation theorists argue that there is no single representational system or language of thought which cognition draws on in the planning and control of action, including language, and which justifies the kinds of semantic analysis typical of linguistics. Instead, the psychological architecture supporting reference and other cognitive tasks harnesses the perceptual modality appropriate to particular referents. If this thesis is confirmed, it will carry major implications for the methodology of linguistic semantic research.

3.6 The regress problem

One of the fundamental roles of meaning and hence of concepts in a theory of language is to explain the patterns of reference and inference which comprise use: words have the use they have in virtue of the meanings they express. Along with syntax and pragmatics, semantics has the role of accounting for these patterns. A further challenge for conceptualism arises from the observation that there is nothing in any traditional conceptual representation which determines a particular pattern of use: any given concept, as the mental structure activated during language use, can support an indefinite range of different and incompatible uses.

This emerges most clearly when, in the context of reference, semanticists speak of representations "matching" or "corresponding" to their referents. English speakers are hypothesized to have a conceptual representation of the meaning of, say, *fire*, and match this representation to real-world situations of fire to achieve reference. We lack, however, an account of how this matching happens. What principles determine when a representation matches a real-world situation and how are these principles applied? This apparently innocent question opens a Pandora's box which might cast doubt on the very explanatory viability of explicit representations like concepts in a theory of cognition. If concepts are attributed to cognizers as part of the explanation for their intelligent action, then they also must have the capacity to apply the concept to situations. This capacity in turn requires us to attribute to them a whole new set of principles specifying the way in which this application happens, which themselves then require further principles for *their* own interpretation, and so on *ad infinitum*. In a tradition that goes back at least to Wittgenstein (1953), many researchers have worried that this question opens an explanatory regress: the regress problem and ones like it are often advanced as an argument against the classical understanding of cognition as a symbolic, rule-governed process of symbol manipulation (cf. Kripke 1982; Dreyfus 1985, 1992; Block 1990; Searle 1992; Riemer 2005).

4 Future directions

Having surveyed some considerations pro and contra internalist semantics, we can ask what future directions internalist semantic research might take, and what alternatives may exist to a theory that places concepts – in the strong sense – at the centre of the explanation of meaning. Given the complexity and lack of resolution in the areas mentioned in this chapter, there is not a single one that would not benefit from sustained and foundational research. This is even more the case since various currents of enquiry offer completely different accounts of the internal states corresponding to meaning, and therefore constitute a decisive challenge to linguistic semantics. Prime among these would be the statistical approach to many of the phenomena addressed by traditional conceptualist theories, exemplified by Landauer and Dumais (1997). On these views, linguistic phenomena can be theorized without any appeal to internal conceptualist structures. Another important strand of research is constituted by simulation-based theories of cognitive processes (Barsalou 2008; Prinz 2002; see Chapter 8) mentioned in the previous section. Playing these theories off against those that involve concepts in the strong sense must constitute an urgent task for future investigations into meaning (see e.g. Chaterjee 2010).

Beyond that, the challenge posed by broadly phenomenologically inspired theories of semantics also demands the attention of the field. Semanticists have traditionally presupposed that the meanings they are analysing are essentially more principled analogues of dictionary definitions. However, work like that of Cadiot et al. (2006) and Zlatev (2010) leads us to ask whether a mode of representation that is less abstract and arguably closer to the grain of experience might not provide a better way of capturing facts about meaning. There needs to be a dialogue between traditional semantics and the kinds of alternative analysis proposed by researchers like these.

This challenge draws attention to the present lack of agreement on questions of semantic analysis. Current linguistic research into meaning is characterized by a profusion of different theoretical approaches, with little or no effort being paid to questions of theory evaluation or assessment of rival hypotheses. Of existing semantic theories, it is mainly the Natural Semantic Metalanguage theory that has been the object of sustained challenge on the level of its concrete analyses of meaning (see Geeraerts 2010 for references). While there are plenty of critiques of research in, for instance, Cognitive Semantics, these have largely been directed at the theory's high-level background, and despite some notable controversies like the debate over *over*, rather little effort has been devoted to assessing the adequacy of the particular accounts of meaning it furnishes. If – *if* – semantic research should aim at consensus, then an immediate priority for the discipline must be a concerted attempt to compare different theories and to resolve the numerous differences of approach presently practised. Whether such a project is feasible, however, is far from clear (see the Introduction).

Among the most urgent other priorities must be clarification of the descriptive/expressive distinction. This is, as we have seen, a fundamental distinction in semantic analysis, but one that is currently ill understood. Illuminating the difference between the two genera of meaning would constitute substantial explanatory progress (see Chapter 27).

Further reading

Jackendoff, Ray 1989. What is a concept, that a person may grasp it? *Mind and Language* 4: 68–102. Outlines the role of concepts in a naturalistic theory of cognition.

Riemer, Nick 2013. Conceptualist semantics: explanatory power, scope and uniqueness. *Language Sciences* 35: 1–19. Explores alternatives to concepts in semantic analysis and suggests a clarification of the expressive/descriptive distinction.

Murphy, G. 2002. *The Big Book of Concepts*. Cambridge, MA: MIT Press. A compendium of psychological research on conceptualization.

Schwarz-Friesel, Monika 2007. *Sprache und Emotion*. Tübingen & Basel: A Francke. The most complete account of emotional factors in language. Chapter 4 includes an illuminating discussion of the relation between cognition and emotion in language.

References

Adams, F. 2003. Semantic paralysis. *Behavioral and Brain Sciences* 26: 666–667.
Aizawa, K. and C. Gillett 2009. The (multiple) realization of psychological and other properties in the sciences. *Mind & Language* 24: 181–208.
Allan, Keith 2001. *Natural Language Semantics*. Oxford: Blackwell.
Aquinas, Thomas 1962. *Aristotle: On Interpretation* (Jean T. Oesterle, tr.). Milwaukee, WI: Marquette University Press.
Barsalou, L. 1999. Perceptual symbol systems. *Behavioral and Brain Sciences* 22: 577–660.
Barsalou, L. 2008. Grounded cognition. *Annual Review of Psychology* 59: 617–645.
Bechtel, W. and J. Mundale 1999. Multiple realizability revisited: Linking cognitive and neural states. *Philosophy of Science* 66: 175–207.
Berkelely, G. 1998 [1710]. *A Treatise Concerning the Principles of Human Knowledge*. Oxford: Oxford University Press.
Bierwisch, Manfred and Robert Schreuder 1992. From concepts to lexical items. *Cognition* 42: 23–60.
Binder, J.R., Rutvik H. Desai, William W. Graves and Lisa L. Conant 2009. Where is the semantic system? A critical review and meta-analysis of 120 functional neuroimaging studies. *Cerebral Cortex* 19: 2767–2796.

Block, Ned 1990. Mental pictures and cognitive science. In William Lycan (ed.) *Mind And Cognition. A Reader*. Oxford: Blackwell, 577–607.

Burge, Tyler 1979. Individualism and the mental. In Peter A. French et al. (eds) *Midwest Studies in Philosophy IV*. Minneapolis, University of Minnesota Press, 73–121.

Cadiot, Pierre, Franck Lebas, and Yves-Marie Visetti 2006. The semantics of motion verbs: action, space, and qualia. In Maya Hickmann and Stéphane Robert (eds) *Space in Languages*. Amsterdam: Benjamins, 175–206.

Chaterjee, Anjan 2010. Disembodying cognition. *Language and Cognition* 2: 79–116.

Churchland, Patricia M. 1986. *Neurophilosophy: Toward a Unified Science of the Mind-Brain*. Cambridge, MA: MIT.

Bruno and Maylis Couillaud 2004. *Thomas d'Aquin, Commentaire du* Peryermenias (Traité de l'interprétation) *d'Aristote*. Paris: Les Belles Lettres.

Coupland, Nikolas 2001. Language, situation, and the relational self: theorizing dialect style in sociolinguistics. In Penelope Eckert and J.R. Rickford (eds) *Style and Sociolinguistic Variation*. Cambridge: Cambridge University Press, 185–210.

Cummins, Robert 2000. "How does it work?" vs. "What are the laws?" Two conceptions of psychological explanation. In Keil, F. and R. Wilson (eds) *Explanation and Cognition*. Cambridge, MA: MIT, 117–145.

Damasio, Antonio 1994. *Descartes' Error: Emotion, Reason and the Human Brain*. New York: Putnam.

Damasio, Antonio 2000. *The Feeling of What Happens*. London: Random House.

Di Lollo, Vincent 2012. The feature-binding problem is an ill-posed problem. *Trends in Cognitive Sciences* 16: 317–321.

Dreyfus, Hubert 1985 [1980]. Holism and hermeneutics. In R. Hollinger (ed.) *Hermeneutics and Praxis*. Notre Dame: University of Notre Dame Press, 227–247. Originally in *Review of Metaphysics* 34: 3–24.

Dreyfus, Hubert 1992. *What Computers Still Can't Do*. Cambridge, MA: MIT Press.

Eckert, Penelope 2000. *Linguistic Variation as Social Practice*. Oxford: Blackwell.

Egan, Frances 1992. Individualism, computation, and perceptual content. *Mind* 101: 443–459.

Egan, Frances 1995. Computation and content. *Philosophical Review* 104: 181–203.

Evans, Vivian and Melanie Green 2006. *Cognitive Linguistics: an Introduction*. Edinburgh: Edinburgh University Press.

Farkas, Katalin 2008. *The Subject's Point of View*. Oxford: Oxford University Press.

Fodor, J. 1974. Special sciences (or: the disunity of science as a working hypothesis). *Synthese* 28: 97–115.

Fodor, J. 1975. *The Language of Thought*. Cambridge, MA: Harvard University Press.

Fodor, J. 1981. *Representations*. Cambridge, MA: MIT Press.

Fodor, J. 1987. *Psychosemantics*. Cambridge, MA: MIT Press.

Fodor, 1990. *A Theory of Content and Other Essays*. Cambridge, MA: MIT Press.

Fodor, J. 2008. *LOT2. The Language of Thought Revisited*. Oxford: Oxford University Press.

Fortis, J.-M. 1996. La notion de langage mental: problèmes récurrents de quelques théories anciennes et contemporaines. *Histoire Épistémologie Langage* 18: 75–101.

Funkhouser, E. 2007. Multiple realizability. *Philosophy Compass* 2: 303–315.

Geeraerts, D. 2010. *Theories of Lexical Semantics*. Oxford: Oxford University Press.

Givón, T., 1995. *Functionalism and Grammar*. Amsterdam: Benjamins.

Goddard, Chris and Anna Wierzbicka (eds) 2002. *Meaning and Universal Grammar – Theory and Empirical Findings*. Two volumes. Amsterdam: Benjamins.

Gunther, Y.H. 2003. Emotion and force. In Y.H. Gunther (ed.) *Essays on Nonconceptual Content*. Cambridge, MA: MIT Press, 279–288.

Hinzen, W. and D. Poeppel 2011. Semantics between cognitive neuroscience and linguistic theory. *Language and Cognitive Processes* 26: 1297–1316.

Hooijmans, M. and F. Keijzer 2007. Robotics, biological grounding and the Fregean tradition. *Pragmatics and Cognition* 15: 515–546.

Hooker, C.A. 1981. Towards a general theory of reduction. Part III: Cross categorical reduction. *Dialogue* 20: 496–529.
Hummel, John E. 2013. Object recognition. In Daniel Reisberg (ed.) *The Oxford Handbook of Cognitive Psychology*. New York: Oxford University Press, 32–45.
Jackendoff, Ray 2002. *Foundations of Language: Brain, Meaning, Grammar, Evolution*. Oxford: Oxford University Press.
James, William 1884. What is an emotion? *Mind* 9: 188–205.
Jasperson, Robert, Makoto Hayashi, Barbara Fox 1994. Semantics and interaction: three exploratory case studies. *Text* 14: 555–580.
Kamp, Hans and Reyle, Uwe 1993. *From Discourse to Logic*. Dordrecht, Kluwer.
Kripke, Saul 1980. *Naming and Necessity*. Oxford: Blackwell.
Kripke, Saul 1982. *Wittgenstein on Rules and Private Language*. Oxford: Blackwell.
Lakoff, George 1987. *Women, Fire and Dangerous Things: What Categories Reveal about the Mind*. Chicago: University of Chicago Press.
Landauer, Thomas K. and Susan T. Dumais 1997. A solution to Plato's problem: The latent semantic analysis theory of acquisition, induction, and representation of knowledge. *Psychological Review* 104: 211–240.
Langacker, Ronald 1997. The contextual basis of cognitive semantics. In Jan Nuyts and Eric Pederson (eds) *Language and Conceptualization*. Cambridge: Cambridge University Press, 229–252.
Lillard 1998. Ethnopsychologies: Cultural variations in theories of mind. *Psychological Bulletin* 123: 3–32.
Locke, J. 1691 [1979]. *An Essay Concerning Human Understanding*. Oxford: Clarendon Press.
Marr, David 1982. *Vision*. New York: Freeman.
Mendola, J. 2008. *Anti-externalism*. Oxford: Oxford University Press.
Mill, J.S. 1875. *A System of Logic, Ratiocinative and Inductive*. 9th ed. London: Longmans, Green, Reader, and Dyer.
Murphy, G.L. 2011. How words mean: Lexical concepts, cognitive models, and meaning construction. By Vyvyan Evans [review]. *Language* 87: 393–396.
O'Regan, J.K. and A. Noe 2001. A sensorimotor account of vision and visual consciousness. *Behavioral and Brain Sciences* 24: 939–1011.
Palmer, Stephen E. 1999. *Vision Science: Photons to Phenomenology*. Cambridge, MA: MIT Press.
Patterson, K., Peter J. Nestor and Timothy T. Rogers 2007. Where do you know what you know? The representation of semantic knowledge in the human brain. *Nature Reviews Neuroscience* 8: 976–987.
Peirce, Charles Sanders 1868 [1991]. Some consequences of four incapacities. In James Hoopes (ed.) *Peirce on Signs*. Chapel Hill: University of North Carolina Press, 67–71.
Peterson, Mary A. and Ruth Kimchi 2013. Perceptual organization in vision. In Daniel Reisberg (ed.) *The Oxford Handbook of Cognitive Psychology*. Oxford: Oxford University Press, 9–31.
Pietroski, Paul 2003. The character of natural language semantics. In Alex Barber (ed.) *Epistemology of Language*. Oxford: Oxford University Press, 217–256.
Port, R. and T. van Gelder (eds) 1995. *Mind as Motion: Explorations in the Dynamics of Cognition*. Cambridge, MA: MIT Press.
Potts, Christopher 2007. The expressive dimension. *Theoretical Linguistics* 33: 165–197.
Prinz, Jesse 2002. *Furnishing the Mind: Concepts and their Perceptual Basis*. Cambridge, MA: MIT Press.
Prinz, Jesse 2004. *Gut Reactions*. Cambridge, MA: MIT Press.
Putnam, Hilary 1975. The meaning of 'meaning'. In K. Gunderson (ed.) *Language, Mind and Knowledge. Minnesota Studies in the Philosophy of Science*, vol. 7. Minneapolis: University of Minnesota Press, 131–193.
Pylyshyn, Zenon W. 1984. *Computation and Cognition: Toward a Foundation for Cognitive Science*. Cambridge, MA: MIT Press.
Riemer, Nick 2005. *The Semantics of Polysemy. Reading Meaning in English and Warlpiri*. Berlin: Mouton de Gruyter.

Riemer, Nick 2013. Conceptualist semantics: explanatory power, scope and uniqueness. *Language Sciences* 35: 1–19.
Rumelhart, D.E., J.L. McClelland and The PDP Research Group 1986. *Parallel Distributed Processing: Explorations in The Microstructure of Cognition. Vol 1. Foundations*. Cambridge, MA: MIT Press.
Salmelin, Riitta and Tom Mitchell 2012. Tracking neural coding of perceptual and semantic features of concrete nouns. *NeuroImage* 62: 451–463.
Sanford, A.J. 2002. Context, attention and depth of focussing during interpretation. *Mind and Language* 17: 188–206.
Schilling-Estes, Natalie 2007. Sociolinguistic fieldwork. In Robert Bayley and Ceil Lucas (eds) *Sociolinguistic Theory. Theories, Methods, and Applications*. Cambridge: Cambridge University Press, 165–189.
Schwarz-Friesel, Monika 2007. *Sprache und Emotion*. Tübingen & Basel: A Francke.
Searle, John 1992. *The Rediscovery of the Mind.* Cambridge, MA: MIT Press.
Sperber, D. and D. Wilson 1995. *Relevance. Communication and Cognition*. 2nd ed. Oxford: Blackwell.
Stevenson, C. 1937. The emotive meaning of ethical terms. *Mind* 46: 14–31.
Gustavo, Dean Pomerleau, Mark Palatucci, Leila Wehbe, Alona Fyshe, Riitta Salmelin and Tom Mitchell. 2012. Tracking neural coding of perceptual and semantic features of concrete nouns. *NeuroImage* 62: 451–463.
Van Gelder, T. 1998. The dynamical hypothesis in Cognitive Science. *Behavioral And Brain Sciences* 21: 615–665.
Viberg, Åke 1984. The verbs of perception: a typological study. In B. Butterworth, B. Comrie and Ö. Dahl (eds) *Explanations for Language Universals*. Berlin: Mouton de Gruyter, 123–162.
Vigliocco, Gabriella, Lotte Meteyard, Mark Andrews and Stavroula Kousta 2009. Toward a theory of semantic representation. *Language and Cognition* 1: 219–247.
Waskan, Jonathan A. 2006 *Models and cognition. Prediction and explanation in everyday life and science*. Cambridge, MA: MIT Press.
Wierzbicka, Anna 1999. *Emotions Across Languages and Cultures*. Cambridge: Cambridge University Press.
Wikforss, Åsa 2008. Semantic externalism and psychological externalism. *Philosophy Compass* 3: 158–181.
Wittgenstein, Ludwig 1953. *Philosophical Investigations*. Oxford: Blackwell.
Zlatev, Jordan 2010. Phenomenology and cognitive linguistics. In Gallagher and Schmicking (eds) *Handbook of Phenomenology and Cognitive Science*. Dordrecht: Springer, 415–443.

Related topics

Chapter 1, (Descriptive) Externalism in semantics; Chapter 5, Cognitive semantics; Chapter 7, Categories, prototypes and exemplars; Chapter 8, Embodiment, simulation and meaning; Chapter 12, Lexical decomposition; Chapter 27, Expressives.

3
A history of semantics

Keith Allan

1 Naming

Human beings name things in their environment. The name helps to distinguish and identify the denotatum (thing named) and is essential to communication with fellow humans about such denotata. (Denotation is the relation between language expressions and things or events in worlds – not just the world we live in, but any world and time that may be spoken of.) Reference is a speaker's use of a language expression in the course of talking about its denotatum (Allan 2014; Strawson 1950). In Plato's *Cratylus* (Plato 1997) c. 385 BCE, Socrates advances the hypothesis that the earliest name-giver selected a name that captures the essence of its denotatum that is in some way iconic (as with onomatopoeic bird names like *cuckoo*). On this hypothesis the meaning of a word would be 'natural' because directly recognizable from the form of the word. Many of the Ancients sought to demonstrate that names are far more descriptive than the facts allow. For example, Socrates in *Cratylus* 406c derives the name Dionusos (god of Bacchanalia) from *didous ton oinon* 'giving wine'. He recognizes the implausibility of such accounts (426b–427b, 434e–435c), but a clear statement that names are symbols that denote by convention is first found some 25 years after *Cratylus* in Aristotle's *On Interpretation* 16a3, 16a20 (Aristotle 1984).

It is generally accepted today that language expressions have meaning by convention, but this invites the question: How does the convention get established? The most acceptable explanation is the Kripke (1972) notion of 'baptism', i.e. the initiation of a name-using practice, which is a variation on a long-established view that a history of conventional usage characterizes the vocabulary in the language and allows successive generations to communicate easily.

Before we leave the matter of proper names, Peter Abelard (1079–1142), Walter Burley (c. 1275–1345), John Stuart Mill (1806–1873), and a handful of today's philosophers believe that proper names and indexicals (determined by the situation of utterance) make 'direct reference'; that is, that they have no semantic content but directly pick out the referent. By contrast, common names refer distributively to individuals, while collectives (*herd*, *pair*) and quantified nominals (*three ducks*) pick out distributively a contingently determined set of individuals. This ignores the fact that in every language most personal proper names identify characteristics of the referent: *Elizabeth* is appropriate to females and not males and is of European origin, *Měi* 美 is appropriate to females only and is of Chinese origin, *Kofi* is of Akan origin and it is appropriate to males not females. So, most proper names do have a minimal semantics that identifies some basic characteristics of the typical name bearer. However, Frege (1892) was wrong to attribute encyclopaedic information about a particular name bearer (such that Aristotle was the tutor of Alexander) as the semantics of the name. There is still controversy about the status of proper names in linguistic semantics, but the notion that names make direct reference and have no semantic content extinguishes the semantic difference between *Cicero is Cicero* and *Cicero is Tully* which have the same truth value and make identical reference.

2 Realism vs. nominalism

Around 200 CE Alexander of Aphrodisias adopted Aristotle's suggestion (*On Interpretation* 16a3) that the relation of words to their denotata is mediated through the mind, a view championed by Boethius (c. 480–524) as a major influence on the medieval Latin tradition in philosophy. Another contention of Alexander is that universals (*all dogs*, *all coal*) do not exist in reality but only in the mind. Some thoughts derive from real entities, but universals don't, they are mental abstractions: here's a controversy that echoes through the Middle Ages into the modern era. Boethius added a twist of his own by claiming that the mental abstractions derive from reality by application of intelligence, reason, imagination, or the senses.

Peter Abelard (1079–1142) promulgated the doctrine that universals are mere words (*nomina*), i.e. he is a nominalist (see King (2004)). He rejected Boethius' mentalistic criterion for universals on the basis that it could only derive from an aggregation of individuals, yet there could be no prior criterion for such aggregation. According to Abelard, natural kinds are ordained by God and could have been otherwise: frogs could have had reason, men could have been amphibians. He concludes that universality is not a feature of real-world objects, it is merely linguistic: humans speak of similarities that they perceive distributed among individuals referred to using the same noun or verb. Sentences refer to the world and not to someone's understanding of the world, thus *If something is human it is animal* is a truth about the world such that an individual can understand the concept human without previously entertaining the concept that the human is animal. Language is not a medium for the transmission of ideas from one human to another, but conveys information about the world – a position taken up later by Gottfried Leibniz (1646–1716) and Noam Chomsky (b. 1928, see Chomsky 1975). Abelard recognized that true entailments necessarily follow from true premises. *If Socrates is a human being then Socrates is an animal* is necessarily true since 'whatever the species is predicated of, so too is the genus' (Rijk 1970: 323).

William of Ockham (c. 1285–1349) identified two kinds of signification: 'primary', which allows for correct reference, and 'secondary', which applies to predicates that denote their nominal counterparts, for instance *brave* denotes bravery. There was also *suppositio* 'supposition', which identifies what kinds of reference are made by the speaker using the nominals within a proposition and consequently figure in the statement of truth conditions. For Ockham, as for Abelard, mental language is primary, spoken language secondary, written language tertiary. The truth of a proposition and true synonymy are defined only for mental language (see Spade 2002). On universals Ockham was a nominalist who began with ideas similar to Abelard, but came to believe that universals simply predicate something of many individuals; thus he recast the universal *all men are animal* in terms of a particular: *if something is a man, it is animal* (a move directly echoed in Discourse Representation Theory, Kamp 1981). The medieval view was that 'understanding is of universals, but sense-data derive from particulars' (Spade 2002: 162). For Abelard and Thomas Aquinas (1225–1274), knowledge was the effect of sense-data (*species*) transmitted from entity to mind, but Ockham rejected this on the ground that universals would necessarily have to exist in the entities, which is impossible because everything but God is contingent.

Walter Burley/Burleigh (c. 1275–1345) was a realist critical of Ockham's nominalism. For Burley semantic distinctions derive from ontological differences between the entities denoted. Individuals are the *significata* of singular names and universals are the *significata* of general names. *Man* applies as a general term to all men because it denotes the universal *humanity* that is present in and essential to each man in the real world. *Humanity* has no extension distinct from that of *man*. (The extension of a language expression designates something that exists in a particular world.) After 1324, Burley no longer claimed that universals are constitutive parts of the individuals of which they are predicated, though they do reveal the substantial nature of the particular. Each particular is a token for a universal such that the extension of a general name is a set of such particulars. Propositions are the creation of cognitive acts; they relate to the real world by combining the things to which their constituents refer. The truth of *man is animal* is a fact about the real world because the denotata of *man* and *animal* exist in the real world. In *De puritate artis logicae* 1324–8 Burley discusses the difference between *Twice you ate a loaf of bread* in which 'loaf of bread' refers to two loaves fused for this mode of expression and the fallacious *A loaf of bread you ate twice*, which refers to a particular loaf that cannot be eaten twice (Burley 2000: §93). Today, the first of these would be dealt with in event-based semantics (see below). Burley noticed problems with sentences such as *Every man who has a donkey sees it* (Burley 2000: §130–32; Seuren 2006; Geach 1968; Kamp 1981; Groenendijk and Stokhof 1991). As Burley points out, a man who owns two donkeys might see only one of them, thus allowing for the truth of *some man who has a donkey doesn't see it* leading to the contradictory consequence *therefore some man who has a donkey is not a man who has a donkey*. Clearly something here needs to be explained. I return to the modern treatment of the semantics of donkey sentences later.

John Locke (1632–1704) in his *Essay Concerning Humane Understanding* reiterated the notion that language is conventional, disclaiming any inherent or necessary link between a word and its denotatum (Locke 1700: III.ii.1). 'Ideas' provide the mind with representations of objective qualities of objects (such as size, shape, or weight) and also secondary qualities such as colour, taste, or smell which are subjective (*ibid.* Book II). To understand thinking and knowing one must understand language as the means of thought and communication (Book III). Locke claimed that words only mean what they are understood to mean; consequently, usage must be the sole arbiter of meaning (III.ii.2). Linguistic forms represent the ideas of things and not the things themselves (III.ii.5). Sometimes words are used even when there are no ideas corresponding to them as with generic terms and universals – which Locke suggests are creations of the mind, through abstraction; they denote 'nominal essences'. Like Alexander of Aphrodisias, Abelard, Ockham, and Thomas Hobbes (1588–1679) before him, Locke was a nominalist (Locke 1700: III.iii.11f). Locke's views on universals (and many other things) were challenged in Leibniz's *Nouveaux Essais sur l'entendement humain* (Leibniz 1981 [1765]).

3 The earliest forays into lexical semantics

In the Western Classical Tradition of linguistics (see Allan (2010)), lexical semantics began with etymologies and glossaries of literary works that gave way to word lists with attributed meanings (both monolingual and bilingual) resembling modern dictionaries. The *Lexeis* ('Glossary') of Aristophanes of Byzantium (c. 257–180 BCE) offered glossaries of poets and dramatists (Aristophanes of Byzantium 1986). The most celebrated Renaissance dictionary was Ambrogio Calepino's (c. 1450–1510) *Cornucopiæ* first published in 1502. A milestone in modern lexicography was Samuel Johnson (1755). Today, the application of lexicographical techniques to digitized corpora has revolutionized lexicography (see Hanks (2013)). However, attempts at the systematic representation of dictionary meanings by e.g. Russian lexicographers Jurij Apresjan (2000) and Igor Mel'cuk (1984–1991) in terms of semantic primitives have not been widely adopted.

The interesting aspect of ancient etymologies like Isidore of Seville's *Etymologiae* (Isidore 1850) is that, unlike etymologists since Ménage (1650) who seek to map the diachronic development of the meanings and forms of the word, the ancients sought to explain the meaning of the word in terms of its perceived component forms (Robins 1997: 27). They assumed that knowledge is embodied in word meanings and can be elucidated via reference to the original meaning; hence the original forms and meanings of words in what would today be called the proto-language were, supposedly, finessed. Although the explanations in ancient etymologies are most often faulty, they do focus attention on the meaning of the word and on the existence of lexical networks based partly on the semantic relations among listemes (language expressions whose meaning is not determinable from the meanings – if any – of their constituent forms but which have to be memorized as a combination of form and meaning). Today's version of such lexical relations is the wordnet; see www.globalwordnet.org.

Modern use of the term *semantics* stems from an article by Michel Bréal (1832–1915) in which he defined it as 'the science of significations' (Bréal 1883: 133). The term gained much wider currency with the publication of *Essai de sémantique: Science de significations* (Bréal 1897) translated as *Semantics: Studies in the Science of Meaning* (Bréal 1900). He regarded semantics as an essential but neglected part of linguistic study. A hearer 'goes straight to the thought behind a word' modulating the sense (decontextualized meaning) so as to capture the intention of the speaker (*ibid.* 107). Bréal agreed with William Whitney (1875: 87) that speakers understand language without recourse to etymology; so, the search for mythical 'true meaning' gave way to a search for the patterns and causes of semantic change. Words are signs of thoughts, and meanings change in line with speakers' needs to communicate; cf. Whitney (1867: 20). Old words are used in new contexts, and thereby their meanings subtly change: the 'customary office of a word [is] to cover, not a point, but a territory, and a territory that is irregular, heterogeneous, and variable' (Whitney 1875: 110). This opens the way for prototype and stereotype semantics (see below). For Bréal, semantic change has to be studied with an eye to the contexts and uses of terms in former times. The system operates through rational inference. He was unusual in looking not only at lexical meaning but also language functions (Bréal 1897: 189). Like Hermann Paul, whose *Prinzipien* Bréal (*ibid.* 307) was praised for its contribution to semantics, Bréal sees the multiple meanings in decontextualized language reducing to one meaning or 'valeur' in reference. The use of *value* by Whitney and Bréal is tied to referential import, whereas Saussure (1916) uses the term to mean 'differential value' within the semantic field as part of the language system. For Bréal, language doesn't merely describe or narrate; it is used in a variety of what today would mostly be called illocutionary functions (commanding, taking possession, persuading, pleasing, promising, questioning, and exclaiming).

4 Componential analysis

In the seventeenth century there were many attempts to identify a 'philosophical language' common to all mankind (Lodwick 1972 [1647–1686]; Dalgarno 1661; Wilkins 1668; Leibniz

1765). These prefigure twentieth-century proposals for universally applicable semantic primitives and the notion of componential analysis, which seeks to identify the sense of a listeme in terms of one or more semantic components. The principal means of accomplishing this has been through the structuralist method of contrastive distributional analysis (see Chapter 12), though there is no consistent one-to-one correlation between semantic components and the morph(eme)s of any language. Listemes that share semantic components are semantically related. Semantic components reflect the characteristics of typical denotata, hence there is a hierarchy of semantic components which corresponds to perceived hierarchies among denotata. For instance, FELINE is a semantic component of *cat* and entails the semantic component ANIMAL which is also, therefore, a component of *cat*. This suggests a thesaurus-like structure for semantic components. It follows that the set of semantic components for a language can be discovered by identifying all the relationships that can be conceived of among the denotata of listemes. In practice, this could be everything in all worlds, actual and non-actual. There have been numerous attempts to carry out such a task; among the most successful was *An Essay Toward a Real Character and a Philosophical Language* (Wilkins 1668) although this had no demonstrable influence on twentieth-century componential analysis. Since the nineteenth century, anthropologists had been comparing widely differing kinship systems in culturally distinct societies by interpreting them in terms of universal constituents that equate to semantic components (see Kroeber (1909)). Two of the earliest articles in the componential analysis of meaning, Lounsbury (1956) and Goodenough (1956), appeared consecutively in the same issue of the journal *Language* and both were analyses of kin terms. They showed that semantic analysis could be carried out using approved methods of structural analysis, similar to those used to filter out the phonetic components of the Sanskrit stop phonemes. For instance, Lounsbury's paper begins with a comparison of Spanish and English kin terms: *ti-o, hij-o, abuel-o, herman-o* ('uncle', 'son', 'grandfather', 'brother') vs. *ti-a, hij-a, abuel-a, herman-a* ('aunt', 'daughter', 'grandmother', 'sister'). English has no gender morphs corresponding to the Spanish suffixes *-o* and *-a*, but gender is nonetheless a significant component in the meaning of the English kin terms. Their covert gender must be compatible with the sex of the person denoted; consequently, it is anomalous to call one's uncle *aunt*, or one's sister *brother*. Hence, too, the anomaly of **My brother is pregnant*. And when the terms *aunt* and *uncle* are extended as terms of respect to an older generation, they are assigned according to the sex of the referent. There are syntactic consequences: the personal pronoun anaphoric to *uncle* is *he/him*; the one for *aunt* is *she/her*. *Father*, *uncle*, and *aunt* have in common that they are FIRST_ASCENDING_GENERATION. *Father* and *uncle* additionally have in common that both are MALE, whereas *aunt* is FEMALE. *Aunt* and *uncle* are both COLLATERAL, whereas *father* is LINEAL. The meaning relationships between *father*, *uncle*, and *aunt* can be seen from the semantic components identified.

Componential analysis in semantics was influenced by the adaption of distinctive feature analysis based on the methodology of Prague school phonology to morphosyntax. Roman Jakobson (1936) identified the distinctive 'conceptual' features of each case in Russian. Zellig Harris (1948) analysed the verb paradigm of Hebrew using the categories of tense, person, and gender on a distributional basis that corresponds to Jakobson's analysis in terms of conceptual features. A third strand in the development of componential analysis was semantic field theory. The semantic field of a listeme is determined from the conceptual field in which its denotatum occurs; its structure is the structure of the conceptual field. The notion of semantic field is found in Humboldt (1836) and it was later developed by Trier (1931), Porzig (1950), Weisgerber (1950), and Geckeler (1971). In *Structural Semantics*, Lyons (1963) examined the meanings that can be ascribed to words such as *téchnē* 'skill', *epistḗmē* 'knowledge', *sophía* 'wisdom', *aretḗ* 'virtue', etc. in the semantic fields of knowledge and skill in Plato's works. Lyons was motivated by Trier's survey of the shifting field of High German *wîsheit*, *kunst*, and *list* but unlike Trier's subjective speculations, Lyons presents a rigorous analysis using techniques derived from works such as Saussure (1916), Harris (1951), and Chomsky (1957). Few scholars have undertaken extensive analysis of a semantic field, but Bendix (1966) analysed the field of *have* and its counterparts in Hindi and Japanese, Lehrer (1974) analysed the fields of cooking and sound, and Backhouse (1994) is an extensive study of taste terms in Japanese. A conceptual field such as colour, kinship, or cooking terms is covered by a number of listemes in a language, each denoting a part of the field. Different languages, and at different times in history any one language, may divide the field differently among listemes. The differential value (Saussure's 'valeur') of a listeme is that part of the conceptual field that it denotes in contrast with the part denoted by other listemes in the same semantic field. To generalize: when new objects and new ways of doing things come into existence there is a change in the conceptual field that leads to a change in the semantic field resulting from the adding of listemes or the semantic extension of existing ones. Seemingly closed fields such as case inflexions or kin terms should permit exhaustive componential analysis in which every term within the field is characterized by a unique subset of the universal set of semantic components defining the field. However, these systems invariably leak into other fields when meaning extensions and figurative usage are considered. Furthermore, an exhaustive componential analysis of the entire vocabulary of a language is probably unachievable, because it proves impossible to define the boundaries, and hence all the components, of every field.

Semantic primes and their interpretations constitute the vocabulary of the semantic metalanguage. We may suppose that semantic components are composed from semantic primes, but what are these primes and how many are there? A semantic prime is reminiscent of Morris Swadesh's 'basic vocabulary' created to plot diachronic relationships between unwritten languages. It consists of names for things common to the experience of all human communities: the sun, human body parts and functions, etc. (Swadesh 1955).

Proponents of Natural Semantic Metalanguage (NSM) believe that semantic primes (originally named *primitives*) and their elementary syntax exist as a minimal subset of ordinary natural language (Goddard 1994: 10). Seventeenth-century seekers after a universal language including Lodwick (1652), Dalgarno (1661), and Wilkins (1668) had proposed primitive semantic components. Arnauld and Nicole (1996 [1662]) recognized that the meanings of most words can be defined in terms of others, but that ultimately there are some undefinable semantically primitive words. Uriel Weinreich (1962: 36) identified a discovery procedure for a semantic metalanguage built upon natural language. The idea was to stratify the language into (a) a central core of semantic primes whose members are definable only circularly and by ostensive definition such as 'colour of the sky' in the entry for *blue*. (b) The next stratum out uses items whose definitions contain only core items without (further) circularity. (c) Each more peripheral stratum uses items from the preceding strata without circularity. Anna Wierzbicka has been carrying out this programme in a cross-language context since 1972, searching for a universal set of semantic primes expressed principally through the vocabulary of English, but also other languages. The number of semantic primes has grown from 14 in Wierzbicka (1972) to 63 in Goddard (2009).

It is important to consider the playoff between the effectiveness of a semantic definition and its accuracy. This requires that the purpose of the semantic analysis be identified. For whom or what is the resulting semantic specification designed? NSM semantic definitions are not designed to be used by machines that simulate language understanding; they are intended to be easily accessible to a non-native speaker of the language. But every such person will already know what, say, a cup is, so a brief description would be sufficient (see Cruse (1990: 396); Allan (2001: 280f)).

Componential semantics presupposes a checklist of properties to be satisfied for the correct use of the decomposed expression (Fillmore 1975: 123). For example, the default denotatum of *bird* is bipedal, has feathers, and is capable of flight. But there are several species of flightless birds (e.g. emus, penguins); a downy chick and a plucked chicken are featherless, but nonetheless birds; and a one-legged owl and a mutant three-legged hen are also birds. So the notion of a checklist of essential properties for the denotatum is problematical (see Chapter 12). Prototype and stereotype semantics are alternatives to checklist theories of meaning.

5 Prototype and stereotype semantics

The prototype hypothesis is that some denotata are better exemplars of the meaning of a lexeme than others, therefore members of the category denoted by the lexeme are graded with respect to one another. For example, a bird that flies, such as a pigeon, is a better exemplar of the category of birds than a penguin, which doesn't (see Chapter 7).

How are prototypes discovered? Battig and Montague (1969) asked subjects to list as many vegetables, or fruits, or diseases, or toys, etc. as they could in 30 seconds. They hypothesized that the most salient members in each category would be (a) frequently listed and (b) high on the list. They found, for instance, that a carrot is the prototype for vegetable, i.e. the best exemplar of the category because it was listed frequently and early. A tomato belongs to two categories: it is a vegetable in folk belief and technically a fruit. On the Battig and Montague scale, a tomato ranked 6th as a vegetable and 15th as a fruit. George Lakoff (1972) interprets such rankings in terms of fuzzy sets of objects with a continuum of grades of category membership between 0.0 and 1.0. The carrot is the best instance with a value 1.0, a tomato has the value 0.68 (and 0.14 membership in the fuzzy set 'Fruit'), and a pickle is graded only 0.006 of 'Vegetable'. Any entity assigned a value greater than 0.0 is a member of the category, i.e. the pickle is a vegetable no less than the carrot. What the fuzzy set membership value indicates is how good or bad an exemplar of the category a certain population of speakers perceives that entity to be. A tomato is vegetable-like because it is eaten, often with other vegetables, as part of an hors d'oeuvre or main course. It is not eaten, alone or with other fruits, for dessert. A tomato is fruit-like because it grows as a fruit well above the ground and not on or below it. Also, it is often eaten raw and the extracted juice is drunk like fruit juices. It is our practice of eating tomatoes as if they are vegetables rather than fruit that explains their relative ranking in each category (see Chapter 7).

Eleanor Rosch carried out a series of experiments on prototype semantics summarized in Rosch (1978). Rosch (1973) found that the common cold is a very poor exemplar of 'Disease' – which conflicts with the Battig and Montague finding. The discrepancy between the two findings is explained by the fact that Rosch gave her subjects only six diseases to rank (cancer, measles, malaria, muscular dystrophy, rheumatism, cold) and a cold is the mildest of them. Obviously, establishing the prototype depends upon the experiences and beliefs of the population investigated. Consequently, the claimed prototypicality ranking is valid for the community surveyed, but not for all speakers of the language, or even the same subjects on a different occasion.

Ludwig Wittgenstein (1953: §§66–71) wrote of some categories being defined not by a checklist of properties but by 'family resemblances'. George Lakoff (1987) adopted this notion into prototype theory identifying chains of similarities among members of a category. Take the example of the word *mother* and the category 'Mother'. The prototypical mother is the woman who produces the ovum, conceives, gestates, gives birth to and then nurtures a child (giving rise to the traditional definition of *mother*). Radiating from this are more peripheral attributes of a *mother*. The natural or biological mother produces the ovum, conceives, gestates, and gives birth to the child. The genetic or donor mother supplies the ovum to a surrogate mother in whose womb the genetic mother's ovum is implanted and in whose body the foetus develops through to birth. The nurturant mother may be the genetic mother, a surrogate mother, adoptive mother, or foster mother. In addition there is a *stepmother*, a *mother-in-law*, while polygamous societies and other social systems offer additional complexities. Figurative extensions arise: e.g. the prototypical or natural mother is the source for *necessity is the mother of invention*. There is a set of identifiable resemblances among these uses and meanings of the word *mother*, but no set of properties common to all of them. Some extended meanings are figurative (e.g. *mother superior*), and a very important development in late twentieth-century studies of meaning was the general acceptance, following Lakoff and Johnson (1980), that metaphor and metonymy are all-pervasive in language and not clearly demarcated from 'literal' meaning.

Hilary Putnam (1975) proposed a stereotype semantics such that the meaning of a language expression is a minimum set of stereotypical facts constituting a mental image, mental construct, or Gestalt with the attributes of the typical denotatum, including pragmatic connotations (see Allan (2007)). Putnam expressly allows for experts to have considerably more knowledge at their command than their fellows – which raises the question: Do the words *elm* and *beech* have the same stereotype and meaning for a botanist as they do for an inner-city dweller who can't distinguish an elm from a beech? Presumably not. However, if the botanist were to point out and name an elm, the inner-city dweller would know that referent is not a beech, even if s/he could still not recognize another elm thereafter.

How is 'a (stereo-)typical denotatum of *e*' distinguishable from 'as-good-an-exemplar-as-can-be-found among the class of things denoted by *e*'? Presumably, the stereotype properly includes the prototype. For instance, whatever the stereotype of *vegetable* may be, it properly includes the prototype carrot and the peripheral onion. The stereotypical *vehicle* includes the prototypical car and/or bus together with the peripheral horse-drawn wagon. We should, therefore, favour the stereotype in giving the semantics of language expressions, despite the fact that most adherents to prototype semantics often incorrectly subsume stereotype semantics and ignore Putnam.

6 Frame semantics

Frames (Goffman 1974; Fillmore 1982) identify the characteristic features, attributes, and functions of a denotatum, and its characteristic interactions with things necessarily or typically associated with it. For example, a restaurant is a public eating-place; its attributes are: (1) business premises where, in exchange for payment, food is served to be eaten on the premises; consequently, (2) a restaurant has a kitchen for food preparation, and tables and chairs to accommodate customers during their meal. Barsalou (1992: 28) describes attributes as slots in the frame that are to be filled with the appropriate values. The frame for *people* registers the fact that people have the attributes of age and sex. The attribute sex has the values male and female. It can be represented formally by a function BE_SEXED applied to the domain D={x:x is a person} to yield a value from the set {male, female}. The function BE_AGED applies to the same domain to yield a value from a much larger set. Knowledge of frames is called upon in the proper use of language. Attributes for events include participants, location, and time of occurrence, e.g. the verb *buy* has slots for the attributes buyer, seller, merchandise, payment: these give rise to the thematic structure (valencies, case frames) of the verb (see Chapter 23). An act of buying occurs in a certain place at a certain time (a world~time pair with values relevant to evaluation of truth, see below). The 'lexical semantic structures' of Pustejovsky (1995) can, hypothetically, systematically describe semantic frames for every listeme. To sum up, frames provide a structured background derived from experience, beliefs, or practices, constituting a conceptual prerequisite for understanding meaning. The meaning of a language expression relies on the frames, and it is these that relate listemes one to another.

7 Semantics within syntactic structures

Most semantic relations extend beyond listemes to the syntactic structures that combine them. Although the semantics of propositions has been considered within philosophy since Plato, Aristotle, and the Stoics, the first step within linguistics was undertaken by a philosopher, Jerrold J. Katz and a cognitive scientist, Jerry A. Fodor in Katz and Fodor (1963) 'Structure of a semantic theory'. It was Katz who was largely responsible for establishing semantic theory as one component of a transformational generative grammar. The principal semantic component was the 'semantic marker', which names a concept that any human being can conceive of; hence, the theory is applicable to all natural languages (Katz 1967, 1972).

Katz sought to establish a theory of meaning (sense) that would do all of the following: define what it is; define the form of lexical entries; relate semantics to syntax and phonology by postulating semantic theory as an integral component of a theory of grammar; establish a metalanguage in which semantic representations, properties, and relations are expressed; ensure the metalanguage is universal by correlating it with the human ability to conceptualize; identify the components of meaning and show how they combine to project meaning onto structurally complex expressions. Essentially, these are goals that should be met by any semantic theory – though what is meant by 'component of meaning' and the integration of semantics with phonology and syntax may be radically different within different theories. Missing from Katz's conditions is the requirement that the meaning of language expressions needs to be related to the real and imaginary worlds people speak and write of. Furthermore, Katz's theory offered no account of utterance or speaker meaning.

Katz's semantic theory is interpretative. The earliest version was geared to the syntactic model of Chomsky (1957) and was fatally flawed (see Bolinger (1965); Weinreich (1966)). In later versions Katz's theory was designed to assign meanings to the output of autonomous syntactic rules of a transformational generative grammar of the kind described in Chomsky (1965) but he never updated it to accommodate later developments in generative syntax. Nor did Katz ever validate the vocabulary and syntax of his theory, and we can only learn to interpret his metalanguage by abduction from his examples, among which there is little consistency, and so his semantic markers remain only partially comprehensible. There were at least five differently structured semantic readings for *chase* given by Katz himself (Katz 1966, 1967, 1972, 1977b; Katz and Nagel 1974) and an additional two in Janet Fodor (1977) (see Allan (1986) for extensive discussion). We can interpret Katz's semantic markers for *chase*, for instance, because they use English words whose meanings we combine to match up with our existing knowledge of its meaning (something like *X is quickly following the moving object Y with the intention of catching it*). Katz has claimed (as have others) that the English used in the semantic metalanguage is not English, which is used only as a mnemonic device. However, the only way to make any sense of the metalanguage is to translate it into a natural language. That is why analysing *bachelor* into {(Human), (Adult), (Male), (Single)}, as did Katz and Nagel (1974: 324), is a more enlightening semantic analysis than, say, {(48), (41), (4D), (53)}. Formalism, especially unconventional formalism, can only be justified if it increases explicitness of statement and rigour of analysis, and promotes clarity of expression.

Katz's semantic theory was the first to try to comprehensively integrate linguistic semantics with syntax. Logicians had taken steps in this direction since the Stoic period, and Prague school linguists had studied aspects of functional sentence perspective a decade or so earlier but, in spite of its shortcomings, Katz's conception of the syntax~semantics interface was far more wide-ranging and influential, and it did identify the parameters that other theories needed to engage with. A major limitation was the absence of any proper treatment of pragmatics and no obvious extension beyond sentences to texts. These faults are also to be found in most of its rivals.

8 Alternatives to Katzian semantics

Noam Chomsky was educated in the Bloomfieldian school that eschewed semantic theory as speculative subjectivism. For him semantics was at best an add-on for the syntactic base, a position affirmed by Katz and later by Ray Jackendoff. The *Aspects* theory developed in Chomsky (1965) had a level of deep structure at which the meaning of each sentence constituent was syntactically specified and the meaning 'projected' upwards through nodes in the phrase marker to semantically interpret the sentence. Deep structure was separate from a level of surface structure at which the form of the sentence (as used in everyday utterance) was specified. This conception of grammar leads naturally to the view that pairs of formally distinct but semantically equivalent expressions arise from the same deep structure by different transformations, e.g. (a) *X caused Y to die* and *X killed Y* or (b) *X reminds me of Y* and *X strikes me as similar to Y* or (c) *my mother* and *the woman who bore me*. In generative semantics (the term was first used by Lakoff in 1963 [Lakoff (1976)], the earliest published use is Bendix (1966: 12)), the initial structures in a grammar are semantic rather than solely syntactic. It grew directly from reaction to the 'standard theory' of Katz and Postal (1964) and Chomsky (1965) with its emphasis on syntactic justification. Lakoff (1965), originally conceived as an extension of standard theory, postulates phrase markers that terminate in feature bundles like those in *Aspects*; Lakoff differs from Chomsky in proposing that listemes be inserted into only some terminal nodes, the rest functioning as well-formedness conditions on lexical insertion and semantic interpretation, which preceded other transformations. Gruber (1965) contains lexical structures that have most of the syntactic characteristics of standard theory trees, but some terminal nodes are semantic components. Some transformations operate prior to lexical insertion. For instance, from the prelexical structure VP[V[MOTIONAL, POSITIONAL] PrepP[Prep[ACROSS] . . .]], lexical insertion will put either the verb *go* under the V node and the lexeme *across* under the Prep node, or alternatively map the single verb *cross* into a combination of both the V and Prep nodes. The latter was a radical innovation: because semantic interpretation is made before transformations such as passive apply, semantics and syntax are interdependent. A similar conclusion was reached in Postal (1966, 1970, 1972) and Lakoff and Ross (1976 [1967]). Weinreich (1966) and McCawley (1968a) showed that lexical insertion is semantically governed and that syntactic structure is merely the skeleton for semantics. Thus, in generative semantics, initial symbols represent semantic components set into structures that are a hybrid of predicate logic and natural language syntax – both well-established conventional systems. These structures could be rearranged in various ways by transformations before lexical forms were mapped onto them. Meaning is determined directly from the initial semantic structure.

9 Conceptual semantics

For Ray S. Jackendoff, semantics is a part of conceptual structure in which linguistic, sensory, and motor information are compatible (see Jackendoff (1983, 2007)). Jackendoff, although not subscribing to prototype or stereotype semantics, believes that word meaning is a large, heterogeneous collection of typicality conditions (i.e. what's most likely the case, such as that a bird typically flies) with no sharp distinction between lexicon and encyclopaedia. According to Jackendoff, every content-bearing major phrasal constituent of a sentence corresponds to a conceptual constituent. S expresses STATE or EVENT. NP can express almost any conceptual category. PP expresses PLACE, PATH, and PROPERTY. Jackendoff is principally interested in the semantic structure of verbs, with a secondary interest in function-argument structures in the spatial domain. He makes no attempt to decompose nouns semantically, treating them as semantic primitives. In his view, only kin terms and geometric figures admit of satisfactory semantic decomposition. By contrast, he finds that verbs decompose into comparatively few classes (as also in Role and Reference Grammar, see Van Valin (1993, 2005)).

Jackendoff's vocabulary of semantic primitives is very much larger than the set used by NSM researchers (see above). The syntax of his lexical conceptual structure (LCS) is a configuration of functions ranging over arguments. For instance,

(1) *Bill drank the beer* $[_{Event}CAUSE([_{Thing}BILL]^{\alpha}_{A\text{-actor}}, [_{Event}GO([_{Thing\text{-liquid}}BEER]_{A\text{-theme}}, [_{Path}TO([_{Place}IN([_{Thing}MOUTH\ OF([_{Thing}\alpha])])])])])]$

Conceptual semantics shows that a semantic decomposition of verbs making extensive use of just a few primitives is a feasible project. The syntax of LCS is a function-argument structure similar to that of predicate calculus, so that someone acquainted with predicate calculus can construct a lexical conceptual structure despite the fact that Jackendoff does not employ standard logical formulae. Although LCS makes no use of logical connectives, some of the more complex formulae imply conjunction between the function-argument structures in a lexical conceptual structure. There are a score of primitive verbs so far identified, so although the set of functions is restricted, the vocabulary of primitive arguments is unbounded. Conceptual semantics integrates with a version of Chomskyan syntactic theory.

10 The importance of truth conditions

Donald Davidson (1967b: 310) said that 'to give truth conditions is a way of giving the meaning of a sentence'. Truth is dependent on worlds and times: *Marilyn Monroe would have been 74 on June 1, 2000* is true (she was born June 1, 1926). McCawley (1968a, b) was one of the first linguists to adopt and adapt truth conditions and predicate logic into grammar (see McCawley (1993 [1981])). The importance of truth conditions had often been overlooked by linguists, especially those focusing on lexical semantics. Hjelmslev (1943), Lyons (1968), and Lehrer (1974) all suggest that the nine listemes *bull, calf, cow, ewe, foal, lamb, mare, ram, stallion* – which constitute a fragment of a semantic field – can be contrasted with one another in such a way as to reveal the semantic components in Table 3.1.

The basis for claiming that BOVINE or MALE is a semantic component of *bull* cannot be a matter merely of language. It is a relation speakers believe exists between the denotata of the terms *bull* and *male* and *bovine* (i.e. things in a world that these terms may be felicitously used to refer to). Doing semantic analysis of listemes, it is not enough to claim that (2) is

Table 3.1 A componential table

BOVINE	bull	cow	calf
EQUINE	stallion	mare	foal
OVINE	ram	ewe	lamb
	MALE	FEMALE	YOUNG
	ADULT		

linguistic evidence for the claim that MALE is a semantic component of *bull*, because (3) is equally good until a basis for the semantic anomaly has been established that is independent of what we are seeking to establish – namely the justification for the semantic components identified in Table 3.1.

(2) A bull is male.
(3) A bull is female.

The only language-independent device available is an appeal to truth conditions, and this takes us to the denotata of *bull* and *male*. In fact what we need to say is something like (4).

(4) In every admissible possible world and time an entity which is a bull is male and in no such world is an entity which is a bull a female.

Note that the semantic component MALE of Table 3.1 must be equivalent to the relevant sense of the English word *male*. Thus, the assumption is that semantic components reflect characteristics of typical denotata as revealed through their intensions across worlds and times. In any case, they provide the justification for postulating the semantic components in Table 3.1 as a set of inferences such as those in (5).

(5) For any entity x that is properly called a *bull*, it is the case that x is adult and x is male and x is bovine.

In fact it is not part of a general semantic characterization of *bull* that it typically denotes adults; one can, without contradiction, refer to a *bull calf*. Rather, it is part of the general naming practice for complementary sets of male and female animals. Nor is *bull* restricted to bovines; it is also used of male elephants, male whales, male seals, male alligators, etc. The initial plausibility of Table 3.1 and (5) is because it describes the (stereo)typical bull. The world of the English speaker is such that *bull* is much more likely to denote a bovine than any other species of animal, which is why *bull elephant* is usual, but *bull bovine* is not. This reduces (5) to something more like (6).

(6) For any entity x that is properly called a *bull*, it is the case that x is male and probably bovine.

What is uncovered here is that even lexical semantics is necessarily dependent on truth conditions together with pragmatically probable conditions (see Chapter 1).

11 The development of formal semantics

Charles Sanders Peirce (1839–1914) is celebrated for being a founder of pragmatics, but he also made extensive and highly original contributions to mathematical logic. He introduced into logic the material-conditional operator and operators like NAND and NOR. Peirce (1870) invented the notion of a variable and a syntax for the logic of relations of arbitrary adicity. By 1883 he had developed a syntax for quantificational logic. However, it is Gottlob Frege (1848–1925) who usually gets the credit for developing the first system of formal logic using a metalanguage modelled on the language of arithmetic (Frege 1879). The distinction made in Frege (1892) between *Sinn* ('sense') and *Bedeutung* ('denotation; reference') is comparable with Arnauld and Nicole's (1965 [1662]) comprehension~extension, Hamilton's (1876) intension~extension, or John Stuart Mill's (1843) connotation~denotation though it is uncertain whether he was directly influenced by any of these. Frege noted that $a = a$ and $a = b$ are obviously statements of different cognitive value, as we can see from the fact that although *the morning star* refers to Venus and *the evening star* also refers to Venus, the two phrases differ in sense and intension. Frege distinguished senses from ideas (concepts), which some of his followers have failed to do. Ideas are particular to individual language users, senses form 'a common store of thoughts which is transmitted from one generation to another'. Although he doesn't say so, this view is compatible with sense being a property of the language itself, which is, of course, transmitted across generations. The fact that truth is assigned to the reference of propositions led him to raise questions about what have come to be called opaque and intensional contexts.

In *Foundations of Arithmetic* Frege asserts (echoing James Harris and Jeremy Bentham) that words have meaning only in virtue of being constituents of sentences that have sense (Frege 1884: 70). In other words, meaning is a function of context. This context principle is the top-down counterpart to the bottom-up principle of compositionality often assigned to Frege, e.g.

> [E]very sentence, no matter how complicated, can be seen as the result of a systematic construction process which adds logical words one by one.
>
> (Gamut 1991 I:15)

And it is found in Frege (1963 [1918]: 1), which states that we can 'distinguish in the thought corresponding to parts of a sentence, so that the structure of the sentence serves as an image of the structure of the thought'. But it is a principle that goes back at least as far as Plato's *Sophist*.

It became clear during the twentieth century that an indefinite noun phrase requires the hearer to create a subset x from a set y such that $x \subset y$ as in *Two coffees, please* (a set of two from the set of all possible coffees relative to the context of discourse). Bertrand Russell (1905) presented a theory of definite descriptions in which a sentence such as (7) has the logical translation (8) for some x such that x is a lamb, and for every y such that if y is a lamb then y is identical to x, such that x is sick.

(7) The lamb is sick.
(8) $\exists x(Lx \,\&\, \forall y(Ly \rightarrow y=x) \,\&\, Sx)$

The definite indicates a readily identifiable referent by equating set x with set y (perhaps by naming it) such that a definite article is similar to a universal quantifier. This has become known as the quantificational reading of the definite article and some people believe that the referential use of a definite description rests on prior understanding of its quantificational meaning (Kripke 1977; Bach 2004). There is a contrary view, refuting the quantificational analysis in favour of direct reference, that effectively sees the use of definites as analogous with pointing, thus rendering the definite unanalysable (Kaplan 1978; Devitt 2007). The controversy shows no sign of abating.

Since about the time of Cresswell (1973) and Keenan (ed.) (1975), there have been many linguists working in formal semantics. Formal semantics interprets formal systems, in particular those that arise from the coalescence of set theory, model theory, and lambda calculus with philosophical logic – especially the work of Richard Montague (Montague 1974; Dowty et al. 1981), and the tense logic and modal logic such as Prior (1957) and Kripke (1963, 1972). By and large, formal semantics has ignored the semantics of listemes such as nouns, verbs, and adjectives – which are typically used as semantic primes (but see Dowty 1979). It does, however, offer insightful analyses of secondary grammatical categories like number and quantification, tense, and modals.

Event-based semantics was initiated by Davidson (1967a). The idea is to quantify over events, thus *Ed hears Jo call out* is a complex of two events as shown in (9), where there is the event e of Jo's calling out and the event e' of Ed hearing e.

(9) $\exists e[\text{call out}(\text{Jo}, e) \ \& \ \exists e' \ \text{hear}(\text{Ed}, e, e')]$

Following a suggestion of Parsons (1980, 1990) participant roles can be incorporated as in (10), *Max drinks the beer*.

(10) $\exists e[\text{drink}(e) \ \& \ \text{agent}(e, \text{Max}) \ \& \ \text{patient}(e, \text{the beer})]$

This facilitates the nonspecification of the characterizing statement *Max drinks* in (11).

(11) $\exists e[\text{drink}(e) \ \& \ \text{agent}(e, \text{Max})]$.

There is always the question of how the meanings of complex expressions are related to the simpler expressions they are constructed from: this aspect of composition is determined by model theory in Montague semantics, which is truth conditional with respect to possible worlds. Where traditional predicate and propositional logic was concerned only with extension (existence) in the (real) world, intensional logics allow for existence in a possible (hypothetical) world. Just as intensions are comparable with 'sense', extensions are comparable with 'reference' or, better, denoting something within a particular model or set of models (see Chapter 4).

12 Dynamic semantics

As a rule, any two successive references to an entity involve some kind of change to it on the second reference. For instance:

(12)   Catch [a chicken$_1$]. Kill [it$_2$]. Pluck [it$_3$]. Draw [it$_4$]. Cut [it$_5$] up. Marinade [it$_6$]. Roast [it$_7$]. When you've eaten [it$_8$], put [the bones$_9$] in the compost.

All nine subscripted NPs refer to the creature identified in 'a chicken$_1$', which refers to a live chicken. After 2 it is dead, after 3 featherless, after 5 dismembered, after 7 roasted, and after 8 eaten. 9 refers to the chicken's bones after the flesh has been stripped from them. Thus 7, for instance, refers not to the chicken in 1, but to the caught, killed, plucked, drawn, cut up, and marinaded pieces of chicken. Heim (1983, 1988) described this as updating the file on a referent. These successive states of the chicken are presented as updates in the world~time pair spoken of. The dynamic aim is similar in Discourse Representation Theory (DRT) (Kamp 1981; Kamp and Reyle 1993) where the interpretation of one in a sequence of utterances (a discourse) is dependent on co-text such that the next utterance is an update of it. DRT has been especially successful in capturing the complex semantics of so-called donkey sentences (see above). For instance, (13) (in a move presaged by Ockham) paraphrases as (14).

(13) Every girl who owns a pony loves it.
(14) If a girl owns a pony, she loves it.

A discourse representation structure (DRS) for (14) is (15). The arrow ⇒ indicates that the second box is a consequence of the first. The left-hand box is interpreted first, then the right-hand box. Notice that the anaphor for a-pony-loved-by-the-girl-who-owns-it is z, and it does not occur in the left-hand box. The DRS for (13) is (16).

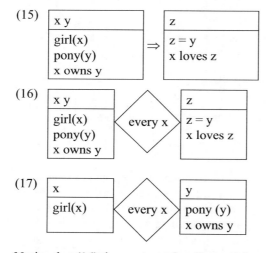

Notice that (16) does not say that *Every girl owns a pony*, whose DRS is (17). DRT is undergoing extensions in the twenty-first century; see Asher and Lascarides (2003), Jaszczolt (2005, 2009).

13 Conclusion

This essay has sketched a history of semantics, but much is omitted. I began with concerns about what names are and where they come from, then turned to the persistent realist vs. nominalist controversy as it concerns universals. I reviewed various opinions about the relationship between human minds, language expressions, and aspects of their meanings such as sense and intension, reference and extension. In the Western Classical Tradition, lexical semantics began with etymologies and glossaries of literary works that gave way to word lists with attributed meanings (both monolingual and bilingual) resembling modern dictionaries. Study of semantic relations among listemes gave rise to lexical semantics.

Componential analysis began in the eighteenth century but in its modern form from the mid-twentieth. There have been very few exhaustive studies of the semantic components in any semantic field and componential analysis is moribund. There is also a serious problem determining what counts as a semantic prime, despite the efforts of proponents of the Natural Semantics Metalanguage. Prototype semantics, stereotype semantics, and frame semantics complement rather than replace componential analysis. The contribution of syntax to the meaning of utterances was at last incorporated into semantic theory, though the efforts of Katz and Jackendoff really need to be augmented by the techniques of dynamic semantics. And the contribution of pragmatics has been completely ignored in this essay (see Allan (2001, 2010)).

Further reading

Allan, Keith 2010. *The Western Classical Tradition in Linguistics* (Second expanded edition). London: Equinox. [First edn 2007.]. Chapter 13, 'Linguistic semantics and pragmatics from earliest times', surveys the history of semantics.

Allan, Keith 2013. *The Oxford Handbook of the History of Linguistics.* Chapter 23 'The logico-philosophical tradition' by Pieter M. Seuren; Chapter 24 'Lexical semantics from speculative etymology to structuralist semantics' by Dirk Geeraerts; Chapter 25 'Post-structuralist and cognitive approaches to meaning' by Dirk Geeraerts. Oxford: Oxford University Press. These chapters deal with the topics named in the chapter titles.

Nerlich, Brigitte 1992. *Semantic Theories in Europe, 1830–1930: From Etymology to Contextuality.* Amsterdam/Philadelphia: John Benjamins. The early history of modern linguistic semantics.

References

Allan, Keith 1986. *Linguistic Meaning*. 2 vols. London: Routledge and Kegan Paul.
Allan, Keith 2001. *Natural Language Semantics*. Oxford & Malden MA: Blackwell.
Allan, Keith 2007. The pragmatics of connotation. *Journal of Pragmatics* 39: 1047–57.
Allan, Keith 2010. *The Western Classical Tradition in Linguistics* (Second expanded edition). London: Equinox. [First edn 2007.].
Allan, Keith 2014. Referring to 'what counts as the referent': a view from linguistics. In Alessandro Capone, Franco Lo Piparo and Marco Carapezza (eds) *Perspectives on Pragmatics and Philosophy*. Berlin: Springer Verlag, 263–84.
Apresjan, Juri D. 2000. *Systematic Lexicography*. Transl. by Kevin Windle. Oxford: Oxford University Press.
Aristophanes of Byzantium 1986. *Aristophanis Byzantii Fragmenta*. Post A. Nauck collegit, testimoniis ornavit, brevi commentario instruxit William J. Slater. Berlin: De Gruyter.
Aristotle 1984. *The Complete Works of Aristotle. The Revised Oxford Translation.* Ed. by Jonathan Barnes. Bollingen Series 71. Princeton: Princeton University Press.
Arnauld, Antoine and Pierre Nicole 1965. *La Logique, ou L'art de Penser: contenant, outre les règles communes, plusieurs observations nouvelles propres à former le jugement.* Éd. critique par Pierre Clair et François Girbal [based on the final 1683 version]. Paris: Presses universitaires de France.
Arnauld, Antoine and Pierre Nicole 1996. *The Logic or the Art of Thinking. Containing, Besides Common Rules, Several New Observations Appropriate for Forming Judgment.* Transl. by Jill V. Buroker. Cambridge: Cambridge University Press.
Asher, Nicholas and Alex Lascarides 2003. *Logics of Conversation*. Cambridge: Cambridge University Press.
Bach, Kent 2004. Descriptions: points of reference. In Marga Reimer and Anne Bezuidenhout (eds) *Descriptions and Beyond*. Oxford: Oxford University Press, 189–229.

Backhouse, Anthony E. 1994. *The Lexical Field of Taste: A Semantic Study of Japanese Taste Terms*. Cambridge: Cambridge University Press.

Barsalou, Lawrence W. 1992. Frames, concepts, and conceptual fields. In Eva Kittay and Adrienne Lehrer (eds) *Frames, Fields, and Contrasts*. Norwood NJ: Lawrence Erlbaum, 21–74.

Battig, William F. and William E. Montague 1969. Category norms for verbal items in 56 categories. *Journal of Experimental Psychology Monograph 80*.

Bendix, Edward H. 1966. *Componential Analysis of General Vocabulary: The Semantic Structure of a Set of Verbs in English, Hindi, and Japanese*. Bloomington IN: Indiana University Press.

Bolinger, Dwight 1965. The atomization of meaning. *Language* 41: 555–73.

Bréal, Michel 1883. Les lois intellectuelles du langage: fragment de sémantique. *Annuaire de l'Assocaition pour l'encouragement des études grecques en France* 17: 132–42.

Bréal, Michel 1897. *Essai de sémantique: Science de significations*. Paris: Hachette.

Bréal, Michel 1900. *Semantics: Studies in the Science of Meaning*. Transl. by Mrs Henry Cust, with a preface by John P. Postgate. London: W. Heinemann.

Burley, Walter 2000. *On the Purity of the Art of Logic: The Shorter and the Longer Treatises*. Transl. by Paul V. Spade. New Haven: Yale University Press.

Chomsky, Noam 1957. *Syntactic Structures*. The Hague: Mouton.

Chomsky, Noam 1965. *Aspects of the Theory of Syntax*. Cambridge MA: MIT Press.

Chomsky, Noam 1975. *Reflections on Language*. New York: Pantheon Books.

Cresswell, Max J. 1973. *Logics and Languages*. London: Methuen.

Cruse, D. Alan 1990. Prototype theory and lexical semantics. In Savas L. Tsohatzidis (ed.) *Meanings and Prototypes: Studies in Linguistic Categorization*. London: Routledge, 382–402.

Dalgarno, George 1661. *Ars Signorum, Vulgo Character Universalis et Lingua Philosophica*. London: J. Hayes. [Menston: Scolar Press Facsimile. 1968.].

Davidson, Donald 1967a. The logical form of action sentences. In Nicholas Rescher (ed.) *The Logic of Decision and Action*. Pittsburgh: University of Pittsburgh Press, 81–94 [Reprinted in Donald Davidson 1980 *Essays on Actions and Events*. Oxford: Oxford University Press, 105–21].

Davidson, Donald 1967b. Truth and meaning. *Synthese* 17: 304–23. Reprinted in Jay Rosenberg and Charles Travis (eds) 1971, *Readings in the Philosophy of Language*. Englewood Cliffs NJ: Prentice Hall, 450–65.

Devitt, Michael 2007. Referential descriptions and conversational implicatures. *European Journal of Analytic Philosophy* 3: 7–32.

Dowty, David R. 1979. *Word Meaning and Montague Grammar: The Semantics of Verbs and Times in Generative Semantics and in Montague's PTQ*. Dordrecht: Reidel.

Dowty, David R., Robert E. Wall and Stanley Peters 1981. *Introduction to Montague Semantics*. Dordrecht: Reidel.

Fillmore, Charles J. 1975. An alternative to checklist theories of meaning. In Cathy Cogen et al. (eds) *Proceedings of the First Annual Meeting of the Berkeley Linguistics Society*. Berkeley: Berkeley Linguistics Society, 123–31.

Fillmore, Charles J. 1982. Towards a descriptive framework for spatial deixis. In Robert J. Jarvella and Wolfgang Klein (eds) *Speech, Place, and Action: Studies in Deixis and Related Topics*. Chichester: John Wiley, 31–59.

Fodor, Janet D. 1977. *Semantics: Theories of Meaning in Generative Grammar*. New York: Thomas Crowell.

Frege, Gottlob 1879. *Begriffsschrift, eine der arithmetischen nachgebildete Formelsprache des reinen Denkens*. Halle: Louis Nebert.

Frege, Gottlob 1884. *Die Grundlagen der Arithmetik: eine logisch-mathematische Untersuchung über den Begriff der Zahl*. Breslau: W. Koebner.

Frege, Gottlob 1892. Über Sinn und Bedeutung. *Zeitschrift für Philosophie und philosophische Kritik* 100: 25–50. Reprinted as 'On sense and reference'. In Peter Geach and Max Black (eds) 1960, *Translations from the Philosophical Writings of Gottlob Frege*. Oxford: Blackwell, 56–78.

Frege, Gottlob 1963. Compound thoughts. *Mind* 72: 1–17.

Gamut, L.T.F. 1991. *Language Logic and Meaning*. Vol. 1, *Introduction to Logic*. Vol. 2, *Intensional Logic and Logical Grammar*. Chicago: Chicago University Press.

Geach, Peter T. 1968. *Reference and Generality: An Examination of Some Medieval and Modern Theories*. Emended edn. Ithaca: Cornell University Press [First edn 1962].

Geckeler, Horst 1971. *Strukturelle Semantik und Wortfeldtheorie*. München: W. Fink.

Goddard, Cliff 1994. Semantic theory and semantic universals. In Cliff Goddard and Anna Wierzbicka (eds), *Semantic and Lexical Universals: Theory and Empirical Findings*. Amsterdam: John Benjamins, 7–29.

Goddard, Cliff 2009. The 'communication concept' and the 'language concept' in everyday English. *Australian Journal of Linguistics* 29: 11–26.

Goffman, Erving 1974. *Frame Analysis: An Essay on the Organization of Experience*. New York: Harper and Row.

Goodenough, Ward H. 1956. Componential analysis and the study of meaning. *Language* 32: 195–216.

Groenendijk, Jeroen A.G. and Martin J.B. Stokhof 1991. Dynamic predicate logic. *Linguistics and Philosophy* 14: 39–100.

Gruber, Jeffrey S. 1965. *Studies in Lexical Relations*. PhD thesis. Massachusetts Institute of Technology. Published by the Indiana University Linguistics Club (Bloomington) in 1970. Revised version in Gruber 1976, *Lexical Structures in Syntax and Semantics*. Amsterdam: North Holland, 1–210.

Hamilton, (Sir) William 1876. *Lectures on Metaphysics and Logic*. Vol. II *Logic*. Edited by the Rev. Henry L. Mansel and John Veitch. New York: Sheldon and Co. [First published Edinburgh and London: W. Blackwood, 1859–60].

Hanks, Patrick 2013. Lexicography from earliest times to the present. In Keith Allan (ed.) *Oxford Handbook of the History of Linguistics*. Oxford: Oxford University Press, 503–35.

Harris, Zellig S. 1948. Componential analysis of a Hebrew paradigm. *Language* 24: 87–91.

Harris, Zellig S. 1951. *Methods in Structural Linguistics*. Chicago: University of Chicago Press.

Heim, Irene R. 1983. File change semantics and the familiarity theory of definiteness. In Rainer Bäuerle, Ch. Schwarze and Arnim von Stechow (eds) *Meaning, Use, and the Interpretation of Language*. Berlin: De Gruyter, 164–89.

Heim, Irene R. 1988. *The Semantics of Definite and Indefinite Noun Phrases*. New York: Garland.

Hjelmslev, Louis 1943. *Omkring Sprogteoriens Grundlaeggelse*. Copenhagen. Reprinted as *Prolegomena to a Theory of Language*. Trans. Francis J. Whitfield. Madison: University of Wisconsin. 1961.

Humboldt, Wilhelm von 1836. *Einleitung. Über die Verschiedenheit des menschlichen Sprachbaues und ihren Einfluss auf die geistige Entwickelung des Menschengeschlechts. In Über die Kawi-Sprache auf der Insel Java*. Erster Band. Berlin: Druckerei der Königlichen Akademie der Wissenschaften.

Isidore 1850. Etymologiarum. In Jacques-Paul Migne (ed.) *Patrologiae Cursus Completus, Patrologiae Latinae Tomus LXXXII*. Paris: J-P Migne, 73–847.

Jackendoff, Ray S. 1983. *Semantics and Cognition*. Cambridge MA: MIT Press.

Jackendoff, Ray S. 2007. *Language, Consciousness, Culture: Essays on Mental Structure* (Jean Nicod Lectures). Cambridge MA: MIT Press.

Jakobson, Roman 1936. Beitrag zur allgemeinen Kasuslehre. Travaux du Cercle Linguistique de Prague 6: 240–88. ['Contribution to the general theory of case' in Chapter 22 of Linda R. Waugh and Monique Monville-Burston (eds) 1990. *Roman Jakobson On Language*. Cambridge MA: Harvard University Press, 332–85.]

Jaszczolt, Kasia (Katarzyna) M. 2005. *Default Semantics: Foundations of a Compositional Theory of Acts of Communication*. Oxford: Oxford University Press.

Jaszczolt, Kasia (Katarzyna) M. 2009. *Representing Time: An Essay on Temporality as Modality*. Oxford: Oxford University Press.

Johnson, Samuel 1755. *A Dictionary of the English Language: In which the Words are Deduced From their Originals, and Illustrated by Examples from the Best Writers. To which are prefixed, a history of the language, and an English grammar*. 2 vols. London: W. Strahan.

Kamp, Hans 1981. A theory of truth and semantic representation. In Jereon A.G. Groenendijk, Theo M.V. Janseen and Martin B.J. Stokhof (eds) *Formal Methods in the Study of Language*. Amsterdam: Mathematisch Centrum, 277–322.

Kamp, Hans and Uwe Reyle 1993. *From Discourse to Logic: Introduction to Modeltheoretic Semantics of Natural Language, Formal Logic and Discourse Representation Theory*. Dordrecht: Kluwer.

Kaplan, David 1978. Dthat. In Peter Cole (ed.) *Syntax and Semantics 9: Pragmatics*. New York, 221–43.

Katz, Jerrold J. 1967. Recent issues in semantic theory. *Foundations of Language* 3: 124–94.

Katz, Jerrold J. 1972. *Semantic Theory*. New York: Harper and Row.

Katz, Jerrold J. and Jerry A. Fodor 1963. Structure of a semantic theory. *Language* 39: 170–210.

Katz, Jerrold J. and Richard I. Nagel 1974. Meaning postulates and semantic theory. *Foundations of Language* 11: 311–40.

Katz, Jerrold J. and Paul M. Postal 1964. *An Integrated Theory of Linguistic Descriptions*. Cambridge MA: MIT Press.

Keenan, Edward L. (ed.) 1975. *Formal Semantics of Natural Language: Papers from a Colloquium Sponsored by the King's College Research Centre*. Cambridge: Cambridge University Press.

King, Peter 2004. Peter Abelard. In Edward N. Zalta (ed.) *Stanford Encyclopedia of Philosophy*: http://plato.stanford.edu/entries/abelard.

Kripke, Saul 1963. Semantical considerations on modal logic. *Proceedings of a Colloquium on Modal and Many-valued Logics. Helsinki, 23–26 August, 1962*. Helsinki: Acta Philosophica Fennica.

Kripke, Saul 1972. Naming and necessity. In Donald Davidson and Gilbert Harman (eds) *Semantics of Natural Language*. Dordrecht: Reidel, 253–355. Republished separately as *Naming and Necessity* 1980. Oxford: Blackwell.

Kripke, Saul 1977. Speaker's reference and semantic reference. In Peter A. French, Theodore E. Uehling and Howard K. Wettstein (eds) *Contemporary Perspectives in the Philosophy of Language*. Minneapolis: University of Minnesota Press, 6–27.

Kroeber, Alfred L. 1909. Classificatory systems of relationship. *Journal of the Royal Anthropological Institute* 39: 77–84.

Lakoff, George 1965. *On the Nature of Syntactic Irregularity*. Report NSF-16. Cambridge MA: The Computation Laboratory of Harvard University. Reprinted as *Irregularity in Syntax* 1970. New York: Holt, Rinehart and Winston.

Lakoff, George 1972. Hedges: a study of meaning criteria and the logic of fuzzy concepts. In Paul M. Peranteau, Judith N. Levi and Gloria C. Phares (eds) *Papers from the Eighth Regional Meeting of the Chicago Linguistics Society*. Chicago: Chicago Linguistics Society, 183–228. Revised version in D. Hockney, W. Harper, and B. Freed (eds) 1972. *Contemporary Research in Philosophical Logic and Linguistic Semantics*. Dordrecht: Reidel, 221–71.

Lakoff, George 1976. Toward generative semantics. In James D. McCawley (ed.) *Syntax and Semantics 7: Notes from the Linguistic Underground*. New York: Academic Press, 43–61. [First circulated 1963.]

Lakoff, George 1987. *Women, Fire, and Dangerous Things*. Chicago: University of Chicago Press.

Lakoff, George and Mark Johnson 1980. *Metaphors We Live By*. Chicago: University of Chicago Press.

Lakoff, George and John R. Ross 1976. Is deep structure necessary? In James D. McCawley (ed.) *Syntax and Semantics 7: Notes from the Linguistic Underground*. New York: Academic Press, 159–64. [First circulated in 1967.]

Lehrer, Adrienne 1974. *Semantic Fields and Lexical Structure*. Amsterdam: North Holland.

Leibniz, Gottfried W. 1765. *Œuvres philosophiques latines et francoises de feu Mr. De Leibnitz*. Amsterdam: Rudolf Raspe.

Leibniz, Gottfried W. 1981. *New Essays on Human Understanding*. Transl. and edited by Peter Remnant and Jonathan Bennett. Cambridge: Cambridge University Press. [Nouveaux Essais sur L'Entendement Humain, written 1704, first published in Oeuvres Philosophiques latines et francoises de feu Mr. De Leibnitz, Amsterdam: Rudolf Raspe, 1765.]

Locke, John 1700. *Essay Concerning Humane Understanding*. 4th edn, with large additions. 4 vols. London: Printed for Awnsham and John Churchil et al. [First edn, 1690.].

Lodwick, Francis 1652. The groundwork or foundation laid, (or so intended) for the framing of a new perfect language and an universall or common writing. In Vivian Salmon (ed.) 1972. *The Works of Francis Lodwick: A Study of his Writings in the Intellectual Context of the Seventeenth Century*. London: Longman, 203–22.

Lodwick, Francis 1972. *The works of Francis Lodwick: a study of his writings in the intellectual context of the seventeenth century*. Ed. by Vivian Salmon. London: Longman.

Lounsbury, Floyd G. 1956. A semantic analysis of the Pawnee kinship usage. *Language* 32: 158–94.

Lyons, (Sir) John 1963. *Structural Semantics: An Analysis of Part of the Vocabulary of Plato*. Oxford: Blackwell.

Lyons, (Sir) John 1968. *Introduction to Theoretical Linguistics*. London: Cambridge University Press.

McCawley, James D. 1968a. Lexical insertion in a transformational grammar without deep structure. In Bill J. Darden, Charles-James N. Bailey and Alice Davison (eds) *Papers from the Fourth Regional Meeting of the Chicago Linguistic Society*. Chicago: Chicago Linguistic Society, 71–80. James D. McCawley 1973. *Grammar and Meaning*. Tokyo: Taikushan, 155–66.

McCawley, James D. 1968b. The role of semantics in a grammar. In Emmon Bach and Robert T. Harms (eds) *Universals in Linguistic Theory*. New York: Holt, Rinehart and Winston, 124–69. Reprinted in James D. McCawley 1973. *Grammar and Meaning*. Tokyo: Taikushan, 59–98.

McCawley, James D. 1993. *Everything That Linguists Have Always Wanted to Know about Logic, But were Ashamed to Ask*. 2nd edn. Chicago: University of Chicago Press. [First edn 1981].

Mel'cuk, Igor A. et al. 1984–1991. *Dictionaire Explicatif et Combinatoire du Français Contemporain*. 3 vols. Montréal: Les Presses de l'Université de Montréal.

Ménage, Gilles 1650. *Les Origines de la langue françoise*. Paris: Augustin Courbé.

Mill, John S. 1843. *A System of Logic, Ratiocinative and Inductive: Being a Connected View of the Principles of Evidence and the Methods of Scientific Investigation*. 2 vols. London: John W. Parker.

Montague, Richard 1974. *Formal Philosophy*. Ed. by Richmond Thomason. New Haven: Yale University Press.

Parsons, Terence 1980. Modifiers and quantifiers in natural language. In Francis J. Pelletier and Calvin G. Normore (eds), *New Essays in Philosophy of Language*. Guelph: Canadian Association for Publishing in Philosophy, 29–60.

Parsons, Terence 1990. *Events in the Semantics of English: A Study in Subatomic Semantics*. Cambridge MA: MIT Press.

Peirce, Charles S. 1870. Description of a notation for the logic of relatives, resulting from an amplification of the conceptions of Boole's calculus of logic. *Memoirs of the American Academy of Sciences* 9: 317–78.

Plato 1997. *Complete Works*. Ed. by John M. Cooper. Indianapolis: Hackett.

Porzig, Walter 1950. *Das Wunder der Sprache; Probleme, Methoden und Ergebnisse der modernen Sprachwissenschaft*. Bern: A. Francke.

Postal, Paul M. 1966. On so-called 'pronouns' of English. In Francis P. Dinneen (ed.) *Report of the Seventeenth Annual Round Table Meeting on Linguistics and Language Studies*. Washington DC: Georgetown University Press. Reprinted in David A. Reibel and Sanford A. Schane (eds) 1969. *Modern Studies in English: Readings in English Transformational Grammar*. Englewood Cliffs NJ: Prentice Hall, 201–26.

Postal, Paul M. 1970. On the surface verb 'remind'. *Linguistic Inquiry* 1: 37–120.

Postal, Paul M. 1972. The best theory. In Stanley Peters (ed.) *Goals of Linguistic Theory*. Englewood Cliffs NJ: Prentice Hall, 131–70.

Prior, Arthur N. 1957. *Time and Modality*. Oxford: Clarendon Press.

Pustejovsky, James 1995. *The Generative Lexicon*. Cambridge MA: MIT Press.

Putnam, Hilary 1975. The meaning of 'meaning'. In Keith Gunderson (ed.) *Minnesota Studies in Philosophy*. Minneapolis: University of Minnesota Press. Reprinted in *Mind, Language, and Reality: Philosophical Papers Vol. 2* 1975. Cambridge: Cambridge University Press, 215–71.

Rijk, Lambert M. de 1970. *Dialectica: Petrus Abaelardus; first complete edition of the Parisian manuscript*. 2nd revised edn. Assen: Van Gorcum.

Robins, Robert H. 1997. *A Short History of Linguistics*. 4th edn. London: Longman. [First edn 1967].
Rosch, Eleanor 1973. On the internal structure of perceptual and semantic categories. In Timothy E. Moore (ed.) *Cognitive Development and the Acquisition of Language*. New York: Academic Press, 111–44.
Rosch, Eleanor 1978. Principles of categorization. In Eleanor Rosch and Barbara B. Lloyd (eds) *Cognition and Categorization*. Hillsdale NJ: Lawrence Erlbaum, 27–48.
Russell, Bertrand 1905. On denoting. *Mind* 14: 479–93. Reprinted in Robert C. Marsh (ed.) 1956 *Logic and Knowledge*. London: Allen and Unwin, 39–56.
Saussure, Ferdinand de 1916. *Cours de linguistique générale*. [Publié par Charles Bally et Albert Sechehaye; avec la collaboration de Albert Riedlinger.]. Paris: Payot.
Seuren, Pieter A.M. 2006. Donkey sentences. In E. Keith Brown (ed.) *Encyclopedia of Language and Linguistics*. 2nd edn, 14 vols. Oxford: Elsevier, 763–66.
Spade, Paul V. 2002. *Thoughts, Words, and Things: An Introduction to Late Mediaeval Logic and Semantic Theory*: http://pvspade.com/Logic/docs/thoughts1_1a.pdf.
Strawson, Peter F. 1950. On referring. *Mind* 59: 320–44. Reprinted in Jay Rosenberg and Charles Travis (eds) 1971. *Readings in the Philosophy of Language*. Englewood Cliffs NJ: Prentice Hall, 175–95.
Swadesh, Morris 1955. Towards greater accuracy in lexico-statistic dating. *International Journal of American Linguistics* 21: 121–37.
Trier, Jost 1931. *Der Deutsche Wortschatz im Sinnbezirk des Verstandes: Von den Anfängen bis zum Beginn des 13. Jahrhunderts*. Heidelberg: C. Winter.
Van Valin, Robert D. Jr 2005. *Exploring the Syntax-Semantics Interface*. Cambridge: Cambridge University Press.
Van Valin, Robert D. Jr (ed.) 1993. *Advances in Role and Reference Grammar*. Amsterdam: John Benjamins.
Weinreich, Uriel 1962. Lexicographic definition in descriptive semantics. In Fred W. Householder and Sol Saporta (eds) *Problems in Lexicography: Report of the Conference on Lexicography held at Indiana University November 11–12, 1960*. Bloomington IN: Indiana University Research Center in Anthropology, Folklore and Linguistics, 25–43. [Reprinted in Labov, William and Beatrice S. Weinreich (eds) 1980. *Weinreich on Semantics*. Philadelphia: University of Pennsylvania Press, 295–314.]
Weinreich, Uriel 1966. Explorations in semantic theory. In (ed.) Thomas A. Sebeok *Current Trends in Linguistics 3*. The Hague: Mouton. Reprinted in Labov, William and Beatrice S. Weinreich (eds) 1980. *Weinreich on Semantics*. Philadelphia: University of Pennsylvania Press, 99–201.
Weisgerber, Leo 1950. *Vom Weltbild der deutschen Sprache*. Dusseldorf: Schwann.
Whitney, William D. 1867. *Language and the Study of Language: Twelve Studies on the Principles of Linguistic Science*. New York: Charles Scribner.
Whitney, William D. 1875. *The Life and Growth of Language*. London: Henry S. King.
Wierzbicka, Anna 1972. *Semantic Primitives*. Berlin: Athenaum.
Wilkins, John 1668. *Essay Towards a Real Character and a Philosophical Language*. London: S. Gellibrand and John Martin for the Royal Society [Menston: Scolar Press Facsimile, 1968].

Related topics

Chapter 1, (Descriptive) Externalism in semantics; Chapter 2, Internalist semantics: meaning, conceptualization and expression; Chapter 4, Foundations of formal semantics; Chapter 5, Cognitive semantics; Chapter 10, Semantics and pragmatics; Chapter 12, Lexical decomposition.

Part II
Approaches

4
Foundations of formal semantics

Jon Gajewski

In this chapter, I discuss in broad outlines the ingredients of a theory of formal semantics. Specific phenomena are dealt with in detail in other chapters of this volume. So, by necessity the discussion will be at a high level with little in the way of detail. The goal of the chapter is to sketch the desiderata of a theory of semantics and the formal approaches to them. Where possible, I will highlight the choice points and the options selected by different approaches to formal semantics. In section 1, I introduce the aims of a theory of natural language semantics. In section 2, I sketch the necessary components of a formal theory of semantics. Section 3 is devoted to discussion of issues that bear on the choice of rules of semantic composition. In section 4, the structure of denotation domains in a model is discussed. Section 5 examines two proposals for how formal semantic theories might incorporate aspects of the interaction of meanings with pragmatic contexts.

1 Introduction

The study of the semantics of natural language concerns itself with the aspects of meaning that are linguistically determined. Evidence for the meanings of linguistic expressions come from a variety of sources. One primary source of evidence is the way that sentences relate to each other semantically. For example, judgements of entailment, consistency and contradiction between sentences provide crucial evidence concerning their meaning. In some cases, these relations between sentences depend crucially on properties of the language system and others appear to depend instead on information derived from cognitive systems outside of language.

(1) a   Kim bought a sweater and Chris read a book.
    b   Kim bought a sweater.

(2) a   Katrina is a wombat.
    b   Katrina is a marsupial.

A theory of semantics of natural language seeks to explain English speakers' intuitions about the entailment relationship between sentences (1)a and (1)b. A theory of semantics should also be compatible with an account of intuitions concerning the relation between (2)a and (2)b, but we expect that conceptual knowledge about taxonomies will also play a crucial role.

It is commonly assumed that it is not enough for a theory of semantics, however, to simply give an account of a set of relations between sentences. Language has external significance; speakers use sentences of various types to convey and acquire information about the world, as well as to accomplish actions that change the world. From this perspective, a theory of semantics should specify a connection between linguistic expressions and aspects of the external world. The fundamental concept in this connection is truth. Truth and falsity specify particular relations between sentences and the world. A common idea (the correspondence theory) is that a sentence is true if there is some sense in which the meaning of the sentence corresponds to the facts of the world. There are many ideas about how to specify what is meant by correspondence (e.g. theories about truth makers, see the debate in Armstrong 1989 and Lewis 1992 et seq.). A related notion concerning the connection of language and world is reference, which connects terms to objects in the world. We will return to this and related notions below.

Given this connection, another primary source of evidence for a theory of linguistics meaning is speakers' intuitions about the truth and falsity of sentences in various situations. There is an important connection between these intuitions and the intuitions concerning the semantic relatedness of sentences discussed above. That is, the intuitions concerning semantic relations can be seen as based on intuitions about truth in possible circumstances/situations/worlds. A sentence ϕ entails another sentence ψ just in case in any situation/circumstance/world in which ϕ is true, ψ is true. Two sentences ϕ and ψ are consistent if and only if there is a situation/circumstance/world in which both ϕ and ψ are true. Such basic considerations lead to the idea that truth conditions play an important role in a speaker's linguistic competence concerning meaning. A truth condition provides the necessary and sufficient conditions under which a sentence is true.

(3) Sentence ϕ is true if and only if _____

If a speaker had such knowledge of the truth conditions of all the sentences of her language, then she would be capable of the kind of judgements discussed above – at least in principle. One might know the conditions under which a sentence is true but not be able to obtain the information relevant to making an actual judgement of truth or falsity – indeed such information may not be obtainable. A common view is that such knowledge is also sufficient to ascribe knowledge of meaning to a speaker.

2 Formal semantics

> I reject the contention that an important theoretical distinction exists between formal and natural languages.
>
> Richard Montague, EFL

A theory of formal semantics seeks to give a theory of semantics of the sort described above using a particular set of tools. Montague (1970, 1973) pioneered the interpretation of natural language through the tools of logic and analytic philosophy. First, as set out in the quote above, formal semantics employs notions from the study of formal languages. A **formal language** is nothing more than a set of strings over a finite vocabulary. It is common, however, to study formal languages that are generated by a set of syntactic rules. In the case of the analysis of natural language, the language is given – it is the output of the faculty of grammar. Natural languages have important syntactic structure. As mentioned above, semantic competence in a language consists of knowing the truth conditions for the sentences of the language. It is well known, however, that natural languages are unbounded in the number of well-formed, interpretable sentences that they contain. Consequently, an adequate theory of semantics competence – which seeks to discover what is in the head that permits knowledge of meaning – must be **compositional**. A compositional theory specifies the meaning of complex expressions as a function of the meanings of its parts. Hence a theory of formal semantics must begin with a specification of a formal language $\mathcal{L}$ and its syntactic description.

There is a fact of the matter about the syntactic structure of natural languages. So, ideally, the formal language specified will adequately model the structure of the language being analyzed. There are many different views on the syntactic structure of natural language. The spectrum ranges from theories that take interpretation to be the most important piece of evidence for structure to theories that recognize non-semantic restrictions on structure and countenance evidence for syntactic structure that is not derived from interpretation. The former theories posit a transparent connection between language structure and interpretation; sentences are assembled to be interpreted and can be interpreted directly (Direct or Surface Compositionality, see Barker and Jacobson 2007). The evidence considered by the latter theories often leads to situations in which there are syntax-semantics mismatches. Within these latter approaches, there are many possible responses to syntax-semantics mismatches. Some approaches posit a mechanism by which sentences are paired with more than one syntactic analysis. One of these may be specified as the analysis that is relevant to interpretation (this is the sentence's Logical Form, see May 1977, 1985) or the interpretation could depend on features of more than one of the structural analyses. Alternatively, a theory might postulate readjustment rules within the semantics that change the meanings of parts to be deployed in cases of mismatches (Type-shifting, Partee 1987). These alternatives are not mutually exclusive and are often deployed in one and the same theory.

The formal language selected $\mathcal{L}$ serves as input to a mechanism that pairs sentence of the language with truth conditions. As said above, the pairing cannot be direct – a language speaker cannot have an infinite list of sound meaning correspondences in her head. So, a compositional strategy mediated by syntactic structure must be adopted. An important approach to this problem is to describe a function that assigns **semantic values** to all the syntactic units of a language, including its sentences. This process involves a number of component parts. The input to this function is our language $\mathcal{L}$, but now we must specify its possible outputs. To do so is to specify a model for interpreting the language. A **model** consists of (i) a specification of semantic domains – the possible semantic values for syntactic units, and (ii) a function that maps the basic units of the language $\mathcal{L}$ to objects in the semantic domains. Thus, a model specifies both what there is as far as the language is concerned – that is, its ontology – and an interpretation of the minimal units of the language. The minimal units are the vocabulary items of the language. These are the words or morphemes of the language.

The semantic domains of the model will typically include a set of truth values as well as a domain of individuals. There are different approaches to the former domain, but generally the set is assumed to be {0,1} where 0 customarily stands for falsity and 1, truth. Sets containing three or four values are also common. The domain of individuals, on the other hand, contains those individuals that serve as the referents of individual constants and terms. These domains can be extended to domains of more complex objects using set theory. For example, one might specify a domain of sets of individuals or of functions from individuals to truth values. As we shall see, these semantic denotation domains differ in the extent to which they are structured. The set of truth values {0,1} is naturally ordered by the less than or equal to relation on natural numbers. This structure has linguistic significance. The domain of individuals, on the other hand, might plausibly be viewed as unordered, though we will see reason to reconsider this below. Finally, a fully intensional semantics must also include domains for indices of interpretation, including possible worlds and times. These may serve as denotation domains for terms of the language or only contribute indirectly to the more complex intensional domains as in Montague (1970, 1973).

The **interpretation function**, conventionally written in circumfix form as $[\![\cdot]\!]$, maps syntactic units to elements of the semantic domains. The interpretation function carries a model M as a parameter, $[\![\cdot]\!]^M$. Among the basic vocabulary expressions, some, the logical/functional expressions, receive the same interpretation in all models. Others, the non-logical/content expressions, receive varying semantic values in different models. Within a compositional theory, the semantic values of syntactically complex expressions will be calculated recursively from the meanings of these basic expressions using a restricted set of semantic composition principles. Montague proposed a system of rule-by-rule interpretation in which each syntactic rule of the formal language has a specific corresponding rule of interpretation. Others have argued for an abstraction of interpretation principles away from the specific syntactic structures; see for example Klein and Sag's (1985) view of Type-driven interpretation. Indeed, Frege (1980 [1892]) proposed that the only necessary principle of semantic composition is function application. In a theory that assigns functions as semantic values, the rule of function application says that if an expression is composed of two expressions such that one denotes a function and the other an object in the domain of the first, then the whole expression denotes the output of applying the function to the object.

(4) Function application

If an expression α is composed of immediate constituents β and γ where $[\![\beta]\!]$ is a function whose domain includes $[\![\gamma]\!]$, then $[\![\alpha]\!] = [\![\beta]\!]([\![\gamma]\!])$.

A Fregean approach to predication in simple sentences like Kim smokes would look as follows, assuming a model in which D_e is the domain of individuals ("e" for "entity") and D_t the domain of truth values. Suppose the model specifies semantic values like those in (5) for the vocabulary items Bill and smokes.

(5) a $[\![\text{Kim}]\!]^{M_1} = \text{Kim}$
    b $[\![\text{smokes}]\!]^{M_1} = f: D_e \to D_t$
        for all $x \in D_e$, $f(x) = 1$ if and only if x smokes

(6) $[\![\text{Kim smokes}]\!]^{M_1} = [\![\text{smokes}]\!]^{M_1}([\![\text{Kim}]\!]^{M_1})$
    = 1 if and only if Kim smokes

(In fact the entry in (5)b is more of a rule for associating semantic values with the expression *smokes* than the actual semantic value in a given model. In a particular model, the semantic value of *smokes* will be a function of the kind [Bill $\to$ 1, Sue $\to$ 0]. In such a case the output of the calculation is a definite truth value as opposed to a statement of truth conditions.)

The precise set of composition principles is a matter of debate. Generally speaking, there is a tendency wherever possible to minimize the set of composition principles and build peculiarities into the meanings of particular lexical items. The lexicon is the repository of arbitrary connections that must be learned (although the lexicon has its own organization). Still, semanticists differ on the give and take between syntax and semantics. A simple syntax may necessitate a more complex set of composition principles; on the other hand, complicating the syntax can yield a simpler semantics. A strong theory of Logical Form may get by with little more than function application, while a directly compositional theory incorporates a broader array of composition principles.

Natural languages exhibit **ambiguity**, the phenomenon whereby a surface string of the language is associated with more than one meaning. It is worth considering how to deal with ambiguity in an analysis of language that uses formal languages. A familiar kind of ambiguity is lexical ambiguity, whereby a single string may have multiple meanings because the string contains an item that has two meanings. Within a formal language, this kind of ambiguity is not difficult to model. An ambiguous vocabulary item is analyzed as two separate expressions with identical pronunciation. So, strings that contain these homophonous expressions are in fact not identical as they contain different vocabulary items. It is also not difficult to deal with structural ambiguity. In structural ambiguity, a single string of vocabulary items has two (or more) different syntactic analyses. That is, the string can be derived through different rule applications in the syntax. The semantics as we have described it is sensitive to syntactic structure/derivation. Consequently, the semantics may assign different interpretations to a string under its different analyses. Other putative cases require a different approach. Consider the sentence below.

(7) He influenced Chris.

This sentence can be used to express different propositions. In one context, it may express that Kim influenced Chris, in another context, that Mark did. A semantic theory needs a way to incorporate this dependence on the context of use.

A common way (cf. Cooper 1979, inspired by Montague) to approach this is to relativize the interpretation of an expression to a function that represents the intentions of a speaker to use a pronoun to refer to a particular individual. This function is a **variable assignment**. Within the language, some expressions, such as pronouns, are singled out as variables. These variables are introduced into the language bearing a natural number as an index. The variable assignment then is a partial function from natural numbers to individual in the models domain of individuals. The variable assignment is a parameter of interpretation in addition to the model, representing a feature of the context of use. This leads to a rule like the following for the interpretation of pronouns.

(8) If α is a pronoun bearing index i and g a variable assignment whose domain includes i, then $[\![\alpha_i]\!]^{M,g} = g(i)$

There is an alternative to this view that suggests that pronouns that receive their interpretation from context are not free variables whose value is supplied by a variable assignment, but instead denote identity functions.

(9) If α is a pronoun, then $[\![\alpha]\!]^M = f: D_e \to D_e$
for all $x \in D_e$, $f(x) = x$

Note that in sentence (7) above, on this view, the pronominal subject and the predicate could not semantically compose by function application. The subject denotes a function from individuals to individuals and the predicate influence Chris denotes a function from individuals to truth values. Such a view then requires an additional principle of composition. The idea is that sentences with pronouns that receive their interpretation from context do not denote truth values. Instead, such sentences denote a function from individuals to truth values. A truth value is obtained by applying this function to a salient individual. Such a function can be obtained from the parts described above via function composition.

(10)   Function composition: f ∘ g = f(g(x))

The pronoun takes an individual as an argument and gives an argument as output. This individual can in turn serve as input to the predicate, which maps it to a truth value.

The two approaches are quite similar in effect. It is possible to view the variable-based approach as deriving functions from variable assignments to truth values as the denotations of sentences. A truth value is only obtained when such a function is applied to an appropriate variable assignment; that is, one whose domain includes the indices of all free variables. The difference between the two proposals depends on the way they embed with an analysis of further phenomena including bound variable readings of pronouns and the interpretation of displacement in syntax.

At this point it is worth noting another way in which function composition can be implemented in the semantics. Rather than adding a principle of composition that allows for different ways of combining the meanings of two expressions, we can introduce a unary operation that lifts the type of one expression and allows for function application to take place. Geach's Rule (Geach 1972) is such a rule. The Geach Rule maps a function f to a new function that takes functions into f's domain and maps them to functions into f's range. At this point, it will be useful to introduce some pieces of notation that will facilitate formulating the Geach Rule. First, below we extend the notation for denotation domains to functional domains. A domain of type $<\sigma,\tau>$ contains functions from D_σ to D_τ. Second, we introduce the lambda notation for naming functions.

(11)   Type domains
    a D_e is the domain of individuals
    b D_t is the domain of truth values
    c $D_{<\sigma,\tau>}$:= the domain of functions from $D\sigma$ to $D\tau$

(12)   Lambda notation
    [λx: α . β] := the function from the individuals x that satisfy α to β

With this notation we can formulate the Geach Rule more perspicuously.

(13)   Geach Rule
    For any function f∈ $D_{<\sigma,\tau>}$, $G_\rho(f)$ is the function g∈ $D_{<<\rho,\sigma>,<\rho,\tau>>}$, where g = [λh:h∈$D_{<\rho,\sigma>}$.[λy:y∈$D_\rho$. f(h(y))]]

For example,

(14)   a   [λx:x∈D_e. x influenced Chris]
    b   [λx:x∈D_e. x]
    c G_e((14)a) = [λh:h∈$D_{<e,e>}$.[λy:y∈D_e. [λx:x∈D_e. x influenced Chris](h(y))]]
                   = [λh:h∈$D_{<e,e>}$.[λy:y∈D_e. h(y) influenced Chris]]
    d   [λh:h∈$D_{<e,e>}$.[λy:y∈D_e. h(y) influenced Chris]](λx.x) = [λx:x∈D_e. x influenced Chris]

3 Rules, binding and quantification

3.1 Binding

As mentioned above, pronouns have uses in which their interpretation does not depend on the context of utterance, but instead depends on syntactic context. Consider for example the "bound variable" readings of pronouns. In sentence (15) below, the caller argument of the main predicate and the child argument of the relational noun mother co-vary and range over the relevant students that the subject quantifies over. In this case, we say the pronoun is bound by the quantificational subject. A formal theory of semantics must determine how such connections of binding are established.

(15) a) Every student called his mother.
b) For every student x, x called x's mother.

Recall that on the variable-based theory, the pronoun carries an index and depends on the variable assignment for its interpretation. Consequently, what we need is (i) to supplement the structure with another index that makes the connection between binder and bindee and (ii) to formulate a new rule that manipulates the variable assignment as directed by the binding index. In the formulation of this rule, I follow Büring's (2003) recipe for beta binding. Büring, in turn, follows the Derived VP Rule of Partee (1975). On this view, β indices are freely insertable in the syntax.

(16) Logical Form for (15)
Every student β1 [called his1 mother]

The interpretation of the beta binder is as follows. Note that beta binders do not change the type of their sisters. Instead, they modify the variable assignment that under which their sister is interpreted and identify the argument of the predicate with interpretation of the bound variable under the modified assignment.

(17) Beta Binding
$[\![β_n \ XP]\!]^g = λx.[[\![XP]\!]^{g[n→x]}(x)]$

(18) A modified variable assignment
$g[n→x]$ is the same as g except that $g[n→x]$ maps n to x.

Applying this analysis to (16), we obtain the results below.

(19) $[\![β_1 \ [\text{called his}_1 \ \text{mother}]]\!]^g =$
$λx:x∈D_e.[\![\text{called his}_1 \ \text{mother}]\!]^{g[1→x]}(x) =$
$λx:x∈D_e.$ x called x's mother

This is the appropriate type for an argument of a quantifier and has established the appropriate connection between the co-varying argument positions. Following the insights of Generalized Quantifier Theory (Barwise and Cooper 1981), a quantificational noun phrase denotes a set of sets. In type-theoretic terms, a generalized quantifier denotes a function of type $<<e,t>,t>$. For example, with our quantifier every student above has the following semantic value.

(20) $[\![\text{every student}]\!] = [λf:f∈D_e.\text{for every student x, } f(x)=1]$

Similar results can be obtained in variable-free framework through the use of wider array of compositional principles and/or type shifts. The Geach Rule is an effective way of passing along dependence on an input, but cannot on its own account for the kind of binding that we observe in the example (16). Rather we need a rule that maps a function that maps individuals to functions on individuals to a function that can take functions from individuals to individuals to a function on individuals. This rule, which is quite similar in form to the Geach Rule and is given the name Z by Jacobson (1999), is given below.

(21) Z Rule
For any function $f \in D_{<\sigma,<e,\tau>>}$, $z(f)$ is the function $g \in D_{<<e,\sigma>,<e,\tau>>}$, where $g = [\lambda h: h \in D_{<e,\sigma>}.[\lambda x: x \in D_e. f(h(x))(x)]]$

(22) a ⟦ his mother ⟧ = λx. x's mother
b ⟦ called ⟧ = $[\lambda x: x \in D_e.[\lambda y: y \in D_e$. y called x]]
c $z(⟦$ called $⟧) = [\lambda f: f \in D_{<e,e>}.[\lambda x: x \in De$. x called $f(x)]]$
d $z(⟦$ called $⟧)(⟦$ his mother $⟧) = [\lambda x: x \in D_e$. x called x's mother]]

3.2 Syntactic displacement

An adequate theory of semantics must also have mechanisms for dealing with the phenomenon of syntactic *displacement*. Displacement refers to the phenomenon whereby a syntactic constituent (often a phrase) occurs in a position distinct from that typically occupied by constituents serving the same grammatical function. For example, a noun phrase may serve as the object of a verb, providing the verb with an argument that it requires, but appear in a position that is distinct from the canonical position for objects in the language. A typical and simple example from English is the case of topicalization. Consider the sentence in (23a) below. The verb *admire* requires an object, as can be seen from (23b). And the usual position for an object is after the verb, as seen with the accusative marked object pronoun in (23c).

(23) a Tom, every student admires.
b *I admire.
c I admire him.

The challenge for semantics is to allow the noun phrase *Tom* in this sentence initial position to saturate the internal argument (admiree role) of the verb. One response is to see in such constructions a situation formally similar to that of the binding of pronouns. Under such a view, displacement of a noun phrase results in a variable (with index) being inserted in its canonical position, for example in the object position in (23a). This insertion is thought to be a reflex of *movement* of the noun phrase from object position to the sentence initial position. Such movement presupposes a theory that assigns multiple syntactic representations to a sentence. When the noun phrase lands a binding index is inserted between the noun phrase and its new sister. Again, I follow Büring (2003), who distinguishes movement (μ) indices from other binding indices, like the β indices used in (16). (For a theory that identifies binding and movement indices by arguing that all binding requires movement, see e.g. Heim (1993/1998), developing ideas of Reinhart 1983.)

(24) Logical Form of (23a)
Tom μ_3 [every student admires t_3]

Such structures are interpreted using the rule below. Note that unlike the beta-binding rule, the mu-binding rule does change the type of the constituent it applies to; a beta-binder maps a predicate of type <e,σ> to <e,σ> for any type σ, a mu-binder maps a predicate of type σ to <e,σ>.

(25) Mu Binding
⟦μ$_n$ XP⟧^{g} = λx.⟦XP⟧$^{g[n→x]}$

A variable-free approach takes a different tack on displacement structures. Once again, the addition of function composition plays a role in the analysis. When a predicate lacks an argument to apply to function composition may apply, so long as there is an appropriate type of function around for the lacking predicate to compose with. A full appreciation of an approach of this kind must be supplemented with an appropriate syntax, as may be found in Categorial Grammar, cf. Carpenter 1998 and Steedman 2000, for example. In such a theory, in our example (23a), ⟦ admire ⟧ may either apply to an argument to its right or else compose with a function to its left. Suppose ⟦ admire ⟧ is a function from individuals (D_e) to functions from D_e to truth values {0, 1}; that is, ⟦ admire ⟧ is type <e,<e,t>>. When, in (23a), ⟦ admire ⟧ does not find an argument to its right to apply to it may then compose with the subject quantifier to its left. As shown in (20) above, the quantifier is type <<e,t>,t>.

(26) Function composition
If f and g are functions such that the domain of f includes the range of g, then
f∘g = λx.f(g(x))

(27) ⟦ every student ⟧ ∘ ⟦ admires ⟧ =
λx. ⟦ every student ⟧(⟦ admires ⟧(x)) =
[λx∈D_e. For all y in D_e such that y is a student, y admires x]

This function may then apply to the topicalized object Tom yielding the truth value 1 if every student admires Tom and 0 otherwise.

3.3 Quantification

Closely related to the issue of how to treat syntactic displacement is the issue of how to treat quantifiers that serve as the non-final arguments of multi-place predicates. The simplest examples involve quantifiers in the object position of transitive verbs. In such cases, neither the verb nor the object quantifier may apply to the other. The types do not match for functional application (<e,<e,t>> and <<e,t>,t>).

(28) Kim admires every student.

One possibility is suggested by theories that allow for and interpret syntactic movement. In such theories it is possible to postulate an additional level of syntactic representation, the Logical Form mentioned above. Since movement is a possible way to map from a structure representing the basic grammatical functions of a sentence to its surface representation, as in topicalization, it is hypothesized that movement may also map a surface representation to its Logical Form (May 1977 et seq.). No additional interpretive principles are required. We have already sketched the mechanisms needed to interpret movement.

(29) a Surface
       Kim admires every student.
     b Logical Form
       every student μ$_2$ [Kim admires t$_2$]

(30) $[\![$ every student $]\!](\lambda x. [\![$ Kim admires $t_2]\!]^{g[2 \to x]}) = 1$ iff
$[\![$ every student $]\!](\lambda x.$ Kim admires x)

Variable-free theories that posit direct compositional analyses of the surface representation cannot make use of the concept of "covert" movement, even though such theories possess mechanisms for interpreting displacement – function composition, as we have seen in (27). In such cases, a strategy of type-shifting must be adopted (see, for example, Hendriks (1993)). Either the type of the verb or the type of the quantifier must be adjusted to allow for semantic composition through function application. A common choice is to lift the type of the quantifiers. In this case, it would be necessary to lift the quantifier from $<<e,t>,t>$ to $<<e,<e,t>>,<e,t>>$.

(31) Type-shifting operation
For any quantifier α such that $[\![\alpha]\!] \in D_{<<e,t>,t>}$,
$TS([\![\alpha]\!]) = \lambda f \in D_{<e,<e,t>>}.\lambda x \in D_e. [\![\alpha]\!](f(x))=1$

The type-shifted quantifiers may now apply to a transitive verb yielding a one-place predicate that may either apply to an individual denoted by the subject, or serve as the argument of another quantifier. This rule in (31) resolves the type mismatch in this case but will not suffice as a general solution to the problem. This rule must be a member of a family of rules that will allow for interpretation as the first argument of any n-place predicate and additional rules are required to bring about different scope orders in sentences that contain two or more quantifiers.

Choosing between these two perspectives in particular with respect to quantifier interpretation can be a difficult matter. A phenomenon that is often discussed in this regard is antecedent contained deletion (ACD). An example is given in (32)b. This sentence involves the omission of the overt material "read" present in (32)a.

(32) a   Bill read every book that Fred read.
     b   Bill read every book that Fred did.

Advocates of quantifier raising have argued that ACD involves verb phrase ellipsis – that what is deleted in (32b) is [$_{VP}$ read t]. There is no similar VP in the sentence to license elision of this VP – unless the object quantifier moves and leaves a trace.

(33) every book that Fred ~~read t~~ [Bill read t]

Advocates of variable-free approaches on the other hand argues that what is missing is just a verb. Jacobson (1992) advocates an approach on which the gap is a free preform anaphoric to a transitive verb. More recently, Charlow 2008 proposes a binding account of ACD within variable-free semantics. See Chapter 18 in this volume for further in-depth discussion of quantification.

3.5 Interim summary

In this section, I have endeavoured to give a sketch of how a formal theory of semantics is set up including the specification of a language and its syntax, the specification of a model that includes domains, and in some detail the selection of a set of recursive compositional rules. I hope to have given some sense of how all three of these depend on one another. Certain kinds of approaches to the syntax (CCG vs. LF, for example) favour certain kinds of compositional principles and will require different kinds of entities in the model. In the next section, I will discuss the linguistics significance of the structure of the denotation domains that form part of the models.

4 Structure of models

A linguistically significant property of the models that semanticists propose for natural languages is the structure of the denotation domains they determine. As discussed above, models contain domains of truth values and individuals (and potentially many more including worlds, times, events, numbers/degrees . . .), as well as functional domains defined from the basic domains. The basic domain of individuals may be viewed as an unordered set, or as one that is structured by a part-whole relation. Other domains are naturally viewed as structured. For example, the domain of truth values, when viewed as the set $\{0,1\}$, can be seen as a set of numbers ordered by the less than or equal to relation $\leq$. Similarly, the functional domain $D_{<e,t>}$ of function from individuals to truth values may be seen as a set partially ordered by the subset relation $\subseteq$ (speaking loosely here, given the one-to-one correspondence between functions of type <e,t> and subsets of D_e). In fact, both of these domains may be viewed as having the full structure of Boolean algebra with fully defined operations of meet, join and complementation. In the domain of truth values, these operations are truth-functional conjunction, disjunction and negation. In $D_{<e,t>}$, the operations are intersection, union and set complementation.

4.1 Monotonicity and orderings

The structure imputed to denotation domains has important consequences for a theory of semantics. There are, for example, expressions of natural language that show a sensitivity to the structure of denotation domains and how they are or are not respected by operators of language. Negative polarity items (NPIs) are such a case. A negative polarity item, like English *ever*, must be in an environment that is somehow negative. Sentential negation is the paradigmatic case.

(34) a   *Bill will ever go to Hartford.
     b   Bill won't ever go to Hartford.

Ladusaw (1979) argued convincingly that NPIs are sensitive to a formal property of expressions – monotonicity – that is defined in terms of the structure of the model. This case is discussed in Chapter 17 of this volume. I refer readers there for details.

4.2 Plurals: semilattices

Following Link (1983) it is common to attribute to the domain of individuals the structure of join semilattices. A join semilattice is a set of individuals closed under an operation ($\sqcup$, join) that is associative, commutative and idempotent. This operation corresponds to a non-Boolean interpretation of *and* as in the coordination *Mary and Bill*. The operation maps to individuals, Mary and Bill, to their sum, Mary$\sqcup$Bill. Sum individuals are necessary to deal with the phenomenon of collective predication. This algebraic structure determines a part-whole ordering on the domain of individuals.

(35) For any two individuals a, b ∈ D_e:
 a ⊑ b if and only if a⊔b = b

(36) Bill and Mary are a couple. (≠ Bill is a couple and Mary is a couple.)

Given this ordering, there are individuals that are designated as **atoms**. The atoms of a join semilattice are the individuals that are minimal with respect to the order ⊑.

The ordering of individuals in the domain D_e is linguistically significant, because there are predicates of natural language that are sensitive to the part-whole structure of individuals. For example, a predicate like *have blue eyes* may be predicated of a noun phrase that denotes a complex sum individual, but the truth of the statements is always dependent on the properties of the atomic parts of the sum individual. Link (1983) proposed that the extension of *have blue eyes* is a subset of the atoms of the domain.

(37) ⟦ blue-eyed ⟧ ⊆ {y: y is an atom & y ∈ D_e}

This would not allow such a predicate to apply to sum individuals. To allow for this in statements like (38), a pluralized version of the predicate must be supplied. To this end, Link proposes the pluralizing * operator.

(38) Mary and Bill have blue eyes.
(39) *P = the closure of P under ⊔

Given this operation, the predication will be true just in case the atomic parts of the sum individual Mary⊔Bill are in the extension of the unstarred extension of *have blue eyes*.

(40) *⟦ blue-eyed ⟧(Mary⊔Bill)

4.3 Islands

It would take us too far afield to discuss these proposals in detail, but many interesting semantic accounts of islands have been given by appealing to the structure of denotation domains. Szabolcsi and Zwarts (1993) proposed that some weak island effects could be explained by the fact that some operations, like negation, are not defined in certain denotation domains, like the domain of manners, cf. (41).

(41) *How did Fred not behave?

This is reminiscent of Landman's (1991) claim that individual negation and disjunction do not exist because the domain of individuals lacks full Boolean structure. Fox and Hackl (2006) additionally suggest that negative degree questions are unacceptable due to a crucial property of the structure of the degree domain that interacts with maximalization in questions. The relevant property is density of the ordering on degrees.

(42) *How tall isn't Bill?

Abrusán (2011) revisits both phenomena with a novel view on how exhaustification in questions interacts with the structure of the denotation domains of degree and manner; see section 5.2 below for further discussion of exhaustification.

5 The relation of semantics to context

In this section, we consider how interaction with context enters into the formulation of formal theories of semantics. The reader is referred to Chapters 10 and 11 of this volume for in-depth discussion of the issues.

5.1 Dynamic semantics: context change potentials

There are several problems that theories of formal semantics have faced that have forced a rethinking of the relation between the semantics of a statement and the context in which it is used. One such problem is the phenomenon of intersentential anaphora involving indefinite antecedents. Consider the sequence of sentences in (43).

(43) A woman entered the room. She sat down.

The first sentence introduces existential quantification over women. The second sentence contains a pronoun that one might be tempted to say "refers" back to the woman from the first sentence. The first sentence, however, does not pick out a unique woman who can serve as the referent of the pronoun.

An obvious alternative would be to analyze the relation between the quantifier in the first sentence as one of variable binding, like the cases discussed above in section 3.1. In predicate logic terms, one might suggest the right scope interpretation is the following.

(44) $\exists x \, [\, \text{woman}(x) \wedge \text{entered}(x) \wedge \text{sat\_down}(x) \,]$

This does appear to be an adequate sketch of the meaning of (43). Unfortunately, the project of assigning (43) such an interpretation faces a rather large obstacle. That obstacle is that quantifiers are generally not allowed to take scope beyond the sentences in which they are contained.

(45) No woman entered the room. She sat down.
  [Infelicitous without additional context.]

(46) $\neg \exists x \, [\, \text{woman}(x) \wedge \text{entered}(x) \wedge \text{sat\_down}(x) \,]$

There is no way to interpret this sequence of sentences in the way that seems to be required in the case of (43). The problem, then, is how can an indefinite/existential quantifier like *a woman* take scope over a sequence of sentences when a quantifier like *no woman* may not?

An important response to this, as well as to some related problems in anaphora and presupposition, was to change our fundamental notion about what the meaning of a sentence is. Under traditional views, the meaning of a sentence is identified with its truth conditions. Those truth conditions contain information that, through the utterance of a sentence with the intention to perform a certain speech act, may have an effect on the knowledge and beliefs of the participants of a conversation. Such knowledge and belief form a part of the context in which a sentence is uttered. Under the proposed view, the meaning of a sentence should not be seen as the static truth conditions, but rather as the **dynamic** effect that the utterance of the sentence has on context. Hence the approach is referred to as dynamic semantics; see Dekker 2012 for a recent approach and Chapters 3 and 10 of this volume for additional discussion.

Under the view of dynamic semanticists there is a big difference between expressions like *no woman* and *a woman*. The former is quantificational in the usual sense, but the latter is not. Rather indefinites like *a woman* are simply variables, which in the context of a dynamic semantics will have the effect of the intersentential scope required by (43). There are many different approaches to dynamic semantics from the Discourse Representation Theory of Kamp (see Kamp and Reyle (1993)) to the Dynamic Predicate Logic of Groenendijk and Stokhof (1991). In this section, I will sketch a version of dynamic semantics due to Heim (1982, 1983). Under this view the meaning of a sentence is its Context Change Potential (CCP), a function from contexts to the contexts modified by the content of the sentence.

To see how to specify the meaning of a sentence as the effect that it has on context, we must have some notion of context in mind. Heim makes use of Stalnaker's view. Stalnaker (1974) suggests that at any point in a conversation there is a set of propositions – the Common Ground – that represents the mutually held beliefs of the participants of the conversation – or at least what they are disposed to act as if they believe. This set of propositions determines a set of worlds – the Context Set – in which all of the propositions of the common ground are true. Heim adopts the Context Set as the relevant representation of context for dynamic semantics. In Heim's contexts, each world is paired with a variable assignment, a function from natural numbers into the domain of individuals.

The context potential of a sentence ϕ then is written as "+ϕ" which may then be applied to a context c, conventionally written as "c+ϕ". Let us now consider what the context change potentials of sentences involving indefinites would look like. According to Heim, indefinites are just variables that bear an index. That index must be new in the context (Heim's novelty condition). In other words, the context may impose no restrictions on the index of the indefinite. For example, in a context in which the index 2 is new, the CCP of the first sentence of (43) may be as follows.

(47) c + A woman$_2$ entered the room
      = c ∩ {<g,w>: g(2) is a woman in w and entered in w}
      = c'

This sentence removes from the context c any assignment of world pairs in which the individual assigned to 2 is not a woman or did not enter. Thus, a new context c' is created that has only kept the pairs <g,w> of c where g(2) is a woman who entered in w. This revised context then is the input context to all succeeding sentence in the discourse. The second sentence of (43) may now be analyzed as below. As a pronoun, the index on *she* must have already been used in context, as it was in this case by *a woman* (Heim's familiarity condition).

(48) c + she$_2$ sat down
      = c ∩ {<g,w>: g(2) sat down in w}

When this CCP is applied to c' it further restricts the assignment world pairs, so that the output context, call it c", only contains pairs <g,w> such that g(2) is a woman in w entered in w and sat down in w. In this way, a dependency arises between the expressions in the two separate sentences. All that we need now is to understand where existential force comes from. In Heim's theory, this follows from the definition of the proposition determined by a context.

(49) Let c be a set of assignment world pairs. Then, the proposition determined by c is
      {w: for some g, <g,w> ∈ c}

So, the output context after update by (43) is a proposition that will entail that there exists an individual who is a woman and entered and sat down.

Compare the case of a quantifier like *no woman*. The quantifier is introduced with an index j. This index must also be novel in the context. Note, however, that updating c with a CCP containing *no woman* had no effect on the restrictions imposed on the index j in the output context.

(50) c + *no$_j$ x$_j$ is a woman* A =
  {<g,w>∈c: for every a, if <g[a/j],w> ∈ c + x$_j$ is a woman, then
  <g[a/j],w> ∉ c + x$_j$ is a woman + A}

Consequently the CCP of a quantified statement of this kind does not present the possibility of taking scope over and binding pronouns in succeeding sentences. There are alternative analyses of such anaphoric possibilities. The most common is the non-dynamic E-type pronoun approach; cf. Cooper (1979), Heim (1990), Elbourne (2006).

The dynamic approach to semantics and, in particular, the support that it has drawn from the phenomenon of presupposition projection has been a matter of much recent debate. Schlenker (2007), Fox (2008) and George (2008) have presented approaches to the problem of presupposition projection that do not involve the typical mechanisms of dynamic semantics, such as context change potentials. A primary argument in favour of these proposals is that they offer a depth of explanation of the phenomenon that had not been achieved by dynamic theories. Schlenker (2009) has in more recent work reassessed and refined aspects of the dynamic approaches to achieve more explanatory theories.

5.2 Scalar implicatures: exhaustification operators

Another important phenomenon concerning the interaction of semantics and context that has received much recent attention is that of scalar implicatures. A scalar implicature derives from the assertion of a sentence containing an expression that belongs to a quantity scale. Grice (1975) was the first to discuss the calculation of implicatures. Horn (1972) formulated an influential approach to scalar implicature proposing the existence of conventionalized scales (often called Horn scales) that give rise to implicatures. The general idea is that when a speaker uses an item from a scale (see 51b), their use of that item is automatically compared with statements they could have made with the item's scalemates.

(51) a Bill read some of the articles.
  b <some, many, most, all>   Scale
  c Bill didn't read all of the articles.   Scalar implicature

If they could have chosen an item that would have resulted in a stronger statement (*all* in 51c), they should have used that item (if the additional information is relevant). Given that they did not choose to make the stronger statement (and it was relevant), hearers are entitled to infer that the speaker does not know the stronger statement to be true – or even that the speaker knows it to be false. This line of reasoning relies on Horn's (1972) scales and Grice's (1975) rules for conversation including maxims enjoining speakers to make their contributions as informative as appropriate and to say only that for which they have adequate evidence.

Another perspective has arisen suggesting that, in fact, scalar implicatures are calculated in parallel with the recursive compositional rules of semantics. Here I will discuss only one argument that has been given in favour of this view (cf. Chierchia et al. 2010). Hurford

(1974) observed that disjunctive statements are infelicitous when one of the disjuncts entails the other. Since being a dog entails being an animal, the following sentence is infelicitous.

(52) #Mary saw an dog or an animal.

It has been noticed, however, that in some cases that involve scalar items, disjunctions that have one disjunct entailed by the other can indeed be felicitous. Consider the case of "some or all". Solving all of the problems means solving some of them, and yet (53) is felicitous.

(53) Bill solved some or all of the problems.

Chierchia et al. 2010 argue that this sentence is felicitous because it does in fact satisfy Hurford's constraint. They argue that this is so because there is a reading for the first conjunct that is not entailed by the second. Typical uses of *some* result in a "not all" implicature. Chierchia et al. suggest that a grammatical mechanism is able to apply that makes this implicature part of the meaning of the first disjunct. They propose, specifically, that there is an exhaustification operator O, similar in meaning to *only* that introduces implicatures. Under such a view, it is possible to embed O under the scope of other operators.

(54) Bill read (only) some of the articles.
(55) [O[Bill solved some of the problems] or [Bill solved all the problems]]
      "Bill solved only some of the problems or he solved all of them."

The proposal is controversial and has been the topic of much recent debate. Alternative proposals that do not make use of exhaustification operators have been advanced. For criticisms of this approach and more Gricean alternative see Geurts (2009).

6 Conclusion

In this brief point, I have attempted to give a sketch of the tools and concerns of formal approaches to semantics. Many issues remain to be resolved: the appropriate character of the syntactic input, the dividing line between semantics and pragmatics, the role of models in semantic theory. On the last point, see Zimmermann (2012). One important development within the field of formal semantics has been the attempt to extend the use of these tools to the analysis of less well-studied languages. Important contributions in this domain include Matthewson (2008) et seq. on the cross-linguistic study of the semantics-pragmatics interface and Schlenker et al. (2013) on the formal semantics of sign languages.

Further reading

Jacobson, Pauline 1999. Towards a Variable-Free Semantics. *Linguistics and Philosophy* 22: 117–184.
    Strong statement of the benefits of a surface compositional approach to natural language semantics.
Heim, Irene and Kratzer, Angelika 1998. *Semantics in Generative Grammar*. Oxford: Blackwell. Now classic textbook that has established a lingua franca among formal semanticists, with special attention paid to the rules of interpretation.
Landman, Fred 1991. *Structures for Semantics*. Kluwer: Dordrecht. Still the best introduction to the intricacies of the structure of models for different domains, including events, times and plural individuals.

Dekker, Paul 2011. Dynamic Semantics. In C. Maienborn, K. Von Heusinger and P. Portner (eds) *Semantics: An International Handbook of Natural Language Meaning*, vol. 1. Mouton de Gruyter: Berlin, 229–254. Very clear and up-to-date introduction to the central concepts of dynamic semantics. Includes discussion of the historical development of these concepts.

Chierchia, G., D. Fox and B. Spector 2010. The Grammatical View of Scalar Implicatures and the Relationship between Semantics and Pragmatics. http://semanticsarchive.net/Archive/WMzY2ZmY/CFS_EmbeddedSIs.pdf. To appear in *Handbook of Semantics*, Paul Portner, Claudia Maienborn et Klaus von Heusinger (Eds), Mouton de Gruyter. Important guide to recent developments at the interface of semantics and pragmatics. An emphasis on the analysis of implicatures and their interpretation when embedded.

References

Abrusán, M. 2011. Presuppositional and negative islands: a semantic account. *Natural Language Semantics* 19: 257–321.

Armstrong, D.M. 1989. *A Combinatorial Theory of Possibility*. Cambridge: Cambridge University Press.

Barker, C. and P. Jacobson (eds) 2007. *Direct Compositionality*. Oxford: Oxford University Press.

Barwise, J. and R. Cooper 1981. Generalized quantifiers and natural language. *Linguistics and Philosophy* 4: 159–219.

Büring, D. 2003. Cross-over situations. *Natural Language Semantics* 12: 23–62.

Carpenter, B. 1998. *Type-logical Semantics*. Cambridge, MA: MIT Press.

Chierchia, G. 1989. Anaphora and attitudes de se. In R. Bartsch, J. van Benthem and P. van Emde Boas (eds), *Semantics and Contextual Expression*. Dordrecht: Foris, 1–31.

Chierchia, G., D. Fox and B. Spector 2010. The grammatical view of scalar implicatures and the relationship between semantics and pragmatics. http://semanticsarchive.net/Archive/WMzY2ZmY/CFS_EmbeddedSIs.pdf. To appear in Paul Portner, Claudia Maienborn et Klaus von Heusinger (Eds), *Handbook of Semantics*. Berlin: Mouton de Gruyter.

Cooper, R. 1979. The interpretation of pronouns. In F. Heny and H. S. Schnelle (eds) *Syntax and Semantics, Volume 10*. New York: Seminar Press, 61–92.

Cooper, R. 1983. *Quantification and Syntactic Theory*. Dordrecht: D. Reidel.

Dekker, P. 2012. *Dynamic Semantics*. Dordrecht: Springer.

Elbourne, P. 2006. *Situations and Individuals*. Cambridge, MA: MIT Press.

Fauconnier, G. 1975. Polarity and the scale principle. *Chicago Linguistic Society* 11: 188–199.

Fox, Danny, and Martin Hackl 2006. The universal density of measurement. *Linguistics and Philosophy* 29: 537–586.

Fox, Danny 2008. Two short notes on Schlenker's theory of presupposition projection. *Theoretical Linguistics* 34: 237–252.

Frege, G. 1980 [1892]. Function and concept. Translated by P. Geach. In P. Geach and M. Black (eds. and trans.) *Translations from the Philosophical Writings of Gottlob Frege*. 3rd ed. Oxford: Blackwell, 325–345.

Geach, P. 1972. A program for syntax. In Donald Davidson and Gilbert Harman (eds) *Semantics of Natural Language*. Dordrecht: Reidel, 483–497.

George, Benjamin 2008. Predicting presupposition projection: some alternatives in the Strong Kleene tradition. Ms. UCLA.

Geurts, B. 2009. Scalar implicature and local pragmatics. *Mind and Language* 24: 51–79.

Grice, H.P. 1975. Logic and conversation. In P. Cole and J.L. Morgan (eds) *Speech Acts*. New York: Academic Press, 41–58.

Groenendijk, J. and M. Stokhof 1991. Dynamic predicate logic. *Linguistics and Philosophy* 14: 39–100.

Heim, I. 1982. *The Semantics of Definite and Indefinite Noun Phrases*. PhD thesis. UMass, Amherst.

Heim, I. 1983. On the projection problem for presuppositions. In M. Barlow et al. (eds) *WCCFL 2: Second Annual West Coast Conference on Formal Linguistics*. Stanford, CA: Stanford Linguistics Association, 114–125.

Heim, I. 1990. E-type pronouns and donkey anaphora. *Linguistics and Philosophy* 13: 137–177.
Heim, I. 1998. Anaphora and semantic interpretation: a reinterpretation of Reinhart's approach. In U. Sauerland and O. Percus (eds), *The Interpretative Tract, MIT Working Papers in Linguistics*, vol. 25. Cambridge, MA: MITWPL.
Heim, I. and A. Kratzer. 1998. *Semantics in Generative Grammar*. Malden, MA: Blackwell.
Hendriks, H. 1993. *Studied Flexibility: Categories and Types in Syntax And Semantics*. Universiteit van Amsterdam: Institute for Logic, Language and Computation.
Horn, L. 1972. *On the Semantic Properties of the Logical Operators in English*. Bloomington, IN: Indiana University Linguistics Club.
Hurford, J.R. 1974. Exclusive or inclusive disjunction. *Foundations of Language* 11: 409–411.
Jacobson, P. 1992. Antecedent contained deletion in a variable free semantics. In C. Barker and D. Dowty (eds) *Proceedings of the 2nd Conference on Semantics and Linguistic Theory*. Ohio State University: OSU Working Papers in Linguistics.
Jacobson, P. 1999. Towards a variable-free semantics. *Linguistics and Philosophy* 22: 117–185.
Kamp, H. and Reyle, U. 1993. *From Discourse to Logic*. Dordrecht: Kluwer.
Kaplan, D. 1989. Demonstratives. In Joseph Almog, John Perry, Howard K. Wettstein and David Kaplan (eds.) *Themes from Kaplan*. New York: Oxford University Press, 481–563.
Klein, E. and I. Sag 1985. Type-driven translation. *Linguistics and Philosophy*: 163–201.
Ladusaw, William A. 1979. *Polarity Sensitivity as Inherent Scope Relations*. PhD dissertation. University of Texas, Austin.
Landman, F. 1991. *Structures for Semantics*. SLAP 45. Dordrecht: Kluwer.
Lewis, David 1992. Critical notice of Armstrong, a combinatorial theory of possibility. *Australasian Journal of Philosophy* 70: 211–224.
Link, G. 1983. The logical analysis of plurals and mass terms. In R. Bauerle, C. Schwartze and A. von Stechow (eds) *Meaning, Use and Interpretation of Language*. Berlin: Mouton de Gruyter, 302–323.
Matthewson, L. 2008. Pronouns, presuppositions, and semantic variation. *Proceedings of SALT XVIII*. Ithaca, NY: Cornell Linguistics Club, 527–550.
May, R. 1977. *The Grammar of Quantification*. PhD thesis. MIT.
May, R. 1985. *Logical Form: Its Structure and Derivation*. Cambridge, MA: MIT Press.
Montague, Richard 1970. English as a formal language. In Bruno Visentini et al. (eds) *Linguaggi nella società e nella tecnica*. Milan: Edizioni di Comunità, 189–224. Reprinted in Richmond H. Thomason (ed.) 1974. *Formal Philosophy*. Yale University Press, 188–221.
Montague, Richard 1973. The proper treatment of quantification in ordinary English. In K.J.J. Hintikka, J.M.E. Moravcsik and P. Suppes (eds) *Approaches to Natural Language*. Dordrecht: Reidel, 221–242.
Partee, B. 1975. Montague grammar and transformational grammar. *Linguistic Inquiry* 6: 203–300.
Partee, B. 1987. Noun phrase interpretation and type-shifting principles. In J. Groenendijk, D. de Jong and M. Stokhof (eds) *Studies in Discourse Representation Theory and the Theory of Generalized Quantifiers*. Dordrecht: Foris Publications, 115–143.
Reinhart, T. 1983. *Anaphora and Semantic Interpretation*. London: Croom-Helm.
Schlenker, P. 2007. Transparency: an incremental theory of presupposition projection. In U. Sauerland and P. Stateva (eds) *Presuppositions and Implicatures in Compositional Semantics*. Basingstoke: Palgrave Macmillan.
Schlenker, P. 2009. Local contexts. *Semantics and Pragmatics* 2: 1–78.
Schlenker, P., J. Lamberton and M. Santoro 2013. Iconic variables. *Linguistics and Philosophy* 36: 91–149.
Stalnaker, R. 1974. Pragmatic presuppositions. In M. Munitz and P. Under (eds) *Semantics and Philosophy*. New York: New York University Press, 197–213.
Stechow, Arnim von 2003. Feature deletion under semantic binding: tense, person, and mood under verbal quantifiers. In Makoto Kadowaki and Shigeto Kawahara (eds) *NELS 33*. Amherst Massachusetts: GLSA, 397–403.
Steedman, M. 2000. *The Syntactic Process*. Cambridge, MA: MIT Press.

Szabolcsi, Anna and Frans Zwarts 1993. Weak islands and an algebraic semantics of scope taking. *Natural Language Semantics* 1: 235–284.
Zimmermann, E. 2012. Model-theoretic semantics. In K. v. Heusinger, C. Maienborn and P. Portner (eds) *Handbook of Semantics. Volume 1*. Berlin: de Gruyter Mouton, 762–802.

Related topics

Chapter 1, (Descriptive) Externalism in semantics; Chapter 16, The semantics of nominals; Chapter 17, Negation and polarity; Chapter 18, Varieties of quantification.

5
Cognitive semantics

Maarten Lemmens

1 Introduction

This chapter discusses meaning as it is viewed in cognitive linguistics. The term "cognitive linguistics" will be used here as a cover term to refer to a number of related theories, such as Cognitive Grammar, (Radical) Construction Grammar, Conceptual Metaphor Theory, etc. that each have their own specifics, but essentially adhere to the same general cognitive-functional, usage-based perspective on language. One of the basic tenets of these cognitive theories is that language does not constitute a separate innate faculty of mind (cf. Langacker 1987: 13). Undeniably, human beings have an innate (i.e. genetically determined) predisposition that allows them to learn language; however, the full articulation of the linguistic system depends on experiential factors (physiological as well as cultural) and cognitive abilities that are not unique to language. Nor is it necessarily so that grammatical structure, at a very abstract level, is innate and (thus) universal. The innate, universal nature of grammar (which is in fact an empirical question rather than the theoretical a priori which it often is taken to be, cf. also Tomasello 1995 or Levinson 2003a) is not an issue that is relevant to the current chapter, but grammar's interaction with experiential factors and cognitive abilities is at the heart of what "cognitive semantics" is.

In fact, the term "cognitive semantics" is somewhat misleading, as it may suggest that semantics is a separate module within the linguistic model, next to "cognitive syntax", "cognitive morphology", "cognitive pragmatics", etc. However, cognitive linguistics does not adopt a modular view on language: all structures in language, ranging from morphemes to words to syntactic patterns, are considered as inherently meaningful and, moreover, as being of the same kind, i.e. symbolic form-meaning pairings, called "symbolic units" (Langacker's Cognitive Grammar) or "constructions" (Construction Grammar). More specifically, grammar is defined as a structured inventory of such form-meaning pairs. For lexical items and morphemes, assuming such a form-meaning pair is quite uncontroversial, as it goes back to de Saussure's basic insight on the arbitrariness of the link between the *significant* (signifier) and the *signifié* (signified). However, de Saussure and later (mainstream) linguistic theories (of which generative linguistics is the most salient representative) held the view that, idiomatic constructions notwithstanding, the meaning of *compositional* structures, such as in polymorphemic words or syntactic structures, is not arbitrary since it is derivable from the meanings of the parts. In other words, speakers know how to figure out the meaning of compositional words such as *woodstove* or *windmill* on the basis of (i) the meaning of the parts (*wood* and *stove*, *wind* and *mill*) and (ii) the meaning(s) of the N-N compounds in English.

Similarly, the meaning of a phrase like *a yellow car* can be computed on the basis of the meaning of the parts (*a*, *yellow*, *car*) and the knowledge that in the structure ART-ADJ-N the article "determines" the NP and the adjective is a modifier to the noun, typically referring to some quality that the entity referred to by N possesses (in this case, the colour of the car). Unless there is some idiomaticity to the compositional structure, its meaning will not be stored. Most linguistics models thus adopt what Taylor (2012) has called a "dictionary and grammar" perspective on language: everything that is idiosyncratic and non-computable is stored in the dictionary and everything that is computable is regulated by the grammar that typically is regarded as devoid of meaning.

The cognitive definition of grammar as an inventory of form-meaning pairs actually goes against such a view, saying not only that grammatical patterns are inherently meaningful, but also that the existence of a more general pattern (a "rule") does not exclude storage of instances of these patterns with their (possibly particular) meaning. Langacker has called this the *rule/list fallacy*: it is not necessarily so that because something is regular or computable, it is not, or cannot be, stored. Quite the contrary; it turns out that full compositionality is rare and that speakers store much more than is often assumed, including such compositional structures, some of which may be partially filled with specific lexical items (e.g. Jackendoff's (2008) *constructional idioms*, such as *a N of a man* or *N by N*), whereas others are fully schematic (e.g. the ditransitive construction, such as *Maarten gave Nick a book*). While in other models, the latter would be considered as the products of a grammatical rule devoid of meaning, in cognitive linguistics they, too, would be considered as inherently meaningful. In short, any linguistic unit, be it a morpheme, a lexical item or a larger (grammatical) pattern, is a symbolic unit linking a particular form to a particular meaning (which Langacker calls the *semantic pole*). Clearly, there will be differences between the semantic structure of lexical items, which will be more content-specific, and that of more syntactic patterns (such as the ditransitive construction, the caused motion construction or the setting construction: see Chapter 24) which will have a more schematic meaning.

This chapter will discuss how meaning at all levels is characterised in such a non-modular cognitive model. Clearly, what we present here is but a minimal sketch of the basic tenets of the model (see Geeraerts and Cuyckens (2007) for more elaborate discussions of some of the contexts presented here). The structure of the chapter is as follows. We will first present how cognitive semantics equates meaning with conceptualisation and thus incorporates an encyclopaedic view on meaning (section 2.1). Next, we will present more details on what such semantic structure looks like, talking first about conceptual imagery (section 2.2) and subsequently about the structure of semantic categories (section 2.3). In section 2.4 we briefly discuss metaphor and metonymy, given their central place in cognitive semantics. Section 2.5 rounds off the presentation with a brief sketch of constructional semantics.

2 Critical issues and topics

2.1 Meaning as conceptualisation

In cognitive linguistics, meaning is defined as conceptualisation: "Semantic structure is conceptualization tailored to the specifics of linguistic convention. Semantic analysis therefore requires the explicit characterization of conceptual structure" (Langacker 1987: 99). At first sight, the cognitive view may not seem to be fundamentally different from other theories which consider meanings to be concepts or conceptual representations. However, as becomes clear from what follows, the cognitive view still differs in important ways, such as its encyclopaedic view on meaning as well as its view that meaning is non-truth conditional.

The conceptual structure that provides the conceptual content of linguistic expressions can range from fairly simple concepts or a perceptual experience to complex knowledge clusters, cf. Langacker's (1987, 1991a) *cognitive domains*, Lakoff's (1987) *Idealised Cognitive Models* or Fillmore's *frames* ("unified frameworks of knowledge, or coherent schematizations of experience"; 1985: 223; see Dancygier and Sweetser (2014)). An oft-quoted example is that of the RESTAURANT frame which involves the experience of choosing a restaurant, waiting to be seated, a waiter serving you, choosing from a menu, ordering the food, picking up the bill, etc. Similarly, the meaning of words such as *weekend*, *workday* or *school night* can only be understood in reference to the typical (culture-specific) organisation of our time in weeks consisting of days during which we work (for payment) or go to school, and days when we do not, and the social practices that come with that distinction.

Understanding concepts like *weekend accidents* or *school night* requires quite a bit of cultural knowledge, such as the fact that partying or going out is typically reserved for weekends, as it usually involves staying up late (not ideal if the next day starts early) and a lot of drinking, which thus leads to more (lethal) traffic accidents during the weekend. In a similar vein, our understanding of what a *confession* is crucially relies on received ideas about certain moral standards that may hold in a particular society concerning "sinful" or secretive behaviour that one should own up to if one wants to be morally correct. As may be clear from these examples, the knowledge structures against the background of which we understand the meaning of linguistics items include (shared) cultural beliefs and practices. In other words, cognitive linguistics embraces an encyclopaedic view on meaning in the sense that the concepts constituting the meanings of expressions are often drawn from our general ("encyclopaedic") world knowledge – or at least, it rejects a strict dichotomy between linguistic and encyclopaedic knowledge. Such a dichotomy is, on the other hand, characteristic of "dictionary" views of semantics, in which an expression's linguistically relevant meaning is limited to the minimal literal sense, as recorded in dictionary definitions.

Cognitive linguistics takes an experiential view on conceptualisation and meaning, observing that many of our concepts are grounded in our experience – cultural and physical. Regarding the latter, cognitive linguistics holds the view that our everyday bodily experience plays an essential role in structuring our conceptual world. As Gibbs *et al.* (1994: 233) put it, "Knowledge is seen by many cognitive semanticists [. . .] as being grounded in patterns of bodily experience. These patterns, called *image schemas*, emerge throughout sensorimotor activity as we manipulate objects, orient ourselves spatially and temporally, and direct our perceptual focus for various purposes" (see also Lakoff (1987)). Examples of such image schemas are notions like CONTAINMENT, TRAJECTORY (consisting of SOURCE-PATH-GOAL), SUPPORT, SCALE, or even more basic configurational spatial concepts like FRONT-BACK, UP-DOWN, etc. Conceptual domains that imply such image schemas are said to be embodied (hence, the embodiment of meaning: see Chapter 8). Clearly, not all conceptual domains are embodied, yet even non-experiential domains often receive such embodied structure via metaphorical mappings. Hence, a distinction is often made between "primary domains" that are more directly embodied human experience and "abstract" or "secondary domains" that are not, such as social or mental states or processes; the distinction is, however, not always easy to make. Note that also within primary domains, some domains, such as SPACE, are more anchored to direct (physical) experience than others, such as TIME. As a result, one often finds metaphorical mappings from SPACE to TIME rather than the other way around, even if both are closely intertwined in many of our spatio-temporal experiences.

2.2 Conceptual imagery

As indicated above, conceptual domains are crucial to the meaning of a linguistic item. However, while a conceptual domain provides what Langacker calls the *conceptual content* of an expression, it does not exhaustively define the meaning of that expression. Crucially, linguistic expressions contribute to how the conceptual content is construed; each linguistic expression or construction imposes its own construal. In Langacker's terms, each expression is said to embody "conventional imagery". We will consider three important dimensions of imagery here: (i) vantage point (and subjectification), (ii) figure/ground (or profile/base) alignment and (iii) level of specificity.

Consider the sentences *The lamp is above the table* and *The table is under the lamp*; they may refer to the same situation (i.e. their truth conditions would be the same), yet clearly they each impose their own perspective or vantage point on the scene or, put differently, they frame the situation differently. Given the different conceptual construal, these two sentences are semantically non-equivalent. Many linguistic expressions incorporate such a vantage point: *He will do it tomorrow* implies a temporal viewpoint, *Come here!* implies a deictic viewpoint, and *The ball is behind the tree* implies a spatial viewpoint relative to the speaker/conceptualiser (see Levinson (2003b) for an interesting discussion of such spatial viewpoints). One of the basic claims of cognitive semantics is that much of language can be described as encoding different conceptualisations of experience.

Langacker points out that viewpoint often leads to a subjective construal, which means that the conceptualisation of a scene includes part of the conceptualisation process by the speaker/conceptualiser. Spatial expressions, once again, illustrate such subjectification quite nicely; take Langacker's examples *The balloon rose rapidly* (1991b: 327, ex. 7b) or *Vanessa is sitting across the table* (1991b: 328, ex. 9b). In both cases, the construal of the situation includes a mental scanning from the conceptualiser's point of view, in the vertical and horizontal dimensions, respectively. It is possible to bring the conceptualiser onto the scene, e.g. *Vanessa is sitting across the table **from me***, but this is a more objective construal of the scene where, in Langacker's terms, the conceptualiser is put "on stage". In a subjective construal, the conceptualiser remains off stage, i.e. not in the focus of observation.

Probably the most telling illustration of conceptual imagery is that of the figure/ground (or profile/base) alignment (not unrelated to that of perspective). This is an insight taken over from cognitive psychology, which refers to the basic principle of cognitive and perceptual experience by virtue of which humans perceive (or cognize) entities as standing out against others. This cognitive ability is often called "attention" and it is not exclusive to language. In visual perception, we can also see something as "standing out" from the background (the very notions of *foreground* and *background* when talking about a picture or painting build on this capacity). Similarly, in auditory perception, we can single out a particular sound from a multitude of sounds, such as what your friend is saying to you in a noisy bar, or one particular voice that you can single out from a polyphonic choral piece. Typically, attention is a matter of degree, and some entities possess properties that make them stand out more readily than others; this is often referred to as (cognitive or perceptual) "salience".

Talmy (2000) points out that spatial expressions incorporate a difference of salience where the moving or located entity, the figure, is seen as standing out from another, the ground. For example, *The car drove by the houses* is undoubtedly the most common way of expressing the event, singling out the moving car as most salient, even if this can be overruled (i.e. construed differently), as in *The houses flashed by*. Similarly, in a static location, a (small) movable object will be singled out for attention much more often than its supporting background; hence, we typically say *The cup is on the table* and not *The table is supporting the cup*. Notice that the earlier cited examples about the table and the lamp also differ in typicality of salience: focusing on the lamp as does *The lamp is above the table* is much more typical than singling out the table (*The table is under the lamp*), even if such a more unusual construal of the scene may in some contexts be quite appropriate. These examples illustrate that the general cognitive ability of attention (or salience) manifests itself also in language, as linguistic structures incorporate a focus of attention to certain elements of the conceptual structure that provides the conceptual content of the expression. In Langacker's terms, linguistic expressions impose a profile on a conceptual base, where profiling is defined as "a substructure that is elevated to a special level of prominence within the base" (Langacker 1991b: 5). The profile/base relationship captures the relationship of a concept and the domain relative to which it is understood. One of the examples Langacker gives is that of *hypotenuse* whose meaning can only be understood against the background of a triangle. Or take again the example of *weekend* which profiles a subpart of a base itself designated by *week*.

In cognitive grammar, grammatical oppositions like that between nouns and verbs also receive a semantic definition involving profile and base; for example, the verb *kill* and the noun *killing* are both characterised with respect to the same base, but each imposes a different profile: the noun profiles a thing (a region in one domain) whereas, being a relational predicate, the verb profiles a temporal sequence of interconnections between entities. In fact, the grammatical difference relates to our cognitive capacity for conceptual reification, i.e. our ability to conceive of an array of temporal states as a single unified (abstract) entity. As Lakoff and Johnson (1980) have shown, such conceptual reification underlies much of our metaphorical thinking, as we treat non-discrete abstract entities as if they are discrete and tangible. For example, conceptualising events, which in the real world may not always have a clear beginning and end, as entities with clear boundaries allows us to qualify them, taking or thinking about different aspects just as we would examine different aspects of a concrete object.

The third example of conceptual imagery that we will discuss concerns the *level of specificity* at which we conceive an entity. If you see a dog on the lawn, you might refer to this entity (i.e. conceive of it) as *a German shepherd* (most specific), *a dog* (less specific), *an animal* (unspecific) or *something* (least specific). Notwithstanding this variation, speakers have a tendency to prefer one of these levels of conceptualisation as the default way to think and talk about the given situation (in this example, *dog*) which has been identified as the basic level of categorisation. The motivation for this preference lies in the fact that it is cognitively and communicatively economical, since one item conveys a whole bundle of information that is sufficiently neutral yet not too specific.

2.3 Conceptual networks

As pointed out above, cognitive semantics entails an encyclopaedic view on meaning: knowing what a *school night* is not only requires much more than the juxtaposition of *school* and *night* but also relates to acceptable social behaviour; some linguistic models may consider that as not relevant to semantic characterisation, since related to world knowledge (often considered part of *pragmatics*). In cognitive linguistics, as already noted, a strict distinction between linguistic and encyclopaedic knowledge is rejected. Clearly, some conceptual specifications are quite central to the characterisation of (linguistic) meaning whereas others may be more peripheral and have only minimal importance. What is crucial is that no strict demarcation can be made between what constitutes a relevant semantic (i.e. linguistic) feature and what does not. Such an encyclopaedic view also entails that no strict demarcation is made in cognitive linguistics between semantics and pragmatics, even if, here also, some things may be more semantic (i.e. stored with the linguistic item as part of its meaning) whereas others may be more pragmatic, i.e. determined by the immediate (linguistic or social) context in which an expression is used. For reasons of space, we can unfortunately not elaborate on this issue within the scope of this chapter (but see Chapter 10).

An encyclopaedic view on semantics obviously has important repercussions for the definition of the meaning of, say, a lexical item as stored in the mental lexicon. Trying to account for the meaning of the lexical item *bird* (to take a typical example) will thus not lead to a bundle of distinctive semantic features that represent the necessary and sufficient conditions for any entity to be included under the term *bird*, given that it is difficult, if not impossible, to determine which features are essential to its linguistic meaning and which are accidental, i.e. resulting from our encyclopaedic knowledge of birds (e.g. the colour of their feathers or the shape of their beaks, etc.). Instead, it turns out that some features may be more central to a definition of the word *bird* (or to the definition of the category of entities that we call birds) than others, and therefore that, logically, some birds may be more typical exemplars than others. We will not elaborate here on the idea of prototype categories itself (see Geeraerts (1988), Taylor (2005) for some relevant discussion), but we will briefly discuss how this is relevant to the characterisation of semantic structure at all levels of linguistic organisation (see also Chapter 7).

One of the essential notions of cognitive semantics is that the semantic pole of a linguistic unit represents a (complex) semantic category; as any other conceptual category, this is considered to be a prototype-based category. More specifically, this means that some semantic substructure within that category is more salient than others and thus forms the semantic prototype, or the prototypical meaning of that linguistic structure. For example, the prototypical meaning of the adjective *warm* will be characterised against the domain of temperature (as in *warm water* or *a warm bed*); this will be the meaning that most people will spontaneously think of as the meaning of this adjective. Other meanings, such as those instantiated by *warm feelings*, *a warm colour* or *a warm voice* will be less typical; in this case, they are metaphorically related to the prototype. The semantic pole of the adjective *warm* is not exhaustively defined by the prototype alone, but by the complex network of all the semantic substructures (typically called senses, even if it may not always be clear what constitutes a sense and what not: see Chapter 13). Taken together these senses thus form what Lakoff (1987) has called a "radial (polysemic) network", which can be represented as in Figure 5.1 below, where the filled dot represents the semantic prototype and the broken arrows, the semantic extensions.

The major cognitive operation that underlies the building of such a network is analogy, where an extended meaning is judged sufficiently similar to the prototype to be incorporated into the network. The key to category membership is not a checklist of necessary and sufficient semantic features, but a judgement of similarity (similar to Wittgenstein's idea of family resemblance). As Geeraerts (1988: 223) correctly observes, this is precisely why

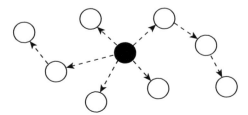

Figure 5.1 Semantic prototype category (radial network)

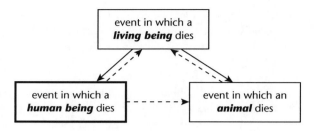

Figure 5.2 Extension, schematisation and instantiation in a schematic network

prototype-structured categories are cognitively advantageous, as they combine "structural stability with flexible adaptability: the categorial system can only work efficiently if it can maintain its overall organisation for some time [. . .]; however, it should be flexible enough to be easily adaptable to changing circumstances".

Langacker's cognitive grammar model also incorporates the idea of prototypical meanings that are cognitively more salient, yet it focuses more on the analogy that underlies category extension leading to *schematic networks*. Let us illustrate that with a simple example, the verb *kill*. When asked to make a sentence with this verb, most speakers will produce a sentence illustrating what can be considered as the prototypical meaning of this verb, roughly defined as an event in which a human being (volitionally) acts upon another human being such that this latter being dies. However, the verb is also used to refer to an event where an animal is the victim. This could be regarded as an extended use of the verb, which is based on the similarity between human beings and animals. This analogy is captured by a more general semantic structure (something like "event in which a living being dies") that neutralises the differences between the two usages. In Langacker's terms, this superordinate structure is a schema and the result is a schematic network, which can be diagrammed as in Figure 5.2. In the Langackarian diagrammatic conventions, both the extension and the schematisation are represented by the broken arrow, as both imply that certain attributes are cancelled out. Once one has such a (low-level) schema, the two usages can be regarded as more specific instantiations said to elaborate the schema; in other words, every schematisation automatically entails instantiation, represented in Figure 5.2 by the solid downward arrows.

The semantic category of *kill* is clearly more complex, as the existence of other kinds of "living" beings, such as plants or micro-organisms, can be halted as well. A more complete diagram of the (literal) domain of *kill* could thus be represented as in Figure 5.3 (adapted from Lemmens 1998: 51).

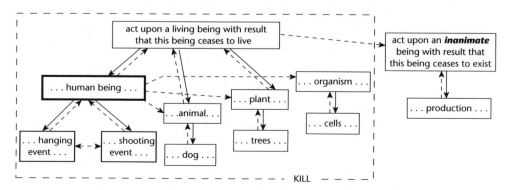

Figure 5.3 A (simplified) schematic network for *kill*

Note that the prototype is not a particular contextual usage of the verb but is itself a schematisation over individual usage events whose specifics may be quite different (in the diagram represented by a hanging event and a shooting event). All of the uses inside the dashed box represent the domain proper of *kill*, whereas metaphorical uses such as *kill the production of the car* or *kill the proposal* cross the domain boundary. Nevertheless, they are motivated by the same mechanism of analogy (or perceived similarity) between the existence of animate and non-animate entities; the schema capturing that similarity would thus be something like "end the existence of an entity". The latter schema does not exhaust the meaning of *kill* (i.e. it cannot be regarded as the definition); it is the entire network that forms the semantic pole of an expression. As Rice (1996: 141) points out, Langacker's model can be regarded as a vertical model, since "outward growth from the prototype tends to co-occur with upward growth"; a radial category would then be more of a horizontal, centre-periphery model.

The description above has been greatly simplified for expository purposes, and clearly in reality things are more complicated. In what follows we will briefly present some important nuances and critical comments.

The first comment is that the definition of what is to be included in the prototype of a category is often not so straightforward. This is typically illustrated by natural kind categories (like BIRD or FURNITURE), but let us illustrate this with a another example, that of the three cardinal posture verbs in Dutch, *zitten* ("sit"), *liggen* ("lie") and *staan* ("stand"), that not only have grammaticalised to basic locative verbs used to express the location of any entity in space (e.g. a bed "standing" in the room, cities "lying" near the sea, or water "sitting" in the bottle), but also have extensive metaphorical and idiomatic uses (see Lemmens (2002, 2006a); Lemmens and Perrez (2010, 2012) for more detailed analyses). The prototypes of these semantic categories are fairly straightforward, *viz.* the representation of the three basic human postures of sitting, standing and lying. Yet, as Newman (2002) correctly observes, these prototypes are in fact more accurately defined as "experiential clusters" of attributes, some of which will motivate particular semantic extensions.

For example, one of the attributes of *staan* is that of a human being resting on its feet which, at least for Dutch, becomes the key element for the highly productive extension to locative use: *staan* will be used to express the location of *any* entity (regardless of its actual vertical dimension) that is resting on its base; logically then, cars, beds, computers, plates or shoes will all be said to be standing when they are (functionally) positioned on their base. In fact, this extension is motivated by a more abstract image schema of a "standing" entity that captures the similarity between a human being on its feet and an inanimate entity resting on its base. Or take the case of *zitten* "sit". One of the features associated with the prototype (but which may possibly not be so salient at first sight) is the idea that there is close contact with and semi-containment in the chair that one is sitting in. This notion has been shown to be the motivating factor to one of the most productive uses of Dutch *zitten* referring to CLOSE CONTAINMENT. Hence, water will be said to "sit" in the bottle, bacteria will "sit" in the blood or sugar will "sit" in my coffee. Significantly, many metaphorical extensions build off these associations that may at first sight not have been central to the prototype. This justifies, once more, an encyclopaedic view on (lexical) meaning.

The second more critical comment is that in both radial and schematic networks, meanings are represented as stable, interrelated entities (dots or boxes); Langacker terms these "established senses"; that is, senses that are sufficiently frequent to have become entrenched in the linguistic system (i.e. they are stored as such). These are not unlike what Croft and Cruse (2004: 126) call "microsenses". They illustrate this with the different microsenses of *knife*:

a type of cutlery, a type of weapon, a type of (medical) instrument, a type of DIY tool, etc. However, this is an idealisation of a reality that most likely is much more fluid. First of all, it is not yet clear to what extent these meanings are indeed clearly identifiable structures stored in the mind of speakers, even if there is evidence from categorisation tasks (see Rice (1996)) that some of them seem to be cognitively real. (The cognitive reality of such networks has been an issue that has long preoccupied cognitive linguists, as nicely illustrated by the title of one of the first publications (Sandra and Rice 1995) addressing this issue, "Network analyses of prepositional meaning: Mirroring whose mind – the linguist's or the language user's?") Similarly, Croft and Cruse nicely illustrate how these microsenses are a linguistic reality to speakers; they point out, for example, that if one does not have a knife at the dinner table but one has a penknife in one's pocket, one would still say that one does not have a knife "of the proper sort" to cut the meat with. Second, the context in which an item is used will invariably adduce some further specifications without these necessarily giving rise to new individualised senses. Croft and Cruse (ibid.) aptly call this "contextual modulation", a concept already introduced in Cruse (1986) who describes it as "each context emphasizing certain semantic traits, and obscuring and suppressing others" (Cruse 1986: 52). To take one of Cruse's own examples, the phrases *The car needs washing* and *The car needs servicing* highlight different parts of the car, yet it is not the case that *car* is referring to something different in these two sentences. While such contextual modulation is probably not stored (note that in this case, they can be explained by metonymy: see section 2.4 below), they might over time lead to different senses provided they stand out sufficiently or occur sufficiently frequently so that they become entrenched as individual instantiations (Taylor (2005) says contextual modulation contains "the seeds of polysemy"). In fact, one could argue, as Langacker does, that the contexts profile another aspect of the (complex) conceptual domain related to cars; in more technical terms, the different contexts are said to profile a different *active zone* (Langacker 1991b: Ch.7; 2000: 62ff.).

A final critical comment is the question of which type of analysis is now to be followed: categorisation by schema or by prototype? Note that the two are not mutually exclusive, as schematic networks incorporate the idea of a prototype (Langacker calls these "experientially based conceptual archetypes"), but they do imply a different perspective. Notice also that schematic networks may present a solution to the conflict between the "lumpers" (a term suggested by Croft (2001) to refer to those who argue for general schematic meanings and relaying the other differences to the context) and the "splitters" (arguing for different individual senses and thus rampant polysemy). Tuggy (1993, 2007) convincingly points out that a schematic network resolves the debate between polysemy (ambiguity) and vagueness:

> The prototypical case of ambiguity is where two semantic structures [. . .] are both well-entrenched (and therefore salient) while there is no well-entrenched and elaboratively close schema. [. . .] Prototypical vagueness, on the other hand, involves meanings which are not well-entrenched but which have a relatively well-entrenched, elaboratively close schema subsuming them.
>
> (Tuggy 1993: 280–1)

Significantly, this difference in salience can be entrenched or contextually determined, and it may change over time.

In the case of clear polysemy (or homonymy), a unifying over-arching schema may not be found for lexical semantic categories, as already observed in an early study by Lindner (1980) on the prepositions *in* and *out*. Dutch posture verbs provide yet again a nice illustration of this difficulty. One of the highly productive uses of Dutch *staan* "stand" is the reference to printed text. It is possible to see some motivation for this, where one could argue that letters are perceived as standing on a line; italics can thus be defined as *schuinstaand* (literally "stand slantingly"). Alternatively, the conceptualisation may be one where letters are perceived as figures standing out in relief vis-à-vis the background (the paper or any other carrier), and thus the vertical scanning giving rise to *staan* is from the paper upward. While both are plausible, the question remains to what extent these motivations are cognitively real and, thus, to what extent there still is a schema uniting this meaning of *staan* with prototypical (or locational) *staan*. It seems quite likely that speakers may simply regard these as unrelated senses (absence of unifying schema). This does not deny that this usage is not well-entrenched, or that it has become in itself a productive source for further extensions, since any printed matter can be said to "be standing", ranging from pictures in a book to icons on my desktop, files on my computer or on the internet, or songs on a record or a CD (conceived as printed on the carrier).

2.4 Metaphor and metonymy

In cognitive (lexical) semantics, metaphor and metonymy play a major role as structuring principles in the semantic category. Importantly, these are not seen as purely linguistic relations, but as conceptual principles. Lakoff and Johnson's (1980) book *Metaphors We Live By*, which laid the basis for Metaphor Theory (and later Blending Theory, cf. Fauconnier (1994), Coulson and Oakley (2001)), is probably the publication that popularised the idea of the cognitive nature of (particularly) metaphor which is said to structure the way we talk, think and act, an idea that had, however, an important precedent in an article from 1954 by the philosopher Max Black.

In cognitive linguistics, the difference between metaphor and metonymy is typically defined in two ways. First, the underlying mechanisms are different: metaphor builds on (perceived) *similarity* where one entity is said to be *understood* in terms of another (e.g. ARGUMENT IS WAR, LOVE IS A JOURNEY, CHANGE IS MOTION, ANGER IS HEAT IN A CONTAINER, etc.). Metonymy, in contrast, is defined in terms of *reference*, where one entity is used to *refer* to another, usually because it is (conceptually) contiguous to it. Physical contiguity motivates the metonymy underlying the use of *door* in *walk through the door* (the aperture in the wall) versus *paint the door* (the board covering that aperture), or that between the container and contained (e.g. *drink a glass of beer*). Conceptual contiguity could be argued to be the motivation for the metonymy POSSESSOR-POSSESSED as the two need not be physically contiguous.

The second difference between metaphor and metonymy that is often invoked (which follows logically from the preceding) is that metaphor concerns a mapping across different domains (or, more accurately, frames), whereas metonymy implies a shift within one and the same domain. For example, the meanings of *kill* in the uses *kill a human being* and *kill life on the planet* can be seen as metonymically related, involving a shift of an instance (a living being) to the larger process (life) yet the relation is not metaphorical since they are both still characterised vis-à-vis the domain of killing proper. A usage such as *kill the peace process* is, however, metaphorical, as it is no longer the domain of taking away life that is at issue. Notice that the same metonymical shift of profile as in the source domain is possible here as well, e.g. *Under economic pressure, Ford decided to kill the **production** of the car* (process) vs. *Under economic pressure, Ford decided to kill the **car*** (product).

A metonymy can thus be defined as a shift of profile within the domain: "the ability of the speaker to select a different contextually salient concept profile in a domain or domain matrix than the one usually symbolized by the word" (Croft and Cruse 2004: 48). Such shifts are often motivated because one is focusing on a particular aspect in a given context; for example, if I say *I see there are some new faces in class today*, I am using *faces* metonymically as it is the part of a person that allows me to recognise them (or not, in this case). Similarly, *a helping hand* focuses on the part of the body that we stereotypically use when helping others. In an earlier study on the verb *abort* (Lemmens 1998: 211ff), I pointed out that ideological reasons may also motivate metonymical shifts: pro-lifers will typically focus on the end-point and thus say *abort a baby/child* whereas pro-choicers often downplay this aspect and use *foetus* or *zygote* or omit the argument altogether (e.g. *A woman has the right to abort, if she so chooses*). More neutral parties often choose a more neutral formulation such as *abort a pregnancy*.

While the difference between metaphor and metonymy will mostly be clear enough, the latter example actually shows that this may not be so. Even if pregnancy and foetus/baby can be argued to be metonymically related, *abort a pregnancy* could equally be regarded as a metaphor since it is an instantiation of *abort a process* (a metaphorical usage), just like *abort a mission* or *abort a takeoff*. The criterion of domain boundary crossing that is often used in cognitive linguistics may not be so helpful either, given the difficulty of defining what a domain is (see, for instance, Clausner and Croft (1999) on this issue); it seems that the decision of boundary crossing is often post hoc, i.e. after one has already decided that a usage is metaphorical. But even then, such a decision may not always be easy to make. Let us again consider the example of the Dutch cardinal posture verbs which are frequently used as basic locative verbs to express the location of any entity in space. If a bottle is said to be standing on the table (motivation: BASE), should such a locative use then be considered as metaphorical or not? Clearly, it is no longer characterised to the postural domain, yet this use of *staan* for inanimate objects is so entrenched and can be applied to such a wide set of objects (computers, phones, printers, cars, trains, plates, dishes, containers, ashtrays, pies, etc.) that it could be considered as a (literal) instantiation of the schema "object resting on its base" of which a human in standing position is a privileged subschema.

The story becomes even more complicated when metonymy is brought in. As noted above, in cognitive linguistics it is common to regard metonymy as an extension mechanism operating *within* a domain. Consider the following examples with Dutch *zitten* "sit":

(1) a   Zij zit in de zetel. ("She sits in the armchair")
    b   Zij zit in de auto. ("She sits in the car")
    c   Zij zit in de kelder. ("She sits in the cellar")

The first usage is clearly one where the person is in a prototypical sitting posture and the context specifies the support that partially surrounds her (hence the use of *in* rather than *op* "on"). The second example implies a metonymical shift away from this support (the seat) to the larger enclosing space (the car), and so does the last example. The difference between the latter two, however, is that the (b) sentence still implies a sitting posture, whereas the (c) example most likely does not (even if not excluded): the sentence can, for example, be used felicitously even when she is walking around in the cellar. Under that interpretation, the usage is no longer committed to a particular posture and should thus be labelled metaphorical (mediated by metonymy). The use of *zitten* as in the last example, expressing the idea of enclosure/containment rather than a sitting posture, is extremely common in Dutch, and not restricted to human beings as any object enclosed in a (narrow) container can be coded with *zitten* such that speakers may consider this to be a non-metaphorical usage. It thus seems that such locational uses straddle the border between (prototypical) postural uses and more metaphorical ones, that relate to abstract location, such as, for example, a mistake that "sits" in your reasoning or someone sitting in a depression.

Despite these issues, it is safe to assume that metaphor and metonymy are cognitive principles that play a role in semantic structure. That a strict demarcation between literal and metaphorical may not always be easy to make follows logically from the prototype-structure of categories where boundaries may not always be very strict (and see also Chapter 11).

2.5 Constructional semantics

So far, the discussion has focused on lexical meaning; it will be recalled that in cognitive linguistics also grammatical structures are considered as inherently meaningful. Given the more general nature of these constructions, their semantic structure will be considered to be more general or, in the more technical terms introduced above, to be more *schematic*. The cognitive principle driving the schematisation is the same, *viz.* that of analogy. Let us illustrate that with one of Jackendoff's pet examples of constructional idioms, the [*V one's X PRT*] construction, as instantiated by expressions such as *work one's head off*, *sing one's heart out* or *cry one's eyes out*. Jackendoff correctly points out that these expressions are idiomatic, as the NP and particle are typically selected from a quite constrained class (see, however, Cappelle (2005: 46ff; 453ff) for an interesting discussion). In addition, the object NP is not licensed by the verb as one cannot say **he sang his heart* or **he worked his head*; in other words, it is the entire construction with the particle that allows for the integration of an object NP, thereby overruling the verb's typical intransitive nature. In Construction Grammar, this phenomenon is called coercion; cf. Michaelis (2004, 2006), Goldberg (2006). Also the semantics of these expressions is to some extent idiomatic (i.e. more than just the sum of the meaning of the parts), as they invariably mean that the action expressed by the verb (working, laughing, crying, etc.) is done to a high degree or even to some excess. In other words, the construction incorporates a particular evaluative (affective) judgement that can be paraphrased as "do X intensively or excessively".

Just like lexical categories, these expressions can be seen as building a schematic network where analogy and schematisation are the structuring principles. Two of the obvious schematisations concern the possessive pronoun and the body part where usages such as *He worked **his ass** off* and *They worked **their heads** off* are both regarded as instantiations of the more schematic structure <NP_i> *work* <$POSS_i$> <BODY PART> *off*. Parts of this schema are open, like the subject NP, while other parts are filled (e.g. *work*, *off*) or semi-open. The latter means that they are (i) syntactically constrained, such as is the case for the possessive pronoun, which should in principle be co-referential with the subject NP (e.g. it would be quite odd to say *The teacher worked the students' heads off*) or (ii) semantically constrained, such as the BODY PART being restricted to certain body parts, as illustrated by the oddness of *work one's eyes off*. The occurrence of a phrase like *bust one's head off* leads to a (low-level) schematisation of the verb, where *bust* and *work* are seen as semantically quite close. Expressions such as *laugh one's ass off*, *lie one's ass off*, *sweat one's ass off*, *dance one's ass off*, etc. push the schematisation even further to <NP_i> <V> <$POSS_i$> <BODY PART> *off*. Figure 4 gives a simplified view of the resulting schematic network. Further levels of schematisation allow the integration of other particles (e.g. *cry one's eyes **out***).

The resulting schematic network captures the common meaning ("do V intensively or excessively") yet also allows for specific semantic elements being incorporated through the lexical items that occur into the different instantiations. Clearly, there are semantic

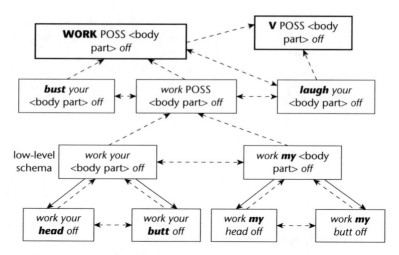

Figure 5.4 A (simplified) schematic network for *work one's X off*

constraints. For example, given the close association between singing and (possibly effortful) breathing, *singing one's lungs out* is quite interpretable as doing intensive singing; similarly, given the conventional link between singing and the expression of emotions, *singing one's heart out* is fairly transparent given the metonymy of heart as a seat for the emotions. However, to say *sing one's arms out/off* is quite difficult (if not impossible) to interpret, given the absence of any transparent link between arms and singing. Surely, repeated use might lead to semantic bleaching which is what has happened to *V one's {head/ass off}* where the choice of verb no longer seems to be constrained by the body part. This takes us back to salience within the category: some instantiations turn out to be more salient (more prototypical instances) than others.

The above discussion has focused on a particular constructional idiom, or rather a family of related idioms, that can be captured under the general schema *V one's X PRT*; one might argue that this could still be regarded as a supra-lexical unit rather than a grammatical structure (see Chapter 24). While indeed the *V one's X PRT* construction remains somewhat more specific in some respects, it should be clear that a similar analysis can be suggested for more general grammatical patterns, such as the Ditransitive construction, e.g. *John gave Mary a book*, the Caused Motion construction (e.g. *She put the book on the table*) or the Intransitive motion construction (e.g. *He went into the room*). These are also considered as symbolic form-meaning pairs where a particular form is paired with a particular (highly schematic) meaning. For example, the Ditransitive construction couples a particular syntactic pattern (NP V NP NP) to a meaning which can be roughly paraphrased as X CAUSES Y TO RECEIVE Z; as such it is considered semantically different from the *to*-dative construction (NP V NP *to* NP, e.g. *John gave the book to Mary*) whose meaning can be paraphrased as X MOVES Y TO Z. (See Stefanowitsch and Gries (2003) for corpus-based evidence (via collostructional analysis) on this difference and the repercussion on the different types of verbs that occur in these constructions.)

Notice that here also the meaning of the construction may change the meaning of the verb that occurs in it (a case of coercion). For example, the verb *break* is a lexical causative referring to a change of state where motion is backgrounded (if considered part of the verb's meaning at all), yet it saliently refers to a motion event in *She broke the eggs into the bowl* (caused motion) or in *The sun broke through the clouds* (see Lemmens (2006b) for some discussion of these uses of *break* and other lexical causatives). The meaning of the construction also guides the interpretation of novel verbs; if one were to say of the author of the present chapter that *He lemmensed into the room*, it will be clear, thanks to the meaning of the Intransitive Motion construction, that the verb refers to a particular manner of motion even if it may not be clear what that manner is (nor would we care to specify that here).

In its ambition to prove that such grammatical schemas are also meaningful, the cognitive linguistic literature (especially in Construction Grammar) may have overemphasised the quest for, or the existence of, highly schematic constructions that unify all the members of the category. However, as with lexical semantic categories, it need not be the case that such high-level schemas exist; in fact, some recent studies (see, among others, Perek (2015), Lemmens and Perek (2009)) show that it may be more accurate to pitch the constructional generalisations at a lower level. For example, Perek (2015) points out that there may not be such a thing as one single conative construction that unites all the instances (e.g. *Bill kicked at the ball*, *She gulped at the whisky*, *He pulled at the wagon*), but rather a number of low-level schemas that generalise over semantically related verbs and also have their own semantic properties.

3 Conclusions

If one were pushed to summarise cognitive semantics in a number of keywords, some proper candidates would be *conceptualisation* (which entails *encyclopaedic*), *construal* (the cognitive capacity to conceptualise experience in alternate ways), *image schemas* (schematic patterns of bodily experience) and *prototype-structured categorisation*. These principles are not restricted to lexical items, but underlie linguistic structures at all levels, ranging from morphemes, lexical items and semi-open idioms, to semantically highly schematic grammatical patterns.

Further reading

Croft, William and Alan Cruse 2004. *Cognitive Linguistics*. Cambridge: Cambridge University Press. Introductory textbook that offers a clear introduction to some of the basic tenets of cognitive linguistics.

Geeraerts, Dirk 2010. *Theories of Lexical Semantics*. Oxford: Oxford University Press. Comprehensive overview of the major traditions of word meaning research in linguistics, charting the evolution of the discipline from the mid-nineteenth century to the present day.

Geeraerts, Dirk and Hubert Cuyckens 2007. *The Oxford Handbook of Cognitive Linguistics*. Oxford: Oxford University Press. Probably the most complete presentation of cognitive linguistics with contributions detailing many of the issues presented in this chapter (embodiment, construal, schematic networks, entrenchment, Idealised Cognitive Models, image schemas, metaphor, metonymy, etc.).

References

Black, Max 1954. Metaphor. *Proceedings of the Aristotelian Society* 55: 273–294.
Cappelle, Bert 2005. *Particle Constructions in English. A comprehensive coverage*. PhD thesis, K.U. Leuven.
Clausner, Timothy and William Croft 1999. Domains and image schemas. *Cognitive Linguistics* 10: 1–35.
Coulson, Seana and Todd Oakley 2001. Blending basics. *Cognitive Linguistics* 11: 175–196.

Croft, William 2001. *Radical Construction Grammar. Syntactic Theory in Typological Perspective*. Oxford: Oxford University Press.
Croft, William and Alan Cruse 2004. *Cognitive Linguistics*. Cambridge: Cambridge University Press.
Cruse, Alan 1986. *Lexical Semantics*. Cambridge: Cambridge University Press.
Dancygier, Barbara and Eve Sweetser 2014. *Figurative Language*. Cambridge: Cambridge University Press.
Fauconnier, Gilles 1994. *Mental Spaces: Aspects of Meaning Construction in Natural Language*. Cambridge: Cambridge University Press.
Fillmore, Charles 1985. Frames and the semantics of understanding. *Quaderni di Semantica* 6: 222–254.
Geeraerts, Dirk. 1988. Where does prototypicality come from? In Brygida Rudzka-Ostyn (ed.) *Topics in Cognitive Linguistics*. Amsterdam and Philadelphia: John Benjamins, 207–229.
Geeraerts, Dirk and Hubert Cuyckens 2007. *The Oxford Handbook of Cognitive Linguistics*. Oxford: Oxford University Press.
Gibbs, Raymond W., Dinara A. Beitel, Michael Harrington and Paul E. Sanders. 1994. Taking a stand on the meanings of stand: bodily experience as motivation for polysemy. *Journal of Semantics* 11: 231–251.
Goldberg, Adèle E. 1995. *Constructions: A Construction Grammar Approach to Argument Structure*. Chicago: Chicago University Press.
Goldberg, Adèle E. 2006. *Constructions at Work. The Nature of Generalization in Language*. Oxford: Oxford University Press.
Jackendoff, Ray 2008. Construction after construction and its theoretical challenges. *Language* 84: 8–28.
Lakoff, George 1987. *Women, Fire and Dangerous Things*. Chicago: Chicago University Press.
Lakoff, George and Mark Johnson 1980. *Metaphors We Live By*. Chicago: Chicago University Press.
Langacker, Ronald W. 1987. *Foundations of Cognitive Grammar. Vol. I: Descriptive Application*. Stanford: Stanford University Press.
Langacker, Ronald W. 1991a. *Foundations of Cognitive Grammar. Vol. II: Descriptive Application*. Stanford: Stanford University Press.
Langacker, Ronald W. 1991b. *Concept, Image, and Symbol*. Berlin and New York: Mouton de Gruyter.
Langacker, Ronald W. 2000 *Grammar and Conceptualization*. Berlin and New York: Mouton de Gruyter.
Lemmens, Maarten 1998. *Lexical Perspectives on Transitivity and Ergativity. Causative Constructions in English*. [Current Issues in Linguistic Theory 166]. Amsterdam and Philadelphia: John Benjamins.
Lemmens, Maarten 2002. The semantic network of Dutch *zitten*, *staan*, and *liggen*, In John Newman (ed.) *The Linguistics of Sitting, Standing, and Lying*. Amsterdam and Philadelphia: John Benjamins, 103–139.
Lemmens, Maarten 2006a. Caused posture: experiential patterns emerging from corpus research. In A. Stefanowitsch and S. Gries (eds) *Corpora in Cognitive Linguistics. Corpus-Based Approaches to Syntax and Lexis*. Berlin: Mouton de Gruyter, 261–296.
Lemmens, Maarten 2006b. More on objectless transitives and ergativization patterns in English, *Constructions*. http://elanguage.net/journals/constructions/article/view/2821.
Lemmens, Maarten and Florent Perek 2009. Getting at the meaning of the English *at*-construction: the case of a constructional split, *CogniTextes* 5. http://cognitextes.revues.org/331.
Lemmens, Maarten and Julien Perrez 2010. On the use of posture verbs by French-speaking learners of Dutch: a corpus-based study. *Cognitive Linguistics* 21: 315–347.
Lemmens, Maarten and Julien Perrez 2012. A quantitative analysis of the use of posture verbs by French-speaking learners of Dutch, *CogniTextes* 8. http://cognitextes.revues.org/609.
Levinson, Stephen C. 2003a. Language and mind: let's get the issues straight! In Deirdre Gentner and Susan Goldin-Meadow (eds), *Language in Mind: Advances in the Study of Language and Cognition*. Cambridge, MA: MIT Press, 25–46.
Levinson, Stephen C. 2003b. *Space in Language and Cognition: Explorations in Cognitive Diversity*. Cambridge: Cambridge University Press.

Lindner, Susan 1982. What goes up doesn't necessarily come down: the Ins and outs of opposites. *Chicago Linguistic Society* 18: 305–323.
Michaelis, Laura A. 2004. Type shifting in construction grammar: an integrated approach to aspectual coercion. *Cognitive Linguistics* 15: 1–67.
Michaelis, Laura A. 2006. Construction grammar. In K. Brown (ed.) *The Encyclopedia of Language and Linguistics*, Second edition, Volume 3. Oxford: Elsevier, 73–84.
Newman, John (ed.) 2002. *The Linguistics of Sitting, Standing, and Lying*. Amsterdam and Philadelphia: John Benjamins.
Perek, Florent 2015. *Argument Structure in Usage-Based Construction Grammar: Experimental and Corpus-Based Perspectives*. Amsterdam/Philadelphia: Benjamins.
Rice, Sally 1996. Prepositional prototypes. In René Dirven and Michael Pütz (eds), *The Construal of Space in Language and Thought*. Berlin and New York: Mouton de Gruyter, 135–165.
Sandra, Dominiek and Sally Rice 1995. Network analyses of prepositional meaning: mirroring whose mind – the linguist's or the language user's? *Cognitive Linguistics* 6: 89–130.
Stefanowitsch, A. and Gries, S. Th. 2003. Collostructions: investigating the interaction of words and constructions. *International Journal of Corpus Linguistics* 8: 209–243.
Talmy, Leonard 2000. *Toward a Conceptual Semantics* (Vol. I and II). Cambridge, MA: MIT Press.
Taylor, J. R. 2005. *Linguistic Categorisation*. Oxford: Oxford University Press.
Taylor, J. R. 2012. *The Mental Corpus: How Language is Represented in the Mind*. Oxford: Oxford University Press.
Tomasello, Michael 1995. Language is not an instinct. *Cognitive Development* 10, 131–156.
Tuggy, David 1993. Ambiguity, polysemy, and vagueness. *Cognitive Linguistics* 4: 273–290.
Tuggy, David 2007. Schematicity. In Dirk Geeraerts and Hubert Cuyckens (eds) *The Oxford Handbook of Cognitive Linguistics*. Oxford: Oxford University Press, 82–116.

Related topics

Chapter 2, Internalist semantics; Chapter 6, Corpus semantics; Chapter 7, Categories, prototypes and exemplars; Chapter 8, Embodiment, simulation and meaning; Chapter 10, Semantics and pragmatics; Chapter 13, Sense individuation; Chapter 15, Semantic shift; Chapter 24, Compositionality.

6

Corpus semantics

Michael Stubbs

The term "corpus semantics" is a shorthand way of referring to a combination of data, methods and theory: empirical observational evidence from large computer-readable corpora is used to formulate hypotheses about meaning. The data-intensive methods depend on the ability to store and search large text collections for lexical and grammatical patterns. One of the most significant findings has been the pervasiveness, in all kinds of texts, of predictable collocations, and a major theoretical puzzle has been how best to model multi-word units of meaning.

Computer technology was used in the 1960s and 1970s to do preliminary work on word frequency and on collocations (Kučera and Francis 1967; Sinclair et al. 2004 [1970]; Allén 1975). However, it was only by the mid-1980s that computers became powerful enough to make realistic contributions to the construction of the first corpus-based dictionary (Cobuild 1987), and only from around the mid-1990s that the widespread availability of large corpora and user-friendly software made the data and methods available to scholars with no expertise in computing.

1 Data, definitions and initial examples

All unattributed examples of attested language use below are from the BNC (British National Corpus). This consists of 100 million words of contemporary English from over 4000 text samples, and can be accessed at http://www.natcorp.ox.ac.uk and via various user-interfaces (Hoffmann et al. 2008; Fletcher 2003). A clear advantage of empirical methods is that readers can check my findings in this corpus. Even better, of course, would be to check them in other independent corpora.

Double quotation marks are used for terms and quotations. Single quotation marks are used for meanings. *Word-forms* are in lower-case italic. *LEMMAS* and *WORD FAMILIES* are in upper-case italic. The term "lemma" is traditionally used for a class of a basic word-form plus its inflected forms which are all the same part of speech, e.g. the verb *drink, drinks, drank, drunk, drinking*. A "word family" (Bauer and Nation 1993) is a word plus both its inflected and derived forms, e.g. *drink, drinker*. But the form *drink* can be a verb or noun, and *drunk* can be a verb, adjective or noun. Empirical studies of corpus data have shown that different forms of a lemma often pattern in different ways from each other, and that members of a word family often pattern in a similar way.

Diamond brackets enclose collocates of a word-form or lemma, e.g. *DRINK <beer, coffee, tea, wine* etc.>. Square brackets, as in [A B], make a claim that this is a linguistic unit, not merely a linear sequence of words. A slash, as in [A/B], indicates that the linear sequence is variable. For example, the following occurrences are evidence of a unit [*HEAVY/DRINK*] which is realized not only by variable forms of lemmas (as traditionally defined), but also by verbs and nouns (*drank*, *drinker*), and by adjectives and adverbs (*heavy*, *heavily*), in variable linear sequences and variable spans (in the sense of a window of orthographic words to the left and right).

> she thought he drank too heavily
> he was drinking heavily
> he was a heavy drinker and smoker
> both were heavy red-wine drinkers

This example confirms the view that multi-word units are "the biggest single problem that the lexicon presents for language analysis" (Hanks 2013: 61) and therefore constitute some of the most intractable problems in semantics: What are the basic units of meaning in a language? How can they be reliably and objectively identified and consistently and formally described? How are different units related? For example, are *heavy drinker*, *heavy drug-user*, *heavy gambler* and *heavy smoker* variants of a more general unit, in which *heavy* denotes 'a lot' and connotes the speaker's disapproval of socially undesirable behaviour?

The combinations **heavily drunk* and **heavy eater* (in the sense of 'glutton') both sound odd to me, but both occur in many texts by native speakers in the Web. No two speakers use their language in exactly the same way, and a comparison of corpus-based dictionaries, prepared by experienced lexicographers, shows frequent disagreement about word meanings, especially connotations (Stubbs 2007). Since there is no sharp boundary between normal and unusual, the problem is to achieve the correct level of generalization about usage (Hanks 2013: 411), and a constant background question is whether a corpus can ever, strictly speaking, provide semantic data, since intuition is always required to interpret the data.

Kilgarriff (1997: 137) provides a good summary of the balance required. Semantic analysis can never be entirely objective, but corpora allow us to study language "with a degree of objectivity [. . .] where before we could only speculate".

2 Historical perspectives

The layperson's notion of basic units of meaning – at least for speakers of European languages – has long been the "word". Dictionaries list words, and in several Germanic languages they are simply called "word-books" (e.g. German *Wörterbuch*). This looks like a case of speakers being misled about the general nature of language by the nature of their own writing systems. If we ignore complications such as hyphenated words, the writing systems of languages such as English, German and Russian signal word boundaries by spaces. Other languages do things differently: for example, in written Chinese each character represents a single syllable morpheme, but word boundaries are not marked.

In addition, dictionaries (for English, German, Russian, etc.) generally present language units (word-types) out of context in an alphabetic sequence that is irrelevant to both their semantic relations and their use in communication. This contributes to the odd but widespread notion that each word has a "literal meaning"; that is, a basic inherent meaning when it is not being used to communicate anything (Toolan 2008: 156).

A very different view, that the meaning of words depends on their verbal environment, was already clear, from the Middle Ages onwards, to the scholars who constructed concordances. Ordering concordance lines alphabetically by given search words facilitates finding instances, but what is listed is not word-types, but word-tokens along with their co-text. Cruden (1737) defines the function of his famous biblical concordance thus:

> A Concordance is a Dictionary, or an Index [. . .], wherein all the words used [. . .] are ranged alphabetically, and the various places where they occur are referred to, to assist us in [. . .] comparing the several significations of the same word.

It would be more helpful to distinguish between a concordance and a dictionary. A concordance sets out the data in a convenient form which allows patterns of co-occurrence to be seen. But this is only the evidence that must be interpreted by the dictionary-maker. A slogan often quoted in this connection, and usually attributed to much later work by Wittgenstein (1958, §43) and Austin (1962), is "meaning is use". This is a convenient slogan, but a more precise formulation would be that patterns of use, especially patterns of recurrent collocation, provide empirical observational evidence of meaning.

The first scholar to use technology for constructing concordances was Roberto Busa. In 1948, in collaboration with IBM, he began converting the complete works of Thomas Aquinas into digital form, initially on 11 million punch cards. Twenty million lines of text were published as the *Index Thomisticus*, nowadays available in an online version with a powerful search engine. For many, his work in the 1940s defines the starting point of computer-assisted text analysis. Busa (2007) provides his own account of this work.

Ideas are often proposed independently by different researchers at approximately the same time. The idea that the distribution of a word – specifically its co-occurrence frequencies with typical collocates – can disambiguate word senses was put forward in various places in the 1950s and 1960s. In a paper on machine translation, Weaver (1955) used the term "statistical semantics" to mean that probabilistic patterns of language usage in large text collections can provide evidence of what words mean. This is similar to the well-known statement by Firth (1957a: 11) that "you shall know a word by the company it keeps" and that part of the meaning of a word is its "habitual collocation" with other words. Detailed examples were provided by McIntosh (1961), still several years before corpus resources became generally available. He predicts that nouns that follow the adjective *molten* will be similar in meaning, though it would be "laborious" to list them. With modern methods, of course, it is not at all laborious, and findings from the BNC confirm his predictions exactly. The top noun collocates, immediately to the right of *molten*, with a frequency of 5 or more, include superordinate *metal* along with several hyponyms:

> *metal* 31, *rock* 26, *lava* 15, *iron* 14, *lead* 10, *glass* 9, *material* 9, *gold* 8

McIntosh further argues that we learn the meanings of words from our experience of them in different contexts, and this can also be illustrated from corpus data. The following occurrences of *molten* provide partial paraphrases of the word in the immediate co-text: something that is molten is "red hot", can "flow", can "cool" from its molten state, and so on.

- *seem to glisten, as if they were red hot, molten*
- *placed in moulds for molten lead to flow around them*
- *the basalt cooled from its original molten state*
- *as the powder passes through the flame, particles can become molten*

Finally, he points out that the co-text influences the meaning of a word: for example, *pig* in the phrase *molten pig iron*. McIntosh (1961: 330–31) thus sets out major principles that have been thoroughly documented by corpus study: "the lexical item and the word are not co-extensive" and the collocates of a word go "a long way towards constituting [its] meaning".

Sinclair (1998: 8) makes more explicit the significance of the *pig iron* example via the descriptive category he calls "reversal": "the precise meaning of a word is determined more by the verbal environment of a word [than by] the parameters of a lexical entry". That is, most words are ambiguous in isolation, but their potential meanings are restricted – and often determined – by their phraseology. Sinclair's example is that *white* in *white wine* denotes a colour specific to wine, often pale green, and not what *white* might seem to mean out of context (when it is not being used to communicate anything).

Computers do not, of course, understand meanings: all they can do is identify and count recurrent sequences of characters. This is, however, essential to linguistic analysis, and studying recurrent strings across large amounts of text (especially with the help of computer-generated concordance lines) has made visible new kinds of evidence of extended phrasal units. As Harris (1988: 19) puts it:

> [T]he very essence of language seems to depend on the possibility of regular recurrence of verbal items of various kinds. [. . .] Any general analysis of how language works is thus forced to tackle the notion of linguistic units.

This was explicitly recognized in early computer-assisted work by Allén et al. (1975: vol 3, xxxiii). In their investigation of a one-million-word Swedish newspaper corpus, the "first level of description" was "all collocations having at least two identical instances" in the corpus. Recurrence was "the methodological foundation of the investigation". This characteristic of language was also widely recognized in the British Firthian tradition of functional linguistics which led directly to modern corpus linguistics. Halliday (1978: 4), Firth's student, argues that "in real life, most sentences are not uttered for the first time" and that "a great deal of discourse is more or less routinized". In the first computer-assisted study in this tradition, Sinclair – Firth's student and Halliday's colleague – studied the relation "between statistically defined units of lexis and postulated units of meaning" in a 135,000-word corpus of spoken texts (Sinclair et al. 2004 [1970]: 6).

Nevertheless, until the development of corpus methods, most linguists greatly underrated the role of recurrent phraseology in modelling language use. There have long been dictionaries of clichés, catch phrases and the like, which contain thousands of examples of idioms that are not semantically transparent (e.g. *axe to grind*, *bee's knees*, *can of worms*, etc.). But the wider phraseological tendency of language in use, and the cultural functions of these phrasal units, was initially recognized by only a few scholars, such as Bolinger (1976) and Pawley and Syder (1983), who argue that native speakers know thousands of idiomatic units, which vary only slightly in form, and which are conventional labels for culturally recognized concepts.

Many ideas are described as new or ground-breaking, whereas they have long histories. It is often impossible to find the first mention of an important concept, and some of the basic ideas in this field were put forward over long periods of time, forgotten about and independently rediscovered, often much later. However, more important than mere mention is the development of a concept into a systematic research programme. It is this recognition – of the theoretical significance of phraseology – that has developed rapidly since the 1960s.

3 Current contributions and research

3.1 The discovery problem

Research on the phraseological tendency of language in use must be approached from two directions: software can automatically extract data from large corpora, but the linguist's intuition is necessary to interpret these data. The following concepts have proved useful in providing initial evidence, as far as possible automatically, of phrasal units of meaning.

(1) "N-grams" are fixed sequences of orthographic word-forms. For example, the 4-grams *at the end of* and *at the same time* are frequent in the BNC, and are easy for software to identify, but they are only raw surface data. Another 4-gram is *that there is a*, but we probably would not want to claim linguistic status for it, even though it occurs frequently. The 4-gram [*on the other hand*] seems a much better candidate for a linguistic unit: it is also frequent, it is a fixed phrase, its meaning is non-compositional (i.e. not predictable from the meaning of the individual words), and it is listed separately in many dictionaries as a discourse marker. However, if we specify search parameters in advance, we may find only what we are looking for, since a recurrent n-gram may be only part of a longer more abstract unit. For example, *in no uncertain terms* is a 4-gram with rare internal variation, but it is usually preceded by the verb *TELL*, by one of its hyponyms (e.g. *EXPLAIN*, *REPLY*, *URGE*), or by a roughly synonymous word or phrase:

> were told in no uncertain terms
> informed them in no uncertain terms
> put him right in no uncertain terms
> were shown the door in no uncertain terms

N-gram data are useful, but have to be carefully interpreted.

(2) "Skip-grams" are n-grams such as A x B or A B x C, where x = one or more variable word-forms. (Cf. Fletcher (2003) on "phrase-frames" and Renouf and Sinclair (1991) on "collocational frameworks".) For example, *at the* x *end of* is a 5-skip-gram, whose variants include *at the far end of* and *at the top end of*. But again, if we search for skip-grams of a fixed length, we will miss examples such as *at the very cheap end of the market*; *at the as yet unfashionable end of the terrace*. These seem – intuitively – to be variants of the same phrasal unit, and illustrate a very general problem. There is a difference between recurrent word strings and what we would intuitively regard as more abstract semantic units. Also, *a* x *of* is very frequent. Frequent realizations include: *a number of*; *a series of*; *a great deal of*; *a wide range of*; *a large number of*. This raises the interpretative problem of how to make valid semantic generalizations about the variable words. Many involve measurements, but not all (e.g. *a result of*; *a matter of*; *a kind of*).

(3) "Concgrams" (Cheng et al. 2006; Greaves 2009) are units that allow three different parameters of variation in the recurrent association of two or more words: their realization (different forms of a lemma or word family), their linear sequence and their span (e.g. A B, B A, A x B, A x y B, A B C, B C A, etc.). Cheng et al. (2009) study variants and their frequencies of the two-word concgram [*PLAY/ROLE*]. The BNC has over 3,800 occurrences of [*PLAY/ROLE*] in a span of 5, of which around 12 per cent are [*PLAY/ROLE/important*], for example:

> will play a crucially important role
> playing an active and important role
> may play important and unanticipated roles
> have an important role to play
> one important role which typifications play
> the important and unacknowledged role which women had to play

Other approximate synonyms of *important* occur (e.g. *crucial, major, key, leading, vital*), and it is relatively easy in this case to agree on 'important' as a superordinate semantic label. Variants such as *play a minor role* occur much less frequently, and are often signalled to be against expectation. However, in addition, [*PLAY/PART/important*] also occurs over 400 times, with many of the same adjectives. The occurrence of *ROLE* and *PART* in the same context is distributional evidence that they are related in meaning. But this leaves the problem of how best to summarize the main patterns without being swamped by details. We have to decide whether [*PLAY/ROLE/important*], [*PLAY/PART/crucial*] etc. are all variants of a more abstract pattern.

(4) "PoS-grams" (Fletcher 2003) are sequences of parts of speech. This concept allows us to identify frequent ADJ-NOUN pairs (e.g. *long time*), NOUN-NOUN pairs (e.g. *world war*), ADV-ADJ pairs (e.g. *most important*), etc. These patterns lie outside what are usually regarded as "collocations" in the sense of frequent lexical co-occurrences, but PoS-grams are realized by n-grams. For example, the top 4-PoS-gram in the BNC is:

preposition + determiner + singular noun + *of*

Its top realizations are: *at the end of, as a result of, in the case of.*

Clearly PoS-grams can be identified only in a grammatically tagged corpus where we can look only for sequences defined by the tag-set used. Sinclair (2004: 190–91) is therefore sceptical of such annotation and favours a "plain text policy" which avoids the potential circularity of tagging the corpus (possibly using pre-corpus assumptions) and then searching for the tags. This might well reveal recurrent sequences of old categories, but will not reveal any new categories.

N-grams and similar linear strings can be found rapidly and accurately with software, but – as illustrated above – they are often realizations of more abstract patterns which can be recognized only via the linguist's intuitions.

(5) "Collocations" are defined in many ways and are only recognizable to software if operationalized. Firth (1957a) seems equivocal as to whether collocation is an observable linear sequence of orthographic words ("quite simply the mere word accompaniment", p. 11), or an abstract psychological relation of order ("mutual expectancy", p. 12). It seems most obvious to interpret his famous definition (Firth 1957b: 196) as referring to word families:

> Meaning by collocation is an abstraction at the syntagmatic level [. . .] One of the meanings of *night* is its collocability with *dark*, and of *dark*, of course, collocation with *night*.

But he does not make explicit the possible variability in sequence, span and word-form, which – as I have shown above – can be documented with data on concgrams:

> one <u>dark</u> and stormy <u>night</u>
> on the <u>dark</u>est of <u>night</u>s
> belonged to <u>dark</u>ness and the <u>night</u>
> the dull day was <u>dark</u>ening into a cold <u>night</u>
>
> <u>night</u> <u>dark</u>ened the cup of the valley
> the <u>night</u>-<u>dark</u>ness of his hair and eyes
> through the lonely <u>night</u> in pitch <u>dark</u>ness
> at <u>night</u>fall just as the sky <u>dark</u>ened

Nor does Firth recognize that different forms of a lemma often pattern differently: see Sinclair (1991: 53–64, 154) on *YIELD*, and Stubbs (2001: 28) on *SEEK*.

Second, collocations can be semantically transparent or not. Palmer's (1933) famous definition seems ambiguous in this respect: "a succession of two or more words that must be learnt as an integral whole and not pieced together from its component parts". Sinclair therefore argues that words do not merely co-occur, but that they are co-selected: a single choice of two or more apparently independent words can "constitute a single choice" (Sinclair 1991: 112), and therefore create a new meaning. This is the main evidence that they are components of the same lexical item. A widely cited example is *naked eye* (Sinclair 1996) which is hardly ever used in the sense of 'unprotected eye', but has a non-compositional meaning, and is used when talking of something which is 'difficult to see without a telescope/microscope etc', in uses such as:

– *just about visible with the naked eye and easily seen with binoculars*
– *because they are so faint not a single one is visible to the naked eye*

Corpus study has shown that the Fregean concept of compositionality applies much less widely than is often assumed. The most frequent noun-noun combinations in the BNC include the following, none of which are entirely semantically transparent: *world war, interest rates, world cup, health service, trade union*. For example, *world cup* means 'an international football (soccer) championship that takes place every four years between men's teams from different countries'.

(6) The term "collostruction" denotes a unit identified by measuring the attraction or repulsion of words to slots in grammatical constructions (Stefanowitsch and Gries 2003; Gries and Stefanowitsch 2004). This documents one of the essential claims of corpus analysis, that it is impossible to separate lexis and syntax, since different meanings of words are associated with distinctive formal patternings.

In a quantitative study of collocations (Stubbs 1995), I showed that the lemma *CAUSE* is used overwhelmingly to talk about undesirable states of affairs. Characteristic collocations, averaged across several independent corpora, included:

CAUSE <problems, death, trouble, damage, cancer, difficulties>

With data mainly from small corpora of only 3.3 million words, I used two simple statistical tests to check probabilities of co-occurrence of word-forms. Barnbrook et al. (2013: 156–61) replicate my analysis on a corpus of 450 million words, and corroborate my basic findings. However, Klotz (1997) points out that purely lexical data miss a generalization about the relation between lexis, syntax and semantics. We can say: *X caused problems. X caused* *cancer. X caused him problems.* But not: **X caused him cancer.* That is, lexis interacts with grammar: words for illnesses and diseases do not occur in the ditransitive construction. This point is further refined by Stefanowitsch and Gries (2003) who use statistical methods to distinguish between three syntactic structures in which *CAUSE* occurs:

transitive: *X caused problems*
prepositional dative: *X caused harm to Y*
ditransitive: *X caused Y distress*

They argue (p. 222) that

> The transitive construction occurs exclusively, and the prepositional dative predominantly, with external states and events; in contrast, the ditransitive construction encodes predominantly internal (mental) states and experiences.

Hunston (2007: 251–53) agrees that *CAUSE* occurs with negatively evaluated situations when human self-interest is involved, but points out that the expression of speaker attitude interacts with text-type, and that there is often no negative evaluation in scientific and technical texts (e.g. *The effect of the tides is like a brake, causing the spin of the earth to slow*). Finally, Smith and Nordquist (2012) compare Early Modern and Present-day English and show that the negative semantic associations of *CAUSE* have developed over time.

This shows the power of empirical methods. An initial study is checked against a much larger independent corpus, missing details are filled in, partial counter-examples are discovered and explained, and more refined methods are developed.

3.2 Sinclair's model

Underlying any theory of language are assumptions about social interaction, but much linguistic description ignores both topic (what speakers are talking about) and communicative function (why they are talking about it). Harris (2003: 166) refers to Chomsky's "perverse rejection of the notion that languages are forms of communicational activity identified with particular communities".

One of the best worked-out models of multi-word semantic units, which attempts to relate language form and communicative function, is proposed by Sinclair (1996, 1998). His model consists of an obligatory core, plus four parameters. Collocation and colligation define the form of the unit. Semantic preference defines its propositional relation to its co-text, and semantic prosody defines its communicative function (the reason for phrasing something in this way at this point in the text). In more detail:

(1) Collocation is a relation between co-occurring word-forms. It can be identified on largely objective observable evidence of concrete word-tokens, although it is often useful to group word-forms into abstract lemmas and word families.
(2) Colligation is a relation between words and co-occurring abstract grammatical classes (e.g. passive or negative) which it is often possible to identify automatically. However, grammar shades into semantics. For example, both grammatically

negative and positive clauses can express the same idea (he *would not move* versus *he refused to move*).
(3) Semantic preference is a relation between co-ordinated topical choices in text. It concerns propositional content, and can be identified by co-occurring lexis, but only if the analyst understands what the text is about (its topic) and has an intuitive knowledge of semantic fields.
(4) Semantic prosody expresses the speaker's motivation or communicative purpose. It is similar to illocutionary force. It can be identified only if the analyst has an intuitive understanding of speakers' evaluations and attitudes. Here semantics shades into pragmatics.

As we move from (1) to (4), we move from features that are objectively observable to features that require the analyst's subjective interpretation: from (mere) surface sequence to underlying (theoretical) order.

For various reasons these relations were not previously recognized. The units do not refer to independent things or events in the external world. Their realizations are typically variable and discontinuous. Their constituents have different strengths of internal attraction. The semantic prosodies often have no traditional labels.

Sinclair's model can be summarized even more simply as follows:

collocation and colligation:	strings of words/grammar	FORM
semantic preference:	reference and predication	CONTENT
semantic prosody:	purpose, speaker intention	FUNCTION

This now looks very similar to the original definition by Searle (1969: 23–24) of a speech act, which has an internal structure of acts of different kinds:

utterance act:	mere strings of words	FORM
propositional act(s):	reference and predication	CONTENT
illocutionary act(s):	purpose, speaker intention	FUNCTION

There are also similarities with models proposed in construction grammar, though Sinclair and Mauranen (2006: 31) regard the differences as substantial since construction grammar takes little account of the linearity of text.

Sinclair's model can compactly describe empirical data. Here is an example (from Atkins and Rundell 2008: 376), which illustrates recurrent lexical patterns around the core *CONSIGN . . . to . . .*:

will be consigned to the dustbin of history
have been consigned to the rubbish heap
should be consigned to the scrap heap of history
was soon consigned to the wannabes pile
have been consigned to oblivion
will be consigned straight to hell
he was now consigned to outer darkness
has been consigned to the dustbin as a forgotten tradition
simply consigning him to a museum of dead ideas
would consign 100,000 workers to the dole queues

(1) Collocation. Frequent collocates are: *dustbin, history, oblivion, rubbish, scrap*.
(2) Colligation. The verb is usually passive. It is not always easy to distinguish sharply between propositional content and evaluative attitude (and perhaps especially here since the most frequent collocates have unpleasant denotations), or to find appropriate labels for attitudinal meanings. However:
(3) Semantic preference. The meaning is occasionally neutral: something is moved from one place to another (*suitcases were consigned to his office for safe-keeping*). But most often by far, the change is for the worse. Something no longer wanted is being disposed of, or someone is being marginalized or condemned to an unpleasant fate, usually permanently (Rundell 2002). The set of collocates is open-ended, but most denote 'the past' (e.g. *history books, museum*), or 'rubbish' (e.g. *wannabes pile, scrap heap*), or some very unpleasant place (e.g. *hell, perdition, outer darkness*).
(4) Semantic prosody. In addition, the speaker is often conveying a critical attitude towards this move and/or sympathy for who/whatever is to be disposed of and forgotten about. If it is reported that old people are "consigned to institutional care" the implication is that this is not their choice.

Out of context, some uses seem positive (*Isabella was consigned to comfortable retirement*). But the wider co-text reveals that Isabella is a queen who has been arrested, and the next sentence reports that Mortimer, arrested at the same time, was executed (BNC text F9L, history book). Any analytic method displays some things and hides others. A concordance is a visualization technique: it rips texts into fragments, and presents them in ways that show otherwise invisible patterns. This is its purpose: to show things from a different point of view. However, leaving concordance lines as isolated fragments divorces them from their communicative function in the original texts, and can imply that language consists of independent formal structures.

Through their linear syntagmatic organization, extended lexical units contribute to textual cohesion. They integrate lexical, syntactic and textual analysis (Sinclair and Mauranen 2006: 155). Therefore, if we combine quantitative and qualitative methods, and study how the lexical item [*CONSIGN* x *to* 'an unpleasant fate'] is used in texts, we see that it often emphasizes a textual contrast between an earlier desirable state and a later undesirable state. In the following examples there are contrasts between achievements/oblivion, life/death, along with other markers of textual contrast (e.g. *if . . . then . . .; in that case . . . rather than . . .*).

> *If the achievements of the Thatcher years were not to be <u>consigned to</u> oblivion, then a tactical retreat was necessary.* (BNC text AHN, broadsheet newspaper.)
>
> *In that case, the electorate might well prefer to be Red and live to fight another day rather than be <u>consigned to</u> a nuclear crematorium.* (BNC text ABA, book on world affairs.)

Consigning something/someone to the dustbin/to oblivion does not have a purely discourse-external reference. It has reality as a social construct: the kind of event that has been talked about frequently in the past (all good things come to an end?). Francis (1993: 141, 155) emphasizes the cultural functions of such units, and thereby tackles the complex web of intentions, beliefs and social values which characterize language use:

> [W]e can compile a grammar of the typical meanings that human communication encodes [. . .] the ways in which we typically evaluate situations [. . .] how difficult or easy life is made for us, how predictable things are, and how well we understand what is going on.

Extended lexical units are ideal types: coherent gestalts with a formal structure and logical relations between the parts. Their function is textual (they make texts hang together), intertextual (they create discourse objects) and social (they encode cultural schemas).

More generally, Sinclair's model operationalizes Morris's (1938) classic definition of the relations between syntax, semantics and pragmatics. Collocation and colligation relate signs to other signs: this is the traditional definition of syntax. Semantic preference relates signs to the world: this is the traditional definition of semantics. Semantic prosody relates signs to speakers: this is the traditional definition of pragmatics. The model therefore meets a major criterion of the significance of an idea, by relating things that were previously often not clearly related, namely lexis, syntax, semantics and pragmatics.

The model is based on a large amount of data, but on close study of only a small number of cases, perhaps a few dozen. Some of the more widely cited case studies include Louw (1993), Stubbs (1995), Channell (2000), Partington (2004) and Hunston (2007). It is not yet clear how many such items there are – presumably there are thousands – how variable they can be, and how the model can be tested. It is easy to obtain confirming instances, but unclear what would constitute a counter-example, or even whether the concept of counter-example is fully applicable when the analysis is based on probabilities.

3.3 More on semantic prosodies

The feature of Sinclair's model that immediately attracted attention was "semantic prosody". The first use of the term in print was by Louw (1993), following the first example of a prosody around the phrasal verb *SET in* by Sinclair (1991: 74), who comments:

> The most striking feature of this phrasal verb is the nature of subjects. In general, they refer to unpleasant states of affairs. [A few] refer to the weather; a few are neutral, such as *reaction* and *trend*. The main vocabulary is *rot, decay, malaise, ill-will, decadence, impoverishment, infection, prejudice, vicious (circle), rigor mortis, numbness, bitterness, mannerism, anticlimax, anarchy, disillusion, disillusionment, slump.* [. . .] The subjects of *set in* are also [. . .] largely abstractions: several are nominalizations of another part of speech.

The term "prosody" derives from Firth's work on phonology, where he argued that a single phonetic feature can stretch across several units, as traditionally defined. For example, since the vowel in the word *man* occurs between two nasals, it will itself be nasalized. In the words, *limp, lint* and *link*, the final consonant clusters consist of two bilabials, two alveolars or two velars. English has no words such as *limt or *linp. It is therefore misleading to regard the consonant clusters as consisting of two phonemes: both are selected together as one unit. In analogy, "semantic prosody" refers to a single semantic feature instantiated across several words which are simultaneously co-selected.

It might seem more helpful to label this "pragmatic prosody" or "discourse prosody", since it has communicative and text cohesive functions. However, Sinclair's term "semantic prosody" emphasizes that the evidence is not inferred from non-linguistic knowledge about the social context, but is observed in the co-text. Other literature argues that the term is not clearly defined, and tries to distinguish more clearly between "semantic prosody" and "connotation" and/or between "semantic prosody" and "semantic preference" (Morley and Partington 2009). Hunston (2007) distinguishes between the implied attitudinal meaning of a word and Sinclair's own use of "semantic prosody" to refer to the discourse function of a unit of meaning. Stewart (2010) provides a book-length attempt to define the term, and a comprehensive list of previous work, but discusses "semantic prosody" independently of the model of which it is only one parameter, and reaches no clear conclusions about a better definition.

Debates about terminology and definitions risk missing the essential point that the most important thing is empirical description, and that much previous work neglected the fact that co-occurrence phenomena, and the resulting evaluative prosodies of extended lexical units, are much more extensive than previously realized.

3.4 The vexed question of statistics

Raw frequencies alone cannot identify semantic units. For example, if a word is itself infrequent, then clearly the collocations in which it occurs cannot be frequent, and would be missed if raw frequency was our only search criterion. The lemma *QUESTION* occurs over 42,000 times in the BNC. The word *vexed* occurs only 165 times, but when it does occur, it has nearly a one-in-three chance of occurring in the 2-gram *vexed question(s)*. Less frequent 2-grams include the approximately synonymous *vexed problem* and *vexed topic*. That is, the attraction is asymmetrical: *vexed* predicts *QUESTION* much more strongly than *QUESTION* predicts *vexed*. However, for several reasons, I am more interested in what corpus data can tell us about the nature of extended units of meaning than with statistical methods.

First, many different statistics have been used to measure the strength of association between co-occurring word-forms (Clear 1993, Stubbs 1995, Evert 2008), and there is considerable disagreement about which statistical methods are appropriate. The log-likelihood test is widely regarded as more reliable than some other tests, since it takes into account the relative frequency of words: it ignores chance combinations of high-frequency words, and also combinations of rare words (Dunning 1993; Rayson 2012). However, like many other statistical measures of collocational strength it also fails to distinguish symmetrical and asymmetrical relations (Gries 2013).

Second, there is more general disagreement about whether such statistics are appropriate at all. At one end of the debate are scholars such as Gries (2010), who laments the lack of statistical sophistication amongst (many) corpus linguists. At the other end are those such as Sinclair (2008: 28), who argues that all the statistics used assume the possibility of randomness and, since this never holds for words in texts, statistics are largely irrelevant in the study of meaning. In words often attributed to Ernest Rutherford (1871–1937), "if your experiment needs statistics, you ought to have designed a better experiment".

Third, whatever methods are used, the linguist still has to interpret the data generated. There is sometimes a suspicion that analysts try out different statistics, and then select the one which supports their intuitions (which is like shooting an arrow at the barn door and painting a bull's eye around where the arrow lands).

4 Future directions

Corpus semantics is essentially diachronic and sociolinguistic (Teubert 2005), in so far as we analyze not what could hypothetically be said, but what frequently has been said in the past, by many different speakers in many different kinds of texts. The focus is on "normal, central, typical usage" (Hanks 2013: 7). The essential problem for analysis is variability. Many phrasal units have a well-defined core and canonical realizations, but fuzzy peripheral features and boundaries. In addition to the variables discussed above (frequency, linear sequence, span, word-form/lemma), further variables are only beginning to be studied and pose problems of choosing the appropriate level of descriptive delicacy. Only a few representative studies are noted below.

Many years ago Firth (1935) showed that different units occur in different text-types. More recent studies (e.g. Gray and Biber 2013) compare n-grams in different written and spoken genres. Studies by Hoey (2005) and Mahlberg (2009) show that different phraseology tends to occur at different places in texts and thereby has text-organizing functions (which they call textual colligation). Change over time is documented in many corpus-based studies of grammaticalization (e.g. Lindquist and Mair 2004, Hoffmann 2005), which analyze the role of frequency in the emergence of phrasal units. The development of semantic prosodies over time is studied by Smith and Nordquist (2012). The extent to which semantic units and their prosodies might be universal or comparable across languages has only just begun to be studied, but see Lewandowska-Tomaszczyk (1996) and Xiao and McEnery (2006) on Polish and Chinese. The extent to which automatic recognition of phrasal units is possible is discussed by Sinclair et al. (1997) who have designed language-independent software.

The most extensive applications have been in lexicography. Since the late 1980s, the compilation and analysis of large corpora has had a major influence on methods used to compile English-language dictionaries and grammars, especially monolingual dictionaries for advanced learners. Many of the principles are set out by Sinclair (1987) and Hanks (2013). By 1995 other major British dictionary publishers (Chambers, Cambridge University Press, Longman, Macmillan and Oxford University Press) had followed Cobuild (1987) and were also using corpus data and methods.

Applications in other areas have been relatively modest. They include the following. Cotterill (2001) illustrates potential forensic applications by examining the semantic prosodies of words and phrases used to describe domestic violence in the O.J. Simpson trial. Dam-Jensen and Zethsen (2008) illustrate applications in the training of translators by showing how extended lexical units convey evaluations that are not accessible to introspection and which have not been part of traditional dictionary definitions.

5 Conclusions

As often happens in scientific areas, several principles that have turned out to be central to corpus semantics were proposed over a long period of time. Major ideas were proposed, then forgotten about, then rediscovered when circumstances changed – the invention of new technology was often crucial. Scholars from the Middle Ages onwards realized clearly the potential of language use for studying meaning. A series of other ideas then paved the way for rapid development from the 1980s onwards when new technology could help with visualizing patterns in large corpora. However, corpus evidence of meaning is indirect, and the linguist still needs traditional skills to see the wood for the trees in the vast amounts of data that technology makes available.

Further reading

Hanks, P. 2013 *Lexical Analysis: Norms and Exploitations*. Cambridge, Mass.: MIT Press. Dozens of examples from an experienced lexicographer of the implications of corpus analysis for both practice (dictionary making) and theory.

Sinclair, J. 1991. *Corpus Concordance Collocation*. Oxford: Oxford University Press. The now classic book which proposed what quickly became the standard ideas in the field.

References

Allén, S. et al. 1975. *Nusvensk frekvensordbok baserad på tidningstext. Frequency dictionary of present-day Swedish based on newspaper material*. Stockholm: Almqvist & Wiksell.

Atkins, S. B. T. and M. Rundell 2008. *The Oxford Guide to Practical Lexicography*. Oxford: Oxford University Press.

Austin, J. L. 1962. *How to Do Things with Words*. Oxford: Clarendon.

Barnbrook, G., O. Mason, and R. Krishnamurthy 2013. *Collocation: Applications and Implications*. Basingstoke: Palgrave Macmillan.

Bauer, L. and P. Nation 1993. Word families. *International Journal of Lexicography* 6: 253–79.

Bolinger, D. 1976. Meaning and memory. *Forum Linguisticum* 1: 1–14.

Busa, R. 2007. Foreword: perspectives in the digital humanities. In S. Schreibman, R. G. Siemens, and J. Unsworth (eds) *A Companion to Digital Humanities*. Oxford: Blackwell, xvi–xxi.

Channell, J. 2000. Corpus-based analysis of evaluative lexis. In S. Hunston and G. Thompson (eds) *Evaluation in Text*. Oxford: Oxford University Press, 38–55.

Cheng, W., C. Greaves and M. Warren 2006. From n-gram to skipgram to concgram. *International Journal of Corpus Linguistics* 11: 411–33.

Cheng, W., C. Greaves, J. Sinclair, and M. Warren 2009. Uncovering the extent of the phraseological tendency. *Applied Linguistics* 30: 236–52.

Clear, J. 1993. From Firth principles: computational tools for the study of collocation. In M. Baker, G. Francis, and E. Tognini-Bonelli (eds) *Text and Technology*. Amsterdam: Benjamins, 271–92.

Cobuild 1987. *Collins Cobuild English Language Dictionary*. Editor in Chief J. Sinclair. London: HarperCollins.

Cotterill, J. 2001. Domestic discord, rocky relationships: semantic prosodies in representations of marital violence in the OJ Simpson trial. *Discourse and Society* 12: 291–312.

Cruden, A. 1737. *A Complete Concordance to the Holy Scriptures*. London: Frederick Warne.

Dam-Jensen, H. and K. K. Zethsen 2008. Translator awareness of semantic prosodies. *Target*, 20: 203–21.

Dunning, T. 1993. Accurate methods for the statistics of surprise and coincidence. *Computational Linguistics* 19: 61–74.

Evert, S. 2008. Corpora and collocations. In A. Lüdeling and M. Kytö eds. *Corpus Linguistics. An International Handbook*. Berlin: Mouton de Gruyter, article 58.

Firth, J. R. 1935. The technique of semantics. *Transactions of the Philological Society* 34: 36–72.

Firth, J. R. 1957a. A synopsis of linguistic theory 1930–1955. *Studies in Linguistic Analysis*. Oxford: Philological Society, 1–32. Reprinted in F. R. Palmer (ed.) 1968. *Selected Papers of J.R. Firth 1952–1959*. London: Longman.

Firth, J. R. 1957b. Modes of meaning. *Papers in Linguistics 1934–1951*. London: Oxford University Press, 190–215.

Fletcher, W. 2003. *PIE Phrases in English*. http://pie.usna.edu [Accessed April 2015].

Francis, G. 1993. A corpus-driven approach to grammar. In M. Baker, G. Francis, and E. Tognini-Bonelli (eds) *Text and Technology*. Amsterdam: Benjamins, 137–56.

Gray, B. and D. Biber 2013. Lexical frames in academic prose and conversation. *International Journal of Corpus Linguistics* 18: 109–35.

Gries, S. Th. 2010. Methodological skills in corpus linguistics. In T. Harris and M. Moreno Jaén (eds) *Corpus Linguistics in Language Teaching*. Frankfurt am Main: Peter Lang, 121–146.

Gries, S. Th. 2013. 50-something years of work on collocations: what is or should be next . . . *International Journal of Corpus Linguistics* 18: 137–65.

Gries, S. Th. and A. Stefanowitsch 2004. Extending collostructional analysis. *International Journal of Corpus Linguistics* 9: 97–129.

Greaves, C. 2009. *ConcGram 1.0. A Phraseological Search Engine*. Software manual. http://www.benjamins.com/jbp/series/CLS/1/manual.pdf [Accessed Sept. 2009.]

Halliday, M. A. K. 1978. *Language as Social Semiotic*. London: Arnold.

Hanks, P. 2013. *Lexical Analysis: Norms and Exploitations.* Cambridge, Mass.: MIT Press.
Harris, R. 1988. *Language, Saussure and Wittgenstein.* London: Routledge.
Harris, R. 2003. *Saussure and his Interpreters.* 2nd ed. Edinburgh: Edinburgh University Press.
Hoey, M. 2005. *Lexical Priming.* London: Routledge.
Hoffmann, S. 2005. *Grammaticalization and English Complex Prepositions: a Corpus-Based Study.* London: Routledge.
Hoffmann, S., S. Evert, N. Smith, D. Lee, and Y. Berglund-Prytz 2008. *Corpus Linguistics with BNCweb.* Frankfurt am Main: Peter Lang.
Hunston, S. 2007. Semantic prosody revisited. *International Journal of Corpus Linguistics* 12: 249–68.
Kilgarriff, A. 1997. Putting frequencies in the dictionary. *International Journal of Lexicography* 10: 135–55.
Klotz, M. 1997. Ein Valenzwörterbuch englischer Verben, Adjektive und Substantive. *Zeitschrift für Angewandte Linguistik* 27: 93–111.
Kučera, H. and W. N. Francis 1967. *Computational Analysis of Present-Day American English.* Providence: Brown University Press.
Lewandowska-Tomaszczyk, B. 1996. Cross-linguistic and language-specific aspects of semantic prosody. *Language Sciences* 18: 153–78.
Lindquist, H. and C. Mair (eds) 2004. *Corpus Approaches to Grammaticalization in English.* Amsterdam: Benjamins.
Louw, B. 1993. Irony in the text or insincerity in the writer? The diagnostic potential of semantic prosodies. In M. Baker, G. Francis, and E. Tognini-Bonelli (eds) *Text and Technology.* Amsterdam: Benjamins, 157–76.
Mahlberg, M. 2009. Local textual functions of *move* in newspaper story patterns. In U. Römer and R. Schulze (eds) *Exploring the Lexis-Grammar Interface.* Amsterdam: Benjamins, 265–87.
McIntosh, A. 1961. Patterns and ranges. *Language* 37: 325–37.
Morley, J. and A. Partington 2009. A few frequently asked questions about semantic – or evaluative – prosody. *International Journal of Corpus Linguistics* 14: 139–58.
Morris, C. W. 1938. Foundations of the theory of signs. In O. Neurath, R. Carnap, and C. W. Morris (eds) *International Encyclopedia of Unified Science*, vol. 1, no. 2, Chicago: Chicago UP.
Palmer, H. E. 1933. *Second Interim Report on Collocations.* Tokyo: Kaitakusha.
Partington, A. 2004. Utterly content in each other's company: semantic prosody and semantic preference. *International Journal of Corpus Linguistics.* 9: 131–56.
Pawley, A. and F. H. Syder 1983. Two puzzles for linguistic theory. In J. C. Richards and R. W. Schmidt (eds) *Language and Communication.* London: Longman, 191–226.
Rayson, P. 2012. Corpus analysis of key words. In C. A. Chapelle (ed.) *The Encyclopedia of Applied Linguistics.* Oxford: Wiley-Blackwell, 33–71.
Renouf, A. J. and J. Sinclair 1991. Collocational frameworks in English. In K. Ajimer and B. Altenberg (eds) *English Corpus Linguistics.* London: Longman, 128–43.
Rundell, M. 2002. If only they'd asked a linguist. http://www.hltmag.co.uk/jul02/idea.htm [Accessed April 2015].
Searle, J. 1969. *Speech Acts.* London: Oxford University Press.
Sinclair, J. 1991. *Corpus Concordance Collocation.* Oxford: Oxford University Press.
Sinclair, J. 1996. The search for units of meaning. *Textus* 9: 75–106. [Reprinted in Sinclair 2004: 24–48.]
Sinclair, J. (ed.) 1987. *Looking Up.* London: Collins ELT.
Sinclair, J. 1998. The lexical item. In E. Weigand (ed.) *Contrastive Lexical Semantics.* Amsterdam: Benjamins, 1–24. [Reprinted in Sinclair 2004: 131–48.]
Sinclair, J. 2004. *Trust the Text.* London: Routledge.
Sinclair, J. 2008. Borrowed ideas. In A. Gerbig and O. Mason (eds) *Language, People, Numbers.* Amsterdam: Rodopi, 21–41.
Sinclair, J., S. Jones, and R. Daley 2004 [1970]. *English Collocation Studies: The OSTI Report.* ed. R. Krishnamurthy. London: Continuum. [Originally mimeo 1970.]

Sinclair, J., O. Mason, J. Ball, and G. Barnbrook 1997. Language independent statistical software for corpus exploration. *Computers and the Humanities* 31: 229–55.

Sinclair, J. and A. Mauranen 2006. *Linear Unit Grammar*. Amsterdam: Benjamins.

Smith, K. A. and D. Nordquist 2012. A critical and historical investigation into semantic prosody. *Journal of Historical Pragmatics* 13: 291–312.

Stefanowitsch, A. and S. Th. Gries. 2003. Collostructions: investigating the interaction between words and constructions. *International Journal of Corpus Linguistics* 8: 209–43.

Stewart, D. 2010. *Semantic Prosody: A Critical Evaluation*. London: Routledge.

Stubbs, M. 1995. Collocations and semantic profiles. *Functions of Language* 2: 23–55.

Stubbs, M. 2001. *Words and Phrases*. Oxford: Blackwell.

Stubbs, M. 2007. Inferring meaning. In A. Mehler and R. Köhler (eds) *Aspects of Automatic Text Analysis*. Berlin: Springer, 233–53.

Teubert, W. 2005. My version of corpus linguistics. *International Journal of Corpus Linguistics* 10: 1–13.

Toolan, M. 2008. On inscribed or literal meaning. In R. Harris and G. Wolf (eds) *Integrational Linguistics*. Bingley: Emerald, 143–58.

Weaver, W. 1955. Translation. In W. N. Locke and D. A. Booth (eds) *Machine Translation of Languages*. Cambridge, Mass.: MIT Press, 15–23.

Wittgenstein, L. 1958. *Philosophische Untersuchungen*. Frankfurt am Main: Suhrkamp.

Xiao, R. and McEnery, T. 2006. Collocation, semantic prosody, and near synonymy: a cross-linguistic perspective. *Applied Linguistics* 27: 103–29.

Related topics

Chapter 3, A history of semantics; Chapter 10, Semantics and pragmatics; Chapter 14, Sense relations; Chapter 15, Semantic shift; Chapter 24, Compositionality; Chapter 28, Interpretative semantics.

Part III
Meaning and conceptualization

7
Categories, prototypes and exemplars

James A. Hampton

1 Introduction

This chapter describes an approach to theorizing about the meaning of words that is primarily based in the empirical research methods of cognitive psychology. The modern research tradition in this area began with the notion introduced by Tulving (1972) of *semantic memory*. Tulving pointed to an important distinction between the memories that each individual has of their own past (which he termed *episodic memory* – memory for events and episodes of experience), and the general conceptual knowledge of the world that we all share, which he termed *semantic memory*. There is some ambiguity about just how broadly the notion of semantic memory should be taken. For example, does it include all facts you know that are not based on actual experiences, or should it be restricted to conceptual knowledge about what *kinds* of things there are in the world and their properties? Nonetheless, the central contents of semantic memory are quite clear. The semantic memory store contains the concepts that enable us to understand and reason about the world, and as such it provides the knowledge base that underpins the meanings of utterances and individual words in any language. Knowing that a bird is a creature or that chemistry is a science involves a conceptual knowledge network where cultural and linguistic meanings are represented: semantic memory is a combination of a mental dictionary in which words are given definitions and a mental encyclopaedia in which general information concerning the referent of the word is stored.

There is general agreement that semantic memory is largely separate from episodic or other forms of memory (such as memory for motor actions). In particular, people may suffer severe forms of amnesia while retaining their production and comprehension of language.

Semantic memory models of the 1970s were based on two main theoretical ideas. One was to consider semantic memory as a form of network. Collins and Quillian (1969) developed a structural model of semantic memory in which concepts were nodes in a network, joined by labelled links. For example, the word BIRD would be linked by a *superordination* "Is a" link to ANIMAL, and by a *possession* "Has a" link to FEATHERS. In the same way the word would be linked to a range of the properties that it possessed, classes to which it belonged, and subclasses that it could be divided into. Figure 7.1 shows an example for BIRD.

The network provides a neat representation of how the meaning of kinds and their properties could be interrelated. Birds are partly characterized by their possession of feathers, while feathers are partly characterized by being a property of birds. The model also has the

James A. Hampton

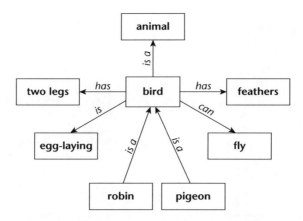

Figure 7.1 A semantic network representation of the meaning of BIRD

advantage of providing an economical way of storing a large amount of information. A property only needs to be stored in the memory structure at the most general level at which it is usually true. It is not necessary to store the fact that birds have skin or that they reproduce, since these properties are true of animals in general. If questioned about whether birds reproduce, the memory system would retrieve the relevant links connecting bird to reproduction in the following way:

(1) A bird is an animal
(2) An animal is a biological organism
(3) Biological organisms reproduce

from which the inference would be drawn that birds reproduce.

Evidence for the semantic network model was in fact weak and the model was quickly superseded, although it has had an extraordinarily enduring presence in the text books. The primary evidence was based on reaction time measures for either judging category membership (A robin is a bird) or property possession (A robin has feathers). Collins and Quillian (1969) reported that response times to true sentences increased with the number of inferential links that needed to be retrieved. Thus "A robin is a robin" was faster than "A robin is a bird" which was faster than "A robin is an animal". The model made predictions based on a search and retrieval process, whereby information was already present in the network, and the time required to retrieve it could be used as an index of the network's internal structure.

Difficulties with the model arose immediately with the response times for false sentences. In the case of false statements such as "A robin is a fish", the more intervening links there are in the network, the *faster* is a correct rejection since people are delayed by similarity between subject and predicate terms for false sentences. For example "A robin is a fish" is slower to falsify than "A robin is a vehicle". It was therefore necessary to introduce a more complex search algorithm, involving the idea of spreading activation. Collins and Loftus (1975) proposed that activation would start at the subject and predicate nodes and then spread with diminishing strength through the network. Dissimilar nodes would lead to a rapid "false" decision as the two streams of activation died away without entering the same link. However, activation of similar nodes, being in the same part of the network, would lead to retrieval of a common path linking them. This path would then have to be checked to see if it warranted the inference that the sentence was true. Slow false responses for close items were explained by the need to do this checking.

Further evidence against the network idea was not long in appearing. Smith et al. (1974) demonstrated how three-level hierarchies of terms could be found in which the distance effect was reversed. For example "A chicken is a bird" was slower to verify than "A chicken is an animal". Since the model requires that the latter is based on an inference from chickens being birds and birds being animals, there was no way to explain this type of result.

An additional problem, familiar in semantic theories, was the question of whether nodes corresponded to words, or to word senses. Should the property node "has four legs" be attached to both horses and chairs, or does the difference in the kind of leg involved require different nodes to reflect each sense of *leg*? Network theorists did not attempt to address these questions, leaving the model very limited in its scope.

Smith et al. (1974) proposed an alternative model based on the notion of semantic features. Semantic features as originally conceived were aspects of a word's meaning. Features like gender and animacy play a role in explaining syntactic acceptability, while linguists also analyzed semantic fields such as kinship terms in terms of their featural components.

Within structuralist linguistics features are typically defined as having three possible values. For example, Number could be singular, not singular (i.e. plural) or unspecified. In Smith et al.'s model, however, the notion was greatly broadened to include more or less any property as a semantic feature. Having a red breast would be a feature of robins, and having a trunk a feature of elephants. Feature models aim to capture the meaning of a word in a very similar way to the network model, but instead of providing a network of connected links, each word is simply represented by a list of its features. Thus BIRD would be represented as in Figure 7.2.

Rather than using search and retrieval as the process underlying semantic verification, the feature model made a different assumption. Focusing on categorization decisions (e.g. a robin is a bird), the model proposed that a decision is based on a comparison of the set of features that defines ROBIN and the set of features that defines BIRD. If robins possess all of the features that are necessary for being a bird, then the sentence will be judged true. Otherwise it will be false.

To recap, when people judge category statements, they are faster to say True when the two words are more similar, and faster to say False when the two words are more dissimilar. To capture this result, Smith et al.'s model proposed two stages in a decision process. In the first stage, overall featural similarity was computed in a quick heuristic fashion. If the result

BIRD
- is alive
- flies
- has feathers
- has a beak or bill
- has wings
- has legs and feet
- lays eggs
- has just two legs
- builds nests
- sings or cheeps
- has claws
- is very lightweight

Figure 7.2 A feature representation of the meaning of BIRD

showed either very high similarity or very low similarity, then a quick True or False decision could be given. However, if the result based on overall similarity was inconclusive, a second stage was required. An inconclusive first-stage result would mean that a true category member lacked some of the characteristic features of the category (e.g. flightless birds such as OSTRICH or PENGUIN), or that a non-member possessed some of those features (e.g. flying mammals such as BAT). To deal with these slow decisions, the second stage required the individual defining features of the category (e.g. BIRD) to be identified and checked off against the features of the possible category member.

Smith et al.'s model was no more successful than Collins and Quillian's, although like the former model it has had great longevity in the literature. The first difficulty with the model was that Rosch and Mervis's (1975) work on prototype concepts revealed that many words did not have a clear set of defining features that could be appealed to for a second-stage decision. The second was that the response time results could be explained more parsimoniously in terms of a single similarity computation.

For example, Hampton (1979) showed that when people make erroneous categorization decisions, they tend to be very slow. According to Smith et al.'s model, errors should only arise in the rapid heuristic first stage – for example, when someone agrees that a bat is a bird on the basis of their similarity without checking the defining features in stage 2. The slow second stage should be more error free, given that the defining features are carefully checked off. In fact, most semantic categories have borderline regions where response times become very slow, and people's responding becomes less consistent (McCloskey and Glucksberg 1978). This pattern of data is more consistent with the Prototype model described below.

The feature model also had little explanation to offer for the verification of properties. The proposal that categorization depends on feature checking would imply that properties should be verified faster than category membership judgements. In fact, the reverse is the case. Hampton (1984) measured verification times for two kinds of sentences: category statements such as *Robins are birds* and property statements such as *Robins have wings*. Sentences were equated for their production frequency in a feature listing task. The category statements were consistently faster to verify, making it implausible that people judge that a robin is a bird by first verifying that it has wings (and other defining features).

This brief historical overview of semantic memory research serves to set the background for more recent theories of how people represent word meaning. Semantic networks have proved the inspiration for very large-scale network analysis of meaning using statistical associations (see e.g. Chapter 6). Feature-based models have been the inspiration for schema-based representations of concepts and meanings, including recent versions of prototype and exemplar models.

2 Word meaning and semantic categories

A function of word meaning, much studied in psychology, is to categorize the world into labelled classes. Although semantics is concerned with the meaning of all language, research in psychology has focused in a rather narrow fashion on nouns, and in particular on semantic categories. The reason for this is that categories such as Sport, Fruit or Science provide a rich test bed for developing theories of concepts and meaning. Notably, (a) they are culturally specific to a degree but also tied to objective reality, (b) they have familiar category "members", subclasses like Tennis, Lemon or Physics, which can be used in experiments on categorization and reasoning, and (c) people can introspect on the basis they use to classify, and can describe general properties of the classes.

With more abstract concept terms like RULE or BELIEF, it is hard for people to reflect on the meaning. Hampton (1981) found that people had difficulty in performing each of the tasks that would allow the construction of a prototype model for abstract concepts. By comparison many studies have shown that people can readily generate both exemplars (i.e. category members) and attributes (i.e. properties) for categories such as Sport or Fruit. These domains therefore provide a good way to test just how the meaning of the category concept is represented psychologically.

2.1 Prototypes

The idea of representing a conceptual meaning with a prototype owes much to the pioneering work of Rosch and Mervis (1975). A prototype represents a kind in terms of its most common and typical properties. However, no individual property need be true of the whole kind (although some may be), so that belonging to the category simply involves possession of a sufficient number of such properties. Exemplars will also differ in typicality as a function of the number of such properties they possess. More broadly, a prototype concept is one whose reference is the set of all exemplars whose similarity to a prototype representation is greater than some threshold criterion.

In a series of highly influential papers Rosch and Mervis presented a large array of empirical work showing that many concepts underlying semantic categories had a prototype structure. A standard methodology to show this structure has evolved, and typically uses all or some of the following steps (each with a different group of participants):

A   People generate exemplars of the category. For example, for SPORTS, participants list all the sports that they can think of.
B   Participants judge the typicality of each of the exemplars. By typicality is meant the degree to which the exemplar is representative of or typifies the category as a whole. For example, football and tennis are considered typical as Sports.
C   The exemplars are listed together with other items from the same domain (e.g. other human recreational activities) and participants make category membership judgements about each item.
D   Participants generate attributes for the category. They list what sports tend to have in common, which differentiates them from other types of thing.
E   Participants judge the "importance" or "definingness" of each of the attributes for the meaning of the category. For example, how important is the attribute "is competitive" for the category of sport?
F   All the exemplars and attributes generated with a certain minimum frequency are placed as rows and columns of a matrix, and participants complete the table with judgements of whether each exemplar possesses each attribute.

When all this has been done, the analysis can then proceed. Prototype structure is revealed in four ways.

(1) The category boundary is found to be vague in (C). There are a significant number of activities which are borderline cases where people cannot agree about the categorization.
(2) There are systematic variations of typicality across category exemplars in (B), which correlate with frequency of generation in (A) and other cognitive measures.

(3) Just as there is no clear set of category members, so there is no clear set of category attributes in (D) and (E). Attributes can be ranged along a continuum of definingness, and people will disagree about whether some attributes should be counted as part of the concept's meaning.
(4) Most importantly, when the matrix of exemplar/attribute possession from (F) is examined, no definition can be offered such that all of the category members and only the category members possess some fixed set of attributes. Being a sport is not a matter of possessing a set of singly necessary and jointly sufficient defining attributes. Rather there is a clear correlation between the number (and definingness) of the attributes that an exemplar possesses and the degree to which it is typical of the category and/or the degree to which people agree that it belongs.

Using this type of methodology in the years following Rosch and Mervis (1975), prototype models were found across a range of different domains, including speech acts like lying, psychiatric categories and personality ascriptions, as well as artefacts, human activities and folk biological kind categories.

There has been much debate about the validity of the prototype model as a theory of concepts. It is therefore worth clarifying the notion. First, the theory should not be confused with the operational methodology used to provide evidence of it. It is not supposed for example that the mind contains a list of attributes in the verbal form in which they are generated. Clearly, meaning has to be grounded (see Chapter 8) in experiential sub-symbolic levels of cognition, so it is unhelpful for a psychological model to give the meaning of one word simply in terms of others unless there is a primitive base of terms that are defined non-verbally (see Chapter 12). Second, while it is true that prototype theory defines the extension of a term in terms of similarity (number and weight of matching versus mismatching attributes), it is not wedded to any particular theory of similarity per se. One proposal is that the degree of category membership and typicality can be associated with the distance from the prototype in a similarity space. However, there are important ways in which similarity does not map into proximity in a space which undermine this proposal. A space assumes that the same dimensions are relevant for all similarity comparisons, but this is clearly not the case – A and B may be similar for different reasons than B and C. In addition, the prototype that represents the category has to be represented at a higher level of abstraction than the prototypes that represent its members. It is for this reason that the prototype is *not* to be equated with the most typical exemplar. The concept of Bird is not equivalent to the concept of Robin. There are attributes of robins (for example, its coloured breast) that do not figure in the more abstract concept of Bird, so that we can agree with "A robin is a bird" and disagree with "A bird is a robin".

The key proposal of prototype theory is that meaning is represented in the mind through an idealized general representation of the common attributes of the extension (the referents) of the term. It is this information that people are able to access when they generate lists of attributes or judge how central an attribute is to the meaning of a term. The reference of a term is then determined by similarity to this prototype representation. This mechanism for determining reference provides prototype theory with an advantage over many other accounts in that it directly explains the vagueness and imprecision of meaning. The vagueness of language has been the source of much debate in semantics (Keefe and Smith 1997), as it presents a serious challenge to the determination of truth for propositions and combinations of propositions in natural language. Traditionally, vagueness has been identified with the problem of determining the truth of statements using scalar adjectives such as TALL or BALD, where on the one hand it is clear that there is some height at which *X is tall* turns from False to True, but on the other hand it seems impossible to identify any particular height as being the critical value except through arbitrary stipulation. Prototype theory shows that similar problems of vagueness can arise with the multi-faceted concepts that underlie noun terms.

Vagueness in noun categories can be expressed in prototype theory by proposing *degrees of membership*. A tomato is a fruit to a certain degree. The relation between graded membership and typicality has also been a source of confusion. According to the theory, as an item becomes increasingly dissimilar from a category prototype, first its typicality declines, although it remains a clear member of the category. Then as it reaches the boundary region of the class, both typicality and degree of membership will decline, until it is too dissimilar to belong to the category at all. It is probably confusing to talk of the typicality of items that are NOT members of a category, although in fact Rosch and Mervis did ask their participants to rate typicality for such items, and people did not apparently object.

2.2 Evidence for prototypes

The primary evidence for prototypes comes from studies using the procedure outlined above. Where a meaning carries many inferences (attributes such as that if X is a bird, X can fly), many of which are probabilistic (not all birds actually fly), and where membership of the category is vague at the boundary, then a prototype is likely to be involved. Paradoxically, however, these are not necessary features of a prototype meaning. If there is a cluster of attributes that are strongly correlated, and if the world happens to contain no cases that would lie near the boundary in terms of similarity, then it is possible that a prototype representation would in fact be compatible with a conjunctive definition and no borderline vagueness. Consider the example that has been used so far of Birds. Birds are the only feathered bipedal creatures, and since their evolutionary ancestors among the dinosaurs became extinct long ago, there are no borderline cases within the folk taxonomy of kinds (which is our primary concern as psychologists). So BIRD has a clear-cut definition – "feathered bipedal creature" – and no borderline cases. But there is no reason to suppose that people represent them differently from bugs, fish and reptiles, which are much less clearly represented as concepts.

A classic study by Malt and Johnson (1992) demonstrated the prototype nature of artefact concepts. They constructed descriptions of unfamiliar objects that might either have the appearance but not the function of a given artefact like a BOAT, or alternatively the function but not the appearance. They were able to show that having the correct function was neither sufficient nor necessary for something to be judged to belong in the category. The absence of a set of singly necessary and jointly sufficient defining attributes is a hallmark of prototype representation.

An immediate worry about the method for finding prototypes is that the outcome may result from averaging and summing across individuals who themselves may have clearer definitions of their meanings. If the linguistic community contained three different clearly defined ideas of what Sport means, then the result of combining the ideas in the procedure will look like a prototype. McCloskey and Glucksberg (1978) were able to show that this is not the case. They asked a group of participants to make category membership judgement for a range of categories. In the list of items were many borderline cases, and this was shown in the degree to which people disagreed about them. The participants were then asked to return some weeks later and repeat their judgements. If it was the case that each individual had their own clearly defined category, then the judgements should have shown high consistency between the first and second occasion. In the event, however, there was a high level of inconsistency for those same items about which people disagreed. There were some stable inter-individual differences, but the main result was that vagueness exists within the individual rather than just between individuals.

Research on prototypes has also demonstrated that people's use of language can often be shown to deviate from logical norms in ways that are readily explained by the theory. The theory uses an internalist account of semantics (see Chapter 2), whereby meaning is fixed by the mental contents of the representation of a concept in memory. In addition, by depending on similarity to determine the reference of a term, the door is opened to various forms of "reasoning fallacy". Similarity is a relatively unconstrained measure, since the basis on which similarity is calculated can shift depending on what is being compared. North Korea may be similar to Cuba in terms of politics, while Cuba is similar to Barbados in terms of climate and location, but there is little or no similarity between North Korea and Barbados. This shifting of the basis for similarity can lead to intransitivity in categorization, as Hampton (1982) showed. If categorization has the logical structure of class inclusion, then it should be transitive. If A is a type of B, and B a type of C, A should be a type of C. In the study people were happy to agree that chairs were a typical type of furniture. They also agreed that ski-lifts and car-seats were kinds of chair, but they did not want to call them furniture. While in logical taxonomies the "Is a" relation is transitive, in natural conceptual hierarchies it is not. Similarity is the culprit. In deciding that a chair is a kind of furniture, people are focused on how well chairs match the attributes typical of furniture. Then when deciding if a car-seat is a kind of chair, they focus on the attributes typical of chairs. As the basis of determining similarity shifts, so the intransitivity becomes possible.

As illustration of the power of the prototype theory to account for a wider range of phenomena, consider the following two reasoning fallacies. Tversky and Kahneman (1983) introduced the famous conjunction fallacy. They described the case of Linda who was involved in liberal politics in college. Participants were then given various statements to rank in terms of their probability. They consistently considered "Linda is a feminist bank teller" as more likely than the plain "Linda is a bank teller" even though the first is a subclass of the second. The results were explained in terms of *representativeness*. People judge probability on the basis of similarity – in this case on the basis of the similarity between what was known about Linda and the two possible categories she was compared with. The subclass relation between bank tellers and feminist bank tellers was never considered.

The second fallacy was reported by Jönsson and Hampton (2006) as a phenomenon we called the *inverse* conjunction fallacy. As with the conjunction fallacy, the issue concerns fallacious reasoning about subclasses. In our study we gave people two universally quantified sentences such as:

All sofas have backrests.
All uncomfortable handmade sofas have backrests.

Different task procedures were employed across a series of experiments, but the general result was that people considered the first sentence more likely to be true, even though the second was entailed by the first. Hampton (2012) argues that people are thinking "intuitively" in terms of intensions. Backrests are a typical property of sofas, but less typical of uncomfortable handmade sofas. In spite of the universal quantifier, this difference in property typicality drives the judgement of likely truth. (Similar effects also occur in inductive reasoning where dissimilarity can undermine people's assessments of the truth of apparently certain inferences.)

Standard semantic theories have difficulty with accounting for these results. Prototype theory explains (and in fact predicts) their occurrence. The effects of conjunction on prototype representations (as in feminist bank teller, or handmade sofa) have been widely studied (see Hampton 2011). The meanings of the two terms interact at the level of individual attribute values so that the meaning of the conjunction is no longer determined in a simple compositional way (see Chapter 24). For example, in the case of the sofa, a backrest implies comfort, whereas the modifier "uncomfortable" implies the opposite. The interaction between these conflicting features throws doubt on whether the backrest will still be there.

2.3 Context effects and prototypes

One possible source of the variability seen in people's prototypes may come from context (see Chapter 11). Clearly, the notion of "sport" is likely to shift in the context of a kindergarten sports day, the 2012 London Olympics or a country house weekend in Scotland. Intuition suggests that there is some common core to the different contextually shifted meanings, but prototype theory would suggest that rather than still retaining some common definitional core, each meaning in fact involves a shift away in a different direction from a common prototype, to the point where there is very little in common across the different senses of "sport".

Studies have shown a strong influence of various contextual factors on how people judge typicality of instances. For example, Roth and Shoben (1983) manipulated the scenario in which a concept appeared (e.g. "the bird crossed the farmyard" or "the trucker drank the beverage"). Instances typical to the context (chickens or beer) were boosted in processing speed. In another study Barsalou and Sewell (1984) showed that if people were asked to adopt the point of view of another social group (e.g. housewives vs. farmers), then their typicality judgements would completely shift. Remarkably, students' agreement about typicalities from the adopted point of view was not much lower than their agreement about their own (the student's) point of view.

Another study notably failed to find any effect of context on categorization. Hampton et al. (2006) provided participants with lists to categorize containing borderline cases (such as whether an avocado is a fruit or whether psychology is a science). Participants were divided into different groups and given different contextual instructions. For example, in the Technical Condition, they were asked to imagine they were advising a government agency such as a Sports Funding Council on what should be considered sport. In the Pragmatic Condition, in contrast, they were asked to imagine that they were devising a library index that would place topics of interest in categories where people would expect to find them. A Control Condition simply categorized the items without any explicit context. Various measures were taken of categorization within each group, including the amount of disagreement, individual consistency across a period of a few weeks, the size of the categories created, the correlation of category probability with an independent measure of typicality, and the use of absolute as opposed to graded response options. Across six categories and two experiments there was very little evidence that the instructions changed the way in which people understood or used the category terms. Overwhelmingly the likelihood that an item would be positively categorized was predicted by the item's typicality in the category in an unspecified context with near perfect accuracy.

It is debatable whether there are in fact stable representations of concepts (and hence word meanings) in memory, or whether concepts are only ever constructed within a particular context. It is fair to say that every use of a concept in language will involve a contextual component – there is no direct window into what is represented. But at the same time it is reasonable to hypothesize that there is some permanent information structure in memory on which the context operates. Prototype representations have the flexibility to allow for contextual modification. On the other hand, exemplar models (see below) provide even greater flexibility with each context driving the concept representation through retrieval of a set of similar previously encountered contexts.

2.4 Critiques of the prototype theory of meaning

Critics of prototype theories of concepts were not long in coming to the fore. Rey (1983) pointed out that all of the problems that have been identified with descriptivist or internalist semantics as an account of concepts apply equally to the prototype theory. If conceptual (or meaning) content is equated with the information represented in a person's mind, then it becomes difficult to provide an account of truth. It does not seem right to say that a person who believes that snakes are slimy (which in fact they are not) is speaking the truth when they utter the statement "snakes are slimy", even though the meaning of snake for them includes its sliminess. If the truth/falsehood of these kinds of sentences were entirely determined analytically in terms of meanings, this would lead to an alarming solipsism. Another issue is the unlikelihood that two people will ever share the same meaning for a word, given the instability and individual variation seen in prototypes, so it is then hard to explain successful communication or disagreement about facts. Once again, each individual is in their own solipsistic world of meaning (see Chapter 2).

Handling these critiques leads into complicated areas. Perhaps the best way through the maze is to point out that in possessing a meaning of a word, the language user is not the person in charge of what the word means. Their prototype has to be connected to two sources of external validation. First, the physical and social world places constraints on conceptual contents. The person with the false belief about slimy snakes will change that belief when they first touch one. Second, people's meanings are constrained by the group of language users to which they belong. There are normative rules about the use of words which get enforced to a greater or lesser extent in the course of everyday conversation and language exchange. More importantly, a person should be willing to accept the "defeasibility" of their conceptual meanings. They should be happy to defer to reality or to social norms when shown they are out of line.

Within psychology, there have been two further developments from the first prototype model proposed by Rosch and Mervis (1975). Ironically perhaps, they have taken the field in two opposite directions, either increasing the representational power of the model or reducing it. The argument in favour of increased representational power was first made in an influential paper by Murphy and Medin (1985). They argued that lexical concepts are not simply classification devices based on similarity, as the prototype account seemed to suggest. Rather, concepts provide a means of understanding and predicting the world that can incorporate deeper theoretical structures. Rather than classifying an instance in the category to which it bears maximum similarity, they suggested that people classify instances in the category that best explains its observable properties. Development of this idea suggests that prototypes are in fact knowledge schemas, interrelated networks of attributes with causal explanatory links between them. For example, birds' lightweight bones together with their wings ENABLE them to fly, which CAUSES them to perch on trees, and ENABLES them to escape predators. This "theory" notion provides an account of how we reason with concepts. There are numerous demonstrations of the power of this approach – particularly in the developmental literature where it has been shown that children quickly learn to go beyond perceptual similarity in forming conceptual classes. In effect, words have to serve many purposes. One is to provide simple names for the things in the world around us so that we can easily communicate about them. Another is to provide the means of cultural transmission of complex ideas that have taken centuries to refine. Words like *mud* or *bug* are of the former kind, and are best modelled as prototypes. Words like *nitrogen* or *polio* refer in a different way, through their role in a deeper theory of the world and its nature.

The alternative development from prototypes has been to reduce the representational assumptions and propose that meanings are represented by sets of stored individual occurrences or exemplars. For example, the meaning of BIRD would be represented through storing memories of individual instances of actual birds such as robins, sparrows and penguins. One clear reason behind this approach is that it captures the way in which children learn language. Only rarely is a word learned by reference to a definition given by an adult or other source. Most of our words are just acquired through hearing them spoken, or reading them in text, and using the context of their use to arrive at the meaning of the word. As more and more contexts are observed, so the meaning becomes more clearly defined. However, it is not necessary to assume any analysis of the meaning into attributes or schema representations. Storing individual occurrences in memory is sufficient to explain the development of an appropriate understanding of the meaning of the word.

2.5 Exemplar theory for word meanings

Exemplar models in psychology began with Medin and Schaffer (1978) from which Nosofsky (1988) later developed the best known model – the Generalized Context Model (GCM). These models were developed to explain the results of experiments in which participants were taught novel classifications of more or less artificially constructed perceptual stimuli. The advantage of such lab-based experiments is that the experimenter has full control over exactly how the stimulus classes are defined, and what learning is provided. Typically, a participant is exposed to a number of repetitions of a learning set, classifying instances in the set as in class A or class B, and receiving corrective feedback on each trial. They are then tested without feedback on a transfer set including new instances that have not previously been seen. Models are tested for their ability to correctly predict the probability that participants will endorse these new instances as an A (or a B).

The relevance of such models for lexical semantics is that they represent a laboratory model of one way in which people may learn new concepts. Hearing a term used on a number of occasions, the speaker then generalizes its use to new occasions. Of course there are many differences between the laboratory task and learning in the wild. Word learning is often achieved without explicit feedback, and most lexical categories are not set up in a way that divides up a given domain into contrasting sets. However, in response, variants of exemplar models have been devised that incorporate unsupervised learning (i.e. learning without error correction) and probabilistically defined classes.

The first advantage of exemplar models over prototype representations is that there is no information loss. If every exemplar and its full context is stored in memory, then not only can the central tendency of a class (e.g. its idealized member) be computed, but also the variability within the class. (Variability can only be captured within prototype theory by the fixing of the level of similarity that is required for categorization. Highly variable classes, such as furniture, would have low similarity criteria, while low-variability classes such as butterflies would require a high threshold for similarity.) Because all exemplars are stored it is also possible with an exemplar representation to retrieve information about the co-occurrence of individual attributes. Small birds tend to sing, while large birds tend to make raucous calls. Prototype representations do not capture these correlations within the category, since the size and type of call are each represented as independent attributes.

A second advantage is that it is possible to represent classes that are not distributed around a single central point. Prototype models assume that there is a central prototypical representation, and that all instances are classified according to their similarity to this representation. In a semantic space, this means that the model assumes that the category boundary is spherical (or hyper-spherical in more than three dimensions). But exemplar models allow that a conceptual category may have more than one similarity cluster within it. For example, sexually dimorphic creatures like pheasants form two similarity clusters around the typical male and the typical female. A creature that was an "average" of these two forms would not be a typical pheasant, even though they would be at the centre of the class. Another example from the literature is the case of spoons. Small metal spoons and large wooden spoons are each more typical than small wooden or large metal spoons. Exemplar models have no difficulty with this, since each encountered spoon is represented and the correlation of size and material is retrievable from the stored cases.

A third advantage of exemplar representations is that they incorporate frequency effects. The more common a given exemplar, then the stronger will be its influence on the categorization of others. Prototype abstraction will also be sensitive to frequency – for example, the most frequent size or most frequent colour will tend to be the most typical. However, the frequency of given combinations of features is lost in the process of prototype abstraction.

Much of the research on exemplar models is of little relevance to lexical semantics. There are, however, some interesting results in support of an exemplar approach to word meaning. Gert Storms and colleagues in the Concat group at the Katholieke Universiteit Leuven have compiled a large database of semantic categories (De Deyne et al. 2008). The database includes a range of biological, artefact and activity categories. The norms provide (among other things) data on how frequently a word is generated as an exemplar of a category, how typical, imageable and familiar it is, what attributes are considered as relevant to category membership with their frequency of generation and rated definingness, and which exemplars possess which attributes. There are also pair-wise similarity judgements for exemplars across all categories.

Using these data, the Leuven group have been able to test prototype and exemplar ideas with data that are much closer to the concerns of lexical semantics. A recent review by Storms (2004) provides a useful summary. Storms first explains that in contrast to the presentation of perceptual stimuli in a laboratory experiment, it is not clear just how to interpret the notion of an exemplar in semantic memory. As described above, the key issue concerns whether categorization and typicality within categories is determined by similarity to the prototype attribute set (the so-called *independent cue model*) or whether it is determined by specific similarity to other exemplars within the category, in which case relational information is also involved (the *relational coding* model). A good fit to a category is not just a question of having enough of the right attributes, it also involves having the right combinations of pairs, triples etc. of attributes. It is the involvement of this relational information that provides the sub-clustering within a category that is characteristic of exemplar representations.

Storms (2004) lists three sources of empirical evidence for exemplar models of lexical semantic concepts. In each case the question relates to whether category typicality (and categorization probability) declines in a smooth continuous fashion with distance from a central prototype, or whether there is evidence for deviations from this pattern. (Full references can be found in Storms (2004).)

A first set of tests relates to the question of Linear Discriminability. According to the prototype model, concepts in semantic memory should be linearly discriminable (LS) from each other on the basis of a simple additive combination of the available attributes. In effect, category membership of an item is based on seeing whether the item has a sufficient number of the relevant category attributes, and only categories that have this structure can be represented with prototypes. Exemplar models are less constrained since weight can be given to certain configurations of features, as in the case of the metal and wooden spoons above. To test the models, researchers taught people artificial categories that either respected the LS constraint required by prototype models, or were non-linearly discriminable. Initial research found that when overall similarity was held constant, categories that respected the LS constraint were no easier to learn than those that did not, although evidence for an advantage of LS categories has since also been reported.

These studies all used artificial category learning methods. Ruts et al. (2004) were the first to investigate the issue using data from semantic categories. The Concat norms were used to map category exemplars into a multi-dimensional semantic space. Proximity in the space represents similarity between exemplars, so that semantic categories form clusters like galaxies in the space. Four different spaces were constructed for each domain of categories using from two to five dimensions to capture the similarity structure with increasing accuracy. Prototype theory was then tested by seeing whether categories could be distinguished from each other within the space by defining a plane boundary between them, as required by the LS constraint. In the case of biological kinds like insects, fish and birds, the categories were easily discriminated even in the low-dimensionality spaces. However, pairs of artefact kinds like cleaning utensils versus gardening utensils, or clothing versus accessories, were not discriminable, even in the highest dimensional space. Ruts et al. concluded that prototypes were sufficient for representing biological kinds, but that artefact kinds did not respect the LS constraint, and so exemplar representations were more appropriate for those kinds.

In a second set of studies demonstrating exemplar effects in semantic memory, Storms and colleagues used the same attribute by exemplar matrices to explore whether the prototype or exemplar model provided a better prediction for four different measures of category structure. Four predictions based on the prototype model were created using different ways of weighting the attributes in the matrix to create a sum of weighted attributes possessed by each exemplar. Predictions from the exemplar model were created by first rank-ordering the exemplars in the category in order of frequency of generation to the category name. (For example, "apple" might be the highest-frequency exemplar generated to the category name "fruit".) Twenty-five different predictors were then created by measuring the average similarity of each exemplar to either the highest one, the highest two or up to the highest 25 exemplars in the list. Finally, the different predictors were correlated with four measures of category structure: rated typicality, categorization time, exemplar generation frequency and category label generation frequency. Overall the results clearly favoured the exemplar model. The optimum number of exemplars involved was between seven and ten. Individual average similarity to the top ten exemplars in a category was generally a better predictor of the different measures than was similarity to an abstracted prototype.

The final source of evidence for exemplar effects is also from the Storms group in Leuven. Two studies looked at how people categorize unknown fresh food products as either fruits or vegetables. Thirty exotic plant foods were presented on plates to twenty participants, and were categorized as fruits or vegetables. Storms and colleagues compared prototype and exemplar model predictions of the resulting categorization probabilities. Prototype predictions were based on ratings of the degree to which each instance possessed the most important features of each category. Exemplar predictions were based on ratings of similarity of each instance to the eight most frequent exemplars of fruits and vegetables respectively. The results showed that the two models did more or less equally well, but that, interestingly, a regression model using both predictors taken together gave a significantly improved fit. In other words, both possession of the right attributes *and* similarity to the most common exemplars contributed to the likelihood of categorization. For the full story of how people represent novel fruits and vegetables, see the discussion in Storms (2004).

2.6 Critique of exemplar models

There have been a number of issues raised with exemplar models, but I will briefly focus on those that are most relevant to semantic memory. The first concerns what is taken to be an *exemplar*. In the classification learning literature there is evidence that each presentation of an individual exemplar is stored, so that there is no account taken of the possibility that it might be the same individual seen on each occasion. For lexical semantics, it is more likely that one should interpret the evidence for exemplar effects in terms of what Heit and Barsalou (1996) called the *instantiation principle*. In a hierarchy of lexical concepts, such as ANIMAL, BIRD, EAGLE, the principle suggests that a particular level such as BIRD is represented as a collection of the concepts at the next level below. So birds are represented by eagles, sparrows and robins, while robins are represented by male robins and female robins. Below this bottom level (i.e. where there are no further familiar subdivisions of the taxonomy), it is unclear whether individual exemplars (meaning actual experiences of an individual in a particular situation) are influential.

A related criticism is the problem of how people learn about lexical concepts that they never experience firsthand. How do we learn to represent the meaning of words like *electron*, *nebula* or *aardvark*? There must be a route to learning meanings that does not involve direct experience of individuals, since, although I have a (rough) idea of what an aardvark is, I don't recall having ever met one. A combination of pictures and written and spoken communication has provided me with all that I know about the concept.

3 Future directions

Psychological studies of lexical semantics form a bridge between different research traditions, and so are well placed to attempt an integration of different sources of evidence. For psychology, the development of mathematically well-defined models of category learning has tended to sacrifice ecological validity for laboratory precision. It is important in the future that the models turn their attention to the different ways in which people acquire categorical concepts in real life. Much of learning, whether in school, college or in apprenticeships, involves the development of concepts – ways of classifying experience, events or objects which provide one with predictive understanding of the world. Certainly there are cases where concepts are learned through experience with exemplars – either with feedback from others about their category membership or (more probably) a mixture of trial and error learning and unsupervised observational learning. But there are also many concepts that are learned first through direct instruction and then incorporated into one's working conceptual repertoire through exercise of the concepts in real cases. Most forms of expertise – be it in finance, medicine or horticulture – are likely to be learned in this way. Concepts (and thus the meaning of the words that label them) are learned through experience in different situations. Knowledge of their logical properties (such as the inferences they support) is stored side-by-side with knowledge of their perceptual/sensory qualities, their emotional valence and their potential for action and achieving goals (Barsalou 2008). Understanding how nouns and verbs contribute meaning to utterances is likely to be dependent on a full treatment of the richness of our conceptual representations.

4 Conclusions

Psychology has generated a number of theoretical models for the concepts that underlie the meanings of nouns. Reviewing the large number of studies that have been done within the field, the conclusion one arrives at is that there is actually good evidence for each of them. In fact, different concept meanings may require different accounts of their representation. Some domains may be represented by linearly discriminable concepts with simple prototype structure. Others may have a *granularity* such that the internal structure of a category has sub-prototypes within it. A closer examination of the differences between prototype and exemplar theories suggests that they are simply different versions of the same model. Barsalou (1990) showed that the models are at either end of a continuum with maximum abstraction at the prototype end, and zero information loss at the exemplar end. Different concepts probably lie somewhere in between, with the degree of abstraction depending on the specific conceptual domain. Highly common and highly similar entities (like raindrops) may be represented as an abstract prototype, while familiar and distinctive classes, like the concept of dog for a dog lover, would be represented in granular fashion as the collection of individual dog breeds, themselves represented perhaps by prototypes.

In addition to these similarity-based models, other concepts involve detailed schematic knowledge of the kind found in science and other academic disciplines, where similarity becomes less relevant and explicit definitions more common.

Given the variety and flexibility of the mind in how it provides meaning to the world, it should not be a surprise to find that our words have similar multiplicity in how their meanings are constructed in the mind. Words are used for many functions, and this necessarily gives rise to a wide range of semantic structures.

Further reading

Barsalou, L. W. 1999. Perceptual symbol systems. *Behavioral and Brain Sciences* 22: 577–609. Barsalou proposes that compositional semantics can be made compatible with an embodied approach to cognition through a symbolic representation system using symbols that preserve some of the perceptual nature of the things they represent.

Hampton, J. A. 2006. Concepts as prototypes. In B. H. Ross (ed.), *The Psychology of Learning and Motivation: Advances in Research and Theory*, Vol. 46. Amsterdam: Elsevier, 79–113. In this chapter I present an overview of the evidence that people represent meanings or words, or concepts, in terms of their most typical features. A prototype is presented as being a structured set of semantic properties which may have different degrees of centrality. A concept's extension is determined in a vague way through similarity of a potential exemplar to the represented prototype.

Hampton, J. A. 2015. Concepts in the semantic triangle. In E. Margolis and S. Laurence (eds), *The Conceptual Mind: New Directions in the Study of Concepts*. Cambridge, MA: MIT Press, 655–676. This chapter presents a discussion of three ways in which meanings can be fixed, in terms of the external world, social convention and psychological representations.

Hampton, J. A. and Jönsson, M. L. 2013. Typicality and compositionality: the logic of combining vague concepts. In M. Werning, W. Hintzen and E. Machery (eds), *Oxford Handbook of Compositionality*. Oxford: Oxford University Press, 385–402. In this chapter we discuss the controversial issue of semantic compositionality. We argue that a strict view of compositionality is incompatible with the evidence of how people combine concepts. We defend a weaker principle that allows for the introduction of background knowledge in the determination of the meaning of a complex phrase.

Murphy, G. L. 2002. *The Big Book of Concepts*. Cambridge, MA: MIT Press. Murphy's book is a classic review of a wide range of psychological studies of concepts, and covers the main theories of categorization. While it is now over 14 years old, it has not been surpassed in the breadth of its coverage and the balanced critique that is offered.

References

Barsalou, L. W. 1990. On the indistinguishability of exemplar memory and abstraction in category representation. In T. Skrull and R. S. Wyer (eds), *Advances in Social Cognition, Volume III: Content and Process Specificity in the Effects of Prior Experiences*. Hillsdale, NJ: Lawrence Erlbaum Associates, 61–88.

Barsalou, L.W. 2008. Cognitive and neural contributions to understanding the conceptual system. *Current Directions in Psychological Science* 17: 91–95.

Barsalou, L. W. and D. R. Sewell 1984. Constructing representations of categories from different points of view. *Rep. No. 2. Emory University, Atlanta GA: Emory Cognition Project*.

Collins, A. M. and E. F. Loftus 1975. A spreading activation theory of semantic processing. *Psychological Review* 82: 407–428.

Collins, A. M. and M. R. Quillian 1969. Retrieval time from semantic memory. *Journal of Verbal Learning and Verbal Behavior* 8: 240–248.

De Deyne, S., S. Verheyen, E. Ameel, W. Vanpaemel, M. Dry, W. Voorspoels and G. Storms 2008. Exemplar by feature applicability matrices and other Dutch normative data for semantic concepts. *Behavior Research Methods* 40: 1030–1048.

Hampton, J. A. 1979. Polymorphous concepts in semantic memory. *Journal of Verbal Learning and Verbal Behavior* 18: 441–461.

Hampton, J. A. 1981. An investigation of the nature of abstract concepts. *Memory and Cognition* 9: 149–156.

Hampton, J. A. 1982. A demonstration of intransitivity in natural categories. *Cognition* 12: 151–164.

Hampton, J. A. 1984. The verification of category and property statements. *Memory and Cognition* 12: 345–354.

Hampton, J. A. 2011. Conceptual combinations and fuzzy logic. In R. Belohlavek and G. J. Klir (eds), *Concepts and Fuzzy Logic*. Cambridge, MA: MIT Press, 209–231.

Hampton, J. A. 2012. Thinking intuitively: the rich and at times illogical world of concepts. *Current Directions in Psychological Science* 21: 398–402.

Hampton, J. A., D. Dubois and W. Yeh 2006. The effects of pragmatic context on classification in natural categories. *Memory and Cognition* 34: 1431–1443.

Heit, E. and L. W. Barsalou 1996. The instantiation principle in natural categories. *Memory* 4: 413–451.

Jönsson, M. L. and J. A. Hampton 2006. The inverse conjunction fallacy. *Journal of Memory and Language* 55: 317–334.

Keefe, R. and P. Smith 1997. Theories of vagueness. In R. Keefe and P. Smith (eds), *Vagueness: A Reader*. Cambridge, MA: MIT Press, 1–57.

Malt, B. C. and E. C. Johnson 1992. Do artifact concepts have cores? *Journal of Memory and Language* 31: 195–217.

McCloskey, M. and S. Glucksberg 1978. Natural categories: well-defined or fuzzy sets? *Memory and Cognition* 6: 462–472.

Medin, D. L. and M. M. Schaffer 1978. Context theory of classification learning. *Psychological Review* 85: 207–238.

Murphy, G. L. and D. L. Medin 1985. The role of theories in conceptual coherence. *Psychological Review* 92: 289–316.

Nosofsky, R. M. 1988. Similarity, frequency and category representations. *Journal of Experimental Psychology: Learning, Memory, and Cognition* 14: 54–65.
Osherson, D. N. and E. E. Smith 1981. On the adequacy of prototype theory as a theory of concepts. *Cognition* 11: 35–58.
Rey, G. 1983. Concepts and stereotypes. *Cognition* 15: 237–262.
Rosch, E. R. and C. B. Mervis 1975. Family resemblances: studies in the internal structure of categories. *Cognitive Psychology* 7: 573–605.
Roth, E. M. and E. J. Shoben 1983. The effect of context on the structure of categories. *Cognitive Psychology* 15: 346–378.
Ruts, W., G. Storms and J. A. Hampton 2004. Linear separability in superordinate natural language concepts. *Memory and Cognition* 32: 83–95.
Smith, E. E., E. J. Shoben and L. J. Rips 1974. Structure and process in semantic memory: a featural model for semantic decisions. *Psychological Review* 81: 214–241.
Storms, G. 2004. Exemplar models in the study of natural language concepts. *Psychology of Learning and Motivation – Advances in Research and Theory* 42: 1–40.
Tulving, E. 1972. Episodic and semantic memory. In E. Tulving and W. Donaldson (eds), *Organization of Memory*. London: Academic Press.
Tversky, A. and D. Kahneman 1983. Extensional versus intuitive reasoning: the conjunction fallacy in probability judgment. *Psychological Review* 90: 293–315.

Related topics

Chapter 2, Internalist semantics; Chapter 5, Cognitive semantics; Chapter 8, Embodiment, simulation and meaning; Chapter 11, Contextual adjustment of meaning; Chapter 12, Lexical decomposition; Chapter 15, Semantic shift; Chapter 16, The semantics of nominals; Chapter 24, Compositionality.

8
Embodiment, simulation and meaning

Benjamin Bergen

1 Introduction

Approaches to meaning differ in ways as fundamental as the questions they aim to answer. The theoretical outlook described in this chapter, the *embodied simulation* approach, belongs to the class of perspectives that ask how meaning operates in real time in the brain, mind, and body of language users. Clearly, some approaches to meaning are better suited to this question than others. Mechanistic models that bridge levels of analysis—from the brain and its computations to the functions and behaviours they support—and that recruit the convergent tools of empirical cognitive science are particularly well equipped. The embodied simulation approach is an example of this type of approach.

The fundamental idea underlying the embodied simulation hypothesis is a remarkably old one. It's the notion that language users construct mental experience of what it would be like to perceive or interact with objects and events that are described in language. Carl Wernicke described the basic premise as well as anyone has since (and with remarkably little modern credit, as Gage and Hickok (2005) point out). Wernicke wrote, in 1874:

> The concept of the word "bell," for example, is formed by the associated memory images of visual, tactual and auditory perceptions. These memory images represent the essential characteristic features of the object, bell.
>
> (Wernicke 1977 [1874]: 117)

This is the essence of simulationism. Mental access to concepts involves the activation of internal encodings of perceptual, motor, and affective—that is, *modality-specific*—experiences. This proposal entails that understanding the meaning of words involves activating modality-specific representations or processes. Wernicke came to this notion through his work on localization of cognitive functions in the brain, and as a result, it should be no surprise that he had a very clear view of what the neural substrate of these "memory images" would be and where it would be housed:

> the memory images of a bell [. . .] are deposited in the cortex and located according to the sensory organs. These would then include the acoustic imagery aroused by the sound of the bell, visual imagery established by means of form and color, tactile imagery

acquired by cutaneous sensation, and finally, motor imagery gained by exploratory movements of the fingers and eyes.

(Wernicke 1977 [1885–1886]: 179)

In other words, the same neural tissue that people use to perceive in a particular modality or to move particular effectors would also be used in moments not of perception or action but of conception, including language use. This, in words now 130 years old, is the embodied simulation hypothesis.

Naturally, this idea has subsequently been developed in various ways. Part of its history involves some marginalization in cognitive science, especially starting in the 1950s with the advent of symbolic approaches to cognition and language. If the mind is a computer, and a computer is seen as a serial, deterministic, modular symbol system, then there is no place for analog systems for perception and action to be reused for higher cognitive functions like language and conceptualization.

But more recent history has seen substantial refinement of the embodied simulation hypothesis, on three fronts. First, cognitive psychologists came to the idea because of the so-called "symbol grounding" problem (Harnad 1990). In brief, the problem is this: if concepts are represented through symbols in the mind, these symbols must somehow be grounded in the real world, or else they don't actually mean anything. For instance, if mental symbols are only defined in terms of other mental symbols, then either there must be core mental symbols that are innate and serve as the basis for grounding meaning (see e.g. Fodor (1975)), or symbols must relate to the world in some meaningful way. Otherwise, they are ungrounded and meaningless. This is a hard problem, and as a result, some cognitive psychologists began to suggest that perhaps what people are doing during conceptualization doesn't involve abstract symbol manipulation, but rather manipulation of representations that are like action and perception in kind (Barsalou 1999). In essence, perhaps the way out of the symbol grounding problem is to get rid of the distance (or "transduction" as Barsalou et al. 2003 argue) between perception and action on the one hand and the format of conceptual representation on the other. (For a more complete account of transduction, see Chapter 2 on internalist semantics.)

A second branch of work that pointed towards embodied simulation came from *cognitive semantics*. This is an approach to analytical linguistics that aims to describe and explain linguistic patterning on the basis of conceptual and especially embodied individual knowledge, experience, and construal (Croft and Cruse 2004). Cognitive semanticists argue that meaning is tantamount to conceptualization—that is, it is a mental phenomenon in which an individual brings their encyclopedic experience to bear on a piece of language. Making meaning for a word like *antelope* involves activating conceptual knowledge about what antelopes are like based on one's own experience, which may vary across individuals as a function of their cultural and idiosyncratic backgrounds. The idea of embodied simulation dovetails neatly with this encyclopedic, individual, experiential view of meaning, and cognitive semanticists (see Chapter 5) were among the early proponents of a reinvigorated embodied simulation hypothesis.

And finally, action-oriented approaches to robotics and artificial intelligence pointed to a role for embodied simulation in language. Suppose your goal is to build a system that is able to execute actions based on natural language commands. You have to build dynamic motor control structures that are able to control actions, and these need to be selected and parameterized through language. In such a system, there may be little need for abstract symbols to represent linguistic meaning, except at the service of driving the motor actions. But the very same architecture required to enact actions can also be used to allow the system to also understand language even when not actually performing actions. The theory of meaning that grew from this work, and its name, *simulation semantics* (Feldman and Narayanan 2004), is one implementation of the embodied simulation hypothesis.

In the past decade, embodied simulation has become a bona fide organized, self-conscious enterprise with the founding of a regular conference, the Embodied and Situated Language Processing workshop, as well as publication of several edited volumes (Pecher and Zwaan 2005) and books (Pulvermüller 2003; Bergen 2012). It's important to note that none of these approaches view simulation as necessary or sufficient for all meaning construction—indeed, one of the dominant ongoing research questions is precisely what functional role it performs, if any. The varied simulationist approaches merely propose simulation as part of the cognitive toolkit that language users bring to bear on dealing with meaning in language.

2 Current research on simulation

While most current work on simulation in linguistic meaning-making is empirical, as the review in this section will make clear, this empirical work is motivated by introspective and logical arguments that something like simulation might be part of how meaning works in the first place.

One such argument derives from the symbol grounding problem, mentioned in the previous section. Free-floating mental symbols have to be grounded in terms of something to mean anything. One thing to tether symbols to is the real world—symbol-world correspondences allow for truth-conditional semantics (Fodor, 1998; see Chapter 1). Another thing to ground symbols in is other symbols—inspired, perhaps, by Wittgenstein's proposal that meaning is use (Wittgenstein 1953). On this account, exemplified by distributional semantic approaches like HAL (Lund and Burgess 1996) and LSA (Landauer et al. 1998), to know the meaning of a symbol, you need only know what company it keeps. However, as Glenberg and Robertson (2000) demonstrate, these word- or world-based approaches to grounding both fail to make correct predictions about actual human processing of language.

Another argument is based on parsimony of learning, storage, and evolution. Suppose you're a language learner. You have perceptual and motor experiences in the world, which are processed using specific brain and body resources that are well tuned and appropriately connected for these purposes. To reuse these same systems in a slightly different mode seems more parsimonious than would be transducing the patterns of activation in these systems into some other representational format (abstract symbols, for instance) that would need to recapitulate a good deal of the same information in a different form. The same argument goes for subsequent storage—storing two distinct versions of the same information in different formats could potentially increase robustness but would decrease parsimony. And similarly, over the course of evolution, if you already have systems for perceiving and acting, using those same systems in a slightly different way would be more parsimonious than introducing a new system that represents transduced versions of the same in a different format.

Finally, from introspection, many people are convinced that something like simulation is happening because they notice that they have experiences of imagery (the conscious and intentional counterpart of simulation) while processing language. Processing the words *pink elephant* leads many people to have conscious visual-like experiences in which they can inspect a non-present visual form with a color that looks qualitatively like it's pink and has a shape that looks qualitatively like that of an elephant, from some particular perspective (usually from the right side of the elephant).

But each of these arguments has its weaknesses, not least of which is that they can't inform the pervasiveness of simulation, the mechanisms behind it, or the functions it serves. To address these issues, a variety of appropriate empirical tools have been brought to bear on the question, ranging from behavioural reaction time experiments to functional brain imaging.

2.1 Behavioural evidence

The largest body of empirical work focusing on simulation comes from behavioural experimentation. For the most part, these are reaction time studies, but there are also eye-tracking and mouse-tracking studies that measure other aspects of body movement in real time as people are using language. Generally, these behavioural studies aim to infer whether people are constructing simulations during language use, and if so what properties these simulations might have, what factors affect them, and at what point during processing they're activated.

Reaction time studies of simulation generally exhibit some version of the same basic logic. If some language behaviour, say understanding a sentence, involves activating a simulation that includes certain perceptual or motor content, then language on the one hand and perception or action on the other should interact. For instance, when people first process language and then have to subsequently perceive a percept or perform an action that's compatible with the implied or mentioned perceptual or motor content, they should be faster to do so than when the percept or action is incompatible. For example, processing a sentence about moving one's hand toward one's body (like *Scratch your nose!*) leads to faster reactions to press a button close to the body. Conversely, sentences about action away from the body (like *Ring the doorbell!*) lead to faster responses away from the body (Glenberg and Kaschak 2002). Similarly, a sentence that describes an object in a vertical orientation (like *The toothbrush is in the glass*) leads to faster responses to an image of that vertical object, while sentences about objects in a horizontal orientation (like *The toothbrush is in the sink*) lead to faster processing of horizontal images of the same object (Stanfield and Zwaan 2001).

Compatibility effects like these demonstrate that language processing primes perceptual and motor tasks, in ways that are specifically sensitive to the actions or percepts that language implies. Similar designs have demonstrated that comprehension primes not only the direction of action and orientation of objects, but also the effector used (hand, foot, or mouth), hand shape, direction of hand rotation, object shape, direction of object motion, visibility, and others (see Bergen (2012) for a review).

One of the most interesting features of this literature is that there are various experiments in which the priming effect appears—superficially—to reverse itself. For example, Richardson et al. (2003) found that language about vertical actions (like *The plane bombs the city*) lead to slower reactions to circles or squares when they appear along the vertical axis of a computer monitor (that is directly above or below the center of the screen) while language about horizontal actions (like *The miner pushes the cart*) lead to slower reactions along the horizontal axis. Other experiments have reported findings of this same type (Kaschak et al. 2005; Bergen et al. 2007).

At the surface, this might seem problematic, but a leading view at present is that these two superficially contradictory sets of findings are in fact consistent when the experimental designs are considered closely. In fact, they may reveal something important about the neural mechanisms underlying the different effects. Richardson et al.'s (2003) work is a good case study. In their experiment, a circle or square was presented on the screen with only a slight delay after the end of the preceding sentence (50–200msec). With the time it takes to process a sentence, this meant that the participant was still processing the linguistic stimulus when the visual stimulus was presented. So the two operations—comprehending the sentence and perceiving the shape—overlapped. That's design feature number one. Second, the objects described in the sentences in this study (such as bombs or carts) are visually distinct from the circles and squares subsequently presented. That is, independent of where on the screen they appeared, the mentioned objects did not look visually like the mentioned objects. Other studies that find interference effects (Kaschak et al. 2005; Bergen et al. 2007; Yee et al. 2013) have the same design features—the language and the visual stimulus or motor task have to be dealt with simultaneously, and in addition, the two tasks are non-integrable—they involve the same body-part performing distinct tasks (Yee et al. 2013) or distinct visual forms (Kaschak et al. 2005).

Interference findings like these are often interpreted as suggesting that the two tasks (language use on the one hand and perception or motor control on the other) use shared neural resources, which cannot perform either task as efficiently when called upon to do two distinct things at the same time. By contrast, compatibility effect studies, like those that present language followed at some delay by an action or image that matches the implied linguistic content, do not call on the same resources to do different things at the same time, and as a result, do not induce interference but rather facilitation of a matching response.

One major weakness of reaction time studies like these is that they present a perceptual stimulus or require a physical action that matches the linguistic content or not. This raises the concern that it might only be this feature of the experimental apparatus that induces simulation effects. That is, perhaps people only think about the orientation of toothbrushes in the context of an experiment that systematically presents visual depictions of objects in different orientations. Perhaps the experiment induces the effects.

One way to methodologically circumvent this concern is with the use of eye-tracking. Several groups have used eye-tracking during passive listening as a way to make inferences about perceptual processes during language processing. For instance, Spivey and Geng (2001) had participants listen to narratives that described motion in one direction or another while looking at a blank screen, and while the participants believed the eye-tracker was not recording data. The researchers found that the participants' eyes were most likely to move in the direction of the described motion, even though they had been told that this was a rest period between the blocks of the real experiment. Another study (Johansson at al. 2006) first presented people with visual scenes and then had them listen to descriptions of those scenes while looking at the same scene, looking at nothing, or looking at nothing in the dark. They found that people's eye movements tracked with the locations of the mentioned parts of the scene. Both studies suggest that even in the absence of experimental demands to attend to specific aspects of described objects, actions, and scenes, people engage perceptual processes. This is consistent with the idea that they perform simulations of described linguistic content, even when unprompted by task demands.

2.2 Imaging

Behavioural evidence provides clues that people may be activating perceptual and motor knowledge during language use. Brain imaging research complements these findings, by allowing researchers to ask where in the brain there is differential activity when people are using language of one type or another. Modern models of functional brain organization all include some degree of localization of function—that is, to some extent there is neural tissue in certain locations that performs certain computations that contribute differently to cognition than other neural tissue does. For example, there are parts of the occipital lobe, such as primary visual cortex, that are involved in the calculation of properties from visual stimuli, and parts of the frontal lobe, like primary motor cortex and premotor cortex, that are involved in controlling motor action. Brain scanning, such as functional magnetic resonance imaging (fMRI), permits a measure to be taken of where activity is taking place in the brain—in the case of fMRI, this is blood flow, which increases as a consequence of neuronal firing. By comparing the fMRI signals obtained while people are performing different tasks, it's possible to localize differences in how the brain responds across those tasks.

Dozens of brain imaging studies have looked at what happens in people's brains when they're presented with language that has different semantic content, and the findings are relatively clear. When people are processing language about motor actions, there's an increased signal in motor areas, as compared with language not about motor actions. This signal in the motor system observed during motor language processing is weaker than when people are actually moving their bodies, and overlaps but may not be fully co-extensive with the area in which a signal is observed while people are performing intentional imagery of motor actions (Willems et al. 2010). But the signal is present even when people are not asked to think deeply about the meanings of the sentences they're presented with. Similarly, language that describes visual scenes leads to an increased signal coming from the brain's vision system. For instance, language about motion leads to increased activity in the medial temporal lobe, which houses a region implicated in the visual processing of motion (Saygin et al. 2010).

Brain imaging techniques are often criticized for their limitations—for instance, the subtractive approach they typically adopt doesn't afford insight into the actual function of the implicated brain areas, their temporal resolution is often poor (with fMRI, it's on the order of seconds) and they can only be used to compare grossly contrasting stimuli, like language about motion versus static language. But they are a critical component of a methodologically triangulating approach to meaning. Behavioural methods can reveal details of timing and functional interaction between different cognitive mechanisms, but they can only indirectly reveal anything about location, which is imaging's strength. To complete the story, we need to know not only where and when, but also how. And that's what we'll turn to next.

2.3 Neuropsychology

Traditionally, the best type of evidence on what functions certain brain and body systems are used for—that is, what precisely they do for a particular behaviour—comes from localized brain damage. When damage to a particular part of the brain is accompanied by a cognitive impairment, but damage to some other area does not lead to the same cognitive impairment, that suggests that the first brain region but not the second is mechanistically involved in that particular cognitive behaviour. This logic—known as a *dissociation*—is the form of evidence that first led pathologists like Paul Broca and Carl Wernicke to be able to pair brain regions involved in language use with hypothesized functions in the nineteenth century. And it has been used consistently since then as the gold standard for localization of function in the human brain.

Despite the appeal of neuropsychological studies, they have clear limitations. Because it's not possibly to ethically induce brain lesions in humans, researchers are restricted to those brain insults that occur naturally due to stroke, traumatic brain injury, etc., which often leave damage that is distributed across the brain. As a result, neuropsychological studies often include participants who have lesions to similar or overlapping brain regions, but no two lesions will be the same. In addition, most patients are studied some time after the injury, which means that there will have been brain changes over the course of recovery that obscure the organization at the time of damage.

These limitations notwithstanding, there have been a few dissociation studies focusing on language use that differentiated across language with different content. For instance, Shapiro et al. (2005) showed that damage to the left temporal cortex, a region implicated in visual recognition of objects, often leads patients to lose the ability to access nouns describing physical objects. But damage to the left frontal cortex, an area dedicated to motor control, tends to lead to difficulties with verbs describing actions. This evidence is suggestive that parts of the brain used for perceiving objects and performing actions also underlie meanings of words.

2.4 Transcranial magnetic stimulation

Although it's not possible to lesion living human brains, techniques are available that temporarily disrupt activity in a particular region. Transcranial Magnetic Stimulation (TMS) is one of these—it involves the application of a strong electromagnet to the scalp, inducing a field that enters the cerebral cortex and modifies neuron behaviour locally. TMS is often used as a transient proxy for lesion studies—it can be applied to a specific brain area, and if doing so impairs some behaviour (and if applying TMS to other brain regions does not impair this same behaviour), then this is effectively a dissociation.

Several studies have reported on the result of applying TMS to specific brain regions during language processing, in the hope of determining whether access to motor or perceptual processes plays a mechanistic role in using language about action or percepts. For instance, Shapiro et al. (2001) found that applying TMS to motor regions interferes with producing verbs but not nouns. Verbs often describe actions, while nouns are less likely to do so. So it could be that the reason people have more trouble producing verbs when motor cortex is interfered with is that accessing knowledge about how to move the body is part of the machinery people use to produce verbs, more so than for nouns.

2.5 Adaptation

The inferential logic of dissociations is so useful that there's even some behavioural work that tries to harness it, but without relying on naturally incurred brain damage or artificially induced brain changes from applied magnetic fields. Instead, it's based on *adaptation*. When people perform certain behaviours continuously for a long enough duration, the neural structures that they rely on come to be less active over time. A classic example of this is motion adaptation effects—when you look at something moving in one direction for long enough, and then look away, the world appears to be moving in the opposite direction (the *waterfall illusion*). Recent studies have attempted to use adaptation paradigms to knock out certain brain structures and potentially also language processing capacities, to determine what functional role these structures play in language use.

For instance, Glenberg et al. (2008) had people move 600 beans by hand in a single direction—either towards or away from their body. They then had to make judgements about sentences that described motion towards or away from their body. And surprisingly, people were slower to make judgements about sentences that described motion in the *same* direction in which they had just moved the 600 beans. In other words, first adapting to a particular action makes people take longer to process language about a similar action.

2.6 Computational modeling

So there's a good deal of experimental evidence that simulation—or something like it—occurs during language use and even some indication that it might play a functional role. An experimental approach is one way to address the viability of the simulation hypothesis. In cognitive science, similar claims are often assessed in a second way as well, through computational modeling. By implementing a proposed model of how the proposed mechanism would work—in this case, simulation—and then observing how a system that incorporates that mechanism behaves, it's possible to ask a slightly different question: would this mechanism do what it's supposed to do? That is, a model can provide a practical proof-of-concept. Another side benefit of computational implementation is learning in detail about other mechanisms that would need to be in place for a system to actually do whatever it is supposed to do—for instance, understand language.

There has been some modeling work using simulation as part of a language comprehension system. The most extensively developed uses a particular model of grammar (Embodied Construction Grammar—Bergen and Chang 2005; 2013) as an interface between language processing and simulation. There's been a good deal of work in this paradigm, implementing simulation using dynamic computational control schemas and deploying those schemas to compute and propagate inferences for both literal and metaphorical language (Narayanan 1997).

Among the things that have been hammered home from modeling efforts like this one is that it's critical for the language processing system to implement an organizational interface between linguistic form and simulation. The fundamental issue is that to simulate usefully, a system has to know what to simulate. And to generate instructions to simulation, that system will need to take cues not only from the linguistic input but also context and world knowledge. An example might help clarify this point. Suppose you're dealing with a verb like *jump*. There are different simulations appropriate to different types of jumping. If *jump* appears in a sentence like *The high-jumper jumped*, that jumping will be different from *The triple-jumper jumped*. And both will be very different from *The train jumped* or *The cat jumped*. For a simulation to appropriately reflect the inferred intent of the speaker/writer, it has to be sensitive to contextual factors, and this implicates a process of assembling the cues from language and extralinguistic context. Different theorists have labeled this assembly process as "meshing" (Kaschak and Glenberg 2000) or "analysis" (Bergen and Chang 2005).

3 Toward a simulation semantics

Empirical evidence suggests that processing words and sentences leads to perceptual and motor simulation of explicitly and implicitly mentioned aspects of linguistic content. This could have consequences for theories of semantics, but not without raising a series of fundamental questions. What and how might words contribute to simulation? Does this differ as a function of properties of the word? (Perhaps words with more concrete referents like *dog* involve simulation differently from ones with more abstract referents, like *God*.) How do linguistic elements other than words contribute to and constrain meaning, including linguistic elements like idioms or grammatical constructions? And for that matter, what are the effects of context, including the linguistic and physical environment as well as the current belief and knowledge state of the language user? Current work attempting to develop a simulation-based theory of meaning has made some limited progress on these questions.

3.1 Limits of simulation

Based on the evidence presented in the previous section, it might be tempting to equate simulation with meaning—perhaps words are associated with specific but varied sensorimotor experiences, and the internal re-enactment of these experiences constitutes the meaning of those words (see e.g. Pulvermüller (2003)). But while there is indeed a great deal of evidence for such associations, this simplest account would fail to capture fundamental aspects of meaning.

To begin with, many words have syncategorematic meaning properties—their meaning depends on the words they co-occur with. The sensorimotor features that *big* contributes to a described scene are non-overlapping in *big dog* versus *big run*, for instance, not to mention more abstract uses like *big headache* or *big problem*. An even bigger problem is presented by well-known examples like *safe*, which evokes a relatively abstract frame and doesn't specify roles within it. A *safe beach* can be one on which one is unlikely to be in danger (for instance, from a dangerous shore break), but it can also be a beach that itself is not in danger (perhaps from erosion). Not only is it hard to pin down shared sensorimotor properties of these different uses of *safe*; more troublingly, the comprehender has to decide whether the noun it modifies is the thing that threatens safety of something else (and if so, what) or is itself under threat (and again, if so, of what).

These complications aren't limited to parade examples like these. As discussed in the previous section, even words with clear, low-level sensorimotor associations like *jump* display rampant polysemy and vagueness. And this can in principle only be navigated using contextual information, from low-level grammatical details to high-level expectations generated from situations of use. As a consequence, it appears to be that in general, meaning construction is an active process that involves the interplay of knowledge of context, encyclopedic knowledge, and prior expectations. All of this conspires to constrain what goes into the content of simulation. None of this is compatible with an account in which word-associated simulation *is* the meaning of a word.

Instead, there appear to be a variety of processes at play as people attempt to construct meaning from perceived language. (The emphasis in the literature on simulation has been placed on comprehension, since this is far easier to study than language production, and I continue with that bias here, though there's certainly much to say about simulation in language production; see, for instance, Hostetter and Alibali (2008), Sato (2010), and Parrill et al. (2013).) Simulation may play a role in meaning. But what role is still to be ascertained. And its role may vary as a function of factors like the comprehender's relation to the language. (Is it highly conventional? Is the comprehender paying close attention? Is she listening or reading to deeply understand, to act, or to get through the page as quickly as possible?)

Processes other than simulation are clearly at play, including superficial statistical ones—some words are more likely to invite a particular interpretation in some contexts than others. Knowledge about how grammar constrains combinatorial semantics is also in play. And beyond these are still higher-level pragmatic issues, like what a language user can infer about why a speaker would use a particular word or produce a particular utterance, what's presupposed, and implied, and so on.

3.2 Linguistic and extralinguistic sources of simulation

Simulation can be systematically affected by words, especially open-class words. There's now ample evidence that a noun or verb contributes content to be simulated. For instance, one study (Bergen et al. 2007) manipulated just whether a noun or a verb was associated with up or down, as in the examples below (the up- or down-associated words are italicized). The presence of just one such word in a sentence affected participants' ability to subsequently perceive a circle or square in the upper or lower part of the screen, which is interpreted as a consequence of location-specific simulation.

(1) a   The *sky* darkened.
    b   The *grass* glistened.
    c   The chair *toppled*.
    d   The mule *climbed*.

Much more generally, the presence of an open-class word can often be solely responsible for the appearance of a category of thing or event in simulation—a sentence that includes *toothbrush* will result in simulation of a toothbrush and possibly brushing of teeth.

But context—both linguistic and physical context—can affect the content of simulation. We've already seen that the words surrounding a given content word can affect the details of the simulation that corresponds to what it denotes—the orientation of a simulated toothbrush, for instance, depends on whether it's described in language as being found in the sink or a cup. There's also clear evidence that physical context affects simulation as well. It's been shown, for example, that when a person has seen an object in a particular configuration (for example, a vertical versus a horizontal toothbrush), their subsequent language-driven simulation processes are affected—it takes longer for someone who has previously seen a horizontal toothbrush in an unconnected task to read a sentence that implies a vertical toothbrush (Wassenburg and Zwaan 2010).

So at the minimum, simulation is sensitive to physical and lexical context. But it also appears that grammatical context plays a role in configuring simulation. Consider the difference between an action described using progressive versus perfect aspect, or active versus passive voice. Grammatical choices like these needn't change the details of the action itself, but they might change the simulation language users produce in response to them. Recent work shows that progressive aspect increases simulation of the nucleus of a described event (Bergen and Wheeler 2010), while perfect aspect augments endstate simulation (Madden and Zwaan 2003). Similarly, active voice might increase and passive voice might suppress simulation from the perspective of the agent (Bergen 2012). These effects of grammar constitute second-order contributions to simulation—they dictate not what to simulate but how to simulate it—what perspective to adopt or what part of the simulated event to focus on.

And it also appears that the goals of the language user or task-specific demands imposed on them affect simulation. Simply stated, people can approach language with different degrees of attention to semantic details. In experimental setups where they know that after a sentence, they'll be asked to decide whether an image depicts something mentioned in the sentence, people appear to activate more perceptual detail in simulation, as compared with situations where they are not asked to compare images with sentence content (Rommers et al. 2013). So the language user's orientation towards language—what they expect to need to do with it—can affect the richness of the perceptual simulations they construct (see Chapter 29 on semantic processing).

3.3 Simulation and abstract concepts

There are a number of obvious limits to what simulation might do for language use. Perhaps chief among these, simulation seems best suited to representing concrete perceptual or motor concepts, and less well suited for abstract concepts. Even if we're willing to stipulate that there's a case to be made that something in the semantics of *cat* or *jump* involves perceptual or motor simulation, the case seems much harder to make for *justice* or *truth* or *value*. Acknowledging this concern, some theorists have argued that concepts live on a cline from concrete to abstract, where the most abstract will have no use for simulation (Dove 2009; Chatterjee 2010).

But there are other perspectives worth discussing. The first, articulated by Barsalou and Wiemer-Hastings (2005), among others, argues that abstract concepts may be fleshed out through simulations of the situations in which those concepts are grounded. For instance, perhaps understanding the concept denoted by *truth* involves simulating the common experience of holding in mind a belief about the world, which is confirmed by observation of the world. For example, my experience of it being true that I'm writing this chapter on a laptop involves holding both the belief in mind that I'm writing on a laptop and the perceptual observation of the laptop in front of me. That match between belief and observation might ground my experience of what *truth* denotes. The experience is both situated and perceptually grounded in that it involves perceptual predictions and perceptual observations, and perhaps understanding the word *truth* involves running a simulation of a relevant prediction-perception match. Other senses of *truth* might involve not belief but assertions about the world, but the general form of the story would be similar. In sum, abstract concepts might be grounded through perceptual and motor simulations of their situations of use.

A second, more deeply explored view sees abstract concepts as grounded metaphorically in concrete ones (Lakoff and Johnson 1980). There's a long and rich tradition of linguistic research on metaphorical language—it's well documented that we frequently and conventionally speak about abstract concepts in concrete terms—in terms of physical objects (**doling out** *justice*; *a* **morsel** *of truth*) or physical space (**high** *value*). The embodied metaphor hypothesis proposes that we similarly conceive of abstract concepts in terms of concrete concepts (Gibbs 2006). That is, perhaps accessing the meanings of *justice* or *truth* involves brain systems dedicated to representing physical objects, and perhaps understanding the meaning of *value* involves brain systems dedicated to perceiving changes in vertical position.

Psychologists of language have been pursuing this hypothesis since the 1990s, and neuroscientists began joining the action about ten years later, along with social psychologists. To summarize these distinct literatures briefly, at present we know certain things. First, processing metaphorical language primes the actual source domain (for instance, reading about someone *blowing his stack* primes heat; Gibbs et al. 1997) and the reverse is also true (performing a grasping action speeds processing of *grasp an idea*; Wilson and Gibbs 2007). Second, brain systems specialized for perception and action sometimes do and sometimes do not become measurably active when people passively read metaphorical sentences like *He kicked the habit* (compare Aziz-Zadeh and Damasio 2008 with Tettamanti et al. 2005). One of the factors at play appears to be familiarity—less familiar metaphorical expressions induce greater activation in perception and action systems than more familiar expressions do (Desai et al. 2012). And finally, even in the absence of metaphorical language, there appear to be deep-seated connections that show up in real-world judgements and decision making. For instance, just as people who are kind and generous are often described metaphorically as *warm*, holding a warm coffee cup leads people to judge others as more kind and generous (Williams and Bargh 2008). We metaphorically describe morality as cleanliness and people not only show an increased preference for cleansing products after describing an immoral act they've performed, but also act as though the moral transgression has been washed away after physically cleaning their hands (Zhong and Liljenquist 2006). In sum, if not incontrovertible, there are several strands of research that converge on the conclusion that there are conceptual connections across domains that are connected through linguistic metaphor.

Clearly, there's much more to know about meaning and metaphorical and abstract language. And there are hints that a full account of how it works might involve simulation. Some might take this as a case of taking one of the most glaring weaknesses of a simulation-based account and turning it into a strength.

4 Current and future directions

Many questions remain about how simulation relates to meaning, and in this section I highlight several areas of continuing research.

4.1 Functions of simulation

While there is substantial evidence of simulation during language use, less is known about exactly what function it serves, if any. What role, mechanistically, does simulation serve in meaning-making?

A variety of possibilities have been entertained in the literature. Perhaps simulation serves as a representational format for semantics—that is, perhaps Mentalese or the Language of Thought is in fact articulated in terms of perceptual and motor simulations. Another possible use for simulation is to generate inferences. For instance, connecting the dots between *A colony of nudists moved in next door to Tristan* and the subsequent sentence *He decided to build a wall* involves a logical connecting step. Understanding the causal connection between the two propositions might involve simulating the visual details. Another possibility is that people might simulate to prepare to act. Upon hearing the word *scalpel*, a comprehender's belief about what's intended by that utterance might modulate the simulation they perform. If they believe they're being asked to hand someone the object, then they might prepare to do so by simulating manual interactions with it. But if they're merely being asked to point to the image of the object in a book, they might simulate that pointing action instead.

It's also possible that, while pervasive, simulation plays no functional role in meaning, as argued, for instance, by Pavan and Baggio (2013). On this account (Mahon and Caramazza 2008), simulation effects are epiphenomenal: meaning is constructed using abstract symbols that have no perceptual or motor substance, but which are connected to motor and perceptual systems such that activation spreads to those systems during language use. So what appear to be simulation effects are merely the consequence of non-functional downstream activation that results from and doesn't affect or play a role in meaning-making.

This deflationary account provides a useful counterweight to the enthusiasm generated by a stream of apparently confirmatory results indicating that systems for perception, motor control, and affect are also engaged during language use. It highlights the sorts of inference that can be reasonably drawn from studies using different methodologies. Facilitatory priming and brain imaging results cannot adjudicate between a causal and epiphenomenal role for simulation in meaning. But other methods discussed above, especially neuropsychological dissociation, magnetically induced impairments, and behavioural adaptation, do have the potential to address the functional role of simulation.

At present, however, those types of study are only starting to be applied systematically to different language functions to ask precisely what simulation does for meaning and under what circumstances. One tantalizing question remains—if simulation isn't necessary or sufficient for meaning, then what other processes are involved? How do people make meaning without simulation, and how does simulation coordinate with other meaning-related processes?

4.2 Simulation and gesture

If simulation involves generating an internal facsimile of actual perception and action, then how does it relate to the actual perception and action that people engage during communication through gesture? A number of papers have recently proposed that the production and perception of paralinguistic gesture might relate to simulation in a variety of ways. For one, gesture of certain types might be an external manifestation of simulation, enacted either when simulation surpasses some threshold for actual action (Hostetter and Alibali 2008) or for targeted communicative purposes—to affect the comprehension, including the simulated content, of the understander (Marghetis and Bergen 2014). On either of these accounts, gesture might be a tool that can be used to indirectly measure the presence or nature of simulation (Parrill et al. 2013). On the language perceiver's side, perceived gestures might indeed affect ongoing simulation, but the reverse is also possible—ongoing or prior simulation might affect how particular gestures are interpreted. In short, there may be ample room for productive work studying interactions between simulation and gesture.

4.3 Simulation and individual differences

One key component of the simulation account is that the capacity to simulate specific perceptual, motor, or affective experiences in response to language is the product of the individual's experiences. It follows that different experiential histories will produce different capacities and tendencies to simulate. This variation could in principle arise within a culture as the result of idiosyncratic or systematic intra-cultural variation or interculturally as a function of those precise dimensions along which culturally contingent experiences differ.

A second way that people might differ with respect to simulation involves individual differences, driven not by culturally contingent experience but differential cognitive styles and cognitive capacities. People with greater capacity for verbal working memory or a preference for verbal-auditory processing might simulate differently from people whose preferences and capacities lie more in the visual domain (Bergen 2012).

Promising early findings suggest that both experience and cognitive style predict differences in how language users simulate. For instance, cultural practice (for example, how many hands to use when transferring small objects to social superiors) produces motor simulation differences in Americans versus Koreans (Dennison and Bergen 2010). Experience playing hockey affects the use of the motor system while people are listening to descriptions of hockey actions (Beilock et al. 2008). And visualizers show greater visual simulation effects during language processing than verbalizers (Dils and Boroditsky 2010).

4.4 Limits of simulation

It's uncontroversial that there is a lot about meaning that simulation cannot account for. Metalinguistic intuitions—for instance, the feeling that the word *one* means precisely and not approximately one—are not easily dealt with through simulation alone. Simulation is clearly not sufficient for meaning, any more than visual perception is sufficient for what we know about objects. Work thus far has focused on expanding what we know about when simulation happens and what it does, while relatively less scrutiny has attended to what has to surround it—what other mechanisms must be in place alongside and integrated with simulation to account for all that humans do with respect to meaning. These appear to be productive directions in which the field is headed.

Further reading

Barsalou, L. W. 1999. Perceptual symbol systems. *Behavioral and Brain Sciences* 22: 577–660. This seminal article defines simulation and its potential role in language and other cognitive functions.

Bergen, B. 2012. *Louder than words: the new science of how the mind makes meaning*. New York: Basic Books. This book summarizes work on simulation and language, with sections on grammar, timing, abstract concepts, and individual and cross-linguistic differences.

Pecher, D. and Zwaan, R. A. (eds) 2005. *Grounding Cognition: The Role of Perception and Action in Memory, Language, and Thinking*. Cambridge: Cambridge University Press. This edited volume presents a collection of chapters from leaders in the field on core theoretical topics in embodied cognition and language.

Pulvermueller, F. 2002. *The Neuroscience of Language: On Brain Circuits of Words and Serial Order*. Cambridge: Cambridge University Press. This book proposes a unified theory of embodied grounding of language, based on well-understood principles of neurocomputation.

References

Aziz-Zadeh, L. and Damasio, A. 2008. Embodied semantics for actions: findings from functional brain imaging. *Journal of Physiology (Paris)* 102: 35–39.

Barsalou, L. W. 1999. Perceptual symbol systems. *Behavioral and Brain Sciences* 22: 577–660.

Barsalou, L. W., W. Kyle Simmons, A. K. Barbey and C. D. Wilson 2003. Grounding conceptual knowledge in modality-specific systems. *Trends in Cognitive Sciences* 72: 84–91.

Barsalou, L.W. and K. Wiemer-Hastings 2005. Situating abstract concepts. In D. Pecher and R. Zwaan (eds), *Grounding Cognition: The Role of Perception and Action in Memory, Language and Thought*. New York: Cambridge University Press, 129–163.

Beilock, S. L., I. M. Lyons, A. Mattarella-Micke, H. C. Nusbaum and S. L. Small 2008. Sports experience changes the neural processing of action language. In *Proceedings of the National Academy of Sciences USA*, 105: 13269–13273.

Bergen, B. K. 2012. *Louder than Words: The New Science of how the Mind Makes Meaning*. New York: Basic Books.

Bergen, B. 2007. Experimental methods for simulation semantics. *Methods in Cognitive Linguistics* 18: 277.

Bergen, B. and N. Chang 2005. Embodied construction grammar in simulation-based language understanding. In Jan-Ola Östman and Miriam Fried (eds), *Construction Grammars: Cognitive Grounding and Theoretical Extensions*. Amsterdam: John Benjamins, 147–190.

Bergen, B. and N. Chang 2013. Embodied construction grammar. In Thomas Hoffmann and Graeme Trousdale (eds), *Oxford Handbook of Construction Grammar*. Oxford: Oxford University Press, 168–190.

Bergen, B. K., S. Lindsay, T. Matlock and S. Narayanan 2007. Spatial and linguistic aspects of visual imagery in sentence comprehension. *Cognitive Science* 315: 733–764.

Bergen, B. and K. Wheeler 2010. Grammatical aspect and mental simulation. *Brain and Language* 112: 150–158.

Chatterjee, A. 2010. Disembodying cognition. *Language and Cognition* 2: 79–116.

Croft, W. and D. A. Cruse 2004. *Cognitive Linguistics*. Cambridge: Cambridge University Press.

Dennison, Heeyeon and Benjamin Bergen 2010. Language-driven motor simulation is sensitive to social context. *Proceedings of the 32nd Annual Meeting of the Cognitive Science Society*, 901–906.

Desai, R. H., J. R. Binder, L. L. Conant, Q. R. Mano and M. S. Seidenberg 2012. The neural career of sensorimotor metaphors. *Journal of Cognitive Neuroscience* 239: 2376–2386.

Dils, A. T. and L. Boroditsky 2010. A visual motion aftereffect from understanding motion language. In *Proceedings of the National Academy of Sciences USA*, 107: 16396–16400.

Dove, G. 2009. Beyond perceptual symbols: a call for representational pluralism. *Cognition* 1103: 412–31.

Feldman, J. and S. Narayanan 2004. Embodied meaning in a neural theory of language. *Brain and Language* 892: 385–392.

Fodor, J. 1975. *The Language of Thought*. New York: Crowell.

Fodor, J. A. 1998. *Concepts: Where Cognitive Science Went Wrong*. Oxford: Clarendon Press.

Gage, Nicole and Gregory Hickok 2005. Multiregional cell assemblies, temporal binding and the representation of conceptual knowledge in cortex: a modern theory by a classical neurologist, Carl Wernicke. *Cortex* 41: 823–832.

Gibbs, R. W. 2006. Metaphor interpretation as embodied simulation. *Mind and Language* 213: 434–458.

Gibbs, R. W., J. M. Bogdanovich, J. R. Sykes and D. J. Barr 1997. Metaphor in idiom comprehension. *Journal of Memory and Language* 37: 141–154.

Glenberg, A. M. and M. P. Kaschak 2002. Grounding language in action. *Psychonomic Bulletin and Review* 93: 558–565.

Glenberg, A. M. and D. A. Robertson 2000. Symbol grounding and meaning: a comparison of high-dimensional and embodied theories of meaning. *Journal of Memory and Language* 43: 379–401.

Glenberg, A. M., Sato, M. and L. Cattaneo 2008. Use-induced motor plasticity affects the processing of abstract and concrete language. *Current Biology* 18: R290–R291.

Harnad, S. 1990. The symbol grounding problem. *Physica D: Nonlinear Phenomena* 42: 335–346.

Hostetter, A. B. and M. W. Alibali 2008. Visible embodiment: gestures as simulated action. *Psychonomic Bulletin and Review* 153: 495–514.

Johansson, R., J. Holsanova and K. Holmqvist 2006. Pictures and spoken descriptions elicit similar eye movements during mental imagery, both in light and in complete darkness. *Cognitive Science* 306: 1053–1079.

Kaschak, M. P. and A. M. Glenberg 2000. Constructing meaning: the role of affordances and grammatical constructions in sentence comprehension. *Journal of Memory and Language* 43: 508–529.

Kaschak, M. P., C. J. Madden, D. J. Therriault, R. H. Yaxley, M. Aveyard, A. A. Blanchard and R. A. Zwaan 2005. Perception of motion affects language processing. *Cognition* 94: B79–B89.

Lakoff, G. and M. Johnson 1980. *Metaphors We Live By*. Chicago, IL: University of Chicago Press.

Landauer, T. K., P. W. Foltz and D. Laham 1998. An introduction to latent semantic analysis. *Discourse Processes* 25: 259–284.

Lund, K. and C. Burgess 1996. Producing high-dimensional semantic spaces from lexical co-occurrence. *Behavior Research Methods, Instruments and Computers* 28: 203–208.

Madden, C. J. and R. A. Zwaan 2003. How does verb aspect constrain event representations? *Memory and Cognition* 31: 663–672.

Mahon, B. Z. and A. Caramazza 2008. A critical look at the embodied cognition hypothesis and a new proposal for grounding conceptual content. *Journal of Physiology (Paris)* 1021: 59–70.

Marghetis, T. and B. Bergen 2014. Embodied meaning, inside and out: the coupling of gesture and mental simulation. In Cornelia Müller, Alan Cienki, Ellen Fricke, Silva H. Ladewig, David McNeill and Sedinha Tessendorf (eds.), *Body-Language-Communication*. New York: Mouton de Gruyter.

Narayanan, S. 1997. *KARMA: Knowledge-based active representations for metaphor and aspect*. Unpublished doctoral dissertation. University of California, Berkeley.

Parrill, F., B. Bergen and P. Lichtenstein 2013. Grammatical aspect, gesture and conceptualization: using co-speech gesture to reveal event representations. *Cognitive Linguistics* 241: 135–158.

Pavan, A. and G. Baggio 2013. Linguistic representations of motion do not depend on the visual motion system. *Psychological Science* 242: 181–188.

Pecher, D. and R. A. Zwaan 2005. *Grounding Cognition: The Role of Perception and Action in Memory, Language and Thinking*. Cambridge: Cambridge University Press.

Pulvermüller, F. 2003. *The Neuroscience of Language: On Brain Circuits of Words and Serial Order*. Cambridge: Cambridge University Press.

Richardson, D. C., M. J. Spivey, L. W. Barsalou and K. McRae 2003. Spatial representations activated during real-time comprehension of verbs. *Cognitive Science* 27: 767–780.

Rommers, J., A. S. Meyer, F. Huettig and J. Rommers 2013. Object shape and orientation do not routinely influence performance during language processing. *Psychological Science* 24: 2218–2225.

Sato, M. 2010. Message in the "body": effects of simulation in sentence production (Doctoral dissertation, University of Hawaii).

Saygin, A. P., S. McCullough, M. Alac and K. Emmorey 2010. Modulation of BOLD response in motion-sensitive lateral temporal cortex by real and fictive motion sentences. *Journal of Cognitive Neuroscience* 2211: 2480–2490.

Shapiro, K., F. M. Mottaghy, N. O. Schiller, T. D. Poeppel, M. O. Fluss, H. W. Muller, A. Caramazza and B. J. Krause 2005. Dissociating neural correlate for verbs and nouns. *Neuroimage* 24: 1058–1067.

Shapiro, K. A., A. Pascual-Leone, F. M. Mottaghy, M. Gangitano and A. Caramazza 2001. Grammatical distinctions in the left frontal cortex. *Journal of Cognitive Neuroscience* 136: 713–720.

Spivey, M. and J. Geng 2001. Oculomotor mechanisms activated by imagery and memory: Eye movements to absent objects. *Psychological Research* 65: 235–241.

Stanfield, R. A. and R. A. Zwaan 2001. The effect of implied orientation derived from verbal context on picture recognition. *Psychological Science* 12: 153–156.

Tettamanti, M., G. Buccino, M. C. Saccuman, V. Gallese, M. Danna, P. Scifo, F. Fazio, G. Rizzolatti, S. F. Cappa and D. Perani 2005. Listening to action-related sentences activates fronto-parietal motor circuits. *Journal of Cognitive Neuroscience* 17: 273–281.

Wassenburg, S. I. and R. A. Zwaan 2010. Readers routinely represent implied object rotation: the role of visual experience. *The Quarterly Journal of Experimental Psychology* 639: 1665–1670.

Wernicke, C. 1977 [1874]. Der aphasische Symptomenkomplex: eine psychologische Studie auf anatomischer Basis. In G. H. Eggert (ed.), *Wernicke's Works on Aphasia: A Sourcebook and Review*. The Hague: Mouton, 91–145.

Wernicke, C. 1977 [1885–1886]. Einige neuere Arbeiten ueber Aphasie. In G. H. Eggert (ed.), *Wernicke's Works on Aphasia: A Sourcebook and Review*. The Hague: Mouton, 31–40.

Willems, R. M., I. Toni, P. Hagoort and D. Casasanto, 2010. Neural dissociations between action verb understanding and motor imagery. *Journal of Cognitive Neuroscience* 22: 2387–2400.

Williams, L. E. and J. A. Bargh 2008. Experiencing physical warmth influences interpersonal warmth. *Science* 322: 606–607.

Wilson, N. L. and R. W. Gibbs, Jr. 2007. Real and imagined body movement primes metaphor comprehension. *Cognitive Science* 31: 721–731.

Wittgenstein, L. 1953. *Philosophical Investigations*. G. E. M. Anscombe and R. Rhees (eds.), G. E. M. Anscombe (trans.). Oxford: Blackwell.

Yee, E., E. Chrysikou, E. Hoffman and S. L. Thompson-Schill 2013. Manual experience shapes object representation. *Psychological Science* 246: 909–919.

Zhong, C. B. and K. Liljenquist 2006. Washing away your sins: threatened morality and physical cleansing. *Science* 313: 1451–1452.

Related topics

Chapter 2, Internalist semantics; Chapter 5, Cognitive semantics; Chapter 7, Categories, prototypes and exemplars; Chapter 26, Acquisition of meaning; Chapter 29, Semantic processing.

9
Linguistic relativity

Daniel Casasanto

1 Introduction

According to the theory of linguistic relativity, language shapes the way people think; as a result, speakers of different languages may think differently, in predictable ways. This proposal, often associated with the writings of Benjamin Whorf (1956; see also von Humboldt (1988); Sapir (1929)), has generated decades of controversy among linguists, psychologists, philosophers, and anthropologists. Many scholars believe the theory of linguistic relativity to be "wrong, all wrong" (Pinker (1994: 57); see also Bloom and Keil 2001), and some have sought to convince readers that research on the "Whorfian" question is pseudoscience (e.g. Pullum 1991). But, for a moment, imagine you are unaware of the history of this embattled idea. Imagine you are coming to the question, "Does language influence how we think?" for the first time, and reasoning from first principles. You might posit that: (1) Language is a nearly omnipresent part of the context in which we use our minds. (2) Thinking depends on context. (3) Therefore, language could have pervasive influences on how and what we think.

Does it? If so, *how* does language shape thought? Which parts of language influence which aspects of cognition or perception, and by what mechanisms? For much of the twentieth century, scholars despaired of answering these questions, pointing to two stumbling blocks for linguistic relativity. Some suggested that the "Whorfian" question was inherently circular, because tests of the influence of language on thought were contaminated by participants' use of language during the tests (Gleitman and Papafragou 2013; Pullum 1991). Others argued that, after decades of trying, proponents of linguistic relativity had only managed to produce evidence of "weak" and "banal" effects of language on thought (Pinker 1994: 65; see also McWhorter 2014). Yet, in the early twenty-first century, theoretical and experimental advances have reinvigorated efforts to understand how language influences our cognition and perception, and how people who speak different languages think differently as a consequence.

This chapter will focus on studies that have begun to address the two perennial concerns about research on linguistic relativity mentioned above. One set of studies overcomes the problem of circularity by showing patterns of behavior that differ as a function of linguistic experience, but which cannot be explained by the use of language during the test. The second set of studies overcomes concerns about the magnitude of the impact language can have on cognition, suggesting that words found in some languages but not others can radically transform people's minds, and have reshaped the world we live in.

To focus on studies that address these persistent causes of skepticism, I will omit discussion of a great deal of influential research on linguistic relativity that preceded them, including the many studies on color categories by Paul Kay and colleagues (e.g. Kay and Regier 2006), studies on ontological categories by John Lucy and colleagues (e.g. Lucy 1996), and studies on spatial frames of reference by Stephen Levinson and colleagues (e.g. Levinson 2003). Also, space precludes discussion of all of the variants of linguistic relativity that have been articulated; Whorf, himself, never stated any unitary "Whorfian hypothesis" (for discussion see Kay and Kempton (1984); Lucy (1992)).

2 Are Whorfian effects limited to effects of "thinking for speaking"?

Dan Slobin (1996: 75–76) proposed an influential version of linguistic relativity, arguing that language should affect cognition during the process of encoding our thoughts into words, or "thinking for speaking":

> There is a special kind of thinking that is intimately tied to language – namely, the thinking that is carried out, on-line, in the process of speaking. [. . .] "Thinking for speaking" involves picking those features of objects or events that . . . are readily encodable in the [speaker's] language.

Different languages may guide speakers to specify different kinds of information in their speech. Therefore, different languages may cause their speakers to activate different information in memory when recounting the same episode, or to highlight different information about the perceptible world when inspecting or describing the same scene.

Slobin (1996) gives the example that English and Spanish bias their speakers to specify different kinds of information in the verb when describing motion events. English motion verbs tend to specify a *manner* of motion (e.g. *running*, *flying*, *rolling*), whereas Spanish verbs more often specify a *path* of motion (e.g. *entering*, *exiting*). Although English typically includes path information in other parts of speech (e.g. in prepositions, as in "the bird flew *down* from the nest"), Spanish and other "path languages" like Korean often omit manner information altogether.

Slobin's PhD student, Kyung-ju Oh, tested whether differences in the linguistic encoding of path and manner can influence Koreans' and US English speakers' memories for motion events (Oh 2003). Monolingual participants, tested in their home countries, watched videos of people performing activities like strolling out of a building or trudging along a path, and described what they saw. Later, they received a surprise memory test probing details of these events. English and Korean speakers did not differ in their memory for path-relevant details, consistent with the salient encoding of path information across both languages, nor did they differ in their memory for control aspects of the events (e.g. the color of an actor's shirt). Yet the English speakers remembered more manner-relevant details than the Korean speakers, consistent with manner being more frequently encoded in the English speakers' event descriptions than in the Koreans'.

Oh's experiment showed a correlation between the way people talked about events and the way they remembered them later, suggesting that the way people code their experiences into language can influence performance on subsequent nonlinguistic tasks. Yet, on a skeptical interpretation of these results, it is possible that speakers used language to reconstruct the events from memory when asked to recall them, reactivating verbal descriptions consciously or unconsciously. If so, although Oh's memory task was "nonlinguistic," the results could be considered to be a type of thinking-for-speaking effect, provided that "speaking" includes covertly encoding experiences into words (i.e. speaking to one's self). Consistent with this possibility, subsequent studies suggest that language-specific differences in event representation disappear when participants perform a concurrent verbal task that interferes with using language online to encode the events (but not when they perform a concurrent non-verbal task; Trueswell and Papafragou 2010).

This pattern of results is not limited to tests of how language influences event representation. Across a variety of experimental paradigms, effects of language on cognition or perception are readily explained as effects of overt or covert thinking for speaking. Some of the most thoroughly studied effects of language on thought are extinguished under verbal interference conditions (e.g. effects of color vocabulary on color judgements; Winawer et al. (2007)). Such results have led some researchers to conclude that linguistic relativity effects are limited to thinking-for-speaking effects (cf. Slobin 2003), and even to argue that effects of language on thought may be strictly limited to circumstances that encourage participants to use language strategically to perform a task (Papafragou et al. 2008).

Some scholars have speculated that when people are *not* thinking for speaking, linguistic relativity effects should disappear (Clark 2003; Papafragou et al. 2007; Landau et al. 2010). For example, Eve Clark predicted that if truly nonlinguistic tests of linguistic relativity could be devised, their results should differ dramatically from the results of thinking-for-speaking-driven experiments:

> [W]e should find that in tasks that require reference to representations in memory that don't make use of any linguistic expression, people who speak different languages will respond in similar, or even identical, ways. That is, representations for nonlinguistic purposes may differ very little across cultures or languages.
>
> (2003: 22)

Clark added:

> Of course, finding the appropriate tasks to check on this without any appeal to language may prove difficult.
>
> (2003: 22)

3 Beyond thinking for speaking: Whorfian psychophysics

Casasanto and colleagues developed a strategy for meeting Clark's challenge: the "Whorfian psychophysics" paradigm. Psychophysics, one of the oldest branches of experimental psychology, is the study of how precisely organisms can encode, discriminate, or reproduce simple physical stimuli (e.g. the length of a line or the brightness of a flash of light). In our studies, differences between languages predicted differences in their speakers' mental representations, but these predictions were tested using psychophysical stimulus-reproduction tasks with nonlinguistic stimuli and responses.

The first set of experiments built upon a task that Casasanto and Boroditsky (2008) developed to investigate relationships between mental representations of time and space. In the original experiments, English speakers saw objects that varied in their spatial or temporal extents. In the canonical version of the task, lines of different spatial lengths and durations "grew" gradually across a computer screen, and disappeared when they had reached their maximum extent in both space and time. Participants were then asked to reproduce either the spatial or temporal extent of the stimulus by clicking the mouse to indicate the beginning and ending points of either the spatial or temporal interval. Participants were unable to ignore the spatial dimension of the stimuli when reproducing the temporal dimension: for lines of the same average duration, those that traveled a longer distance were judged to take a longer time, and those that traveled a shorter distance to take a shorter time. Numerous versions of this task showed the effect to persist over variations in perceptual, attentional, and mnemonic factors, in children and adults (see Bottini and Casasanto (2013) for a review). It appears that the tendency to conceptualize duration in terms of spatial distance is a robust aspect of temporal cognition – at least for English speakers.

3.1 Time in one or three dimensions

Like many other languages, English tends to describe duration in terms of one-dimensional spatial length (e.g. a *long* time, like a *long* rope; Alverson (1994); Evans (2004)). This unidimensional mapping has been assumed to be universal: a consequence of the unidirectional flight of time's arrow, and of universal aspects of our bodily interactions with the environment (Clark 1973). It is hard to avoid using uni-dimensional spatial metaphors when talking about the durations of events in English. Try replacing the word "long" in the phrase "a *long* meeting" with a synonym. Words like *lengthy*, *extended*, *protracted*, or *drawn out* would suffice – all of which express time in terms of linear extent.

In contrast with English speakers, however, Greek speakers tend to express duration in terms of volume or amount (e.g. a *lot of* time (*tr. poli* ora), like a *lot of* water (*tr. poli* nero)). Rather than "a *long* night," Greek speakers would say "a *big* night" (*tr. megali* nychta) to indicate that the night seemed to last a long time. Greek speakers *can* express duration in terms of linear extent, just as English speakers can make use of volume or amount expressions, but volume metaphors are more frequent and productive in Greek, whereas linear extent metaphors are more frequent and productive in English (Casasanto et al. 2004; Casasanto 2008; 2010).

Does the tendency to talk about duration in terms of one-dimensional or three-dimensional space influence the way people tend to think about it? To find out, in one set of experiments we gave English and Greek speakers a pair of nonlinguistic psychophysical tests of their ability to estimate duration in the presence of irrelevant length or volume information (Casasanto et al. 2004; Casasanto 2008; 2010). In the length interference task, participants were asked to reproduce the durations of lines that gradually extended across the screen while trying to ignore the lines' spatial length, as described above. In the volume interference task, participants reproduced the durations for which they saw a container gradually filling up, while trying to ignore the container's fullness.

As before, English speakers had difficulty screening out interference from spatial distance when estimating duration: lines that traveled a longer distance were mistakenly judged to take a longer time than lines of the same duration that traveled a shorter distance. But their time estimates were relatively unaffected by irrelevant volume information. Greek speakers showed the opposite pattern. They had more difficulty screening out interference from volume, so fuller containers were judged to remain on the screen for more time than emptier containers, but their judgements were relatively unaffected by the spatial extent of lines. The pattern of distance and volume interference in these nonlinguistic psychophysical tasks reflected the relative prevalence of distance and volume metaphors for duration in English and Greek. Similar patterns were found in speakers of Indonesian (a "distance language") vs. speakers of Spanish (a "volume language"; Casasanto et al. 2004).

In these experiments, participants were informed before each trial whether they would need to reproduce the spatial or temporal dimension of the stimulus. Is it possible that these results were due to participants covertly labeling the relevant dimension of the stimuli as they perceived or reproduced it? If so, these experiments would be subject to the same inferential limitations of previous studies whose results can be explained by the online use of language: an effect of thinking for covert speaking. Fortunately, this skeptical possibility is ruled out by the design of the experiments. We cannot know whether participants *tried* to label the stimuli (e.g. using words like "long" and "short" covertly), but we can definitively rule out the possibility that the observed effects were due to such verbal labeling. In each experiment there were nine different levels of duration (the durations ranged from 1 to 5 seconds, increasing in 500-millisecond increments), which were fully crossed with nine different levels of length or volume (e.g. the lengths ranged from 100 to 500 pixels, increasing in 50-pixel increments). Due to the crossing of these levels (i.e., pairing each level of space with each level of time), space and time were orthogonal: there was no correlation between the spatial and temporal magnitudes of the stimuli.

Because of this feature of the experimental design, it is impossible that labeling the relevant dimension could produce the predicted effect of interference from the irrelevant dimension – which varied orthogonally. Consider, for example, a participant who labeled all of the long-duration lines "long" and the short duration lines "short" during the time estimation trials. This labeling strategy, if it affected time estimates at all, would only work *against* the effect of spatial length on time estimation, given that spatial length was orthogonal to time. Even if participants attempted to label durations of the stimuli as "long" or "short" (etc.), the experimental design ensured that the predicted effects of space on time estimation occurred in spite of this labeling strategy, not because of it.

3.2 Beyond a language-thought correlation

The cross-linguistic comparison between Greek and English speakers shows a correlation between temporal language and temporal thinking. Can language play a causal role in shaping nonlinguistic time representations? To test whether using volume metaphors in language can change the way people think about duration, the experimenters trained English speakers to use Greek-like metaphors for time (Casasanto 2008; 2010). After about 20 minutes of exposure to these new metaphors, the effect of irrelevant volume information on English speakers' nonlinguistic duration estimates was statistically indistinguishable from the effect found in native Greek speakers. Together, these data show that people who use different temporal metaphors in their native languages conceptualize time the way they talk about it, even when they are not using language. Furthermore, linguistic experience can play a causal role in shaping mental representations of time. Producing or understanding spatio-temporal language like a Greek speaker, even for a few minutes, can cause English speakers to think about time differently, using a different kind of spatial scaffolding.

3.3 Alternative spatial metaphors for musical pitch

The Whorfian psychophysics paradigm used to establish cross-linguistic differences in temporal thinking has been extended to probe language-based differences in people's mental representations of musical pitch. Like English, Dutch describes pitches as "high" (*hoog*) or "low" (*laag*), but this is not the only possible spatial metaphor for pitch. In Farsi, high pitches are "thin" (*nāzok*) and low pitches are "thick" (*koloft*). Dutch and Farsi speakers' performance on nonlinguistic pitch reproduction tasks reflects these linguistic differences (Dolscheid et al. 2013). Participants were asked to reproduce the pitch of tones that they heard in the presence of irrelevant spatial information: lines that varied in their height (height interference task) or their thickness (thickness interference task). Dutch speakers' pitch estimates showed stronger cross-dimensional interference from spatial height, and Farsi speakers' from the thickness of visually presented stimuli. This effect was not explained by differences in accuracy or in musical training between groups. When Dutch speakers were trained to talk about pitches using Farsi-like metaphors (e.g. a tuba sounds *thicker* than a flute) for 20–30 minutes, their performance on the nonlinguistic thickness interference task became indistinguishable from native Farsi speakers'. Experience using one kind of spatial metaphor or another in language can have a causal influence on nonlinguistic pitch representations.

These space-pitch interference studies used a similar design to the space-time interference studies described above: nine levels of space were crossed with nine levels of pitch. Therefore, the experimental design rules out the possibility that labeling pitches with spatial words (e.g. "high" or "low") could produce the observed effects; on the contrary, using such verbal labels for pitch during the task could only work against the predicted effects of height or thickness on pitch reproduction. To underscore the point that differences between Dutch and Farsi speakers' pitch reproduction were not caused by using language online (i.e., by thinking for speaking to one's self), Dolscheid et al. (2013) asked Dutch speakers to do the height interference task while performing a secondary verbal suppression task that prevented them from encoding the stimuli verbally. If the effect of height on pitch were driven by covertly labeling the stimuli using spatial words, then it should disappear under verbal interference. However, we hypothesized that this effect was not due to online use of spatial metaphors for pitch in language, but rather to the activation of an implicit association between nonlinguistic representations of space and pitch in memory: a *mental metaphor* (Casasanto 2010; Lakoff and Johnson 1999). If so, the effect of height on pitch should persist under verbal interference. Consistent with this prediction, the effect of height on pitch reproduction in Dutch speakers was equally strong with and without concurrent verbal suppression.

3.4 The role of language in shaping mental metaphors

What role does spatial language play in shaping nonlinguistic representations of time and pitch? Is language creating cross-domain associations, or is linguistic experience modifying pre-linguistic mental metaphors? Pre-linguistic infants appear to intuit a link between more duration and more spatial extent (Srinivasan and Carey 2010), and also between more duration and more size (Lourenco and Longo 2011). Thus, both the distance-duration mapping that is most prevalent in English and the volume-duration mapping that is most prevalent in Greek may be present pre-linguistically. Likewise, infants as young as four months old are sensitive to the height-pitch mapping found in Dutch-speaking adults (but not in Farsi-speaking adults), and also to the thickness-pitch mapping found in Farsi-speaking adults (but not in Dutch-speaking adults; Dolscheid et al. (2014)). There is no need, therefore, to posit that using linguistic metaphors causes people to construct these mappings *de novo*.

Together, these infant and adult data support a developmental story with two chapters. First, children represent duration via a family of spatial mappings, which includes mappings from both spatial length and volume. Likewise, they represent pitch via mappings from both height and thickness. These initial mappings may be universal, based either on innate cross-domain correspondences (Walker et al. 2010) or on early-learned correlations between source and target domains in children's experience with the physical world (Lakoff and Johnson 1999). The distance-duration and volume-duration mappings could be learned by observing that more time passes as objects travel farther distances and as quantities accumulate in three-dimensional space. Height-pitch mappings could be learned from seeing (or feeling) the larynx rise and fall as people produce higher and lower pitches with their voices. Thickness-pitch mappings could be learned from observing the natural correlation between the size of an object or animal and the sound that it makes (imagine the sound made by banging on a soda can vs. an oil drum).

Later, linguistic experience modifies these pre-linguistic source-target mappings. Suppose each time speakers use a linguistic metaphor like "a *long* meeting" or "a *high* soprano" they activate the corresponding mental metaphor. Repeatedly activating one source-target mapping instead of another (e.g. height-pitch instead of thickness-pitch) should strengthen the activated mapping and, as a consequence, weaken the competing mapping via competitive learning (Casasanto 2008; Dolscheid et al. 2013). This process of strengthening one spatial mapping during language use, at the expense of the alternative spatial mapping, may explain how universal space-time and space-pitch mappings in infants become language-specific mappings in adults.

On this account, our mental metaphors are structured hierarchically (Casasanto and Bottini 2014). Specific mappings, conditioned by linguistic experience, are selected from families of mappings conditioned by relationships between source and target domains in the natural world. This hierarchical structure may help to explain how source-target mappings can be important for our representations of target domains but also surprisingly flexible. For example, perhaps Dutch speakers could be trained to think like Farsi speakers so quickly because they did not have to *learn* the thickness-pitch mapping during their 20–30 minutes of using Farsi-like linguistic metaphors. Rather, this linguistic training strengthened the association between thickness and pitch that was present in participants' minds from infancy (as indicated by data from Dutch four-month-olds), but which had been weakened as a consequence of their frequent use of height-pitch metaphors in language.

One prediction of this account (called Hierarchical Mental Metaphors Theory; Casasanto and Bottini (2014)) is that specific source-target mappings should be easy to activate via linguistic training so long as they are members of a family of nonlinguistic source-target mappings encoded in our minds (over either phylogenetic or ontogenetic time) on the basis of observable source-target correspondences in the world. Mappings that are not members of a pre-linguistically established family – and that do not reflect correlations between source and target domains in the natural world – should be relatively hard to activate via training, because these mappings would need to be created, not just strengthened.

In a test of this prediction, Dutch speakers were trained to use a thickness-pitch mapping that is the reverse of the mapping found in Farsi, and in the natural world: thin=low and thick=high. These "reverse-Farsi"-trained participants received the same amount of training as the participants trained to use the Farsi-like mapping. Whereas Farsi-like training had a significant effect on participants' nonlinguistic pitch representations, reverse-Farsi training had no effect (Dolscheid et al. 2013). Thus, brief linguistic experience caused Dutch participants to use the thickness-pitch mapping that reflects correlations between thickness and pitch in the world (and is evident in pre-linguistic infants). Yet the same amount of linguistic experience was not effective at instilling the opposite thickness-pitch mapping, which has no obvious experiential correlates, and is therefore not predicted to be among the pre-linguistically established space-pitch mappings.

3.5 Summary of Whorfian psychophysics findings

It is possible to test Whorfian questions without using words, thereby escaping the circularity that can result from using language as a source of hypotheses about the mind and also as a means to test these hypotheses. Furthermore, it is possible to construct experiments that show influences of language on nonlinguistic mental representations: representations that are "nonlinguistic" insomuch as (a) they are found, in some form, in pre-linguistic infants, (b) they are continuous and difficult to describe adequately using the lexical categories available in ordinary non-technical speech, and (c) they can be activated without using language overtly or covertly, and persist in the presence of a verbal suppression task.

In the cases of space-duration and space-pitch mappings, it appears that the role of linguistic experience is to modify the strength of pre-linguistically available cross-domain associations. As a result of using one kind of verbal metaphor or another repeatedly, speakers who rely on different metaphors in language subsequently activate different mental representations of time and pitch, scaffolded by different kinds of spatial representations. These results provide the first evidence that using language can have *offline effects* on speakers' mental representations – that linguistic relativity effects are not limited to thinking-for-speaking effects.

4 When are the effects of language on thought "important"?

The psychophysical studies reviewed above suggest that experience using language can cause people to form systematically different mental representations, even if they are not using language online, at the moment they form them. These studies address one longstanding concern about linguistic relativity effects: circularity. Yet they do not fully address a second longstanding concern: are these language-induced cognitive differences *important*? Some researchers have concluded that they are not: either because the effects are context-dependent (Gleitman and Papafragou 2013), or because cross-linguistic differences do not appear to radically change the way speakers of different languages perceive or understand their world (McWhorter 2014). This conclusion appears to emerge from three common beliefs about linguistic relativity research or about how our minds work, more broadly – beliefs that bear reexamination.

4.1 Belief no. 1: if mental representations are flexible, they must not be very important

Some researchers suggest that because effects of language on thought "are malleable and flexible," they "do not appear to shape core biases in . . . perception and memory" (Trueswell and Papafragou (2010), writing about effects of language on motion event representation). Indeed, all of the Whorfian effects mentioned so far are flexible: influences of motion descriptions on event representations and influences of color words on color judgements are modulated by verbal interference. Influences of spatial metaphors on nonlinguistic representations of duration and pitch can be rapidly changed by new patterns of experience using linguistic metaphors. However, the fact that these representations are flexible and context-dependent does not make them unimportant: if this were the case, then *all mental representations* would be "unimportant."

In the twentieth century, cognitive scientists took seriously the notions that our minds contain a mental dictionary of word meanings (e.g. Johnson-Laird 1987) and a mental encyclopedia of concepts (e.g. Pinker 1999). These technical metaphors have a misleading entailment. Entries in a dictionary or an encyclopedia are essentially unchanging: once written, the entries are simply looked up subsequently. Any aspect of a concept or word meaning that can change, then, is often deemed peripheral: not part of the true, "core" entry in our dictionary or encyclopedia. Yet the idea that thoughts are fixed entities in a mental repository, which are simply accessed when needed, is incompatible with what we know about brains. Thoughts (i.e. concepts, percepts, feelings, word meanings) are instantiated in brains, and brains are always changing; therefore, thoughts are always changing. Although space prohibits elaboration of this argument (see Casasanto and Lupyan (2015); Spivey (2007)), it should be unsurprising that the mental representations people form during linguistic relativity experiments are context-dependent; our mental representations are flexible and context-dependent – arguably, without exception (see Besner et al. (1997); James (1890); and see Chapter 2).

4.2 Belief no. 2: the goal of relativity research is to demonstrate differences between minds, therefore relativity effects are only important if they show radical differences

If the primary goal of relativity research were to show that people with different experiences think differently, then the more dramatic the between-group differences were, the more important the results would be. For many researchers, however, demonstrating cross-linguistic differences in thinking is a means to an end – not an end in itself.

The most fundamental goal of linguistic relativity research is to determine whether and how language shapes thought: that is, whether language merely reflects our conceptualizations of the world, or whether it also contributes to those conceptualizations. If the latter, then language can provide part of the answer to myriad questions about how cognition and perception develop, and how they change throughout the lifetime on various timescales. Comparing ways of thinking across language groups, to determine whether people who talk differently also think differently, is one powerful way to work toward the more basic goal of determining how language shapes thought. Tests of linguistic relativity can advance our scientific understanding of the origins and structure of our knowledge *whether or not* they show that members of different groups form radically different mental representations when presented with the same stimuli.

4.3 Belief no. 3: there's no evidence that cross-linguistic differences can produce radical differences between minds

Before the twenty-first century, there may have been no evidence for any *single* cross-linguistic difference that produces radical differences in speakers' thoughts. Yet dramatic differences in thinking could arise from the combination of many subtle differences between languages. So far, cross-linguistic differences in thinking have been reported across many fundamental domains of human experience. Language not only influences representations of *motion events* (e.g. Oh 2003), *duration* (e.g. Casasanto et al. 2004), *color* (e.g. Thierry et al. 2009; Winawer et al. 2007), and *pitch* (Dolschied et al. 2013), but also representations of *spatial relationships* (e.g. Levinson and Brown 1994; McDonough et al. 2003), *concrete objects* (e.g. Boroditsky et al. 2003; Lucy and Gaskins 2001; Srinivasan 2010), *theory of mind* (e.g. Lohmann and Tomasello 2003; Papafragou 2002, cf., Papafragou et al. 2008), *causation* (e.g. Fausey and Boroditsky 2011; Wolff et al. 2009), and *number* (e.g. Frank et al. 2008; Spelke and Tsivkin 2001).

Some aspects of language may have pervasive effects on thought. For example, applying grammatical gender to nouns can influence mental representations of their referents (e.g. Boroditsky et al. 2003). Naming an object like a table with a masculine noun (*il tavolo* in Italian) or a feminine noun (*la table* in French) can influence how people conceptualize these objects, causing speakers of different languages to endow the objects with stereotypically masculine or feminine qualities. The influence of gender on each object may be subtle, but since gender is applied to every noun (and often reiterated on verbs and adjectives), the collective effect of arbitrarily sexing every nameable object in one's lexicon could be substantial – whether or not such an effect is available to introspection. Moreover, when the pervasive effects of gender on object representations are combined with the effects of many other aspects of language on many other aspects of thought (such as those listed above), the aggregate of their individual effects could be that speakers of different languages tend to activate manifestly different conceptions of the same objects and events. It may be shortsighted, therefore, to dismiss apparently non-radical effects of language on thought as unimportant, theoretically or practically.

Furthermore, twenty-first-century research on language and thought provides evidence of at least one example of a radically mind-altering effect of language on thought. Language appears to transform our minds by playing a crucial role in creating the domain of *large exact number*, causing the thoughts entertained in some language communities to be incommensurable with the thoughts entertained in others. This cognitive transformation, in turn, has wrought immeasurable changes on the world as we know it.

4.4 Effects of language that transform mind and world

Imagine showing an adult a tray with four apples on it, taking it away, then showing them another tray with five apples on it and asking which tray held more apples: could they tell you? The answer appears to be: only if their language provides words for "four" and "five."

Children are not born with the capacity to represent "large" exact quantities, meaning quantities greater than three, nor do they develop this capacity through universal aspects of physical and social experience. They develop the capacity to mentally represent "exactly four," or "exactly seventeen," studies suggest, only if they are exposed to a list of counting numbers in their language. It is easy to take the existence of a verbal count list for granted, since they are found in the languages used by all modern, industrialized cultures. Yet counting systems like ours are recent and rare in human history, and are still unknown to people in many cultures (Dehaene 1999).

Human infants start out with two systems for representing quantity that they share with non-human animals: a system for individuating small collections of objects (up to three), and a system for representing and comparing large approximate quantities (Carey 2004; 2009; Dehaene 1999; Feigenson et al. 2004). The first *parallel individuation* system allows children to determine whether a box contains two toys or three, but does not enable them to reliably distinguish three toys from four. The second *approximate number* system allows them to distinguish larger collections of objects from one another so long as their ratio is sufficiently large. Infants under six months old can only discriminate quantities if their ratio is 1:2 (Feigenson et al. 2004). Eventually, the approximate number system becomes attuned to closer ratios, but discrimination performance remains probabilistic even in adults who rely on this system, and never attains the precision needed to reliably discriminate nine objects from ten, or to entertain an idea like "exactly 78." Separately and together, the parallel individuation and approximate number systems lack the power to represent number as we know it, or even to represent positive integers – something that seems to come naturally to Western children from their earliest years of school.

Carey (2004; 2009) posited that learning the list of counting words in their native language is what allows children to exceed the representational capacities of their primitive number systems, over a lengthy developmental process. Children first learn to say the numbers in order as a word game (typically the numbers one through ten in Western cultures), much like they learn nonsensical nursery rhymes: they can recite the numbers in order, but they do not understand them. Through having the spoken numbers matched with fingers or collections of objects, children start to understand that each number word refers to a precise quantity. First they learn that "one" refers to one object. Weeks or months later they learn that "two" refers to two objects. At this stage of being a "two-knower," children asked for "two marbles" can deliver the correct number, but when asked for "three marbles" or "four marbles" they will respond with some small collection of marbles greater than two. Eventually, after a period as "three-knowers," children induce how counting works; number becomes a productive system, where each number word in the count list refers to a unique numerosity, and successive number words refer to numerosities that differ by exactly one. (Acquiring the semantics of natural language quantifiers may contribute to the acquisition of small exact number concepts (Barner et al. 2007). This claim is distinct from the claim discussed here, that a verbal count list is essential for the acquisition of large exact number concepts.)

Some details of the process by which children learn to map number words to numerosities remain unclear, but there is now compelling evidence that language is essential for the acquisition and use of large exact number concepts. It appears that in the absence of a count list in language, people do not develop the capacity to enumerate exact quantities greater than three. Initial evidence for this radical claim came from a study by Peter Gordon (2004), who tested the numerical abilities of an Amazonian people known as the Pirahã. The Pirahã have no words for exact numbers. They quantify collections of things using the terms *hói* (about one), *hoí* (about two), and *baágiso* (many; see Frank et al. 2008). When Gordon (2004) asked members of the Pirahã tribe to perform a set of simple counting tasks their responses suggested a surprising lack of numerical competence. In one task Gordon asked each of his Pirahã participants to watch him drop up to nine nuts into a can. He then withdrew the nuts one by one and asked the participant to indicate when the can was empty. If the participants were counting nuts, this task would be easy. Yet the participants were unable to evaluate the number of nuts correctly. Some participants responded incorrectly even when there were only two or three nuts in the can. About half of the participants responded incorrectly when there were four nuts in the can, and the majority responded incorrectly when there were more than four nuts. On the basis of results like these, Gordon (2004: 498) concluded that "the Pirahã's impoverished counting system truly limits their ability to enumerate exact quantities when set sizes exceed two or three items," thus advancing two radical claims: (1) The Pirahã are unable to mentally represent exact numbers greater than three and (2) They lack this representational capacity because they lack number words. The first claim challenges the universality of humans' basic numerical competence, and the second supports a radical version of linguistic relativity, often called linguistic determinism: the limits of one's vocabulary can determine the limits of one's conceptual repertoire.

Although both of Gordon's (2004) claims have been supported by subsequent studies, initially they were strongly criticized, not only by opponents of linguistic relativity (Gelman and Gallistel 2004) but also by its proponents (Casasanto 2005; Frank et al. 2008). Limitations of the data from this pioneering study preclude drawing any conclusions about the Pirahã's numerical competence, and limitations of the experimental design preclude drawing conclusions about a causal role for language in shaping numerical abilities.

Concerning the data, the Pirahã not only failed tasks that rely on exact enumeration, like the nuts-in-a-can task, they also failed simpler tasks that can be completed without drawing on exact number representations greater than one. In one task, Gordon (2004) placed a stick on a flat surface to delineate the experimenter's side from the participant's side. He then arranged batteries in a row on his side of the partition and asked the participants to arrange batteries on their side so as to "make it the same" (p. 497). In another version of this task, the experimenter drew lines on a piece of paper, and asked participants to copy them. Crucially, these and other similar tasks do not require exact enumeration. It would be possible to create a matching array of batteries, for example, by aligning them spatially, placing batteries on the surface in one-to-one correspondence with the example array. The fact that the Pirahã did not do this suggests that they did not understand the goal of the task. It is informative that the Pirahã did not respond randomly; the number of batteries (or lines or nuts) in their responses were correlated with the number of items in the stimuli, suggesting that they were producing an *approximate match*, using their approximate number system. They appear to have been performing a different task from the one the experimenter intended.

The fact that the Pirahã failed to create matching arrays even on tasks that could be completed successfully without exact enumeration renders their failures on the other exact-number-requiring tasks completely uninterpretable. The one-to-one matching tasks served as a *manipulation check*: an experimental condition that allows the experimenter to verify that the tasks are working as planned (e.g. that the participants understand the instructions and the goal of the task). If participants fail the manipulation check, then their failures on the conditions of interest cannot be interpreted with respect to the experimental hypothesis. Put simply, if participants fail the manipulation check, the experiment is a failure, and it teaches us nothing. In this case, the Pirahã rarely gave the correct answer on tasks that could be solved by one-to-one matching or spatial alignment. Therefore, we cannot interpret their failures on tasks that require exact enumeration as evidence that they lack large exact number concepts.

Fortunately, this weakness of the data was addressed by a subsequent study. Michael Frank and colleagues (Frank et al. 2008) returned to the Pirahã and performed five tasks that were similar to Gordon's: two tasks could be solved via one-to-one matching, and therefore served as manipulation checks. The remaining three tasks could only be performed correctly by creating a representation of an exact number. This time, the data provided clear evidence that the Pirahã understood the tasks; they passed the manipulation checks, matching the number of objects that the experimenter presented with almost perfect accuracy for arrays of up to ten objects. Yet they failed to reproduce the correct number of objects when the tasks required exact enumeration (e.g. nuts in a can). As in Gordon's (2004) data, the Pirahã's responses approximated the target number, but participants rarely gave the correct answer for quantities greater than four. Since they passed the manipulation checks, these failures cannot be explained away as failures to understand the task. Rather, these data show that the capacity to represent "exactly four" as distinct from "exactly five" is not a human universal, validating Gordon's (2004) first claim and supporting a foundational assumption of Carey's (2004; 2009) model of how large exact number competence is acquired through language.

Yet for both Gordon's (2004) and Frank and colleagues' (2008) study, limitations of the experimental design preclude any claims about a causal role for language in shaping number concepts. These studies each reported data from only one group of participants, but implicitly the studies were cross-cultural comparisons between the Pirahã and Western adults (who were shown subsequently to perform almost perfectly on these simple enumeration tasks (Frank et al. 2012)). Therefore, the studies used a *quasi-experimental* design: participants were not randomly assigned to treatment and control groups, as they would be in a study using a *randomized-controlled* experimental design (i.e. participants were not assigned to be "treated" with number words or not). Quasi-experiments, no matter how well executed, cannot support causal inferences; they can only show correlations. In these studies, the experimental design was capable of showing a correlation between people's number vocabularies and their capacity for exact enumeration. The studies were not capable of showing a causal role for language in shaping number representations; thus, they were not capable, even in principle, of supporting a claim for linguistic determinism.

It is often challenging to implement randomized-controlled experiments in the field, and researchers must settle for constructing correlational studies so as to rule out alternative explanations for the correlations they observe. In the case of the studies by Gordon (2004) and by Frank et al. (2008), there was a looming alternative to the suggestion that language shapes numerical abilities; perhaps *culture* shapes numerical abilities. Cultures that have a counting system in language differ from cultures that lack such a system in many ways, making it difficult to isolate the role of language. The Pirahã results suggest that keeping track of large exact quantities is not critical for getting along in Pirahã society. In the absence of any environmental or cultural demand for exact enumeration, perhaps the Pirahã never developed this representational capacity – and consequently, they never developed the words (Casasanto 2005). On this view, perhaps being part of a numerate society is what drives the development of exact number concepts in individuals' minds: not language.

This skeptical possibility was addressed in a study by Elizabet Spaepen and colleagues (Spaepen et al. 2011) who tested numerical competence in Nicaraguan homesigners: deaf individuals who do not have access to any working model of language, oral or manual, and who have developed an idiosyncratic set of gestures to communicate, called *homesigns*. Although deprived of language, these homesigning adults are nevertheless functional members of a numerate society, and are exposed to opportunities and motivations to enumerate things exactly. Nevertheless, the homesigners could not consistently match target sets greater than three. Like the Pirahã, the homesigners were capable of approximating the target numbers (e.g. extending approximately the same number of fingers as the experimenter had shown them), but not matching them exactly. Thus, even when integrated into a numerate society, individuals do not spontaneously develop representations of large exact numerosities without input from a conventional language with a counting system.

Together, these findings provide compelling evidence that the capacity to represent exact numerosities greater than three is not a human universal. They also strongly suggest that a counting system in language may be necessary for the development of large exact number concepts. The data, to date, are correlational and cannot demonstrate a causal role for language in the development of number concepts, but no credible alternative has been advanced in light of the evidence that enculturation in a numerate society is not sufficient to drive the development of numeracy in individuals (Spaepen et al. 2011).

People exposed to number words develop a new representational capacity, and can entertain thoughts that are unthinkable by people who lack this linguistic experience: not only thoughts like, "What's the 12th digit of Pi?" but also thoughts like, "I'll have a dozen eggs" or "Take four steps forward." The capacity to represent and manipulate exact numbers is fundamental to the world as we know it, underlying the science and engineering that produced the buildings we live in, the medicines we take, the cars we drive, and the computers at our fingertips. Without exposure to a count list in language, it appears that the large exact number representations in our minds would not exist; without large exact number, our modern, technological world would not exist. As such, it seems reasonable to suggest that large exact number provides an example of one conceptual domain in which language has a dramatic and transformative effect on thought (cf. Pinker 1994; Bloom and Keil 2001; McWhorter 2014).

5 Varieties of linguistic relativity effects

How does language shape thought, over what timescale, by what mechanism, and how dramatic are the effects? There are no single answers to these questions. There are many parts of language, many aspects of cognition and perception, and many possible ways in which they can interact. This chapter illustrated how the grammatical packaging of information about motion events can *direct attention* to different aspects of the perceptible world, influencing what people remember about their experiences, at least so long as they can encode these experiences in words. Using different spoken metaphors can *strengthen some implicit associations in memory while weakening others*, leading to differences in the mental representation of time and musical pitch that can be found even when people are prevented from using language. Linking nouns with gendered determiners can *highlight certain features of objects or ideas*, making these features more salient for speakers of one language than for speakers of another, thus changing mental representations of nouns' referents in ways that may be subtle but pervasive. Finally, by serving as placeholders in an ordered sequence, number words can help to *create a new representational capacity*: one that radically changes our mind and world. When researchers arrive at different answers to questions about linguistic relativity this may be due, in part, to their examining different kinds of language-thought interactions, which operate over different timecourses, by different mechanisms.

Acknowledgements

This research was supported in part by grants from Junta de Andalucía, the European Regional Development Fund (P09-SEJ-4772), and the Spanish Ministry of Economy and Competitiveness (PSI2012-32464), and by a James S. McDonnell Foundation Scholar Award (220020236).

Further reading

Carey, S. 2004. Bootstrapping and the origin of concepts. *Daedalus* 133, 59–68. A brief overview of Susan Carey's proposal that number words play a critical role in the development of number concepts.

Casasanto, D. 2008. Who's afraid of the Big Bad Whorf? Cross-linguistic differences in temporal language and thought. *Language Learning* 58: 177, 63–79. A rebuttal to an influential critique of linguistic relativity.

Dolscheid, S., S. Shayan, A. Majid, and D. Casasanto 2013. The thickness of musical pitch: psychophysical evidence for linguistic relativity. *Psychological Science* 24: 613–621. An illustration of "offline" effects of language on thought, showing that previous linguistic experience can influence subsequent thinking.

Frank, M. C., D. L., Everett, E. Fedorenko, and E. Gibson 2008. Number as a cognitive technology: evidence from Pirahã language and cognition. *Cognition* 108: 819–824. Evidence that an indigenous Amazonian group has neither exact number words nor exact number concepts.

Whorf, B. L. 1956. *Language, Thought, and Reality: Selected Writings of Benjamin Lee Whorf*. Edited by John B. Carroll. Cambridge, MA: MIT Press. A collection of Benjamin Lee Whorf's writings on relationships between language and thought.

References

Alverson, H. 1994. *Semantics and Experience: Universal Metaphors of Time in English, Mandarin, Hindi, and Sesotho*. Baltimore: Johns Hopkins University Press.

Barner, D., D. Thalwitz, J. Wood, and S. Carey 2007. On the relation between the acquisition of singular-plural morpho-syntax and the conceptual distinction between one and more than one. *Developmental Science* 10: 365–373.

Besner, D., J. A. Stolz and C. Boutilier 1997. The Stroop effect and the myth of automaticity. *Psychonomic Bulletin and Review* 42: 221–225.

Bloom, P. and F. C. Keil 2001. Thinking through language. *Mind and Language* 164: 351–367.

Boroditsky, L., L. A. Schmidt and W. Phillips 2003. Sex, syntax, and semantics. In D. Gentner and S. Goldin-Meadow (eds) *Language in Mind: Advances in the Study of Language and Thought*. Cambridge, MA: MIT Press, 61–79.

Bottini, R. and D. Casasanto, 2013. Space and time in the child's mind: metaphoric or ATOMic? *Frontiers in Cognition*. doi: 10.3389/fpsyg.2013.00803

Carey, S. 2004. Bootstrapping and the origin of concepts. *Daedalus* 133: 59–68.

Carey, S. 2009. *The Origin of Concepts*. New York: Oxford University Press.

Casasanto, D. 2005. Crying "Whorf!" *Science* 307: 1721–1722.

Casasanto, D. 2008. Who's afraid of the Big Bad Whorf? Cross-linguistic differences in temporal language and thought. *Language Learning* 58 Suppl 1: 63–79.

Casasanto, D. 2010. Space for thinking. In V. Evans and P. Chilton (eds) *Language, Cognition and Space: State of the Art and New Directions*. London: Equinox Publishing, 453–478.

Casasanto, D. and L. Boroditsky 2008. Time in the mind: using space to think about time. *Cognition* 1062: 579–593.

Casasanto, D., L. Boroditsky, W. Phillips, J. Greene, S. Goswami, S. Bocanegra-Thiel et al. 2004. How deep are effects of language on thought? Time estimation in speakers of English, Indonesian, Greek, and Spanish. In K. Forbus, D. Gentner, and T. Regier (eds) *Proceedings of the 26th Annual Conference Cognitive Science Society*. Hillsdale, NJ: Lawrence Erlbaum Associates, 575–580.

Casasanto, D. and R. Bottini 2014. Mirror reading can reverse the flow of time. *Journal of Experimental Psychology: General* 1432: 473–479.

Casasanto, D. and G. Lupyan 2015. All concepts are ad hoc concepts. In E. Margolis and S. Laurence (eds) *The Conceptual Mind: New Directions in the Study of Concepts*. Cambridge: MIT Press, 543–566.

Clark, E. 2003. Languages and representations. In D. Gentner and S. Goldin-Meadow (eds) *Language in Mind: Advances in the Study of Language and Thought*. Cambridge: MIT Press, 17–23.

Clark, H. H. 1973. Space, time, semantics and the child. In T. E. Moore (ed.) *Cognitive Development and the Acquisition of Language*. New York: Academic Press, 27–63.

Dehaene, S. 1999. *The Number Sense: How the Mind Creates Mathematics*. New York: Oxford University Press.

Dolscheid, S., S. Hunnius, D. Casasanto, and A. Majid 2014. Prelinguistic infants are sensitive to space-pitch associations found across cultures. *Psychological Science*. doi: 10.1177/0956797614528521.

Dolscheid, S., S. Shayan, A. Majid, and D. Casasanto 2013. The thickness of musical pitch: psychophysical evidence for linguistic relativity. *Psychological Science* 245: 613–621.

Evans, V. 2004. *The Structure of Time: Language, Meaning and Temporal Cognition*. Amsterdam: John Benjamins.

Fausey, C. M. and L. Boroditsky 2011. Who dunnit? Cross-linguistic differences in eye-witness memory. *Psychonomic Bulletin and Review* 18: 150–157.

Feigenson, L., S. Dehaene, and E. Spelke 2004. Core systems of number. *Trends in Cognitive Sciences* 8: 307–314.

Frank, M. C., D. L. Everett, E. Fedorenko, and E. Gibson 2008. Number as a cognitive technology: evidence from Pirahã language and cognition. *Cognition* 108: 819–824.

Frank, M. C., E. Fedorenko, P. Lai, R. Saxe, and E. Gibson 2012. Verbal interference suppresses exact numerical representation. *Cognitive Psychology* 64: 74–92.

Gelman, R. and C. R. Gallistel 2004. Language and the origin of numerical concepts. *Science* 306: 441–443.
Gennari, S. P., S. A. Sloman, B. C. Malt, and W. Fitch 2002. Motion events in language and cognition. *Cognition* 83: 49–79.
Gleitman, L. and A. Papafragou 2013. Relations between language and thought. In D. Reisberg (ed.) *Handbook of Cognitive Psychology*. New York: Oxford University Press, 504–523.
Gordon, P. 2004. Numerical cognition without words: evidence from Amazonia. *Science* 306: 496–499.
James, W. 1890. *Principles of Psychology*. Vol. 1. New York: Holt.
Johnson-Laird, P. N. 1987. The mental representation of the meaning of words. *Cognition* 25: 189–211.
Kay, P. and W. Kempton 1984. What is the Sapir-Whorf hypothesis? *American Anthropologist* 86: 65–79.
Kay, P. and T. Regier 2006. Language, thought and color: recent developments. *Trends in Cognitive Sciences* 10: 51–54.
Lakoff, G. and M. Johnson 1999. *Philosophy in the Flesh: The Embodied Mind and its Challenge to Western Thought*. Chicago: University of Chicago Press.
Landau, B., B. Dessalegn, and A. Goldberg 2010. Language and space: momentary interactions. In V. Evans and P. Chilton (eds) *Language, Cognition and Space: The State of the Art and New Directions. Advances in Cognitive Linguistics Series*. London: Equinox, 51–78.
Levinson, S. C. 2003. *Space in Language and Cognition: Explorations in Cognitive Diversity*. Vol. 5. Cambridge: Cambridge University Press.
Levinson, S. C. and P. Brown 1994. Immanuel Kant among the Tenejapans: anthropology as empirical philosophy. *Ethos* 22: 3–41.
Lohmann, H. and M. Tomasello 2003. The role of language in the development of false belief understanding: a training study. *Child Development* 74: 1130–1144.
Lourenco, S. F. and M. R. Longo 2011. Origins and development of generalized magnitude representation. In S. Dehaene and E. M. Brannon (eds.) *Space, Time and Number in the Brain: Searching for the Foundations of Mathematical Thought*. London: Academic, 225–244.
Lucy, J. A. 1992. *Language Diversity and Thought: A Reformulation of the Linguistic Relativity Hypothesis*. Cambridge: Cambridge University Press.
Lucy, J. A. (ed.) 1996. *Grammatical Categories and Cognition: A Case Study of the Linguistic Relativity Hypothesis*. Cambridge: Cambridge University Press.
Lucy, J. A. and S. Gaskins 2001. Grammatical categories and the development of classification preferences: a comparative approach. In M. Bowerman and S. C. Levinson (eds) *Language Acquisition and Conceptual Development*. Cambridge: Cambridge University Press, 257–283.
McDonough, L., S. Choi, and J. M. Mandler 2003. Understanding spatial relations: flexible infants, lexical adults. *Cognitive Psychology* 46: 229–259.
McWhorter, J. H. 2014. *The Language Hoax: Why the World Looks the Same in Any Language*. Oxford: Oxford University Press.
Oh, K. J. 2003. *Language, Cognition, and Development: Motion Events in English and Korean*. Doctoral dissertation, University of California, Berkeley.
Papafragou, A., C. Massey, and L. Gleitman 2002. Shake, rattle, 'n' roll: the representation of motion in language and cognition. *Cognition* 84: 189–219.
Papafragou, A., J. Hulbert and J. Trueswell 2008. Does language guide event perception? Evidence from eye movements. *Cognition* 10: 155–184.
Papafragou, A., P. Li, Y. Choi, and C. H. Han 2007. Evidentiality in language and cognition. *Cognition* 103: 253–299.
Pinker, S. 1994. *The Language Instinct: How the Mind Creates Language*. New York: Harper.
Pinker, S. 1999. *Words and Rules: The Ingredients of Language*. New York: Basic Books.
Pullum, G. K. 1991. *The Great Eskimo Vocabulary Hoax and Other Irreverent Essays on the Study of Language*. Chicago: University of Chicago Press.
Sapir, E. 1929. The status of linguistics as a science. *Language* 5: 207–214.
Slobin, D. I. 1996. From "thought and language" to "thinking for speaking." In J. J. Gumperz and S. C. Levinson (eds) *Rethinking Linguistic Relativity*. Cambridge: Cambridge University Press, 70–96.

Slobin, D. I. 2003. Language and thought online: cognitive consequences of linguistic relativity. In D. Gentner and S. Goldin-Meadow (eds) *Language in Mind: Advances in the Study of Language and Thought*. Cambridge: MIT Press, 157–192.

Spaepen, E., M. Coppola, E. S. Spelke, S. E. Carey, and S. Goldin-Meadow 2011. Number without a language model. *Proceedings of the National Academy of Sciences* 10: 3163–3168.

Spelke, E. S. and S. Tsivkin 2001. Language and number: a bilingual training study. *Cognition* 78: 45–88.

Spivey, M. 2007. *The Continuity of Mind*. Oxford: Oxford University Press.

Srinivasan, M. and S. Carey 2010. The long and the short of it: on the nature and origin of functional overlap between representations of space and time. *Cognition* 11: 217–241.

Srinivasan, M. 2010. Do classifiers predict differences in cognitive processing? A study of nominal classification in Mandarin Chinese. *Language and Cognition* 2: 177–190.

Thierry, G., P. Athanasopoulos, A. Wiggett, B. Dering, and J. R. Kuipers 2009. Unconscious effects of language-specific terminology on preattentive color perception. *Proceedings of the National Academy of Sciences* 106: 4567–4570.

Trueswell, J. C. and A. Papafragou 2010. Perceiving and remembering events cross-linguistically: evidence from dual-task paradigms. *Journal of Memory and Language* 63: 64–82.

von Humboldt, W. 1988. *On Language: The Diversity of Human Language-Structure and its Influence on the Mental Development of Mankind*. Cambridge: Cambridge University Press.

Walker, P., J. G. Bremner, U. Mason, J. Spring, K. Mattock, A. Slater, and S. P. Johnson 2010. Preverbal infants' sensitivity to synaesthetic cross-modality correspondences. *Psychological Science* 21: 21–25.

Whorf, B. L. 1956. *Language, Thought, and Reality: Selected Writings of Benjamin Lee Whorf*. Edited by John B. Carroll. Cambridge: MIT Press.

Winawer, J., N. Witthoft, M. C. Frank, L. Wu, and L. Boroditsky 2007. Russian blues reveal effects of language on color discrimination. *Proceedings of the National Academy of Science* 104: 7780–7785.

Wolff, P., G. H. Jeon, and Y. Li 2009. Causers in English, Korean, and Chinese and the individuation of events. *Language and Cognition* 1: 167–196.

Related topics

Chapter 2, Internalist semantics; Chapter 5, Cognitive semantics; Chapter 7, Categories, prototypes and exemplars; Chapter 8, Embodiment, simulation and meaning; Chapter 25, The semantics of lexical typology; Chapter 26, Acquisition of meaning.

Part IV
Meaning and context

10
Semantics and pragmatics

John Saeed

1 Introduction

From a certain traditional perspective the distinction between semantics and pragmatics is clear. Semantics is the study of the literal meaning encoded by correctly constructed sentences in a language. Pragmatics, on the other hand, is the study of the role of language in social action, in particular how communication is reliant on mutual understanding of intentions, goals and social relationships. This view of pragmatics covers a wide range of lines of enquiry, including those concerned with the impacts of linguistic communication on participants like Austin's (1975) Speech Act Semantics and Habermas's (1979) Universal Pragmatics. Other orthogonal forms of enquiry such as anthropological linguistics and sociolinguistics investigate the role of language in mediating and constructing cultural and social practices. However, debates about the relations and boundary between semantics and pragmatics have been a lively part of the literature for several decades. Interest in the topic quickened in linguistics in particular in the 1970s, spurred on by work in a number of areas. One was the empirical work by linguists on the nature of presupposition, for example Jackendoff (1972), Karttunen (1974) and Kempson (1975). A speaker's choice of lexical items or syntactic structures was seen to relate to their judgements about knowledge shared with their interlocutors. The question arose of how syntactic and semantic rules could incorporate non-linguistic contextual factors like whether information was currently considered known, new or in focus. The question was whether presuppositions are to be seen as properties of sentences, utterances or speakers. A related line of enquiry investigated the distinction between ambiguity and vagueness or under-determination, especially in how negation works in language (Zwicky and Sadock 1975; Atlas 1977; Kempson 1979). Perhaps the most influential impetus came from Grice's (1975, 1978) investigation of how a speaker's intended meaning may be more than or different from the literal meaning of an uttered sentence. Grice's theory of implicatures requires a proposition derived from what is said in order to trigger the inferences to get to the speaker's intended meaning. This propositional content was for Grice the semantic content of the utterance. The problem, as it emerged over successive years of enquiry, is that there is not only a gap between the propositions expressed and what the speaker means by them but also a gap between the form of the utterance and the propositions that might be expressed by or derivable from it. While there is far from consensus on the exact nature or form of propositions (Soames 2012), it is assumed that they have truth-conditions and so may participate in inference and reasoning generally. They are viewed as having psychological validity (Kintsch 1998) and many scholars assign them a key role in cognition and communication. The issue for linguistics is: how are they produced? If there need to be processes of fleshing out between the linguistic form of an utterance with its conventional meanings and the resulting propositions, are these semantic or pragmatic processes? This has been one of the key areas of frontier dispute and we look at the debate in more detail.

Our discussion will concentrate on the view from linguistics. Semantics, as part of the study of language, belongs to everyone and is of concern to a wide range of neighbouring disciplines, including of course philosophy, psychology and informatics. Modern linguistics has been particularly open to influences from philosophy and much of the debate about the relations between semantics and pragmatics has reflected ideas from the philosophy of language. Often there is no clear disciplinary distinction in the discussions. To keep within reasonable bounds we concentrate on issues that currently loom largest from the linguistics side of the fence.

2 Grice's conversational implicature

Within contemporary linguistics debate about the relation between pragmatics and semantics has been strongly influenced by Grice's (1975, 1978, 1989) distinction between "what is said" in an utterance and what a speaker means by an utterance. This is often characterised (see for example Carston (2004)) as a distinction between "what is said" as propositional, or truth-conditional, content, and what is intentionally implied by the speaker's utterance. Grice was not concerned to provide a tight definition of this notion of "what is said", but in addition to following the grammatical and semantic rules of the language his discussions of the derivation of this level of meaning include fixing reference, assigning values to deictic expressions and resolving ambiguous expressions (Grice 1975). A speaker's intended meaning may be more than "what is said" because of the intended communication of conversational implicatures: implications that are not part of the conventional meaning of the utterance, as in a typical (invented) example (1):

(1) A: Would you like another drink?
     B: I've an early start in the morning.

Here B's reply may in the right context be interpreted to implicate a refusal or simply "no".

Grice's work suggests the following distinction between semantics and pragmatics: semantics is concerned with the proposition expressed while pragmatics is concerned with the implicatures of the utterance. His assumptions about semantics reflect the dominance in twentieth-century linguistics of truth-conditional and formal approaches. The twentieth-century philosophical analysis of language placed propositions and their truth-conditions centre stage in the search for semantic content. Grice's work builds on this to open up the prospect of an inferential pragmatics that explores the gap between the semantic content of the speaker's utterance, when viewed analytically, and what listeners seem to understand as the speaker's meaning. Pragmatic processing relies on the predictability of inferential behaviour, seen by Grice as depending on cooperative principles underlying communication (Grice 1975, 1978). His cooperative principle in (2) and maxims in (3) below predict that the listener assumes, and the speaker relies on this, that the speaker is speaking truthfully, relevantly and appropriately, including assessing what the hearer knows, selecting the right degree of clarity, etc. Clearly this not a claim that speakers always behave in this way; rather it is a claim that inferential strategies seem to rely on such assumptions.

(2) Grice's Cooperative Principle (see Grice (1989: 26))
     "Make your contribution such as is required, at the stage at which it occurs, by the accepted purpose or direction of the talk exchange in which you are engaged."

Semantics and pragmatics

(3) Grice's maxims (see Grice (1989: 26–6))
    i The Maxim of Quality
       Try to make your contribution one that is true, i.e.
       a do not say what you believe is false
       b do not say that for which you lack adequate evidence.
    ii The Maxim of Quantity
       Make your contribution as informative as is required for the current purposes of the exchange (i.e. not more or less informative).
    iii The Maxim of Relation
       Make your contributions relevant.
    iv The Maxim of Manner
       Be perspicuous, and specifically:
       a avoid ambiguity
       b avoid obscurity
       c be brief
       d be orderly.

Grice suggested that conversational implicatures must be capable of being worked out, i.e. a reasoning process must be identifiable, even if it is not deduction. For every implicature one should be able to predict a process of calculation involving "what is said" (the literal meaning), the cooperative principle and context. A characteristic Gricean formulation is:

(4) "Working out schema for conversational implicatures
    a The speaker (S) has said that p.
    b There is no reason to think that S is not observing the maxims.
    c S could not be doing this unless he thought that q.
    d S knows (and knows that the hearer (H) knows that he knows) that H can see that he thinks that the supposition that he thinks q is required.
    e S has done nothing to stop H from thinking that q.
    f S intends H to think, or is at least willing to allow H to think, that q.
    g And so, S has implicated that q." (Grice 1975)

Grice used the term non-natural meaning (meaning$_{NN}$) for interactional communication between mutually aware participants to distinguish it from simpler forms of signification. He provided an initial characterisation of this as below:

(5) Grice's Meaning$_{NN}$ (Levinson 2000: 13)

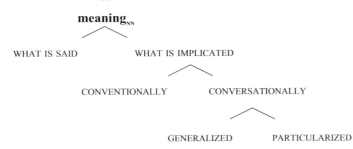

Though Grice never quite puts it in these terms, the distinction in (5) between "what is said" and "what is implicated" might be taken to reflect the Gricean division between semantics and pragmatics, since "what is said" is presumably the truth-conditional content. That is, the distinction between what is said and what is implicated corresponds to the line drawn between truth-conditional and non-truth-conditional meaning. The notion of conventional implicature has proved problematic in subsequent work: for many there is something intuitively odd about expressions that have conventional, learned meanings but which are understood by inference. An example often used is English *but*, which as shown below in addition to linking clauses consistently carries a meaning of unexpectedness or contrast:

(6) a He's a politician but he's honest.
 b Jack Sprat is thin but his wife is fat.
 c But you know I'm allergic to shellfish!

Despite this degree of conventionality, the contrastive meaning of *but* is excluded from "what is said" because the difference between it and *and* does not affect the truth-conditions of the proposition expressed. Subsequent work in this general framework has found ways to re-analyse these effects (Bach 1999; Blakemore 2002).

The pragmatic inferences called conversational implicatures are claimed to have specific features, for example being non-conventional, cancellable and reinforceable. Non-conventionality captures the fact that the inference is not encoded in the linguistic form of the utterance, as is clear from examples like (1) earlier, where there are a number of ways in which the reply in (1) could have been expressed to communicate the same indirect response. They are cancellable by context or by explicit statement, as we can see in (7) below. The sentence (7a) when uttered would carry for Grice an implicature of temporal sequence that is then cancelled in (7b) without causing anomaly:

(7) a I go to work, come home and have a beer.
 b I go to work, come home and have a beer, but not necessarily in that order.

This contrasts with a semantic relation like entailment as shown in (8). The sentence (8a) has the entailment in (8b), assuming constancy of reference; and (8c) shows that cancelling it produces anomaly:

(8) a The president was assassinated yesterday.
 b The president is dead.
 c The president was assassinated yesterday but he's not dead.

Gricean implicatures are reinforceable without causing redundancy, so the sentence (9a) may carry the implicature in (9b) and explicitly stating this does not cause redundancy in (9c).

(9) a Some of my friends are anarchists.
 b Not all of my friends are anarchists.
 c Some of my friends are anarchists but not all of them.

Once again this contrasts with entailment where the sentence *The president was assassinated yesterday and he is dead* seems to involve redundancy.

To complete the Gricean taxonomy in (5): particularised conversational implicatures (PCIs) depend completely on specific context of utterance: they are one-off inferences. Generalised conversational implicatures (GCIs) are context dependent but range over contexts, like a default. They only fail if blocked by inconsistency with context. Carston (2004), following Levinson (2000), provides the following example to illustrate the difference:

(10) A: Did the children's summer camp go well?
B: Some of them got stomach 'flu.
GCI: Not all the children got stomach 'flu.
PCI: The summer camp didn't go as well as hoped.

3 Detaching sentence meaning from truth-conditions

Bach (1994) develops a version of Grice's approach that also distinguishes between sentence meaning on the one hand and utterance meaning on the other, where the latter is what a speaker means by uttering a sentence. In this view sentence meaning is only part of the evidence for utterance meaning. A speaker may use a sentence figuratively to communicate a different meaning or may intend to produce indirect meanings by inference on the part of the addressee. The sentence may or may not express a proposition even when relativised to context by the resolution of deictic elements. The uttered sentences may be less than explicit because they are incomplete and, in this view, cannot express a proposition, as in (11) where "fast enough for what?" is left unexpressed:

(11) John isn't fast enough.

In other cases the sentence may express a proposition but needs to be expanded to express what the speaker really intended. Bach (1994: 267) gives the example (12) below, where (12a) is said by a mother comforting a child with a cut finger; (12b) is the content of (12a), the basic proposition, and (12c) is the expanded and intended content:

(12) a   You are not going to die, Peter.
    b   There is no future time at which you will die, Peter.
    c   You are not going to die from this cut, Peter.

For Bach in both (11) and (12a) the speaker is not being fully explicit. In recognising that the semantic representation is incomplete in truth-conditional terms, Bach abandons the view that the semantic content of a sentence must be a truth-bearing proposition. The expansion of sentences to make them more explicit, and thus propositional, forms a level of what he terms *implicitures* to distinguish them from implicatures. These implicitures are then neither a part of the semantics of the uttered sentence nor conversational implicatures but a middle level of meaning that belongs to pragmatics. Semantics in this view then is the purely linguistic study of sentence meaning, regardless of whether the product can bear truth-conditions. Pragmatics, on the other hand, is the study of utterance meaning, involving the production of implicitures and implicatures.

4 The growth of contextualism

4.1 Neo-Gricean theories

Other writers in the broadly Gricean enterprise have further developed the view, known as contextualism, that substantial context-dependent processes are necessary to arrive at "what is said" as opposed to "what is implicated". This enquiry is characterised by revisions of Grice's original maxims and by an ongoing debate about the relationship between linguistic form and pragmatic processes. Along the way different characterisations of the interface between semantics and pragmatics emerge. Horn (1984, 1989, 2004), for example, argues for a reworking of the Gricean maxims into two basic pragmatic principles, briefly outlined below:

(13) Horn's Q- and R-principles (Horn 1984, 1989)
    a   The Q-principle
         Make your contribution sufficient;
         Say as much as you can (given the R-principle)
    b   The R-principle
         Make your contribution necessary;
         Say no more than you must (given the Q-principle)

Horn's Q-principle conflates Grice's Quantity maxim and parts 1 and 2 of Grice's Manner maxims and can basically be paraphrased as "say the most that you are licensed to say". Alternatively, taking the hearer's point of view in mind, it could be paraphrased as "maximise the informational content of what you say". On the other hand, the R-principle is a speaker-oriented economy principle. The two, speaker versus hearer economy principles, are held to be in tension. The best-known application of the Q-principle is the Q or Horn scales of strength, which are designed to account for the generalised conversational implicatures produced by some linguistic expressions. They are shown schematically below:

(14) Q scale/Horn scale (Huang 2007: 38)
      For <S, W> to form a Q or Horn scale,
    i $A(S)$ entails $A(W)$ for some arbitrary sentence frame A:
    ii S and W are equally lexicalised, of the same word class, and from the same register; and
    iii S and W are "about" the same semantic relation, or from the same semantic field.

Thus Horn scales are typically scales of alternates, ordered strong to weak, for example:

(15) a   <all, some>
       b   <identical, similar>

The Q-maxim operating on scales ensures that the use of a weaker alternate implies the negative of a stronger:

(16) a   "Some of the audience paid for their tickets" implicates "not all did"
       b   "Their answers were similar" implicates "Their answers were not identical"

Levinson (2000) proposes a similar but distinct revision where Grice's conversational maxims are replaced by three pragmatic principles governing pragmatic inferences, called heuristics: the Q-, I- and M-heuristics. The Q-heuristic, which corresponds to Grice's Maxim of Quantity 1, can be described either from the point of view of the speaker or the addresses, and is given in simplified form below:

(17) Levinson's Q-heuristic (Huang 2007: 41)
    Speaker: Do not say less than is required (bearing in mind the I-principle)
    Addressee: What is not said is not the case.

Levinson's I- and M-heuristics concern economy. His I-heuristic, which corresponds to Grice's Maxim of Quantity 2, is in (18) and the countervailing M-heuristic is in (19):

(18) Levinson's I-heuristic
    Speaker: Do not say more than is required (bearing in mind the Q-heuristic)
    Addressee: What is said simply is meant to be interpreted stereotypically.

(19) Levinson's M-heuristic
    Speaker: Do not use an unusual expression without reason.
    Addressee: What is said in an unusual way signals an unusual situation.

The Q-heuristic, like Horn's Q-principle, gives rise to scales. In addition to the simple scales as in (15) above, Levinson identifies more complex cases of alternate sets, for example clausal sets, where the alternates are distinguished by the stronger entailing its subparts and the weaker not entailing its components, as in (20):

(20) Example of Levinson Q-$_{clausal:}$ conditionals
    a <since p then q>, <if p then q>
    b "Since he's here, he can play" entails "He is here"; and "He can play"
    c "If he's here, he can play" does not entail "He is here" or "He can play"

In this example, "since p then q" entails p, and entails q, as shown in (20b). However, "if p then q" does not entail p, and does not entail q, as shown in (20c). Because of this relationship, by uttering "If he's here, he can play" the speaker, by excluding the stronger, implicates: "Maybe he's here; maybe not; therefore maybe he can play; maybe not" i.e. uncertainty. The I-heuristic is used to explain the how speakers employ or assume defaults and stereotypes to narrow to specific interpretations so that a *cheese board* is for cutting cheese, not made of cheese, and a *kitchen knife* is used in kitchens, not for cutting kitchens. It is also used for the examples of strengthening implications mentioned earlier, for example the occasion when conjunctions like English *and* can imply temporal and causal sequence as in (21); *if* is strengthened to be interpreted as "if and only if" as in (22): and the strengthening of negation as when (23a) implicates (23b):

(21) They ran out of the bank and the police opened fire.

(22) If you pass your examinations, I'll buy you a car.

(23) a John doesn't like sushi.
    b John dislikes sushi.

The M-heuristic explains speakers' use of unusual expressions to avoid defaults and stereotypes. It seeks to account for the pragmatic effects of negative asymmetry, where (24a) below will be interpreted differently from (24b); or where the use of a periphrastic expression carries a distinction of meaning as in (25):

(24) a I don't dislike Henry.
     b I like Henry.

(25) a Mandy fired the gun.
     b Mandy caused the gun to fire.

An important part of Levinson's (2000) proposal is the elaboration of Grice's generalised conversational implicatures as defaults triggered by linguistic structure. Levinson identifies three levels at the semantics-pragmatics interface: sentence meaning (semantics proper), utterance-type meaning (defaults) and utterance-token meaning (produced by pragmatic inference). The defaults are defeasible (i.e. cancellable) pragmatic inferences, which are seen as part of a wider class of presumptive meanings or preferred interpretations. They are not produced as one-off contextual inferences but are enrichments of the semantic representation automatically triggered by linguistic forms. They serve to determine the proposition expressed in a number of ways, including the kind of lexical narrowing and strengthening outlined above. These defaults form an independent level between semantics and pragmatics but that interfaces with both.

In Levinson's account the default inferences will only be subsequently cancelled if they clash with context. As we noted, Grice's original position seemed to assume that reference resolution, the determination of deictic elements and disambiguation are necessary to determine "what is said". Levinson (2000) proposes to add defaults to this so that there is a level of semantic representation that is even more clearly dependent on pragmatic processes, even if these are unconscious and automatic. This level then gives rise to conversational implicatures produced by conscious inference. So although in this view implicature straddles the division between what is said and what is implied, and in traditional terms the semantics/pragmatics border, the old border is still there in a sense in the division between the types of pragmatic process involved. In fact Levinson discusses a more complicated interaction involving interleaving of levels, because of examples like (26) and (27) below, where the truth-conditional operations of the conditional and comparison only work if the pragmatic default (or GCI) is part of the meaning:

(26) If they got married and had a child, their parents will be pleased, but if they had a child and got married their parents will not be pleased. (*and* implicates *then*)
(27) It is better to eat some of the cake than it is to eat it all. (*some* implicates *not all*)

In this view a pragmatic process inferentially enriches the underdetermined aspects of the semantic representation on the basis of the default assumptions given by the heuristics (a pragmatic level 1). Then the semantics provides semantic interpretations that will determine truth-conditions, entailments and other classic semantic relations. Subsequently this enriched semantic representation gives rise to particularised conversational implicatures (a pragmatic level 2). Levinson describes this interleaving of levels as *pragmatic intrusion* or, alternatively, *presemantic and postsemantic pragmatics*.

4.2 Relevance theory

A more radical departure in the Gricean tradition is provided by Relevance Theory (Sperber and Wilson 1995; Carston 2002; Wilson and Sperber 2012), which situates its account of the inferential interpretation of meaning within a psychologically oriented model of communication based on relevance (see Chapter 11). Relevance is, as a property of both cognition and communication, characterised as two principles:

(28) Cognitive Principle of Relevance (Sperber and Wilson 1995: 260)
Human cognition tends to be geared towards the maximisation of relevance.

(29) Communicative Principle of Relevance (Sperber and Wilson 1995: 158)
Every act of overt communication conveys a presumption of its own optimal relevance.

The cognitive principle proposes that a characteristic of human cognition is to seek to achieve as many cognitive effects as possible for as little processing cost as possible. The communicative principle claims that making an utterance communicates a kind of guarantee: that the utterance is relevant enough to be worth the addressee's effort to process it and is moreover the most relevant one the speaker could make in the circumstances. Relevance is gauged by the effects on the cognitive environment of the addressee in the specific context; that is, by various modifications to the addressee's knowledge or beliefs. Clearly the effects will vary from one context to another. If the principles license the inferential behaviour of hearers, the balance between contextual cognitive effects and processing effort acts as a limit to the inferential process. This account then switches the behavioural basis of communication from Grice's principles of language usage (possibly learned by speakers) to unconscious psychological principles wider than language.

Relevance theorists share with other contextualist accounts the view that linguistic form underdetermines meaning and that contextual processes are required to enrich the semantic output from linguistic rules towards a propositional status. However, this approach is characterised by the view that the same relevance-based inferential process is employed both to enrich the underspecified semantic forms and to derive conversational implicatures from richer propositional representations (see Chapter 11). The linguistic rules of a language produce semantic representations that are too sketchy to support propositions, and presumably to register in consciousness. Relevance theorists recognise a range of processes including disambiguation, reference assignment and enrichment that allow the formulation of more compete representations from these underdetermined schemas. Richer representations that support truth-conditional propositional meaning are called *explicatures*. Clear cases of enrichment involve ellipsis and sentence fragments. In the exchange below, in a reasonable context, A might reconstruct (31) from the exchange in (30):

(30) A: Who stole the armadillo?
B: Roger.

(31) Roger stole the armadillo.

This seems a straightforward case of the contextually most accessible information being used to fill gaps in the linguistic input. But relevance theorists propose that similar processes allow listeners to enrich the linguistic input for unexpressed information about time, sequence and causation, among other semantic parameters. Wilson and Sperber (2012: 179) discuss their now well-known examples:

(32) I have had breakfast.
(33) I have been to Tibet.

All that's available from the linguistic input is that the speaker has had breakfast, or been to Tibet, at some point in time before the utterance. In practice, the presumption of relevance will lead the listener not to assume that (32) is intended to communicate that the speaker has had breakfast at some time in her life, but to try to construe it as maximally relevant, i.e. that she has had food recently enough for it to be worth mentioning, i.e. recently enough not to need to eat breakfast again. Note that this assumes a kind of reasonable context: it is quite possible for (32) to be used in another context to communicate that the speaker has eaten breakfast at some time in her life. For (33) we can imagine a situation where the relevant time frame might be the speaker's lifetime.

Similar processes are held to explain the sequential and causal interpretations constructible for connectives like *and* seen above, for example:

(34) "It's always the same at parties: either you get drunk **and** no one will talk to you or no one will talk to you **and** you get drunk." (Blakemore 1992: 80)

Thus the neo-Gricean category of generalised conversational implicatures forms in this account part of the explicatures of the utterance.

The explicatures created by enriching a linguistically encoded semantic representation may be embedded under markers of the speaker's stance that do not affect the truth-conditions of the proposition. An example is illocutionary adverbs such as *seriously*, *frankly*, etc. that modify the type of speech act performed, as in (35):

(35) a Confidentially, he's a bit of a crook.
     b Frankly, I don't know the answer.
     c Seriously, we have to get out of here.

These are said to form *higher-level explicatures* of the utterance. Explicatures as propositional representations give rise to contextual effects, i.e. implicatures of various types, which represent non-truth-conditional intended meaning.

Relevance Theory thus situates the border between semantics and pragmatics at the border between linguistically encoded meaning on the one hand and what is explicated and implicated on the other. Or to put it another way: semantics is concerned with decoded linguistic meaning and pragmatics with inferential meaning. Consequently pragmatic processes are clearly required to obtain propositional truth-conditional representations. A recent focus has been the application of this approach to word meaning as part of supplementing lexical semantics with a lexical pragmatics (see Chapter 11).

4.3 Recanati's truth-conditional pragmatics

Recanati (e.g. 2010) proposes a strong version of the contextualist position that a truth-conditional "what is said" is always produced by pragmatic processes. In this account these processes are different in kind from the inferences that produce implicatures, being more automatic and unconscious. They include linguistically triggered saturation, where reference is fixed and deictic elements are assigned values, and free enrichment, which is not linguistically triggered and which makes more explicit some unexpressed information. A typical example is (36) where the intended referent of *she* is fixed by saturation and a causal and temporal relation may be understood, depending on context, by enrichment.

(36)   She went to MIT and studied linguistics.

Recanati views the unexpressed comparators of an adjective like *tall* in (37) or the understood information *ready for what* in (38) as examples of saturation:

(37)   Your son is tall.
(38)   Sonja is ready.

In this view saturation produces a proposition, or conversely, omitting this process would result in an open sentence unable to support truth-values. Free enrichment is optional but unlike the inferences that produce implicature does affect truth-conditions. The result is an augmented proposition. In Recanati's view saturation is a "bottom-up" process since it is motivated by the linguistic form while enrichment is a "top-down" process since it is motivated by the hearer's desire to create an interpretation of the speaker's meaning. Free enrichment is part of a more general process of modulation, which is the contextual localisation or grounding of the context-independent meaning of expressions. In Recanati's view free (as in not linguistically constrained) pragmatic enrichment to propositional content is an all-pervasive feature of language that enables a limited resource to be adapted to a very large number of situations.

5 Restricting context

A number of proposals, in particular from philosophers of language, have sought to restrict the contribution of context to truth-conditional semantic representations. One approach is to limit the pragmatic processes leading to truth-conditional representations by insisting that they have to be linguistically licensed by constituents of the sentence itself. These would include deictic elements like pronouns, demonstratives, and temporal and locational adverbs. In short, to use Recanati's terms discussed above, this is to include saturation in semantics but to exclude free enrichment and other forms of modulation. The result is a conservative contextualism that is characterised, for example, by Cappelen and Lepore (2005). In this view the utterance of a sentence produces a basic proposition that is produced across all contexts it is uttered in, with other different propositions being derived from it that will vary from context to context, depending on pragmatic processes. Thus there are two levels of meaning: a minimal semantic content that is propositional and a richer contextualised speech act content.

Borg (2004, 2007) argues for a similar position, Minimal Semantics, where a minimal proposition is provided by semantics and then supplemented by intuitive utterance content, given by pragmatics. Sentences in this view have truth-conditions even if a speaker cannot tell for any given situations whether they are true. The mapping between an uttered sentence and a real-life situation is in this account a process of verification of truth-conditions rather than the formal semantic assignment of truth-conditions to a sentence. As part of her aim of "capturing the repeatable, code-like, normative aspects of linguistic meaning" (2004: 310) Borg proposes that semantic representations are derived by formal computational operations alone, with no reference to "subjective" parameters such as speaker intentions, goals, etc., while pragmatic content on the other hand can have access to non-formal, abductive processes. Borg proposes minimal propositions that will neither be typically communicated nor necessarily psychologically accessible to speakers and hearers, as with the proposition (39b) suggested as produced by the (uttered) sentence (39a) (2004: 228):

(39) a   Jill can't continue.
     b   Jill can't continue something.

It is unlikely that the hearer will understand (39b) as the communicated meaning, but this objection has little bite if propositions are not readily mentally accessible. Atlas (2011), among others, has objected to the truth-conditional implications of asserting the existence of "something" in the truth-conditions in (39b).

Since relevance theorists assume a very reduced semantic representation produced by the grammar, the difference between Borg's position and theirs may be less dramatic than that suggested by the contextualist-minimalist debate. The difference comes down to how minimal the semantic representation is. Relevance theorists propose a sub-propositional schema from which pragmatics allows the derivation of propositions. Borg proposes a minimal proposition that will often not correspond to the proposition expressed by the speaker. This point is made Wedgwood (2007) in his comparison between Cappelen and Lepore (2005) and Relevance Theory. From this angle relevance theorists might be characterised as "radical semantic minimalists".

6 Dynamic semantics

There is a tendency in the approaches discussed so far to follow the philosophical tradition of viewing sentences as static, independent constructs that are individually mapped to semantic forms. Much of language structure, however, reveals that sentences naturally form part of larger structures that are produced through an interactive process among speakers. Speakers use pronouns, for example, to link references to entities between sentences and between sentences and the context. These links shift as the conversation progresses and new entities are talked about. Speakers often use elliptical or partial forms, relying on their hearers' ability to supply the missing elements. A number of formal approaches have been developed to capture the dynamic nature of language, including File-change Semantics (Heim 1983), Dynamic Predicate Logic (Groenendijk and Stokhof 1991), Update Semantics (Veltman 1996), and Discourse Representation Theory (Kamp et al. 2011). These approaches have sought to formalise a process of updating information states, as a model of communicated assumptions about context. Discourse Representation Theory (DRT), for example, provides a formal model of the introduction and tracking of reference to entities in discourse by, for example, indefinite noun phrases and pronouns (see also Chapters 3 and 4). In this account a sentence's meaning is characterised as an update operation on a context rather than directly as a set of truth-conditions. Each sentence is interpreted in a context with the result being a new context. DRT formalises at least two aspects of the discourse context: the referential discourse history of entities and the related presuppositions. In treating semantic content as updating the discourse context, DRT merges information from across the traditional semantics/pragmatics divide.

The main form of representation is a Discourse Representation Structure (DRS), usually presented in a box format, as shown in (41) below. The discourse referents are given in the top line of the DRS, called the universe of the DRS, and below them are conditions giving the properties of the discourse referents. These conditions govern whether the DRS can be embedded into the model of the current state of the discourse. A DRS is true if all of the discourse referents can be mapped to individuals in the situation described in such a way that the conditions are met. These DRSs are built up by construction rules from the linguistic input, sentence by sentence. If we take the sentences in (40) as a mini-discourse, where the subscript *i* marks co-reference, the first will be represented by the DRS in (41) and the second will update the first to create the DRS in (42):

(40) a Rotwang built a robot$_i$.
     b It$_i$ was beautiful.

(41)
```
| x y
| ROTWANG (x)
| ROBOT (y)
| BUILD (x, y)
```

(42)
```
| x y z
| ROTWANG (x)
| ROBOT (y)
| BUILD (x, y)
| z = y
| BE BEAUTIFUL (z)
```

In this brief example the DRT account shows how an indefinite noun phrase can be used to introduce an entity (a robot) into the discourse context and how this can then be referred to by a subsequent pronoun (*it*). However, not all uses of an indefinite nominal introduce an entity into the context in this way, for example when the nominal occurs in a negative context:

(43) a Rotwang did not build a robot$_i$.
     b ?It$_i$ was beautiful.

In DRT the anomaly in (43b) is reflected by recognising that certain scope elements, such as negation, create a subordinate construction within a DRS, a sub-DRS, and specifying that elements within the sub-DRS are inaccessible to relations like anaphora. Thus the sentence (43a) is represented by the DRS (44) below:

(44)
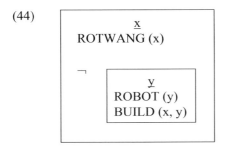

Here the DRS contains one discourse referent and two conditions: the first is the usual naming relation, ROTWANG (x), and the second is a second DRS embedded in the first and marked by the logical negation sign ¬. The satisfaction of this second condition is that there is not a robot such that Rotwang built it. This contained DRS is said to be subordinate to the containing DRS and is triggered by the construction rules for negation. Adding the second sentence (43b) results in the DRS in (45):

(45)
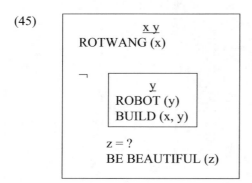

Here the question mark in the identification of an antecedent for y (i.e. *it*) is because the only possible antecedent for y (a robot) is not accessible since it occurs in the subordinate DRS box under negation. The effect of this is that discourse referents introduced within a subordinate DRS under the scope of negation do not enter the discourse context and are thus inaccessible to pronouns in subsequent stages of the DRS.

In this theory the DRSs are elaborated to explore the referential behaviour of noun phrases in a range of syntactic configurations, and under negation and quantification. Since these DRSs form a level of mental representations reflecting the hearer's process of updating the discourse as it progresses, this theory proposes a psychologically based account of meaning interpretation as a computation over representations. As noted earlier, the integration of the (rather minimal) contextual information of the discourse itself with semantic information blurs the traditional distinction between literal meaning and pragmatics. Developments of DRT have extended the integration of discourse contextual parameters, such as Layered DRT (Maier 2009), which incorporates further presuppositional behaviour, and Segmented DRT (Asher and Lascarides 2005), which integrates rhetorical structure.

7 Cognitive semantics

Cognitive linguistics is a very wide field of enquiry but in general scholars in this approach reject the correspondence theory of truth, and resulting truth-conditions, as a means of representing meaning. Lakoff (1989) describes two assumptions deriving from the dominant tradition in twentieth-century philosophy of language that he believes must be rejected in a cognitive approach to language. The first is objectivism, characterised as:

(46) The Objectivist Commitment. The commitment to the view that reality is made up, objectively, of determinate entities with properties and relations holding among those entities at each instant. This is a commitment to a view that reality comes with a preferred description, and it is a commitment as to what reality is like. (1989: 56)

The second is a truth-based account of meaning that he traces back to Frege:

(47) The Fregean Commitment. The commitment to understand meaning in terms of reference and truth, given the objectivist commitment. Semantics is taken as consisting in the relationship between symbols and the objectivist world, independent of the minds of any beings. An example would be to define meaning in terms of Tarski's truth convention *T*, which in turn defines the truth of logical forms in terms of what their elements refer to in a set-theoretical model of the world. (1989: 56)

For Lakoff, as for other linguists in this general paradigm, these assumptions are inconsistent with a cognitive approach to language and must be replaced with a model of embodied cognition (Gibbs 2005) wherein meaning reflects conceptualisation and individual utterances reflect speakers' choices of construal. Langacker (2008) identifies categories of construal that include specificity, focusing, prominence and perspective. Specificity reflects decisions about levels of precision and granularity. Focusing describes the selection of content for linguistic communication and its arrangement into foreground and background, including distinctions of information structure. Prominence or salience reflects decisions about the selection of a conceptual domain and attention to relations or positions within it. Perspective is the speaker's choice of vantage point to report a scene, for example, and between alternate characterisations of temporal relations. These construal processes are inherently context dependent and so cognitive linguists view the division between semantics and pragmatics as an artefact of the mistaken assumptions in (46) and (47).

Cognitive linguists have proposed a range of conceptual structures that underpin linguistic communication, including image schemas (Johnson 1987; Lakoff 1987, 1989; Hampe 2005), frames (Fillmore 1982), idealised cognitive models (Lakoff 1987) and mental spaces (Fauconnier 1994, 1997). Image schemas are basic structures deriving from bodily experiences of vision, space, motion and forces that combine to build up richer and more abstract conceptual structures. Schemas like PATH, UP-DOWN and CONTAINER have been used to characterise topographical concepts that underlie spatial language such as prepositions. Idealised cognitive models (ICMs) explore the implications for language of research in cognitive psychology on prototype effects in categorisation (Rosch 1973, 1975; Rosch and Mervis 1975; Rosch et al. 1976). Like frames, ICMs are higher-level conceptions that incorporate knowledge about the world. So the ICM BACHELOR is made up of prototypical assumptions that make the Pope an untypical bachelor. Mental spaces are mental representations that reflect aspects of dynamic discourse context. They reflect how participants manage reference to states of affairs and entities within them, for example allowing mapping between the current context of discourse and temporally distinct, hypothetical or counterfactual scenarios. All of these forms of representation reflect cognitive processes that are identified as wider than language and that incorporate information from a range of sources including bodily experience, cultural knowledge and the specific context of utterance.

This lack of distinction between encyclopaedic and linguistic knowledge characterises the cognitive linguistic approach to word meaning. In this view lexical items are conceptual categories whose cognitive function is the object of study. They form information structures that mediate the speaker's encounters with the world (Geeraerts 1995). The meaning attached to a word is a prompt for a process of meaning construction in context. This local lexical grounding or modulation (Cruse 1986) takes account of any form of knowledge contextually available. This encyclopaedic usage-based approach moves away from the traditional analogy of a dictionary for knowledge of word meaning: a mental lexicon. Instead encyclopaedic knowledge is accessed by the use of words in context so the distinction between semantics and pragmatics has no theoretical weight (see Chapter 5).

8 Conclusion

Grice's proposal was for a theory of pragmatics, starting where linguistic form itself leaves off. However, explorations in this paradigm have led to re-evaluation of semantics itself and its relation to pragmatics, in particular for those who seek to maintain a traditional role for truth-conditions in semantic content. Such an enterprise faces the problem that semantic content underdetermines propositional content. There are a number ways of dealing with this. One, the consensus perhaps in current linguistics, is to abandon the applicability of truth-conditions to sentences and their semantics. Truth-conditions and propositions are then only indirectly related to the output of grammar. Consequently language is part of their generation but, as Relevance Theory suggests, a wider theory of cognition and communication is required to give a full account of how speakers and hearers arrive at a communicated meaning. A conservative response, mainly from philosophers, is the attempt to limit the contextual contribution to propositions to overt linguistic triggers. This approach has the problem of finding a principled way to define such a set of triggers. Dynamic approaches like DRT place a level of mental representation between language and truth-conditions and admit contextual features into the representation. This shifts the focus of interest to the point where information of different sorts is integrated in the interpretation of meaning. For cognitive linguists, who have generally rejected the distinction between semantics and pragmatics, the growing evidence of contextual effects does not pose a problem. Scholars in this approach have long discounted the correspondence theory of truth as a basis for semantic analysis and have instead proposed cognitive representations that freely draw on all types of available knowledge. It is possible to see in this continuing debate a move within linguistics to a greater interest in the relationship between semantic and conceptual representations (see Chapter 2) and in dynamic and cognitive approaches to meaning in which the semantics/pragmatics border is not an important focus of enquiry.

Further reading

Geeraerts, Dirk 2010. *Theories of Lexical Semantics*. Oxford: Oxford University Press.
This book sets the cognitive semantics approach to lexical semantics against the background of other approaches.
Kamp, H., J. van Genabith and U. Reyle 2011. Discourse representation theory. In: D. M. Gabbay and F. Guenther (eds) *Handbook of Philosophical Logic*. Second edition. Dordrecht: Springer, 125–394. This work provides a comprehensive outline of Discourse Representation Theory.
Recanati, F. 2010. *Truth Conditional Pragmatics*. Oxford: Oxford University Press. This philosophically oriented work provides arguments for a contextualist position.
Wilson, D. and D. Sperber 2012. *Meaning and Relevance*. Cambridge: Cambridge University Press. This is an overview of and update on developments in Relevance Theory.

References

Asher, N. and A. Lascarides. 2005. *Logics of Conversation*. Cambridge: Cambridge University Press.
Atlas, J. D. 1977. Negation, ambiguity, and presupposition. *Linguistics and Philosophy* 1: 321–336.
Atlas, J. D. 2011. Whatever happened to meaning? Remarks on contextualists and propositionalisms. In K. Turner (ed.) *Making Semantics Pragmatic*. Bingley, UK: Emerald Group, 19–48.
Austin, J. L. 1975. *How to Do Things with Words*. Second edition. Oxford: Clarendon Press. (First published 1962.)
Bach, K. 1994. Semantic slack: what is said and more. In S. L. Tsohatzidis (ed.) *Foundations of Speech Act Theory: Philosophical and Linguistic Perspectives*. London: Routledge, 267–291.

Bach, K. 1999. The myth of conventional implicature. *Linguistics and Philosophy* 22: 326–366.
Blakemore, D. 1992. *Understanding Utterances: An Introduction to Pragmatics*. Oxford: Blackwell.
Blakemore, D. 2002. *Relevance and Linguistic Meaning: The Semantics and Pragmatics of Discourse Markers*. Cambridge: Cambridge University Press.
Borg, E. 2004. *Minimal Semantics*. Oxford: Oxford University Press.
Borg, E. 2007. Minimalism versus contextualism in semantics. In G. Preyer and G. Peter (eds) *Context-Sensitivity and Semantic Minimalism*. Oxford: Oxford University Press, 339–359.
Cappelen, H. and E. Lepore 2005. *Insensitive Semantics*. Oxford: Blackwell.
Carston, R. 2002. *Thoughts and Utterances: The Pragmatics of Explicit Communication*. Oxford: Blackwell.
Carston, R. 2004. Truth-conditional content and conversational implicature. In C. Bianchi (ed.) *The Semantics/Pragmatics Distinction*. Stanford, CA: CSLI, 65–100.
Cruse, D. A. 1986. *Lexical Semantics*. Cambridge: Cambridge University Press.
Fauconnier, G. 1994. *Mental Spaces: Aspects of Meaning Construction in Natural Language*. Second edition. Cambridge: Cambridge University Press.
Fauconnier, G. 1997. *Mappings in Thought and Language*. Cambridge: Cambridge University Press.
Fillmore, C. J. 1982. Frame semantics. In The Linguistic Society of Korea (ed.) *Linguistics in the Morning Calm*. Seoul: Hanshin, 111–138.
Geeraerts, D. 1995. Representational formats in Cognitive Linguistics. *Folia Linguistica* 39: 21–41.
Gibbs, R. W. 2005. *Embodiment and Cognitive Science*. Cambridge: Cambridge University Press.
Grice, H. P. 1975. Logic and conversation. In P. Cole and J. L. Morgan (eds) *Syntax and Semantics. Vol. 3: Speech Acts*. New York: Academic Press, 43–58.
Grice, H. P. 1978. Further notes on logic and conversation. In P. Cole (ed.) *Syntax and Semantics. Vol. 9: Pragmatics*. New York: Academic Press, 113–128.
Grice, H. P. 1989. *Studies in the Way of Words*. Cambridge, MA: MIT Press.
Groenendijk, J. and M. Stokhof 1991. Dynamic predicate logic. *Linguistics and Philosophy* 14: 39–100.
Habermas, J. 1979. *Communication and the Evolution of Society*. Translated by T. McCarthy. Boston, MA: Beacon.
Hampe, B. (ed.) 2005. *From Perception to Meaning: Image Schemas in Cognitive Linguistics*. Berlin: Mouton de Gruyter.
Heim, I. 1983: On the projection problem for presupposition. In M. Barlow, D. P. Flickinger and M. T. Westcoat (eds) *Proceedings of the West Coast Conference on Formal Linguistics*, Vol 2. Stanford: Stanford Linguistics Association, 114–125.
Horn, L. R. 1984. Toward a new taxonomy for pragmatic inference: Q-based and R-based implicatures. In D. Schiffrin (ed.) *Meaning, Form and Use in Context: Linguistics Applications*. Washington, DC: Georgetown University Press, 11–42.
Horn, L. R. 1989. *A natural history of negation*. Chicago: University of Chicago Press.
Horn, L. R. 2004. Implicature. In L. R. Horn and G. Ward (eds) *The Handbook of Pragmatics*. Oxford: Blackwell, 3–28.
Huang, Y. 2007. *Pragmatics*. Oxford: Oxford University Press.
Jackendoff, R. 1972. *Semantic Interpretation in Generative Grammar*. Cambridge, MA: MIT Press.
Johnson, M. 1987: *The Body in the Mind: The Bodily Basis of Meaning, Imagination, and Reason*. Chicago: University of Chicago Press.
Kamp, H., J. van Genabith and U. Reyle. 2011. Discourse representation theory. In D. M. Gabbay and F. Guenther (eds) *Handbook of Philosophical Logic*. Second edition. Dordrecht: Springer, 125–394.
Karttunen, L. 1974. Presupposition and linguistic context. *Theoretical Linguistics* 1: 181–193.
Kempson, R. M. 1975. *Presupposition and the Delimitation of Semantics*. Cambridge: Cambridge University Press.
Kempson, R. M. 1979. Presupposition, opacity and ambiguity. In C.-K. Oh and D. A. Dinneen (eds) *Syntax and Semantics 11: Presupposition*. New York: Academic Press, 283–297.
Kintsch, W. 1998. *Comprehension: A Paradigm for Cognition*. New York: Cambridge University Press.

Lakoff, G. 1987. *Women, Fire and Dangerous Things*. Chicago: University of Chicago Press.
Lakoff, G. 1989. Philosophical speculation and cognitive science. *Philosophical Psychology* 2: 55–76.
Langacker, R. W. 2008. *Cognitive Grammar: A Basic Introduction*. Oxford: Oxford University Press.
Levinson, S. C. 2000. *Presumptive Meanings: The Theory of Generalized Conversational Implicature*. Cambridge, MA: MIT Press.
Maier, E. 2009. Proper names and indexicals trigger rigid presuppositions. *Journal of Semantics* 26: 253–315.
Recanati, F. 2010. *Truth Conditional Pragmatics*. Oxford: Oxford University Press.
Rosch, E. 1973. Natural categories. *Cognitive Psychology* 4: 328–350.
Rosch, E. 1975. Cognitive reference points. *Cognitive Psychology* 7: 532–547.
Rosch, E. and C. Mervis 1975. Family resemblances: studies in the internal structure of categories. *Cognitive Psychology* 7: 573–605.
Rosch, E., C. Mervis, W. Gray, D. Johnson and P. Boyes-Braem 1976. Basic objects in natural categories. *Cognitive Psychology* 8: 382–439.
Soames, S. 2012. Propositions. In G. Russell and D. G. Fara (eds) *The Routledge Companion to the Philosophy of Language*. London: Routledge, 209–220.
Sperber, D. and D. Wilson. 1995. *Relevance: Communication and Cognition*. Second edition, with a new Postface. Oxford: Blackwell.
Veltman, F. 1996. Defaults in update semantics. *Journal of Philosophical Logic* 25: 221–261.
Wedgwood, D. 2007. Shared assumptions: semantic minimalism and Relevance Theory. *Journal of Linguistics* 43: 647–681.
Wilson, D. and D. Sperber 2012. *Meaning and Relevance*. Cambridge: Cambridge University Press.
Zwicky, A. and J. Sadock 1975. Ambiguity tests and how to fail them. In J. P. Kimball (ed.) *Syntax and Semantics 4*. New York: Academic Press, 1–36.

Related topics

Chapter 1, (Descriptive) Externalism in semantics; Chapter 2, Internalist semantics; Chapter 5, Cognitive semantics; Chapter 11, Contextual adjustment of meaning; Chapter 15, Semantic shift; Chapter 29, Semantic processing.

11
Contextual adjustment of meaning

Robyn Carston

1 Introduction: sentence meaning and speaker meaning

It is generally much easier to say what a speaker means when she utters a particular sentence in the course of a communicative exchange than it is to say what the sentence itself means in the abstract (or what any of the specific words or phrases within it mean). Consider the following exchange between two university lecturers, focusing on what Amy means (or communicates) by her utterance:

(1) Bill: Did the staff-student meeting go well?
    Amy: We gave up – the students wouldn't engage.

Clearly, what Bill takes Amy to be communicating depends on a rich background of assumptions that Amy assumes are accessible to him, but we all have access to some of these assumptions (based on general and cultural knowledge) and can surmise that she has communicated at least the following two propositions (or very similar ones):

(2) a Amy and the other staff members at the meeting *gave up* on their attempt to discuss certain issues with the students who were at the meeting because those *students would not engage* with these issues.
    b The meeting did not go well (from the point of view of Amy).

The key point is that there is a pretty massive gap between what is communicated here and the meaning of the two sentences employed for the purpose, "We gave up," and "The students wouldn't engage," both of which could be used, whether singly or together, in other conversational exchanges to communicate very different information. What about the meaning of the sentences themselves, abstracted from any particular use or context? The range of communicative possibilities achievable with these sentences goes hand in hand with their having a quite meagre meaning or semantic character in and of themselves. I won't attempt to specify here what that is in any detail, but whatever it is, it has to accommodate the fact that, for instance, "we" is used to refer to a salient group of individuals which includes the current speaker, whoever that may be, and "engage" can be used to convey a wide range of quite distinct meanings as in "engage with a problem," "engage an audience," "engage a plumber," "engage the gears of a car," "get engaged to someone," etc.

The gap between sentence meaning and speaker meaning is a perfectly general phenomenon. The nature of this gap and how we bridge it constitutes the domain of a pragmatic theory, a theory concerned with how it is that hearers are able to recover rich specific messages on the basis of utterances of linguistic expressions that radically underdetermine those messages (see Chapter 10). There are many different manifestations of this linguistic underdetermination of what the speaker meant (or communicatively intended): ambiguities (lexical and structural); referential indeterminacies such as "we" and "the students" in Amy's utterance above; unspecified quantifier domains as in "*Everyone* left early"; incomplete expressions as in "The students didn't *engage*" or "Mary is *ready*"; vague expressions like "He is *young*" or "They live *nearby*"; implicit clausal connections like the causal relation between the two parts of Amy's utterance above, approximations like "He has a *square* face"; non-literal uses as in metaphorical and/or ironical uses of "Susan is a *saint*"; and illocutionary indeterminacies as in "You will meet Bill tomorrow," which could be a prediction, a promise, a request or a bet.

The focus of this chapter is cases where the meaning provided by a lexical item has to be adjusted in context to recover the concept the speaker intended, as in the cases of "engage," "square" and "saint" just mentioned. Before directly addressing this issue, however, it is worth setting out some relevant background, so in the next section I provide a brief review of two pairs of terms: semantics and pragmatics; explicature and implicature. In section 3, some different kinds of pragmatic enrichment are described: saturation, "free" pragmatic enrichment, unarticulated constituents. Then, with these parts of the bigger picture in place, we move, in section 4, to the main topic of how it is that hearers are able to grasp the intended occasion-specific meanings of words, and, in section 5, to an overview of the debate about exactly what lexical meanings are (whether full-fledged concepts or something more schematic and semantically underspecified). The chapter ends with a brief conclusion in which these views on word meaning are related to the overarching theoretical positions of minimalism, contextualism and pragmaticism.

2 Linguistic communication: semantics and pragmatics

2.1 Semantics: truth conditions and/or encoded linguistic meaning?

According to long tradition, the core notion of semantics is that of "truth conditions". Philosophers of language take a fundamental property of language to be its "aboutness", that is, its capacity to represent, or say things about, the external world. The conditions that make a sentence a true representation are what connect linguistic representations to the external world. On this basis, we can be said to have semantic knowledge of a language to the extent that we grasp the truth conditions of the sentences it generates (see Chapter 1). However, coming from a more recent cognitive-scientific perspective, there is another way of construing the semantic component of a language: as the meaning that is encoded in the linguistic system, that is, the stable context-independent meaning of the basic elements (morphemes or words) together with the meaning relations determined by its syntactic structures. An interesting question concerns the extent to which these two conceptions of semantics – as truth-conditional content and as encoded meaning – coincide.

It is obvious that there is not a perfect coincidence as there are words in every natural language (as opposed to human-made logical languages) which are intrinsically context-dependent. These are the familiar pronouns and demonstratives (or "indexicals"), e.g. the encoded context-independent meaning of the word "that" is something very minimal (and difficult to specify) which enables it to be used to mean (or "refer to") an indefinite range of individuals, properties or situations. Thus, the sentence "That's good" does not have a fully specifiable set of truth conditions unless it is relativized to a particular context of use. The question is whether context-dependence is confined to a small set of words of this sort (as "semantic minimalists" maintain) or is a much more widespread feature of language (as "semantic contextualists" maintain). The truth-conditional semantics programme for natural language sentences can accommodate some limited context-dependence especially if it can be handled by a determinate set of contextual parameters like the speaker, the hearer, the day, time and place of utterance, which allow for a direct rule-based mapping from context-dependent word (e.g. "I", "you", "today", "now") to entity referred to ("semantic value", as it is sometimes put).

However, if context-dependence extends to descriptive words like nouns, verbs and adjectives, the programme looks less promising. Even more problematic, if sentence meanings are not fully propositional, even once the context-particular values of indexical words (pronouns, demonstratives) have been determined, then truth conditions cannot be given for natural language sentences but only for the propositions (or thoughts) they are used to communicate on a specific occasion of use. On the basis of cases like those discussed in section 1, this does seem to be the case: while the occasion-specific thought(s) communicated by "We gave up" or "The students wouldn't engage" or "Mary is ready" or "Everyone left early" are fully truth-conditional, it is far from obvious (and has proved difficult to establish) that the sentences themselves have a propositional content. According to the position known as "contextualist semantics", it is not sentence types or even tokens of sentences (relativized to a narrow set of contextual parameters) but speech acts or utterances that have truth-conditional contents, and those contents are, to a greater or lesser extent, dependent on the context in which they are used, where the context involved is broad, encompassing general and cultural background knowledge as well as the immediate situation of utterance.

If contextualism is right and the semantic minimalist account of sentence meaning in truth-conditional terms cannot be sustained, what is to be said about sentence semantics? It seems that the linguistic semantic enterprise becomes not the provision of truth conditions, but a specification of the kind of meaning-relevant information provided by (encoded by) linguistic expressions as abstracted from any contextual specifics. In the case of lexical items, this might include concepts (perhaps the lexical form "dog", for instance, maps to a mental concept DOG, which provides a repository for our accumulated knowledge about dogs; see Chapter 2) and procedures or processing constraints (perhaps the word "but", for instance, tells us something about how we are to relate the sentence that follows it to the one that precedes it). In the case of syntactic structures and an array of functional words and morphemes (e.g. certain prepositions, case marking, inflectional affixes) the account would have to specify the relationships and connections they contribute to the meaning of sentences in which they appear. The output of this linguistic semantics is not a propositional entity (a thought) but a rich set of conceptual, structural and other clues that constrain and guide the processes of recovering the thoughts that constitute the communicated content of speakers' linguistic utterances. On this sort of picture, then, there are two rather distinct semantic enterprises: there is a "translational" semantics, which explicates the mapping of natural language expressions onto mental representations that play the evidential role just described, and there is what some see as "real" semantics, which relates representations to the aspects of the external world that they represent, a truth-conditional semantics of thoughts (or sentences in Mentalese, the language of thought (Fodor 1975)). For further discussion of linguistic underdeterminacy and of the two kinds of semantics, see Carston (2002: 48–64).

2.2 Pragmatics: implicature and explicature

The role of pragmatics is to take the output of the translational linguistic semantics as just described and use it, together with contextual assumptions, to infer the speaker's meaning. These pragmatic inferential processes are constrained and guided by principles that are specific to utterance interpretation and based on the presumed rationality of the communicative process, that is, that speakers meet particular standards of informativeness, relevance and orderliness (Grice 1975, Wilson and Sperber 2004).

As noted in the discussion of Amy's utterance in (1) above, it seems natural to think of speakers as communicating two kinds of propositions or thoughts, one that takes the encoded linguistic meaning as a kind of template (see (2a) above) and the other whose content seems to be quite separate from the linguistic meaning (see (2b) above). This latter component of communicated meaning is pretty universally known as "conversational implicature," but the first component, a fleshing out of the skeletal linguistic meaning, has been given a number of different labels: "what is said (pragmatic)" or "what is said (intuitive)", as distinct from semantic construals of what is said; primary speaker meaning; "impliciture", which captures the fact that some of its content is only "implicit" in what is said (semantically construed); "explicature", which highlights the distinction with "implicature" while allowing for a range of pragmatic contributions (hence varying degrees of explicitness). In what follows, I will use the term "explicature" which has been defined as follows within the relevance-theoretic pragmatic framework: An assumption/proposition which is communicated (speaker-meant) and is developed out of one of the encoded logical forms (semantic representations) of the sentence uttered (Sperber and Wilson 1995 [1986]: 182). Any other assumptions (or propositions) that are communicated (speaker-meant) are implicatures.

An important constraint on utterance interpretation is that the derivation process should be inferentially sound, which entails that any implicated conclusions should follow logically from the explicature (and contextual assumptions). Recall again the implicature of Amy's utterance above: "The staff-student meeting didn't go well." This clearly does not follow from the schematic linguistic meaning of the sentences she uttered: "We gave up", "The students didn't engage", not even after the referents of "we" and "the students" have been provided. Further processes of pragmatic enrichment of the decoded meaning are necessary, as indicated in the representation of the explicature in (2a). The different kinds of pragmatic enrichment that may be involved in developing a decoded linguistic meaning into an explicature are discussed in the next section.

3 Pragmatic enrichment

Consider again the two sentences from the conversation in (1), repeated here for convenience:

(3) We gave up. The students wouldn't engage.

When either or both of these are uttered, recovery of the speaker's explicature requires a variety of pragmatic enrichments. Some of these are overtly required by the linguistic form used and others are not. When the pragmatic process of supplying a specific contextual content or value is linguistically indicated, it is known as a process of "saturation," and when it is not, it is known as "free" enrichment (Recanati 1993). The contrast is between pragmatic processes that are linguistically controlled or mandated, and so obligatory (they must take place in all contexts of use), and those that are "free", that is, not linguistically controlled, hence optional (they need not take place in all contexts). Such linguistically "free" processes are entirely a matter of pragmatics, that is, of recovering an interpretation that meets prevailing presumptions about the relevance (or informativeness) of intentional communicative behaviour.

3.1 Saturation

The most obvious case of saturation in (3) is the assigning of a referent to the pronoun "we", which overtly sets up a slot or variable to be contextually filled. Arguably, however, there are slots that are not marked by such audible or visible linguistic forms, that is, they are cases of covert indexicals/variables or implicit arguments. The following are plausible cases involving saturation of a linguistically present but imperceptible constituent, such that the contextually supplied content answers the bracketed question:

(4) a Paracetamol is better.   [than what?]
    b It's the same.   [as what?]
    c He is too young.   [for what?]
    d It's hot enough.   [for what?]
    e The winners each get £1,000.   [winners of what?]

These are all, arguably, semantically incomplete (subpropositional) until the constituent is contextually supplied. In each case, there's a lexical item which, as a matter of its meaning, requires completion: *better*, *same*, *too x*, *x enough*, *winner*. This may also be the case for components of the sentences in (3): the delimitation of the group of students or the activities which are taken to be the objects of "give up" and "engage." If these are cases of saturation, then there must be some linguistic indication or other that the pragmatic process is required: in the case of the verb forms, it might be that their lexical entries specify an obligatory object; for the definite description "the students," it might be some formal indication on the definite article or on the predicate "students" or the phrase as a whole (see Stanley (2002) for discussion of these options).

3.2 Unarticulated constituents

There are instances of pragmatic enrichment that seem to be "free" in the sense outlined above: they do not seem to be indicated by anything in the linguistic form employed by the speaker and they are not required to ensure minimal propositionality. Consider the following:

(5) a It'll take time for your knee to heal.
    b She has a brain.
    c Something has happened.

Once reference is assigned (to "your" and "she" and to any temporal variables), these examples are semantically complete (propositional) but, without further pragmatic adjustment, they are banal obvious truths (any process takes place over a span of time, all human beings have a brain as part of their physical makeup, etc.). In virtually no instance would a speaker of these sentences intend to express that uninformative, irrelevant proposition; rather, she would intend an enriched or elaborated proposition which is relevant, that is, which interacts fruitfully with the addressee's accessible contextual assumptions.

It has been argued that these are cases where a pragmatic process supplies an unarticulated constituent of content to the explicature. Let's be clear what is meant by this notion since the pragmatically supplied constituents of content in (4) above are also "unarticulated" in one sense of this expression: they have not been given phonetic expression by the speaker. But the concept of unarticulated constituent (UC) at issue here is a more restrictive one according to which absence of linguistic articulation means absence of any formal indication at all, hence neither any overt audible/visible linguistic expression nor any covert (phonetically unrealised) linguistic element in the logical form of a sentence. It is only when this is the case that we have "free" pragmatic enrichment.

This sort of linguistically unmandated enrichment arguably applies to a much wider range of cases than the banal truisms above in (5). The following are plausible cases:

(6) a Jack and Jill went up the hill [*together*].
    b Mary left Paul and [*as a consequence*] he became clinically depressed.
    c She took out her gun, went into the garden and killed her father [*with the gun, in the garden*].
    d I'll give you £10 if [*and only if*] you mow the lawn.
    e Louise has always been a great lecturer [*since she's been a lecturer*].

Without the bracketed material, each of these is fully propositional (truth-evaluable) and is not an obvious truth, but in a great many contexts it is the propositional form enriched with the bracketed constituent that is the one communicated. It is this enriched proposition that is taken by addressees to be the content of what is asserted, that is, the basis upon which the speaker is judged to have spoken truly or not and the content that serves as a key premise in the inferential derivation of implicatures. Without these developments of the logical form (in addition to disambiguation and saturation), in many contexts the interpretation of the utterance would not meet the presumed pragmatic standard of sufficient informativeness or relevance. Such "free" enrichment processes are like implicatures in that both are linguistically unarticulated and whether they are derived or not is entirely a pragmatic matter: they are supplied only if they are needed to reach an inferentially sound interpretation that satisfies pragmatic constraints. For further discussion of free enrichment and examples of unarticulated constituents, see Carston (2002), Hall (2008) and Recanati (2002, 2012).

It is sometimes not clear whether we are dealing with a case of an unarticulated constituent or saturation of a covert indexical/variable element and arguments are needed to establish which is in operation. Among the contended cases are the following, where the constituent in brackets is not pronounced in the utterance:

(7) a Everyone [*at such and such a party*] left early.
    b It's raining [*in Oslo*].
    c We've eaten [*dinner*].

While advocates of free enrichment would argue that the constituents given in italics are entirely pragmatically motivated (Carston 2002; Recanati 2002), others (let's call them "formalists") maintain that these components of explicature content are underwritten by a covert linguistic element (Stanley 2000; Stanley and Szabó 2000; Martí 2006). This debate remains unresolved with a lack of definitive arguments one way or the other and with both sides facing an issue of potential overgeneration: the advocate of free enrichment has to show that the process is adequately constrained by pragmatics alone (Hall 2014) and the formalist has to convince us that the (many) imperceptible elements he posits are really there. While this particular debate may seem both arcane and intractable, it has important implications and needs to be resolved. For the formalist, unarticulated constituents are a particularly unappealing prospect as they cause problems for any orthodox principle of semantic compositionality, which aims to provide an algorithm for composing the (truth-conditional) meaning of any sentence out of its basic components and their combinatorics. For the free enrichment advocate, unarticulated constituents are a manifestation of the power of pragmatics in utterance interpretation, making it not just an optional add-on to linguistic decoding but an independent determinant of the speaker's explicitly communicated meaning.

There is another kind of pragmatic enrichment or adjustment that occurs in developing the encoded sentence meaning into the explicature. This is the process of modulating or adjusting literal (encoded) word meanings, as in, for instance, adjusting the meaning of the verb "engage" in (3) above in determining the specific concept the speaker intended (paraphraseable as "give focused attention and thought [to an issue or problem]"). An interesting question is whether this is a linguistically controlled pragmatic process or a "free" pragmatic process. It appears strikingly different from the process of indexical saturation, but whether it qualifies as free rather than linguistically controlled (in some way or other), so whether it is an optional pragmatic process rather than an obligatory one, depends entirely on the nature of encoded lexical meanings. If lexical meanings are fully conceptual (hence can contribute directly to truth-conditional content, thus to explicature) then contextual adjustments of word meaning are optional and the pragmatic process is, in this sense, free, but if they are some more schematic kind of mental entity (hence semantically underspecified), the process of word meaning adjustment is one of specifying the concept expressed and is obligatory. I return to this issue in section 5 where views on the nature of encoded word meaning are discussed. In the next section, we look at the pragmatic processes of word meaning modulation.

4 Occasion-specific word meanings

4.1 Lexical adjustment and ad hoc concepts

Several accounts of word meaning adjustment in context have been developed in recent years by pragmatic theorists who take different approaches to the process. Two prominent accounts are those of François Recanati (2004) and relevance theorists (e.g. Wilson and Carston 2007). There is considerable overlap of outlook: both agree that a word may contribute to the explicature of an utterance a constituent of content that is different from its literal encoded meaning. However, their views on the actual processes responsible for these meaning adjustments diverge markedly (for discussion, see Carston 2007, Recanati 2007). On Recanati's contextualist approach, "the interpretation that eventually emerges ... results from a blind, mechanical process.... The dynamics of accessibility does everything and no 'inference' is required. In particular, there is no need to consider the speaker's beliefs and intentions" (Recanati 2004: 32). The relevance-theoretic account, on the other hand, is fully inferential and the hearer's interpretive process is guided by the assumption that the speaker is a rational communicator whose utterance meets a standard of "optimal relevance", that is, her addressee can expect to derive a range of beneficial cognitive effects from attending to the utterance and to not be put to any unnecessary effort in the process (see Wilson and Sperber (2004) for the full account). Here, I outline the relevance-theoretic account of word meaning adjustment in terms of a pragmatic inferential process of *ad hoc* concept construction.

Consider the following examples, taking them to be utterances about a man in his forties, Boris, who has been married for many years:

(8) a Boris is a man.
    b Boris is a child.
    c Boris is a bachelor.

In (8a), the linguistically encoded content is a trivial uninformative truth, hence does not meet the standard of optimal relevance. The addressee's process of trying to grasp the speaker's meaning, a process guided by his expectation of relevance, leads to the encoded concept MAN being narrowed down so as to encompass just men of some kind. Depending on the specifics of the context, it could be narrowed down to "typical man" or "ideal man" and, of course, what constitutes a typical man or an ideal man will itself vary from context to context. The outcome of this process is an occasion-specific sense (or "*ad hoc*" concept) MAN*, whose denotation is a proper subset of the set of individuals that fall under the original encoded concept MAN. In (8b), we have the opposite phenomenon: the encoded concept CHILD is adjusted so as to mean roughly "person who behaves in certain childish ways", and the result is a concept CHILD* which is broader than the lexically encoded concept – as well as children, it includes some adults. Then, if we take (8c) as an utterance by Boris's wife, who has long endured his affairs with other women and general lack of commitment, the concept BACHELOR* which is communicated is, arguably, both a broadening of the lexical concept BACHELOR (it includes *married* men who behave in certain ways) and a narrowing of it (it excludes *unmarried* men who don't behave in this stereotypic way).

These *ad hoc* concepts, which are marked by an asterisk to distinguish them from lexically encoded concepts, are composed into the explicature and play a key role in warranting implicatures of the utterance. So, for (8c), for instance, the interpretation ultimately derived looks something like the following:

(9) Explicature: BORIS$_x$ IS A BACHELOR*
    Implicatures: BORIS$_x$ DISLIKES EMOTIONAL COMMITMENT
                   BORIS$_x$ PREFERS TO AVOID DOMESTIC RESPONSIBILITIES
                   BORIS$_x$ ENJOYS GOING OUT WITH HIS FRIENDS AND MEETING NEW WOMEN

Without going into the details of the cognitive and communicative principles proposed in relevance theory (see Wilson and Sperber (2004) and Chapter 10), I will briefly outline the account given within this framework of how a hearer reaches this interpretation of (8c). Let us assume, in line with the theory, that a hearer follows a path of least effort in accessing interpretations and accepts the first one that yields a satisfactory array of implications (or other cognitive effects) while requiring no gratuitous processing effort from him. When the lexical form /bachelor/ is recognized, it activates a lexical concept BACHELOR along with a range of associated encyclopaedic information about bachelors, including bundles of assumptions that make up stereotypes of certain kinds of bachelors, one for the carefree, fast living, undomesticated sort, another for the elderly, fussy, woman-averse sort. In the context, which includes the fact that it is Boris's wife who is the speaker, it is likely that the first of these bundles of stereotypic information is more highly activated than the second and that the definitional information that bachelors are unmarried men is either very low in activation or, if initially highly activated, is rapidly suppressed, given its inconsistency with Boris's married status. On this basis, perhaps together with further contextual assumptions about

Boris, the hearer forms hypotheses about the speaker's meaning, which may well include propositions such as those given above as implicatures of the utterance: Boris is uncommitted, irresponsible, etc. The claim is that the explicature (which develops out of the decoded linguistic meaning) and the implicatures are derived in parallel and there are processes of mutual adjustment between them that go on until the interpretation settles into a sound inference pattern and meets the presumption of optimal relevance. What that entails in this case is the adjustment of the encoded concept BACHELOR to yield the concept BACHELOR* which warrants the hypothesized implications and no others.

4.2 Metaphor and other non-literal uses of words

An interesting further proposal made within the relevance-theoretic approach to lexical pragmatics is that exactly the same process of *ad hoc* concept construction as outlined in the previous subsection applies in the comprehension of metaphorically used words (Wilson and Carston 2007, 2008; Sperber and Wilson 2008). So, for example, in figuring out what the speaker means by an utterance of the sentence "Boris is a chameleon", the interpretive process would be one of accessing highly activated components of information associated with the concept CHAMELEON. Given contextual constraints, including that the subject, Boris, is a human being, the information accessed would include the assumptions that chameleons change their appearance and behaviour according to the environment they are in, that they are thereby able to evade detection, etc. (and would exclude the information that they are lizards, brightly coloured, with rapidly darting tongues, etc.). This readily accessible information is used in forming a hypothesis about the intended implications of the utterance and adjusting the lexical concept to the *ad hoc* concept CHAMELEON* so as to warrant just those implications.

Underlying this account is the assumption that metaphorical uses are simply one kind of loose use of language and lie on a continuum with other varieties of loose use, including approximations, category extensions and hyperbolic uses. Although the *ad hoc* concepts derived in cases of what are pre-theoretically labelled metaphors are likely to involve a more radical broadening of the encoded literal meaning than these other cases of loose use, there is no difference in kind and nothing special about the mechanism involved in metaphor interpretation. Consider, for instance, the following uses of the word "marathon":

(10) a Mary ran the London marathon this year.
 b I'm going to run a marathon for charity.
 c My morning jog is a marathon.
 d The presidential election campaign is a marathon.

While (10a) is a strictly literal case (that is, the running event referred to is 26 miles and 385 yards), (10b) may be an approximation where the use of "marathon" could include runs that are somewhat less than 26 miles but which are still considered long and demanding. Then, with regard to (10c), let's suppose it is uttered by a rather unfit person who has only recently embarked on the activity of jogging round her small local park; this would be a case of hyperbolic use and the information associated with the encoded concept MARATHON that it would activate would be to do with the physical effort expended by the runner, the resulting fatigue, etc. and not to do with the run being of considerable length. Finally, for (10d), an apparent case of metaphorical use, the information about physical distance and physical running would not be accessed while that concerning the psychological and emotional stamina required would be. The idea, then, is that for each of these uses, a different subset of the mass of information associated with the lexical concept MARATHON is the most highly activated one and plays an instrumental role in determining which particular *ad hoc* concept the speaker intended.

There are some challenges to this very "deflationary" view of metaphor. First, although the on-line *ad hoc* concept construction process seems to work fine for these simple lexical cases, which are typical of spontaneous face-to-face conversation, one might wonder how adequate it is to capture more creative, complex or extended cases of metaphor, especially those that occur in poetry and seem to require sustained reflective processing (see Carston (2010a)). Second, for many theorists, metaphor, even though a pervasive use of language, is not to be assimilated to a more general class of loose uses of language but employs its own distinctive processing mechanism. A view held by many cognitive linguists is that metaphor is first and foremost a cognitive (rather than a communicative) phenomenon and humans manipulate a wide range of *conceptual* metaphors which effect mappings between disparate cognitive domains, so, for example, there is a conceptual metaphor <HUMANS ARE ANIMALS> which provides mental mappings from the domain of animals to the domain of human characteristics and behaviour (see Lakoff (1993) and Chapter 5). This would underlie the utterance of "Boris is a chameleon" discussed above and the many other metaphorical uses of animal terms ("pig", "dog", "cow", "bear", "wolf", "fox", etc.). One possibility is that conceptual metaphors, if they exist, are one of the sources of encyclopaedic information used in the relevance-theoretic account of *ad hoc* concept formation (Tendahl and Gibbs 2008).

4.3 Ad hoc concepts – open issues

The work on *ad hoc* concepts is relatively recent and there are many questions raised by the notion. The first is whether these entities are to be thought of as internally structured (decompositional) or unstructured (atomic) (for discussion of this distinction, see Chapter 12). *Prima facie*, these pragmatically derived concepts appear likely to be structured: the *ad hoc* concept BACHELOR* expressed by the use of "bachelor" in (8c) above seems to consist of a combination of other concepts along the lines of: MAN WHO IS IRRESPONSIBLE, UNCOMMITTED, PROMISCUOUS, etc. However, many relevance theorists are committed to an atomic view of lexical concepts and would like this to carry over to the *ad hoc* concepts derived from them; the idea would be that, for this use of "bachelor," the highly activated concepts IRRESPONSIBLE, UNCOMMITTED, PROMISCUOUS, etc. trigger an atomic concept BACHELOR* which functions as a basic component in thought (a "word" in Mentalese).

A second question that has been raised is the extent to which these "*ad hoc*" components of communicated meaning are really novel or occasion-specific; after all, at least some of them are quite familiar, even standardized, uses of the words concerned, e.g. the application of "chameleon" to an unreliable, fickle person, or "child" to an adult who is behaving in an immature way. This is undeniably right; these contextually conditioned word meanings may already be active components of the hearer's cognitive repertoire so, as used here, "*ad hoc*" cannot be taken to mean new or one-off. What it means is that the concept is *pragmatically derived* as opposed to lexically decoded and even here there may be differences across individuals – for someone who has only been exposed to the use of "chameleon" for a certain kind of human behaviour and is ignorant of the lizard species, this human-applicable concept might be the one it encodes. One of the strengths of this pragmatic account of how we can communicate a wide range of distinct concepts across contexts is that it allows for considerable individual differences in lexical knowledge.

Third, the question arises whether, in cases of genuine novelty, the *ad hoc* meaning derived is always a full-fledged concept or something less determinate. Consider in this regard the following attested example, focusing on the novel use here of the word "topspin":

(11) *Theatre critic discussing a new play on in London:*
"The gold standard performance comes from McDiarmid. Vocally, he is spell-binding, giving lines dextrous *topspin* and unexpected bursts of power."

Sunday Times (04/09/11) *Culture* section, p. 23

With some fairly minimal knowledge of the nature and effects of hitting a ball with topspin in games like cricket and tennis, one can grasp enough implications of the critic's description of McDiarmid's vocal performance to be able see the relevance of the utterance. Plausible implicatures are the following:

(12) McDiarmid speaks his lines in a way that compels attention
His changes of pitch and rhythm are unusual and remarkable
The other actors may find it hard to match his verbal skill

But what about the novel "concept" communicated here, the *ad hoc* component of meaning that would replace the literal encoded concept TOPSPIN in the explicature of the utterance? This use of the word "topspin" may have been entirely new for many readers, as it was for me, and it may well be that we would not be able to employ it with any confidence in a new context, even though it clearly supports implications such as those in (12) and so does the job quite adequately in this particular instance. The thought here, then, is that a reader, who has essentially understood this utterance, may nevertheless not have formed a complete concept TOPSPIN* (which is locked to a property in the world) but rather just a metarepresentational mental entity "TOPSPIN"*, marked as not fully understood, something which may or may not become fully conceptualized at a later date. For discussion of the three issues just sketched, see Carston (2010b) and Hall (2011).

A final point of interest here is whether the account of pragmatic contributions to explicature really needs both *ad hoc* concepts (resulting from word meaning modulation) and unarticulated constituents (UCs), as discussed in section 3.2. It seems that quite a number of the cases discussed in the literature on UCs might be better thought of as cases of word meaning modulation. Consider again some of the examples given earlier as involving UCs:

(13) a She has a [*good*] brain.
b Jack and Jill went up the hill [*together*].
c She took out her gun, went into the garden and killed her father [*with the gun*, *in the garden*].
d I'll give you £10 if [*and only if*] you mow the lawn.
e It's raining [*in Oslo*].

Some of these seem easily conceptualized as cases of deriving an enriched or narrowed *ad hoc* concept, e.g. "good brain" is a specifization of "brain"; "kill with a gun" is a manner specification of "kill." Perhaps, then, these are really lexical adjustments that would appear in the explicature as the atomic concepts BRAIN* and KILL*. Whether this can be extended to all cases of putative UCs (such as the location phrases in (13c) and (13e)) is another open question. It might not seem to matter much one way or the other but, as with the debate about UCs and covert indexicals mentioned in section 3.2, it is interesting for its impact on "semantic compositionality". Either way, some kind of enriched construal of compositionality is needed, but in the case of UCs this is much more problematic because a new component of structure appears to be derived without any linguistic basis, while in the case of lexical adjustments the *ad hoc* concept simply occupies the structural position of the linguistically encoded concept.

In this section, we have been assuming that words encode concepts, so the pragmatic process of lexical modulation takes one concept as its input and delivers another as its output. This assumption is questioned in the next section.

5 Encoded word meanings: concepts or semantically underspecified?

It is widely held by philosophers, psychologists, linguists and pragmaticists that descriptive words (nouns, verbs, adjectives) encode concepts, that is, mental symbols that (i) function as components of thoughts and (ii) denote entities, properties or situations in the world, hence are fully semantic entities in the truth-conditional sense. There has been a long debate about whether these lexical concepts are internally structured (hence composed of more basic components) or are themselves the primitives of the representational system (hence are atomic or unstructured). Most relevance theorists have adopted the view of Jerry Fodor that they are atomic, that is, that "cat" means CAT, "green" means GREEN, "open" means OPEN, and so on (for detailed arguments in favour of concept atomism, see Fodor 1998). Whether the atomistic view of lexical concepts or a decompositional position ultimately turns out to be correct, the relevant point here is that these encoded (standing) word meanings are the kind of entity that can be speaker-meant and so can be a constituent of explicatures. It follows that, even though word meanings are typically pragmatically adjusted in context, this is an optional (free) process and the encoded concept may, on occasion, be the very concept the speaker intends to communicate.

Sperber and Wilson (1998) maintain that while most words encode full-fledged concepts, some words encode something more minimal, which they call a "pro-concept", that is, a meaning that does not itself contribute to explicatures (truth-conditional contents) but functions instead as a constraint on the kind of concept that it can be used to express. What the concept expressed is on any occasion of use has to be pragmatically inferred using relevant contextual information. They suggest "my", "have", "near" and "long" as possible instances of words which encode pro-concepts. However, they go on to say: "quite commonly, all words behave *as if* they encoded pro-concepts: that is, *whether or not a word encodes a full concept*, the concept it is used to convey in a given utterance has to be contextually worked out" (Sperber and Wilson 1998: 185; my emphasis (RC)). One of the examples they discuss of a word that encodes a full concept but behaves *as if* it encodes a pro-concept is the verb "open". They note the widely acknowledged fact that it can be used to express a range of different but related concepts, depending on both linguistic and extralinguistic context (e.g. "open the door (with a key/with an axe)", "open a book", "open a bottle", "open one's eyes", "open a shop", "open a conference", and so on). As they say: "A verb like 'open' acts as a pointer to indefinitely many notions or concepts" (1998: 197). However, they assume that "open", like most verbs, encodes a concept and so, on occasion, "it may happen that the intended concept is the very one encoded by the word" (1998: 197). The point of primary interest here is that, according to this account, the linguistic "evidence" or "clue" to the speaker's *intended concept*, which is provided by the encoded meaning of the word and is input to the pragmatic adjustment process described in the previous section, is itself a concept, a full-fledged semantic entity.

There is reason to wonder whether this is the right view of encoded (or "standing") word meaning. First, note that while we can rather easily grasp the specific concepts of opening that we form in understanding the phrases "open one's mouth", "open the window", "open a shop", etc., it is very difficult to get any purchase on the nature of the alleged lexical concept OPEN, which is meant to be distinct from, and more general than, any of these. The question is whether there is any definite component of content there at all or whether any thought about opening must contain one of the more specific concepts (Carston 2012, 2013).

Second, this issue is not confined to a few verbs that happen to have multiple uses, like "open", "stop", "pass", "cut", "run", "rest", "turn". Rather, it applies to virtually all descriptive words, given that, as Wilson and Carston (2007: 231) maintain: "lexical narrowing and broadening (or a combination of the two) are the outcomes of a single interpretive process which fine-tunes the interpretation of *almost every word*." A similar view is taken by the computational linguist Bosch (2007) who, working in a different framework, observes that the lexical meaning of many words is underspecified and must be developed at a conceptual/pragmatic level for its expressed meaning to be recovered by a hearer. The noun "novel", for example, which he discusses at length, can have the following senses: a complex of ideas/thoughts (when the author is working on it), a text (when it is completed), a publication (e.g. when we talk of an author's most recent novel), a physical object (e.g. when we talk of a suitcase full of novels), and certain combinations, e.g. "Peter is reading the novel he found at the bus-stop" (text and physical object). No particular one of these senses is obviously the encoded meaning or is sufficiently all-encompassing to provide the basis for pragmatically inferring the other senses. As Bosch says, "If we want to maintain just one lexical entry for *novel* it must remain underspecified in many respects" (2007: 68). He discusses a number of other words of various lexical categories (e.g. "work", "rain", "run", "cut", "open", "fast") whose susceptibility to being used to express different concepts, which he calls "contextual concepts," points to the same conclusion: "the lexical semantics should be left underspecified in these cases." However, like relevance theorists, Bosch also talks of "lexical *concepts*" and likens his position to that of Fodor and Lepore's (1998) "disquotational" view of the lexicon, that is, lexical forms map directly to atomic concepts, which constitute their standing meaning (ibid: 13).

The question here is: if words quite generally behave as if they don't encode concepts, why maintain that they do encode concepts? There are other possibilities for what encoded word meanings might consist of: (a) they might be schematic entities (which, while not conceptual themselves, function as constraints on the range of concepts they can be used to express), (b) they might be rich arrays of information (so that some of their meaning features have to be filtered out on any occasion of use), or, the most radical position, (c) there might be no encoded word meanings at all, but only an accumulation of memory traces of previous uses of a word, which provide the input to pragmatic processes of occasion-specific word meaning determination. The nature of standing (encoded) word meaning is currently a hotly debated topic and each of these positions has its advocates (see, for instance, Bosch (2009), Carston (2013), Pritchard (forthcoming), Rayo (2013)).

Recall the question raised at the end of section 3, whether the pragmatic process of modulating word meanings is obligatory or optional. If encoded word meanings are not fully conceptual but are instead semantically underspecified, as suggested here, the pragmatic process is obligatory: whether enriching a schematic lexical meaning or selecting from an array of lexically provided information or traces of previous uses, this process of recovering the concept the speaker expressed must take place across all contexts of use. If this is right, it may turn out that there are, after all, no "free" pragmatic processes involved in the recovery of the speaker's explicature.

6 Conclusion: contextual adjustment of meaning and pragmaticism

There is little doubt that the level of explicitly communicated content (the explicature or "intuitive" truth-conditional content of an utterance) often receives considerable pragmatic input in addition to the meaning that comes directly from the linguistic system. This chapter has reviewed a range of kinds of pragmatic enrichment – saturation, unarticulated constituents and word meaning modulation. The question yet to be resolved is whether all of these processes are required and, in particular, whether there really are free (hence optional) pragmatic processes at this level (implicature derivation being, of course, an unequivocally "free" pragmatic process) or, instead, all pragmatic contributions to explicature are linguistically mandated (hence obligatory).

To finish, I would like to return briefly to the two opposing stances on truth-conditional content: semantic minimalism and semantic contextualism. The main difference between them is their view of natural language semantics; specifically, whether sentences are propositional, hence truth-conditional. It's worth noting that minimalists, as much as contextualists, recognize the explicature/implicature distinction, that is, the distinction between two kinds of speaker meaning (or intentionally communicated content), and both agree that explicature (or "what is said" by a speaker) requires considerable pragmatic input (see the minimalists Borg (2004) and Cappelen and Lepore (2005) on this point). What interests both parties is truth-conditional content ("real" semantics): for minimalists, this starts with *sentences* in a language system, for contextualists it only comes into play with *utterances* of sentences in specific contexts. The implication of this for the level of word meaning is that minimalists have to maintain that encoded or standing word meanings are conceptual – that is, fully semantic entities, which can contribute directly (without pragmatic mediation) to truth conditions (Borg 2012) – whereas contextualism is compatible with the entire range of views, from fully semantic word meanings, through semantically underspecified meanings, to meaning eliminativism (Recanati 2004).

A third general position is pragmaticism, represented by the relevance-theoretic approach discussed in this chapter. It shares with contextualism the view that sentence meaning is schematic, not fully truth-conditional, and that pragmatic input is essential for a hearer to determine a fully propositional entity, but this is not the essence of the position because it is first and foremost a theory of communication rather than a semantic theory. Thus, the focus is on the thoughts that speakers communicate by their linguistic utterances and, in particular, on the processes by which hearers are able to recover these thoughts (Carston 2002, 2009). In this respect, pragmaticism tends to eschew contextualist talk of word meanings being *fixed in or by context* and to focus on the communicative intention of the speaker and the pragmatic principles that guide the hearer in reaching a warranted conclusion about the content of that intention. Accordingly, despite the title of this chapter, it is more appropriate to talk of "pragmatic adjustment" of meaning rather than "contextual adjustment" of meaning. Contexts, as such, are powerless, or, as Bach (2005) aptly puts it, there is no "context *ex machina*". What makes it possible to use a word to communicate a concept that is different from its encoded meaning is the coordinated interaction of two human minds, speaker and hearer.

Further reading

Bach, K. 1994. Conversational impliciture. *Mind and Language* 9: 124–65. A philosopher of language discusses pragmatic processes of "completion" and "expansion", which fall within the broad class of cases of pragmatic enrichment and so contribute to what he calls "impliciture" (similar to "explicature") as opposed to "implicature".

Bosch, P. 2007. Productivity, polysemy, and redicate indexicality. In B. ten Cate and H. Zeevat (eds) *Proceedings of the Sixth International Tbilisi Symposium on Language, Logic & Computation*. Berlin: Springer, 58–71. A computational linguist discusses the wide range of senses a single word may have in different contexts of use and argues that the encoded lexical meaning of such words is univocal and underspecified with the various senses derived in the process of utterance comprehension.

Carston, R. 2010. Explicit communication and 'free' pragmatic enrichment. In B. Soria and E. Romero (eds) *Explicit Communication: Robyn Carston's Pragmatics*. Basingstoke: Palgrave, 217–287. The cognitive-scientific basis of the relevance-theoretic account of explicit communication is set out, distinguishing it from the philosophical account of Paul Grice, and some criticisms of the cognitive approach are addressed.

Recanati, F. 2004. *Literal Meaning*. Cambridge: Cambridge University Press. A philosopher of language makes a strong case for "contextualism" and the essential role of "primary" pragmatic processes which enrich linguistic content and contribute to the truth-conditional content of an utterance (the proposition meant by the speaker).

Wilson, D. and R. Carston 2007. A unitary approach to lexical pragmatics. In N. Burton-Roberts (ed.) *Pragmatics*. Basingstoke: Palgrave, 230–260. The relevance-theoretic account of the pragmatic adjustment of word meaning in context is presented in detail, explaining what triggers the process, the different directions and outcomes it may have, and what determines its stopping point.

References

Bach, K. 2005. Context *ex machina*. In Z. Szabo (ed.) *Semantics Versus Pragmatics*. Oxford: Clarendon Press, 15–44.

Borg, E. 2004. *Minimal Semantics*. Oxford: Oxford University Press.

Borg, E. 2012. *Pursuing Meaning*. Oxford: Oxford University Press.

Bosch, P. 2007. Productivity, polysemy, and redicate indexicality. In B. ten Cate and H. Zeevat (eds) *Proceedings of the Sixth International Tbilisi Symposium on Language, Logic & Computation*. Berlin: Springer, 58–71.

Bosch, P. 2009. Predicate indexicality and context dependence. In P. De Brabanter and M. Kissine (eds) *Utterance Interpretation and Cognitive Models: Current Research in the Semantics/Pragmatics Interface vol. 20*. Bingley: Emerald Group, 99–126.

Cappelen, H. and E. Lepore. 2005. *Insensitive Semantics. A Defense of Semantic Minimalism and Speech Act Pluralism*. Oxford: Blackwell.

Carston, R. 2002. *Thoughts and Utterances: The Pragmatics of Explicit Communication*. Oxford: Blackwell.

Carston, R. 2007. How many pragmatic systems are there? In M-J. Frapolli (ed.) *Saying, Meaning, Referring: Essays on the Philosophy of Francois Recanati*. Houndmills: Palgrave, 18–48.

Carston, R. 2009. Relevance theory: contextualism or pragmaticism? *UCL Working Papers in Linguistics* 21: 17–24.

Carston, R. 2010a. Metaphor: *ad hoc* concepts, literal meaning and mental images. *Proceedings of the Aristotelian Society* vol. 110, part 3: 295–321.

Carston, R. 2010b. Explicit communication and 'free' pragmatic enrichment. In B. Soria and E. Romero (eds) *Explicit Communication: Robyn Carston's Pragmatics*. Basingstoke: Palgrave, 217–287.

Carston, R. 2012. Word meaning and concept expressed. *The Linguistic Review* 29: 607–623.

Carston, R. 2013. Word meaning, what is said and explicature. In C. Penco and F. Domaneschi (eds) *What is Said and What is Not*. Stanford: CSLI Publications, 175–204.

Fodor, J. A. 1975. *The Language of Thought*. New York: Thomas Crowell.

Fodor, J. A. 1990. *A Theory of Content and Other Essays*. Cambridge, Mass.: MIT Press.

Fodor, J. A. 1998. *Concepts. Where Cognitive Science Went Wrong*. Oxford: Clarendon Press.

Fodor, J. A. and E. Lepore. 1998. The emptiness of the lexicon: reflections on Pustejovsky. *Linguistic Inquiry* 29: 269–288.

Grice, H. P. 1975. Logic and conversation. In P. Cole and J. Morgan (eds) *Syntax and Semantics 3: Speech Acts*. New York: Academic Press, 41–58.

Hall, A. 2008. Free enrichment or hidden indexicals? *Mind and Language* 23: 426–456.
Hall, A. 2011. Ad hoc concepts: atomic or decompositional? *UCL Working Papers in Linguistics* 23: 1–10.
Hall, A. 2014. 'Free' enrichment and the nature of pragmatic constraints. *International Review of Pragmatics* 6: 1–28.
Lakoff, G. 1993. The contemporary theory of metaphor. In A. Ortony (ed.) *Metaphor and Thought*, 2nd edition. Cambridge: Cambridge University Press, 202–251.
Martí, L. 2006. Unarticulated constituents revisited. *Linguistics and Philosophy* 29: 135–166.
Pritchard, T. forthcoming. Conditions, constraints, and standing meaning.
Rayo, A. 2013. A plea for semantic localism. *Noûs* 47: 647–679.
Recanati, F. 1993. *Direct Reference: From Language to Thought*. Oxford: Blackwell.
Recanati, F. 2002. Unarticulated constituents. *Linguistics and Philosophy* 25: 299–345.
Recanati, F. 2004. *Literal Meaning*. Cambridge: Cambridge University Press.
Recanati, F. 2007. Reply to Carston. In M-J. Frapolli (ed.) *Saying, Meaning, Referring: Essays on the Philosophy of Francois Recanati*. Houndmills: Palgrave, 49–54.
Recanati, F. 2012. Pragmatic enrichment. In G. Russell and D. Graff Fara (eds) *Routledge Companion to the Philosophy of Language*. London: Routledge, 67–78.
Sperber, D. and D. Wilson 1995 [1986]. *Relevance: Communication and Cognition*. Oxford: Blackwell; Cambridge, Mass.: Harvard University Press. Second edition (with postface) 1995.
Sperber, D. and D. Wilson 1998. The mapping between the mental and the public lexicon. In P. Carruthers and J. Boucher (eds) *Language and Thought*. Cambridge: Cambridge University Press, 184–200.
Sperber, D. and D. Wilson 2008. A deflationary account of metaphors. In R. Gibbs (ed.) *The Cambridge Handbook of Metaphor and Thought*. Cambridge: Cambridge University Press, 84–105.
Stanley, J. 2000. Context and logical form. *Linguistics and Philosophy* 23: 391–434. Reprinted in J. Stanley. 2007: 30–68.
Stanley, J. 2002. Nominal restriction. In G. Preyer and G. Peter (eds), *Logical Form and Language*. Oxford: Oxford University Press, 365–388. Reprinted in J. Stanley, 2007: 111–132.
Stanley, J. 2007. *Language in Context*. Oxford: Clarendon Press.
Stanley, J. and Z. Gendler Szabó 2000. On quantifier domain restriction. *Mind and Language* 15: 219–261. Reprinted in J. Stanley, 2007: 69–110.
Tendahl, M. and R. Gibbs 2008. Complementary perspectives on metaphor: cognitive linguistics and relevance theory. *Journal of Pragmatics* 40: 1823–1864.
Wilson, D. and R. Carston 2007. A unitary approach to lexical pragmatics. In N. Burton-Roberts (ed.) *Pragmatics*. Basingstoke: Palgrave, 230–260.
Wilson, D. and R. Carston 2008. Metaphor and the 'emergent property' problem: a relevance-theoretic treatment. *The Baltic International Yearbook of Cognition, Logic and Communication, vol. 3: A Figure of Speech*. Manhattan, KS: New Prairie Press, 1–40.
Wilson, D. and D. Sperber 2004. Relevance theory. In L. Horn and G. Ward (eds) *The Handbook of Pragmatics*. Oxford: Blackwell, 607–632.

Related topics

Chapter 2, Internalist semantics; Chapter 5, Cognitive semantics; Chapter 10, Semantics and pragmatics; Chapter 12, Lexical decomposition; Chapter 13, Sense individuation; Chapter 28, Interpretative semantics; Chapter 29, Semantic processing.

Part V
Lexical semantics

12
Lexical decomposition

Nick Riemer

1 Introduction

Decompositional approaches to lexical content, which proceed by analysing meanings into smaller components, are a highly common explanatory strategy in semantics. They are found not only in overtly decompositional theories like those discussed in this chapter, but also in prototype theories (see Chapter 7), which presuppose that concepts are characterized by distinct *attributes*, in various computational and cognitive models (Pustejovsky 1991, 1995; Langacker 1987), which distinguish different features within semantic representations, and in neurosemantic studies of online processing, beyond the scope of this chapter (Just et al. 2010; Sudre et al. 2012). In addition, most morphosyntactic and typological theories are predicated on the idea that grammatical categories can be characterized by certain distinct properties (animacy, telicity, stativity, and agency, to name just four), which are easily conceived of as distinct features of meaning (see e.g. Corbett (2012)).

Other parts of this book illustrate many of the particular decompositional theories of meaning current in lexical semantics (see especially Chapters 22, 23, and 25). In this chapter, we address the issue of semantic decomposition more generally. We begin in section 2 by sketching various indicative decompositional strategies and outlining some of the reasons for which a decompositional approach to word meaning might be attractive. Section 3 then discusses some of the most interesting questions and problems decompositional projects pose. As we will see, the considerable heuristic utility of decompositional approaches to meaning is offset by the no less significant problems that attach to decomposition as a theory of underlying semantic structure.

2 Motivations and rationales for decomposition

In everyday metalinguistic discourse, speakers' efforts to clarify the meaning of a definiendum may take the form of a *paraphrase*, that is a string of several other words or phrases, presented as having the same communicative effect (for instance, we might clarify what we mean by *toast* with the paraphrase *grilled sliced bread*). Dictionary definitions, which are an elaboration of this kind of pretheoretical practice, manifest the same essentially analytical logic: the meaning of the definiendum is recast in terms of several defining words which, if the definition is to be explanatorily successful, must each in some sense be simpler than the definiendum or, at least, already understood by the definition's user.

Decompositional theories of lexical semantics rest on the intuition that the analytical structure of definitional paraphrases is not simply heuristic. Meanings should be thought of in essence as complex structures of more basic components, just as the meaning of a sentence must be seen as a compositional function of the meanings of its individual words (see Chapter 24). Phenomenologically, we certainly do not experience what we call a word's meaning as a structure which can be broken down, to use Cruse's formulation, into "the meanings of other words" (Cruse 1986: 16). Peirce's statement about thoughts – "two thoughts are two events separated in time, and one cannot literally be contained in the other" (Peirce 1868: 69) – applies to the experience of meaning as well. Nevertheless, decompositional reasoning is familiar from many common-sense arenas. On a decompositional approach, meanings are comparable to objects that straightforwardly consist of different parts, or of different enumerable intrinsic properties; or they are like temporally unfolding processes, recursively analysable into a series of different phases. As pointed out by Sprengel (1980: 149), a decompositional conception of meaning is implicit in the ancient definition according to which a concept can be divided into a *genus proximum* and a *differentia specifica*, such as "horse" and "female" for "mare". In the modern period, the earliest decompositional theories of word meaning were consciously modelled on decompositional theories of phonology (see Geeraerts (2010) for details). Just as complex articulatory gestures could arguably be factored into a finite set of more basic underlying phonetic properties, so too word meanings were assumed to be constructed from a smaller set of inherent, perhaps primitive, semantic elements (see Lipka (1992: 100ff) for discussion).

Decompositional analysis sees meanings as constituted by different permutations of a fixed set of recurrent components. Semantic "proportions" such as that existing between *beef/cow* and *pork/pig*; *car/garage*, *plane/hangar*, and *boat/shed*; and *circle/sphere* and *square/cube* can be described as involving the presence of identical meaning-constituting parts ("food"/"animal"; "vehicle"/"[storage] place"; "2-dimensional"/"3-dimensional") appearing across all pairs (see (Leech 1981: 91) for discussion). The explanatory benefit of this approach derives from reducing the diversity of a language's vocabulary to permutations of a single less numerous set of elements (see Bendix (1966: 4) for discussion of economy in decompositional systems). Lipka (1992: § 3.3.2) attempts a typology of semantic components – an interesting but necessarily incomplete exercise, given that anything that can appear in a definition can be converted into a component, and that there are therefore no a priori constraints on components other than constraints on what can be expressed in a metalanguage. The following German examples (Wunderlich 1997: 43–4), which go back to Generative Semantics, give a flavour of one of the most common kinds of decompositional analysis, discussed in Chapter 22, which analyses verb meanings as compositionally assembled from underlying primitive predicates:

(1) a   einschlafen "fall asleep"
        Hans schlief ein.
        Hans fell asleep
        BECOME (SLEEP(x))

    b   wecken "wake"
        Hans weckte Maria.
        Hans wakened Maria
        CAUSE (x, BECOME(NON(SLEEP(y))))

c   machen "make"
    Hans machte Maria wutend.
    Hans made Maria angry
    CAUSE (x, BECOME(P(y)))

As these analyses make clear, the units into which meanings are decomposed need not be conceived of simply as autonomous and self-standing: the components in (1) display a combinatorial structure in which each is supplied with a certain number of arguments. (See Fodor (1970) for some important objections to this kind of analysis.)

The motivations for engaging in decompositional analysis can be appreciated by discussing the two tracks by which decomposition entered semantic theory historically: a structuralist track originating in Saussure, which initially embodied a conception of meaning quite at odds with decomposition; and a cognitivist track originating in seventeenth-century philosophical rationalism and revived under the influence of the cognitive turn in linguistics in the second half of the twentieth century (see Chapter 22). The distinction between these two sources of decompositional ideas is not, of course, absolute. In the course of examining these two tracks, we will mention some important examples of decompositional theories.

2.1 Classical structuralism, lexical relations, and semantic difference

Structuralist theories in general stress that "there is no meaning apart from significant differences" (Nida 1975: 32): a word's meaning can only be accurately characterized by considering its place in the network of related terms with which it stands in a relation of paradigmatic choice. As Trier expressed it: "[t]he value of a word is first known if one distinguishes it from the value of neighbouring and opposing words. It only has any sense as part of a whole, for meaning only exists within a field" (1931: 6, quoted by Lyons (1963: 48)). Words are selected by speakers out of a large pool of possibilities – synonyms, antonyms, hyponyms, meronyms etc. – the suitability of any one of which is a function of the message being communicated. The significance of any one word is therefore only appreciated by assessing it in contrast to possible alternatives, each of which instantiates a certain semantic relation with the word actually selected. The set of alternatives from which a word can be chosen constitutes that word's *semantic field*.

Before proceeding, it is important to note that the original structuralist position, inspired by Saussure's (1979 [1916]: 166) insistence that language embodies only differences without positive terms, denied the possibility of any decompositional analysis. For this tradition of research, semantic relations *exhaust* word meaning: there just *is* nothing more to the meaning of a word than the semantic relations it holds to other words.

This commitment to relational rather than intrinsic properties as the essence of meaning cuts strongly against the essentializing habits of mind that have become deeply embedded in contemporary linguistic theorizing. These days, we are likely to think that the only reason words *can* enter into semantic relations with each other at all is that they convey some minimal meaning content over which the various semantic relations are defined: *open*, for instance, could not stand in a relation of antonymy to *shut* if the two words did not contain contrasting semantic information in virtue of which they count as antonyms.

Classical, especially European, structuralists deny this presupposition: for them, "the meaning of a given linguistic unit is defined to be the set of (paradigmatic) relations that the unit in question contracts with other units of the language (in the context or contexts in which it occurs), without any attempt being made to set up 'contents' for these units" (Lyons 1963: 59). In a passage that serves as a telling analogy for the structuralist position on meaning, Reichenbach (1947: 210, quoted by Lyons (1963: 58–9)) asserts the priority of relational over intrinsic qualities in the case of weight:

> What is the weight of a body? It is usually conceived as an abstract property of the body, recognizable from certain physical effects. Using Russell's principle of abstraction we can reduce the concept *weight* to the relation *having the same weight*. The weight of a body is the class of all objects having the same weight as this body. An adept in traditional logic would object that in order to define the same weight we must first define the weight, and then proceed by addition of the different specifica to the genus. But there is no reason to insist on this impractical method. It is admissible to conceive the notion of the same weight as prior to that of weight and to define the latter in terms of the former. This corresponds to the actual procedure used in empirical ascertainment of the weight of a body. The balance is a device which indicates, not the weight, but equality of weight.

Similarly, meaning for classical structuralists needs to be seen as a wholly relational property. Dictionary definitions, which might be thought to precisely express words' core semantic essences, actually do nothing other than state their semantic relations. For instance, the definition of *open* offered by the *Concise Oxford* – "allowing entrance or access, or passage" – can be viewed as a statement that *open* is *synonymous* with the phrase "allowing entrance or access, or passage", and *antonymous* with "closed" or "blocked". Lexical relations, not intrinsic semantic content, are therefore the bedrock of meaning.

This classical structuralist position now commands barely any adherents, even though semantic relations are an ongoing focus of research (Cruse 1986; Murphy 2003; see Chapter 14). However, an analogous denial of the existence of decompositional semantic content is occasionally still found in the hypothesis that "meaning postulates" (Carnap 1952; Katz and Nagel 1974; Fodor et al. 1975) are the bearers of semantic content. Meaning postulates are the kinds of logical relations which terms entertain with each other. Instead of saying that the three components "grilled sliced bread" *constitute* or *are the components of* the meaning *toast*, we might simply say that the *word* "toast" is linked to the phrase *grilled sliced bread* by a meaning postulate specifying that one *entails* the other, such that if something can be referred to as *toast*, then it can necessarily also be referred to as *grilled sliced bread*. On this picture, *toast* doesn't have any underlying semantic decomposition: its meaning may be atomic (Fodor 1998), but its privileged relation with the phrases taken to define it arises from its participation in the relevant meaning postulate.

Not least among the disadvantages of the idea that semantic relations or meaning postulates exhaust meaning is the fact that such approaches have nothing to say about the properties in virtue of which terms can break out of the circle of their linguistic relations so as to refer to extralinguistic entities: accounting for reference, indeed, is the central motivation for postulating intrinsic semantic contents. Nevertheless, the idea that meaning has to be assessed contrastively, in the context of semantically related words, was taken up by American anthropologists and linguists, who initiated decompositional analysis in the form that became institutionalized in twentieth-century linguistics. Consideration of lexical fields like kinship terms (Goodenough 1956; Lounsbury 1956) and many others gives rise to the impression that words' meanings are structured by minimal recurrent differences: the difference between *mother* and *father*, for example, is exactly the same as that between *daughter* and *son*, or between *aunt* and *uncle*: in each case, the first term includes the information

Lexical decomposition

that the referent is female, the second that it is male. "Female" and "male" can therefore be extracted as recurrent components of the meanings of these terms. (Alternatively, and on the model of phonological analysis, we might posit only one feature – "female" – and mark it as either present or absent – [+female], [–female] – in the underlying decompositions.) Similarly, features expressing generational difference [ascending/descending generations], and directness of relation (by blood or marriage) are extracted until every non-synonymous word in the semantic field has received a unique array of features. The analysis posits only enough underlying features to distinguish every word from every other in the semantic field or contrast set (see Chapter 25).

Componential analysis of this sort has been applied beyond kinship vocabulary – for example, to terms for artefacts (Pottier 1964, 1965), to verbs of possession (Bendix 1966) and to perceptual (Baldinger 1984) and dimension vocabulary (Greimas 2002), to name only a few domains (see Nida (1975) for extensive discussion). Figure 12.1 shows a possible array of semantic features along these kinds of lines for fourteen kinds of marine "vessel", distinguished through seven features, for which they may be unspecified (when marked by "ø").

This is certainly not the only decompositional analysis that it might be possible to advance for this set of words: as in any other domain of empirical investigation, theories are underdetermined by the evidence for them, in the sense that the same set of data is in principle open to multiple analyses, even within the same overall explanatory framework. Some researchers, however, have worried that componential analyses like those in Figure 12.1 are particularly arbitrary (Burling 1964: 26). However this may be, as the feature grid in Figure 12.1 suggests, terms from many fields of the vocabulary are much messier in their feature decompositions than kinship vocabulary is. Exactly how far a decompositional analysis could be pursued has never been fully tested: in contrast to the exhaustive analyses of phoneme repertoires, componential analysis has never been taken far enough by

	primarily transports freight	mainly for leisure	has single main form of propulsion	human source of propulsion	used in conjunction with another vessel	more than one hull	flat bottomed
rowboat	–	ø	+	+	–	–	–
dinghy	–	ø	+	+	+	–	–
ferry	–	–	+	–	–	–	–
yacht	–	+	–	–	–	–	–
barge	+	–	+	–	–	–	+
cargo ship	+	–	+	–	–	–	–
catamaran	–	+	–	–	–	+	–
buoy	–	–	–	–	+	–	+
punt	–	+	+	+	–	–	+
cruise ship	–	+	+	–	–	–	–
sail-board	–	+	+	–	–	–	+
tug-boat	–	–	+	–	+	–	–
trawler	–	–	+	–	–	–	–
pedal-boat	–	+	+	+	–	ø	ø

Figure 12.1 Componential analysis of some English words for marine vessels

217

researchers to provide anything like a representation of the meanings of the entire vocabulary, or even of a representative part of it.

Notice also that the seven features required to distinguish the terms in Figure 12.1 do not always coincide either with the information that would be represented in a dictionary entry, or with the information we would intuitively seize on to describe the meaning of the words: singularity of the form of propulsion, for instance, isn't an obvious part of the meaning of *cargo ship*. This is characteristic of componential analysis grounded in semantic fields: since the point of the decomposition is to minimally distinguish each member of the field from the others, the analysis will often be couched in terms of criteria that appear peripheral from a definitional point of view, but which pick out minimal differences of exactly the kind needed. Furthermore, none of the features conveys the fact that the "vessels" are used on water. Since all of the vessels have this feature, it isn't required to distinguish any of these words from the others. However, such a feature would be used to distinguish words for vessels with words for land or air vehicles. Feature arrays like those in Figure 12.1 are thus only ever a partial representation of the semantic components necessary to fully specify the contrastive relations within the whole of the lexicon.

2.2 Decomposition and the cognitive turn

As componential analysis drew further away from its structuralist origins, a second rationale for undertaking it loomed larger: the desire to ground meaning analysis in a level of semantic primitives, i.e. a set of indefinable, elementary concepts presumed to form the basis of the conceptual, and hence semantic, system. Semantic primitives were thought necessary as a response to the problem of definitional circularity – the fact that, since definitions are couched in other words, it is impossible to give fresh definitions of *every* word in a language, because sooner or later the same terms end up being both used as definienda and in the definitions themselves. Seventeenth-century philosophical rationalism had been alive to this kind of problem (see Maat (2004)):

> we should not try to define all words, because this would often be useless. It would even be impossible .... For in order to define a word it is necessary to use other words designating the idea that we want to connect to the word being defined. And if we then wished to define the words used to explain that word, we would need still others, and so on to infinity. Consequently, we necessarily have to stop at primitive terms which are undefined. It would be as great a mistake to try to define too many words as not to define enough, because in both cases we would fall into the confusion which we are claiming to avoid.
>
> (Arnauld and Nicole 1996 [1683]: 64)

The new cognitive sciences (Boden 2006) interpreted linguistic ability, like many other cognitive capacities, as the manifestation of an underlying mental rule-system. Language production and understanding were the product of the rule-governed, formal manipulation of a finite repertoire of mental symbols. Katz and Fodor (1963) represent an early attempt to characterize the semantic component of such a rule-system in a decompositional manner. (Note that Fodor has subsequently abandoned this commitment to semantic decomposition, now arguing that word meanings are atomic, and to be explained externalistically: Fodor (2008); see Chapter 1.) Katz and Fodor's account differentiates between semantic markers and semantic distinguishers. The markers, such as "male", "human", and "animal", are semantic components which "reflect whatever systematic relations hold between that item and the rest of the vocabulary of the language" (Katz and Fodor 1963: 187). As we have already seen, many words participate in sex-antonymy contrasts like that between *bachelor* and *spinster*: "male" therefore marks one term within a systematic semantic opposition. By contrast, the distinguishers do not participate in any regular contrasts: they are idiosyncratic aspects of meaning (such as the fact that *bachelor* can refer to someone who holds the lowest university degree) for which the semantic theory offers no general account. This contrast represents a move away from the tight relation between decomposition and lexical relations that motivated the earliest versions of decompositional theory. (See Bolinger (1965) for a criticism of the marker/distinguisher split, and of a number of other aspects of Katz and Fodor's analysis.)

Katz and Fodor's theory was specifically intended to integrate with generative grammar. Subsequent important attempts to pursue formal decompositional analyses broadly compatible with generative linguistics can be found in Pustejovsky (1991) and Jackendoff (1989; 1991). These decompositional theories, like all those discussed so far, do not necessarily presuppose that the semantic components into which meanings are analysed are themselves lexicalized in individual words. This is particularly the case for Jackendoff's decompositional system, Conceptual Semantics, on which Jackendoff has been working, largely independently, since the 1970s (Jackendoff 1983; see Chapter 3). Conceptual semantics involves highly abstract primitives, arrived at in pursuit of an avowedly internalist (see Chapter 2) decompositional logic aspiring to reveal elementary universal cognitive operations within what he calls "conceptual structure" (see especially Jackendoff (1989); Jackendoff's theory is discussed in Riemer (2010: 262–70); its mentalist assumptions are critically examined by Gross (2005); Taylor et al. (2011) provide a cognitive model broadly compatible with Jackendovian and with other feature systems). Conceptual Semantics primitives display a complex combinatorial structure, possessing arguments in a way that allows them to map on to syntactic structure (Jackendoff 1987). *John opened the door*, for instance, is attributed the following structure, paraphrased as "John caused [CAUSE] the coming into being [INCH] of a state [BE] where the door has the property of being open" (see Chapter 22 for more details):

[$_{Event}$ CAUSE ([$_{Thing}$ JOHN], [$_{Event}$ INCH ([$_{State}$ BE ([$_{Thing}$ DOOR], [$_{Property}$ OPEN])])])]

Jackendoff is not committed to the idea that the particular components involved in analyses like this one are absolutely primitive, i.e. not open to further decomposition. Further investigation may reveal ways of breaking down the existing components further.

Unlike conceptual semantics, the Natural Semantic Metalanguage theory (NSM; Wierzbicka 1996; Goddard and Wierzbicka 2002; see Chapter 25) does precisely assume that the primitive components at the root of the semantic system *are* individually lexicalized. NSM takes seriously the problem of definitional circularity discussed above, postulating the existence of a corpus of undefined – and indefinable – primitive concepts, out of which other lexical meanings are constructed. The novelty of the theory is the postulation that semantic primitives are universally given phonological expression: in other words, that every language has an "exponent" of every primitive meaning, i.e. some morpheme by which that meaning is expressed. This means that the vocabulary of every natural language contains words or other morphemes expressing the 60-odd primitive concepts that NSM sees as constituting the root of all other meanings. (A consequence of this is that there is no decompositional analysis that can be advanced of these 60 words in the terms of the theory.)

Decomposition in the NSM framework involves prose paraphrases of meanings: here, for instance, is the decomposition of *break*:

Someone X broke Something Y:
Someone X did something to Something Y,
because of this, something happened to Y at the same time
it happened in one moment
because of this, after this Y was not one thing anymore
people can think about it like this: "it can't be one thing anymore"

(Goddard 2010: 465)

All the words used in this definition are primitives. The claim of naturalness embodied in NSM rests on the assertion that paraphrases like this can be translated perfectly into any natural language. This claim has been contested, as have most other aspects of the NSM programme (see Riemer (2006) and Geeraerts (2010) for some discussion), but NSM's heuristic utility as a tool for the exploration of meaning is beyond doubt.

The more cognitively oriented a theory, the less likely it is to explicitly ground decomposition in the analysis of lexical fields. Instead, the focus will be on capturing lexical items' intrinsic semantic content, understood as the minimal information always conveyed by a word in every context in which it occurs. The fact that most words cannot be characterized as having any unique informational content that is invariant across all contexts is the rationale for seeing them as polysemous (see Chapter 13). The invariant informational content conveyed by a term can be captured by considering the *entailments* of propositions expressed using the term in question. Entailment can be defined as a *necessary* inferential connection between two propositions. A proposition p entails another proposition q if whenever p is true q must also be true: "this is a potato" entails "this is a vegetable" because there is no way the first can be true and the second false. Considering entailments gives us a way of identifying semantic components: given the relation between potato and vegetable, we are justified in concluding that part of the meaning of *potato* is "vegetable", and that "vegetable" is, as a result, a semantic component of *potato* (see Cruse (1986: 14–15) for discussion of entailment). Entailment relations, and hence decompositional structure, can be inferred from diagnostic frames as in (2):

(2) a *It's a potato, but it's not a vegetable.
    b *It's a potato, but it's a vegetable.
    c   It's a potato, so it's a vegetable.

(2a) is a contradiction; (2b) contains in *but* an implication of contrast inconsistent with the compatibility of *potato* and *vegetable*; (2c) concludes vegetablehood from potatohood. These facts are explained if we conclude that "x is a vegetable" is *inherently* conveyed by the phrase "x is a potato" – if, in other words, "vegetable" is a component of *potato* (see Lipka (1992: 116) for discussion). For verbs, equivalent tests might be as follows, establishing "move" as a component of *run*:

(3) a *They're running but they're not moving/without moving.
    b *They're running but they're moving.
    c   They're running so they're moving.

See Lipka (1992) and Cruse (1986) for exploration of these tests.

2.3 A typology of decompositional theories

The preceding sketch allows us to advance some criteria for a typology of decompositional semantic theories. First, we can ask whether a decompositional theory necessarily grounds its decomposition in a semantic field, or whether it analyses meanings on an individual basis. Burling (1964: 20) exemplifies the first trend: for him:

> Componential analysis is applied to a set of terms which form a culturally relevant domain and proceeds by recognizing semantic distinctions (components) which apportion the terms of the set into contrasting sub-sets, such that every item is distinguished from every other item by at least one component.

Bendix (1966: 4), on the other hand, rejected "strict delimitation of a lexical domain" as an "essential first step in any semantic investigation", feeling "that entry into the continuous semantic system can be gained at any arbitrary point".

Second is the question of whether the theory is committed to asserting the primitive status of the components into which meanings are factored, or whether the meaning components postulated as underlying a particular meaning or semantic field might prove to be susceptible to further analysis. We can then distinguish between theories – usually the older ones – whose components do not come supplied with any formalized combinatorial structure and those – Jackendoff's Conceptual Semantics, NSM, event structure theories (see Chapter 22) – where they do. A fourth criterion is supplied by whether the components are assumed to be universal (in the sense of valid for the semantic analysis of every language), and a fifth by whether they are necessarily able to be lexicalized in every language (as they are for NSM but not for any others). Finally, a sixth criterion specifies whether componential analysis is uniquely targeted at putatively necessary and sufficient elements of meaning, or whether features discerned in a word's semantic makeup may be present to varying extents, or only be optionally present. This latter possibility is not the case in any of the theories we have exemplified so far, but is found in prototype theory (see Chapter 7), and in the approach developed by Cruse (1986), where semantic components ("traits") are defined as showing varying degrees of necessity – "criterial, expected, possible, unexpected and excluded" (1986: 16).

3 Questions and problems

Despite the precedents for decompositional strategies that have sometimes been claimed in other domains of cognitive explanation (see Tversky (1977: 329)), it is not self-evident that meanings are the kinds of things which can be broken down in this way. As we have already observed, decompositional structuring is not a feature of our experience of meaning (see e.g. chapter 6 of Merleau-Ponty (1945)). Even among its proponents, disclaimers about the limits of decompositional analysis are not infrequent (see e.g. Bendix (1966: 3)). There are, in particular, numerous areas of the vocabulary which seem ill-suited to a decompositional approach. For instance, it is hard to imagine how one might identify features involved in words for colours, smells, and sounds. Jackendoff responds to this problem by postulating that some meaning-constituting components might be what we could call direct "plug-ins" from the perceptual system (Jackendoff 1989; 2002). As Nida points out, there are also words which seem to differ purely in degree or intensity, and which do not therefore lend themselves very easily to decompositional treatment. Nida mentions *toss* and *hurl*. "Both", he says, "may be regarded as types of throwing, but the major difference is one of intensity, and accordingly one must reckon with a continuum on which there is no fixed boundary between the two" (Nida 1975: 63). Nevertheless, the main challenges to decompositional analysis do not arise from obstacles encountered while trying to apply it to the explanation of particular kinds of meaning, but from doubts about quite general conditions of its applicability. We will explore these under three main headings, concentrating on the issues of analyticity, the definability of metasemantic terms, and the question of compositionality and Gestalts.

The most acute attacks on decompositional semantics have found fault with a presupposition that is foundational for many more semantic theories than just decompositional ones: the very contention that word meaning consists in *descriptions* (cf. Russell (1910–11)), in other words in complex informational representations quite generally. Since any semantic decomposition can be restated as a definition or as a meaning postulate, this objection targets accounts of semantics based on decomposition, meaning postulates and definitions indifferently. In what follows, we will follow conventional practice in these discussions and often use "definition" to cover all three kinds of description.

3.1 Components and analyticity

A general challenge to the view of meaning as consisting in descriptions capturable by definitions is derived from the philosopher W.V.O Quine's well-known critique of the existence of analyticity (Quine 1951). Analyticity is a central notion for semantics, analytic truths being those that follow from the *meanings* of the terms in which they are expressed. Analyticity requires that some propositions be entailments – "analytic inferences" – of others: "x is a vegetable", for instance, analytically follows from "x is a potato". Another way of putting this is to say that, if analytic inferences really exist, then it just *has* to be the case that "vegetable" is part of the *meaning* of *potato* – it's impossible to imagine a way of revising the meaning of *potato* in a way that would eliminate "vegetable". Analyticity is the root of semantics, so if it can be shown that there *are* no analytic truths, then semantics as traditionally conceived is unceremoniously put out of business. Quine's argument is precisely that there are no analytic inferences: no part of meaning, even the part we think of as most essential to a word's semantics, is absolutely immune from revision.

Quine is led to this conclusion for the following reasons. All our beliefs – that is, the propositions we think are true – are linked to each other in a seamless web, and it's possible to revise even fundamental beliefs as long as we make substantial enough alterations to *other* beliefs elsewhere in the system. For example, given radical enough alterations to our theories of plant matter, it might turn out that potatoes aren't actually vegetables – just as it has recently become false that Pluto is a planet, thanks to a reclassification by the International Astronomical Union. No matter how unlikely, it's at least conceivable that as a result of a revolution in our understanding of plants, potatoes might turn out to belong to some entirely new, distinct biological category. In that case, we would not want to say that the literal meaning of *potato* had changed, particularly since the word's extension – the actual objects to which it refers – would obviously still be the same. But we would no longer draw the analytic inference "x is a vegetable" from "x is a potato", and would have to discard "vegetable" from our analysis of *potato*'s meaning. Examples like this suggest that there is, in fact, *no* information which is *necessarily* entailed by a word: even though some beliefs seem very hard to revise, the holistic (interconnected) nature of our belief system means that any information putatively analytically entailed by a word is, like "vegetable" for *potato*, actually dispensable, given radical enough alterations to other beliefs. To adopt terminology more familiar in linguistics, this critique of analyticity amounts to a complete rejection of the dictionary-encyclopaedia distinction (Haiman 1980; see Chapter 10), and to a defence of the view that *everything* in language is pragmatic (encyclopaedic).

Quinean arguments have been particularly directed by Fodor against various proposals for decompositional analyses in lexical semantics. After an earlier period in which, as we have seen, Fodor participated in decompositional projects, he now accepts the case against analytical inference. As a result, he defends an atomic view of semantic content. There is no such thing as semantic information per se; all the apparently analytic inferences we draw, such as the inference that *if x walked, then x moved*, are in fact simply facts about the way the world seems to be, not about language (see Horsey (2000) for discussion). Fodor and Lepore (1998) point out, however, that not all of the entailments of a word are meaning-constituting: *two* entails "prime", since two is necessarily a prime number, but it is simply implausible that "prime" is part of the *meaning* of *two*. Similar remarks apply to the inference from *square* to "not circular". An account of meaning that depends on analytical inference is therefore obliged to state what it is that determines which entailments are meaning-constituting and which are not. This has never, however, been done.

3.2 The failure of definitions

A second argument against decomposition points to the signal failure of any satisfactory definitional (decompositional, meaning postulate) account of meaning. Despite centuries of effort, there has not yet been any successful definition offered of even a single word, in the sense of a description or set of descriptions which show complete substitutivity for the definiendum in every literal context. Consider, for instance, the meaning of the adjective *tired*. A natural first inclination would be to define this as "wanting or needing to sleep" – but this soon falters when we realize that one can easily be tired but not want or need to sleep. Nor can *tired* mean "feel as though one would sleep if the conditions were right", because it is perfectly possible (i.e. non-contradictory) to say *I'm tired, but I feel as though I still wouldn't sleep if the conditions were right*; nor, for similar reasons, can it be analysed as "being about to sleep". It proves, indeed, notoriously difficult to advance definitions for vocabulary which do capture exactly the same meaning as the definiendum. As Fodor et al. (1975: 530) speculate, "[p]erhaps the reason that semantic representations have proved to be so elusive is simply that, after all, there aren't any".

Two main kinds of response have been made to this criticism. The first, offered for example by Jackendoff (1989), consists in denying that the way in which components are composed into single lexical meanings is the same as the way in which *whole words* are composed into definitions: this means that "it will often be impossible to build up an expression of conceptual structure phrasally that completely duplicates a lexical concept" (Jackendoff 1989: 96). In other words, definitions aren't even all *meant* to work, since they put concepts together in an entirely different way from how these are combined within single word meanings. Accepting this vindicates definitional semantics, since discrepancies between definitions and meanings are to be expected (see Bierwisch and Schreuder (1992) for some further discussion). In reply to Jackendoff, a critic of definitions will say that allowing discrepancies between definitions and meaning renders the definitional hypothesis unfalsifiable and therefore useless.

3.3 The definition of metasemantic terms

The second response to the failure of definitions would be to claim that definitions, like any other generalization about the lexicon, "are statistically significant regularities, so individual counterexamples to them don't necessarily undermine them" (Johnson 2004: 342). Once again, this would have the effect of defusing cases of apparent definitional failure, since it requires that definitions as stated must accurately capture meaning most of the time, i.e. in a statistically significant set of cases. However, this response runs into an objection that goes to the heart of semantic analysis: the fact that there is no objective way to determine when a metalinguistic analysis does actually fit the definiendum (see Fodor and Lepore (2005: 353)). We explore this problem in the present section.

Take for example "stativity", a semantic feature frequently appealed to in linguistic analysis, particularly in studies of lexical aspect (see Chapter 19). This feature is important because it figures in generalizations about morphosyntax – specifically, the proposal that predicates whose decomposition includes the feature "state" resist progressive markers. The nub of Fodor and others' criticism of definitional accounts of semantic content can be captured by observing that the decision to attribute or withhold the feature "state" from the decomposition of a predicate is not subject to any objective constraints (Fodor and Lepore 1998: 277) and cannot therefore form part of any serious empirical venture. If it is simply in the investigator's gift whether a particular definition should be considered to apply to a particular definiendum, and if disagreements between different researchers are not open to objective settling, but are essentially a matter of individual intuition, we would seem to be dealing with a significantly different kind of theoretical enterprise from the one that most linguists presuppose.

An important factor in this problematic is the *autoexemplificational* character of semantic analysis (McGilvray 1998: 255). Autoexemplificationality is the fact that definitions and decompositions both use language itself as its own medium of analysis: we analyse a definiendum using *other* words of the same or a different language, with appropriate typographical notice, such as when we define *dog* as DOMESTIC CANINE, or [+ canine] [+domestic], etc.

The autoexemplificational character of semantic analysis introduces a significant paradox. As we have seen, one basic aim of semantics in general, and of decompositional theories in particular, is to reveal the underlying mechanisms that enable the designative relationship between expressions and aspects of the environment. We want to understand what it is about the word *coat*, for instance, that enables it to refer to actual coats. (This is not, of course, the only phenomenon of interest to semantics. We also want an account of the mechanisms that license the inferential relationships that expressions contract among themselves, such as the inference from *coat* to *clothing*.) As native speakers, we are typically – though not, of course, invariably – confident in the lexical choices we make to accomplish acts of reference. On the whole, these choices command a high degree of intersubjective agreement: more often than not, we will agree whether a particular article of clothing can be referred to as a *coat*, and this is also true of many other objects, events, properties, or relations, which are just as likely to receive an identical linguistic categorization by different speakers. If this were not the case, indeed, language could not serve as an effective medium of coordinated action in the world (Riemer 2013a).

However, the picture changes substantially when we try to analyse the underlying cognitive operations which explain this referential uniformity – when, for instance, we try to decompose the meanings of ordinary expressions in search of primitive elements of which they may be composed. This project involves establishing a second designative relationship to explain the first. To explain why the word *coat* designates actual coats, we hypothesize that its meaning can be analysed as a configuration of more primitive components – in illustrative componential terms, [+ clothing], [+ for upper body], [– underwear], and so on – each of which instantiates some primitive (or, at least, more basic) element of mental content. To refer to these primitive elements of content, we adopt some special notational convention, such as the square brackets used in componential analysis, small capitals, etc. This establishes a second designative relationship: just as *coat* designates actual coats, a semantic primitive like [+clothing] or [state] designates an item of internal mental content – whatever facet of mental architecture it is that is activated in the linguistically relevant circumstances. Let's refer to these two designative relationships as the relationship of *referential designation* for the relationship between the word *coat* and the actual objects it denotes, and *metalinguistic designation* for the relationship between a semantic component like [clothing] or [state] and the relevant aspect of mental architecture that it names.

Importantly, the metalinguistic designation relationship must, of necessity, be situated at a "lower" explanatory level, and be different in kind, from the referential designation relationship. We cannot, in other words, allow our explanatory theoretical terms like [state] to have *identical* designative conditions to the ones that obtain for their referential designation equivalents. If we don't respect this condition, we will find ourselves in a purely circular venture which wouldn't offer any explanatory advantage: our use of the "[state]" operator to explain meanings on the level of metalinguistic designation would simply mirror the way we use the *noun* "state" on the referential-designative level. Clearly, such a situation wouldn't be explanatory: we're trying to *explain* the designative capacities of the vocabulary, not to simply *mirror* those capacities on a lower level.

The insistence that metalinguistic designation must generally be separate from referential designation leaves decompositional semantic analysis in a delicate position. As we have just seen, this separation is a precondition of the explanatory utility of semantic decomposition. But the consequence of this is that it leaves us with no criteria by which to decide when one of the primitive terms is appropriately seen as present. The primitive terms on the level of metalinguistic designation have no criteria of application: only our basic-level linguistic practices on the referential-designative level themselves do. Hence the paradox: we can only apply primitive metalinguistic terms objectively (or, at least, in a manner that commands intersubjective agreement) by *identifying* them with object-language terms, whose use conditions are uncontroversial. But, of course, it is these very object-language terms whose meaning we want an account of – and we do not get one simply by reinstating these very object-language terms in the metalanguage, even if we dress them up in small capitals, surround them with brackets, or employ other kinds of typographical signal to designate them as metalanguage terms.

Another way of capturing the paradoxical character of semantic decomposition would be to observe that it is *only* our ordinary linguistic practices that are characterized by the intersubjectivity required for scientific analysis – but it is exactly these practices that we want to clarify. (A point very similar to this emerges from the later Wittgenstein (1953): there is no more primitive level of explanation than that of our everyday linguistic practices; as a result, it is futile to try to break these down into *more* primitive constituents, since in doing so we deprive ourselves of the only designative relationship on which consensus exists: the referential-designative one between words and objects of the environment.) These considerations have the effect of undermining the viability of decomposition even further: if the application of the metasemantic terms in which decompositional analyses are couched is essentially unconstrained, then we have even less reason for confidence in them.

3.4 Decomposition, context and Gestalts

The motivating assumption of decompositional approaches is the idea that the component parts or features which constitute a meaning are psychologically less complex than the meaning as a whole, and are therefore *prior*, temporally or logically, to the whole semantic representations which they jointly form. Another challenge to decomposition arises from the observation that Gestalt phenomena, which reverse this dependence of wholes on parts, appear to be widespread psychologically. Gestalt effects are observed in the frequent – perhaps the most frequent – cases in which our perception of an object is not brought about bottom up, by first perceiving a set of independent parts which are subsequently assembled into a single whole, but rather in the opposite direction, first perceiving the whole before any analysis into parts is possible (see Hergenhahn (1992: chapter 14) for details). Many psychologists and philosophers, mostly working outside linguistics itself, have thought that word meaning is a Gestalt phenomenon (Merleau-Ponty 1945). One observation that is consistent with this is that in many, if not most instances, the interpretation of a semantic component appears to depend on prior identification of the whole meaning to which it belongs. Take the component [for sitting], which plausibly enters into the decomposition of many words for furniture, distinguishing chairs, stools, and sofas from beds and cupboards. How can we tell whether the component [for sitting] matches a particular referent? What is it, for instance, that makes [for sitting] present in the case of a stool, and absent in the case of a bed, even though, as a matter of fact, beds are in many ways much better for sitting on than stools are? The answer, it would seem, is that the appropriateness of the component is a function of whether the referent *as a whole* counts as a chair, stool, sofa, or other piece of furniture intended for sitting, or not. In other words, identification of the *component* seems to depend on prior identification of the *whole concept*: in François Rastier's terms (see Chapter 28), the global determines the local, and not the other way round. But this is exactly the opposite of the direction required by a decompositional approach. (Bierwisch and Schreuder 1992 draw an interesting parallel with the way that phonological features are interpreted differently phonetically in different environments.)

3.5 Decomposition and discourse context

Decompositional analysis, like most other kinds of semantic investigation, presupposes that there is a unique analysis of meaning which is always invoked on every occasion of a word's use. However, this assumption ignores the fact that every other dimension of linguistic structure consists of "a range of unselfconscious and more self-conscious varieties" (Schilling-Estes 2007: 174). The amount of attention a speaker pays to their speech – their self-consciousness while speaking – has been recognized as an influence on output since at least Labov (1972) and psycholinguists have recently started to hypothesize that semantics is also influenced by this parameter. According to Sanford (2002: 189): "those things that are attended to receive deeper, more extensive [semantic] processing" – as he notes, "a common enough idea in the psychology of attention".

To think about the influence of attention on semantics, we can distinguish two different modalities of language use: planned and free. (This distinction is related, but not identical to, a number of well-known distinctions basic to the study of linguistic variation (Labov 1972; Eckert 2000; Coupland 2001; Schilling-Estes 2007).) Planned language use occurs in those contexts in which speakers are consciously paying attention to the communicative effectiveness of their words and where, as a result, they are more consciously aware of the normative constraints to which their language is subject (Verschueren 1999). Conversely, in free or unplanned contexts, participants are not paying any particular attention to these factors: they are speaking spontaneously and without special care.

The interest of the free/planned distinction lies in the following claim: decompositional analyses of descriptive meaning like those standardly advanced in semantics are most psychologically real for planned language use. In planned contexts, speakers are consciously aware of the factual and communicative constraints to which their words are subject, and deliberately strive to satisfy them; in so far as definition-like structures capture these constraints, the decompositional analyses theorists advance of words' meanings can have some relation to the actual structures speakers consciously draw on to plan and regulate their utterances. In free contexts, by contrast, speakers are unlikely to be deliberately subjecting their language to these constraints; as a result, the psychological reality of consolidated, decompositional analyses of meanings is diminished.

In some contexts, then – planned ones – speakers and hearers probably do use definitions and similar representations to plan and regulate their language use. As the speaker's desire to guarantee the effectiveness of their words increases, the amount of planning they devote to their linguistic expression increases. Frequently, this planning will not be conscious: the speaker will simply be aware of speaking slowly or deliberately, but they won't be aware of the decisions occurring subconsciously in the lead-up to their utterance. Occasionally, however, the speaker may bring the planning process to the level of consciousness by making it deliberately verbal: the speaker may think through their words "in language", bringing explicit verbal paraphrases to mind, with which they refer to the various aspects of meaning they wish to convey (see Prinz (2002: 150) for discussion). The calling to mind of the definition constitutes a kind of "rehearsal" by which the speaker can simulate the probable effects of different word choices. Similarly, if the hearer doesn't seem to understand, the speaker can verbalize a definition as part of a semantic repair strategy. In these cases, speakers arguably do invoke definitional structures consciously in planned language use.

These considerations allow us to clarify the influence of context on the psychological status of decompositional analyses of meaning like those traditionally advanced in semantics. On the suggestion we have been entertaining here, such analyses become psychologically real in two kinds of planned contexts. First, language users consciously bring minimal verbal definitions to mind to help them plan their utterances. Second, speakers can explicitly verbalize these definitions to the hearer, as part of a process of semantic repair.

Planned contexts, then, confer a certain degree of psychological reality on the decompositional representations traditionally offered in semantics. As the degree of planning decreases, two things happen. First, the diminishing necessity of explicit attention means that the speaker does not need a highly specific representation of the referent. The further away we get from planned discourse the more minimal, holistic and preprogrammed the representations underlying speech can be. Entrenchment, Gestalt effects, routinization, and other factors all diminish the extent to which consolidated, elaborated structures subtend speech (cf. Langacker (1987); Givón (1995); Verschueren (1999); Bybee (2010)).

Second, as the context becomes less planned and more free, connotational, emotional, or "expressive" content comes to the fore (Potts 2007). As the speaker's attention to explicit normative constraints is relaxed, the affective/emotional dimension of meaning becomes more determinative of the discourse sequences in which words figure and, to a lesser extent, of reference. The less attention I am paying to normative considerations, the freer the inferences and other connections I will make.

I have suggested, then, that a kind of "internal context", namely the degree of planning brought to the utterance, affects the kinds of meanings communicated and, in particular, the extent to which decompositional analyses of these meanings are apt. If true, this removes the surprising immunity of semantics to the influence of contextual variables known to affect other levels of linguistic structure. If other dimensions of language are affected by the amount of conscious attention the speaker brings to their utterance, it is not surprising that semantic differences are also found. See Binder and Desai (2011) for broadly compatible suggestions, and Riemer (2013b) for more detailed discussion.

4 Conclusion

We will conclude with some remarks on the explanatory effectiveness of decompositional analysis by invoking some general considerations about the explanation of cognitive phenomena.

For Cummins (2000: 126), the extent to which a proposed explanation of a cognitive phenomenon like meaning is actually explanatory can be assessed against three criteria: how far the explanation (a) involves less sophisticated elements than the explanandum, (b) is different in kind from the explanandum, and (c) doesn't tacitly push back a lot of explanatory jobs to other parts of the organism. How does a standard decompositional analysis fare on these measures? Let's examine a classic decompositional conceptual analysis, such as the proposal that the meaning "wake" is a mental representation consisting of four conceptual elements, a "cause" operator, a "become" operator, a negative operator, and an "asleep" operator, such that "wake" corresponds to the complex concept "cause to become not asleep".

The first requirement – that the analysis be less sophisticated than the analysandum – is easy to apply in many cases outside language. For example, the cognitive theory of vision (Marr 1982) sets out to explain our ability to detect edges and other features of the observed environment from certain mathematically primitive operations. This is a clear case of a highly sophisticated human capacity being explained through an ensemble of much more elementary operations. In this light, are "cause", "become", and "not asleep" "less sophisticated" than "wake", taking "sophisticated" to mean something like "more easily represented and/or computed"? Unfortunately, we simply have no idea how to measure differences in ease of representation or computation of this kind: in the absence of any robust theory of cognitive processes, the question is entirely open.

Before addressing Cummins' second criterion, we can observe that this highlights another problem Cummins mentions: the fact that we have no independent way to describe psychological capacities other than by the analyses we offer of them. The only way we have to capture what it is to understand the meaning "wake" is to offer some kind of intensional description of that meaning in other terms, such as, precisely, "cause to become not asleep". But if we then go on to claim that "cause to become not asleep" actually represents the *underlying conceptual structure* concerned, we have advanced an extra claim for which other evidence is needed.

On Cummins' second criterion – difference in kind from the explanandum – it is equally unclear whether we have achieved any explanation. "Asleep", "become", and "cause", like "wake" itself, are all meanings and, on the face of it, meanings of a similar order of complexity. It may be true that we can often (or at least sometimes) use the expression "cause to become not asleep" as an alternative to the expression "wake", but this does not show that the former is the analysis of the latter.

On the third criterion, too, we are not much better off: we are presupposing an ability to correctly apply the concepts "cause", "become", and "not asleep", but without an account of what this ability consists in. In particular, there is a pressing question about how the cognitive system determines when the conditions for applying a concept are satisfied (see Chapter 2). Most words in natural language are vague, in that whether they can be accurately predicated of a particular referent is not a simple yes/no matter, but admits of degrees.

On Cummins' criteria at least, it would seem that decompositional strategies in semantics are of dubious explanatory utility. Nevertheless, there seems to be no currently available alternative within the ambit of traditional linguistics. Non-decompositional computational models like Landauer and Dumais (1997), which model likelihood of occurrence statistically, abandon the hypothesis of lexical content and therefore fall outside the scope of semantics as normally conceived. As long as one approaches semantic analysis with the aim of distinguishing a variety of semantic properties within a lexeme, some form of decomposition is the most likely theoretical model, even if it is presently unclear how far it meets some reasonable criteria of explanatory utility. An alternative response would be to reconceive the epistemological framework in which semantic analysis is undertaken: rather than holding it to the same criteria as the natural sciences – the ultimate source of Cummins' criteria – we might choose to see it instead as a fundamentally hermeneutic exercise closer to the interpretative textual disciplines (see Chapter 28 and Riemer (2005: chapter 7)). Such a reorientation would have the advantage of not holding the existing explanatory strategies of semantics to a standard they are manifestly unable to uphold, while at the same time offering a way to conceive of them which accounts for the intuition of explanatory progress that many investigators feel while pursuing them. See the Introduction to this volume for more suggestions in this spirit.

Further reading

Katz, Jerrold J. and Jerry A. Fodor 1963. The structure of a semantic theory. *Language* 39: 170–210. An influential early presentation of many issues in component semantics, intended to be compatible with generative grammar.
Nida, E. 1975. *Componential Analysis of Meaning*. The Hague: Mouton and Cruse, D.A. 1986. *Lexical Semantics*. Cambridge: Cambridge University Press. Two very full book-length treatments, from differing perspectives, of many of the issues arising in lexical decomposition.
Lyons, John 1977. *Semantics*. Oxford: Oxford University Press. Section 9.9 valuably discusses many important points.
Geeraerts, D. 2010. *Theories of Lexical Semantics*. Oxford: Oxford University Press. Gives the context of the development of componential analysis in linguistics.

References

Arnauld, Antoine and Pierre Nicole 1996 [1683]. *Logic or the Art of Thinking*. Cambridge: Cambridge University Press.
Baldinger, Kurt 1984. *Vers une sémantique moderne*. Paris: Klincksieck.
Bendix, Edward H. 1966. *Componential Analysis of General Vocabulary: The Semantic Structure of a Set of Verbs in English, Hindi, and Japanese*. Bloomington: Indiana University Press.
Bierwisch, M. and R. Schreuder 1992. From concepts to lexical items. *Cognition* 42: 23–60.
Binder, J. and R.H. Desai 2011. The neurobiology of semantic memory. *Trends in Cognitive Sciences* 15: 527–536.
Boden, Margaret 2006. *Mind as Machine. A History of Cognitive Science*. 2 volumes. Oxford: Clarendon.
Bolinger, Dwight 1965. The atomization of meaning. *Language* 41: 555–573.
Burling, R. 1964. Cognition and componential analysis: God's truth or hocus pocus? *American Anthropologist* 66: 20–28.
Bybee, J. 2010. *Language Usage and Cognition*. Cambridge: Cambridge University Press.
Carnap, R. 1952. Meaning postulates. *Philosophical Studies* 3: 65–73.
Corbett, Greville 2012. *Features*. Cambridge: Cambridge University Press.

Coupland, Nikolas 2001. Language, situation, and the relational self: theorizing dialect style in sociolinguistics. In P. Eckert and J.R. Rickford (eds) *Style and Sociolinguistic Variation*. Cambridge: Cambridge University Press, 185–210.

Cruse, D.A. 1986. *Lexical Semantics*. Cambridge: Cambridge University Press.

Cummins, R. 2000. "How does it work?" vs. "What are the laws?" Two conceptions of psychological explanation. In F. Keil and R. Wilson (eds) *Explanation and Cognition*. Cambridge, MA: MIT Press, 117–145.

Eckert, P. 2000. *Linguistic Variation as Social Practice*. Oxford: Blackwell.

Fodor, J. 1970. Three reasons for not analyzing kill as cause to die. *Linguistic Inquiry* 1: 429–438.

Fodor, J.D., J.A. Fodor and M.F. Garrett 1975. The psychological unreality of semantic representations. *Linguistic Inquiry* 6: 515–531.

Fodor, J. 1998. *Concepts: Where Cognitive Science Went Wrong*. Oxford: Oxford University Press.

Fodor, J. and Ernie Lepore 1998. The emptiness of the lexicon: reflections on James Pustejovsky's "The Generative Lexicon". *Linguistic Inquiry* 29: 269–288.

Fodor, J. 2008. *LOT2. The Language of Thought Revisited*. Oxford: Oxford University Press.

Geeraerts, D. 2010. *Theories of Lexical Semantics*. Oxford: Oxford University Press.

Givón, T. 1995. *Functionalism and Grammar*. Amsterdam: Benjamins.

Goddard, Cliff 2010. The natural semantic metalanguage approach. In Bernd Heine, Cliff Goddard, and Anna Wierzbicka (eds.) 2002. *Meaning and Universal Grammar – Theory and Empirical Findings*, vol. 1. Amsterdam, Philadelphia: John Benjamins.

Haiman, John 1980. Dictionaries and encyclopedias. *Lingua* 50: 329–357.

Heine, B. and Narrog, H. (eds) *The Oxford Handbook of Linguistic Analysis*. Oxford: Oxford University Press, 459–484.

Goodenough, Ward H. 1956. Componential analysis and the study of meaning. *Language* 32: 195–216.

Greimas, Algirdas Julien 2002. *Sémantique structurale*. 3rd ed. Paris: PUF.

Gross, Steven 2005. The nature of semantics: on Jackendoff's arguments. *The Linguistic Review* 22: 249–270.

Hergenhahn, B.R. 1992. *An Introduction to the History of Psychology*. 2nd ed. Belmont: Wadsworth.

Horsey, Richard 2000. Meaning postulates and deference. *University College London Working Papers in Linguistics* 12. http://www.ucl.ac.uk/psychlangsci/research/linguistics/publications/wpl/00papers/uclwpl12.

Jackendoff, R. 1983. *Semantics and Cognition*. Cambridge, MA: MIT Press.

Jackendoff, R. 1987. The status of thematic relations in linguistic theory. *Linguistic Inquiry* 18: 369–411.

Jackendoff, R. 1989. What is a concept, that a person may grasp it? *Mind and Language* 4: 68–102.

Jackendoff, R. 1991. Parts and boundaries. *Cognition* 41: 9–45.

Jackendoff, R. 2002. *Foundations of Language*. Oxford: Oxford University Press.

Johnson, Kent 2004. From impossible words to conceptual structure: the role of structure and processes in the lexicon. *Mind & Language* 19: 334–358.

Just, Marcel Adam, Vladimir L. Cherkassky, Sandesh Aryal and Tom M. Mitchell 2010. A neurosemantic theory of concrete noun representation based on the underlying brain codes. *PLoS ONE* 5: 1–15.

Katz, Jerrold J. and Jerry A. Fodor 1963. The structure of a semantic theory. *Language* 39: 170–210.

Katz, Jerrold J. and Richard I. Nagel 1974. Meaning postulates and semantic theory. *Foundations of Language* 11: 311–340.

Labov, W. 1972. *Sociolinguistic Patterns*. Philadelphia: University of Pennsylvania Press. Landauer, Thomas K. and Susan T. Dumais 1997. A solution to Plato's problem: the latent semantic analysis theory of acquisition, induction, and representation of knowledge. *Psychological Review* 104: 211–240.

Langacker, Ronald 1987. *Foundations of Cognitive Grammar*, vol. I. Stanford: Stanford University Press.

Leech, G. 1981. *Semantics*. 2nd ed. Harmondsworth: Penguin.

Lipka, Leonhard 1992. *An Outline of English Lexicology*. 2nd ed. Tübingen: Niemeyer.

Lounsbury, Floyd 1956. A semantic analysis of Pawnee kinship usage. *Language* 32: 158–94.

Lyons, John 1963. *Structural Semantics*. Oxford: Blackwell.

Lyons, John 1977. *Semantics*. Oxford: Oxford University Press.
Maat, Jaap 2004. *Philosophical Languages in the Seventeenth Century: Dalgarno, Wilkins, Leibniz*. Dordrecht: Kluwer.
Marr, D. 1982. *Vision*. New York: Freeman.
McGilvray, J. 1998 Meanings are syntactically individuated and in the head. *Mind & Language* 13: 225–280.
Merleau-Ponty, M. 1945. *La phénoménologie de la perception*. Paris: Gallimard.
Murphy, M. Lynne 2003. *Semantic Relations and the Lexicon. Antonymy, Synonymy and Other Paradigms*. Cambridge: Cambridge University Press.
Nida, E. 1975. *Componential Analysis of Meaning*. The Hague: Mouton.
Peirce, Charles Sanders 1868. Some consequences of four incapacities. In James Hoopes (ed.) 1991, *Peirce on Signs*. Chapel Hill: University of North Carolina Press, 54–84.
Pottier, B. 1964. Vers une sémantique moderne. *Travaux de linguistique et de litterature* 2: 107–137.
Pottier, B. 1965. La définition sémantique dans les dictionnaires. *Travaux de linguistique et de litterature* 3: 33–39.
Potts, C. 2007. The expressive dimension. *Theoretical Linguistics* 33: 165–198.
Prinz, Jesse 2002. *Furnishing the Mind: Concepts and their Perceptual Basis*. Cambridge, MA: MIT Press.
Pustejovsky, James 1991. The generative lexicon. *Computational Linguistics* 17: 409–441.
Pustejovsky, James 1995. *The Generative Lexicon*. Cambridge, MA: MIT Press.
Quine, W.V.O 1951. Two dogmas of empiricism. *Philosophical Review* 60: 20–43.
Reichenbach, H. 1947. *Elements of Symbolic Logic*. New York: Macmillan.
Riemer, N. 2005. *The Semantics of Polysemy. Reading Meaning in English and Warlpiri*. Berlin: Mouton.
Riemer, N. 2006. Reductive paraphrase and meaning. A critique of Wierzbickian semantics. *Linguistics and Philosophy* 29: 347–379.
Riemer, N. 2010. *Introducing Semantics*. Cambridge: Cambridge University Press.
Riemer, N. 2013a. Conceptualist semantics: explanatory power, scope and uniqueness. *Language Science* 35: 1–19.
Riemer, N. 2013b. Sous-minimalité, planification et effets de contexte sur la représentation sémantique. *Corela* [Online], HS-14. http://corela.revues.org/3424.
Russell, B. 1910–11. Knowledge by acquaintance and knowledge by description. *Proceedings of the Aristotelian Society* (New Series) 11: 108–128. Reprinted in *Mysticism and Logic*, London: George Allen and Unwin, 1917, and New York: Doubleday, 1957.
Sanford, A.J. 2002. Context, attention and depth of focussing during interpretation. *Mind and Language* 17: 188–206.
Saussure, F. de 1979 [1916]. *Cours de linguistique générale*. Paris: Payot.
Schilling-Estes, Natalie 2007. Sociolinguistic fieldwork. In Robert Bayley and Ceil Lucas (eds) *Sociolinguistic Theory. Theories, Methods, and Applications*. Cambridge: Cambridge University Press, 165–189.
Sudre, Gustavo, Dean Pomerleau, Mark Palatucci, Leila Wehbe, Alona Fyshe, Riitta Salmelin and Tom Mitchell 2012. Tracking neural coding of perceptual and semantic features of concrete nouns. *NeuroImage* 62: 451–463.
Sprengel, Konrad 1980. Über semantische Merkmale. In Dieter Kastovsky (ed.) *Perspektiven der lexikalischen Semantik*. Bonn: Bouvier Verlag Herbert Grundmann, 145–177.
Taylor, K.I., B.J. Devereux and L.K. Tyler 2011. Conceptual structure: towards an integrated neuro-cognitive account. *Language and Cognitive Processes* 26: 1368–1401.
Trier, Jost 1931. *Der deutsche Wortschatz im Sinnbezirk des Verstandes: Die Geschichte eines sprachlichen Feldes I. Von den Anfängen bis zum Beginn des 13. Jhdts*. Heidelberg: Winter.
Tversky, Amos 1977. Features of similarity. *Psychological Review* 84: 327–352.
Verschueren, Jef 1999. *Understanding Pragmatics*. London: Arnold.
Wierzbicka, A. 1996. *Semantics. Primes and Universals*. Oxford: Oxford University Press.

Wierzbicka, A. and Cliff Goddard 2002. *Meaning and Universal Grammar. Theory and Empirical Findings*. Amsterdam: John Benjamins.
Wittgenstein, L. 1953. *Philosophical Investigations*, G.E.M. Anscombe and R. Rhees eds., G.E.M. Anscombe trans. Oxford: Blackwell.
Wunderlich, D. 1997. Cause and the structure of verbs. *Linguistic Inquiry* 28: 27–68.

Related topics

Chapter 2, Internalist semantics; Chapter 5, Cognitive semantics; Chapter 7, Categories, prototypes and exemplars; Chapter 14, Sense relations; Chapter 22, Event semantics; Chapter 25, The semantics of lexical typology; Chapter 28, Interpretative semantics, Chapter 29, Semantic processing.

13
Sense individuation

Dirk Geeraerts

In the first week of March 2013, immediately after the Italian parliamentary elections, the cover of the magazine *The Economist* bore a composite picture featuring Silvio Berlusconi and Beppe Grillo, under the caption *Send in the clowns*. Semantically speaking, lots of things are going on here. Both men are clowns in a derived sense only, if we take the literal meaning of *clown* to be "fool, jester, as in a circus or a pantomime; performer who dresses in brightly coloured unusual clothes and whose performance is meant to make the audience laugh". Grillo entered parliament as the leader of the anti-establishment Five Star Movement, but as he originally is an actor and a comedian, the relevant sense of *clown* could be paraphrased as "comic entertainer", i.e. as a slightly looser, more general reading of the central meaning. Berlusconi on the other hand is a clown in a figurative sense: his populist political antics characterize him as a man acting in a silly and foolish way – a metaphorical buffoon, in short. But while we readily recognize that *clown* applies in different ways to Grillo and Berlusconi, this creates a problem when we try to define the precise meaning of the word in *Send in the clowns*. The plural suggests that there is a single sense of *clown* that applies to both men, but then what would that meaning be, given the differences that we just discussed? Should we define a meaning at all that covers both "comic entertainer" and "metaphorical buffoon", or should we rather say that the simultaneous presence of two distinct senses underlies the punning effect of *Send in the clowns*?

From the point of view of semantic theory, this simple example illustrates a crucial methodological question: we perceive the differences between the three interpretations of *clown* – "jester in a circus or pantomime", "comic entertainer in general", "someone acting so silly as to make a fool of himself" – but what arguments exactly do we have to say that these are different meanings of the word, and how do we determine what the meaning is in the context of a specific utterance? How, in other words, do we establish the polysemy of a word, or any other linguistic expression?

This chapter introduces a major change that has taken place over the last quarter century in the way linguists think about the problem of polysemy. Roughly speaking, semantic theory has moved from a static conception of polysemy, in which senses are well-defined linguistic units (just like, say, phonemes or morphemes are discrete elements within the structure of a language) to a much more flexible and dynamic view of meaning. The chapter consists of three main parts. In the first part, we gradually zoom in on the central questions of polysemy research. We then present an overview of the arguments that have led semanticists to abandon a static conception of polysemy. In the third part, we have a look at the various ways, theoretical and methodological, in which semantic theory has incorporated the new view. The chapter concludes on a prospective note: it will be argued that the challenge posed by the new conception of meaning has not yet been adequately answered but rather defines a research programme for further investigations.

1 Drawing distinctions

To get a grip on the issues involved in the study of polysemy, we first need to introduce two sets of distinctions: that between polysemy, vagueness, and ambiguity on the one hand, and that between utterance meaning and systemic meaning on the other.

1.1 Polysemy, vagueness, ambiguity

The first distinction is important because in linguistic semantics (and specifically in lexical semantics, which will be our main focus throughout the chapter), the concept of polysemy contrasts with the notion of vagueness. More specifically, the distinction between polysemy and vagueness involves the question whether a particular semantic specification is part of the semantic structure of the item, or is the result of a contextual, pragmatic specification. For instance, *neighbour* is not considered to be polysemous between the readings "male dweller next door" and "female dweller next door", in the sense that the utterance *our neighbour is leaving for a vacation* will not be recognized as requiring disambiguation in the way that *she is a plain girl* does. In the latter case, you may be inclined to ask whether *plain* is meant in the sense of "ugly" or "unsophisticated, simple". In the former case, you may perhaps wonder whether the neighbour in question is a man or a woman, but you would not be inclined to ask something like: "In which sense do you mean *neighbour* – male neighbour or female neighbour?" The semantic information that is associated with the item *neighbour* in the lexicon does not, in other words, contain a specification regarding gender; *neighbour* is vague (or "unspecified", as is sometimes said) as to the dimension of gender, and the gender differences between neighbours are differences in the real world, not semantic differences in the language. This notion of *conceptual underspecification* has to be kept distinct from three other forms of semantic indeterminacy. Since at least some of these alternative forms of indeterminacy may themselves be referred to as *vagueness*, we need to be aware that the discussion of vagueness (as contrasting with polysemy) is beset by terminological pitfalls.

First, conceptual underspecification as just illustrated differs from the *referential indeterminacy* that may characterize the individual members of a category, as illustrated by a word like *knee*. It is impossible to indicate precisely where the knee ends and the rest of the leg begins, and so each individual member of the category *knee* is not discretely demarcated.

Second, referential indeterminacy may relate to entire concepts rather than just their individual members. Such *categorical indeterminacy* involves the fuzzy boundaries of conceptual categories, as illustrated by any colour term. In the same way in which we can think of the category *knee* as the set of all real and possible knees, we can think of a colour like *red* as the set of all individual hues that could be called *red*. But then, it will be very difficult to draw a line within the spectrum between those hues that are a member of the category *red* and those that are not: where exactly does the boundary between *red* and *orange* or *red* and *purple* lie (see Chapter 7)?

Third, the conceptual underspecification of individual meanings differs from the *interpretative indeterminacy* that occurs when a given utterance cannot be contextually disambiguated. For instance, when the intended interpretation underlying *she is a plain girl* cannot be determined on the basis of the available information, the interpretation is indeterminate, and the utterance is said to exhibit ambiguity. Ambiguity, in other words, may result from contextually unresolved polysemy.

1.2 Utterance meaning and systemic meaning

A second distinction that is necessary to get a clear view on the problem of polysemy is that between meaning at the level of the linguistic utterance, and meaning at the level of the linguistic system – between the meaning, in other words, that is a stable part of the system of the language, and the meaning that is realized in the context of a specific speech situation. In a simple model, the distinction between polysemy and vagueness coincides with that between utterance meaning and systemic meaning. As the case may be, in the actual situation in which the sentence is uttered, *our neighbour is leaving for a vacation* might call up the idea of a man or a woman, when all involved know who is being talked about. But although the concepts "male dweller next door" or "female dweller next door" would then indeed be activated in the context of the utterance, we would still not say that they add to the polysemy of *neighbour*. We could call "male dweller next door" or "female dweller next door" the utterance meaning of *neighbour*, but the systemic meaning would just be "person who lives next door": the systemic meaning belongs to the level of semantics, the utterance meaning to the level of pragmatics.

Does this imply that we can forget about utterance meaning? In the Saussurean, structuralist framework, the core of linguistic enquiry is the system of the language, and in the Chomskyan, generative framework, it is the mental representation of language, the way language is represented in the mind. So both of these traditions (and they are, apart from the post-Chomskyan functional-cognitive approaches, the dominant traditions in the history of contemporary linguistics) naturally favour focusing on systemic meaning. But while there may be a traditional theoretical motivation for looking at systemic meanings alone, methodologically speaking this can only be maintained if we have direct access to the mental lexicon. Some theorists do indeed assume that we can introspectively establish the meaning of linguistic expressions, at the level of the linguistic system. A highly articulate voice in this respect is Wierzbicka's (1985 and multiple other publications; see Chapter 25 for more discussion). She argues that to state the meaning of a word, one must introspectively study the structure of the concept that underlies and explains how the word can be used, and to understand the structure of the concept means to discover and describe fully and accurately the internal logic of the concept, through methodical introspection and thinking, rather than through experimentation or empirical observation of the scope of application of the item. To the extent that they understand language, language users have direct, unmediated access to the meaning of the linguistic expressions. The method of semantics, then, consists of attentively tapping into that immediate knowledge.

Such an idealist methodological position needs to be treated with caution, though (for a more extensive discussion of criticism voiced with regard to Wierzbicka's views, see Geeraerts 2010: 127–137). First, as a rather down-to-earth rebuttal, we may consider the way in which such an introspective exercise would actually work. In practice, one would likely imagine different contexts in which the targeted expression is used, and determine the definition of the word on that basis: if you want to know what *clown* means, you imagine circumstances in which you would use the word, and try to find a common denominator for those usages. But that, of course, is basically a roundabout way of grounding the analysis in contextualized language use: rather than a direct access to systemic meaning or mental representations, introspection then merely provides an indirect access to utterance meaning. Second, we could ask the question how an introspective method can be validated, i.e. how can we establish that it is a valid method, without simply assuming that it is? One possibility could be to compare the results of an introspective strategy with actual usage data: is the meaning that is intuitively identified the same that is activated in actual usage? But then again we would obviously be back to square one: we would again be using utterance meaning as a point of comparison, and we'd need to establish what those utterance meanings are.

So, unless we can be more convinced of the possibility of a direct access to systemic meaning, including utterance meaning in the investigation is a methodological prerequisite: utterance meaning is the primary observational basis of semantics.

2 Blurring the lines

The conceptual exploration in the previous section reveals that the sense individuation issue has two dimensions: the level at which the individuation takes place, and the criteria to be used for individuation. In this section, we take a closer look at each of these dimensions. First, we will see how a critical scrutiny of the traditional polysemy tests tends to blur the distinction between vagueness and polysemy. Second, we will show that a closer look at the levels of analysis has a similar result, i.e. to blur the distinction between utterance meaning and systemic meaning.

2.1 Polysemy tests

An examination of different basic criteria for distinguishing between polysemy and vagueness reveals, first, that those criteria are in mutual conflict (in the sense that they need not lead to the same conclusion in the same circumstances), and second, that each of them taken separately need not lead to a stable distinction between polysemy and vagueness (in the sense that what is a distinct meaning according to one of the tests in one context may be reduced to a case of vagueness according to the same test in another context). (See Geeraerts (1993) for a fuller treatment.) In general, three types of polysemy criterion can be distinguished.

First, from the *truth-theoretical* point of view taken by Quine (1960: 129), a lexical item is polysemous if it can simultaneously be clearly true and clearly false of the same referent. Considering the readings "harbour" and "fortified sweet wine from Portugal" of *port*, the polysemy of that item is established by sentences such as *Sandeman is a port* (in a bottle), *but not a port* (with ships). Anticipating on the discussion in section 3.2, we may say that this criterion basically captures a semantic intuition: are two interpretations of a given expression intuitively sufficiently dissimilar so that one may be said to apply and the other not?

Second, *linguistic* tests involve syntactic rather than semantic intuitions. Specifically, they are based on acceptability judgements about sentences that contain two related occurrences of the item under consideration (one of which may be implicit). If the grammatical relationship between both occurrences requires their semantic identity, the resulting sentence may be an indication for the polysemy of the item. For instance, the identity test described by Zwicky and Sadock (1975) involves "identity-of-sense anaphora". Thus, *at midnight the ship passed the port, and so did the bartender* is awkward if the two lexical meanings of *port* are at stake. Disregarding puns, it can only mean that the ship and the bartender alike passed the harbour, or conversely that both moved a particular kind of wine from one place to another. A mixed reading in which the first occurrence of *port* refers to the harbour, and the second to wine, is normally excluded. By contrast, the fact that the notions "vintage sweet wine from

Portugal" and "blended sweet wine from Portugal" can be combined in *Vintage Noval is a port, and so is blended Sandeman* indicates that *port* is vague rather than polysemous with regard to the distinction between blended and vintage wines.

Third, the *definitional* criterion (as informally stated by Aristotle in the *Posterior Analytics* II.xiii) specifies that an item has more than one lexical meaning if there is no minimally specific definition covering the extension of the item as a whole, and that it has no more lexical meanings than there are maximally general definitions necessary to describe its extension. Definitions of lexical items should be maximally general in the sense that they should cover as large a subset of the extension of an item as possible. Thus, separate definitions for "blended sweet fortified wine from Portugal" and "vintage sweet fortified wine from Portugal" could not be considered definitions of lexical meanings, because they can be brought together under the definition "sweet fortified wine from Portugal". On the other hand, definitions should be minimally specific in the sense that they should be sufficient to distinguish the item from other non-synonymous items. A maximally general definition covering both *port* "harbour" and *port* "kind of wine" under the definition "thing, entity" is excluded because it does not capture the specificity of *port* as distinct from other words.

The existence of various polysemy tests is nontrivial for two fundamental, interlocking reasons. First, the three types of criteria may be in mutual conflict, in the sense that they need not lead to the same conclusion in the same circumstances. In the case of autohyponymous words, for instance, the definitional approach does not reveal an ambiguity, whereas the Quinean criterion does. *Dog* is autohyponymous between the readings "Canis familiaris", contrasting with *cat* or *wolf*, and "male Canis familiaris", contrasting with *bitch*. A definition of *dog* as "male Canis familiaris", however, does not conform to the definitional criterion of maximal coverage, because it defines a proper subset of the "Canis familiaris" reading. On the other hand, the sentence *Lady is a dog, but not a dog*, which exemplifies the logical criterion, cannot be ruled out as ungrammatical.

Second, each of the criteria taken separately need not lead to a stable distinction between polysemy and vagueness, in the sense that what is a distinct meaning according to one of the tests in one context may be reduced to a case of vagueness according to the same test in another context. Without trying to be exhaustive, let us cite a few examples involving the linguistic criterion. Contextual influences on the linguistic test have been (implicitly or explicitly) noted by several authors. In fact, the recognition occurs relatively early in the literature on the subject. When Lakoff (1970) introduced the *and so*-construction as a criterion for polysemy, he argued that *hit* is ambiguous between an intentional and an unintentional reading, because *John hit the wall and so did Fred* would constitute an anomalous utterance in situations in which John hit the wall intentionally but Fred only did so by accident, or the other way round. Catlin and Catlin (1972), however, noted that the sentence could easily be uttered in a context involving imitation. A situation in which John hits his head against the wall after stumbling over his vacuum cleaner and is then comically imitated by Fred might very well be described by the sentence in question. Nunberg (1979) further drew the attention to sentences such as *The newspaper has decided to change its size*, which features intuitively distinct senses of newspaper ("management, board of directors" and "material publication").

Similar cases can be found involving coordination rather than anaphora. For instance, Norrick (1981: 115) contrasted the decidedly odd sentence *Judy's dissertation is thought provoking and yellowed with age* with the perfectly natural construction *Judy's dissertation is still thought provoking though yellowed with age*. If the coordination generally requires that *dissertation* be used in the same sense with regard to both elements of the coordinated predicate, the sentences show that the distinction between the dissertation as a material product and its contents may or may not play a role. Cruse (1982) noted that none of the following series of sentences containing coordination produces feelings of oddity: *John likes blondes and racehorses – John likes racehorses and fast cars – John likes cars and elegant clothes – John likes elegant clothes and expensive aftershave – John likes expensive aftershave and vintage port – John likes vintage port and marshmallows*. Coordinating the first item in the series with the last, however, does produce an awkward sentence. So, while the awkwardness of *John likes blondes and marshmallows* would normally be taken as evidence for the polysemy of *like*, the pairings mentioned above suggest that there is a continuum of meaning rather than a dichotomy. Cruse concludes that readings that are close together can be coordinated without oddity, but if they are sufficiently far apart, they are incompatible. If this picture is correct, it does not make sense to ask how many senses of *like* there are: "There is just a seamless fabric of meaning-potential" (1982: 79).

From these and similar publications (Taylor 1992; Tuggy 1993; Kilgarriff 1997; Allwood 2003) it appeared, in other words, that the contextual flexibility of meaning may take radical forms: it does not just involve a context-driven choice between existing meanings, or the on-the-spot creation of new ones, but it blurs and dynamizes the very distinction between polysemy and vagueness. To come back to our initial example, Grillo is a clown in one sense but not in the other, and the reverse holds for Berlusconi, but in the right context, both seemingly incompatible senses can be combined.

2.2 Levels of analysis

The distinction between systemic meaning and utterance meaning may be made more specific in two ways: as a distinction between conventional meaning and occasional meaning, and as a distinction between stored meaning and derived meaning. If we look more closely into these two distinctions, it will become clear that they blur the equation of "polysemy versus vagueness" and "systemic meaning versus utterance meaning".

The distinction between conventional and occasional meaning was first made explicit by Hermann Paul at the end of the nineteenth century: the conventional meaning (*usuelle Bedeutung*) is the established meaning as shared by the members of a language community; the occasional meaning (*okkasionelle Bedeutung*) involves the modulations that the usual meaning can undergo in actual speech (1920: 75). If the "usuelle Bedeutung" is like the semantic description that would be recorded in a dictionary (fairly general, and in principle known to all the speakers of a language), then the "okkasionelle Bedeutung" is the concretization of that meaning in the context of a specific utterance. To mention just one of the examples listed by Paul, the word *corn* used to be a cover term for all kinds of grain, but was differently specialized to "wheat" in England, to "oats" in Scotland, and to "maize" in the United States, depending on the dominant variety of grain grown in each of these countries: the context of use triggers the specialized meaning. But crucially, there exists a dialectic relationship between language system and language use: occasional meanings that are used very often may themselves become usual, i.e. they may acquire an independent status. So, on the one hand, usual meanings are the basis for deriving occasional ones, but on the other, the contextualized meanings may become conventional and decontextualized. The clearest criterion for a shift from the occasional to the usual level is the possibility of interpreting the new meaning independently. If *corn* evokes "wheat" without specific clues in the linguistic or the extralinguistic environment, then we can be sure that the sense "wheat" has become conventionalized (see Chapter 15).

This dialectic relationship precludes a simple equation of "conventional meaning versus occasional meaning" with "polysemy versus vagueness". To the extent that occasional meanings are just easily traceable contextual specifications, they fall under the heading of "vagueness", and their relevance for linguistics is minimal. However, to the extent that occasional meanings might be on their way to becoming conventionalized, "conventional" becomes a graded notion: meanings may be more or less conventional (and hence, more or less interesting from the systemic point of view). More generally, if we want to get a good idea of language change, occasional utterance meanings cannot be discarded as in principle less interesting: all changes of conventions begin as occasional changes on the utterance level. (For a contemporary formulation of the interplay between system and usage in polysemy research, see Hanks 2013.)

The distinction between conventional meaning and occasional meaning takes a predominantly social perspective on language: it looks at what is common in a community of speakers, and how those common patterns change over time. By contrast, we may look at language as an individual phenomenon as represented in the head of the language user. Within such a psychological perspective (a perspective that has been dominant in contemporary linguistics ever since Chomsky's definition of language as a cognitive phenomenon), economy of representation is often mentioned as an important criterion: a mental representation of the language that is parsimonious is supposed to be superior, and more specifically, linguistic phenomena that can be derived by some kind of generative, rule-based mechanism need not be stored separately in the mental representation. Applied to semantics, this implies that meanings that can be contextually derived need not be mentally stored as such. For instance, *chocolate* has two meanings: "food made from cacao beans, with a brown colour and a hard but brittle substance" and "hot drink made from milk and powder containing chocolate (as defined before)". It could then be argued that in the context *a cup of chocolate*, the presence of *cup* automatically triggers the second interpretation. The pattern *a cup of* ___ assumes that a mass noun will fill the slot, and specifically, a mass noun referring to a liquid. The meaning of *chocolate* is then, so to speak, automatically liquefied. In terms of representation, if we know what *chocolate* means in its basic reading and what *a cup of* ___ demands of its slot filler, it would seem that it is not necessary to separately list the second meaning of *chocolate* in the mental lexicon: instead of selecting the meaning from a list of stored readings, the meaning is computed by applying the expectations that are activated by *cup* to the stored basic meaning of *chocolate*.

This kind of model, aiming at a parsimonious distinction between stored meanings and contextually derived meanings, appears in various theoretical quarters, from Ruhl's largely descriptive approach (1989) over Evans' version of cognitive semantics (2009) to Pustejovsky's formalized Generative Lexicon model (1995). Two problems are relevant in the present context.

First, how important is it really to keep listed meanings and derived meanings separate? A parsimonious approach makes a distinction between semantic information that is stored in the (mental) lexicon, and readings that are derived pragmatically, in context. But if we take into account language change, such a strict distinction between what is stored and what is derived cannot be preserved. Pragmatic, context-dependent meanings have to be able to permeate to the level of semantics, in the way in which Paul's *okkasionelle Bedeutung* can over time be promoted to the status of *usuelle Bedeutung*. This is not just a social process of conventionalization; it is also an individual psychological process: one of the cognitive phenomena to be accounted for is the fact that some uses of a word may become psychologically more salient than others. Such a process requires that a reading that is at one point pragmatically derived leaves a trace in the mental lexicon of the language user: language users remember hearing/reading or saying/writing it, and the more they use it, the more cognitively entrenched it becomes. Just like in the case of conventional and occasional meanings, a strict separation between stored and derived readings (what Langacker (1991) refers to as the "rule/list fallacy") is difficult to maintain.

Second, even if we were able to strictly keep up the distinction, it would not help us with the problem of sense individuation. The distinction between stored meanings and derived meanings does not coincide with that between conventional meanings and occasional meanings, nor does it coincide with that between polysemy and vagueness. Even if the "hot drink" meaning of *chocolate* can be derived contextually, it is still considered a different reading (and a conventional one at that). In fact, it is precisely *because* it is considered a different reading that it makes sense to explore how it can be most economically represented, by listing it or by computing it. As a consequence (and this is a point that cannot be sufficiently emphasized), assuming a dynamic model of meaning distinguishing between listed and computed meanings does not as such solve the question how to distinguish vagueness from polysemy.

So, a closer look at the opposition between utterance meaning and systemic meaning brings to light that like the distinction between vagueness and ambiguity, it is not a strict dichotomy, and in addition, that care needs to be taken with equating it with the latter distinction. At the same time, the discussion reinforces the methodological idea that utterance meaning is the observational basis of polysemy research. If meanings at the level of the linguistic system are postulated to explain the appearance of utterance meanings, we have to be clear about those utterance meanings first. Theoretical models that incorporate a generative or inferential semantic mechanism in the linguistic system as such will have to be clear about the division of labour between stored and derived readings, but as long as it is not established on independent grounds what the total set of meanings is that has to be accounted for, it will be difficult to decide which meanings are going to be stored and which ones will be computed (or both), and by means of which mechanisms. If we want to build a theoretical model of a given phenomenon, we need a set of observations: if we want to know whether the food eaten by chickens influences the colour of the yolk of their eggs, we need to observe chickens with different diets, and in the same way, if we want to compare theoretical models of the mental lexicon (with different degrees of parsimony, with different derivational mechanisms etc.), we need an observational basis as a testing ground and a point of comparison.

3 Exploring the consequences

In the past two decades, the observed vagueness of the borderline between vagueness and ambiguity has contributed to two developments. Theoretically speaking, models of meaning were suggested that try to live up to the idea of systemic meaning as "meaning potential". Methodologically speaking, alternative forms for observing meaning and meaning differences were deployed.

3.1 Theoretical developments

The breakdown of the traditional model of systemic senses as discrete entities that are straightforwardly activated in usage led to the development of alternative models that try to capture the flexibility and fuzziness of meanings. A detailed presentation of these models is beyond the scope of this chapter: see Geeraerts (2010) for a full overview. Analytically speaking, three features constitute the basis of these models:

- *prototypicality effects*, i.e. the recognition that a distinction needs to be made between central and peripheral readings of an item (see Chapter 7);
- *schematicity*, i.e. the idea that the flexibility of meaning includes cases in which a distinction between readings that is relevant in one context is neutralized in another (as, for instance, in the example with which we started the chapter);
- *mechanisms of semantic extension*, i.e. the observation that the flexibility of meaning rests on specific ways of getting from an existing reading to a new one, like metaphor, metonymy, generalization, specification, similarity (see Chapter 15).

Of these three features, prototypicality on the one hand, and metaphor and metonymy on the other, have received most attention from researchers. From a sense individuation point of view, we may note that the influence of the classical model diminished only gradually. For instance, initial models like Brugman's (1988) for the semantic structure of *over* (a preposition that functioned as a rallying point for the comparison of different representational models) took the form of radial networks of very specific readings that were easily mistaken to have the same status as classical, discrete senses. But the nodes in such a network were not meant in the traditional way to begin with, and later studies like Geeraerts (1992) and Dewell (1994) emphasized that the dimensions underlying the various readings provide more insight into the structure of the category than the individual points in the network. Over time, a consensus seems to have grown that an adequate model corresponding to a nonclassical view of meaning takes the form of a structured feature pool from which subsets are selected or derived in a given context.

At the same time, no standard representational format has emerged, and the representational models generally do not address the sense individuation issue directly. Distinguishing between utterance meanings and systemic meanings, for instance, is not a central point of concern, nor is the way in which individual senses are to be identified made explicit. An exception in this respect is Tyler and Evans (2001), who formulate guidelines for the demarcation of senses as well as for the determination of prototypes. The procedure they suggest is at its core a variant of the definitional criterion mentioned above (to the extent that new senses are only to be posited when they are not already covered by a given sense). Although the proposal includes collocational behaviour (see below) as one of the criteria for distinguishing senses, it is not a full-fledged answer to the methodological challenge posed by the difficulties of the classical polysemy tests.

3.2 Methodological developments

The emergence of new models of polysemy (or perhaps we should use a neutral term like "semantic variation" to avoid the suggestion that we adhere to a clear distinction between vagueness and polysemy) was paralleled by shifts in the methodology of semantic research. To understand the importance of methodology, we may go back to the discussion of levels of analysis. We noted that a complete model of linguistic meaning cannot be achieved without systematic attention to differences in contextualized meanings as they appear in actual usage – a "usage-based approach" in the sense of Langacker (1991). But utterance meaning is clearly no more immediately transparent than stored meanings. Recall our opening example: it will not be easy to come up spontaneously with a definition of the meaning realized in *Send in the clowns*. Or consider the example *We are out of fruit*. We know that various features are associated with *fruit*: fruit is generally sweet, juicy, it is commonly used as a dessert, and technically it is the seed-bearing part of a plant. But it is unlikely that all those features are activated in the mind when someone utters the statement *We are out of fruit*. In the context of *A lemon is a fruit*, only a subset of features is activated and conversely, others are backgrounded: a lemon is not sweet, and it is not used as a dessert. But how would that mechanism of foregrounding and backgrounding work in *We are out of fruit*? When you use that phrase when you are drawing up your grocery list, the idea of a certain type of food will probably be prominent in your mind, but apart from that, is the idea of fruit that you have in your head at that point so clear that you can ascertain whether the fact that fruits are dominantly sweet was on your mind or not? Or perhaps you weren't thinking of fruit in terms of an abstract concept with definitional features, but you were thinking of it in terms of a collection of things like apples, strawberries and bananas? But then again, is what passed through your head so clear that you would be able to tell without a doubt whether, for instance, oranges were part of the set you were thinking of (see Chapter 11)?

The difficulty of such direct, introspective analyses strengthens the need for indirect measures of meaning: instead of studying meaning directly, we can study the behavioural correlates of meaningful language use, and base our analysis on those. Three major perspectives for doing this have come to the foreground in the past two decades (see also Stefanowitsch (2010)): an experimental, a referential, and a distributional corpus-based approach.

(1) *Experimental research* (involving reaction time experiments, naming tasks, association tasks, similarity judgements, self-paced reading, lexical decision tasks, sentence completion, eye tracking, neuro-imaging etc.) constitutes the standard methodological paradigm in psycholinguistic research. Through the work of Rosch (1975) on category structure, this type of work had an indirect but considerable influence on the adoption of prototype models in linguistics (see Chapter 7), but linguists themselves only gradually moved to experimental and interdisciplinary studies of semantic issues. Linguistically, the approach is now most conspicuous in the context of research into metaphor, imagery, and embodiment (see Gibbs (2007), Bergen (2007)), more so than in the context of polysemy and prototypicality research.

(2) A *referential method* takes its starting-point in the objects or events that a linguistic expression refers to. For instance, Geeraerts et al. (1994) study Dutch clothing terms on the basis of images and pictures as may be found in magazines and the like. The items referred to by means of a given word are subjected to a componential description, and this description is then used to analyze the boundaries and the internal structure of the clothing words (see Chapter 12). So, for instance, the loanword *legging(s)* is analyzed by describing depicted leggings in terms of length, tightness, presence of a crease, material, function, and gender of the wearer. The frequencies and co-occurrences of these features allow the prototype and the range of the concept to be identified. A referential approach of this kind is so far relatively uncommon (see Anishchanka et al. forthcoming, (2015) for a further example).

(3) The *distributional corpus-based method* is without argument the most influential methodological innovation in linguistic semantics (see Chapter 6). Initiated in the 1980s by Sinclair's lexicographical work (Sinclair 1991), it now takes three main forms. (For a more extensive treatment, see Geeraerts (2010: 165–178, 263–266).) First, most directly related to the tradition pioneered by Sinclair, statistical methods are used for identifying semantically relevant contextual clues in the corpus (collocations, i.e. co-occurring words, and colligations, i.e. syntactic patterns). These distributional data are then usually interpreted manually to arrive at a semantic characterization of the words and expressions under investigation (see Stubbs (2002) for examples). Second, the "behavioural

profile" approach follows the converse path: the corpus utterances in which a word occurs are coded manually or semi-automatically for potentially relevant features, and statistical techniques are then applied to classify the occurrences into distinctive senses and usages. Various statistical techniques are used. For example, Grondelaers et al. (2002) apply a logistic regression analysis to the Dutch particle *er*, Gries (2006) uses hierarchical cluster analysis to group occurrences of the verb *to run* into different senses, and Glynn (2010) performs a correspondence analysis to visualize groups of occurrences of the verb *to bother*. Third, a "semantic vector space" approach as illustrated in Heylen et al. (2012) maximizes the use of quantitative techniques: both the identification of contextual clues and the clustering of occurrences into semantic classes based on those clues is done in a statistical way.

The relationship between these different methods is nontrivial. To a large extent, they seem to capture different, non-overlapping phenomena. The referential method, for instance, will work best for material objects, events, and processes, but a lot of the information that will be revealed by taking such a referential perspective may be absent from the corpus. The information that is encoded in texts is probably not all the information that language users rely on, and specifically, the kind of features that are prominent in a referential approach (like the shape of objects) may not be explicitly expressed in textual data. How easy, for instance, would it be to retrieve information from the corpus about the average length of leggings, or the dominant shades of a colour term like *navy*? In a similar way, at least some of the psycholinguistic experimental methods are able to gather information about on-line processing that is inaccessible to the off-line perspective of a referential or a distributional method.

It is no surprise, then, to see scholars switch to mixed and interdisciplinary methods. Particularly for the semantic analysis of constructions, the combination of corpus data and experimental data is an emerging trend (see Gilquin and Gries (2009)). But although these studies generally show a convergence of the different types of evidence, there is no reason to assume that this will be automatically the case. Schmid (2010), for instance, argues that corpus frequencies need not directly reflect the psychological entrenchment of linguistic expressions. The relationship between the three methods could thus also be one of conflict and not just complementarity. If we look at this possibility with some distance, divergences between the different methods should in fact not come as a surprise. Note to begin with that the three methodological perspectives are crucially similar to the three traditional polysemy tests we distinguished earlier.

- The definitional test resembles the referential approach, to the extent that it too primarily looks at the extralinguistic situation that is referred to by the words.
- The linguistic test, like the corpus-based distributional method, looks at syntagmatic patterns in which a word occurs (but with a much narrower scope than the contemporary corpus approach, to be sure).
- Like the logical test, the experimental psycholinguistic methods explore the subjectively cognitive understanding of the language user.

Given the similarity among the newer empirical methods and the older polysemy tests on the one hand, and the divergences among the three classical tests on the other, divergences among the three successor models (if we may call them that) will have to be seriously reckoned with. As such, an immediate challenge for polysemy research consists of a systematic comparison of the three methods.

4 Defining a programme

In the foregoing we saw, first, how the traditional tests for polysemy exhibit mutual divergences and contextual inconstancy, and so cast doubt on the stability of the distinction between vagueness and polysemy. Second, it became clear that a methodologically sound approach to the problem of sense individuation needs to get a good grip on utterance meaning, even if the goal is to capture systemic meanings. And third, the three traditional polysemy tests, which relied heavily on intuition, were each succeeded by a more sophisticated empirical approach that continues the perspective of the original test in a methodologically more solid manner. But we have no clear picture yet of the possible divergences among those three new approaches, or of the success they have in identifying utterance meanings.

A research programme follows from these conclusions, but it needs to be formulated with caution. If we were simply to ask which method is the best at identifying utterance meanings, we should be aware by now that formulating the question in that way may be deceptive. Validating the methods in a straightforward way is only possible if we have an independent way of identifying utterance meanings – but that was the difficulty to begin with. In addition, if we think of the various methods as tools for identifying precisely delineated utterance meanings, we may well be repeating the mistake that originally came with the traditional model of systemic polysemy. We have given up the idea of discrete systemic meanings, but aren't we still thinking of utterance meanings as clear and distinct entities? Methodologically speaking, we are trying to get a clear picture of utterance meaning, but what if the thing we try to picture is intrinsically unclear? Are we looking at something through a fog, or is the fog the thing we are looking at?

So let us go back to basics: what is it that we do when we describe semantic variation? Given that each utterance is different to begin with, what we are doing when we look for different meanings at the level of utterances is identifying equivalence classes, i.e. sets of utterances that are identical or near-identical from the point of view of meaning. But the equivalence classes that we find may be influenced by the method we use and the specific parameters we include in the application of that method. If we don't hypostatize meaning, then the research programme will have to address the following questions.

First, to what extent do the various methodological approaches correlate with each other? This is the question that emerged at the end of the previous section: under which contextual conditions and parameter settings do the different methods show divergence or convergence?

Second, what external phenomena do the resulting classifications of meaning correlate with? If a given method yields a specific set of equivalence classes among utterances, for which other aspects of linguistic behaviour is that specific classification relevant? For instance, it could be that a distributional analysis yields a classification of semantic verb classes that plays a significant role in the choice of auxiliaries with those verbs, whereas a classification resulting from experimental association data has explanatory value in a multimodal analysis of the spontaneous gestures accompanying language. These are imaginary examples, but the point will be evident: a large-scale exploration of such correspondences should be pursued.

Third, is meaning a unitary phenomenon? If there is no one-to-one correspondence between the results of the methods, we could say that there are aspects of meaning that are identified by method A and others that we measure with method B, but we will have to leave open the possibility that the phenomena under scrutiny will eventually be recognized as different entities altogether, rather than as different aspects of the same phenomenon.

To get a better grip on what is at stake here, we may refer to well-known examples from the exact sciences. On the one hand, meaning could be like light, which has to be conceived in terms of particles or waves depending on the kind of experiment with which its properties are investigated. In physical theory light is still, ontologically speaking, thought of as one thing, but under the perspective of different methods, different properties are foregrounded. How those apparently contradictory properties can be reconciled into a single theoretical model of light is another matter, but that difficulty does not detract from the fact that light is considered a unitary phenomenon. On the other hand, meaning could be like the notion of a vital force, which in large parts of pre-twentieth-century biology was believed to be a unitary principle of life underlying the full spectrum of biological phenomena. Within a reductionist biochemical framework, however, that spectrum is resolved in different, ontologically distinct systems, like metabolism and evolutionary selection, each with its own appropriate methods of investigation. The current situation in semantics could then be described as undecided between these two models: is meaning a unitary phenomenon appearing in different guises according to the perspective we take, or should it be broken down into a complex of distinct phenomena? The question is open for investigation: send in the semanticists . . .

Further reading

Geeraerts, Dirk 1993. Vagueness's puzzles, polysemy's vagaries. *Cognitive Linguistics* 4: 223–272. Systematic discussion of polysemy criteria, and the difficulties associated with them.

Tuggy, David 1993. Ambiguity, polysemy, and vagueness. *Cognitive Linguistics* 4: 273–290. Discusses the representational issues following from the difficulties faced by polysemy criteria.

Glynn, Dylan and Kerstin Fischer (eds.) 2010. *Quantitative Methods in Cognitive Semantics*. Berlin: De Gruyter Mouton, and Glynn, Dylan and Justyna Robinson 2014. *Corpus Methods in Semantics*. Amsterdam: Benjamins. Two representative collections illustrating contemporary methods in polysemy research (and semantics more broadly).

Hanks, Patrick W. 2013. *Lexical Analysis. Norms and Exploitations*. Cambridge, Mass.: MIT Press. Focuses on polysemy from the lexicographer's point of view.

References

Allwood, Jens 2003. Meaning potentials and context: some consequences for the analysis of variation in meaning. In Hubert Cuyckens, René Dirven and John Taylor (eds), *Cognitive Linguistic Approaches to Lexical Semantics*. Berlin: Mouton de Gruyter, 29–66.

Anishchanka, Alena, Dirk Speelman and Dirk Geeraerts forthcoming 2015. Usage-related variation in the referential range of blue in marketing context. *Functions of Language* 22: 20–43.

Bergen, Benjamin 2007. Experimental methods for simulation semantics. In Monica Gonzalez-Marquez, Irene Mittelberg, Seana Coulson and Michael J. Spivey (eds), *Methods in Cognitive Linguistics*. Amsterdam: John Benjamins, 277–301.

Brugman, Claudia 1988. *The Story of 'Over'. Polysemy, Semantics and the Structure of the Lexicon*. New York: Garland.

Catlin, Jane-Carol and Jack Catlin 1972. Intentionality: a source of ambiguity in English? *Linguistic Inquiry* 3: 504–508.

Cruse, D. Alan 1982. On lexical ambiguity. *Nottingham Linguistic Circular* 11: 65–80.

Dewell, Robert B. 1994. 'Over' again: on the role of image-schemas in semantic analysis. *Cognitive Linguistics* 5: 351–380.

Evans, Vyvyan 2009. *How Words Mean. Lexical Concepts, Cognitive Models, and Meaning Construction*. Oxford: Oxford University Press.

Geeraerts, Dirk 1992. The semantic structure of Dutch 'over'. *Leuvense Bijdragen. Leuven Contributions in Linguistics and Philology* 81: 205–230.
Geeraerts, Dirk 1993. Vagueness's puzzles, polysemy's vagaries. *Cognitive Linguistics* 4: 223–272.
Geeraerts, Dirk 2010. *Theories of Lexical Semantics*. Oxford: Oxford University Press.
Geeraerts, Dirk, Stefan Grondelaers and Peter Bakema 1994. *The Structure of Lexical Variation. Meaning, Naming, and Context*. Berlin: Mouton de Gruyter.
Gibbs, Raymond W. 2007. Why cognitive linguists should care more about empirical methods. In Monica Gonzalez-Marquez, Irene Mittelberg, Seana Coulson and Michael J. Spivey (eds), *Methods in Cognitive Linguistics*. Amsterdam: John Benjamins, 2–18.
Gilquin, Gaëtanelle and Stefan Th. Gries 2009. Corpora and experimental methods: a state-of-the-art review. *Corpus Linguistics and Linguistic Theory* 5: 1–26.
Glynn, Dylan 2010. Testing the hypothesis. Objectivity and verification in usage-based Cognitive Semantics. In Dylan Glynn and Kerstin Fischer (eds), *Quantitative Methods in Cognitive Semantics: Corpus-Driven Approaches*. Berlin/New York: De Gruyter Mouton, 239–269.
Gries, Stefan Th. 2006. Corpus-based methods and cognitive semantics: the many senses of 'to run'. In Stefan Th. Gries and Anatol Stefanowitsch (eds), *Corpora in Cognitive Linguistics. Corpus-based Approaches to Syntax and Lexis*. Berlin: Mouton de Gruyter, 57–99.
Grondelaers, Stefan, Dirk Speelman and Dirk Geeraerts 2002. Regressing on 'er'. Statistical analysis of texts and language variation. In Anne Morin and Pascale Sébillot (eds), *6ièmes Journées internationales d'Analyse statistique des Données Textuelles – 6th International Conference on Textual Data Statistical Analysis*. Rennes: Institut National de Recherche en Informatique et en Automatique, 335–346.
Hanks, Patrick W. 2013. *Lexical Analysis. Norms and Exploitations*. Cambridge, Mass.: MIT Press.
Heylen, Kris, Dirk Speelman and Dirk Geeraerts 2012. Looking at word meaning. An interactive visualization of semantic vector spaces for Dutch synsets. In Miriam Butt, Sheelagh Carpendale, Gerald Penn, Jelena Prokic and Michael Cysouw (eds), *Visualization of Language Patters and Uncovering Language History from Multilingual Resources. Proceedings of the EACL-2012 joint workshop of LINGVIS & UNCLH*. Avignon: Association for Computational Linguistics, 16–24.
Kilgarriff, Adam. 1997. I don't believe in word senses. *Computers and the Humanities* 31: 91–113.
Lakoff, George 1970. A note on vagueness and ambiguity. *Linguistic Inquiry* 1: 357–359.
Langacker, Ronald W. 1991. A usage-based model. In Ronald W. Langacker (ed.), *Concept, Image, and Symbol. The Cognitive Basis of Grammar*. Berlin: Mouton de Gruyter, 261–288.
Norrick, Neal R. 1981. *Semiotic Principles in Semantic Theory*. Amsterdam: John Benjamins.
Nunberg, Geoffrey 1979. The non-uniqueness of semantic solutions: polysemy. *Linguistics and Philosophy* 2: 143–184.
Paul, Hermann.1920. *Prinzipien der Sprachgeschichte*. 5th ed. Halle: Max Niemeyer Verlag.
Pustejovsky, James. 1995. *The Generative Lexicon*. Cambridge, Mass.: MIT Press.
Quine, Willard V.O. 1960. *Word and Object*. Cambridge, Mass.: MIT Press.
Rosch, Eleanor and Carolyn B. Mervis 1975. Family resemblances: studies in the internal structure of categories. *Cognitive Psychology* 7: 573–605.
Ruhl, Charles 1989. *On Monosemy. A Study in Linguistic Semantics*. Albany: State University of New York Press.
Schmid, Hans-Jörg 2010. Does frequency in text instantiate entrenchment in the cognitive system? In Dylan Glynn and Kerstin Fischer (eds), *Quantitative Methods in Cognitive Semantics: Corpus-Driven Approaches*. Berlin/New York: De Gruyter Mouton, 101–133.
Sinclair, John M. 1991. *Corpus, Concordance, Collocation*. Oxford: Oxford University Press.
Stefanowitsch, Anatol 2010. Empirical cognitive semantics: some thoughts. In Dylan Glynn and Kerstin Fischer (eds), *Quantitative Methods in Cognitive Semantics: Corpus-Driven Approaches*. Berlin/New York: De Gruyter Mouton, 355–380.
Stubbs, Michael 2002. *Words and Phrases. Corpus Studies of Lexical Semantics*. Oxford: Blackwell.
Taylor, John R. 1992. How many meanings does a word have? *Stellenbosch Papers in Linguistics* 25: 133–168.

Tuggy, David 1993. Ambiguity, polysemy, and vagueness. *Cognitive Linguistics* 4: 273–290.
Tyler, Andrea and Vyvyan Evans 2001. Reconsidering prepositional polysemy networks: the case of 'over'. *Language* 77: 724–765.
Wierzbicka, Anna 1985. *Lexicography and Conceptual Analysis*. Ann Arbor: Karoma.
Zwicky, Arnold and Jerry Sadock 1975. Ambiguity tests and how to fail them. In John Kimball (ed.), *Syntax and Semantics 4*. New York: Academic Press, 1–36.

Related topics

Chapter 2, Internalist semantics; Chapter 5, Cognitive semantics; Chapter 6, Corpus semantics; Chapter 7, Categories, prototypes and exemplars; Chapter 11, Contextual adjustment of meaning; Chapter 12, Lexical decomposition; Chapter 15, Semantic shift; Chapter 29, Semantic processing.

14
Sense relations

Petra Storjohann

1 Introduction

The notion of sense relations is linked with terms such as semantic relations, meaning relations and lexical relations, as well as paradigmatic/syntagmatic relations. The traditional field of sense relations was concerned with paradigmatic relations such as hyponymy, antonymy, synonymy, etc. Paradigmatic relations hold between lexical items which are thought to be intersubstitutable in a given position in a syntagm. In addition to the fine-grained classificatory accounts offered by Cruse (1986), a great number of traditional descriptions and historical guides on sense relations have been supplied in the past (cf. Lyons (2002); Cruse (2002a, 2002b); Lehrer (2002)). General descriptions of conventional classifications have prevailed, e.g. Cann (2011), although research on relations such as antonymy and synonymy has changed with the availability of new computational possibilities and experimental techniques, as well as the development of corpus-guided semantic models (e.g. Sinclair (1991); (Hoey 2005)) and cognitive theoretical frameworks (e.g. Croft and Cruse (2004); Paradis (2005)).

Corpus-guided approaches to meaning and particularly examinations of co-occurrences have provided a substantial contextual understanding of lexical behaviour (see Chapter 6). At the same time, the cognitive account has taken on a comprehensive usage-based view of linguistic structures, leaving behind the division between lexis and grammar and focusing on the interplay between them as, for example, observed in constructions, and viewing meaning in terms of knowledge representation and conceptualisation (see Chapters 5 and 24). Overall, a more empirical and cognitive grounding to sense relations has emerged, offering new methodologies, evidence and hypotheses. It is within the latter context that this chapter will explore sense relations holding between words, concepts and/or constructions. This chapter will focus on recent developments within lexical semantics that have started to explore the most exemplified relations of contrast/opposition (antonymy) and identity/equivalence (synonymy), and will primarily examine the two phenomena by employing corpora and psycholinguistic experimental techniques with respect to English and German.

2 Historical perspective

Within the European context of linguistics in the twentieth century, the treatment of sense relations was long bound up with different traditions from Structuralist and post-Structuralist strands. Their approaches are generally regarded as the most influential in the study of meaning and lexical paradigms. The Structuralist view was based on the assumption that lexical meaning is constituted by the relations lexemes hold with other lexemes in the same lexical-semantic paradigm. Structuralists argued that language is a unique autonomous self-contained and relational system, with clearly recognisable stable structures exposing inherent semantic properties of lexical items that can be decomposed and described (see Chapters 3 and 12). Sense relations are characteristic of a vocabulary that was considered to be an integrated relational system. Words have their positions within the lexical network and they exhibit primitive and universal principles of language structuring. Relations such as antonymy and synonymy were conceived as relations holding between lexemes or lexical units simply by virtue of their meaning or sense.

Studies by Lyons (1968, 1977), Lutzeier (1981), Lehrer and Lehrer (1982) and Bierwisch (1989) accomplished systematic examinations of lexical fields and developed definitions and classifications of paradigmatic relations which were deeply rooted in philosophical categories. Adopting a more contextualised approach, Cruse (1986) provided the most exhaustive taxonomy and a stringent terminology of sense relations. The use of the term "sense relation" suggests a commitment to Structuralist methodologies and the belief that language is structured in a stable relational system. Cruse and Togia (1995) advanced the treatment of sense relations from a traditional post-Structuralist perspective, bringing a cognitive aspect into their theory of meaning. The first attempt at shedding new light on the phenomenon of sense relations within a fully cognitive approach was made by Croft and Cruse (2004), who also made ample use of the keyword "sense relation" within this new theoretical framework. Sense relations were treated as "semantic relations not between words as such, but between particular contextual construals of words" (Croft and Cruse 2004: 141), which were considered to be flexible and dynamic. The ground for a more dynamic explanation of contextually flexible relations and a more compatible semantic model within lexical semantics was established, but without incorporating sufficient empirical evidence to substantiate this elaborate hypothesis.

Although corpus linguistics established empirical research in the study of meaning by examining linguistic structures and patterns in terms of syntagmatic lexical analysis, the subject of binary contrast/opposition and sameness of meaning was not initially a central aspect of the new methodological paradigm. A pioneering comprehensive corpus-based investigation of English antonymy was presented by Jones (2002), who proposed an empirically driven view encompassing structures of language use. Opposite pairs were re-examined by adopting corpus-linguistic methodologies such as statistically analysing patterns and studying examples of textual evidence. This work reopened the chapter on lexical-semantic relations of opposition/contrast, as well as semantic sameness/identity.

3 Critical issues

The Structuralistist and post-Structuralist approaches provided neither a theory that accommodates flexibility in how lexico-semantic relations are used in actual discourse nor one based on a large amount of empirical evidence. Empirical research into lexico-semantic relations revolutionised the linguistic perspective on the dynamic nature and behaviour of antonymy and synonymy in discourse and presented copious evidence that meanings do not have a definitional structure with distinct boundaries. The data-driven investigation of text material has brought up new evidence and insights and pointed out the discrepancy between semantic models and textual structures. Today, a critical view is taken of traditional classifications and the division between syntagmatic vs. paradigmatic structures, as well as the notion of lexical vs. conceptual relations.

3.1 Traditional categories

Classifying types of sense relation to describe the structure of a stable, integrated but dissectible linguistic system, and searching for a rigorous terminology, has been the endeavour and accomplishment of Lyons (1968), Cruse (1986) and Lutzeier (1981). These offered truth-conditionally definable sets fulfilling certain logical criteria of inclusion or exclusion for a detailed categorisation of sense relations. In this way, a comprehensive fine-grained system of sense relations was established and illustrated by introspective examples, which were at first decontextualised, and later more contextualised (Cruse 1986). The categories enabled linguists to group and identify lexical-semantic relations. For example, the relation of binary opposition (traditionally subsumed under the cover term antonymy) was divided into complementaries (e.g. *dead-alive*, *hit-miss*), gradable contraries/antonyms (e.g. *long-short*), reversives (e.g. *fall-rise*) and converses (e.g. *buy-sell*). We will characterise each in turn, before describing the relation of synonymy.

3.1.1 Oppositeness (antonymy)

Complementarity is a logical relation of binary contradiction. Non-gradable terms referring to two concepts are complementaries when they bisect a conceptual domain into two discrete, mutually exclusive sections. If *X is not dead* it necessarily follows that *X is alive* and vice versa. Hence, *X is dead* and *X is alive* cannot both be true at the same time.

Gradable antonymy is a relation of contrast where there is a range of values or degrees along the scale of the variable property (e.g. length, speed, weight). Gradable antonyms (or, simply, antonyms in the strict sense of the word) are terms, often adjectives, which express opposite parts of a scale denoting different degrees of this variable dimension. As a result, gradable antonyms are contraries but not contradictories (cf. Lyons (1977: 272)). *X is long* entails *X is not short* and vice versa, but the statement *X is not long* does not entail *X is short*, and similarly, *X is not short* does not entail *X is long*.

Reversives such as *fall* and *rise* or *up* and *down* are terms that denote movement or changes of a body in opposite directions along a potential path. The contrary directions are established by referring to specific reference points or points of orientation of a moving body. While one item refers to change from A to B, the other signifies change from B to A.

Converseness is a relation of logical equivalence and is restricted to elements with relational character (temporal or spatial) where two elements refer to different perspectives of one event. For pairs such as *above-below*, the relation can be expressed for two objects A and B in the following way: A is above B or B is below A. Converse relations are also common for terms referring to reciprocal social roles (e.g. *parent-child*, *doctor-patient*).

Problems of strict categorisation with regard to relations of opposition and exclusion have been identified by Philpotts (2001) for a number of English and German adjectives which were expected to demonstrate default antonymic readings. Philpotts examines a wide range of data and supplies ample evidence for different types of hybrid relations, such as the fact that in some contexts one member of the antonym pair showed that it is coercible to a complementary interpretation or vice versa. Similarly, Proost (2010), who investigates German verbs denoting speech acts in a decompositional fashion, encounters classification problems.

Sense relations

Her analysis provides evidence that some of the verbs in antonym pairs lack typical attributes associated with specific subtypes of opposite and do not fulfil the traditional truth-conditional tests (cf. Cruse (1986); Lyons (1995)) necessary to establish a relation of complementarity or gradable opposition. Discrepancies and limits of traditional categories of lexico-semantic relations also include pairs with a morphologically derived negated form such as German *intelligent/unintelligent* ("intelligent/unintelligent"), *gefährlich/ungefährlich* ("dangerous/ undangerous"). These often cannot unanimously be classified as either (gradable) antonyms or non-gradable complementaries. The negated element *ungefährlich* does not indicate a degree of some property but an absolute state (compare the typical phrase *absolut ungefährlich*). It does not have inflectional comparative forms, and therefore appears to belong to the category of complementary opposites. In contrast, the unmarked item *gefährlich* refers to a gradable state as, for example, demonstrated by the pattern *relativ gefährlich*. It has inflectional comparative forms and can be coerced to an antonymic reading (cf. Cruse 2004: 164). While it has been assumed that negated forms are not readily gradable, such possibilities occur in actual language use as attested in corpora (Storjohann 2011) and through experimental techniques (Philpotts 2001).

Assessing the strength of antonym affinity is the focus of a study carried out by Paradis et al. (2009). Antonym affinity (also referred to as canonicity) reflects the degree to which antonyms are semantically related and conventionalised and hence entrenched as pairs in language and memory. Paradis et al.'s work is based on experimental methods and corpus-linguistic investigations where they show how opposites in use are judged differently by speakers ranging in their strength of affinity from salient to less salient opposition and are hence perceived as good (canonical) or bad (non-canonical). The classical system with its logical incompatibilities fails to define some of the less salient opposites and cannot account for this variability and flexible use of binary opposites in discourse. A definition was therefore needed that encompasses antonymy simultaneously as a lexical, semantic, conceptual and discourse phenomenon as well as antonymy in terms of logical incompatibility which involves similarity and differences.

3.1.2 Synonymy

Traditionally, **synonymy** has been formally divided into absolute/complete (e.g. *sofa/settee* in Cruse (1986: 269)), partial/propositional (e.g. *fiddle/violin* in Cruse (2004: 155)) as well as cognitive (e.g. *infant/baby* in Cruse (1986: 275)) categories, mainly depending on the degree of meaning difference in terms of expressive, stylistic or discursive traits or with regard to collocational preferences (cf. Cruse (1986: 273)), and depending on formal truth-conditional implications (cf. Lyons (1968: 450)). The typologies of synonyms reflect a continuum of meaning identity and vary in the literature (for a detailed overview see Adamska-Sałaciak (2013)). The central problem surrounds the key notion of presupposed properties exhibited by potentially synonymous pairs and formal-logical conditions regarding distributional identity and interchangeability. Smaller studies of English synonymy (Partington 1998; Murphy 2003), and of German synonymy (Storjohann 2009, 2010; Marková 2012) demonstrate how speakers adapt linguistic patterns to specific communicative needs in actual language use. Synonyms too vary in language use as identified for different degrees of synonymy, irrespective of their alleged type or degree of sameness of meaning. The evidence suggests that semantic equivalence is contextually construed, as shown in example (1) between *sauber/ rein* ("clean/immaculate") or modified by neutralising possible semantic differences which are, alternatively, emphasised in example (2).

(1) *Die Gänge sind, wie der Lokalaugenschein zeigt, sauber. Nicht so rein sind hingegen die Schächte der U-Bahnen.* (*Die Presse*, 16.03.1996, Mißachtetes Rauchverbot: "The underground passageways are, as close inspection reveals, clean. The tunnels of the underground, on the other hand, are not as immaculate.")
(2) *Sydney, die kosmopolitische Millionenstadt, wirkt so herausgeputzt, daß sie nicht nur sauber ist, sondern rein.* (*Die Tageszeitung*, 27.01.1988, S. 7: "Sydney, a cosmopolitan metropolitan city, is so spruced up that it is not just clean but immaculate.")

Meaning identity is an emergent construal marked by concrete forms of linguistic realisations and exemplifying cognitive mechanisms as well as using specific knowledge for particular comparative or inclusive purposes. As illustrated in 4.1.2, the relation of synonymy is dynamic and a product of different types of cognitive equivalence (cf. Adamska-Sałaciak (2013)).

3.2 Syntagmatic vs. paradigmatic relations

Semanticists have traditionally referred to lexico-semantic relations in terms of paradigmatic vs. syntagmatic structures, implying strict distinctions between them. Sense relations and hence primarily paradigmatic relations such as synonymy, antonymy, hyponymy, meronymy etc. were perceived to be related words that constitute a set of potentially substitutable expressions within the same lexical paradigm. A paradigmatic approach to sense relations implies focusing on the semantic properties that define such paradigmatic sets (or sometimes entire lexical fields). A syntagmatic approach, on the other hand, is concerned with lexical items surrounding the lexeme in question in terms of collocation and co-occurrence to describe the meaning of a word in a specific context (cf. Lyons (2002)). Cognitive and corpus-linguistic models have revealed the advantage of focusing on situations where items from the same paradigm co-occur in a single syntagm, adopting a critical perspective on the treatment of antonymy, in particular, as a paradigmatic opposition. Studies of English antonymy (cf. Justeson and Katz (1991); Mettinger (1994); Fellbaum (1995); Jones (2002)) and Swedish (Willners (2001)) as well as Japanese antonyms (Muehleisen and Isono (2009)) have established the view that antonymy is realised in co-text through specific contextual syntagmatic frames. Empirical evidence has also been put forward to support the view that antonym items occur in the same lexico-grammatical environment based on regular intrasentential co-occurrence more often than chance would allow (see details in 4.1.1).

4 Current methodologies, approaches and accounts

Investigations of sense relations are currently carried out through the use of computationally enabled corpus procedures, on the one hand, and different psycholinguistic techniques, on the other. Both have contributed profitably to insights into the nature of paradigmatics by implying a usage-based view of language structures. Conclusions are based on mass data which account for the recurrence, variability and distribution of patterns. The linguistic objectives have changed too and researchers from different linguistic schools and approaches share an interest in contextualised, dynamically construed meaning and in the grounding of language use in cognitive and social-interactional processes. A number of linguists, mostly in English and Swedish linguistics and with a particular interest in the subject of antonymy, have reopened the chapter on lexico-semantic relations, offering new perspectives, employing new methodologies and using empirical evidence (cf. Philpotts (2001); Willners (2001);

Jones (2002); Murphy (2003, 2006); Murphy et al. (2009); Paradis et al. (2009)). Their ideas have inspired other linguists with the same interest in antonymy (e.g. Muehleisen and Isono (2009)) and they have also been adopted by semanticists with an interest in the subject of German synonymy (e.g. Storjohann (2010); Marková (2012)).

4.1 The corpus-linguistic account

In the tradition of British Contextualism, the Firthian hypothesis "You shall know the meaning of a word by the company it keeps" (Firth 1957: 179) was central to lexical studies of meaning. Consequently, it is studies on the English language in particular that have succeeded in advancing theories about lexico-semantic relations.

4.1.1 Contrast and opposition: antonymy

Employing a larger corpus and statistical procedures, Jones (2002) investigates sententially co-occurring pairs expressing opposition. He identifies different lexico-grammatical frames that contextually embed antonym pairs and he demonstrates how these behave distributionally over a corpus. Jones's work (2002) is based on a 280-million-word corpus of written English (later also applied to spoken English, cf. Jones (2002)), and it offers the first systematic and comprehensive analysis of the discourse functions and distributional behaviour of antonyms. The claim that antonymy is linguistically realised in regular phrasal templates as co-occurring pairs in a greater than chance fashion is supported by the large amount of empirical evidence he presents. He also argues that antonyms accomplish various discourse functions, both in written text and in speech. These discourse functions typify antonym pairs according to their immediate grammatical context within a regular syntagm and are not based on logical formal truth-conditional principles. The most frequent discourse functions (examples from Jones (2002) and Jones et al. (2012)) are:

Coordinated Antonymy (*X and/or Y, both X and Y, (n)either X nor Y, either Y or Y, X and Y alike, X as well as Y*):

> *It would be good to hear all experiences, good as well as bad.*
> *Like all of us, athletes need to find a way of rationalising both failure and success.*

Ancillary Antonymy (sentential two-pair contrast between *X/Y* and *A/B*):

> *However, it is the scale of Labour success, not of Conservative failure, that stands out.*
> *The teacher is active and the student is passive.*

Comparative Antonymy (*more X than Y, X is more than Y, X rather than Y, X as . . . as Y*):

> *In every part of the country, more people think badly of him than think well.*
> *It is temporary, I would say it's more temporary than permanent.*

Negated Antonymy (*X not Y, X instead of Y, X as opposed to Y*):

> *Sponsors want to invest in success, not failure.*
> *That's not making it clean, that's making it dirty.*

Distinguished Antonymy (*between X and Y, separating X and Y, X differ from Y*):

> To them, [. . .], the distinction between fact and fiction or good and bad is not always so obvious.
> But then, crowds do not discriminate any too nicely between guilt and innocence.

Transitional Antonymy (*from X to Y, turning X into Y, X gives way to Y*):

> How easy to slip from the legal to the illegal trade, especially when the law is so patchy and the temptation so great.
> But it's been strangely quiet in Twickenham over the last week or two, and I must say my optimism is turning to pessimism.

These frames exhibit specific lexico-syntactic properties but are not necessarily unique to antonymy. Language users may contextually construe a contrast using such templates even in cases in which two incompatible items do not normally express a semantic contrast in nature. The semantic distinction is neutralised, for example, in conjoined patterns such as *X and Y alike*. In this way, specific discourse functions are semantically attributed to each individual phrasal template. As these frames are associated with meaningful components, they could be interpreted as constructions in the sense of Construction Grammar (see details in 4.3).

4.1.2 Semantic similarity/equivalence: synonymy

Corpus-assisted research into synonymy is characterised by two strands: investigating semantic differences in near-synonyms on the one hand, and observing constructional aspects and identifying conceptual processes in the construal of meaning identity in context, on the other. Computational methodologies, such as the statistical analysis of collocations, help linguists to examine fine-grained differences in textual co-occurrences and selectional restrictions between near-synonyms. This has been successfully demonstrated by Partington (1998), by looking at collocations of *sheer/pure/complete/absolute*, by Taylor (2003), who looks at *tall/high* and by Moon (2013), who investigates *brave/courageous* in English. For German, Marková (2012) reviews corpus evidence for *kalt/kühl* ("cold/cool") and *schön/hübsch* ("beautiful/pretty"). Such studies aim to analyse near-synonyms by measuring the degree of collocational overlap to identify the precise circumstances in which a lexical item can be substituted by a semantically similar item.

The discussion of meaning identity has also moved on to a debate where synonymy is viewed as a conceptual relation. Corpus data helps to identify linguistic structures which illuminate how similarity of concepts is conventionally encoded and externalised. In the case of German synonymy, Storjohann (2006, 2010) shows that a number of synonyms also frequently combine in close proximity and recur in combinational sequences. In analogy to Jones's (2002) description of antonyms, they can partly be classified according to their lexico-syntactic behaviour reflecting discourse-functional categories. These are:

Coordinated Synonymy (*X and Y, X or Y, X as well as Y, X and Y alike*):

> *Der Streit im Abgeordnetenhaus um die Auflösung der Westberliner Akademie der Wissenschaften [. . .] müßte "von unabhängigen und neutralen Gerichten" entschieden werden, erklärte die ASJ gestern.* (DeReKo: "The debate in the

parliament on closing the research academy in West Berlin [. . .] must be decided 'by independent and neutral courts'.")

Synonym Clusters (*X, Y, Z; X and Y and Z as well*):

Das Volk der Deutschen muss beweglicher, flexibler, agiler werden, verlangt sein grosser Häuptling in Bonn, der trotz seiner Leibesfülle erstaunlich leichtfüssig geht. (DeReKo: "Germans should become more mobile, flexible and agile, demands the big chief in Bonn.")

Die neutrale, freie, unabhängige Schweiz passt nicht in die neue Weltordnung. Denn das Ziel der UNO ist: Globalisierung auf allen Ebenen - Zentralismus. (DeReKo) ("A neutral, free and independent Switzerland does not fit into the new world order.")

Subordinated Synonymy (*X, which means Y; X, meaning Y; X, which is Y*):

In der ersten schnellen Runde baut sich bei uns eine um etwa zehn Grad kühlere Temperatur auf. Ist sie dann im grünen Bereich, dann ist der Reifen aber schon so abgefahren, daß nicht mehr der optimale, sprich bestmögliche, Haftwert erreicht wird. (DeReKo: "If the temperature is about right, the tyre is already so worn that the optimal, that is the best possible, adhesion can no longer be achieved.")

Corpus data indicates that synonym pairs favour a coordinated phrasal template in everyday language. A conjoined framework is an economical way of conveying as much information as possible, including slight semantic shades of difference between the synonyms. By using such frames, language users who produce repetition signal semantic inclusion as well as exhaustiveness and try to express a specific concept exhaustively by employing variation of expression, thus communicating slightly different pragmatic information. Another effect of such patterning might be that the synonyms involved become more alike as each contaminates the other's semantic interpretation, although this depends on how conventionalised the conjoined pairing is. Speakers characteristically employ subordinating structures where an explanation or clarification is made explicit, as is often the case in technical language use.

Storjohann (2010) investigates larger contexts where German synonyms (e.g. *Gefahr-Risiko* "danger-risk") co-occur within a span of two sentences. Typically, these exemplify sameness of meaning concerning the terms in question (see German example (3), and similarly, English example (4)).

(3) *Die Gefahr, in unmittelbarer Nähe des Atommeilers Krümmel bei Geesthacht an Leukämie zu erkranken, ist für Erwachsene noch höher, als in einer Studie bisher bekanntgeworden war. Die neue Studie über das Risiko für Erwachsene, in der Nähe des Atomkraftwerkes Krümmel bei Geesthacht an Leukämie zu erkranken, enthält mehr Brisanz als bisher angenommen.* (DeReKo: "The danger of developing leukemia in the immediate surroundings of the nuclear reactor 'Krümmel' near Geesthacht is even higher for adults than previously stated in a study. A new study on the risk of developing leukemia in the neighbourhood of the nuclear power plant 'Krümmel' near Geesthacht contains more explosive information than had been assumed.")

(4) *The deputy governor of the Bank of England warned yesterday that the financial crisis could wreak further damage and that there were dangers in rushing to*

overhaul regulation. [. . .] "There is a risk that we have run ahead of ourselves in deciding how we got here and what we should do about it," Mr Tucker added. (*The Independent*, 28 March 2009, p. 52)

Besides attestations of contexts where both synonyms can be substituted within specific constraints, corpus data reveals relations between the items where specific types of conceptual entailment or inclusion are indicated through the use of lexico-grammatical patterns. This is particularly the case for synonyms in close proximity. For example, as indicated by the frames *X implies Y, X because of Y, X otherwise Y* (alternatively *X also means Y, X is nothing but Y, X simultaneously/always means Y, X includes Y*) in sentences (5)–(7), a relation of semantic (causal) implication is expressed by the templates in which *Risiko* ("risk") and *Gefahr* ("danger") occur.

(5) *Wer von "Risiko" spricht, impliziert Gefahr.* (DeReKo: "Those who speak of 'risk' imply 'danger'.")
(6) *"Hunde sind weniger ein Problem,"* sagt Stefanie Gomez, *"aber Katzen gelten wegen der Gefahr einer Toxoplasmoseübertragung als Risiko."* (DeReKo: "Dogs are less of a problem," Stefanie Gomez says, "but cats are considered more of a risk because of the danger of transmitting toxoplasmosis.")
(7) *"Ich werde kein zu großes Risiko eingehen, sonst besteht die Gefahr, dass wir uns für mehrere Wochen schwächen,"* sagt Stephan Krautkremer. (DeReKo: "I will not take too big a risk, as otherwise there is danger that we will be weakened for weeks," Stephan Krautkremer says.)

In other cases, two synonyms lexicalise concepts as mutually dependent or semantically implied/associated in the following way: cause-effect (*X because of Y*), conditional relations (*if X then Y*), relations focusing a purpose-goal orientation (*X in order to Y*), part-of-whole relations (*X as part of Y*) and semantic entailment by superordination (hyperonymy, see section 5). All of these semantic relations illustrate semantic closeness on the basis of different conceptual properties which might be perceived as similar enough to construe sameness of meaning. Consequently, a relation of synonymy can be construed because the lexical items involved are semantically firmly included, associated with or entrenched in each other to appear similar enough to be used as meaning equivalents in specific contexts. This knowledge is shared by speakers.

Croft and Cruse claim that intuitively, speakers operate with a complex notion of synonymy, with different conceptions for different purposes, which are dependent on prototypical situations and on "contingent facts about the world" (2004: 165). This flexibility accounts for synonymy being a conceptual relation, as the knowledge represented by such contexts is stored in the mental lexicon and used to create sameness of meaning when communicatively necessary as the relation of cause-effect or conditionality is taken for implicit conceptual knowledge or as a "contingent fact about the world". As Murphy (2003: 168) points out, "what actually counts as synonymous is constrained by the demands of communicative language use and the context in which this language use occurs". It is the level of specificity of relevant properties that affects how similar the meanings of two words seem (cf. Murphy (2003: 139)). Knowledge of semantic closeness and semantic specificity is available to speakers in situations of use. The stronger the association of one concept with the other becomes, the more likely that a synonymous relation can exist between their lexicalisations, but with the restriction that "construability is not infinitely flexible" (Croft and Cruse 2004: 144). A traditional classification of synonymy cannot sufficiently cover necessary context-sensitive properties. A rather broad pragmatic view of synonymy, as proposed by Murphy (2003: 150), better reflects the linguistic construal of contextual meaning identity. She suggests that two lexical items are taken to be synonyms, "as long as their differences are slight enough that, in context, the two words' meanings contribute the same context-relevant information".

4.2 Psycholinguistic methods in the study of antonymy

The subject of antonym canonicity (affinity) has been addressed using psycholinguistic and corpus methods. Antonym canonicity expresses the degree of conventionalisation in language and the extent of entrenchment in the minds of speakers (Murphy 2003). Questions of canonicity are concerned with the degree of strength of lexico-semantic pairings and why some pairs are strongly associatively connected and hence considered better opposites than others. The use of judgement experiments, elicitation tests, priming experiments and word recognition tasks as ways of assessing the degree of canonicity has been central to the work of Paradis et al. (2009) for English, and Willners and Paradis (2010) for Swedish. Their underlying hypothesis was that people judge pairs as either non-antonymous, somewhat antonymous or as good antonyms. A point of departure for judgement and elicitation tests was the assumption that well-known antonyms co-occur contextually significantly more often than antonyms that are less conventionalised in language use. The aim of the study was to find out if antonym pairs with the highest significance of co-occurrence are also judged and identified as the most conventionalised. Their findings have contributed to the development of a theoretical cognitive framework (see 4.4).

First, the experiments demonstrated that there is a strong correlation between antonym frequency and co-occurrence in a corpus and the degree of canonicity of antonym pairs. High-scoring antonym pairs from psycholinguistic test sets are the same as those that occurred most frequently in the British National Corpus, as single lexical items and as co-occurring pairs. Standard deviation is low for antonyms that were classified as canonical a priori and higher for non-canonical pairs. Speakers largely agree on canonical antonyms. The list of elicited antonyms suggests a scale of canonicity, exhibiting an established antonym canon and ranging from good matches to test items with no clearly preferred partners. Second, there is no significant difference relating to the preference of ordering antonyms or the influence on the judgement of goodness-of-antonymy. Third, the results of the tests point towards canonicity being a gradable property existing along a scale in the sense of a continuum of goodness-of-antonymy. Participants in the elicitation tests were asked to give the best possible opposite for a number of stimulus words, as single words without context. The elicitation experiment showed that a number of antonym seed words favoured only one response antonym word (e.g. *good-bad*, *narrow-wide*, *rapid-slow*), while others had a varying number of different antonym counterparts (e.g. stimulus adjectives such as *delicate-robust/strong/tough*). More frequent and salient adjectives, for example, elicit fewer different adjectival antonyms than less frequent adjectives do. Overall, findings from judgement and elicitation experiments support the view that antonyms should be treated as a conceptual relation instead of being defined as a lexical-categorial relation.

4.3 The constructionist account

Murphy (2006) proposes treating canonical antonym pairings as constructions in the sense of Construction Grammar (cf. Goldberg (1995); Fillmore and Kay (1995); see Chapter 24). A canonical antonym pair is a "complex lexical construction consisting of two lexical items ready for insertion into constructions that require two items of the same part of speech"

(Murphy 2006: 17). Certain specific characteristics of Construction Grammar allow for the treatment of antonym relations as lexical components of grammatical and textual patterns. Construction Grammar posits that constructions are basic linguistic units in terms of form-meaning pairings which make little distinction between their lexical and syntactic constituents. This position is particularly compatible with the view that a relation such as antonymy is realised in syntagmatic structures which constitute a lexical-grammatical pattern which frames antonymous items repeatedly. These templates are more than just a two-member semantic structure. They are syntagmatic forms with specific discourse functions (cf. Jones (2002)) and they have meaningful associations and can thus be interpreted as form-meaning pairs which become linguistically realised in discourse as constructs. For example, in sequences such as *X and Y*, or *X and Y alike* with antonyms *hot* and *cold* as X and Y, an exhaustiveness of a gradable property is indicated and both ends of the two opposite states of a scale as well as all states in between the poles are implied at the same time. Part of the meaning of constructions such as *X and Y* alike is "that it unites and neutralizes contrasting categories, and thus any two words that appear in this construction are interpreted as opposites" (Jones et al. 2012: 107).

Construction Grammar does not rely on a context-free phrase structure grammar and does not separate individual constituents. The view is shared that constructs can interact within larger constructs and unify with each other. Word pairs in a relation of antonymy are treated as "discontinuous lexical items that are compatible with unifiable slots in other constructions" (Jones et al. 2012: 126). Construction Grammar allows for considerations of structures at most linguistic levels, from the morphological to the textual level. That means antonym constructs can appear outside the specific boundaries of particular constituents. This fact is well suited to explain why antonyms can co-occur in constructions such as *hot and cold* as well as in frames such as *from hot to cold*. Antonym constructs and their underlying lexico-grammatical constructions are referred to as contrastive constructions (Jones et al. 2012: 108).

Although there are fewer attestations that synonyms constitute specific lexical form-meaning pairings, smaller corpus studies have demonstrated that a number of meaning equivalents occur in regular sentential patterns (e.g. in coordinated phrasal templates) in a higher-than-chance frequency too (cf. Gries and Otani (2010)). Synonym pairings which are observed to co-occur in specific discourse frames can thus also be treated as constructions. Part of their constructional meaning is that it semantically unites and signals semantic inclusiveness and exhaustiveness. Synonym constructs and their underlying lexico-grammatical constructions could be labelled as inclusive/implying constructions. Overall, the argument for acknowledging highly conventionalised antonyms or synonyms as a constructional phenomenon is based on their grammatical and lexical characteristics as well as on their high degree of conventionalisation.

4.4 The dynamic construal account

An elaborate theoretical explanation of the nature of sense relations concerns opposites (cf. Jones et al. 2012), where all kinds of antonym relations from highly conventionalised lexico-semantic couplings to strongly contextually motivated pairings are accommodated by the cognitive construal approach (Croft and Cruse 2004). Sense relations are treated as semantic relations between "particular contextual construals of words" (Croft and Cruse 2004: 141). This model seeks to explain how antonymy is construed and why some pairs are "better" than others (Paradis 2010). The implication of this treatment of antonymy is that this lexico-semantic relation is primarily conceptual in nature and that it is dynamically construed. So far, the construal account offers a theoretical explanation of all semantic and pragmatic mechanisms that are involved when language users express contrast/opposition. Paradis (2001, 2005) extends the cognitive model by incorporating results from empirical psycholinguistic and corpus-guided studies of antonyms which employ usage-based methodologies. She puts forward an integrated descriptive usage-based proposal of antonymy as a conceptual relation and a construal, adopting a perspective referred to as Lexical Meaning as Ontologies and Construals (LOC). It provides a way of investigating how antonymy can be construed in any pair of lexical items in terms of the configuration of specific semantic content, and exactly why some pairs are perceived to be "better" antonyms than others. For example *good-bad*, *strong-weak*, *rich-poor* are highly conventionalised and hence canonical antonyms, as these are adjectives with meanings referring to properties of salient dimensions of high generality. As Jones et al. (2012: 139–140) point out, meanings that

> lend themselves to conventionalise binary opposition typically profile properties where not more than two possibilities are given. The two possibilities are properties within a simple conceptual dimension that is configured as two parts divided by a boundary or two poles of a single scale structure.

On the other hand, a number of different antonyms are suggested for *calm*, e.g. *stressed*, *stormy*, *rough*, *excited* etc. (examples from Jones et al. 2012: 140). As *calm* does not refer to a single property or a straightforward meaning structure (antonym schema) in a canonical way, different ontological meanings are described. Antonyms do not rely on inherent salient properties but are contextualised through their collocational profiles. The creation of antonymy is a result of construal processing operating with basic ontological categories (also called configurations) such as SCALE, DEGREE, BOUNDEDNESS, comprising semantic components and properties for example LENGTH (e.g. *long-short*), SIZE (e.g. *big-small*), MERIT (e.g. *good-bad*) or GENDER (e.g. *male-female*) etc. This means that opposition used in context implies "cognitive processes that operate on ontological structures when we use language to create meaning" (Jones et al. 2012: 130).

According to the construal account, antonymy is defined as a construal of binary contrast which in effect is a construal of comparison, grounded in perceptual and cognitive processing. Binarity is a schema in conceptual space (e.g. DEGREE/SCALE). The two opposing sides of the domain are divided by a boundary, looking at antonymy with a specific categorical focus. The prerequisites for constituting antonym use are a combination of configuring the boundary of a domain category and using cognitive processes (construals) such as contextual focusing, comparison of the two sides and profiling of a specific dimension. Thereby, specific content is categorised into two antonymic parts and contrasted irrespective of the salience of these parts. The strength of antonymous affinity or method of configuration and thus its salience largely depend on the complexity of the basic conceptual content structures as SCALE or BOUNDEDNESS.

Compared to Structuralist definitions, today, a broad, more pragmatic definition of antonymy is suggested by Jones et al. (2012). It brings together insights from corpus and psycholinguistic studies and applies to all types of opposites referring to "a pair-wise relation of lexical items in context that are understood to be semantically opposite" (2012: 2). This means that antonymy is broadly understood as form-meaning pairings that are used in binary opposition in language use. Words have different antonyms in different contexts depending on which of the item's semantic properties are relevant to contrast within a specific use.

Data-driven research on German synonymy shows indicative evidence that this sense relation can be treated sufficiently within the dynamic contextual construal theory too (Marková 2012). Presumably, similar categorisation principles, configuration and construal processes such as COMPARISON play a vital role in the negotiation of sameness of meaning in language use. However, further evidence from different complementary methodologies is needed to draw convincing theoretical conclusions.

5 Hyponymy, incompatibility and meronymy

Within the traditional paradigmatic viewpoint, sense relations such as hyponymy, meronymy and incompatibility have been described in terms of truth-conditional relations between words or alternatively between meanings/senses. Within a cognitive account, hyponymy (relation of inclusion e.g. between *apple* and *fruit)*, partonymy, also referred to as meronymy, (relation of part-whole, e.g. *finger-hand*) and incompatibility (the relation of exclusion between co-hyponyms, e.g. *dog-cat-mouse*) are treated as semantic relations between particular contextual construals of words with specific boundaries and constraints.

5.1 Hyponymy

Hyponymy is regarded as simple class inclusion and unilateral entailment and is "one of the most important structuring relations in the vocabulary of a language" (Cruse 2004: 148). The meaning of *It's an apple* entails but is not conversely entailed by the meaning of the expression *It's a fruit*. Classical definitions refer to *fruit* as the hyperonym representing a superordinate concept in a branching taxonomic system. A hyponym (*apple*), on the other hand, is a specific type or representative of the overall class of fruits. As long as prototypical notions are related to each other, default interpretations are triggered which generally follow the necessary truth-conditions of inclusion. However, a number of problems of defining hyponymy as a truth-conditional and logically transitive relation of entailment have been pointed out. These concern cases which fail the test of logical transitivity, as soon as non-prototypical hyponyms are assigned as types of commonly known superordinates (see example taken from Cruse (2004: 149)).

(8) *A car seat is a type of seat.*
    A seat is a type of furniture.
    **A car seat is a type of furniture.*

Similarly difficult are the relations between *dog-animal* and *dog-pet*. *It's a dog* entails *It's an animal* and this indicates that *dog* is a hyponym of *animal*. Apart from this first test frame for entailment, normality in a second diagnostic frame *X and other Ys*, as in *dogs and other animals*, further supports a hyponym relation between *dog* and *animal*. However, the expression *dogs and other pets* is also perfectly possible while in most people's judgement *It's a dog* does not necessarily entail *It's a pet*. Is *pet* therefore a superordinate of *dog* or is it not? The relation between *dog* and *animal* might more easily be accepted as hyponymy because *dog* might be a prototypical hyponym of the more prototypical hyperonym *animal*. However, in actual language use, speakers intuitively construe contexts where hyponymous items are connected which are not prototypical (such as between *dogs* and *pets*) and where specific domains instead of default readings are triggered. The cognitive strand allows pairs of lexical items related by hyponymy to be treated as dynamic relations. It accounts for hyponym variation and for hyponymy as a context-bound relation whereby the construability of contextual boundaries and variation of boundary placement affects the interpretation of hyponym pairs. *Dogs and pets*, just like *dogs and animals*, can be considered as related by hyponymy where construed meanings have been adjusted to specify a proper subclass of animals and where a specific domain and different semantic boundaries or domains have been established.

5.2 Incompatibility

If a superordinate/hyperonym such as *animal* has more than one hyponym (e.g. *dog*, *cat*, *mouse* etc.), these are linked as incompatibles (co-hyponyms). Incompatibility (co-hyponymy) exists between members of sets of the same hierarchical level and therefore holds between items referring to the same semantic field or domain. They form sets of terms denoting specific kinds of their common superordinate. These sets designate disjunct classes between which no member is shared. No two terms of different sets can be used simultaneously without implying contradiction. If something is a dog, it is implied that it is not a cat or a mouse and vice versa. Co-hyponymy, like hyponymy, has been of interest to semanticists for the description of the structure of the vocabulary. However, incompatibility does not simply signify a difference of meaning. As repeatedly pointed out by Cruse, this sense relation is "an important and rather special one" (Cruse 2004: 162). A corpus-assisted re-evaluation of the phenomenon of incompatibility with respect to German co-hyponyms and their functions in text and discourse has been propounded in Storjohann (2007). It has been argued that the relation in question can function as a discourse marker provided the incompatibles of a lexical item such as *Globalisierung* ("globalisation") refer to a socially and politically controversial notion. Incompatibles occur in close contextual proximity and participate in regular syntagmatic frames (e.g. conjoined patterns such as *Globalisierung und Deregulierung* "globalisation and deregulation" or *Globalisierung und Kapitalismus* "globalisation and capitalism"). The various incompatibles of *Globalisierung* show crucial evidence for thematic diversity within a specific (critical) discourse. They focus on discursive aspects and illustrate a spectrum of semantic nuances. Therefore, it is claimed that they exhibit a pragmatic-discursive force and that they reveal a sense-constructing function, as they contribute to facets of contextual meaning.

a   Incompatibles denoting global economic states or developments: *Deregulierung* ("deregulation"), *Flexibilisierung* ("flexibilisation"), *Freihandel* ("free trade"), *Privatisierung* ("privatisation") . . .
b   Incompatibles denoting socio-political effects and characteristics of globalised societies and their political actions: *Arbeitslosigkeit* ("unemployment"), *Demokratie* ("democracy"), *Gerechtigkeit* ("justice"), *Migration* ("migration"), *Neoliberalismus* ("neoliberalism") . . .
c   Incompatibles denoting communication and technology: *Computerisierung* ("computerisation"), *Digitalisierung* ("digitalisation"), *Informationsrevolution* ("information revolution"), *Kommunikation* ("communication") . . .

5.3 Partonymy/meronymy

Partonymy/meronymy is a part-whole/portion-whole relation applying to two individual entities that are linked to illustrate the notion of containment (e.g. *finger-hand*). Following the cognitive framework as suggested by Croft and Cruse (2004), meronymy is defined as follows:

If A is a meronym of B in a particular context, then any member a of the extension of A maps onto a specific member b of the extension of B of which it is construed as a part, or it potentially stands in an intrinsically construed relation of part to some actual or potential member of B.

(Croft and Cruse 2004: 160)

Finger is an intrinsic part of a *hand,* not just an attachment, whereas *lake* can be imposed as a part of a *park* but it is not a necessary part of it. Cruse (1986) and Croft and Cruse (2004) have provided a detailed account of the category PART including classes such as part, portion, piece, segment and element, which can be judged differently by speakers as parts of a whole. As Croft and Cruse (2004: 155–156) point out, as an example, how speakers' judgements differ as to whether a *battery* and a *bulb* are equally parts of a *flashlight*, although both are contained in the body of it. Conventionally, the bulb is included whereas a battery is not part of a flashlight as it is expected to be bought separately. A clear definition of meronymy is difficult, as it remains open where the boundaries of a whole entity are.

6 Future directions

Evidence has been put forward to establish that semantic classifications based on formal or logical principles are not always compatible with data emerging from corpus-driven or psycholinguistic studies. Sense relations as contextually construed in discourse are flexible and dynamic and can often not be assigned to rigid logical formulas. The study of opposition in particular provides a solid basis for the development of a larger semantic theory, not by illuminating features of meaning, but by looking at dynamic contextual behaviour, discourse functions and linguistic realisation as patterns in language use, and by examining constructions for hints of underlying cognitive mechanisms.

While a number of linguistic issues have been revisited recently, some research questions remain unexplored or deserve further exploration, since some aspects of the nature of sense relations remain unknown. These mainly concern the ways in which lexico-semantic relations are conventionalised, stored and exploited. First, a number of specific questions address issues of negation as well as differences between affixal and non-negated antonymous adjectives; for example, why the lexical item *natural* co-occurs significantly with opposites such as *artificial* and *man-made* but not with its morphologically derived form *unnatural*. Similar evidence is found for German *normal* ("normal") which co-occurs with *krankhaft* ("morbid") and *verrückt* ("crazy"), but far less frequently with its derivates *unnormal/abnormal*. Second, another interesting aspect of antonymy is that co-occurring antonyms tend to show a specific preference in their order of sequence in constructions (*long > short, good > bad* rather than *short > long, bad > good*). Exhaustive research is needed with regard to the ordering and symmetry of antonyms. Third, another central question is whether the collocation profile of antonym items and the degree to which pairs modify the same nominal meanings affect their degree of antonym affinity. Finally, the subject of hyponymy, incompatibility and meronymy deserve greater attention from a variety of angles. This also implies examinations of relational constructions in various genres and, more importantly, in spoken language. Only then can the phenomena of hyponymy, incompatibility and meronymy be accounted for satisfactorily in contemporary theories. To answer some of the open questions, cross-linguistic investigations contributing to the understanding of lexical typology can also provide valuable insights. With the further development of computational techniques capable of linguistically more precise and more comprehensive data searches, further findings should be expected.

Further reading

Croft, W. and D. A. Cruse 2004. *Cognitive Linguistics*. Cambridge: Cambridge University Press. In section 6 and 7 a cognitive account of sense relations is propounded and hyponymy and relations of contrast are discussed as dynamic, context-sensitive construals.

Cruse, D. A. 1986. *Lexical Semantics*. Cambridge: Cambridge University Press. A contextual approach to lexical semantics with detailed descriptions of lexical-semantic relations.

Jones, St., L. M. Murphy, C. Paradis and C. Willners 2012. *Antonyms in English. Construals, Construction and Canonicity*. Studies in English Language. Cambridge: Cambridge University Press. Provides an extensive investigation of English antonyms and offers an innovative model of how we mentally organise concepts and how we perceive contrast between them.

Paradis, C. 2005. Ontologies and construal in lexical semantics. *Axiomathes* 15: 541–573. Proposes a usage-based model of lexical meaning in terms of properties of ontologies in conceptual space. This theory is the basis of a new antonymy model (see Jones et al. (2012)).

Storjohann, P. (ed.) 2010. *Lexical-Semantic Relations: Theoretical and Practical Perspectives*. Amsterdam/Philadelphia: Benjamins. A collection of articles demonstrating the construction of sense relations in different languages based on corpus-linguistic and psycholinguistic analyses.

References

Adamska-Sałaciak, A. 2013. Equivalence, synonymy, and sameness of meaning in a bilingual dictionary. *International Journal of Lexicography* 26: 329–345.

Bierwisch, M. 1989. Dimensional adjectives: grammatical structure and conceptual interpretation. In M. Bierwisch and E. Lang (eds) *Dimensional Adjectives: Grammatical Structure and Conceptual Interpretation*. Berlin: Springer, 71–261.

Cann, R. 2011. Sense relations. In C. Maienborn, K. von Heusinger and P. Portner (eds) *Semantics. An International Handbook of Natural Language Meaning*. Berlin/Boston: Mouton de Gruyter, 456–479.

Croft, W. and A. D. Cruse 2004. *Cognitive Linguistics*. Cambridge: Cambridge University Press.

Cruse, A. D. 1986. *Lexical Semantics*. Cambridge: Cambridge University Press.

Cruse, A. D. 2002a. Paradigmatic relations of inclusion and identity: synonymy. An overview. In A. D. Cruse, F. Hundsnurscher, M. Job and P. R. Lutzeier (eds) *Lexikologie. Ein internationales Handbuch zur Natur und Struktur von Wörtern und Wortschätzen*. Berlin/New York: Walter de Gruyter, 485–497.

Cruse, A. D. 2002b. Paradigmatic relations of exclusion and opposition: reversivity. An overview. In A. D. Cruse, F. Hundsnurscher, M. Job and P. R. Lutzeier (eds) *Lexikologie. Ein internationales Handbuch zur Natur und Struktur von Wörtern und Wortschätzen*. Berlin/New York: Walter de Gruyter, 507–510.

Cruse, A. D. 2004. *Meaning in Language: An Introduction to Semantics and Pragmatics*. Oxford: Oxford University Press.

Cruse, A. D. and P. Togia 1996. Towards a cognitive model of antonymy. *Journal of Lexicology* 1: 113–141.

DeReKo: das Deutsche Referenzkorpus. Mannheim: Institut für Deutsche Sprache. http://www.ids-mannheim.de/kl/projekte/korpora.

Fellbaum, C. 1995. Co-occurrence and antonymy. *International Journal of Lexicography* 8: 281–303.

Fillmore, C. J. and P. Kay 1995. Construction grammar. Ms., University of California, Berkeley.

Firth, J. R. 1957. *Papers in Linguistics 1934–1951*. London/New York: Oxford University Press.

Goldberg, A. E. 1995. *Constructions: A Construction Grammar Approach to Argument Structure*. Chicago: University of Chicago Press.

Gries, S. T. and N. Otani 2010. Behavioral profiles. A corpus-based perspective on synonymy and antonymy. *ICAME Journal*, 34: 121–150.

Hoey, M. 2005. *Lexical Priming. A New Theory of Words and Languages*. London/New York: Routledge.

Justeson, J. S. and S. M. Katz 1991. Co-occurrence of antonyms adjectives and their contexts. *Computational Linguistics* 17: 1–19.
Jones, S. 2002. *Antonymy: A Corpus-Based Perspective*. London/New York: Routledge.
Jones, S., L. M. Murphy, C. Paradis and C. Willners 2012. *Antonyms in English. Construals, Construction and Canonicity*. Studies in English Language. Cambridge: Cambridge University Press.
Lehrer, A. J. 2002. Paradigmatic relations of exclusion and opposition: gradable antonyms and complementarity. An overview. In A. D. Cruse, F. Hundsnurscher, M. Job and P. R. Lutzeier (eds) *Lexikologie. Ein internationales Handbuch zur Natur und Struktur von Wörtern und Wortschätzen*. Berlin/New York: Walter de Gruyter, 499–507.
Lehrer, A. J. and K. Lehrer 1982. Antonymy. *Linguistics and Philosophy* 5: 483–501.
Lyons, J. 1968. *Introduction to Theoretical Linguistics*. Cambridge: Cambridge University Press.
Lyons, J. 1977. *Semantics*. Cambridge: Cambridge University Press.
Lyons, J. 1995. *Linguistic Semantics: An Introduction*. Cambridge. Cambridge University Press.
Lyons, J. 2002. Sense relations: an overview. In A. D. Cruse, F. Hundsnurscher, M. Job and P. R. Lutzeier (eds) *Lexikologie. Ein internationales Handbuch zur Natur und Struktur von Wörtern und Wortschätzen*. Berlin/New York: Walter de Gruyter, 466–472.
Lutzeier, P. R. 1981. *Wort und Feld. Wortsemantische Fragestellungen mit besonderer Berücksichtigung des Wortfeldbegriffes*. Tübingen: Niemeyer.
Marková, V. 2012. *Synonyme unter dem Mikroskop: eine korpuslinguistische Studie*. Tübingen: Narr.
Mettinger, A. 1994. *Aspects of Semantic Opposition*. Oxford: Clarendon.
Moon, R. 2013. Braving synonymy: from data to dictionary. *International Journal of Lexicography* 26: 260–278.
Murphy, L. M. 2003. *Semantic Relations and the Lexicon. Antonymy, Synonymy and other Paradigms*. Cambridge: Cambridge University Press.
Murphy, L. M. 2006. Antonyms as lexical constructions: or, why paradigmatic construction is not an oxymoron. *Constructions, Special Volume* 1/8: 1–37. http://sro.sussex.ac.uk/701.
Murphy, L. M., C. Paradis, C. Willners and S. Jones 2009. Discourse functions of antonymy: a cross-linguistic investigation of Swedish and English. *Journal of Pragmatics* 41: 2159–2184.
Muehleisen, V. and M. Isono 2009. Antonymous adjectives in Japanese discourse. *Journal of Pragmatics* 41: 2185–2203.
Paradis, C. 2001. Adjectives and boundedness. *Cognitive Linguistics* 12: 47–66.
Paradis, C. 2005. Ontologies and construal in lexical semantics. *Axiomathes* 15: 541–573.
Paradis, C. 2010. Good, better and superb antonyms: a conceptual construal approach. *The Annual of Texts by Foreign Guest Professors*. Vol. 3. Charles University Prague, Faculty of Philosophy and Arts: 385–402. http://lup.lub.lu.se/luur/download?func=downloadFile&recordOId=1583460&file OId=1590145.
Paradis, C. 2011. A dynamic construal approach to antonymy. *Selected papers from the 19th International Symposium of Theoretical and Applied Linguistics*. Thessaloniki: Monochromia, 33–42.
Paradis, C., C. Willners and S. Jones 2009. Good and bad opposites: using textual and experimental techniques to measure antonym canonicity. *The Mental Lexicon* 4: 380–429.
Partington, A. S. 1998. *Patterns and Meanings: Using Corpora for English Language Research and Teaching*. Amsterdam: Benjamins.
Philpotts, V. 2001. *A Comparative Analysis of Antonymy and Hybrid Anto-Complementarity in English and German within a Cognitive Framework*. PhD Dissertation University of Manchester.
Proost, K. 2010. Antonymy relations: typical and atypical cases from the domain of speech act verbs. In P. Storjohann (ed.) *Lexical-Semantic Relations: Theoretical and Practical Perspectives*. Amsterdam/Philadelphia: Benjamins, 95–114.
Sinclair, J. 1991. *Corpus, Concordance, Collocation*. Oxford: Oxford University Press.
Storjohann, P. 2006. Kontextuelle Variabilität synonymer Relationen. Mannheim: Institut für Deutsche Sprache. http://pub.ids-mannheim.de/laufend/opal/opal06-1.html.

Storjohann, P. 2007. Incompatibility: a no-sense relation? In *Proceedings of the 4th Corpus Linguistics Conference, Birmingham*. http://www.birmingham.ac.uk/documents/college-artslaw/corpus/conference-archives/2007/36Paper.pdf.

Storjohann, P. 2009. Plesionymy: a case of synonymy or contrast? *Journal of Pragmatics* 41: 2140–2158.

Storjohann, P. 2010. Synonymy in corpus texts – conceptualisation and construction. In P. Storjohann (ed.) *Lexical-Semantic Relations. Theoretical and Practical Perspectives*. Amsterdam/Philadelphia: Benjamins, 69–94.

Storjohann, P. 2011. Paradigmatische Konstruktionen in Theorie, lexikografischer Praxis und im Korpus. In A. Klosa (ed.) *elexiko. Erfahrungsberichte aus der lexikografischen Praxis eines Internetwörterbuchs*. Tübingen: Narr, 99–129.

Taylor, J. 2003. Near synonyms as coextensive categories: 'Tall' and 'high' revisited. *Languages Sciences* 25: 263–284.

Willners, C. 2001. *Antonyms in Context: A Corpus-Based Semantic Analysis of Swedish Descriptive Adjectives*. (*Travaux de l'Institut de Linguistique de Lund* 40). Lund: Lund University Department of Linguistics.

Willners, C. and C. Paradis 2010. Swedish opposites. A multimethod approach to antonym canonicity. In P. Storjohann (ed.) *Lexical-Semantic Relations: Theoretical and Practical Perspectives*. Amsterdam/Philadelphia: John Benjamins, 15–47.

Related topics

Chapter 5, Cognitive semantics; Chapter 6, Corpus semantics; Chapter 10, Semantics and pragmatics; Chapter 17, Negation and polarity

15
Semantic shift

John Newman

1 Introduction

Semantic shift is most immediately associated with the change in meaning that can be observed at different historical stages of a language in the way one might trace semantic shifts of words from Middle English to Modern English. This is semantic shift on the grand stage of history. But semantic shift can also be understood in ways which make it manifest in very ordinary kinds of language activity as happens in our lived experience, without reference to the historical stages of a language spanning centuries. It is this kind of semantic shift that will be the focus of this chapter, even if the study of semantic shifts of meaning change on the grand scale can still contribute, importantly, to this approach.

As a simple example of shifting that has occurred in the course of the author's lifetime, consider the well-known changes that have occurred in computer terminology. The advent of computers has given rise to a prolific and ongoing recruitment of words to describe new ways of interacting with computers. Familiar words have come to be used in innovative ways to serve this domain of experience: *hardware, application, programme, browser, desktop, navigate, search, domain, flame, memory, virus,* and, of course, many more. The semantic shifts evident in these words are well established in English. Lexicographic practice, as seen in contemporary dictionaries, typically accords these semantic shifts the status of full-fledged meanings (leaving aside the question of whether such practice agrees with what a semanticist might determine, following a particular theory of polysemy: see Chapter 13). But one can point to other more isolated and less permanent kinds of semantic shifts that are less often remarked upon and less likely to find their way into the codified language described by dictionaries. I recently happened to hear the following snippet of speech (from a single speaker, a veterinarian) on a radio program, in reference to how doctors and veterinarians should see themselves: "We are all veterinarians; it's just that some of us specialize in human populations." It was a funny and thought-provoking way of trying to lead listeners to rethink and re-examine how they prioritize veterinarians vis-à-vis doctors and the animal kingdom vis-à-vis humans. The snippet of speech, at the moment I heard it, required some semantic shifting of the word *veterinarian* in my mind (and presumably in the minds of others if they were listening as attentively as I was) from the sense of "a medically trained person who specializes in animals" to "a medically trained person".

These two types of semantic shift have very different consequences in terms of the impact made on the English language. The former is so widespread it has become codified in modern

English, as reflected in the changes made to entries such as *virus* in modern dictionaries. The latter, on the other hand, remains a relatively fleeting experience on the part of some speakers, without any obvious lasting effect on language usage for the vast majority of speakers. Clearly, there is a great difference in the acceptance of these shifts and their spread through society, but this difference in the social impact and the time span of the shifts should not distract us from the commonality of the semantic shifting that underlies both phenomena. They are both semantic shifts that I, for one, have experienced within my lifetime; they form part of my genuinely lived experience of language. This chapter considers key issues that arise for theorizing about language when one makes such phenomena a focus of study. Given that semantic shift, as understood here, is such a commonplace, even mundane, phenomenon, a linguistically naïve person might well expect that the phenomenon would be central to, and hence readily accommodated, in any sophisticated theorizing about language. In point of fact, the phenomenon has not always been the focus of interest in contemporary linguistics that one might have expected it to be and a conceptual framework for adequately dealing with it has yet to be fully developed.

2 Critical issues

In this section I will review a few critical issues that arise in discussions of semantic shift: (i) the flexibility of meaning, (ii) the construction of meaning as a dynamic, cognitive process, and (iii) the context of use.

The observations in section 1 point to a profoundly important characteristic of meaning in reference to natural language: meaning is *flexible*. Semantic shift, in this view, is an undeniable and ubiquitous facet of our ordinary experience of language. In the words of Lichtenberk (1991: 477):

> Word meanings are not fully determinate; they are open-ended, flexible. This is what allows words to be applied to new experiences, to express newly perceived relations among phenomena and thus to form new categories or to alter the make-up of existing categories, and to relate to each other phenomena from different cognitive domains.

The flexibility of meaning lends support to viewing language more as an ongoing, never-to-be completed work in progress, rather than as a static state of affairs – a viewpoint that sits uncomfortably with much of linguistic theorizing that prefers to assume a more fixed, synchronic state of language. In the early twentieth century, Saussure (1959: 100) had elaborated on what he considered to be a necessary conceptual move in studying language synchronically:

> An absolute state is defined by lack of change. But since languages are always changing, however minimally, studying a linguistic state amounts in practice to ignoring unimportant changes. Mathematicians do likewise when they ignore very small fractions for certain purposes, such as logarithmic calculations.

According to Saussure, then, just as mathematicians may sometimes need to round off fractions to whole numbers, so linguists need to ignore unimportant fluctuations in language over the period of time they choose for the synchronic state. *Unimportant* is a critical word in the quote above, since the decision as to what is important or unimportant is the key to what kind of language practices, acts, facts, etc. will be studied. As seen in the quote above, Saussure well understood the ever-changing nature of language but considered it necessary to "fix" language in some absolute, stable state to proceed with a practical description of language. The assumption of a stable language state has been fundamental to most theorizing about language in the post-Saussure era, along with the correlate that language should be conceived of as a fixed object of study.

Inevitably, changing the focus to flexibility of meaning, rather than stability of meaning, means that *human cognitive processes* will occupy centre stage in discussions of semantic shift, rather than the notion of an *abstract stable system*. A congenial home for researchers choosing to make meaning construction and associated human cognitive processes a focal point can be found in the sub-field of pragmatics and the body of research known as Cognitive Linguistics, especially its sub-field Cognitive Semantics (see Chapters 5, 10, and 11). For many researchers working within these approaches, the semantic side of the traditional linguistic unit of the word has been re-conceptualized so that the word is no more than a "prompt" or "trigger" for what the intended meaning might be, leaving it to the listener/reader to construct the fully elaborated meaning (cf. Fetzer's (2011: 25) description of meaning as "not a product and given, but rather dynamic, multifaceted and negotiated in context"). Each use of a word is understood in its larger context, quite possibly a new context in which the word has not been used before, and the listener/reader will associate that word with a fuller meaning, depending on their prior language experience, the immediate linguistic context in which the word appears etc. The idea that meanings emerge in the minds of language users when various cognitive processes are applied is by no means new and some version of this idea is commonplace in linguistics. Making this aspect of language a centre-point and focus for linguistic theorizing is, however, what distinguishes the above approaches.

Addressing the realities of the meanings associated with words like *desktop* and *veterinarian* requires us to recognize that our understanding of a word is closely tied to the *context of use* of that word and how we interpret the whole context of use, a perspective that lies at the core of the pragmatics tradition in linguistics. An earlier and careful statement of this reality is to found in Stern (1931), a volume that still repays close reading. Stern (1931: 68) distinguished two kinds of word meanings: *lexical meaning* (the meaning we ascribe to an isolated word or phrase) and *actual meaning* (the meaning of the word in actual speech). Lexical meaning, for Stern, was a distinctly odd notion, citing the Cambridge psychologist James Ward approvingly:

> We never – except for the sake of this very inquiry [i.e. an academic exercise, JN] – attempt to fix our minds . . . upon some isolated concept; in actual thinking ideas are not in consciousness alone and disjointedly, but part of a context.
> (Ward (1918: 299), cited in Stern (1931: 68))

In Stern's view, it was a mistake to speak of lexical meanings as if they existed on their own, independent of linguistic context. Recognition of linguistic context of usage as a critical factor in any attempt to account for word meaning was also a central tenet for Firth who, as is well known, had pronounced: "you shall know a word by the company it keeps" (Firth 1957: 11). Recent decades have seen the rise of newer approaches in the study of context. These include corpus-based approaches in linguistics whereby the preceding and following linguistic environments (sometimes called "co-text") of a word in use are made readily apparent (see Chapter 6). It is not just the linguistic co-text of a word that is relevant to constructing the meaning of that word, however. Rather, it is the whole context of use that must be considered relevant. This includes listener/reader expectations, discourse topic, the physical setting of the communication act, etc. The word *veterinarian*, for example, did fleetingly undergo semantic shift to "a medically trained person" for me, but this only happened under the circumstances described above, during a radio program, knowing the background of the speaker, and given the immediate co-text of the use of the word.

3 Conceptual tools

No one contemporary linguistic theory does full justice to all the issues raised in section 2. As indicated above, however, Cognitive Linguistics is one framework that can comfortably accommodate semantic shift and I will adopt that framework in what follows. Here I will focus on two influential ideas that have helped to shape much of the work relating to semantic shift within this field. The first relates to extension of meanings as represented in Cognitive Grammar; the second concerns the notion of conceptual blending.

Langacker's Cognitive Grammar (Langacker 1987, 1988, 2008) is a sympathetic framework in which to explore and represent semantic shift (see Chapter 5). For a start, Cognitive Grammar incorporates a dynamic view of meaning, summarized succinctly by Langacker (2008: 30) in the following terms:

> [m]eaning is not identified with concepts but with **conceptualization**, the term being chosen precisely to highlight its dynamic nature. Conceptualization is broadly defined to encompass any facet of mental experience. It is understood as subsuming (1) both novel and established conceptions; (1) not just "intellectual" notions, but sensory, motor, and emotive experience as well; (3) apprehension of the physical, linguistic, social, and cultural context; and (4) conceptions that develop and unfold through processing time (rather than being simultaneously manifested). So even if "concepts" are taken as being static, conceptualization is not.

This underlying view of meaning as a dynamic kind of conceptualization and part of mental experience makes Cognitive Grammar an attractive theory for accommodating and representing the relatedness of a word's senses and the ever-present potential for some semantic shift within the meaning of a word. Figures 15.1 and 15.2 illustrate the core notion of semantic shift as commonly represented in this theory. Figure 15.1 shows a number of key semantic relations, at a very general level, in the diagrammatic form favoured by Langacker. It shows a schematic network in which senses are categorized with respect to other senses. A sense may have the status of a SCHEMA, i.e. a sense so general that it completely encompasses other senses; these other senses, in turn, elaborate the schematic sense and are indicated by solid arrows extending from the schema. Another kind of semantic relationship exists when one sense is perceived as being an EXTENSION, which is to say extended from another sense – the PROTOTYPE. A dashed line is used to indicate the extension from a prototype. In so far as the prototype is the basis for the extension, we may speak of the prototype as sanctioning the extension. Figure 15.2, it must be emphasized, purports to represent no more than Langacker's own judgement about part of the schematic network for *fruit* (cf. Langacker (1987: 74)). In this case, the semantic shift can be attributed, in part, to the increased awareness about the scientific classification of tomatoes as fruit and incorporating that new awareness into a revision of an existing folk belief. Not all semantic shifts on the part of individuals have to be so motivated, of course; semantic shifts can be triggered by any number of factors (simply an imaginative leap, for example). The APPLE, PEAR, and

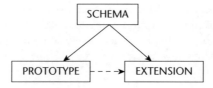

Figure 15.1 The core concepts underlying semantic shift in Cognitive Grammar (adapted from Langacker (1988: 140))

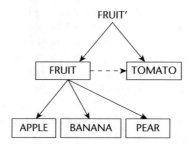

Figure 15.2 Core concepts applied to a semantic shift in fruit (adapted from Langacker (1987: 74))

BANANA senses that appear in Figure 15.2 are categorized as instantiations, or elaborations, of a relatively schematic sense FRUIT. The less familiar, more technical categorization of tomatoes as fruits can be accommodated as an extension from the earlier schematic category. As a network extends horizontally, one would expect the network to also grow upwards since there are likely to be increasingly general schemas encompassing old and new senses. So, an extension of an earlier FRUIT sense to include tomatoes goes hand in hand with the creation of a new, even more encompassing schematic sense, designated by FRUIT'. The concepts of schema, prototype, and extension, as used in Figures 15.1 and 15.2, are the core concepts underlying Langacker's approach to understanding and representing semantic shift and Figures 15.1 and 15.2 do no more than introduce these concepts and the accompanying notation. More complex examples of schematic networks building on these representational devices can be found in Langacker ((1987: 383) for *tree*, (1988: 135) for *run*). Extensions may form a radial network in which all extensions radiate from a single prototype, or they may form a chain such that one extension becomes a local prototype for a new extension, or they may form a network that combines such patterns.

The basic elements invoked in the representation of semantic shift in Figures 15.1 and 15.2 provide the means to accommodate, in a representational way, the all-important flexibility of word meaning. While Cognitive Grammar is attractive for this very reason, there are certainly issues that can be raised with respect to this approach. For one thing, there is the question of deciding just how many senses of a word to recognize, even granting that the analysis purports only to represent a single speaker's intuitions. Arriving at some shared understanding on how to identify vagueness (implying one sense) as opposed to polysemy (implying many individual senses) remains a highly contentious issue in semantics (cf. Chapter 13). A common strategy adopted by linguists has been to proceed to differentiate interpretations of words in context, regardless of whether one treats the differences as vagueness or polysemy. Distinguishing word senses is an issue in any approach to word semantics, quite independently of the presence of any semantic shift, and it is no less an issue when it comes to constructing or evaluating the semantic networks in the Figures above. The construction of semantic networks like those shown in Figure 15.2, as far as current practice in Cognitive Grammar is concerned, relies upon a speaker's own judgement about different senses and how they are related and so take the differentiation of senses to be a "given" or at least something that the speaker or linguist could arrive at through introspection and reflection. Even when a speaker might intuit some semantic relatedness in the many uses of, say, the noun *head* in English (head of the bed, head of the department, head of lettuce), the task of representing these intuitions as schemas, prototypes, and extensions in a diagram like that in Figure 15.2 is not something that can be simply reduced to intuitions.

In recent years, attention has become focused on a kind of semantic shift referred to as *conceptual blending* or *conceptual integration*, as described in publications such as Fauconnier and Turner (1998) and Fauconnier (2009). Very briefly, conceptual blending refers to a cognitive operation in which elements from structures in two different mental spaces are integrated, giving rise to a new blended structure distinct from the two input structures. Fauconnier and Turner (1998: 137) describe mental spaces as "small conceptual packets constructed as we think and talk, for purposes of local understanding and action. Mental spaces are very partial assemblies containing elements, and structured by frames and cognitive models". The use of *desktop* to refer to an entity on a computer, referred to above, exhibits conceptual blending of the mental space associated with a traditional three-dimensional desktop and the mental space associated with a computer screen (an example discussed at some length by Fauconnier and Turner (1998: 156–157)). Conceptual blending is to be thought of as a dynamic cognitive process, underlying countless instances of production and interpretation of expressions that invoke different "frame structures" from two inputs. Conceptual blending comfortably allows for, and indeed encourages, a focus on the actual moment in time when a blend comes about as a cognitive process, having as its outcome a new kind of pairing of form and meaning. Conceptual blending is pervasive in language and other realms in which the human mind is exercised.

The idea of a semantic network incorporating semantic shifts can also be applied to units of language besides words. Indeed, in Cognitive Grammar, morphemes, words, and larger constructional assemblies of morphemes and words are all instances of the same kind of symbolic entity in which there exists a pairing of form and meaning. Just as we may discern semantic shift in a word, so, too, we may discern it in these other kinds of units. One can equally well inquire into the relations among the senses of a suffix like *–er* (agentive sense in *builder*, instrumental in *ruler* etc.), the question tag *hey?* as used at the end of some utterances in colloquial English, or the various senses of a *V1 and V2* construction (reflecting the different kinds of semantic relations that hold between the verbs in conjoined structures such as *go and sit*, *wait and see*, *try and come*, etc.).

Figures 15.1 and 15.2 are intended to capture, in very summary form, the process of semantic shift without any attempt to incorporate details of the actuation or spread of the shift. Figure 15.2, for example, says nothing about the circumstances under which the semantic extension originally took place or just how widespread this conceptualization of *fruit* is. It is not common practice to document the actuation of semantic shifts, with linguists preferring to see their task more in terms of identifying the beginning and end stages of such shifts and what those stages may share. And when there is such discussion, it is often speculative rather than authoritative, and therefore viewed as less than scientific. But there can be satisfying accounts of the origin of semantic shifts, even if they must be labelled "speculative". Wells' (1975) analysis of how *fine$_1$* (as in *be sure to read the fine print*) might have given rise to *fine₂* (as in *it's a fine day*) is a case in point. For Wells (1975: 210), the challenge with a pair of meanings like this, where the meanings could *possibly* overlap, is to imagine a plausible scenario whether there was indeed a *probable* overlap. Wells imagines a process involving a speaker (a salesclerk) and the hearer (a prospective buyer) and where the hearer is examining cloth. The speaker might use *fine* to refer to fine-grained cloth while at the same time (through gesture, expression, and manner) indicate that the speaker admires the cloth and that the hearer is expected to admire the cloth. In this particular case, then, the semantic shift originates in acts of communication in which the speaker intends his utterance one way and the hearer, upon hearing the utterance in a particular context, understands it another way (Wells 1975: 205). Stern (1931) has extended discussion of similar cases where some mismatch between intended and understood meanings might have arisen in acts of communication, e.g. the shift in the meaning of *want* from "to be in want of something, to be lacking something" to "to desire something". Stern uses the terms *equivocal* and *equivocation* to describe the condition which holds when either one of two meanings could be present simultaneously in communication. For Stern, the choice of one meaning over another in such situations was the result of a change in attention focus such that "if the speaker turned his attention to the matter, either of the two possible meanings might emerge as the one really intended" (Stern 1931: 356). Equivocation is by no means the only kind of circumstance, or even the most common kind of circumstance, in which semantic shift can take place (there does not need to be any "misunderstanding" on anybody's part, for one thing). It represents one type of unintentional semantic shift only, ignoring the large class of deliberate semantic shifts that take place (and see the chapter on a general theory of sense change in Stern (1931: 162–191) for an attempt at a comprehensive overview). Nevertheless, equivocation, as illustrated by the *fine* example above, is a good example of how semantic shift can be intertwined with the act of communication (and dependent on the larger context) and how, within that act of communication, semantic shifts can "develop and unfold through processing time" (Langacker 2008: 30). Many semantic shifts leading ultimately to grammaticalization also have their origin in subtle shifts of understanding in the act of communication. Bybee et al. (1994: 268) discuss a range of examples based on conversational implicatures of the type *going to X* "be travelling to a destination X" implying a future event and in turn giving rise to the use of *be going to* as an auxiliary-like verb indicating futurity. Acts of communication, it should be said, play a critical role not just in the actuation of a semantic shift but also in the spread of semantic shifts through a population.

4 Empirical methods

While the concepts introduced in section 3 provide some scaffolding for thinking about and representing semantic shift within contemporary linguistics, those concepts remain, for the most part, relatively (or entirely) subjective in their approach. Above all, the components that make up the semantic networks proposed above and how those components relate to each other are in need of more empirically grounded support to be entirely satisfying. This section introduces some of the methods that are relevant to a more empirically based approach to studying semantic shift.

Most of the research described in this section is not concerned directly with establishing the presence or absence of semantic shift as such, but rather with the goal of finding empirical support for miscellaneous kinds of relations existing between the senses of a word. This research can still inform our understanding of semantic shift, albeit in indirect ways. So, for example, Figure 15.2 above represents some senses (APPLE, BANANA, PEAR) as a sub-group in their own right as part of a larger semantic network, but how much empirical support can be found among speakers or in language usage for such a grouping? Here I will focus on a few key methods for establishing the reality of different aspects of the semantic networks, drawing upon empirical research in experimental psychology, dictionary practice, corpus linguistics, and linguistic typology.

4.1 Experimental methods

One class of empirical results relates to subjects' understanding of prototypical vs. non-prototypical senses of a word, sometimes couched in terms of central vs. non-central senses or uses. Descriptive terms like *central* and *prototypical* in such research may not always be equivalent to how *prototypical* is used in Cognitive Grammar (as seen in Figures 15.1 and 15.2), and one must bear this in mind. However, the psycholinguistic research suggests fruitful lines of research into the different status of senses of a word with some senses being more prominent for a speaker than other sub-senses. A number of studies have preferred to work with the relation of dominance of one sense over another (here, more salient in the mind of the language user), without requiring that a dominant sense be the one and only central sense within a semantic network, e.g. Brisard et al. (1997). As part of the preliminaries required for their actual psycholinguistics study, these authors identified dominant and subordinate senses for a set of Dutch (polysemous and homonymous) adjectives using the following method. Participants had to produce for each adjective as many nouns as possible, nouns understood here as being those that might occur in the adjective + noun frame. The resulting nouns were then classified into semantic types by three judges. The two most frequent semantic domains represented in these semantic types were the basis for identifying the dominant and subordinate meanings for each item. In this study, the dominant senses for polysemous words averaged at 86% for frequency of the semantic domains, the subordinate at 14%, pointing to a clear division between dominant and subordinate types of senses. While the results of these and the many other experiments constructed along similar lines do not necessarily confirm or disconfirm the kind of representation of an individual's awareness of semantic shift in terms of schema, prototype, and extension (as in Figures 15.1 and 15.2), they do point to ways in which more empirically grounded research can throw light on the different status of the senses in such semantic networks.

4.2 Dictionary-based methods

Some methods for exploring the relatedness of word senses draw upon the prior work of lexicographers as reflected in dictionary-making practice. Williams (1992), for example, turned to the *Collins Cobuild English Language Dictionary* (1987) to establish tentative central vs. non-central meanings, as a preliminary step in setting up a series of psycholinguistic experiments. Williams relied on the relative ordering of the two sub-senses, A and B, in a dictionary entry to determine dominance, where the order A–B is taken to reflect the relative centrality of A and non-centrality of B. In this way, the adjective *deep* was found to have a central sense of "low" and a non-central sense of "profound", *awkward* was found to have a central sense of "clumsy" and a non-central sense of "embarrassing", etc. Obviously, this approach to determining the status of word senses depends directly upon whatever principles have been adopted in the dictionary. In the case of the particular dictionary chosen by Williams, the relative ordering involved considerations of frequency of usage (as established through a corpus-based approach to lexicography) and semantics (the more concrete sub-sense would usually be ordered before an abstract sub-sense).

A more sophisticated exploitation of existing dictionary entries can be seen in the work of Venant (2006). Venant was able to build upon the previous work on French synonyms that had been completed as part of the online *Dictionnaire électronique des synonymes* (DES), described in Doualan (2011). The key step in Venant's approach is to construct a set of *cliques* for the word under investigation. A clique is formed by chaining together words which can replace one another in all contexts of use maintaining the relevant sense of the replaced word and without notably changing the meaning of the whole. Dictionaries (of the conventional kind) are the source for establishing cliques in this approach. The basic idea is that word A will enter into a clique with word B if word A appears as one sense of word B or vice-versa. As an example, consider the following selection of cliques for English *book*, retrieved from the electronic dictionary of English synonyms constructed along similar lines to the DES (http://dico.isc.cnrs.fr): {*book, ledger, register*}, {*book, daybook, ledger*}, {*book, log, record, register*}, {*book, playscript, script*}, {*book, manuscript, script*}. Clearly, some pairs of cliques in this list have more in common than other pairs, suggesting two main sub-groupings of the cliques into a "record of accounts" and "script". It is possible to quantify the distance between any two cliques associated with a word in a more formal, algorithmic way which is necessary to establish a more objective basis for sub-grouping of senses. Venant (2006), following Ploux and Victorri (1998), opts for the chi-squared distance measure for this purpose. This metric takes into account not just how many synonyms are shared between two cliques, but also the overall number of cliques a synonym enters into and the overall number of synonyms a clique has. Once the distances between all the cliques associated with a word have been calculated, one can construct a two-dimensional representation of this semantic space by a principal components analysis, in effect carrying out a "correspondence analysis" on the data (see the plots in the works just cited for intriguing examples). In this way, the researcher is able to arrive at graphic representations of semantic networks (not unlike Figure 15.2 above), where the clusterings of sub-senses (operationalized as cliques) are determined not by subjective intuitions but by algorithmic methods. As with other dictionary-based methods, ultimately it is lexicographic practice (and the particular kinds of intuitions that are part and parcel of that practice) that underlies Venant's approach.

4.3 Corpus-based methods

Corpus-based methods in linguistics have become increasingly popular as a consequence of the availability of relatively large corpora and the increased interest in usage-based approaches (see Chapter 6). Corpora, and frequencies of occurrence of words, enter into some of the methods alluded to above, e.g. the identification of central and non-central senses of a word in Williams (1992). The corpus allows the researcher to systematically note co-occurring patterns, not just patterns of co-occurring words, but more importantly patterns of co-occurrence of all kinds of linguistic properties, relating to morphology, syntax, semantics, pragmatics, etc. With a dataset constructed in this way, one can proceed to apply quantitative methods, especially multifactorial methods, to discover tendencies that might not be apparent otherwise. The study of the senses of the English verb *run* in Gries (2006) is especially relevant in the current context. Gries distinguished around 50 different senses of *run*, based on an examination of dictionaries and WordNet entries, and then constructed an impressive amount of co-occurring data relating to each of these senses, based on corpora. The data included morphological properties (such as tense, aspect, and voice), syntactic properties (such as transitivity, whether the verb is used in a main clause or a subordinate), semantic properties (whether the subject is animate, human, abstract), and many others. Gries was then able to apply clustering algorithms to this dataset (similar to what Venant had done with her dataset of cliques), establishing groupings of senses that would not easily be apparent to the researcher without the aid of such quantitative techniques. To be clear, though, Gries takes the sense distinctions as given and it is only clustering of senses that the algorithm leads to, not the individuation of senses.

4.4 Lexical typological methods

Historical and cross-linguistic studies of the lexicon provide further kinds of empirical evidence for attested semantic shifts. The field of lexical typology, in particular, can enrich our understanding of how semantic networks can vary and the limits on how they can grow (see Chapter 25). Wilkins' (1996) research on semantic shift associated with body-part terms is a good example of this kind of research, systematically exploring cross-linguistic tendencies, leading to insights such as, to choose but one, how the natural direction of change is for a body-part term referring to a visible part to come to refer to the visible whole, but not vice-versa.

François (2008) has proposed one highly effective method for constructing a kind of semantic map of polysemies. The starting point for François' analysis is the identification of the senses of a word and he adopts a very practical way of proceeding. The researcher first selects a word, like English *straight*, and identifies, in a preliminary and tentative way, the senses associated with it ("rectilinear", "frank", "honest", "heterosexual", etc.). To avoid arbitrariness in making such decisions, the analyst turns to a second language to determine which additional senses need to be recognized. This procedure is repeated over many languages resulting in the most defensible separation of senses, based on the language under consideration. François illustrates the application of this method for the concept "breathe" (and its nominal counterpart "act of breathing") to produce a number of visually striking maps. Figure 15.3 is François' semantic map for Russian "breathe/breath" (noun- and verb-like senses are combined in the same map). Language-specific semantic maps for one concept will all share a common grid in which all relevant senses have been arranged in such a fashion that there will be a continuous chain of network nodes as part of any extension of meaning. So, for example, a semantic shift from "act of BREATHING" to "whisper" is claimed to proceed via the sense of "(someone) blow". The shaded area surrounded by a bold, continuous line represents the "territory" occupied by senses of Russian *dux*. The shaded area contains examples of "strict co-lexification" whereby the senses attach to the morphological base form, e.g. "act of BREATHING" and "(human) puff of breath". The network nodes outside of the shaded area surrounded by a dashed line, on the other hand, represent "loose co-lexification" referring to senses that are found with cognate, derived and compound forms of *dux*, e.g. *zaduvat* "(wind) start blowing; (someone) blow (candle)". Still other senses lie outside of any enclosed area, indicating semantic shifts that have been attested in some language but not Russian, e.g. "whisper". One should bear in mind that as more languages are considered, more senses may need to be added or existing senses may need to be subdivided, so that the task of drawing such maps must always remain open-ended, awaiting further confirmation or disconfirmation. The resulting "isolectal" maps give some indication of the possible paths of semantic shifts of "breathe" and contribute to a better understanding of attested and unattested kinds of shifts.

Zalizniak (2008) outlines a project designed to produce a *Catalogue of Semantic Shifts* which, like François's cross-linguistic approach just described, combines data from across languages and language families to identify patterns of relatedness of senses. In Zalizniak's case, though, both synchronic polysemy and diachronic shifts are taken into account, based

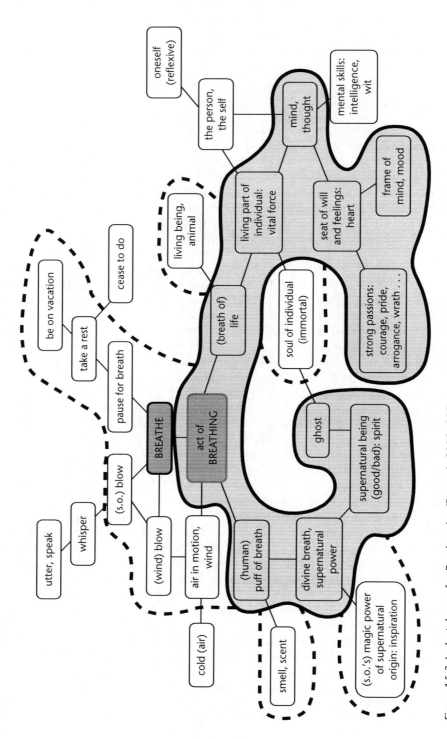

Figure 15.3 Isolectal map for Russian *dux* (François 2008: 208)

on a number of different kinds of relatedness of forms/senses. Polysemy of a single linguistic form would be taken into account, but so too would diachronic semantic evolution of a single linguistic form in a language or between a parent language and a descendant language, as well as senses of cognate words in related languages. And, as with François' approach, the sense of a linguistic form as part of a derived word or a compound word can also be taken into account. So, for example, an entry for the semantic shift "to grasp" → "to understand" is supported by the data in (1).

(1) a   Old Russian *pojati* "to grasp" > Russian *ponjat* "to understand" [semantic evolution within the history of Russian]
    b   Latin *capere* "to get" > Italian *capire* "to understand" [semantic evolution from a parent language to a descendant language]
    c   German *greifen* "to grasp" > *begreifen* "to understand" [semantic shift in a derived word]
    d   French *saisir* "to grasp; to understand" [semantic shift within one polysemous word]

5 Future directions

The overview of semantic shift offered above has repeatedly emphasized the dynamic nature of language, one manifestation of which is the flexibility of meaning. Promising lines of future research on semantic shift may well be found, therefore, in the various strands of research that elaborate the dynamic dimensions of language. One vision for a highly dynamic conceptualization of language is Thorne and Lantolf's (2006) notion of a "linguistics of communicative activity", a vision of linguistics that is far-ranging and diametrically opposed to a narrower view of language as a fixed system. For Thorne and Lantolf, communicative activity lies at the core of how language should be studied:

> [a linguistics of communicative activity] ... is based on a view of language as a historically contingent emergent system, one that provides a repertoire of semiotic devices that people can use to realize their communicative intentions, to interpret the communicative intentions of others and, perhaps most importantly, to foster the conditions of possibility for transforming self and community.
>
> (Thorne and Lantolf 2006: 189)

Thorne and Lantolf set out to "disinvent" language as an object and reinvent it as activity – a position that is highly compatible with the research reviewed above. Thorne and Lantolf are not alone in arguing for this view of language; indeed, to some extent they are merely restating a trend observable in much contemporary research (cf., for instance, Langacker's description of the dynamic nature of Cognitive Grammar above). In their particular vision, the repurposing of words such as *desktop* to accommodate and facilitate new lifestyles is not some marginal aberration of language use, but a reflection of the core, emergent nature of language. Thorne and Lantolf's particular vision for linguistics extends well beyond just an academic interest in issues like semantic shift; they speak of the linguistics of communicative activity as creating conditions leading to *transformations of the self and community*. Somewhat related to the Thorne and Lantolf work is the body of research labelled variously as *complex adaptive systems* research or *dynamic systems* research. As the names suggest, this research puts adaptation and dynamic change at the very core of theorizing about language, and more generally, cognitive processes. De Bot and Larsen-Freeman (2011) provide a helpful characterization of dynamic systems as they understand them which includes as some of the key concepts: change of the system through internal reorganization and interaction with the environment; constant change, with chaotic variation sometimes; nonlinearity in development; and extensive interconnectedness.

Spivey (2008) draws together a vast amount of research in psychology and computational modelling, all of which is concerned with the mind as a dynamic, flexible system. Spivey is particularly interested in the cognitive processes that are evident over extremely small durations of time and this can include the cognitive processes that underlie judgements about the categories that make up the meaning of *fruit*, for example. Among the myriad results that Spivey reports upon in his stimulating book, he includes some discussion of the "semantic saturation" effect (Spivey 2008: 24–25). The essence of this idea is that if you look at the written word (his example is *giraffe*) and read it out aloud about once per second, for a minute, then the meaning of the word seems to fade away. In the course of fading away, and this is the interesting part of this effect for our purposes, the meaning of the word is subject to change. For example, a subject might become conscious of new semantic associations of the word *giraffe*, causing the word to seem more like *raffle, Dan Jurafsky, draft, jejune, gauche* etc. The relevance to the present discussion is not that eventually the meaning of such repeated words seems to disappear altogether for the speaker, but that it seems to take on different meanings in the course of the degradation of the original meaning. There is a trajectory of movement in and around multiple senses that can attach, however briefly, to a word subjected to this experiment. It is semantic shift on a tiny timescale of seconds, rather than on the scale of centuries. Clearly, the phenomenon described above is a process associated with a particular kind of thought experiment and is not anything that is observed and recorded as meaning change in, say, a dictionary. Nevertheless, the phenomenon illustrates an interesting kind of semantic shift that is real and is recognized as a psychological reality. It is evidence of the inherent flexibility and, indeed, precariousness of meaning.

Further reading

Geeraerts, Dirk 1997. *Diachronic Prototype Semantics: A Contribution to Historical Lexicology*. Oxford: Oxford University Press. A thorough discussion of issues relating to the actuation and spread of meaning change, as well as the principles governing meaning change.

Geeraerts, Dirk and Hubert Cuyckens (eds) 2007. *The Oxford Handbook of Cognitive Linguistics*. Oxford: Oxford University Press. This volume contains chapters on many of the topics dealt with above, especially schemas, prototypes, and conceptual blending.

Glynn, Dylan and Kerstin Fischer (eds) 2010. *Quantitative Methods in Cognitive Semantics: Corpus-driven Approaches*. Berlin and New York: de Gruyter. This volume introduces a range of new corpus-based methods for exploring semantics.

Rice, Sally 1996. Prepositional prototypes. In R. Dirven and M. Pütz (eds), *The Construal of Space in Language and Thought*. Berlin and New York: Mouton de Gruyter, 135–165. Rice reviews a number of empirical methods relating to the study of semantic networks.

References

Brisard, Frank, Gert van Rillaer and Dominiek Sandra 1997. Processing polysemous, homonymous and vague adjectives. In Hubert Cuyckens and Britta Zawada (eds), *Polysemy in Cognitive Linguistics: Selected Papers from the Fifth International Cognitive Linguistics Conference*. Amsterdam and Philadelphia: John Benjamins, 261–284.

Bybee, Joan, Revere Perkins and William Pagliuca 1994. *The Evolution of Grammar: Tense, Aspect and Modality in the Languages of the World.* Chicago: Chicago University Press.

de Bot, Kees and Diane Larsen-Freeman 2011. Researching second language development from a dynamic systems theory perspective. In Marjolijn H. Verspoor, Kees de Bot and Wander Lowie (eds), *A Dynamic Approach to Second Language Development: Methods and Techniques.* Amsterdam and Philadelphia: John Benjamins, 5–23.

Collins Cobuild English Language Dictionary 1987. London and Glasgow: Collins.

Doualan, Gaëlle 2011. Introduction à une approche instrumentée de la synonymie: L'exemple du Dictionnaire Electronique des Synonymes. *Cahier du CRISCO* 32. Université de Caen. http://www.crisco.unicaen.fr/IMG/pdf/Cahier_du_CRISCO_no_32.pdf

Fauconnier, Gilles 2009. Generalized integration networks. In Vyvyan Evans and Stéphanie Pourcel (eds), *New Directions in Cognitive Linguistics.* Amsterdam and Philadelphia: John Benjamins, 147–160.

Fauconnier, Gilles and Mark Turner 1998. Conceptual integration networks. *Cognitive Science* 22: 133–187.

Fetzer, Anita 2011. Pragmatics as a linguistic concept. In Neal R. Norrick and Wolfram Bublitz (eds), *Handbook of Pragmatics.* Berlin: De Gruyter Mouton, 23–50.

Firth, J.R. 1957. *Papers in Linguistics 1934–1951.* London: Oxford University Press.

François, Alexandre 2008. Semantic maps and the typology of colexification: intertwining polysemous networks across languages. In Martine Vanhove (ed.), *From Polysemy to Semantic Change: Towards a Typology of Lexical Semantic Associations.* Amsterdam and Philadelphia: John Benjamins, 163–215.

Gries, Stefan Th. 2006. Corpus-based methods and cognitive semantics: the many meanings of *to run*. In Stefan Th. Gries and Anatol Stefanowitsch (eds), *Corpora in Cognitive Linguistics: Corpus-based Approaches to Syntax and Lexis.* Berlin and New York: Mouton de Gruyter, 57–99.

Langacker, Ronald W. 1987. *Foundations of Cognitive Grammar. Vol. 1, Theoretical Prerequisites.* Stanford, CA: Stanford University Press.

Langacker, Ronald W. 1988. A usage-based model. In Brygida Rudzka-Ostyn (ed.), *Topics in Cognitive Linguistics.* Amsterdam and Philadelphia: John Benjamins, 127–161.

Langacker, Ronald W. 2008. *Cognitive Grammar: A Basic Introduction.* Oxford: Oxford University Press.

Lichtenberk, Frantisek 1991. Semantic change and heterosemy in grammaticalisation. *Language* 67: 474–509.

Makoni, Sinfree and Alastair Pennycook 2006. Disinventing and reconstituting languages. In Sinfree Makoni and Alastair Pennycook (eds), *Disinventing and reconstituting languages.* Clevedon: Multilingual Matters, 1–41.

Ploux, S. and B. Victorri 1998. Construction d'espaces sémantiques à l'aide de dictionnaires de synonymes. *Traitement Automatique des Langues* 39: 161–182.

Saussure, Ferdinand de 1959. *Course in General Linguistics.* New York: McGraw Hill.

Spivey, Michael 2008. *The Continuity of Mind.* Oxford: Oxford University Press.

Stern, Gustaf 1931. *Meaning and Change of Meaning: With Special Reference to the English Language.* Bloomington IN: Indiana University Press.

Thorne, Steven L. and James P. Lantolf 2006. A linguistics of communicative activity. In Sinfree Makoni and Alastair Pennycook (eds), *Disinventing and Reconstituting Languages.* Clevedon: Multilingual Matters, 170–194.

Venant, Fabienne 2006. Représentation et calcul dynamique du sens: exploration du lexique adjectival du français. Doctoral dissertation, EHESS, Lattice.
http://tel.archives-ouvertes.fr/docs/00/06/79/02/PDF/these_Venant.pdf

Ward, J. 1918. *Psychological Principles.* Cambridge: Cambridge University Press.

Wells, Rulon S. 1975. Metonymy and misunderstanding: an aspect of language change. In Roger W. Cole (ed.), *Current Issues in Linguistic Theory.* Bloomington, IN and London: Indiana University Press, 195–214.

Wilkins, David 1996. Natural tendencies of semantic change and the search for cognates. In Mark Durie and Malcom Ross (eds), *The Comparative Method Reviewed*. New York and Oxford: Oxford University Press, 264–304.

Williams, John N. 1992. Processing polysemous words in context: evidence for interrelated meanings. *Journal of Psycholinguistic Research* 21: 193–218.

Zalizniak, Anna A. 2008. A catalogue of semantic shifts: towards a typology of semantic derivation. In Martine Vanhove (ed.), *From Polysemy to Semantic Change: Towards a Typology of Lexical Semantic Associations*. Amsterdam and Philadelphia: John Benjamins, 217–232.

Related topics

Chapter 5, Cognitive semantics; Chapter 6, Corpus semantics; Chapter 7, Categories, prototypes and exemplars; Chapter 11, Contextual adjustment of meaning; Chapter 13, Sense individuation; Chapter 25, The semantics of lexical typology.

Part VI
Semantics of specific phenomena

16
The semantics of nominals

Sebastian Löbner

1 Nouns and noun phrases

1.1 The scope of this chapter

This chapter deals with the semantics of nouns and noun phrases (NPs) and the complex apparatus of semantic operations that build NPs out of nouns. It will not examine predicative NPs and generic NPs, as both would require extra discussion. Also, the chapter will disregard those aspects of NPs that relate them to their sentential context. These include linking means such as case, scope properties of NPs (see Chapter 18) and the role of NPs in the information structure of the sentence.

1.2 The nominal onion

The discussion will be organized by following the functional layers of an NP, a structure that I have dubbed the "nominal onion" elsewhere (Löbner 2013: 90). The functional structure is not identical to the syntactic structure of the NP, although it is often reflected in it to some degree. Rather, the NP has an internal structure of functional layers that presuppose each other in a certain order from the nucleus to the outside.

Nuc The core of the structure is the **Nucleus**, an expression of the lexical category N, or a lexical full NP such as a proper name or a personal pronoun in English.

Rel The **Relation** layer serves the specification of a relation between the noun referent and some correlate, e.g. a possessor. Relation specifications at the nucleus are implemented by possessive affixes, possessor complements and other means. In addition, a language may have possessor specifications on the Definiteness layer (e.g. left possessives in English such as *his book, Ed's book*).

Qual The **Quality** layer adds restrictive attributes to the nucleus, typically by means of adjectives, relative clauses or adjoined adverbials.

Unit The **Unit** layer serves the formation of countable units or complex sums for reference. Grammatical number, numeral classifiers and measure terms belong to this layer.

Qt The **Quantity** layer specifies the quantity of the referent(s) by using numerals or vague quantity specifications such as *much, many, several* or *a few*.

Ord	The **Ordering** layer locates the referent relative to others with respect to some ordering; it employs expressions such as *next, last, following*, ordinal numerals and superlatives.
Def	The **Definiteness** layer marks the nominal as definite or indefinite. Adnominal demonstratives, articles, (in)definiteness affixes and determiner possessives belong here.
Qf	The **Quantification** layer proper applies after determination. It produces a quantifying NP with scope, to interact with a predication in a particular way. The layer employs operators such as *every, each, all* or *both*. Plain quantity specification on the layer Qt is not subsumed here.

A similar structure for functional NP layers is assumed in Rijkhoff (2002: 218–231): Quality, Quantity (including our Unit and Quantity) and Location (comprising Relation and Definiteness). Rijkhoff (2002) does not mention Order and Quantification proper as layers in their own right. He deals with ordinal numerals in his Quantity layer, and quantifiers proper are not discussed. Van Valin (2008) applies a similar system. He treats Rel as the topmost layer of Nucleus, to which also restrictive Qual operators apply. The Unit layer, called "nominal aspect", operates on the Nucleus, establishing the NP layer of "Core"; our Qt operations number and quantity specification operate on Core, along with negation; definiteness and deixis apply to the NP layer (our Def); the layers Ord and Qf are not mentioned.

I disagree with Generalized Quantifier Theory (Barwise and Cooper 1981 and a lot of following work, see Chapter 18). GQT disregards the layered structure of the NP by considering all NPs, including proper names, pronouns, bare NPs, indefinites and definites, as cases of quantification. In this chapter, the notion of quantification is restricted to what I am calling "quantification proper" (see section 3.7).

For the sake of convenience, I will refer to all layers except Quality as "determination", as I did in Löbner (2011). Note that the Definiteness layer (with capital D) comprises both definiteness (with lower case d) and indefiniteness. The layers of determination are ordered by relative scope, as will become clear in the discussion to follow. Following Abbott (2010), I refer to the level to which Def applies as "CNP" ("common noun phrase"); the levels resulting from Def and Qf are referred to as "NP".

Nominal nuclei are subject to conceptual distinctions in three independent dimensions: relationality, countability and inherent uniqueness. They will be distinguished by three features [±R], [±C] and [±U], respectively. These features are not immediate meaning components, but describe conceptual properties of nominal meanings. The features do not only apply at nucleus level. Rather, they carry through to the NP level. Passing through the machinery of determinational operations, these features may or may not change. In fact, the main function of determinational operations is to manipulate these characteristics of nominals. The Rel layer manipulates the feature [±R], Unit and Qt work on [±C], Def and Qf on [±U].

2 The nucleus

When dealing with lexical meaning, one has to keep in mind that almost all nouns are polysemous, with more than one lexicalized meaning variant (see Chapter 13). It is tacitly presupposed in the following that whenever we talk of "nouns", we actually relate to nouns in a particular lexical meaning variant. In addition, the compositional contribution of the nucleus noun to a complete NP may differ from its lexical meaning, due to meaning shifts coerced by NP-internal operations, or later in the sentential or discourse context (see Chapter 15).

We will not treat lexical properties of the nucleus such as gender, noun class or other lexical classifications, as these do not bear on the semantics of the determinational mechanisms to be discussed.

2.1 Relationality

The distinction between relational nouns (*daughter*) and absolute nouns (*girl*) is conceptual. Relational nouns have a referential argument and in addition one or more relational arguments. We will confine the discussion here to nouns with one relational argument. With *my daughter*, the relational argument is specified as the speaker, while the speaker's daughter is the referential argument. Relational concepts describe their referents in terms of a criterial relationship to a correlate; in addition, the concept may add sortal characteristics to the description of the referent and/or the correlate. The relationships between referent and correlate(s) are manifold, as witnessed by examples such as *daughter* (kinship), *head* (body part), *boss* (social relation), *baggage* (being carried), *birth* (event), *name* (verbal correlate), *age* (property), etc.

The referent of an NP with a relational nucleus can only be determined if the correlate is specified, or retrieved from context, or if the relational concept is shifted to an absolute concept. Explicit specification of the relational argument usually takes the form of a possessive construction, whence we will refer to the correlate as the "possessor".

Absolute noun concepts describe their potential referents independently of any correlates to be specified. The description may involve implicit correlates, but these are not necessary for fixing the referent. The majority of common nouns are absolute. To see the difference, consider the minimal pair ›daughter‹ (relational) and ›female person‹ (absolute). The two concepts have the same extension; however, a "female person" is a female person by virtue of properties she has in her own right; a "daughter" is a daughter only by virtue of standing in a child-relationship to a parent.

We will use the descriptive feature [+R] for relational nouns and [–R] for nonrelational nouns.

2.2 Countability

The discussion of the distinction between mass and count nouns, and mass and count NPs, is very complex. For the purpose of this chapter, the following essentials are crucial.

The distinction is conceptual. The mass-count distinction, again, applies at the conceptual level: there are mass concepts and count concepts. At the Nuc level, this distinction is a dichotomy, notwithstanding polysemy (e.g. *stone* has both mass and count senses). At the NP level, nouns of either lexical type may have count as well as mass uses, due to shifts during NP formation. The same ontological entities may be described with mass concepts and with count concepts. For example, the count concept ›hair$_{count}$‹ defines its referents as single threads of hair, while the mass concept ›hair$_{mass}$‹ refers to the total body of hairs (on the scalp) constituting a physical object with properties like density or a particular haircut. Plural *hairs*$_{count}$ may refer to the same as *hair*$_{mass}$.

Count concepts are integrative. The referents of count concepts are conceived of as bounded wholes. These wholes may be complex and consisting of constitutive parts, but the parts will not themselves be in the extension of the concept. Examples of nouns with count concept meanings are *pebble* (no constitutive parts), *student* (body part mereology), *piano* (an artefact with a complex mereology of constitutive parts, such as keys and strings) or *orchestra* (a group of musicians playing together on instruments). Count concepts are "integrative" predicates with respect to their referential argument.

(1) A predicate p is INTEGRATIVE with respect to a given argument x iff it is true/false of it as an integral whole. (Löbner 2000: 237)

Something is a "pebble" or not if and only if it is so as a whole object; a group of people is an orchestra or not if and only if it is so as a whole, functioning as a group to make music together as one body of sound. There may happen to be members of the group which form another, smaller orchestra, but this fact would be independent of the question whether the whole group is an instance of "orchestra".

Mass concepts are summative. Mass concepts are not integrative; they denote some kind of homogeneous matter in the widest sense, to be taken as something consisting of parts of the same description as the whole referent. Mass concepts are "summative" predicates about their referential argument. A summative predicate is true of an argument if and only if it is true of all elements of some partition of x, where a partition is a set of parts that add up to the whole.

(2) A predicate p is summative with respect to a given argument x iff: p is true/false for x iff there is a partition of x such that p is true/false for every part in it. (Löbner 2000: 237)

Note that "parts" are restricted to parts *within the domain of the predicate* because the predicate has to be applicable to the parts; the domain D(p) of a predicate is the set of things for which the predicate returns a truth value, either TRUE or FALSE. Due to summativity, the referents of mass nouns are not conceived of as bounded, whence mass concepts fail to define units of reference. There may or may not be minimal elements in D(p). For example, the domain of ›furniture‹ consists of whole objects and collections of whole objects that can be said to be a piece, or pieces, of furniture; of these, the single objects are minimal, and a collection of such objects is a potential referent of *furniture* if and only if each such object is a piece of furniture. Material parts of pieces of furniture, like legs of chairs, are not within the domain of the noun. Other mass predicates do not conceive of their referents as consisting of minimal parts, e.g., ›water‹, ›air‹ or ›poison‹. Yet other concepts may contain a criterion of granularity and of the particles the matter consists of, cf. ›rice‹, ›sand‹, ›garbage‹, ›hair$_{mass}$‹. Even so, with this type of mass concept, the particles will not matter individually, they will just form a "mass". The difference between the types of mass concept represented by ›water‹, ›sand‹ and ›furniture‹ will not matter for determination as discussed below.

Plural count concepts are summative. Plural count concepts are summative, too. The referents of a plural count noun are sums of potential referents of the singular noun. Due to the summativity of plural count concepts, the major distinction is between integrative singular concepts, henceforth "singular concepts", on the one hand and summative mass or plural concepts on the other.

The mass-count distinction in Mandarin. Mandarin is a language that lacks grammatical number marking as well as definite and indefinite articles (Li and Thompson 1981: 104–131). A bare NP can therefore have definite or indefinite singular, plural or mass reference. Also, all nouns can only combine with a numeral when a classifier is added to it. It has therefore been argued that all nouns in Mandarin are mass nouns. This, however, is due to a confusion of the lexical level Nuc and the syntactic level NP. We follow Cheng and Sybesma (1999) in assuming that, at the Nucleus level, Mandarin nouns are either count or mass, due to their respective lexical meaning. The equivalents of count nouns in languages such as English, e.g., *fángzi* "house", are lexically count, integrative concepts. When used as bare NPs, they are number-neutral NPs and hence present a *summative* description of the (possibly complex) NP referent: the description fits its referent if and only if it fits all the singular instances of the concept that make up the referent. As will be argued below, plural reference of Mandarin count nouns is the result of applying a "sums" operation Σ that remains morphologically unmarked.

The features [C] and [Pl]. The three groups of nouns discussed can be distinguished by means of two descriptive binary features. The countability feature [C] directly corresponds to integrativity, [Pl] to plurality. As [+Pl] entails [−C] (plurals are summative), the combination [+C][+Pl] is excluded; thus, there are three classes of concepts at level Nuc:

(3) types of nominal concepts in terms of [C] and [Pl]
    [−C][−Pl]   mass concepts: *water, sand, poison, furniture*
    [+C][−Pl]   singular count concepts: *house*, Mandarin *fángzi* "house", *orchestra*
    [−C][+Pl]   plural count concepts: *houses, people*

In classifier languages such as Mandarin, there are at least two properties that distinguish count nouns from mass nouns: count nouns combine with different classifiers (count classifiers as opposed to mass classifiers, section 3.3); in addition, they allow integrative predication that relates to singular referents in their denotation. (4) illustrates the relevance of the [±C] distinction for the application of the integrative predicate ›small‹:

(4)   a   count   small house, small houses, *xiǎo fángzi* [Mandarin, "small house(s)"]
      b   mass   ?small water, ?small sand

2.3 Inherent uniqueness

Some types of concept are inherently unique in that they describe their referents as something that is uniquely determined in the given situation. Examples are concepts such as ›sun‹ (in the sense ›sun round which the earth orbits‹), unique-role concepts like ›pope‹ (in the sense ›head of the Roman Catholic Church‹), concepts for institutions such as ›main station‹ and concepts for givens like ›weather‹ (in a given context of utterance, which includes a particular place and time) or ›date‹ (day, month and year). Being inherently unique is not necessarily a matter of the richness of conceptual content. A minimal pair of a unique and a nonunique concept are the Japanese noun *otoko* for male persons, children or adults, and the pronoun *kare* "he" that is used for persons only. The two concepts have the same descriptive content, but differ in *kare* being inherently unique. In logical terms, their meanings can be distinguished as follows:

(5)   a   ›kare‹   ιx (person(x) ∧ male(x))
                    "the unique x such that x is a person and x is male"
      b   ›otoko‹   λx (person(x) ∧ male(x))
                    "is a person and male"

We will include personal pronouns and proper names in the discussion because they may partake in determination processes such as definiteness marking. Proper names are considered concepts of a form like the following for a person's name:

(6)   ›Liza‹   ιx (person(x) ∧ name(x) = *Liza*)

We will use the descriptive feature [+U] for inherently unique nouns. While [+U] nouns have exactly one referent in a given context (if the context supports the existence of a referent), [–U] concepts may have any number of referents, none, one or more.

The [U] feature is independent of the [R] feature. In accordance with Löbner (2011), I use the following terminology for nouns, and concepts in general:

(7)   Conceptual types

	[–U] nonunique	[+U] unique
[–R] nonrelational	sortal concept	individual concept
[+R] relational	relational concept	functional concept

In the context of this twofold opposition, "relational (in the narrower sense)" means "relational and nonunique". Functional concepts are relational and inherently unique. They are functional because they provide a function in the mathematical sense that, for any appropriate type of situation, returns exactly one referent for every possessor. There are four semantic subclasses of functional nouns: correlate concepts (›mother‹, ›king‹); part concepts (e.g. body part terms), unique property concepts (›temperature‹, ›price‹, ›size‹, ›colour‹) and related event concepts (›birth‹, ›end‹, ›invention‹).

The [U] and [R] distinctions are both independent of the countability distinction. These are mass nouns of the four types: *water* [–U][–R], *air* [+U][–R], *baggage* [–U][+R] and *skin* [+U][+R].

3 The layers of determination

3.1 Relation

The Relation layer deals with the [R] feature of the NP. Nominal nuclei start out as either [–R] or [+R], but argument NPs necessarily end up as [–R], because [+R] means an open possessor argument, which would preclude determining the referent of the nominal. One exception is NP-external possessive constructions that contain an unsaturated relational noun, such as the "raised possessor" construction in (8):

(8)   German (Germanic, Indo-European)
      ich   habe   mir [*raised possessor*]   das   Bein [+R]   gebrochen
      I   have   1SG.DAT   DEF   leg   broken
      "I   have broken my leg"

The Relation layer hosts operations that take [–R] to [+R], [+R] to [+R] and [+R] to [–R]. We will introduce the matter by discussing Relation in Koyukon, an Athabaskan language spoken in Alaska. Unlike English, Athabaskan handles relationality and absoluteness in a very transparent way. The discussion is based on Thompson (1996).

3.1.1 Relation in Koyukon

In Koyukon, relational nouns can only be used with a possessor specification or a derelationalizing affix (9a). A possessor can be specified by a preceding NP (9b) or a possessor prefix

(9c). If the noun *kkaa'* is to be used absolutely, just referring to a foot without relating it to its possessor, Koyukon uses the prefix *k'e-* (9d). Both, possessor specification and derelationalization, take the nucleus from [+R] to [−R].

(9) Koyukon (Thompson 1996: 666 f.)

     a   *kkaa'   b   gguh   kkaa'   c   ne-   kkaa'
          foot   rabbit   foot   2SG-   foot
                                  "rabbit's foot"   "your$_{SG}$ foot"

     d   k'e-   kkaa'
          DEREL-foot
          "a/the foot"

The semantic effect of derelationalization is existential saturation of the possessor argument. The general mechanism is this:

(10) derelationalization:
[+R] λx λy R(x,y) → [−R] λx ∃y R(x,y)

If an absolute noun is to be used with a possessor specification, it first has to be shifted to [+R] with a relationalizing suffix –e'. The suffix takes, for example, [−R] ›dog‹ to [+R] ›dog of‹; possessor specification takes that concept back to [−R] ›[possessor]'s dog‹ (11b, c).

(11) Koyukon (Thompson 1996: 655)

     a   łeek   b   Dick leeg-   e'   c   se-   leeg- e'
          dog   Dick dog-   REL   1SG-   dog- REL
                          "Dick's dog"   "my dog"

For relational nouns that have been taken to [−R], secondary possession is possible. In such cases, k'e- is prefixed to the result of the first shift to [−R], resulting in re-establishing [+R] for the nucleus; a possessor prefix is then added to the result:

(12) Koyukon (Thompson 1996: 667)

     a   ne-   k'e-   gguh   kkaa'   b   ne-   k'e-   k'e-   kkaa'
          2SG-   REL-   rabbit   foot   2SG-   REL-   DEREL- foot
          "your rabbit's foot"   "your [animal's] foot"

Koyukon reveals two important points: (i) relational nouns are in need of possessor saturation for referential use; (ii) possessive constructions with [−R] nouns require a preceding step of relationalization, i.e., a shift from [−R] to [+R]; (i) then applies to the result. In English, the same semantic operations are at work in the corresponding constructions even though they are not overtly expressed. Thus, English ›my foot‹ in the sense of Koyukon *ne-k'e-k'e-kkaa'*, too, is the result of three [R] operations: (1) derelationalizing ›foot‹ by existential saturation of the semantic possessor argument, (2) adding a pragmatic relation of possession, (3) specifying the new possessor as the speaker.

Koyukon belongs to a wide range of languages that mark possession with [+R] and [−R] concepts in different ways. The phenomenon is known as (in)alienability splits. So-called "inalienable possession" occurs with [+R] nouns; "alienable" possession is applied to [–R] nouns. As a rule, the expression of inalienable possession is morphosyntactically less complex. The examples from Koyukon illustrate this point: [+R] nouns immediately take possessor specifications by juxtaposition (9b) or prefix (9c), whereas [–R] nouns receive an additional relationalizing affix (11b, c). For an overview on (in)alienability, see Chapell and McGregor (1996).

Whereas for [+R] nouns the relation of the referent to the possessor is written into their meanings, [–R] nouns do not provide the possessive relation; rather, it has to be retrieved from context and world knowledge. For possible readings of English genitive constructions, see Vikner and Jensen (2000).

3.1.2 Operations of the relation layer

From [–R] to [+R]: relationalization. The only productive mechanism of this type is relationalization as discussed in (11) and (12) above. In Koyukon, it is realized by *k'e-*; in English it is covert.

From [+R] to [+R]: relational possessor. If a [+R] nominal receives a possessor specification, the open possessor argument is replaced by the possessor concept. The possessor specification may itself be [+R]. This may give rise to possessive chains such as in (13). A possessive chain is completed only if a [+R]-to-[–R] operation is applied, e.g., if a [–R] possessor is added, or derelationalization applied, to the last element.

(13)   the secretary [+R] of the head [+R] of the department [+R] of . . .

From [+R] to [–R] (1): absolute possessor. The main operation that turns a [+R] nominal into [–R] is the specification of the possessor argument, e.g. by a possessive affix, a [–R] possessor NP or a possessive determiner. Possessive affixes (cf. (11c) and (12)) specify a [+U] possessor in the same terms as personal pronouns, e.g. person and number. Possessor NPs combine with the nucleus (14a), the CNP (14b) or the NP as a whole (14c):

(14) a   N: wife *of John*
      b   CNP: *John's* two kids
      c   NP: (Mandarin, Sino-Tibetan)
                  wǒ   de   zhè   xiē   dòng   xiǎo   fángzi
                  I   gen   dem   pl   cls   little   house
                  "these my little houses"

A fourth alternative is possessive determiners, as in English or Italian:

(15) a   my friend
      b   una   mia   amica   (Italian, Romance, Indo-European)
          INDEF.F   1SG. POSS.F   friend
          "a [female] friend of mine"

In Italian, the possessive determiner just specifies the possessor, leaving definite or indefinite determination open; the possessive operates at a level lower than CNP. English Saxon genitives and possessive determiners lead to definite determination for referential NPs (this does not hold for predicative NPs, see Löbner 2011: 304f); like articles, they operate at the level of CNP. This is a widespread phenomenon still waiting for an explanation: if a possessor specification is grammatically complementary with definiteness marking, the interpretation is definite (Haspelmath 1999). In the languages concerned, these possessives have a combined function on the Rel and Def layers. We will deal with them in section 3.6.

From [+R] to [−R] (2): existential possessor. A second mechanism of shifting [+R] to [−R] is derelationalization by existential saturation of the possessor argument, as discussed in (9b) and (10). In English, this operation is covert, in Koyukon it is overtly realized with the derelationalization prefix *k'e*.

From [+R] to [−R] (3): contextual possessor. There is a third mechanism, found with associative anaphora, such as *the author* in (16):

(16) This is an interesting book. By the way, I happen to know the author.

Here, the possessor is determined anaphorically, or more generally, it is retrieved from context. Note that in this case the implicit possessor is definite.

The overall picture. The diagram in Figure 16.1 displays the possible operations; elements with dotted lines around them represent semantic operations that, depending on the type of language, may be covert. Bypassable operations are optional. Thus, a [−R] or [+R] nucleus may pass through the Rel layer without semantic change. [+R] possessor saturation may be iterated. This figure and those to follow are to be read as a flow diagram; any sequence of operations is possible that results from following lines in the direction of the arrows.

3.2 Quality

The primary function of the Quality layer is to add a property or specification to the nucleus concept. Quality operators are attributes that take the form of adjectives, adjoined adpositional phrases or relative clauses. At this level, the attributes are applied immediately to the nucleus. They are restrictive. Nonrestrictive attributes apply at higher levels of the nominal and will not be considered. "Establishing relative clauses" will be dealt with on the Def layer in section 3.6.1. Being restrictive, Quality attributes require a [−U]

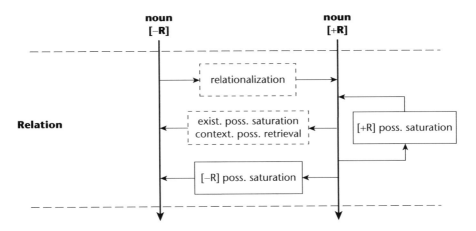

Figure 16.1 Operations of the Relation layer

nucleus that allows for alternative referents. If a restrictive attribute is applied to a [+U] nucleus, the noun needs to be shifted to [−U]. Consider two possible readings of (17):

(17) Obama is a popular president.

The functional concept ›president‹ has a possessor argument and a time parameter, by default the evaluation time t_e, as in (18a, c). In one reading of (17), the possessor argument is retrieved from context and fixed as the US; to enable the comparison required by the concept ›popular‹, the time parameter of ›president‹ is existentially saturated, yielding [−U] status for the resulting meaning ›president$_1$‹ in (18b) meaning ›president of the US at some time‹; as a result, Obama is compared in popularity to former US presidents. In another reading, Obama may be compared to contemporary presidents of other countries; the possessor argument is existentially saturated, again yielding [−U] status.

(18) a ›president‹ $\lambda x\, \lambda y\, (x = \text{president}(y, t_e))$
      b ›president$_1$‹ $\lambda x\, \exists t < t_e\, (x = \text{president}(US, t))$
      c ›president$_2$‹ $\lambda x\, \exists y\, (x = \text{president}(y, t_e))$

There are attributes that transfer [−U] to [+U] concepts; these will be discussed on the Order layer. [−U] to [−U] operators can be applied repeatedly. They form a loop on [−U] concepts. I will not discuss restrictions on the order of adjectives, or the different ways in which restrictive adjectives interact with the nominal (see Demonte (2012), Hole (2015: 1296–1303) and Svenonius (2008) for recent surveys).

3.3 Unit

The discussion here is aimed at covering the Unit and Quantity layers in English as a typical number language and Mandarin as a typical classifier language. All operations on the Unit and Quantity layers require the operand to be [−U] to allow for an open number of referents. If a quantity specification is to be applied to a [+U] concept, it has to be shifted to [−U] first; for example, the functional concept ›president‹ would have to undergo a shift like one of those in (18b, c) to allow for the interpretation of ›three presidents‹.

The Unit layer primarily serves to allow the manipulation of the [C] feature. There are three basic operations: sums formation, application of a count classifier and application of a mass classifier.

From [±C] to [−C]: sums. The sums operation Σ takes a concept N to the concept ΣN for sums of referents of N. The result is a summative concept and hence [−C], independent of the [C] feature of the operand. Applied to [+C] nominals, it yields plural concepts. They will be marked plural in English, but are mostly left unmarked in Mandarin (except for personal pronouns). Covert Σ application is responsible for the number-neutral quality of bare count NPs in Mandarin. Σ on [+C] nouns produces [−C] [+Pl] concepts. The [Pl] feature will bear on the Quant, Def and Qf layers. Plural concepts are eligible to another (covert) application of Σ and, being [−C], to mass classification. Examples of double Σ and of Σ applied to mass nominals will be discussed below in section 3.7.

From [+C] to [+C]: count classifiers. Count classifiers, also called "sortal" classifiers, are applied to [+C] concepts such as Mandarin *fángzi* "house" to form [+C][−Pl] concepts. They are integrative predicates that define a unit of counting, where the unit coincides with a potential referent of the nucleus concept. The classifier may add features such as shape or social meaning to the nominal concept. Thai has a great number of "repeaters" (Allan 1977: 292f). These are count classifiers identical to the classified noun; Allan (1977: 292) quotes Thai *khon si-khon* ("people 4-CLS-for-people"). These cases show that the essential function of a count classifier is to restrict the nominal to singular reference, rather than *creating* a unit. For languages with restricted number marking, count classifiers are functional as singularizers, a prerequisite for applying numerals. In number languages such as English, the singularizing step would not be functional; singular is expressed by the singular form of the noun which is in opposition to its plural form. Classifiers in Mandarin are not only used in combination with numerals, but also with demonstratives, to indicate singular reference.

Allan (1977) gives a survey of semantic types of classifiers. Among the most frequent count classifiers are "material" classifiers for [+C] categories of objects, such as ›human‹, ›small animal‹, ›vessel‹, and shape classifiers such as ›longish‹ (one-dimensional), ›flat‹ (two-dimensional), ›round‹ (three-dimensional). Many classifier languages have a general count classifier; in Mandarin it is *gè* 个.

From [−C] to [+C]: mass classifiers. Mass classifiers, misleadingly also called "massifiers", take concepts of type [−C][±Pl] to [+C][−Pl]. Mass classifiers are integrative predicators. A mass classifier supplies a boundary criterion for the separation of referents. These operators include classifiers for shapes of loose aggregates (›heap‹, ›bunch‹, ›flock‹), shapes of coherent quanta (›loaf‹, ›piece‹, ›puddle‹), containers (›box‹, ›bag‹, ›bowl‹), action-related quanta (›mouthful‹, ›shovel‹) and measures (›inch‹, ›acre‹, ›litre‹, ›gram‹, ›kilowatt‹, ›hour‹, etc.). They are applicable to both mass and plural CNPs. For the application to [+Pl] concepts there are classifiers for pairs (*shuāng*), groups (*bāng*), rows (*pái*), piles (*duī*), etc. Most of them can also be used for mass nouns. English has mass-to-count shifts such as the portion shift underlying the count use of the mass noun *beer* in *she only had one beer for breakfast*. Such shifts function as covert mass classifiers. Some measure classifiers like ›cup‹ derive from concepts for containers by multiple steps of abstraction. For a case study of this process in Russian, see Partee and Borschev (2012).

3.4 Quantity

There are two kinds of quantity specifications available, vague quantity specifications (vagQ) and cardinal numerals. Unlike numerals, vagQ like *much/many* do not require unit formation. In number languages like English, there will be a distinction between vagQ for [−Pl] and [+Pl] numerals: *much*, *little*, *a bit* etc. are applied to [−Pl], *many*, *(a) few* and *several* are used for [+Pl]; there are also vagQ used for both, e.g., *more*, *most* and *some*. In classifier languages like Mandarin, no such distinction is to be observed.

Numerals apply after unit formation, which is either lexical (English) or effected by the application of a classifier. In Mandarin, the classifier is attached to the numeral and both precede the noun:

(19) sān dòng xiǎo fángzi
     3 CCLS small house   [CCLS count classifier]
     "three small houses"

The numeral is applied to a singular concept, whose reference is multiplied by the numeral. There are also number languages such as Hungarian in which all numerals are combined with singular nouns (20b); the plural marking in number languages like English can be attributed to a mechanism of semantic agreement between the numeral and its operand.

(20) a (Mandarin)
       zhè   dòng   fángzi
       DEM   CCLS   house
       "this house"

   b (Hungarian, Ugric, Uralic)   c (Hungarian)
       két   ház   a   ház-ak
       2   house.SG   DEF   house-PL
       "two houses"   "the houses"

If a Qt operation is applied, the nominal acquires a feature [+Q] which corresponds to a quantity attribute in the nominal concept for which a value is specified; note that Σ is not a Qt, but a Unit operation. The feature [+Q] makes the nominal eligible for quantificational use (see section 3.7.2). Without a quantity element, the nominal may take on simple indefiniteness marking (if the language provides any, see section 3.6.1); the nominal will carry a [C] and a [Pl] feature, resulting from its Nucleus properties and operations at the level Unit.

Figure 16.2 gives the overall picture of the operations and features involved on the Unit and Quantity layers. According to the diagram, bare nominals in languages without articles and number distinction may be [−C] or [+C] with or without Σ application.

3.5 Order

A criterion of order can be applied to a nominal at the stage reached now, based on various types of ordering. These include:

- numerical order   *first, second, . . .*
- temporal order   *next, former, first, last, new, old*
- order by a specific scalar criterion   superlatives
- order by subjective preference   *favourite*

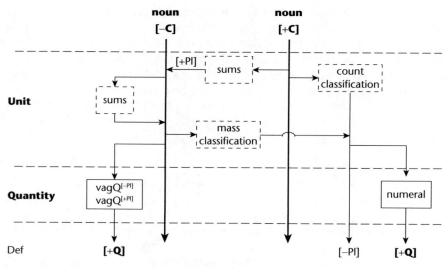

Figure 16.2 Operations of the levels Unit and Quantity

Any type of ordering requires an operand concept denoting a *set* of entities to be ordered; the operands must hence be [−U]. Ordering conceptually identifies one element in the set; therefore, the result of applying an ordering operator to a [−U] operand is [+U]: concepts such as ›third/next/best/favourite book(s)‹ are inherently unique. If the operand is [−Pl], the entities to be ordered are singular referents; if the operand is [+Pl], the ordered entities are sum referents. The operand may carry quality and quantity specifications such as in (21):

(21) the   first/best/next   two   Iranian movies
      her   favourite   two   Iranian movies
      Def   Ord   Qt   Qual   Nuc

The operators ›new‹ and ›old‹ in the list above have to be taken in the sense given in (22a), not as restrictive adjectives on the Qual layer (22b):

(22) a   The new pope is more popular than the old one.
     b   This T-shirt is still quite new/already very old.

The operator ›favourite‹ requires an experiencer argument; it thus adds a [+R] quality to the nominal. Among the operators mentioned, *favourite* and *new* have been analysed in Partee and Borschev (2002); on superlatives, see Sharvit and Stateva (2002).

The application of ordinal numerals requires the same path as cardinal numerals. In numeral classifier languages, an ordinal morpheme is attached to the combination of cardinal numeral and classifier, cf. Mandarin *dì* 第 "number" in (23):

(23) dì   sān   dòng   fángzi
     number   CARD   CCLS   house
     "the third house"

3.6 Definiteness

The approach taken here follows the theory of definiteness developed in Löbner (1985) and (2011), where the reader will find the relevant discussion of other theories of definiteness. According to this approach, the basic function of definite and indefinite determination, explicit or implicit, is to invest the NP with [+U] or [−U] status, respectively. In languages without definiteness marking, bare NPs will carry the lexical [U] feature of the nucleus through to the level of the NP. Thus bare nominals with a [−U]/[+U] nucleus will end up indefinite/definite unless they are modified by a covert operation that changes the [U] value.

In addition to Def operators, there are prior operations that affect [U]. These include:

- A shift to [−U] effected by existential possessor saturation.
- Coercion of a lexical shift to [−U] by application of operands of the Qual, Unit or Qt layers.
- Order specifications, which require [−U] and shift to [+U] (section 3.5).

The [U] feature is also affected by possessor specifications in a possessive chain. This complex will be discussed in section 3.6.2.

3.6.1 Definiteness operations on absolute nominals

From [−U] to [−U] (1): simple indefinites. Simple indefiniteness adds no semantic content to the nominal. If overt, it is used on [−U] nominals that do not carry the [+Q] feature; it may depend on the features [C] and [Pl]. French has three simple indefinite markings: *un/ une* for [+C][−Pl], *du/de la* for [−C][−Pl] and *des* for [+Pl]. English only marks [+C][−Pl] with *a(n)*. Mandarin has optional marking of indefinites by *yǒu* 有. *Yǒu* can be attached to a nominal on the Qual level, to a bare classifier plus nominal in colloquial Mandarin (yielding a one-unit meaning), or to a nominal with numeral and classifier. *Yǒu* is not sensitive to the features [C] and [Pl].

From [−U] to [−U] (2): special indefinites. What I would like to call "special" indefinites include the following elements in English:

- unspecific indefinites: *some* (not as a vague quantity specification)
- free choice indefinites: *any*
- negative indefinites: *no*
- interrogative indefinites: *which*

In English, none of these are sensitive to the features [C] and [Pl].

From [−U] to [+U] (1): demonstratives. Adnominal demonstratives are very widespread. We will not discuss their deictic properties (see Diessel 2012), but only their interaction with the [U] feature. Generally, they presuppose the possibility of choice among potential referents of the nominal; thus, they operate on [−U] nominals. The result, however, is [+U]: nominals with adnominal demonstratives have definite reference. In many languages, such as Hungarian, demonstrative determiners combine with definiteness marking, as in

(24)   az   a   ház
        DEM   DEF   house.SG
        "that house"

The shift to [+U] is enabled by an accompanying gesture of pointing, or more abstract processes amounting to the effect of singling out a referent in the given context of utterance.

From [−U] to [+U] (2): pragmatic definites. The most prominent case of applying definite determination is its operation on [−U] nominals such as, e.g., with anaphors.

(25) Sue wrote a letter to Juliet, but the letter never arrived.

I have called this use of definites "pragmatic" because the uniqueness involved with this type of definites is achieved at utterance level by retrieving information from the given context. The information must be such that the resulting concept is of type [+U]; i.e., conceptually enriched so as to yield a unique description. In the example in (25), the semantic concept ›letter‹ of the anaphoric NP *the letter* is enriched to ›letter Sue wrote to Juliet‹ with reference to the same writing event as in the preceding sentence. This amounts to a unique description in the given context. The conceptual enrichment involved can also be effected by a so-called "establishing relative clause" (Hawkins 1978: 131ff), as in (26):

(26)   The letter *that Sue wrote to Juliet* never arrived.

The identifying information retrieved either implicitly from the context or explicitly from the establishing relative clause is to be considered content of the resulting definite NP concept at utterance level, since it is presupposed in both cases. We will therefore represent this shift as an operation involved with pragmatic definites.

From [±U] to [+U]: determiner possessives. In many languages, certain possessive constructions have the combined effect on the possessum of possessor specification and definite determination. This applies to English Saxon genitives and NPs with possessive pronouns, but not to Italian NPs with possessive pronouns (recall (14) and (15)). This operation equally applies to [−U] and [+U] input, i.e., to relational and functional CNPs.

From [+U] to [+U]: semantic definites. Definiteness marking for [+U] nominals is semantically as redundant as simple indefiniteness marking with [−U] nominals; both may serve other functions such as case marking or just syntactic uniformity. I have called definites with [+U] CNP "semantic" definites because the uniqueness requirement for definite NPs is met by the very semantics of the CNP. Many languages, including Mandarin and Russian, do not mark definite NPs. English does mark definiteness, but not for all [+U] nominals, as it does not use a definite article with (most) proper names and personal pronouns. There are also cases of "bare definites" where [+U] nouns receive no definiteness marking, as in *go to school*, *go to bed* or *at night*. For colloquial German and standard Modern Greek, the use of definite articles extends to proper names; Maori, in addition, even marks personal pronouns as definite (Bauer 1993: 108ff.). Some languages distinguish between pragmatic and semantic definiteness. For example, German dialects have "weak" articles that are exclusively used with semantic definites (see Löbner 2011: 318f).

From [+U] to [−U]: quantification proper. This operation will be discussed in section 3.7.

3.6.2 Definiteness operations on relational nominals

As mentioned in section 2.3, [+R] nominals may be [+U] or [−U]. Except for determiner possessives, possessor specifications operate on the nominal on the Rel layer prior to Def. On the Def level, the relational possessum CNP, to be referred to as "REL", undergoes definite or indefinite determination. This step applies independently of the [U] quality of the possessor POSS. If REL is [+U], it is eligible to semantic definiteness marking, e.g., in *the mother of a boy*. If REL is [−U] it can be determined as indefinite, as demonstrative or pragmatically definite. The whole complex of REL+POSS will take on a [U] character that depends on the [U] features of both, REL and POSS, as indicated in (27).

(27)
		REL		POSS		REL+POSS
a	a brother	[−U]	of a boy	[−U]	→	[−U]
b	a brother	[−U]	of the boy	[+U]	→	[−U]
c	the mother	[+U]	of a boy	[−U]	→	[−U]
d	the mother	[+U]	of the boy	[+U]	→	[+U]

REL+POSS is [−U] if REL or POSS is, since all three combinations in (a) to (c) are sortal concepts that allow for an open number of potential referents (for more discussion see Löbner 2011: 301ff on the [U] feature of possessive chains).

3.7 Quantification proper

In this chapter, we will merely discuss the way in which nongeneric ("particular" or "episodic") quantification fits into the whole architecture of determination; for a comprehensive discussion of quantification see Chapter 18.

Nongeneric quantification proper can be considered a differentiation of an underlying summative predication about the domain of quantification, DoQ (see Löbner (2000: 253–277) for an extensive discussion). For nominal quantification, the domain of quantification is a sums domain, as indicated for the underlying nonquantificational predications in (28); this predication applies distributively to the elements of the sum.

(28)   single case   summative predication on the sum of single cases
  a   mass: the coffee [Σ(coffee)] was served in paper cups.
  b   singular: the eggs [Σ(egg)] are broken.
  c   plural: the students [$\Sigma(\Sigma$(student))] gathered in their classrooms.

The arguments of the VP predicate are of type Σ; hence the VP predicate p itself is raised to $\Sigma(p)$. Since sum predicates are summative, they are either true of all elements of their sum argument or false of all elements. Summative predication thus gives rise to truth value gaps for sum arguments that contain both elements for which p is true and ones for which p is false. If, however, quantification is applied to such a case of summative predication, it turns $\Sigma(p)$ into an integrative predication on the DoQ that specifies the quantity of elements in the sum for which the predication is true. Integrative quantification thus fills the functional gap of predicating about possibly "mixed" sum arguments. One option of applying quantification (in some, but not all languages) is by means of nominal determination; the other, crosslinguistically more common way, is by the use of quantificational adverbs such as *partly* or *completely* (Bach 1995: 10). For nominal quantification, there are two options: the use of genuine quantificational determiners and the use of explicit quantity specifications. In both cases, quantificational determination in English is sensitive to the distinction in terms of [C] and [Pl].

3.7.1 Genuine quantifiers

In (29) we apply universal quantification to the sum(mative) predications in (28):

(29)   single case   quantification
  a   mass: All coffee was served in paper cups.
  b   singular: Every/each egg was broken.
  c   plural: All students gathered in their classrooms.

The truth value gaps for mixed domains are now closed: mixed cases just yield falsity. In English, *every*, *each*, *both*, *either* and *neither* are used for Σ(singular) quantification, while *all* applies to Σ(mass) and Σ(plural).

Nongeneric quantification always presupposes reference to the sum DoQ. This becomes apparent if one observes the equivalence of the partitive paraphrases for the sentences in (29); such a paraphrase is always possible with episodic nominal quantification:

(30)   single case   explicitly partitive quantification
  a   mass: All of the coffee was served in paper cups.
  b   singular: Everyone/each of the eggs was broken.
  c   plural: All of the students gathered in their classrooms.

The partitive paraphrases show that quantification actually involves two operations on the definite sum DoQ: (1) a partitive on a [+U][−C] nominal, (2) application of a quantificational determiner. The partitive is an inverse of the sums operation; it yields elements of the sum for application of the quantified predicate. The result is a shift from [+U] to [−U] since quantificational NPs are not definite (recall section 3.6.1).

3.7.2 Partitive indefinites

In addition to genuine quantifiers, quantity operators, i.e., numerals (with classifiers) and vague quantity specifications, can be used as Qf determiners. These operators are nongeneric quantifiers proper if and only if they are construed as partitive indefinites (see Löbner 1987: 190ff, Löbner 2013: 85f).

(31)   single case   [partitive] quantification
  a   mass: Much [of the] coffee was served in paper cups.
  b   singular: Three [of the] eggs were broken.
  c   plural: Many [of the] students gathered in their classrooms.

4 Concluding remarks

The overall picture of [U] determination on the Order, Definiteness and Quantification layers is illustrated in Figure 16.3. In a simplified manner, the diagram also includes the operations on the preceding layers from Relation to Quantity.

The considerations above amount to a complex model of the various semantic operations involved in forming an NP out of a nominal nucleus. The model depicts the relative order of determinational operations, whether they are optional or necessary, and whether they can be covert in a language or not. It also models the way in which the operations of determination interact with the three basic features of nominals—relationality, countability and uniqueness. The model accounts for possible readings of NPs with no overt determinational elements. Such a "bare" nominal may have passed through any series of operations that can be applied covertly; these include derelationalization, contextual possessor identification, relationalization, Σ, count and mass classification, simple indefiniteness and definiteness. If we take a look at the steps not marked as potentially covert, we realize that these coincide with those operations that add content beyond mere determination: explicit possessor specification, quality modification, quantity specification, ordering, deictic relation, special types of indefiniteness and quantification proper.

Of course, the model is only a general frame; it does not capture all possible interactions within it, and it does not tell us how these functional layers are dealt with in syntax. It does, however, offer a way to locate all essential operations of semantic NP formation in one coherent model.

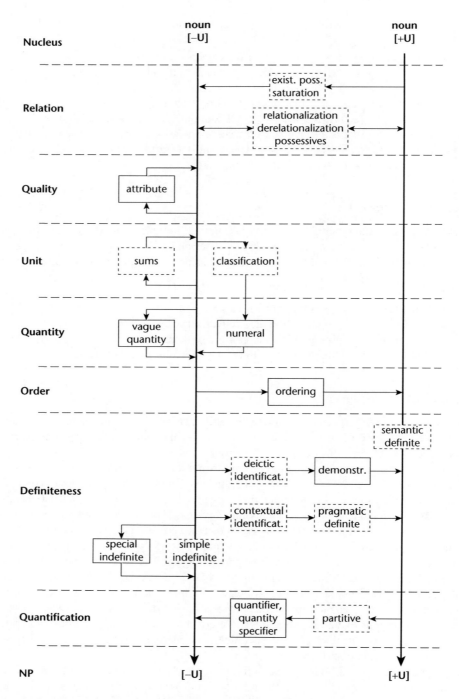

Figure 16.3 Operations of determination on the seven layers

Further reading

Doetjes, J. 2012. Count/mass distinctions across languages. In C. Maienborn, K. von Heusinger and P. Portner (eds), *Semantics: An International Handbook of Natural Language Meaning*, Berlin, New York: De Gruyter, 2559–80. On the mass/count distinction.
Corbett, G. C. 2000. *Number*. Cambridge: Cambridge University Press. On number.
Barker, C. 2011. Possessives and relational nouns. In C. Maienborn, K. von Heusinger and P. Portner (eds), *Semantics: An International Handbook of Natural Language Meaning*. Berlin, New York: De Gruyter, 1109–30. On relational nouns.
Löbner, S. 2011. Concept types and determination. *Journal of Semantics* 28: 279–333. On relationality and inherent uniqueness.
Rijkhoff, J. 2002. *The Noun Phrase*. Oxford: Oxford University Press. For the greater part of the issues discussed, from a typological perspective.
Svenonius, Peter 2008. The position of adjectives and other phrasal modifiers in the decomposition of DP. In L. McNally and C. Kennedy (eds), *Adjectives and Adverbs: Syntax, Semantics, and Discourse*. Oxford: Oxford University Press, 16–42. For a recent survey of approaches to NP-internal layers, and on a subclassification of adnominal adjectives.

References

Abbott, B. 2010. *Reference*. Oxford: Oxford University Press.
Allan, K. 1977. Classifiers. *Language* 58: 285–311.
Bach, E. 1995. Introduction. In E. Bach, E. Jelinek, A. Kratzer and B. H. Partee (eds), *Quantification in Natural Languages*. Dordrecht: Springer, 1–11.
Barker, C. 2011. Possessives and relational nouns. In C. Maienborn, K. von Heusinger and P. Portner (eds), *Semantics: An International Handbook of Natural Language Meaning*. Berlin, New York: De Gruyter, 1109–30.
Barwise, J. and R. Cooper 1981. Generalized quantifiers and natural language. *Linguistics and Philosophy* 4: 159–219.
Bauer, W. 1993. *Maori*. New York, London: Routledge.
Chapell, H. and W. McGregor 1996. Prolegomena to a theory of inalienability. In H. Chappell and W. McGregor (eds), *The Grammar of Inalienability: A Typological Perspective on Body Part Terms and the Part Whole Relation*. Berlin: Mouton de Gruyter, 3–30.
Cheng, L. L.-S. and R. Sybesma 1999. Bare and not-so-bare nouns and the structure of NP. *Linguistic Inquiry* 30: 509–42.
Corbett, G. 2000. *Number*. Cambridge: Cambridge University Press.
Demonte, V. 2012. Adjectives. In C. Maienborn, K. von Heusinger and P. Portner (eds), *Semantics: An International Handbook of Natural Language Meaning*. Berlin, New York: De Gruyter, 1314–40.
Diessel, H. 2012. Deixis and demonstratives. In C. Maienborn, K. von Heusinger and P. Portner (eds), *Semantics: An International Handbook of Natural Language Meaning*. Berlin, New York: De Gruyter, 2407–32.
Doetjes, J. 2012. Count/mass distinctions across languages. In C. Maienborn, K. von Heusinger and P. Portner (eds), *Semantics: An International Handbook of Natural Language Meaning*. Berlin, New York: De Gruyter, 2559–80.
Haspelmath, M. 1999. Article-possessor complementarity: economic motivation in noun phrase syntax. *Language* 75: 227–43.
Hawkins, J. A. 1978. *Definiteness and Indefiniteness*. London: Croom Helm.
Hole, D. 2015. Arguments and adjuncts. In T. Kiss and A. Alexiadou (eds), *Syntax – Theory and Analysis: An International Handbook*. Berlin: De Gruyter, 1284–1320.

Li, C. N. and S. A. Thompson 1981. *Mandarin Chinese. A Functional Reference Grammar*. Berkeley, Los Angeles, London: University of California Press.
Löbner, S. 1985. Definites. *Journal of Semantics* 4: 279–326.
Löbner, S. 1987. Natural language and generalized quantifier theory. In P. Gärdenfors (ed.) *Generalized Quantifiers: Linguistic and Logical Approaches*. Dordrecht: Reidel, 181–201.
Löbner, S. 2000. Polarity in natural language: predication, quantification and negation in particular and characterizing sentences. *Linguistics and Philosophy* 23: 213–308.
Löbner, S. 2011. Concept types and determination. *Journal of Semantics* 28: 279–333.
Löbner, S. 2013. *Understanding semantics*, 2nd edition. New York, London: Routledge.
Partee, B. H. and V. Borschev 2002. Integrating lexical and formal semantics: genitives, relational nouns, and type-shifting. In R. Cooper and T. Gamkrelidze (eds), *Proceedings of the 2nd Tbilisi Symposium on Language, Logic and Computation*. Tbilisi: Tbilisi State University, 229–41.
Partee, B. H. and V. Borschev 2012. Sortal, relational, and functional interpretations of nouns and Russian container constructions. *Journal of Semantics* 29: 445–86.
Rijkhoff, J. 2002. *The Noun Phrase*. Oxford: Oxford University Press.
Sharvit, Y. and P. Stateva 2002. Superlative expressions, context, and focus. *Linguistics and Philosophy* 25: 453–504.
Svenonius, P. 2008. The position of adjectives and other phrasal modifiers in the decomposition of DP. In L. McNally and C. Kennedy (eds), *Adjectives and Adverbs: Syntax, Semantics, and Discourse*. Oxford: Oxford University Press, 16–42.
Thompson, C. 1996. On the grammar of body parts in Koyukon Athabaskan. In H. Chappell and W. McGregor (eds), *The Grammar of Inalienability: A Typological Perspective on Body Part Terms and the Part Whole Relation*. Berlin: De Gruyter, 651–78.
Van Valin, R. 2008. RPs and the nature of lexical and syntactic categories in role and reference grammar. In R. Van Valin (ed.), *Investigations of the Syntax-Semantics-Pragmatics Interface*. Amsterdam/Philadelphia: John Benjamins, 161–78.
Vikner, C. and P. A. Jensen 2000 A semantic analysis of the English genitive. Interaction of lexical and formal semantics. *Studia Linguistica* 56: 191–226.

Related topics

Chapter 18, Varieties of quantification.

17
Negation and polarity

Doris Penka

1 Introduction

Negation is a very basic and central concept in human cognition and language and has been investigated by philosophers and linguists going at least as far back as Aristotle. It is thus far beyond the scope of the present chapter to provide a summary of research on the semantics of negation (see Horn (2001) for a comprehensive overview also on the history of the study of negation). Closely related to negation is the notion of polarity, i.e. whether a statement is negative or affirmative. Expressions that are sensitive to polarity have been a very prominent topic in linguistic research within the framework of generative grammar for the past fifty years. Here, too, I will not be able to do justice to the vast literature on the topic. I will instead focus on recent advances in the analysis of negation and polarity within the framework of formal semantics, hoping to provide the reader with a useful and concise summary of the state of the art.

The topics addressed in this chapter concern different types of negation (sentential, constituent, lexical and metalinguistic negation) as well as the interaction of negation with other semantic operators (so-called neg-raising and negative concord). In the area of negative and positive polarity items, I summarize different proposals for a semantic characterization of the contexts in which they are licensed, discuss varieties of negative polarity items, and address possible sources of polarity sensitivity.

2 Negation

In logic, negation is a one-place operator that reverses the truth-value of a proposition. Negation applied to sentence that is false results in a true statement and vice versa. Thus, sentence (1b) is true in exactly the situations in which (1a) is false.

(1) a   It is raining.
    b   It is not raining.

While from a logical perspective negation as a truth-functional operator is quite a simple notion, the way negation is used and expressed in natural languages paints a highly complex picture that has intrigued linguists for a long time. In the following, I discuss the different ways in which negation occurs in natural languages and how it enters into the semantic composition.

2.1 Types of negation

2.1.1 Sentential negation and constituent negation

Linguists differentiate between (at least) three kinds of negation, depending on the level of clause formation where it enters into the composition. Sentential negation applies to full clauses or complete propositions, constituent negation to a particular part of the clause, and lexical negation at the word level.

(2) a It is not raining.   sentential negation
     b It rained not long ago.   constituent negation
     c unhappy, impossible, non-human   lexical negation

When negation takes scope above the entire clause, we are dealing with a clear case of sentential negation. In this case it is possible to use the paraphrase "it is not the case that . . ." (*It is not raining* for instance can be paraphrased as *It is not the case that it is raining*.) In contrast, a negation that does not refer to the entire clause but only to a particular part of it as in (2b) is a case of constituent negation. Lexical negation applies to a word to yield a meaning that is its opposite (see Chapter 14).

In practice, this tripartite classification is not always easy to apply and there are cases that are not as clear-cut as one would wish. A number of tests to distinguish between sentential and constituent negation were introduced by Klima (1964). They are illustrated in (3) and (4) and classify as sentential negation the negation occurring in sentences that can combine with positive tag questions, *neither* tags and the appositive tag *not even*, and as constituent negation otherwise.

(3) Sentential negation:
John didn't find a job, {
     did he / *didn't he?
     and neither did Mary / *and so did Mary.
     not even a part-time one / *even a part-time one.
}

(4) Constituent negation:
John found a job not far away, {
     didn't he / *did he?
     and so did Mary / *and neither does Mary.
     even a well-paid one / *not even a well-paid one.
}

There are, however, several problems with Klima's tests. First, they are tailored to English and some of them are not applicable to other languages at all. Second, as pointed out by Payne (1985), what these tests really seem to be sensitive to is whether negation is the operator taking widest scope. Finally, it has been questioned whether "constituent negation" is a useful notion at all. Note that instances of so-called constituent negation can usually be paraphrased by a relative clause involving sentential negation, e.g. (4) as (5).

(5) John found a job at a place that is not located far away.

This suggests that what is at the heart of the distinction between sentential and constituent negation is the scope relation between the negation operator and the main predicate. In the case of sentential negation in (3), the main predicate *find* is interpreted in the scope of negation and it is asserted that there was no event of John finding a job (in the time period under consideration). Sentence (4) with constituent negation, on the other hand, asserts that there was an event of John finding a job, and the negation operates on an implicit location predicate. Following Acquaviva (1997), sentential negation can be defined as a negation operator having the main predicate in its scope. Other cases involving a negative particle or adverb can be subsumed under the term of constituent negation.

2.1.2 Lexical negation and antonymy

Certain negative affixes like English *un-* and *in-* contribute negation at the word level. In contrast to sentential negation, lexical negation does not necessarily result in a contradictory opposite but in many cases merely in a contrary opposite (see Horn (2001)). Contrary opposition is defined by the logical Law of Contradiction, according to which the two opposites cannot be simultaneously true while they can be simultaneously false. Contradictory opposition is additionally subject to the Law of the Excluded Middle, which holds that one of the opposed elements must be true. Two statements that are in contradictory opposition thus cannot be true at the same time and they cannot be false at the same time. Sentential negation yields a contradictory opposite, since e.g. the sentences *Mary is happy* and *Mary is not happy* can neither be simultaneously true nor simultaneously false in the same situation. Prefixing *un-*, on the other hand, yields a contrary opposite: the sentences *Mary is happy* and *Mary is unhappy* cannot be simultaneously true, but they can be simultaneously false as witnessed by the fact that *Mary is neither happy nor unhappy* makes a felicitous assertion. This can be explained by the fact that *un-* in this example prefixes to the gradable adjective *happy*, which is associated with a scale. This scale can be partitioned into three segments as shown in (6): the lower part on which unhappy individuals are located, the upper part where happy individuals are located, and in between a neutral interval that contains individuals that are neither happy nor unhappy.

(6)
           unhappy   happy

While the sentence *Mary is unhappy* expresses that Mary is located on the lower, "unhappy" part of the scale, *Mary is not happy* is true if she is located in the complement of the "happy" part, i.e. either the neutral or the "unhappy" interval.

It has also been proposed that in general, the marked term of antonymous pairs of gradable adjectives like *short* (as opposed to *tall*) should be analysed in terms of negation. An open question is whether the decomposition into negation and the unmarked adjective should take place in the syntax or the lexicon (see Heim (2008)).

2.1.3 Metalinguistic negation

While the types of negation considered so far operate on the truth-conditional content, albeit applying at different positions both at the word and clausal level, it has been argued that negation can also be used at a metalinguistic level (see in particular Horn (1985) and (2001)). In this metalinguistic use, negation is not about the truth or falsity of a proposition, but rather about the assertability of an utterance. Rather than denying the truth of the positive counterpart, metalinguistic negation is used to object to its assertability. An example is the following, which does not entail that the object under discussion is not a car. As the continuation makes clear, it conveys that calling it simply a car is inappropriate.

(7) This is not a car. This is a Rolls-Royce.

Another case arguably involving metalinguistic negation is (8), an example that has figured prominently in the philosophical and linguistic literature on presuppositions. Here the second sentence makes prominent a reading of the first sentence where the existence of the king of France is not presupposed.

(8) The king of France is not bald. There is no king of France.

While negation usually does not affect presuppositions, the negation in this example operates on the presupposition triggered by the definite article, namely that there is a king of France. As the continuation makes clear, the first sentence does not deny the truth of the propositional content that the king of France is bald, but rather rejects the assumption that there is a king of France. It would typically be used to reject the previous utterance *The king of France is bald* on grounds of its presupposition.

Metalinguistic negation can be used to object to any aspect of a previous utterance, including its presuppositions (as in (8)), its implicatures (as in (9a)), its pronunciation (as in (9b)), or its style or register (as in (9c)). Cases of metalinguistic negation typically involve an otherwise literal repetition of the utterance objected to, where the word or expression responsible for the felt inappropriateness bears stress. (This is why metalinguistic negation is sometimes also called "echoic").

(9) a   John didn't eat SOME of the cake. He ate all of it.
     b   This is not a para`DOX. It is a `paradox.
     c   Sue did not go to the LOO. She went to the toilet.

Because metalinguistic negation does not operate on the same level as the clause in which it occurs, it does not interact in the same way as sentential negation with other items in the clause. In particular, metalinguistic negation does not license negative polarity items or anti-license positive polarity items (see below). The latter is exemplified in sentence (9a), which involves *some*, which is generally regarded as a positive polarity item and replaced by *any* under negation.

2.2 Interaction of negation and other elements

2.2.1 Negative quantifiers and negative concord

Language can express negation not only by a negation particle or adverb, but also by quantifiers like *nobody*, *nothing* or *no dog*. These also contribute sentential negation, according to the definition introduced above, as they render the main predicate in the scope of negation. (10a), where negation is expressed by a negative quantifier, for instance, is semantically equivalent to (10b) with a negative adverb.

(10) a   John has no dog.
      b   John doesn't have a dog.

Expressions like *no dog*, *nobody* or *nothing* are generally assumed to denote negated existential quantifiers. While this analysis seems appropriate for languages like English, it is problematic for many other languages, where negative quantifiers co-occur with negative adverbs or other negative quantifiers without yielding a reading with double negation. This is illustrated in the following examples from Polish and Italian.

(11) a Nikt   nie   przyszedł.   (Polish)
        nobody   not   came
        "Nobody came." (not: "Nobody didn't come." = "Everybody came.")
    b   Nessuno ha   visto   nessuno.   (Italian)
        nobody   has   seen   nobody
        "Nobody saw anyone." (not: "Nobody saw nobody." = "Everybody saw somebody.")

This phenomenon, where multiple negative constituents in the same clause only contribute one instance of negation to the semantic meaning, is known as negative concord. It is in fact found in the majority of the world's languages. Negative concord poses a challenge to the assumption that expressions like *nessuno*, also dubbed n-words, denote negated existential quantifiers. If the lexical meaning of these expressions is inherently negative, then why do they not always contribute negation to the interpretation? But assuming that they are semantically non-negative is also problematic, as in certain cases they do contribute negation to the semantics. This double-faced nature of n-words is evident in the Italian example (11b), where the first instance of *nessuno* seems to contribute negation, but the second instance does not. Even in languages like Polish, where n-words are generally accompanied by a clause-mate negative particle, there are contexts where n-words by themselves contribute negation, in particular when they are used in isolation as an answer to a wh-question, as in (12).

(12) Kto   przyszedł?   – Nikt.   (Polish)
     Who   came?   – Nobody (="Nobody came.")

In fact, the ability of n-words to be interpreted as negative quantifiers when they are used as fragment answers can be used as diagnostics to differentiate between n-words and so-called negative polarity items, which exhibit a strong affinity to negation without being semantically negative. While a detailed discussion of negative polarity items is deferred to section 3 below, one crucial difference should be mentioned here: in contrast to n-words, negative polarity items always have to co-occur with a negative expression and can never by themselves contribute negation to the interpretation.

Basically, three types of approaches to negative concord have been proposed in the literature. The first takes the ambivalent behaviour of n-words at face value and assumes that they are lexically ambiguous between inherently negative quantifiers and non-negative indefinites. The challenge for such approaches (Herburger 2001) lies in explaining why the distribution of the alleged two lexical items is governed by structural factors (e.g. the first occurrence of *nessuno* in (11b) has to be the negative variant, and the second *nessuno* the non-negative one). The second type of approach maintains that expressions like *nessuno* are semantically negative quantifiers, and extra assumptions are employed to explain that not every negation is factored into the meaning of the sentence. Haegeman and Zanuttini (1996) propose a rule of negative absorption, according to which multiple negation operators are turned into a single one. De Swart and Sag (2002) formalize absorption of negative quantifiers as resumption in a polyadic quantifier framework. The third line of approaches, finally, starts from the opposite assumption and argues that n-words are semantically non-negative. To explain why n-words do in certain configuration contribute negation, these analyses assume that the semantic negation can be realized covertly. Analyses in this spirit can again be divided into different camps. Laka (1990) and Giannakidou (1998 and subsequent) propose that n-words are negative polarity items. A problem with subsuming n-words under negative polarity items is the fact that there are certain crucial differences between n-words and negative polarity items, in particular the above-mentioned ability of n-words to serve as negative fragment answers. Ladusaw (1992) argues that n-words differ from ordinary negative polarity items by their ability of self-licensing, which means that the presence of an n-word is sufficient to trigger a covert negation operator in the clausal structure. This view is fleshed out by Zeijlstra (2004), who analyses negative concord as syntactic agreement and proposes that n-words are (possibly redundant) markers of sentential negation.

There is evidence that even in languages like English, which do not allow negative concord, expressions like *nobody* do not denote negated existential quantifiers. This comes from the fact that the negation they contribute does not always take scope from the same position as the existential quantifier. This is illustrated by the following examples from German and English. As the paraphrases make clear, these sentences give rise to a reading (called the split scope reading) where negation takes scope over the modal predicate, while the indefinite meaning component is interpreted with narrow scope (resulting in a *de dicto* reading).

(13) a   Die   Medizin   muss   kein   Arzt   verabreichen.   (German)
          the   medicine   must   no   doctor   administer
          "It is not necessary that a doctor administers the medicine."
      b   There can be no doubt.
          "It is not possible that there is any doubt."

Considering such split scope readings of negative quantifiers, Penka (2011) proposes to extend Zeijlstra's (2004) analysis in terms of syntactic agreement to languages that do not exhibit negative concord. The different co-occurrence patterns of negative quantifiers and negative adverbs observed in different languages are accounted for by two parameters: (i) whether the negation operator associated with negatively marked indefinites has to be covert or whether it may be realized in the form of a negative adverb or particle; (ii) whether one semantic negation can simultaneously license several negative indefinites or whether there has to be a one-to-one relation between markers and negation operators.

2.2.2 Neg-raising

When negation is combined with certain clause embedding verbs like *believe*, a reading results where negation refers to the embedded clause. Consider (14a), which is usually interpreted as equivalent to (14b). This is stronger than the literal reading *It is not the case that according to what John believes, Mary is sick*, which leaves open the possibility that John has no opinion about Mary's state of health. Other similar verbs like *know* do not behave in this way and (15a) is not equivalent to (15b).

(14) a   John doesn't believe that Mary is sick.
      b   John believes that Mary isn't sick.

(15) a   John doesn't know that Mary is sick.
      b   John knows that Mary isn't sick.

This phenomenon, where the negation appears in the matrix clause while it seems to be interpreted in the embedded clause, is called neg-raising. Other predicates that allow, and in fact, prefer a reading involving neg-raising include *think*, *want* and *seem* (see Horn (1978) for a more comprehensive list).

(16) a   John doesn't think that it will rain today. → John thinks that it will not rain today.
     b   John doesn't want Mary to leave. → John wants Mary not to leave.
     c   It doesn't seem that it will rain today. → It seems that it won't rain today.

Early analyses (starting with Fillmore (1963)) assumed that neg-raising is due to syntactic movement of the negation operator. Semantic and pragmatic accounts in contrast hold that negation is interpreted in its surface position, and that the stronger reading comes about via certain semantic or pragmatic principles. The basic idea, going back to Bartsch (1973), is that neg-raising is due to the Law of the Excluded Middle. That is, it is assumed that a person either believes *p* or that she believes *not-p*. Having no opinion and considering both *p* and *not-p* as possible is excluded. From this assumption, the neg-raising interpretation follows immediately from the literal meaning: "It is not the case that *x* believes *p*" together with "*x* believes *p* or *x* believes *not-p*" entails "*x* believes *not-p*". There are different proposals regarding the source of the assumption of the Excluded Middle. Horn (2001) derives it as an implicature via a general pragmatic principle akin to Grice's Maxim of Relevance, according to which the hearer should read as much as possible into a statement. Gajewski (2005) argues against Horn's proposal because the class of neg-raising predicates does not seem to be entirely determined by their lexical semantics – while e.g. *want* is a neg-raising predicate, *desire* is not. He proposes instead that the Excluded Middle is a lexical presupposition associated exclusively with neg-raising predicates.

3 Negative polarity items

Negative polarity items (NPIs) are words or expressions that can only occur in a limited set of environments, prototypically in the scope of negation. The prime example is English *any*, which is illicit in affirmative sentences like (17a), but fine in negative sentences like (17b).

(17) a   *The burglar left any traces.
     b   The burglar didn't leave any traces.

Other well-known examples of NPIs are the temporal adverb *ever* and certain idiomatic phrases such as *lift a finger* and *drink a drop*.

(18) a   Nobody/*everybody in my family has ever lived abroad.
     b   None/*all of the neighbours lifted a finger to help.
     c   John never/*always drinks a drop.

NPIs can not only occur in the scope of negation and other expressions that are arguably associated with negation, but also in certain other environments. These include, amongst others, the contexts exemplified in (19):

(19) a   Scope of semi-negative quantifiers and adverbs like *few*, *at most*, *rarely*, *hardly* etc.:
         John hardly ever says anything.
     b   Complement clauses of "negative" predicates like *doubt*:
         I doubt that anyone saw anything.
     c   Clauses headed by *without*:
         Sue left without telling anyone.

d   Clauses headed by *before*:
    Mary left before Bill could say anything.
e   Relative clauses modifying a universal quantifier:
    Everyone who saw anything should report to the police.
f   Antecedents of conditionals:
    If the burglar left any traces, we will find them.
g   Comparison clauses:
    Fred is more intelligent than anyone I ever met.
h   Questions:
    Did you see anything unusual last night?

Considering the diverse contexts in (19), the following questions arise:

(20)   i   What notion of "negativity" is common to all the environments where NPIs are licit?
       ii   What precisely are the licensing requirements of NPIs?

There are different ways of viewing the licensing requirements of polarity items, either in terms of environments in which they are licensed, or in terms of expressions that serve as licensors. Instead of (20i) one can alternatively ask what kinds of expressions serve as licensors of NPIs, and this is the way the question has usually been stated (e.g. in Ladusaw 1997). While both perspectives prima facie seem equivalent, the second view also raises questions on the structural relationship between NPIs and their licensors and has triggered a lot of work on the syntactic side of NPI licensing (Progovac 1994; Hoeksema 2000, etc.). See Homer (forthcoming) for arguments that the licensing of polarity sensitive items should be viewed in terms of contexts rather than operators.

The questions in (20) have guided research on NPIs over the past five decades. In his seminal study, Klima (1964) proposed that NPIs are licensed by expressions which he labelled "affective". But giving semantic content to the notion of affectiveness has turned out to be a challenge. There have been attempts to relate affective environments to sentential negation (Baker 1970; Linebarger 1987) such that NPIs are licensed either by a negation operator or via a negative sentence implied by the original utterance. (19b), for example, can be claimed to imply *I don't think that anyone saw anything*. Such approaches, however, suffer from the problem that it is impossible to restrict negative implications to only the sentences in which NPIs are licensed, because there are many entailments of any given proposition and many different representations for those entailments.

3.1 Semantic characterization of licensing contexts

Ladusaw (1979), building on the work of Fauconnier (1979), gave a characterization of the contexts in which NPIs are licensed based on the formal semantic notion of monotonicity or entailment. Most contexts permit inferences from sets to supersets, i.e. from the more specific to the more general. For instance, as a poodle is a specific kind of dog, the inference from (21a) to (21b) is valid. Such kinds of contexts are called upward entailing. Under negation, however, the direction of entailment is reversed, and inferences from sets to subsets are valid. Therefore (22b) follows from (22a). Such contexts where entailment is from the general to the specific are called **downward entailing** (DE) or monotone decreasing.

(21)   a   John owns a poodle.
       b   John owns a dog.

(22) a John doesn't own a dog.
     b John doesn't own a poodle.

A formal definition of downward entailment is given in (24). It is based on a cross-categorial notion of entailment symbolized by "$\Rightarrow$", as defined in (23) (from von Fintel (1999: 100)).

(23) Cross-categorial entailment:
   a For p, q of type t: $p \Rightarrow q$ iff $p = 0$ or $q = 1$.
   b For f, g of type $<\sigma,\tau>$: $f \Rightarrow g$ iff for all x of type σ: $f(x) \Rightarrow g(x)$.

(24) A function f of type $<\sigma,\tau>$ is **downward entailing** if and only if for all x, y of type σ such that $x \Rightarrow y$: $f(y) \Rightarrow f(x)$.

Downward entailment constitutes a generalized notion of negativity, which does not only comprise the scope of negation but many other linguistic contexts. Consider, for example, some of the contexts where NPIs are licensed from (19). They can be shown to be DE by the validity of the following inferences:

(25) Clauses headed by *without*:
     The cat walked across the yard without being caught by a dog. $\Rightarrow$
     The cat walked across the yard without being caught by a poodle.

(26) Relative clauses modifying a universal quantifier:
   a Everyone who owns a dog has to pay a dog licence fee. $\Rightarrow$
   b Everyone who owns a poodle has to pay a dog licence fee.

Ladusaw's hypothesis according to which the crucial property that NPIs are sensitive to is downward entailment has been widely adopted. This analysis, however, requires certain refinements to deal with the full range of cases where NPIs are licensed. There are a number of environments where NPIs are licensed that do not seem to be DE. One case is the scope of *only*, where NPIs are fine, as shown in (27). But intuitively (28b) does follow from (28a).

(27) Only John has ever owned a dog.

(28) a Only John owns a dog.
     b Only John owns a poodle.

The problem is that (28b) conveys that John owns a poodle, which does not follow from (28a). Even if John is the only person owning a dog, it is not guaranteed that John's dog is a poodle. A way out of this problem suggests itself if we take into account that the relevant meaning component of (28b) is generally regarded a presupposition, i.e. it is presupposed that the sentence minus *only* is true. If presuppositions are disregarded when checking for downward entailment, the inference goes through: if we can take for granted that John's dog is a poodle, then (28b) is indeed entailed by (28a). Therefore, von Fintel (1999) proposes that the notion of downward entailment relevant for the licensing of NPIs is one where presuppositions are assumed to be fulfilled. He calls this Strawson downward entailment (inspired by Strawson's (1952) work on presuppositions).

(29) A function f of type $<\sigma,\tau>$ is **Strawson downward entailing** iff for all x, y of type σ such that $x \Rightarrow y$ and $f(x)$ is defined: $f(y) \Rightarrow f(x)$.

While characterizing the contexts where NPIs are acceptable as (Strawson) DE provides an important step towards understanding polarity sensitivity, it still leaves several issues unresolved. For one, the notion of entailment is only applicable to declarative sentences, and it is an open question if and how the DE hypothesis can account for the licensing of NPIs in questions at all (see van Rooy (2003) for a proposal). Moreover, it does not account for the fact that polarity sensitivity does not seem to be a uniform phenomenon. This issue is addressed in the next section.

3.2 Varieties of NPIs

It has been observed that there is considerable variation in the licensing requirements different kinds of NPIs exhibit, both cross-linguistically and within one language. In Modern Greek, for instance, NPIs can also occur in certain contexts that are not DE, in particular in modal contexts as in the following examples (taken from Giannakidou 1998: 59).

(30) a Prepi   na   episkeftis kanenan jatro.   (Greek)
       Must.3SG SUBJ visit   any   doctor
       "You should visit a doctor."
    b Pjene   se   kanenan jatro.
       go.IMP.2SG to   any   doctor
       "Go to a doctor."

To account for these data, Giannakidou (1998 and subsequent) proposes a different licensing condition for NPIs. Following Zwarts (1995), she argues that the relevant semantic property of NPI licensors is nonveridicality, as defined in (31).

(31) A propositional operator f is **nonveridical** iff $f(p)$ does not entail p, for all propositions p.

The sentences in (30), for instance, are nonveridical, as they do not entail that you indeed visit a doctor. The same holds for the DE contexts in (19), where NPIs in English are licensed. Nonveridicality thus provides a weaker notion of negativity than downward entailment, and NPIs in Greek seem to be sensitive to this weaker notion.

But variation in the licensing requirements is not only observed across languages, but also within a language. Consider for instance the distribution of the expressions *in weeks* and punctual *until* in English, illustrated in (32) and (33).

(32) a *I have seen Mary in weeks.
    b I haven't seen Mary in weeks.
    c Nobody has seen Mary in weeks.
    d *At most five people have seen Mary in weeks.

(33) a *I will arrive until Wednesday.
    b I won't arrive until Wednesday.
    c Nobody has arrived until Wednesday.
    d *At most five people have arrived until Wednesday.

While *in weeks* and *until* are excluded from affirmative contexts, they can occur in the scope of negation and negative indefinites, but not in the scope of mere DE expressions such as quantifiers involving *at most*. They thus seem to be pickier and require a stronger kind of negative environment to be licensed. This led Zwarts (1996) and van der Wouden (1997) to propose a hierarchy of negative contexts, where downward entailment constitutes the weakest notion of negative strength, and the strongest corresponds to classical negation. Of intermediate negative strength are anti-additive operators, as defined in (34).

(34) A function *f* is **anti-additive** if and only if for all *x* and *y* in its domain:
$f(x \vee y) \Leftrightarrow f(x) \wedge f(y)$.

According to this definition, negative quantifiers constitute anti-additive operators. Intuitively, this can be verified by checking that (35a) entails (35b) and vice versa.

(35) a   Nobody sings or dances.
     b   Nobody sings and nobody dances.

(36) a   At most five people sing or dance.
     b   At most five people sing and at most five people dance.

In contrast, (36a) and (36b) are not equivalent. ((36b) is true e.g. in a situation in which four people sing and three dance, but (36a) is not.) Therefore, quantifiers involving *at most* do not induce anti-additive contexts and are merely DE. Note that on the other hand being anti-additive entails being DE. This is so because the hierarchy of negative strength is ordered by the subset relation: antimorphic operators, corresponding to classical negation, constitute a proper subset of anti-additive operators, which in turn are a proper subset of DE operators (see Figure 17.1). Corresponding to this hierarchy of negative contexts, Zwarts and van der Wouden distinguish three classes of NPIs: superstrong NPIs are licensed only in strictly negative, i.e. antimorphic contexts, strong NPIs require contexts which are at least anti-additive, and weak NPIs can occur in all kinds of DE contexts. Classifying *any* as a weak NPI, and *in weeks* and *until* as strong NPIs thus accounts for the observed differences in their distribution.

A different perspective on the licensing requirements of strong NPIs is offered by Gajewski (2011). He argues that strong NPIs are not only sensitive to the truth-conditional content of their licensors, but also to the presuppositions and implicatures they induce. Strong NPIs are not licensed in the scope of *only*, for instance, because of the positive presupposition associated with *only*.

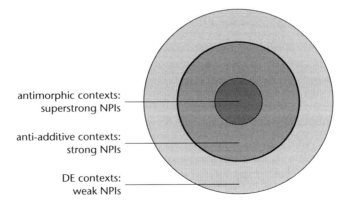

Figure 17.1 Hierarchy of negation and distribution of different classes of NPIs

(37) a   *Only John has seen Mary in weeks.
     b   *Only John arrived until Wednesday.

Gajewski attributes the ungrammaticality of the sentences in (37) to their giving rise to the presuppositions in (38), in which the strong NPIs *in weeks* and *until* do not occur in a DE environment.

(38) a   *John has seen Mary in weeks.
     b   *John arrived until Wednesday.

Similarly, strong NPIs cannot occur in the scope of quantifiers involving *at most*, because these give rise to a positive scalar implicature. The sentences in (39), for example, lead to the scalar implicatures (40), in which the NPI is not in a DE environment.

(39) a   *At most five people have seen Mary in weeks.
         *At most five people have arrived until Wednesday.

(40) a   *Some people have seen Mary in weeks.
     b   *Some people have arrived until Wednesday.

Under this view, the operators that are anti-additive according to Zwarts' classification license strong NPIs because they correspond to the strong endpoint of their scale and thus do not give rise to scalar implicatures. Strong NPIs need to occur in a DE environment in the utterance itself as well as in the presuppositions and implicatures it gives rise to. Weak NPIs, in contrast, only look at the truth-conditional content and require it to be DE.

3.3 The source of polarity sensitivity

An issue we have not addressed so far but which has become central in more recent work on polarity items is the question of what makes a word or expression polarity sensitive. More recent approaches do not content themselves with describing the licensing requirements of NPIs, but strive to explain their limited distribution from their lexical semantics. Adopting the generalization that NPIs are licensed only in contexts that have the semantic property of being DE, they ask why this is so. These approaches start from the observation that a common characteristics of many NPIs cross-linguistically is that they are indefinites (e.g. *any*) or denote minimal amounts or activities (so-called minimizers e.g. *lift a finger* or *drink a drop*), and seek to flesh out the intuition that such expressions add emphasis to a negative statement.

The main idea behind such explanatory approaches has two components. First, using an NPI involves comparing relevant alternatives, i.e. other statements that might have been made instead. Second, an utterance with an NPI can only be used if it is stronger, i.e. more informative than its competitors. In this way, these approaches make sense of the fact that NPIs are licensed exactly in the contexts in which entailment is from the more general to the more specific. Assuming that NPIs denote very general properties, which hold of many entities, using an NPI will make an utterance more informative and thereby strengthen it exactly in those cases where it occurs in a DE context. The different proposals vary in the details of how these two components in the semantics of NPIs are spelled out, i.e. regarding the alternatives against which an utterance with an NPI is considered and the source of the strengthening condition.

In the seminal proposal of Kadmon and Landman (1993), *any* is analysed as an existential determiner inducing domain widening. While the quantificational domain of a quantifier is usually restricted to contextually relevant individuals, the effect of using *any* is that such contextual restrictions are lifted. Consider, for instance, the difference between the sentences in (41). While (41a) states that there were no traces left by the burglar that are relevant in the context, e.g. traces that could be used as evidence by the police, (41b) denies the existence of traces of any kind whatsoever, i.e. even of traces that would not usually be under consideration such as ones that cannot be used by the police.

(41) a   The burglar didn't leave traces.
     b   The burglar didn't leave any traces.

Kadmon and Landman note that domain widening results in a more informative statement precisely in DE contexts. Because entailment in DE contexts is from sets to subsets and all quantifier domains that are more restricted constitute subsets of the widened domain, an utterance where *any* occurs in a DE environment entails all other statements with a more restricted domain of quantification. It is thus in DE contexts where quantifying over a widened domain makes sense, as this will result in a stronger statement. In upward-entailing contexts, in contrast, using *any* yields a less informative statement, one that is entailed by all alternative assertions with a more restricted domain of quantification.

The observation that the use of an NPI yields a stronger statement precisely in DE contexts raises the question why their occurrence is grammatically restricted in a way such that they obligatorily strengthen a statement and can never be used in non-DE contexts. Kadmon and Landman (1993) account for this restriction by stipulating a strengthening condition as part of the lexical meaning of *any*, but this move has been criticized as being non-compositional. Lahiri (1998) derives the strengthening requirement from the conventional implicature associated with the focus particle *even*. His analysis starts from the observation that indefinite NPIs in Hindi are morphologically made up of a predicate meaning 'one' and the particle *bhii*, corresponding to *even* in English. Since *even* is associated with a conventional implicature to the effect that the proposition it applies to is the least likely (or in other words, the most noteworthy), the combination of *even* and a very general predicate leads to a contradiction in non-DE contexts. It has also been suggested that certain English NPIs, in particular minimizers, are associated with a covert *even* (Heim 1984, Guerzoni, 2004).

Krifka (1995) relates the distributional restrictions of NPIs to the mechanism that derives scalar implicatures. As in Kadmon and Landman's and Lahiri's approach, NPIs are assigned denotations that lead to strong statements in DE environments and to weak statements otherwise. According to Krifka, NPIs denote the most general properties and evoke alternatives that denote more specific properties. *Anybody*, for instance, denotes the general property "person" and evokes more specific alternative properties such as "man" or "woman". Krifka furthermore argues that by virtue of evoking alternatives, NPIs trigger the assertion operator that is also responsible for deriving scalar implicatures. The effect of this operator is to deny all logically stronger alternative propositions. If *anybody* occurs in a non-DE context, as in (42a), the assertoric content, in this case that John saw a person, contradicts the implicatures, namely that John did not see a man, a woman etc. It is simply not possible that John saw a person without also seeing someone of whom a more specific property holds.

(42) a   *John saw anybody.
     b   John didn't see anybody.

In contrast, if an NPI occurs in a DE context like (42b), no implicatures arise that could contradict what is asserted. As (42b) asserts that there is no person who John saw, which entails that there is no particular person seen by John, there are no stronger alternative propositions that the implicatures could deny.

This unified perspective on polarity sensitivity and scalar implicatures might also offer the key to solving another long-standing puzzle. Many indefinite expressions that are NPIs seem to lead a double life as so-called Free Choice (FC) items, whose distribution and interpretation differ markedly from the NPI uses. In its FC use, exemplified in (43), *any* seems to be interpreted as a universal quantifier rather than as an existential as in the NPI uses considered so far.

(43)   Any student in my class can solve this problem set.

It is a long-standing question whether the FC and the NPI uses of *any* correspond to separate lexical items, or whether they can be subsumed under a unified analysis. The fact that this double nature is not a peculiarity of English *any*, and is in fact shared by similar expressions in many other languages, provides a strong indication that FC and NPI uses are two sides of the same coin. While earlier attempts at reducing the ambivalent NPI/FC-nature of *any* to existential and generic readings of indefinites have failed (Kadmon and Landman 1993; Lahiri, 1998), Kratzer and Shimoyama (2002) and Chierchia (2006) have paved the way for a unified analysis of polarity sensitivity and FC effects. Assuming that the central semantic property of indefinites that can be used as both NPIs and FC items is domain widening, Kratzer and Shimoyama (2002) argue that strengthening of an utterance as it happens in DE contexts is only one function of domain widening. Another function of domain widening is avoiding false exhaustivity inferences. By instructing the hearer to consider a wide domain of quantification, the speaker might want to signal that he does not want to rule out any conceivable option. The following example, involving the German indefinite *irgendein* in its FC use, for instance, conveys that any doctor whatsoever is a possible option, and thus that Maria is not choosy regarding the identity of her future husband as long as he is a doctor.

(44)   Maria   will   irgendeinen   Arzt   heiraten.   (German)
       Maria   wants   irgendein   doctor   marry
       "Maria wants to marry a doctor and any doctor whatsoever is a conceivable marriage option to her."

Kratzer and Shimoyama (2002) derive this effect of distributing over the entire domain of quantification as a conversational implicature (a so-called anti-exhaustivity implicature). Like other implicatures, it is predicted to disappear in DE contexts. This explains why the indefinite *irgendein* seems to come in two different varieties despite being one lexical item: the FC reading of *irgendein* arises in certain contexts as an implicature, which is not available in DE contexts, where domain widening instead results in strengthening and the NPI use of *irgendein* as in (45).

(45)   Niemand   hat   irgendeinen   Arzt   gesehen.   (German)
       Nobody   has   irgendein   doctor   seen
       "Nobody saw any doctor."

Although semantic/pragmatic theories of polarity sensitivity open up paths of investigation that have not been available before and have become very popular in recent years, they also face challenges. One concerns the question whether they can offer a unified theory of all NPIs. Analyses in the style of Kadmon and Landman (1993), Krifka (1995) and Lahiri (1998) are tailored to explain the polarity sensitivity of expressions that denote low-scale elements like indefinites and minimizers. While cross-linguistically many NPIs fall in this category, not all do, such as English *either*, *in ages*, *yet* and the modal verbs *hoeven* and *brauchen* ("need") in Dutch and German, respectively.

Another problem of semantic/pragmatic analyses is that they derive the limited distribution of NPIs from semantic or pragmatic principles. While pragmatically driven conditions can usually be overridden, this does not seem to be possible in the case of unlicensed NPIs (see Giannakidou (2011)). Moreover, while analyses in the style of Krifka (1995) and Lahiri (1998) predict sentences with unlicensed occurrences of NPIs to be semantically or pragmatically deviant, they are usually considered to be outright ungrammatical. For these reasons, the study of polarity items has figured prominently in recent debates of where to draw the borderline between syntax, semantics and pragmatics and has subsequently led to reconsiderations of the architecture of grammar (see in particular Chierchia (2004, 2006)).

4 Conclusion and open issues

The study of negation and polarity does not only allow crucial insights into the mechanisms underlying interpretation, but it enables drawing conclusions on how semantics is related to other components of the grammar, in particular to syntax and pragmatics. Despite the enormous progress that has been made in this area over the past fifty years, there are still many open questions. One issue that has been addressed in this chapter is the question what makes a word or expression polarity sensitive and how this explains its distribution. While recent accounts that try to explain the distribution of NPIs from general semantic or pragmatic principles seem promising, there is still a long way to go. Another open issue concerns what is often considered the converse of NPIs, namely positive polarity items (PPIs). While the null hypothesis is that PPIs have opposite licensing requirements from NPIs and are thus acceptable in the complement of the environments where NPIs can occur, several facts have been observed that complicate the picture and have stood in the way of a uniform analysis of negative and positive polarity items (for recent discussions of PPIs see Szabolcsi (2004) and Homer (forthcoming)). In general, the question whether sensitivity to polarity is a uniform phenomenon that can and should be captured by a unified analysis is an open one. To make progress in this area, further polarity phenomena in more languages need to be investigated.

Further reading

Horn, Laurence R. 2001. *A Natural History of Negation*. Stanford: CSLI Publications. Originally published 1989 by University of Chicago Press. A comprehensive overview on research undertaken on negation since Aristotle; contains an exhaustive list of references.

Ladusaw, William A. 1997. Negation and polarity items. In S. Lappin (ed.) *The Handbook of Contemporary Semantic Theory*. Oxford: Blackwell, 321–341. The central research questions on polarity sensitivity are laid out in a particularly elucidative manner in this handbook article.

Giannakidou, Anastasia 2011. Negative and positive polarity items. In C. Maienborn, K. von Heusinger and P. Portner (eds) *Handbook of Semantics*. Berlin/New York: de Gruyter, 1660–1712. This handbook article provides a somewhat different perspective on polarity items than the one presented here.

References

Acquaviva, Paolo 1997. *The Logical Form of Negation: A Study of Operator-Variable Structures in Syntax*. New York/London: Garland.
Baker, Carl Lee (1970). Double negatives. *Linguistic Inquiry* 1, 169–186.
Bartsch, Renate 1973. "Negative Transportation" gibt es nicht. *Linguistische Berichte* 27: 1–7.
Chierchia, Gennaro 2004. Scalar implicatures, polarity phenomena and the syntax/pragmatics interface. In A. Belletti (ed.) *Structures and Beyond*. Oxford: Oxford University Press.
Chierchia, Gennaro 2006. Broaden your views. Implicatures of domain widening and the logicality of language. *Linguistic Inquiry* 37: 535–590.
Fauconnier, Gilles 1979. Implication reversal in natural language. In F. Guenthner and S. J. Schmidt (eds) *Formal Semantics and Pragmatics for Natural Languages*. Dordrecht: Reidel, 289–302.
Fillmore, Charles 1963. The position of embedding transformations in grammar. *Word* 19: 208–231.
von Fintel, Kai 1999. NPI licensing, Strawson entailment, and context dependency. *Journal of Semantics* 16: 97–148.
Gajewski, Jon 2005. *Neg-Raising: Polarity and Presupposition*. PhD thesis, MIT.
Gajewski, Jon 2011. Licensing strong NPIs. *Natural Language Semantics* 19: 109–148.
Giannakidou, Anastasia 1998. *Polarity Sensitivity as (Non)Veridical Dependency*. Amsterdam/Philadelphia: Benjamins.
Giannakidou, Anastasia 2011. Negative and positive polarity items. In C. Maienborn, K. von Heusinger and P. Portner (eds) *Handbook of Semantics*. Berlin/New York: de Gruyter, 1660–1712.
Guerzoni, Elena 2004. Even-NPIs in yes/no questions. *Natural Language Semantics* 12: 319–343.
Haegeman, Liliane and Raffaella Zanuttini 1996. Negative concord in West Flemish. In A. Belletti and L. Rizzi (eds) *Parameters and Functional Heads. Essays in Comparative Syntax*. Oxford: Oxford University Press, 117–179.
Heim, Irene 1984. A note on negative polarity and downward entailingness. In C. Jones and P. Sells (eds) *Proceedings of NELS 14*. Amherst: University of Massachusetts, 98–107.
Heim, Irene 2008. Decomposing antonyms? In A. Grønn (ed.) *Proceedings of SuB12*. Oslo: ILOS, 212–222.
Herburger, Elena 2001. The negative concord puzzle revisited. *Natural Language Semantics* 9: 289–333.
Hoeksema, Jack 2000. Negative polarity items: triggering, scope, and c-command. In L. Horn and Y. Kato (eds) *Negation and Polarity*. Oxford: Oxford University Press, 115–146.
Homer, Vincent forthcoming. Domains of polarity items. *Journal of Semantics*.
Horn, Laurence R. 1978. Remarks on neg-raising. In P. Cole (ed.) *Syntax and Semantics 9: Pragmatics*. New York: Academic Press, 129–220.
Horn, Laurence R. 1985. Metalinguistic negation and pragmatic ambiguity. *Language* 61: 121–174.
Horn, Laurence R. 2001. *A Natural History of Negation*. Stanford: CSLI Publications. Originally published 1989 by University of Chicago Press.
Kadmon, Nirit and Fred Landman 1993. Any. *Linguistics and Philosophy* 16: 354–422.
Klima, Edward S. 1964. Negation in English. In J. A. Fodor and J. J. Katz (eds) *The Structure of Language*. Englewood Cliffs, NJ: Prentice-Hall, 246–323.
Kratzer, Angelika and Junko Shimoyama 2002. Indeterminate pronouns: the view from Japanese. In Y. Otso (ed.) *Proceedings of the Third Tokyo Conference on Psycholinguistics*. Tokyo: Hituzi Syobo, 1–25.
Krifka, Manfred 1995. The semantics and pragmatics of polarity items. *Linguistic Analysis* 25: 209–258.
Ladusaw, William A. 1979. *Polarity Sensitivity as Inherent Scope Relations*. PhD thesis, University of Texas at Austin. Published 1980 by Garland, New York.
Ladusaw, William A. 1992. Expressing negation. In C. Barker and D. Dowty (eds) *Proceedings of SALT II. Ohio State Working Papers in Linguistics* 40. Columbus: Ohio State University, 237–259.
Ladusaw, William A. 1997. Negation and polarity items. In S. Lappin (ed.) *The Handbook of Contemporary Semantic Theory*. Oxford: Blackwell, 321–341.
Lahiri, Utpal 1998. Focus and negative polarity in Hindi. *Natural Language Semantics* 6: 57–123.

Laka, Itziar 1990. *Negation in Syntax: On the Nature of Functional Categories and Projections*. PhD thesis, MIT.

Linebarger, Marcia C. 1987. Negative polarity and grammatical representation. *Linguistics and Philosophy* 10: 325–387.

Payne, John R. 1985. Negation. In T. Shopen (ed.) *Language Typology and Syntactic Description*. Cambridge: Cambridge University Press, 197–242.

Penka, Doris 2011. *Negative Indefinites*. Oxford/New York: Oxford University Press.

Progovac, Ljiljana 1994. *Negative and Positive Polarity: A Binding Approach*. Cambridge: Cambridge University Press.

van Rooy, Robert 2003. Negative polarity items in questions: strength as relevance. *Journal of Semantics* 20: 239–274.

Strawson, P. F. 1952. *Introduction to Logical Theory*. London: Methuen.

de Swart, Henriette and Ivan A. Sag 2002. Negation and negative concord in Romance. *Linguistics and Philosophy* 25: 373–417.

Szabolcsi, Anna 2004. Positive polarity – negative polarity. *Natural Language and Linguistic Theory* 22: 409–452.

van der Wouden, Ton 1997. *Negative Contexts. Collocation, Polarity and Multiple Negation*. London/New York: Routledge.

Zeijlstra, Hedde 2004. *Sentential Negation and Negative Concord*. PhD thesis, University of Amsterdam.

Zwarts, Frans 1995. Nonveridical contexts. *Linguistic Analysis* 25: 286–312.

Zwarts, Frans 1996. A hierarchy of negative expressions. In H. Wansing (ed.) *Negation: A Notion in Focus*. Berlin: de Gruyter, 169–194.

Related topics

Chapter 4, Foundations of formal semantics; Chapter 18, Varieties of quantification.

18
Varieties of quantification

Anna Szabolcsi

1 What is a quantifier in natural language?

In his study of the word *both*, the philosopher M. Glanzberg addresses this question in the following way.

> We often think about quantifiers via intuitions about kinds of thoughts. Certain terms are naturally used to express singular thoughts, and appear to do so by contributing objects to the thoughts expressed. Other terms are naturally used to express general thoughts, and appear to do so by contributing higher-order properties to the thoughts expressed. Viewed this way, the main condition on whether a term is a quantifier or not is whether its semantic value is an object or a higher-order property. At least, these provide necessary conditions. [. . .] We also often think about quantifiers in terms of a range of linguistic features, including semantic value, presupposition, scope, binding, syntactic distribution, and many others. [. . .] *[B]oth* appears quantificational by some linguistic standards, and yet appears object-denoting by standards based on intuitions about the kinds of thoughts it expresses. It can appear this way, I shall argue, because the notion of quantification in natural language is in fact the intersection of a number of features, which do not always group together in the same ways, and do not always group together precisely in accord with our intuitions about expressing singular and general thoughts.
>
> (Glanzberg 2008: 208)

On this view, which we also share, the subject matter of the study of quantification in natural language is defined and redefined as research progresses; it is not defined by some antecedently conceived distinction in philosophical logic.

Montague (1974), a classic that launched the enterprise of compositional formal semantics, offered an approach that does not force one to start with assigning expressions like *Arach*, *the dragon*, *every dragon*, *both dragons*, and their brothers to different and irreconcilable sides of the quantificational barricade. Montague's theory therefore explained how the above expressions can be grammatically interchangeable in the majority of sentences in which they occur and yet contribute to the truth conditions of those sentences in their own ways. The approach, which crucially used generalized quantifiers as noun phrase denotations, dominated the 1970s and 1980s, and was extended to capture the commonalities in quantification over individuals, events and times (*always*, *usually*, *twice*), and worlds (*must* and *may*, *necessarily*, *probably*, and *possibly*).

The second major wave of research, starting in the 1990s and continuing as we speak, has uncovered complex and thorough-going differences in the behaviour of the above expressions; among them, the differences hinted at in the Glanzberg quote above. Three major classes of expressions emerged: distributive universals, extra-wide scoping plain indefinites, and modified numeral or counting quantifiers. Their ranks have been joined by event-related quantification, exemplified by verbal pluractionality and numeral phrase pluralization. Although many of the new results, once obtained, could be formalized using generalized quantifier theory, other methods have proved more conducive to discovery and to compositional analysis.

The third major wave, starting around 2000, is focusing on quantifier-phrase-internal and even quantifier-word-internal compositionality.

The discussion will track these strands of research. More detailed discussion can be found in Szabolcsi (2010); the relevant chapters will be pointed out.

2 Uniformity: generalized quantifiers

Consider the pairs *Arach* vs. *every dragon*, *on the 1st of May* vs. *always*, and *actually/in the actual world* vs. *obligatorily/must*. The members of each pair have similar grammatical behaviour. In addition, the first member of each pair refers to a particular individual, time, or world, and the second member is classically quantificational. It would be desirable to have an interpretive strategy that is compatible with all these similarities without obliterating the differences. Generalized quantifier theory offers such a strategy. A generalized quantifier is a semantic object (i.e. not a quantifier phrase). It is a set of properties of individuals, events, times, or worlds. Generalized quantifiers serve as a common denominator for the denotations of diverse expressions of the same category, and moreover offer a mechanics of interpretation that is uniformly applicable across several different categories.

(1) *Arach* belches fire.
 the property of belching fire is an element of *the set of properties that Arach has*

(2) *Every dragon* belches fire.
 the property of belching fire is an element of *the set of properties that every dragon has*

(3) *On the 1st of May* Ladro snacked.
 an event of Ladro's snacking is an element of *the set of events that occurred on the 1st of May*

(4) *Always, when he is at home*, Ladro snacks.
 an event of Ladro's snacking is an element of *the set of events that occur whenever Ladro is at home*

(5) Ladro {*actually / in fact*} thieves.
 the fact of Ladro's thieving is an element of *the set of facts that obtain in the actual world*

(6) Ladro *must* thieve.
 the fact of Ladro's thieving is an element of *the set of facts that obtain in every world in which Ladro does what he is obliged to*

Using the lambda operator to perform abstraction, the prose in (1) and (2) can be formalized as follows, in a simplified notation in the style of Heim and Kratzer (1998); analogous representations can be devised for the adverbs and modals in (3) through (6), and for their interaction with other scope-bearing expressions. Double-bracketing, as in ⟦Arach⟧, signifies the denotation of the enclosed expression. *x*, *y*, *z* are variables over individuals (type e), *P* is a variable over properties, extensionally, sets (type ⟨e,t⟩). Notice that the verb phrase's denotation is asserted to be an element (∈) of the subject's denotation, irrespective of whether the subject is a name or a universal.

(7) ⟦Arach⟧(⟦belch_fire⟧) = λx_e. belch_fire(x)=True ∈ $\lambda P_{\langle e,t \rangle}$. P(arach)=True
(8) ⟦every dragon⟧(⟦belch_fire⟧) = λx_e. belch_fire(x)=True ∈ $\lambda P_{\langle e,t \rangle}$. for all dragons y_e. P(y)=True

The same denotations ⟦Arach⟧ and ⟦every dragon⟧ are at work when these expressions occur in the direct object position. The object and the subject denotations combine with properties one at a time. Suppose we have,

(9) Ladro tricked every dragon.
(10) Some troll tricked every dragon.

In the interpretation of (9), the property λx_e. *belch_fire(x)=True* (being one that belches fire) that occurs in (7) and (8) is replaced by λx_e. *trick(ladro, x)=True* (being one that is tricked by Ladro), so that this property is attributed to every dragon. What about (10)? If we use the analogous property λx_e.*for some troll y_e. trick(y, x)=True*, then being tricked by some troll or other is attributed to every dragon. Here the subject finds itself within the scope of the object, because the denotation of the subject is incorporated into the definition of the property that is asserted to be an element of the generalized quantifier that the object denotes. The scope relation between quantifier phrases is mediated by the relation between generalized quantifiers and their elements.

(11) Generalized quantifiers and their elements: operators and their scopes
 A quantifier phrase denotes a set of properties. Its scope is that stretch of the sentence that denotes a property that is asserted to be an element of that set.

The "subject within the scope of the object" reading just discussed has the following semantic constituent structure:

(12)

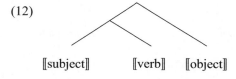

⟦subject⟧   ⟦verb⟧   ⟦object⟧

We haven't said how the properties λx_e. *trick(ladro, x)=True* and λx_e.*for some troll y_e. trick(y, x)=True* are assembled. This is a somewhat technical point which different theories will implement differently: with quantifying-in (Montague 1974), Quantifier Raising (May 1985, Heim and Kratzer 1998), type-lifting applied to verbs (Hendriks 1993), type-lifting applied to quantificational expressions in a continuation semantics (Barker 2002), and so on. Let's say that in the first step λz_e. *trick(z, x_e)=True* is asserted to be an element of ⟦Ladro⟧ or ⟦some troll⟧, i.e. the property of tricking the individual *x* is attributed to Ladro or some troll; subsequently (and this is somewhat sloppy) the variable *x* is abstracted over to form the desired properties.

If, instead, the denotation of the direct object, ⟦every dragon⟧ combines with $\lambda x_e.\ trick(z_e, x)=True$ (the property of being tricked by the individual z), then z can be subsequently abstracted over, forming $\lambda z_e.for\ all\ dragons\ y_e.\ trick(z, y)=True$ (the property of tricking every dragon). If this derivation is chosen, the object *every dragon* will find itself within the scope of the subject. Now the semantic constituent structure will be this:

(13)

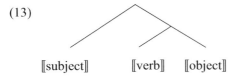

⟦subject⟧   ⟦verb⟧   ⟦object⟧

Generalized quantifier theory does not only provide a uniform interpretation mechanism for a large and varied set of expressions. Generalized quantifiers are semantic objects well suited for the interpretation of the Boolean compounding (conjunction, disjunction, negation) of quantifiers. For example,

(14) ⟦every dragon and some thief⟧ = ⟦every dragon⟧∩⟦some thief⟧ =
$\lambda P_{\langle e,t \rangle}$.(for all dragons x_e. P(x)=True) and (for some thief x_e. P(x)=True)

(15) ⟦on May 1st but not always⟧ = ⟦on May 1st⟧∩(~⟦always⟧)

Generalized quantifiers also facilitate detecting and studying linguistically important semantic properties, again across categories. Consider the licensing of negative polarity items (*any more* . . .):

(16) No dragons belched any more fire.
(17) Arach never belched any more fire.
(18) *Every dragon belched any more fire.

The rough consensus is that downward entailingness (entailment from supersets to subsets) is the semantic property that unites NPI-licensors. This property can be conveniently defined using the denotations we are assuming. Let e be a variable over events (type v), and Q a variable over event-properties (type ⟨v,t⟩).

(19) An expression E is downward entailing iff B∈⟦E⟧ entails A∈⟦E⟧, whenever A⊆B.

(20) $\lambda x_e.fly(x)=True \subseteq \lambda x_e.move(x)=True$

(21) ⟦no dragons⟧ is downward entailing, because
$\lambda x_e.move(x)=True \in \lambda P_{\langle e,t \rangle}.$ for no dragons y_e. P(y)=True entails
$\lambda x_e.fly(x)=True \in \lambda P_{\langle e,t \rangle}.$ for no dragons y_e. P(y)=True.

(22) ⟦never⟧ is downward entailing, because
$\lambda e_v.Arach\_move(e) \in \lambda Q_{\langle v,t \rangle}.$ for no $e_v.Q(e)=True$ entails
$\lambda e_v.Arach\_fly(e) \in \lambda Q_{\langle v,t \rangle}.$ for no $e_v.Q(e)=True$.

(23) ⟦every dragon⟧ is not downward entailing, because
$\lambda x_e.move(x)=True \in \lambda P_{\langle e,t \rangle}.$ for all dragons y_e. P(y)=True does not entail
$\lambda x_e.fly(x)=True \in \lambda P_{\langle e,t \rangle}.$ for all dragons y_e. P(y)=True.

We have just shown that ⟦no dragons⟧ and ⟦never⟧ have the semantic property that licenses NPIs, but ⟦every dragon⟧ does not. Notice that if we were using predicate logic, we might be able to write formulae whose truth conditions match those of the full English sentences, but we would not be able to assign explicit denotations to subsentential expressions and to check their semantic properties.

It is important to see that all the above can be done if we take the denotations ⟦no dragon⟧, ⟦every dragon⟧, and so on to be given; we do not need to know whether they are composed of parts, what the parts are, and what they mean. But in many cases we can go further. The part of the quantifier phrase that determines its denotational semantic properties is what generalized quantifier theory calls a (semantic) determiner. Semantic determiners denote relations between two sets, i.e. properties. For example:

(24) ⟦every⟧(A)(B)=True iff A is a subset of B.
⟦no⟧(A)(B)=True iff the intersection of A and B is empty.
⟦more than one⟧(A)(B)=True iff the intersection of A and B has more than one element.

This description suggests that the sets A and B are on a par. But in fact the relations denoted by natural language determiners are special in that they are restricted by one of the sets, A: in checking the truth of ⟦det⟧(A)(B) one never needs to look beyond the set A. Elements of B that are not in A do not play a role, nor do things that are in neither A nor B. (Technically, restrictedness is a combination of conservativity and extension; see Barwise and Cooper (1981).) It turns out that this set A is the denotation of the nominal segment of the noun phrase, and thus the semantic asymmetry in the roles of the two sets nicely matches the asymmetry in syntactic constituency.

(25)

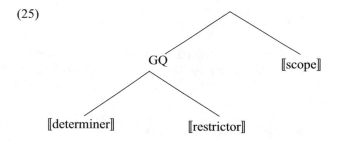

It is to be noted that not all noun phrases denote generalized quantifiers; the dependent character of those underlined in (26) prevents them from doing so; they require extensions of the theory. The same holds for meanings that cannot be built step by step but require, instead, for two or more quantifiers to form a unit and combine with a relation in one fell swoop, illustrated in (27).

(26) The dragons are proud of {themselves/each other}
Every dragon lives in {a different/the same} cave [than/as the other dragons].
Zwerg and Ladro saw two dragons each.

(27) Six bridegrooms led six brides to the altar.
"six couples got married"
Different people have different tastes.
"pairs of people do not/need not have the same taste"

See Barwise and Cooper (1981), Keenan (1996), Keenan and Westerståhl (1997), Barker (2007), and Szabolcsi (2010: chapters 2–5) for discussion of generalized quantifiers as well as the cases above that require extensions of the theory, and Kratzer (1991) and de Swart (1991) for modals and adverbs of quantification.

3 Diversity in the behaviour of quantifiers

The uniform grammatical treatment afforded by generalized quantifier theory is a great advantage, and we have just seen that it correctly preserves differences between expressions that are directly denotational in nature, e.g. whether the expression is downward entailing or not. But at least two natural questions arise now. First, suppose we find differences in the behaviour of noun phrases. Do they fall out from the differences between the generalized quantifiers they denote, in combination with whatever syntax or pragmatics independently contribute to the meaning of the sentence? Second, does the internal composition of semantic determiners matter more than the picture in (24) and (25) suggests?

At least three interesting classes have emerged from the study of differential behaviour: plain indefinites, distributive universals, and modified numerals or counters; distributive numerals then form a bridge to the domain of pluractionality. In what follows we survey some of the most important findings. What is their theoretical consequence for generalized quantifier theory? It turns out that the findings do not follow from the insights that the theory offers, although they could often be encoded as "annotations" on the pertinent lexical items. That means that generalized quantifier theory remains a useful tool for grammars that are satisfied with the granularity that it offers. But it is limited in its ability to guide the research leading to new discoveries, and so current work is often not framed in its terms. See general discussion in Szabolcsi (2010: chapter 6).

The following convention is used in the presentation of examples. When a reading is prefixed with OK or #, that indicates that the given reading is available or unavailable, and does not imply anything about whether the example has other readings. This allows us to list and annotate only those readings of the examples that are relevant to the discussion.

3.1 Plain indefinites

The examples below involve plural indefinites, because only those can illustrate the full range of relevant facts. Definites share many properties with plain indefinites.

Indefinites can take unbounded ("extra-wide") scope, i.e. existential import may extend outside the clause, even the island, that the indefinite is contained in.

(28) If Arach suspects that two dwarves snuck in, he gives out a roar.
    OK   if Arach suspects that there are two dwarves that snuck in . . .
    OK   if there are two dwarves that Arach suspects snuck in . . .
    OK   there are two dwarves such that if Arach suspects they snuck in . . .

Indefinites support discourse anaphora that parallels their existential import. For example, the following discourse is acceptable, but it requires *two dwarves* to have matrix-clausal existential import in the first sentence:

(29) If Arach suspects that <u>two dwarves</u> snuck in, he gives out a roar. {The two dwarves/they} had given him trouble in the past.
    OK   there are two dwarves such that if Arach suspects . . .

Notice that *they* above can refer to just the two particular dwarves, like *the two dwarves* does. It does not have to refer to all dwarves that may have snuck in.

On the other hand, whichever interpretation of (28) we choose, the sentence only entails Arach's giving out of a single roar (per suspicious situation), not one roar per dwarf, altogether two (per suspicious situation). In other words, no matter how broad its existential import, *two dwarves* in (29) cannot make *a roar* referentially dependent. The unbounded "existential scope" (existential import and discourse-referent introducing ability) of plain indefinites contrasts with their clause-bounded "distributive scope".

Within its own clause the plural indefinite is capable of inducing referential variation, observing the hierarchy Subject > Indirect object/Adjunct > Direct object, when neither it nor its target is partitive (see Beghelli (1997) for further details). In (30), quadruples of elves easily vary with dwarves but not with dragons; triples of dragons easily vary with dwarves and/or elves; pairs of dwarves do not vary at all.

(30) Two dwarves reported three dragons to four elves.

Plural indefinites also support collective and cumulative readings:

(31) Two dwarves make a good team.
(32) Two dwarves slayed five dragons between them.

Among singular indefinites, especially the type of *a certain dwarf* has unbounded existential import and supports (singular) discourse anaphora as *two dwarves* does, but given singularity, the question of inducing referential variation and supporting collective or cumulative readings does not arise.

(33) If Arach suspects that <u>a certain dwarf</u> snuck in, he gives out a roar. {<u>The dwarf/he</u>} had given him trouble in the past.

In the past two decades the standard treatment of these properties of plain indefinites has had two crucial components. Their "existential scope" is due to existential closure, effected in a structure-building manner; given that it is syntactically unbounded, it cannot be a product of movement. *Two dwarves* itself denotes a set of two-dwarf pluralities; one of these pluralities is selected by a choice function variable; existential closure applies to this variable. (Alternatively, the value of the choice function variable is supplied by the context and "existential scope" is just an inference.) Their "distributive scope" is due to a distributive operator on the predicate. In other words, plain indefinites are not operators; whatever operator-like behaviour they exhibit is due to the ministrations of some silent helper.

The distributive operator is notated as * and its working is defined in (35).

(34) Two dwarves had a beer.
    $\exists$f. f is a choice function and *⟦had_a_beer⟧(f(⟦two⟧(⟦dwarves⟧)))=True

(35) *P(x)=True if P holds of every atomic part of x; *P(x)=False if P does not hold of any atomic part of x; undefined otherwise.

See Kamp and Reyle (1993), Reinhart (1997), Kratzer (1998), Winter (2001), Schlenker (2006), and Szabolcsi (2010: chapters 7–9) for discussion.

However, various problems have been identified in connection with the use of choice functions in the treatment of unbounded existential scope. Heim (2011) concludes,

> If Schwarz (2001, 2004) is right, we may have to concede what Fodor and Sag (1982) and most subsequent authors wanted to avoid: indefinites are existential quantifiers that enjoy a greater degree of scopal mobility than other kinds of quantificational DPs.
>
> (Heim 2011: 1022)

3.2 Distributive universals

The label serves to set apart *every dragon* and *each dragon* from *all dragons* (a generic of sorts; compare #*All dragons are grouchy today* with *Every dragon is grouchy today*) and from *all the dragons* (a definite plural; compare *All the dragons collided* with #*Every dragon collided*). Singular universal would also be a possible preliminary label, although it is not obvious how it would subsume *every five dragons*. We start with data and then turn to analyses.

Distributive universals of the *each dragon* type do, and those of the *every dragon* type do not, take extra-clausal distributive scope:

(36) Ask someone whether every dragon is dangerous.
  #   for every dragon, ask someone whether it is dangerous

(37) Ask someone whether each dragon is dangerous.
  OK for each dragon, ask someone whether it is dangerous

Neither type supports singular discourse anaphora. However, both have unbounded existential import with respect to their nominal restrictions and support matching plural discourse anaphora, like indefinites do.

(38) {Every / Each} dragon was sitting on a heap. #It was guarding treasure.

(39) Ladro imagined that {every / each} dragon was at home. But they were out.
  OK there was a set of dragons, viz. the set of all dragons, and Ladro imagined that they were at home; but those dragons were out.

Neither type supports collective readings, nor cumulative ones, at least not when in subject position:

(40) *{Every / each} dragon is a good team.

(41) {Every / each} dragon ate ten ponies.
  #   the dragons ate ten ponies between them
  OK the dragons ate ten ponies each

The mere fact that *every / each dragon* supports the distributive "ate ten ponies each" reading is not very remarkable; compare:

(42) {Two dragons / most of the dragons / at most two dragons} ate ten ponies.
  OK . . . ate ten ponies each

Much more interesting are the following facts, which seem to be unique to distributive universals.

Distributive universals enable the sentence-internal reading of singular *a different cave*. The plurals in (44) only support a contextual reading of it.

(43) {Every / each} dragon lives in a different cave.
OK ... in a cave that is different from where the other dragons live

(44) {All the / most / ten / more than five} dragons live in a different cave.
\# ... in a cave that is different from where the other dragons live
OK ... in a cave that is different from one mentioned earlier

Distributive universals support a reading of matrix questions that can be answered with a list of pairs, not only with an individual or functional answer. A word of warning is in order here. Some speakers' initial response may be that (46) can also be answered with a list of pairs and thus the # is incorrect. However, in (46) the list is not a grammatically conditioned answer, merely a cooperative way of spelling out a cumulative answer, and indeed many speakers only accept it if the wh-expression is semantically non-singular (plural *what dishes*, or unmarked *what*).

(45) What dish did {every / each} dwarf want?
OK Zwerg wanted stew, Kerdil a pie, ...

(46) What dish did {the / most / ten / more than five} dwarves want?
\# Zwerg wanted stew, Kerdil a pie, ...
OK A roast.
OK Their own favourite dishes.

The above generalizations are discussed extensively in multiple articles in Szabolcsi (1997a).
Distributive universals support unproblematic "donkey-sentences", i.e. sentences in which an indefinite within the restriction of the quantifier is referred back to with a singular pronoun in the scope of the quantifier (the main clause), as in (47). In contrast, speakers find the plural examples in (48) either unacceptable or confusing in situations where dwarves own multiple donkeys (Kamp and Reyle 1993; Kanazawa 1994, 2001).

(47) {every / each} dwarf who owns <u>a donkey</u> feeds <u>it</u>.
OK every dwarf feeds whatever donkey(s) he owns

(48) ?{The / most / ten / more than five} dwarves who own <u>a donkey</u> feed <u>it</u>.

Brasoveanu (2008, 2010) pulled together the above observations and added new ones, initiating an interesting new line of research. One suggestive example is as follows:

(49) Every dwarf who loaded a donkey with provisions fastened its burden to its back.

We paraphrased (47) using "whatever donkey(s) he owns" – but (49) does not easily lend itself to that treatment. In particular, the interpretation must synchronize individual donkeys, their burdens, and their backs. Brasoveanu (2012) observes that a similar synchronization occurs in conditionals, *when(ever)*-clauses, and classical multiple correlatives in South-Asian and Slavic languages:

(50) "whenever a dwarf loaded a donkey with provisions, that dwarf fastened that donkey's burden to that donkey's back"

We now turn to analyses. Beghelli and Stowell (1997) proposed that *every/each dragon* is similar to *the dragons* in that it contributes only a set of individuals to the interpretation of the sentence. This set is the set of all dragons. It can be computed as the denotation of the nominal restriction of the determiner, *dragon(s)*. *Every/each dragon* and *the dragons* differ in how sentences that contain these expressions obtain their distributive readings. Distributive readings of *the dragons* are due to the * operator that modifies the predicate, exactly as in (34) and (35), but the presence of * is optional. In contrast, *every/each dragon* must associate with a syntactic functional head Dist, whose semantic content, as its name suggests, is a distributive operator. On Beghelli and Stowell's analysis *every* and *each* themselves are not distributive operators; instead, they force the association of their noun phrases with a clause-level distributive operator, much like "negative morphemes" in negative concord items are themselves not negative (*pace* their glosses): instead, they force association with an overt or null clause-level negative operator.

(51) Nikto   nichego   ne   videl.   (Russian)
     nobody   nothing   not   saw
     "Nobody saw anything"

(52) Personne   ∅   a vu   rien.   (French)
     nobody   neg   saw   nothing
     "Nobody saw anything"

For general discussion, see Szabolcsi (2010: chapter 8).

The significant innovation that Brasoveanu (2008, 2010, 2012) introduces pertains to the encoding of distributivity. On Brasoveanu's theory, the domain of quantification in sentences with *every* and *each* is not a set of individuals, but a set of dependencies between individuals (technically, variable assignments, or sequences). The anaphoric connections, pair-list answers, and internal readings of *a different* discussed above all live off of those dependencies.

The core of the analysis revives the early 1980s Kamp/Heim analysis of quantificational determiners in terms of case-quantification, following Lewis's (1975) proposal for adverbs of quantification, where a "case" is an n-tuple of individuals. That analysis was intended to be general, and it was quickly abandoned, because it was marred by the so-called proportion problem. The determiner *most (of the)* counts donkey-owning dwarves; only adverbs count dwarf–donkey pairs. Therefore the truth conditions differ.

(53) Most (of the) dwarves who own a donkey feed it.
(54) {For the most part / usually}, if a dwarf owns a donkey, he feeds it.

The present reincarnation does not involve proportional determiners, and so the same problem does not arise. The unification of a wide range of phenomena that are specific for distributive universals is a remarkable payoff. The compositional aspects of the analysis are not yet obvious, and may not be simple.

3.3 Modified numeral or counting quantifiers

Kamp and Reyle (1993) accorded modified numerals the same quantificational treatment as distributive universals (box-splitting, in DRT terms); Beghelli and Stowell (1997) and Szabolcsi (1997b) keep them apart both from plain indefinites and from distributive universals. The three-way separation is necessary, because noun phrases such as *at least/at most five dragons*, *more/fewer than five dragons*, *five or more dragons*, [$_{Focus}$ *five*] *dragons*, etc. do not have the kind of unbounded ("extra-wide") existential scope that plain indefinites have, and they do not license the singular *a different* or matrix pair-list readings that distributive universals do:

(55) If Arach suspects that more than five dwarves snuck in, he gives out a roar.
  OK if Arach suspects that there are more than five dwarves that snuck in ...
  # if there are more than five dwarves that Arach suspects snuck in ...
  # there are more than five dwarves such that if Arach suspects they snuck in ...

(56) More than five dwarves came from a different village.
  # ... from villages different from each other's

(57) What dish do more than five dwarves want?
  # Zwerg wants stew, Kerdil a pie, ...

They are also poor clause-internal inverse scope takers, at least in the most frequently studied configuration in (58). In this respect they contrast with distributive universals (Liu 1997, Beghelli and Stowell 1997). But the same does not carry over to (59) and (60), as was observed in Takahashi (2006).

(58) Every dragon saw more than five dwarves.
  # there are more than five dwarves that every dragon saw

(59) Tovenaar showed every dwarf to more than five elves.
  OK ... there are more than five elves to whom Tovenaar showed every dwarf

(60) Tovenaar showed more than five dwarves to every elf.
  OK ... there are more than five dwarves that Tovenaar showed to every elf

The most intriguing property of this class is that it lays bare the limitations of a purely truth-conditional account. The class of modified numerals or counting quantifiers cannot be delimited in truth-conditional terms, and even within the class, truth-conditionally equivalent members behave differently. Here is a sampler.

Although *most of the* and *more than 50% of the* are equivalent according to Barwise and Cooper (1981), only noun phrases determined by the latter host binominal *each* (Sutton 1993). Szabolcsi (1997b, 2010: chapter 10) finds that admitting binominal *each* is a good diagnostic of counting quantifiers in English:

(61) *The dragons saw most of the dwarves each.
(62) The dragons saw more than 50% of the dwarves each.

Among counting quantifiers, although *at least two* and *more than one* are logically equivalent, the reciprocal *each other* cares about which is used (Hackl 2002):

(63) At least two dwarves shook hands [with each other].
(64) # More than one dwarf shook hands [with each other].

At most n and *at least n* are epistemic modal varieties of the plain indefinite containing *n*, in contrast to *fewer than n* and *more than n*. This may explain their differences in supporting *namely*-anaphora and in interaction with possibility modals (Geurts and Nouwen 2007):

(65) Ladro invited {at most two / at least two} friends, namely Zwerg and Medve.

(66) ?Ladro invited {fewer than four / more than two} friends, namely Tovenaar, Zwerg, and Medve.

(67) The pony can carry fewer than six sacks.
    OK   not able/allowed to carry more than five
    OK   able/allowed to carry not more than five

(68) The pony can carry at most five sacks.
    OK   not able/allowed to carry more than five
    #   able/allowed to carry not more than five

In addition to such contrasts in acceptability, Koster-Moeller et al. (2008), Hackl (2009), and Lidz et al. (2011) showed that people process some of these expressions differently even if they are logically equivalent. What processing strategies experimental subjects use can be detected by presenting the verification task in different ways that make it easier or more difficult to perform, depending on what strategy the subject uses. When asked to verify statements like *Most/More than half/More than ten of the dots are blue*, experimental subjects were found to persist in using counting strategies that tracked the composition of the expressions, even when that made performing the verification task more difficult. Generalizing, this leads to some version of the following hypothesis:

(69) Interface Transparency Thesis (Lidz et al. 2011: 229):
Speakers exhibit a bias towards the verification procedures provided by canonical specifications of truth conditions.

To be sure, the significance of syntactico-semantic composition that underlies the canonical specifications of truth conditions is probably not particular to counting quantifiers. These expressions make the fact more conspicuous, because they have more varied and more complex structures than some other quantified expressions. Complexity is especially clear in the case of expressions like *more than five dragons* and *the most dragons*, which involve comparisons and degree quantification (Heim 2001; Hackl 2009). Takahashi's (2006) account of the inverse scoping data, cf. (51)–(53), also exploits the syntactic complexity associated with degree quantification. The basic idea is that these expressions comprise two quantifiers that part ways in the course of the syntactico-semantic derivation but may only do so subject to severe constraints. See Szabolcsi (2010: chapters 10 and 11) for further discussion.

Generalized quantifier theory is a good tool for studying those properties of noun phrases that can be captured in truth-conditional terms, but would not be a particularly good tool for studying these newly discovered properties.

3.4 Distributive numerals and pluractionality

The so-called binominal *each* construction in English is clearly related to both distributive quantification and to counting quantifiers. On one hand, it excludes collective ("all together") and cumulative ("between them") readings. On the other hand, as Sutton (1993) observed, it does not suffice for the host to be indefinite; it must be a counting quantifier:

(70) *Three dragons captured {those/most of the} dwarves each.
(71) Three dragons captured {five/few/more than 70%} of the dwarves each.
(72) *Three dragons captured {dwarves/no dwarves} each.
(73) Three dragons captured {one/?a} dwarf each.

The acceptable sentences mean that each dragon captured n (% of the) dwarves, with the addition that they did not capture the same dwarves; i.e. *n (% of the) dwarves* takes narrow scope and exhibits some variation. Although it is interesting that distributivity is marked on the distributed share, in English this seems like the end of the story. In many other languages, however, similar sentences can be true in a wider range of situations. According to Balusu (2005), the Telugu sentence in (74) can be true in any of the situations described in (75).

(74) ii   pilla-lu   renDu renDu   kootu-lu-ni   cuus-ee-ru
     these   kid.pl   two   two   monkey.pl.acc   see.past.3pl
     lit. "These kids saw two two monkeys"

(75) OK these kids saw two monkeys each
     OK these kids (jointly or severally) saw two monkeys at each location
     OK these kids (jointly or severally) saw two monkeys at each interval

What we see is that pairs of monkeys can be distributed over event-participants (kids), but also over contextually individuated spatial or temporal parts of the event. To wit, the following is an equally good sentence in Telugu:

(76) renDu renDu   kootu-lu   egir-i-niyyi
     two two   monkey.pl   jump.past.3pl
     lit. "Two two monkeys jumped"

(77) OK two monkeys jumped at each location
     OK two monkeys jumped at each interval

Balusu analyzes distributive numeral reduplication as the pluralization of the denotation of a numeral phrase, derived by distribution over parts of an event. Balusu also argues that the reading that (76) shares with English sentences like *The kids saw two monkeys each* does not involve direct distribution over kids; instead, it is a special case in which kids and events correspond one-to-one.

Szabolcsi (2010: chapter 8.4) observes that distributive numeral reduplication belongs to the same family of formal devices as the *-ssik* suffix (Korean), *-nka* (Quechua), *-na* (Basque), *po* (Russian), *zutsu* (Japanese), and *jeweils* (German); see the references there. We add here that, when properly spelled out, the interpretation requires the existence of multiple contextually individuated events (event-parts), and therefore locate the phenomenon in an even larger family, the domain of pluractionality.

The term pluractionality refers to event-pluralization, which may manifest itself in multiple event-participants or multiple occurrences of the event over time or at different locations (Lasersohn 1995). Its marking, by inflection, reduplication, or particles, may appear on verbs, on noun phrases, or on numerals; measure phrase split in Japanese seems like another event-pluralizing device (Nakanishi 2007). In ǂHoian, a Khoisan language, the same plural marker applies to verbs and nouns (Collins 2001). Therefore pluractionality offers an especially striking example of the unity of nominal quantification and event quantification.

For both careful cross-linguistic documentation and theoretical analysis, see Matthewson (2000), Zimmermann (2003), Champollion (2012), Cable (2012), and Henderson (2012), among many other pieces in the rapidly growing literature.

4 Compositionality in quantifier words and future directions

Many semanticists intend their research to be guided by the principle of compositionality (see Chapter 24).

(78) The meaning of a complex expression is a function of the meanings of its parts and how they are put together.

In section 2 we saw that generalized quantifier theory gives excellent insights into how the larger constituents (subject, object, etc.) contribute to semantic interpretation. On the other hand, it does not help much with investigating the impact of the internal composition of quantifier phrases; see the discussion in section 3, especially towards the end of 3.3. So different theories offer compositional insights of different granularity. Let us now supplement the above considerations with the following question.

(79) Are (phonological) words the smallest parts that a compositional grammar should take into account? If not, what smaller parts are to be recognized?

Although there is no doctrine that says that word meanings are the minimal building blocks of sentence meanings, in practice semanticists often make that assumption. For example, we readily assign very complex interpretations to quantificational words without specifying how the semantic ingredients are anchored in the components of those words. That practice is probably motivated by the time-honoured lexicalist tradition in syntax. It is therefore of some interest to observe that in the past two decades different lines of research have been converging on the view that words do not have a distinguished status in morpho-syntax; see Distributed Morphology as well as a strand of research in Minimalist Syntax (Julien (2002), Koopman (2005), among others). If that is on the right track, then it does not go without saying that words are minimal building blocks for compositional semantics.

Deconstructing quantifier words has both logical and cross-linguistic motivation, according to Gil's (2008) article in *The World Atlas of Language Structures* (WALS):

> [S]ome semanticists have proposed deriving the interpretations of universal quantifiers from those of conjunctions. For example, in the Boolean Semantics of Keenan and Faltz (1986), conjunctions and universal quantifiers are both represented in terms of set-theoretic intersections.

How well do such semantic representations correspond to the observable lexical and grammatical patterns of languages? . . . [O]ne might suspect that they do not correspond at all well. Thus, in English, the conjunction *and* and the universal quantifier *every* are distinct words with quite different grammatical properties.

However, a broader cross-linguistic perspective suggests that there are indeed widespread lexical and grammatical resemblances between conjunctions and universal quantifiers, thereby lending support to the logicians' analyses . . . .

For the purposes of the [WALS] map, conjunctions are taken to include not only forms with meanings similar to that of *and*, but in addition expressions that are sometimes characterized as **conjunctive operators** or **focus particles**, with meanings resembling those of *also, even, another, again*, and in addition the restrictive *only*. As for universal quantifiers, these are assumed to encompass not only forms with meanings such as those of *every, each* and *all*, but also expressions that are sometimes referred to as **free-choice**.

(Gil 2008, emphases in the original)

To illustrate, consider the Japanese data from Shimoyama (2006) and Kobuchi-Philip (2009):

(80) a nani-mo   "everything/anything" (dep. on stress)
     b jyuu-nin-mo-no gakusei   "as many as ten students"
     c Tetsuya-mo Akira-mo   "both Tetsuya and Akira"
     d Tetsuya-mo   "also/even Tetsuya" (dep. on stress)

In this particular case there is no doubt that *nani-mo* is not a compositional primitive, since both parts lead independent lives in exactly the same sense as they have within *nani-mo*. For example (Shimoyama 2007: 146):

(81) [[[Taro-ga nani-o katta-kara] okotta] hito]-mo heya-o deteitta.
     Taro-Nom what-Acc bought-because got.angry person-MO room-Acc left
     'For every thing x, the people who got angry because Taro had bought x left the room.'

On the other hand, the relationship between (80a) and (80b, c, d) is rarely investigated, Kobuchi-Philip (2009) being one of the remarkable exceptions. It appears that compartmentalization is more of a matter of research habits than an empirical or theoretical necessity. In view of Gil's cross-linguistic observations, unified investigation could be most fruitful. Likeminded work on Japanese *-ka*, Malayalam *-oo*, Sinhala *də*, and Tlingit *sá,* which appear in indefinites, disjunctions, and questions, has been flourishing in recent years; see Cable (2010), Slade (2011), and references therein.

The quantificational elements *more* and *most* have traditionally been analyzed setting aside word boundaries, in generative syntax as well as in recent work in semantics (Heim (2001), Hackl (2009), among many others), and are boosted by new insights from the cross-linguistic patterns of suppletive morphology in comparatives and superlatives (Bobaljik 2012). Szabolcsi (2010: chapter 12; 2015) highlights a range of further results pertaining to compositionality in quantifier words.

Extending compositionality below the word level, especially in quantification as opposed to inflectional morphology, is a new domain of inquiry and no doubt raises many methodological and theoretical questions. But taking this path seems inevitable, even though it must be treaded with appropriate caution.

Further reading

Barker, Chris and Chung-chieh Shan 2014. *Continuations and Natural Language. Oxford Studies in Theoretical Linguistics.* Oxford University Press. A unified theory of scope, binding, reconstruction, and other linguistic phenomena, based on insights offered by computer science.

Keenan, Edward L. and Denis Paperno (eds) 2012. *Handbook of Quantifiers in Natural Language.* Dordrecht: Springer. Questionnaire-based surveys of quantifiers in 17 languages representing altogether 12 language families, written by native speaker or field-worker semanticists.

Steedman, Mark 2011. *Taking Scope: The Natural Semantics of Quantifiers.* Cambridge, MA: The MIT Press. A unified theory of quantifier scope in interaction with other syntactic and semantic phenomena, set in the context of natural language processing by humans as well as computers.

References

Balusu, Rahul. 2005. Distributive reduplication in Telugu. In Christopher Davis, Amy Rose Deal, and Youri Zabbal (eds), *Proceedings of NELS* 36. Amherst: GLSA, 39–53.

Barker, Chris 2002. Continuations and the nature of quantification. *Natural Language Semantics* 10: 211–242.

Barker, Chris 2007. Parasitic scope. *Linguistics and Philosophy* 30: 407–444.

Barwise, Jon and Robin Cooper 1981. Generalized quantifiers and natural language. *Linguistics and Philosophy* 4: 159–219.

Beghelli, Filipppo 1997. The syntax of distributivity and pair-list readings. In Anna Szabolcsi (ed.), *Ways of Scope Taking.* Dordrecht: Kluwer, 349–409.

Beghelli, Filippo and Timothy Stowell 1997. Distributivity and negation: The syntax of *each* and *every*. In Anna Szabolcsi (ed.), *Ways of Scope Taking.* Dordrecht: Kluwer, 71–108.

Bobaljik, Jonathan 2012. *Universals in Comparative Morphology.* Cambridge, MA: The MIT Press.

Brasoveanu, Adrian 2008. Donkey pluralities. *Linguistics and Philosophy* 31: 129–209.

Brasoveanu, Adrian 2010. Decomposing modal quantification. *Journal of Semantics* 27: 437–527.

Brasoveanu, Adrian 2012. Correlatives. *Language and Linguistics Compass* 6: 1–20.

Cable, Seth 2010. *The Grammar of Q.* Oxford: Oxford University Press.

Cable, Seth 2012. Distance distributivity and pluractionality in Tlingit (and beyond). http://www.semanticsarchive.net/Archive/2Y5NzcwZ/.

Champollion, Lucas 2012. *Each* vs. *jeweils*: a cover-based view on distance distributivity. *Logic, Language and Meaning* 251–260.

Collins, Chris 2001. Aspects of plurality in |=Hoan. *Language* 77: 456–476.

Fodor, Janet and Ivan Sag 1982. Referential and quantificational indefinites. *Linguistics and Philosophy* 5: 355–398.

Geurts, Bart and Rick Nouwen 2007. *At least* et al.: The semantics of scalar modifiers. *Language* 83: 533–559.

Gil, David 2008. Conjunctions and universal quantifiers. *The World Atlas of Language Structures Online.* http://wals.info/feature/description/56.

Glanzberg, Michael 2008. Quantification and contributing objects to thoughts. *Philosophical Perspectives* 22: 207–231.

Hackl, Martin 2002. Comparative quantifiers and plural predication. In Karine Megerdoomian and Leora Anne Bar-el (eds), *Proceedings of WCCFL 20.* Somerville, MA: Cascadilla Press, 234–247.

Hackl, Martin 2009. On the grammar and processing of proportional quantifiers. *Most* versus *more than half. Natural Language Semantics* 17: 63–98.

Heim, Irene 2001. Degree operators and scope. In Caroline Féry and Wolfgang Sternefeld (eds), *Audiatur Vox Sapientiae. A Festschrift for Arnim von Stechow.* Studia Grammatica 52. Berlin: Akademie Verlag, 214–240.

Heim, Irene 2011. Definiteness and indefiniteness. In Klaus von Heusinger, Claudia Maienborn, and Paul Portner (eds), *Semantics* (HSK 33.2). Berlin: de Gruyter, 996–1025.

Heim, Irene and Angelika Kratzer 1998. *Semantics in Generative Grammar*. Oxford: Blackwell.
Henderson, Robert 2012. *Ways of Pluralizing Events*. PhD dissertation, University of California, Santa Cruz. http://rmhenderson.squarespace.com/storage/henderson-diss.pdf.
Hendriks, Herman 1993. *Studied Flexibility: Categories and Types in Syntax and Semantics*. PhD dissertation, University of Amsterdam.
Julien, Marit 2002. *Syntactic Heads and Word Formation*. New York: Oxford University Press.
Kamp, Hans and Uwe Reyle 1993. *From Discourse to Logic*. Dordrecht: Kluwer.
Kanazawa, Makoto 1994. Weak vs. strong readings of donkey sentences and monotonicity inference in a dynamic setting. *Linguistics and Philosophy* 17: 109–158.
Kanazawa, Makoto 2001. Singular donkey pronouns are semantically singular. *Linguistics and Philosophy* 24: 383–403.
Keenan, Edward L. 1996. The semantics of determiners. In Shalom Lappin (ed.), *Handbook of Contemporary Semantic Theory*. Oxford: Blackwell, 41–63.
Keenan, Edward L. and Leonard M. Faltz 1986. *Boolean Semantics for Natural Language*. Dordrecht: Reidel.
Keenan, Edward L. and Dag Westerståhl 1997. Generalized quantifiers in linguistics and logic. In J. van Benthem and A. ter Meulen (eds), *Handbook of Logic and Language*. Elsevier: Amsterdam, 837–893.
Kobuchi-Philip, Mana 2009. Japanese MO: universal, additive and NPI. *Journal of Cognitive Science* 10: 172–194.
Koopman, Hilda 2005. Korean (and Japanese) morphology from a syntactic perspective. *Linguistic Inquiry* 36: 601–633.
Koster-Moeller, Jorie, Jason Varvoutis and Martin Hackl 2008. Verification procedures for modified numeral quantifiers. In Natasha Abner and Jason Bishop (eds), *Proceedings of WCCFL 27*. Somerville, MA: Cascadilla Press.
Kratzer, Angelika 1991. Modality. In Arnim von Stechow and Dieter Wunderlich (eds), *Semantics: An International Handbook of Contemporary Research*. Berlin: Walter de Gruyter, 639–650.
Kratzer, Angelika 1998. Scope or pseudo-scope? Are there wide scope indefinites? In S. Rothstein (ed.), *Events and Grammar*. Dordrecht: Kluwer, 163–196.
Lasersohn, Peter 1995. *Plurality, Conjunction, and Events*. Dordrecht: Kluwer.
Lewis, David 1975. Adverbs of quantification. In E. L. Keenan (ed.), *Formal Semantics of Natural Language*. Cambridge: Cambridge University Press, 3–15.
Lidz, Jeffrey, Justin Halberda, Paul Pietroski and Tim Hunter. 2011. Interface transparency and the psychosemantics of *most*. *Natural Language Semantics* 19: 227–256.
Liu, Feng-hsi 1997. *Specificity and Scope*. Amsterdam: John Benjamins.
Matthewson, Lisa 2000. On distributivity and pluractionality. In Brendan Jackson and Tanya Matthews (eds), *SALT X*. Ithaca, NY: Cornell University, 98–114.
May, Robert 1985. *Logical Form: Its Structure and Derivation*. Cambridge, MA: The MIT Press.
Montague, Richard 1974. The proper treatment of quantification in ordinary English. In R. Thomason (ed.), *Formal Philosophy. Selected Papers of Richard Montague*. New Haven, London: Yale University Press, 247–271.
Nakanishi, Kimiko 2007. Measurement in the nominal and the verbal domains. *Linguistics and Philosophy* 30: 235–276.
Reinhart, Tanya 1997. Quantifier scope: how labour is divided between QR and choice functions. *Linguistics and Philosophy* 20: 335–397.
Schlenker, Philippe 2006. Scopal independence: a note on branching and wide scope readings of indefinites and disjunctions. *Journal of Semantics* 23: 281–314.
Shimoyama, Junko 2007. Indeterminate noun phrase quantification in Japanese. *Natural Language Semantics* 14: 139–173.
Slade, Benjamin 2011. *Formal and Philological Inquiries Into the Nature of Interrogatives, Indefinites, Disjunction, and Focus in Sinhala and Other Languages*. PhD dissertation, University of Illinois at Urbana-Champaign.
Sutton, Melody 1993. *Binominal* each. Master's Thesis, UCLA.

Schwarz, Bernhard 2001. Two kinds of long-distance indefinites. In Robert van Rooy and Martin Stokhof (eds), *Proceedings of the 13th Amsterdam Colloquium*. Amsterdam: ICCL, 192–197.
Schwarz, Bernhard 2004. Indefinites in verb phrase ellipsis. *Linguistic Inquiry* 35: 344–353.
Szabolcsi, Anna (ed.) 1997a. *Ways of Scope Taking*. Dordrecht: Kluwer.
Szabolcsi, Anna 1997b. Strategies for scope taking. In Anna Szabolcsi (ed.) *Ways of Scope Taking*. Dordrecht: Kluwer, 109–154.
Szabolcsi, Anna 2010. *Quantification. Research Surveys in Linguistics*. Cambridge: Cambridge University Press.
Szabolcsi, Anna 2015. What do quantifier particles do? *Linguistics and Philosophy* 38: 159–204.
de Swart, Henriette 1991. *Adverbs of Quantification: A Generalized Quantifier Approach*. PhD dissertation, Rijksuniversiteit Groningen.
Takahashi, Shoichi 2006. More than two quantifiers. *Natural Language Semantics* 17: 57–101.
Winter, Yoad 2001. *Flexibility Principles in Boolean Semantics*. Cambridge, MA: The MIT Press.
Zimmermann, Malte 2003. Pluractionality and complex quantifier formation. *Natural Language Semantics* 11: 249–287.

Related topics

Chapter 4, Foundations of formal semantics; Chapter 16, The semantics of nominals; Chapter 17, Negation and polarity; Chapter 23, Event semantics; Chapter 24, Compositionality.

19
Lexical and grammatical aspect

Stephen Dickey

1 Introduction

Verbal aspect is one of three major verbal categories of languages of the world, the other two being tense (see Chapter 20) and modality (see Chapter 21). The commonly accepted definition of the term aspect comes from Comrie (1976: 3, citing Holt (1943: 6)), according to which aspectual categories express "ways of viewing the internal temporal constituency of a situation." Even if there are occasionally quibbles with this formulation, it captures the essence of aspectual categories: they express (relatively objective or subjective) perspectives of the temporal structure of individual events and their relations with each other, without regard to a fixed temporal reference point (usually the time of speech). The latter is the domain of tense.

Since Smith (1997) there has been a consensus that the categories covered by the term *verbal aspect* consist of two distinct sets of phenomena that interact in various ways. The term may, on the one hand, refer to the temporal structures of the default construals of the situations expressed by individual lexical verbs. Such phenomena are generally labelled *lexical aspect*. Lexical aspect is a "covert" linguistic category (cf. Smith (1997: 39)), i.e. it is not directly encoded by grammatical morphemes, but surfaces in various restrictions on the usage of verbal grammatical morphemes in a given language, e.g. their combinability with temporal adverbials. On the other hand, *verbal aspect* may refer to grammatical categories that are explicitly marked by grammatical morphemes in individual languages. Such categories are less tied to default construals of situations, i.e. they tend to reflect more subjective construals of a situation by the speaker. These latter categories fall under the heading *grammatical aspect*.

An examination of the state of aspectology reveals a disjoint field, largely because much of the Germanic and general linguistic literature considers lexical aspect to be the primary domain of investigation, whereas other traditions, such as the Slavistic literature, have focused on the grammatical aspectual categories that are prominent in their linguistic systems (cf. Sasse (2002)). Moreover, within any given tradition there have been disagreements on relatively basic issues. Therefore, this discussion can only provide an overview of some major issues in the study of verbal aspect; due to limits on space only a few aspectual systems can be considered—those of English, Mandarin Chinese and the Slavic languages. Section 2 discusses lexical aspect; section 3 discusses grammatical aspect; section 4 discusses Slavic systems as cases of rich and complex systems; section 5 discusses referential parallels between verbal aspect and nominal categories; and section 6 briefly presents some directions of current approaches and future directions.

2 Lexical aspect

As pointed out above, much of the general aspectological literature focuses on the inherent aspectual properties of the situations expressed by lexical verbs (i.e. verb constellations consisting of verbs and their complements). Thus, such properties are usually referred to as "lexical aspect" (cf., e.g., Filip (2012)). Here I employ the term *situation type*, following Smith (1997).

Vendler's (1957) classification of types of verbal situations remains in widespread use today and is the point of departure for any discussion of situation type. Vendler divided verbs into groups according to two diagnostics: (1) Can a verb occur in the progressive tense in English? (2) Can it collocate with adverbial time phrases of completion such as *in an hour*? These diagnostics combine to produce four types of situations: *states*, *activities*, *accomplishments*, and *achievements*. Vendler's diagnostics reflect different temporal properties, namely whether a situation is durative (i.e. has extension in time), dynamic (i.e. characterized by motion/change as a result of the expenditure of energy), and telic (i.e. proceeding toward an inherent endpoint), as elaborated by Smith (1997). States (e.g. *know*, *believe*) have duration, but are neither dynamic nor telic. Activities (e.g. *push a cart*, *draw*) have duration and are dynamic, but are atelic. Accomplishments (e.g. *build a house*, *draw a circle*) have duration, are dynamic, and are also telic. Achievements (e.g. *reach the summit*, *find an object*) have no duration, as they are momentary situations, but are dynamic and telic.

Achievements, though momentary, tend to allow collocation with time adverbials of completion such as *in an hour* because they often presuppose some preliminary activity leading up to the achievement itself. For example, *He reached the summit in two hours* means that the reaching of the summit occurred after two hours of preliminary activity, i.e. ascent. This feature of achievements is common across languages.

Since Comrie (1976) and especially Smith (1997) Vendler's four-fold typology has been extended to include a second class of momentary situations, *semelfactives*, e.g. *sneeze*, *spit*, *wave*. Semelfactives differ from achievements by being atelic. That is to say, although they are momentary, they are not inherently goal-directed, nor do they produce obvious natural results. The currently accepted typology is given in Table 19.1 (see Chapter 22 for further possible distinctions):

Beyond this basic typology of situations, two other distinctions based on the lexical properties of verb collocations deserve mention. The first is the distinction between *stage-level states* and *individual-level states* (cf. Carlson (1977)). Stage-level states (e.g. *be hungry*, *be available*) last only temporarily (for "stages" of an entity's existence). Individual-level states (e.g. *be tall*, *be intelligent*) are permanent, and last throughout an entity's existence. Individual-level states are maximally static among the situation types. Stage-level states are

Table 19.1 Extended typology of situation type

State	*Activity*	*Accomplishment*	*Achievement*	*Semelfactive*
+ Durative	+ Durative	+ Durative	– Durative	– Durative
– Dynamic	+ Dynamic	+ Dynamic	+ Dynamic	+ Dynamic
– Telic	– Telic	+ Telic	+ Telic	– Telic

similar to activities in that they are situations that typically come to an end (though it must be stressed that they are atelic, i.e. not goal-oriented). However, stage-level states differ from activities in that they are not dynamic (i.e. involve no expenditure of energy).

The second is a three-way division of telic verbs based on the kind of progress toward the goal/end-state profiled by a verb. Tenny (1994) distinguishes incremental-theme verbs, change-of-state verbs, and "route verbs" according to the kind of change involved. In the case of incremental-theme verbs (or verb constellations) such as *eat an apple*, the patient "measures out" the event in that the object is increasingly affected as the event progresses: the scalar change is measured in terms of the increments of apple consumed, which "correspond to the temporal progress of the event" (15) until the apple is completely consumed and the event ends. Incremental-theme verbs always represent accomplishments in Vendler's typology, because a process precedes the endpoint. With change-of-state verbs the change does not necessarily proceed incrementally through the patient; rather, the scalar change often occurs "along measurable degrees of change in some property central to the verb's meaning" (17), e.g., *ripen* (intransitive) and *open* (transitive). Many change-of-state verbs involve multi-valued scalar attributes, e.g. *ripen* or *dry*, and thus represent accomplishments. Other change-of-state verbs involve only two values, e.g. *open* or *die*. As the transitions expressed by such two-valued change-of-state verbs are momentary, this group is a significant source of Vendler's achievements. The path objects of "route verbs" (i.e. motion verbs that take the route as an object) as in *walk the Appalachian trail* measure out the event in a scalar manner in that the increments of the path covered correspond to the temporal progress of the event. As such, they represent accomplishments. However, a difference between route verbs on the one hand and incremental-theme verbs and change-of-state verbs on the other is that the objects of route verbs are not changed by the event, but are simply reference objects.

It must be pointed out that while individual verbs may have default construals with regard to situation type (such as *build* as an accomplishment), situation types cannot be reduced to properties of verbs alone. Thus, whereas *eat* without an object is most likely to be interpreted as an activity (cf., e.g. *eat for fifteen minutes*), the addition of an individuated object, e.g. *eat an apple*, creates an accomplishment. Temporal adverbs can have the same effect: unmodified *see* is quite often a state, whereas *see something suddenly* is an achievement. Thus, the term "lexical aspect" is somewhat of a misnomer; lexical aspect is really a property of verb constellations or clauses. A change in situation type through the addition of arguments and/or adverbials is often termed *aspectual coercion*: *eat* is by default an activity, but the addition of an object (*eat an apple*) "coerces" the predicate into an accomplishment; similarly, sneeze is by default a semelfactive, but adding an adverbial of duration, e.g. *sneeze for a whole minute*, "coerces" the predicate into an activity.

As mentioned in section 1, situation types are covert categories in that they are not directly encoded by specific morphemes. Rather, their existence manifests itself through restrictions on the usage of verbs referring to different kinds of situations. (Languages with aspectual oppositions generally have restrictions similar to those that form the basis for Vendler's diagnostics.) Despite the covert nature of the categories of situation type, they surface in a wide variety of (if not all) languages, and thus must reflect basic principles of human cognition.

3 Grammatical aspect (viewpoint aspect)

Grammatical aspect refers to aspectual categories that are explicitly coded by individual morphemes. Since Smith (1997) grammatical aspect has often been labeled *viewpoint aspect*, which reflects the idea that grammatical aspect is less objective than the categories of situation type, expressing instead subjective construals of a situation as either completed or in progress, etc. Unlike the Vendlerian classes of situation type discussed in section 1 (states, activities, accomplishments, achievements, and semelfactives), which are stable across large numbers of languages (with minor variations), the grammatical categories that fall under the rubric of viewpoint aspect exhibit a much wider variation both in their particular meanings and their morphology. For this reason, it is almost impossible to make cross-linguistic generalizations about viewpoint aspect that also characterize the system of viewpoint aspect in an individual language in anything but the most basic terms.

The grammatical categories that constitute viewpoint aspect consist of meanings that are related to the categories of lexical aspect, but never (or rarely) encode situation type directly. The most common viewpoint categories are *perfective* (PF) and *imperfective* (IMPF). Thus, according to Dahl (1985) the most common aspectual opposition across languages is the PF:IMPF opposition. Dahl (1985: 69) points out that unlike most other tense/aspect/modality categories, which are characterized by quite regular markedness relationships, the PF:IMPF opposition exhibits rather unclear markedness relationships across languages. That is to say, no generalization can be made concerning which member of the opposition tends to be morphologically marked. The reason for this is the aforementioned semantic and morphological diversity of categories of viewpoint aspect.

Following Comrie (1976), the perfective may be defined as expressing a situation that is viewed as a single, complete whole, without distinguishing the individual phases that comprise it. Dahl (1985: 78) describes what might be considered the prototype of a perfective verb: it expresses (a) a "single event, seen as an unanalysable whole," which has (b) a "well-defined result or end-state" and which is (c) "located in the past"; further, the event is (d) "more often than not [. . .] punctual," or at least it is (e) construed as a "single transition from one state to its opposite." Features (b) and (e) reflect the fact that in the default case it is telic situations that are coded perfective, as salient results and end states only exist with accomplishment and achievement predicates. Here it should be pointed out that while perfective verbs (verb forms) are typically telic, atelic perfective verbs (verb forms) occur to varying degrees in various languages. Such atelic perfectives are often called *Aktionsarten* (primarily in the Slavistic literature); common *Aktionsarten* are the delimitative, which limits a situation in time (e.g. Russian *poxodit'* "walk for a while"), and the ingressive, which expresses the inception of a situation (e.g. Russian *zapet'* "[suddenly] start singing"), among many others. Such verb types are also called *procedurals*, as the term *Aktionsart* is often used in the meaning of "lexical aspect" generally.

The imperfective, according to Comrie (1976: 24), focuses on the internal temporal structure of a situation. Dahl (1985: 76) takes issue with this formulation, and questions whether imperfective verb forms such as that in *John was sitting in a chair* necessarily focus on any "internal structure," and whether the totality of the sitting situation is relevant at all. To get around this issue, one might say that the imperfective views a situation without reference to its temporal boundaries or the aforementioned well-defined result/end-state.

The imperfective typically expresses situations that are continuous, ongoing, and/or habitually repeated. The latter two imperfective meanings are often coded directly by grammatical morphemes. Thus, many languages have the *progressive* (PROG) as a category, which views a situation as continuing, but is ordinarily restricted to non-stative (dynamic) situations, cf. English *She is reading a book*. Some languages also have *habitual* as a viewpoint category, which views a habitually repeated situation imperfectively, i.e. as an unbounded macro-situation, cf. English *He used to go out on Friday evenings*.

As Comrie (1976: 27) observes, habitual repetition should be kept distinct from *iterativity* and *distributivity*. Whereas habituality refers to the repetition of a situation on different occasions (e.g. *We usually go out on Friday evenings*), iterativity refers to the repetition of a situation on a single occasion (e.g. *He snapped his fingers three times*). Again, habituality is a subcase of imperfectivity. But iteratively repeated situations easily allow for both the imperfective and the perfective viewpoint, depending on whether the repetitions are viewed as continuing (e.g. *I felt him patting me on the shoulder a few times*) or summarized as a complete, whole situation (e.g. *He patted me on the shoulder a few times and kissed me on the forehead*). Distributivity is a special case of iterativity where an iterated situation is distributed over all of a set of entities, as indicated by universal quantifiers (e.g. *He smashed all of the windows*), and has a high correlation with the perfective viewpoint.

Finally, there is the *perfect*, which views a situation that occurred at some point in time as linked to an ensuing state that is on hand at a later temporal reference point, usually the present, as in the case of the present perfect (e.g. *She has read the book*). A reference point in the past yields the past perfect (e.g. *She had read the book*) and a reference point in the future yields the future perfect (e.g. *She will have read the book*). As the perfect does not really concern the temporal constituency of situations themselves, and is as much a category of grammatical tense as one of aspect, it is not discussed further here (see Chapter 20).

Categories of viewpoint aspect do not generally exist in isolation, but form oppositions with categories expressing either a contradictory or neutral viewpoint. As mentioned above, the most common opposition appears to be the PF:IMPF opposition. In many languages, the PF:IMPF opposition is restricted to the past tense. Thus, in French the primary opposition is between the *passé composé/passé simple* (perfective) and the *imparfait* (imperfective; cf., e.g. Garey (1957)). Further, as Dahl (1985: 82–83) points out, in numerous languages the perfective category is restricted to the past (often termed *aorist*), whereas the imperfective is then subdivided into the present tense and an imperfective past tense (often termed *imperfect*). In such systems the present and the imperfective past share one stem, whereas the perfective past is formed from another. As Dahl points out, this system is common in Indo-European languages (and existed in Proto-Indo-European) as well as in non-Indo-European languages such as Classical Arabic, in which we can see the common elements of the present and the imperfective past quite clearly, as shown in Table 19.2.

A minority of languages do not restrict the PF:IMPF to the past tense. For example, though Classical Greek lacks the opposition in the present and future tenses, it does have separate perfective and imperfective forms in the past tense, the subjunctive, optative, and imperative moods, as well as in all participles. The Slavic languages are another well-known case; they tend to lack the PF:IMPF opposition only in the (actual) present tense and in certain participles. But even in languages that do not restrict PF:IMPF to the past tense, the propensity to mark the PF:IMPF opposition in the past can still be evident. For example, Bulgarian, a Slavic language, has in addition to its derivational PF:IMPF opposition (which is not limited to the past tense) an independent, inflectional *aorist:imperfect* opposition in the past tense. Here it is worth pointing out that languages with a PROG:NON-PROG opposition (such as English) do not commonly restrict it to the past tense (cf. Dahl (1985: 92–93)).

Table 19.2 PF:IMPF in Classical Arabic (Dahl 1985: 83)

PF	*kataba* "he wrote"
IMPF	*yaktubu* "he is writing"
IMPF Past	*ka:na yaktubu* "he was writing"

Regarding the motivation for the tendency for the PF:IMPF opposition to exist primarily in the past tense, it is well known that the present tense is generally incompatible with the perfective aspect, because situations that are ongoing at speech time cannot simultaneously be identified as totalities (completed). (An interesting exception to this incompatibility is the case of performative utterances, in which the completion of the event in question is literally simultaneous to its utterance, as in *I hereby pronounce you man and wife*, cf. Langacker (1990: 90). It should also be pointed out that the lack of the PF:IMPF opposition in the present is primarily characteristic of the *actual present*, i.e. the state of affairs actually on hand at speech time; habitually repeated events in the present are freely coded perfective in many languages.) Thus, the general lack of the PF:IMPF opposition in the present tense is no mystery. In contrast, there has been almost no discussion of why the PF:IMPF opposition is more common in the past than in the future. Klein (1994: 114) simply takes it for granted that "[l]anguages, like old people, have a liking for the past."

However, the tendency to have the PF:IMPF opposition in the past and not in the future can be explained as a result of different cognitive strategies in the two domains of time. As past events have already occurred and thus have ultimately fixed (if nevertheless occasionally unclear or unknown) causal relationships to the state of affairs at the time of speech, people are often interested in "forensically" establishing what events have occurred, what their mutual relationships and ultimately their relationships to the state of affairs at the time of speech are. Moreover, telling about what has already happened includes to no small extent telling about interruptions and unexpected events that occurred while other events were in progress. Conversely, none of the future has occurred, and our statements about the future primarily communicate goal-oriented plans and other idealized speculations about what is yet to happen. A further complication regarding the future is the fact that the anticipated time when the results of future events will be on hand is not the present, but some subsequent, post-event time in the future, so that there are no fixed causal links between future events and the state of affairs at speech time. For these reasons, it seems that there is a lesser need to encode aspectual distinctions in the future tense than in the past.

Of course, complex mutual relations between situations can be relevant in the future, but in the default case humans tend to speak about the future in terms of goal-oriented planning as opposed to what situations will be going on at a particular point in time and what events will be located within those ongoing situations. Thus, it makes sense that languages would be more likely to conventionalize viewpoint aspect oppositions in the past than in the future, and leave the latter to some kind of neutral viewpoint. The assumption that statements about the future are more likely to concern goal-oriented plans and other idealized speculations about future events can also explain why, as Dahl (1985: 93) observes, the English progressive occurs relatively infrequently in the future tense. It can likewise explain why in Russian imperfective verbs occur relatively less frequently in the future tense than they do in the

Table 19.3 Figures for four Russian aspectual pairs by tense and aspect

PF Verb	Past	Future	IMPF Verb	Past	Future
sdelat' "do"	4,088	2,265	*delat'* "do"	2,126	1,018
napisat' "write"	1,557	474	*pisat'* "write"	1,271	173
pročitat' "read"	610	238	*čitat'* "read"	2,055	127
postroit' "build"	357	125	*stroit'* "build"	279	59

past tense. This can be seen in figures taken from the spoken language corpus of the Russian National Corpus (date of searches: 1 December 2013) for four common aspectual pairs of verbs, *delat'/sdelat'* "do," *pisat'/napisat'* "write," *čitat'/pročitat'* "read," and *stroit'/postroit'* "build," given in Table 19.3.

As can be seen from Table 19.3, the perfective future is considerably more frequent than the imperfective future, and chi-square tests for the aggregate tense figures from all four verb pairs (PF past: 6,612; PF future: 3,102; IMPF past: 5,731; IMPF future: 1377) confirm that the relatively higher frequency of the perfective in the future compared to the frequency of the perfective in the past is statistically significant (χ-squared = 331, df = 1, p-value < 2.2e-16), with a small effect size (Cramer's V = 0.14). Thus, the predominance of the English simple future and the Russian perfective future makes sense given that people tend to plan or conceive of future events in their completion and leading to their natural results, as opposed to being in progress and unfinished at a certain point in time, and speakers are thus much more likely to code future events with their default category for completed events.

As examples of viewpoint systems, let us now briefly consider English, Mandarin Chinese, and Russian. English is typologically ordinary in that it has a marked progressive construction *be Xing*. The simple forms in English can be employed in cases where an event is viewed perfectively (e.g. *He wrote the letter and sent it*) and the simple form is often considered to be a marker of perfectivity, e.g. by Smith (1997). However, as Sasse (2002: 258) has pointed out, there are problems with viewing the simple forms as markers of perfectivity: it occurs readily with unbounded states (e.g. *I knew that for a long time*). Further, it is easy to attest in processual contexts (e.g. *As I wrote the letter, my hands started to shake*). Therefore, it is better to consider the English simple forms as aspectually neutral. Put somewhat differently, English does not really have the PF:IMPF opposition, but a PROG:NON-PROG opposition. As mentioned above, in addition to the progressive English also has a habitual construction for the past tense: *used to X*. Thus, it seems that English is relatively rich in imperfective markers, but has no real perfective marker. (The role of the perfect may be ignored here, as it occurs in both perfective contexts, e.g. *He has just crossed the bridge*, and imperfective contexts, e.g. *We have been living here for many years*; it relates a past situation to the speech situation regardless of its temporal constituency.)

Mandarin Chinese appears to have a rich, morphologically heterogeneous system for the marking of viewpoint aspect. According to Xiao and McEnery (2004), in Mandarin Chinese there are four different kinds of perfective markers on the one hand, and four different imperfective markers on the other. An overview with their characterizations of the markers is given in Table 19.4.

Perfective *-le* refers to a situation as a totality that actually occurs prior to some reference point, usually in the past but sometimes in the future; an example is (1).

Table 19.4 Perfective and imperfective markers in Mandarin Chinese

Perfective		Imperfective	
-le	actual	*zhe*	durative
guo	experiential	*zai*	progressive
Reduplication	delimitative	*qilai*	inceptive
Resultative Verb Complements	completion/ result	*xiaqu*	continuative

(1) wo   zuotian   xie-le   yi-feng   xin   (Xiao and McEnery 2004: 96)
    I   yesterday write-PF   one-CLF   letter
    "I wrote a letter yesterday."

(A related particle is sentence-final change-of-state *le*. It is not restricted to the past tense, but occurs in the present and immediate future as well. The relationship between actual *-le* and change-of-state *le* has been subject to debate; see Xiao and McEnery (2004: 90–95) for a discussion.) Experiential *guo* occurs to distance a situation from the present, in a way similar to the English experiential perfect, as in (2).

(2) ta   zai   Lundun   zhu-guo   san-nian   (Xiao and McEnery 2004: 138)
    he   in   London   live-EXP   three-year
    "He [has once] lived in London for three years."

Reduplication in Mandarin Chinese has a delimitative function, i.e. it expresses that a situation continued for some (relatively brief) period of time; reduplication is not incompatible with the perfective marker *-le*, as shown in (3).

(3) ta   xiao-le   xiao   shuo [. . .]   (Xiao and McEnery 2004: 138)
    he   smile-PF   smile   say
    "He smiled a little and said [. . .]"

The last perfective marker consists of the class of resultative verb complements, which are directional adverbs, adjectives, or verbs that typically signal the completion of a situation or the attainment of a resultant state. It is unclear how many resultative verb complements exist, beyond the seven directional resultative verb complements (neither Smith (1997) nor Xiao and McEnery (2004) give any information in this regard). An example of an adjectival resultative verb complement is given in (4).

(4) ta   xi-ganjing-le   yifu   (Xiao and McEnery 2004: 161)
    he   wash-clean-PF   clothes
    "He washed his clothes clean."

According to Xiao and McEnery (2004: 159) resultative verb complements are the most productive way of indicating perfectivity in Mandarin Chinese.

Let us now briefly turn to the four imperfective markers in Mandarin Chinese. Durative *zhe* expresses open-ended situations without any reference to their boundaries, and typically occurs in background predicates, as in (5).

(5) na   haizi   ku-zhe   yao   baba   (Xiao and McEnery 2004: 185)
    that   child   cry-DUR   want   dad
    "While crying, that child called out for her father."

Progressive *zai* differs from durative *zhe* in that it rarely occurs with stative verbs, as the progressive requires dynamic predicates (see the above description of the English progressive); moreover, progressive *zai* does not occur in background clauses (Xiao and McEnery 2004: 207).

The final two imperfective markers are inceptive *qilai* (lit. "get up"), which expresses the beginning of an open-ended situation, and continuative *xiaqu* (lit. "go down"), which expresses continuation of a situation that was previously begun. Examples are given in (6a) and (6b) respectively.

(6) a *shuo-zhe   haiziqi   de   xiao-qilai* (Xiao and McEnery 2004: 224)
       say-DUR   childish   PRT   laugh-INC
       "Having said that, [she] started to laugh like a child."

   b *Wang Hu   kan-le   lianzhang   yi-yan,   you   shuo-le-xiaqu*
       Wang Hu   look-PF   company commander one-CLF   then   say-PF-CONT
                                                       (Xiao and McEnery 2004: 231)
       "Wang Hu took a look at the company commander, and then went on talking."

This cursory description cannot begin to address the complexities of the Mandarin Chinese system of viewpoint aspect. However, it serves to illustrate some basic points that are relevant to the study of viewpoint aspect systems. First, a comparison of the brief descriptions of English and Mandarin Chinese systems of viewpoint aspect shows them to be quite different. The English system may be described as consisting of an asymmetrical inflectional PROG:NON-PROG opposition (without a clear perfective category, and complemented by an inflectional *perfect:non-perfect* opposition), whereas the Mandarin Chinese system consists of a PF:IMPF opposition, though each member of the opposition is marked by four semantically distinct morphemes, which appear to include particles as well as compounded elements (resultative verb complements and the inceptive and continuative markers).

Second, the aspectual status of some of the Mandarin Chinese aspectual markers presented above is less than clear. For instance, though Xiao and McEnery (2004) consider experiential *guo* a perfective, it appears to occur mainly in background material (cf. Ming (2010: 143) and the references cited there), which is a characteristic of imperfective verb forms. Ming also points out that "imperfective" inceptive *qilai* can co-occur with perfective *-le*; note also that continuative *xiaqu* can as well, cf. (6b) above. This raises the question of their precise aspectual value. These and other issues concerning viewpoint aspect in Mandarin Chinese would be less puzzling if there were one or more reliable diagnostic tests for viewpoint perfectivity in Mandarin Chinese, which do not exist as far as I am aware. Failing such diagnostic tests, the assignment of a perfective or imperfective value to a given verb form is ultimately subject to the vicissitudes of different approaches.

The lack of any diagnostic tests for viewpoint perfectivity is a significant problem in aspectology. The lack of any criteria with cross-linguistic validity is surely connected to the fact that the *The World Atlas of Language Structures* (WALS; http://wals.info/chapter/65) characterizes perfective in minimal terms: a verb form is considered perfective if it is "the default way of referring to a completed event" in a given language. This characterization is problematic in the case of English, in which the simple forms are the default means for referring to completion actions, but also easily occur in processual contexts, as pointed out above. Further, if such definitions of the perfective (e.g. Comrie's "a situation viewed as a single, complete whole") really captured the semantic essence of perfective markers, it should be relatively easy to establish a reliable cross-linguistic diagnostic test for viewpoint perfectivity.

Given the apparent inadequacy of the definitions of the perfective based on totality/completion, perhaps the essence of the PF:IMPF opposition lies in the realm of discourse. Hopper (1979) has argued that the cross-linguistic function of aspect is to express the foreground/background distinction (perfective ≈ foreground, imperfective ≈ background). As appealing as this hypothesis is, it encounters problems of its own. First, the correlation between perfective and foregrounding varies from language to language (cf. section 4). Second, the concepts of foreground and background are difficult to define in a falsifiable way, and it is possible that different languages operate with different versions of these categories. Third, the foreground/background distinction is characteristic primarily of narrative discourse, and it is not clear exactly how these concepts are relevant for conversational discourse.

One way around this problem is to analyze viewpoint perfectivity in terms of a cross-linguistically stable prototype (cf. Dahl's description of the "prototypical perfective" given above) with secondary functions in various languages. There is nothing wrong with this approach, but it nevertheless seems relatively trivial, and a prototype approach based on totality/completion may benefit from the addition of a referential notion such as that of a "token of a situation" (see section 5).

The aforementioned problems are a reason why the Slavic aspectual systems will probably never lose their relevance for the study of aspect. In Slavic languages there are two clear diagnostics for perfective verbs: (1) perfective verbs can never be used in answer to the question "What are you doing now?"; (2) perfective verbs can never occur as the complement of a phase verb, e.g. *begin, finish*. Thus, the Slavic languages present an opportunity to examine a system of viewpoint aspect where there is almost no ambiguity about the aspectual value of verb forms. Further, as mentioned above, the Slavic PF:IMPF opposition is not restricted to past-tense forms, but organizes almost the entire verbal system independently of tense and mood. For these reasons, a brief description of viewpoint aspect in Russian is given next, and is followed in section 4 by a discussion of aspectual differences between the Slavic languages.

The PF:IMPF opposition in Russian is expressed not by inflected endings, but by affixation. Perfective verbs typically contain one of seventeen perfectivizing prefixes, e.g. *s-delat'* "do, make," *pere-pisat'* "rewrite"; there is one perfectivizing suffix, semelfactive *-nu-*, cf. e.g. *xoxotnut'* "giggle once/give a giggle." Imperfective verbs either contain no perfectivizing prefix, e.g. *delat'* "do, make," or if they do they contain a specifically imperfectivizing suffix, e.g. *pere-pis-yvat'* "rewrite." Thus, for the vast majority of its verbal lexicon, Russian expresses viewpoint aspect through a system of derivationally related pairs of verbs, as shown in Table 19.5.

Each verb of each aspect has a full paradigm. However, morphologically present-tense perfective verb forms do not express the actual present, but primarily the future and occasionally habitually repeated events; present active participles are limited to the imperfective aspect, and past active and passive participles are limited to the perfective aspect. The indicative tense paradigm for Russian aspectual pairs is given in Table 19.6.

Table 19.5 The Russian system of aspectual pairs

Perfective	*Imperfective*
s-delat' "do, make"	*delat'* "do make"
pere-pisat' "rewrite"	*pere-pis-yvat'* "rewrite"
xoxot-nut' "giggle once"	*xoxotat'* "giggle"

Table 19.6 Russian viewpoint aspect and tense

	Perfective		*Imperfective*
Past	*s-delal* "he made"	Past	*delal* "he was making"
Present/Future	*s-delaet* "he will make/he makes"	Present Future	*delaet* "he is making" *budet delat'* "he will be making"

The derivational nature of Russian aspect might create the impression that it is in fact a type of lexical aspect, i.e. that it merely codes situation type, but nothing could be farther from the truth. Rather, despite their unusual morphological marking, perfective and imperfective verbs are highly sensitive to contextual and discourse factors. This can be seen in examples (7a, b).

(7) a *Segodnja prišel nožik [...] nož super!* (Internet)
       today   arrived.PF little knife knife terrific
       "The pocketknife arrived today [...] the knife is terrific!"

   b *Mne odin nožik uže prixodil, sejčas v zakaze vtoroj.* (Internet)
      me one   little knife already came.IMPF now in order second
      "One pocketknife already came to me, now a second one is on order."

In (7a) the perfective is used because the speaker is interested in the natural result of the event in question, i.e. the qualities of the knife that has arrived. In contrast, in (7b), an imperfective verb is used although it expresses a single, completed action, because the speaker is interested not in the concrete result of the arrival of the knife, but in confirming that knives ordered in that manner do arrive.

The examples in (7) demonstrate the sensitivity of the Russian PF:IMPF opposition to discourse factors (i.e. the concerns of the speaker). In the next section, more Slavic data are adduced to illustrate differences between individual aspectual systems regarding the relationship between lexical and grammatical aspect.

4 Typology versus individual languages: the case of Slavic

In section 3 it was mentioned that systems of viewpoint aspect, and systems with a PF:IMPF opposition in particular, exhibit a wide variation in terms of their morphology and the precise semantic meanings. This section briefly shows that even within the Slavic languages, which are usually considered to represent a single system of viewpoint aspect, there are important differences concerning the interaction between lexical and grammatical aspect as well as the referential functions of perfective and imperfective verbs.

Recall from section 3 that there is a correlation between the perfective viewpoint and telic situation types. Telic situations (accomplishments and achievements) tend to be coded perfective, as are semelfactives; states are consistently imperfective, and activities tend to be coded imperfective. The Slavic languages break down into a western group (Czech, Slovak, Sorbian, and Bosnian/Croatian/Serbian) and an eastern group (Russian, Ukrainian, Belarusian, Bulgarian, and to a lesser extent Polish) with respect to the degree to which these correlations hold. In what follows Russian and Czech are taken as representative of the eastern and western groups (respectively). Recall from example (7b) in the previous section that in Russian a single, completed situation in the past may be coded imperfective in certain discourse contexts. In contrast, in Czech a single, completed action in the past must be coded perfective, as shown in (8).

(8) *Mně jeden kapesní nůž už přišel, druhý mám teď objednaný.*
    me one   pocket knife already came.PF another I have now ordered
    "One pocketknife already came for me, I have ordered another one."

Lexical and grammatical aspect

In the eastern group, the correlation between perfective coding and telic situations is frequently overridden by discourse considerations, whereas this correlation is much stronger in the western group of languages. In other words, situation type is less relevant to the coding of viewpoint aspect in the eastern group than it is in the western group.

Likewise, the correlation between atelic activities and imperfective coding is stronger in the western group, whereas atelic activities can easily be expressed by perfective verbs in the eastern group. This is shown in (9), in which Czech allows an imperfective activity verb in a sequence of events (9a), whereas Russian regularly employs a perfective delimitative verb (9b).

(9) a *Stalin chvíli mlčel, pak se otázal*:
Stalin while was silent.IMPF then REFL asked.PF:
„Má čím válčit?"
has what.INST to wage war

b *Stalin pomolčal, potom sprosil: —U nego est' čem*
Stalin was silent.PF then asked.PF by him is what.INST *voevat'?*
to wage war
"Stalin was silent for a while, then asked: 'Does he have anything to fight with?'"

Again, situation type is less relevant for the coding of viewpoint aspect in Russian, whereas in Czech situation type conditions the coding of viewpoint aspect to a relatively high degree.

If viewpoint aspect in Czech is conditioned by situation type to a relatively higher degree than in Russian, this suggests in fact that viewpoint aspect in Czech and the other western languages is a relatively more objective category (i.e. it is more dependent on default temporal construals of types of situations), whereas viewpoint aspect in Russian and the other eastern languages is relatively more subjective (i.e. the speaker has more choice in his/her construal of a situation in time). The degree of the correlation between the perfective and foregrounding and the imperfective and backgrounding in the two groups of languages supports this idea. For example, in Russian narratives perfective verbs tend to be restricted to sequences of events, whereas in Czech perfective verbs occur frequently in background clauses. This is evident in differences in the coding of viewpoint aspect in contexts of negation. Negation is commonly considered a case of backgrounding, particularly when a predicate is negated over an interval of time. In such contexts, the imperfective is required in Russian, as shown in (10a), whereas Czech allows the perfective, as shown in (10b).

(10) a *Ona nikogda ne priznavalas' v ètom.*
she never not admitted.IMPF in this.
"She never admitted this to him."

b *Nikdy se mu ke svému hladu nepřiznala.*
never SELF him to own hunger NEG.admitted.PF
"She never admitted her hunger to him."

As "admit" is a telic predicate, Czech appears in this case to code the predicate perfective according to its situation type—the perfective verb phrase expresses that no complete event of admitting took place, and the background function of the clause is irrelevant for coding. In contrast, in Russian the temporal diffuseness of a backgrounding clause is more important for the coding of viewpoint aspect than its underlying situation type, and the imperfective is required.

The preceding discussion provides only a glimpse into the aspectual differences between the western and eastern groups of Slavic. It nevertheless shows that even within a single language family, differences in the category of viewpoint aspect can be considerable, and involve differing interrelationships between situation type and viewpoint aspect. It also suggests that there may be a one-way implicational relationship between situation types and the perfective: a language will allow some atelic situations to be coded perfective only if allows telic situations to be coded perfective, but the reverse is not true.

These differences also raise the issue of the adequacy of the typological definitions of the perfective given above. The definition of the perfective as a single, complete whole fairly accurately describes the usage patterns of the Czech perfective, but cannot account for the usage patterns of the Russian perfective. Thus, it seems that in some languages the referential function of viewpoint aspect is considerably more complex than Comrie's definition given in section 3. With regard to Russian, we may say that beyond the expression of events as totalities, a crucial referential function of perfective verbs is to signal that a situation is unique within a given temporal context (for extended discussions, see Leinonen (1982) and Dickey (2000)).

5 Parallels between nouns and verbs

The previous section briefly raised the issue of the referential functions of grammatical aspect. This section continues that line of thinking by pointing out some parallels between the reference of nouns and verbs, first for situation type (based on Mehlig (1996)) and then for viewpoint aspect.

As is well known, there are two types of nouns: count nouns, which refer to discrete, countable entities (e.g. *bicycle*, *chair*), and mass nouns, which refer to uncountable substances (e.g. *milk*, *flour*) (see Chapter 16). The discreteness of the referents of count nouns stems from the fact that they have natural bounds. The referents of mass nouns do not. Thus, the referent of a count noun is heterogeneous, i.e., no subpart of it can be described by that count noun. In contrast, mass nouns are homogeneous, i.e., any subpart of the referent of a mass noun can be described by that mass noun. For example, a part of a bicycle cannot be referred to as *a bicycle*, whereas a portion of a larger quantity of milk can be referred to as *milk*. That is to say, the principle of arbitrary divisibility is valid for mass nouns, but not for count nouns. Further, the principle of cumulativity or additivity is valid for mass nouns: If milk is added to some quantity of milk, the result can still be referred to as *milk*. The principle of cumulativity is not valid for count nouns.

The various situation types show analogous properties: telic situations are bounded by their temporal endpoints in the same way that count nouns are bounded in space. Thus, accomplishment and achievement predicates are discrete and heterogeneous, and the principle of arbitrary divisibility is not valid for them. For example, no subportions or constituent phases of the accomplishment *fix a lock* can be referred to as *fix a lock*. (This is a matter of default construals: reference to subparts, or internal phases, of an accomplishment can be coerced by imperfective categories, e.g. *be fixing a lock*.) Semelfactives such as *sneeze* pattern with telic situations in this regard due to their inherent boundaries. In contrast, atelic situations are unbounded in time in the same way that mass nouns are unbounded in space. They are thus homogeneous, and the principles of arbitrary divisibility and cumulativity are valid for them. For example, any subportion of the activity *sit* can be referred to as *sit*, and someone may sit for just a little longer than they already have, and the whole situation will still be referred to as *sit*. These parallels are summarized in Table 19.7.

Table 19.7 Parallels between nouns and situation type

	Bounded	*Unbounded*
Domain of space	Count nouns	Mass nouns
Domain of time	Telic predicates, semelfactives	Atelic predicates
Principle of arbitrary divisibility	Invalid	Valid
Principle of cumulativity	Invalid	Valid

Thus it seems that situation type and the count/mass distinction reflect the same distinctions applied to the spatial entities that are the referents of nouns and to the temporal entities that are the referents of verbs. That is to say, the concepts of boundedness, homogeneity, and heterogeneity are conspecific to space and time.

Parallels between nominal categories and viewpoint aspect are less straightforward, and there has been far less agreement in this area. One reason is that such comparisons are complicated by the considerable differences in the way we relate to nouns and verbs. As Langacker (2009) observes, nominal and verbal grammatical categories (Langacker's term is *grounding categories*, i.e. grammatical categories that specify the relationship of a lexical unit to the "ground" of the speech situation) are based on "different epistemic concerns": nominal categories function to *identify* instances of a type of object, whereas verbal categories function to *establish the existence/occurrence* of an instance of a type of event. Inasmuch as this is true, verbal categories should generally show a weaker impulse to express the unique identifiability of a situation. However, in recent years there have been attempts to draw parallels between the category of referentiality in nouns (*definite vs. indefinite*) and the PF:IMPF opposition in aspect languages, particularly for Russian aspect. Leinonen (1982) argues that the Russian perfective signals that an event is *temporally definite*, i.e. uniquely locatable in a particular temporal context. More recently, Ramchand (2008) argues that the Russian perfective signals that the event is located by a definite assertion/reference time. A more general approach is taken by Leiss (2000), who suggests that cross-linguistically the shared function of nominal definiteness categories and verbal aspect is to express a TYPE (indefinite noun phrases; imperfective aspect) versus a specific TOKEN (definite noun phrases; perfective aspect). Despite some complications, an approach of this kind allows for a fuller recognition of the prominent discourse functions of aspect in some languages and enables us to make better sense of them. If languages with aspectual systems that lend themselves to a direct comparison with systems of nominal reference are relatively rare, this is due to the aforementioned differences in the way we relate to the referents of nouns and verbs.

6 Current approaches and future directions

Current approaches to aspect understandably vary according to whether the subject is lexical or grammatical aspect. Since Dowty (1979) investigations of lexical aspect have been dominated by studies with formal semantic approaches, e.g. Rothstein (2004) (see Chapter 4). There have also been many formal semantic investigations of grammatical aspect in recent years, e.g. van Lambalgen and Hamm (2005). Similarly, Discourse Representation Theory has found application in the analysis of the discourse effects of aspect systems, cf. e.g. Grønn (2003) for Russian.

In general, recent decades have witnessed a recognition that the discourse effects of grammatical aspect cannot be ignored in a semantic analysis of the category, and analyses of these effects have been made for numerous individual languages. Quantitative methods have been also increasingly employed to provide more accurate empirical bases for analysis; a very recent example is Janda's et al. (2013) study of the nature of prefixation in Russian.

As for future directions, two areas of inquiry that are already proving their importance are psycholinguistic approaches to aspect and studies of the acquisition of aspect in children (see Chapter 26). Psycholinguistic approaches to grammatical aspect are still in their infancy, but aspectual coercion has been the subject of several psycholinguistic investigations, cf. Bott (2010) and the references cited there. On the basis of several experiments, Bott concludes that the interpretation of situation type does not remain underspecified during processing; rather, situation type is immediately determined on the basis of probabilistic information and context. Further, the smallest domain for determining the situation type of a verb is the verb together with its arguments and adverbials. Bott's conclusion supports the idea that situation type is not a matter of verbs but of verb constellations (cf. section 1).

Investigations of the acquisition of aspect have established that situation aspect is grasped by children by the time they are three years old (cf. Wagner (2012) and the sources cited there). They have also established that early on children tend to restrict the perfective forms to telic predicates in the past tense, and restrict imperfective verb forms to atelic predicates in the present tense (cf. again Wagner (2012) and the references cited there). Wagner argues that this is a consequence of lower demands on informational processing that these combinations impose. Similarly, Stoll (2005) establishes that telic perfectives are learned by Russian children earlier than Aktionsart perfectives, such as ingressive verbs, and that the acquisition of the latter is dependent on their narrative competence. While many psycholinguistic studies of verbal aspect and investigations of the acquisition of aspect to date have confirmed pre-existing hypotheses, these approaches will certainly facilitate the resolution of various controversial issues and increasingly result in the development of innovative general hypotheses.

Further reading

Croft, William 2012. *Verbs: Aspect and Causal Structure*. Oxford: Oxford University Press. Croft revisits questions of situation type and aspectual typology from a cognitive perspective.
Michaelis, Laura A. 1998. *Aspectual Grammar and Past-Time Reference*. London: Routledge. Michaelis describes and analyzes the aspectual system of English, with a particular focus on the perfect.

References

Bott, O. 2010. *The Processing of Events*. Amsterdam: John Benjamins.
Carlson, G. 1977. A unified analysis of the English bare plural. *Linguistics and Philosophy* 13: 413–456.
Comrie, B. 1976. *Aspect*. Cambridge: Cambridge University Press.
Dahl, Ö. 1985. *Tense and Aspect Systems*. Oxford: Basil Blackwell.
Dickey, S. 2000. *Parameters of Slavic Aspect: A Cognitive Approach*. Stanford: CSLI.
Dowty, D. 1979. *Word Meaning and Montague Grammar: The Semantics of Verbs and Times in Generative Semantics and in Montague's PTQ*. Dordrecht: Reidel.
Filip, H. 2012. Lexical aspect. In Binnick, R. (ed.) *The Oxford Handbook of Tense and Aspect*. Oxford: Oxford University Press, 721–752.
Garey, H. 1957. Verbal aspect in French. *Language* 332: 91–110.
Grønn, A. 2003. *The Semantics and Pragmatics of the Russian Factual Imperfective*. Unpublished PhD dissertation. University of Oslo.

Hopper, P. 1979. Aspect and foregrounding in discourse. In Givon, T. (ed.) *Discourse and syntax*. New York: Academic Press, 213–241.

Janda, L., A. Endresen, J. Kuznetsova, O. Lyashevskaya, A. Makarova, T. Nesset and S. Sokolova 2013. *Why Russian Aspectual Prefixes Aren't Empty: Prefixes as Verb Classifiers*. Bloomington, IN: Slavica Publishers.

Klein, W. 1994. *Time in Language*. London: Routledge.

Langacker, R. 1990. *Concept, Image, and Symbol. The Cognitive Basis of Grammar*. Berlin: Mouton de Gruyter.

Langacker, R. 2009. *Investigations in Cognitive Grammar*. Berlin: Mouton de Gruyter.

Leinonen, M. 1982. *Russian Aspect, "temporal'naja lokalizacija" and Definite-ness/Indefiniteness*. Helsinki: Neuvostoliittionsttituutin.

Leiss, E. 2000. *Artikel und Aspekt: Die grammatische Muster von Definitheit*. Berlin: Mouton de Gruyter.

Mehlig, H. R. 1996. Some analogies between the morphology of nouns and the morphology of aspect in Russian. *Folia Linguistica* 301–2: 87–109.

Ming, T. 2010. Review of Xiao, Richard and McEnery, Tony. 2004. *Aspect in Mandarin Chinese. A Corpus-Based Study*. *Chinese Language and Discourse* 11: 138–144.

Ramchand, G. 2008. Perfectivity as aspectual definiteness: time and the event in Russian. *Lingua* 118: 1690–1715.

Rothstein, S. 2004. *Structuring Events*. London: Basil Blackwell.

Sasse, H-J. 2002. Recent activity in the theory of aspect: accomplishments, achievements, or just non-progressive state? *Linguistic Typology* 6: 199–271.

Smith, C. 1997. *The Parameter of Aspect*. 2nd edition. Dordrecht: Kluwer Academic Publishers.

Stoll, S. 2005. Beginning and end in the acquisition of the perfective aspect in Russian. *Journal of Child Language* 32: 805–825.

Tenny, C. 1994. *Aspectual Roles and the Syntax-Semantics Interface*. Dordrecht: Kluwer Academic Publishers.

Van Lambalgen, M. and Hamm, F. 2005. *The Proper Treatment of Events*. London: Basil Blackwell.

Vendler, Z. 1957. Verbs and times. *Philosophical Review* 56: 143–160.

Wagner, L. 2012. Primary language acquisition. In Binnick, R. (ed.) *The Oxford Handbook of Tense and Aspect*. Oxford: Oxford University Press, 458–480.

Xiao, R. and McEnery, T. 2004. *Aspect in Mandarin Chinese. A Corpus-Based Study*. Amsterdam: John Benjamins.

Related topics

Chapter 20, Tense; Chapter 21, Modality; Chapter 23, Event semantics; Chapter 24, Participant roles.

20
Tense

Ilse Depraetere and Raphael Salkie

1 Introduction

1.1 Aims

Tense is a very active research field in semantics and philosophy of language. In this chapter we outline some current controversies and theories in the field. Each section indicates some important recent studies where you can find extensive bibliographies. The rest of section 1 sets the scene for the issues and theories covered in sections 2 and 3.

1.2 Tense and time

Compare these two sentences. Example (1) is "in the past tense" (more exactly, it contains two past tense verbs, or alternatively, two past tense morphemes), while (2) is not in the past tense (it does not contain any past tense verbs or morphemes):

(1) Ruby and Joe admitted that they enjoyed eating Marmite.
(2) Ruby and Joe admit that they enjoy eating Marmite.

It is evident that the words *admitted* and *enjoyed* in (1) each contain two morphemes: the verb morpheme *admit* or *enjoy*, and a suffix that appears as *-ed* with regular verbs and is commonly called the past tense suffix, because it typically refers to past time.

Tense is a grammatical term; *time* is not. We all know in practice what time is, though a fuller understanding requires expertise in physics: it's no coincidence that the leading scientist Stephen Hawking named his best-selling book *A brief history of time* (Hawking 1988), and if you are interested in the science of time, that's the place to start. If you want to explore the nature of time further, you had better also read what philosophers have to say about it: a good recent discussion is Dummett (2004); see also section 3.6 below.

Here we are concerned only with the language of time, of which tense is just a part (see Evans (2003) for the bigger picture). In English there are many words and phrases which refer to time: *now, tomorrow, last week, when I was a little child,* and so on. But as well as those, we also have suffixes like the past tense morpheme, along with auxiliary verbs like *have* and *will* which can refer to time. If you want to find out about a word like *tomorrow,* you would consult a dictionary; whereas to learn about suffixes and auxiliary verbs, you would turn to a grammar. Tenses are *time expressions which are part of grammar*. More specifically, tenses are time expressions which:

a   encode time locations relative to other time locations
b   are linked to verbs
c   are part of grammar.

Point (a) just means that tenses indicate when situations happen (following common practice, we use *situation* as a cover term for events, states, actions etc.). The only way to do this is to locate the time of the situation in question (say, Ruby and Joe admitting something) in relation to another time which is already known. So tenses express a relation between (at least) two times. In the default case, the "known time" is the time of speaking, so the past tense usually (but not always) means "past in relation to now". (By the same reasoning, a time word like *yesterday* also expresses a relation between two times: *yesterday* only pinpoints a particular day if you know when "today" is). Tenses that conform to the default and locate the time of a situation relative to the time of speaking are often called *absolute tenses* (also known as *deictic* tenses, as they point to the time of the speech situation); for tenses that depart from the default, the term used is *relative tenses* (Fabricius-Hansen 2006: 567).

Tenses are linked to verbs: with the past tense suffix, that is clear. With auxiliaries like *have* and *will* it is less obvious, and some grammarians are not prepared to call these markers of tense. A word like *yesterday* is not grammatically linked to a verb, so no one would consider it a tense.

1.3 Even the basics are controversial

Tense is a hugely controversial area in linguistics. Consider again examples (1) and (2). We all agree that the verbs in (1) contain two morphemes, but what about (2)? Most grammarians would say that example (2) is "in the present tense", but are there two present tense morphemes in this sentence, one in *admit* and one in *enjoy*? If there are, they are not pronounced: we have to say that the present tense verbs *admit* and *enjoy* contain a suffix which is "covert" or "realised as zero". Alternatively, we could say that the present tense in English is marked by the absence of the past tense morpheme *-ed*.

When we turn to the meanings of tenses, things get even more contentious. In (1), *admitted* is straightforward: it refers to some time in the past. What about *enjoyed*? Well, it is quite likely that what Ruby and Joe said was "We enjoy eating Marmite", which is in the present tense. So using the past tense verb *enjoyed* in (1) seems to communicate that the time of enjoying was present in relation to the (past) time of admitting – alternatively, that the time of enjoying was *simultaneous with* or *included* the time of admitting. So the past tense suffix here conveys the information "simultaneous to another time in the past": it doesn't seem to indicate past time directly in relation to now but only indirectly by its relation to another time – it appears to be relative rather than absolute. Is this another meaning of the past tense, as some grammarians think, or is it the result of other things in the sentence, our knowledge of the world, and the way language is used in real contexts? See section 2.3 for more on this question.

Another observation about example (1) is that in certain circumstances we could just as well have said (3) instead:

(3)   Ruby and Joe admitted that they enjoy eating Marmite.

Example (3) could be a true report of Ruby and Joe saying "We enjoy eating Marmite", just like (1), so long as the speaker of (3) believes that they still enjoy it. In that case, there would be almost no practical difference between saying (1) and saying (3).

What's more, example (1) could also be used to report an utterance of "We enjoyed eating Marmite (when we were little)", with the time of enjoying before (anterior to) the time of admitting. This could suggest yet another relative meaning of the past tense: "anterior to another time in the past".

We will look in more detail at these problems under "tense in reported speech" in section 2.3. We want to emphasise here that examples (1) to (3) illustrate a pervasive and difficult problem in analysing tense: how do we reconcile (a) the most likely meanings of different tenses with (b) the ways they are used. Here is another case which raises the same problem: the meaning and use of the present tense. What could be simpler than "the present tense refers to now"? Well, it is not so simple: (a) To describe an event happening in front of your eyes, you can't just use the present tense in English: if you see a bird singing you don't say "The bird sings" but "The bird is singing". So aspect and tense are intertwined (cf. Chapter 19). (b) The English present tense can be used to refer to future events (*Teaching starts tomorrow*) or past events (*In 1649, King Charles is executed and Cromwell assumes supreme executive power*). The meanings of some tenses (semantics) seem to be different from the way they are used (pragmatics). We will see some more examples of this below. In our view, it is the key problem in analysing tenses.

1.4 Do all languages have tenses?

When we say that a language has tenses, this means that speakers of that language normally must choose a tense in every sentence, even if the tense is redundant as in the sentence *Last year I bought a new car*: Dahl and Velupillai (2011) point out that the words *last year* make it clear that the event took place in the past.

Tense is not a universal: lots of languages don't have tenses at all. In a sample of 1132 languages, 152 (13%) had no tense or aspect inflection (Dryer 2011a). However, if you compare this map with the one at Dryer (2011b), you will see that most of the languages that lack tense or aspect inflection have no inflections of any kind. Even here, though, there is controversy. Mandarin Chinese has often been cited as a language that has no tenses: see Lin (2006) and Smith and Erbaugh (2005) for analyses of Mandarin which assume no tenses and which show how speakers can indicate time relations in other ways. However, Lin (2007) claims that if we accept a Tense Phrase (TP) for English (see section 3.5 below), then we should also accept an abstract TP for Mandarin. Similarly, Matthewson (2006) gives an analysis of St'át'imcets (Lillooet Salish), spoken in British Columbia, Canada, which proposes that although St'át'imcets has no tense suffixes, every finite clause in the language possesses a phonologically covert tense morpheme. At the other end of the spectrum, the Eskimo language Kalaallisut (alias West Greenlandic) has traditionally been said to have up to seven tenses, but recent theoretical work by Shaer (2003) argues that this language is in fact tenseless; from a more descriptive viewpoint, Bittner (2005) takes the same position. For a survey of these issues, see Lin (2012).

1.5 How many tenses?

Tense might look simple. We can distinguish three times in relation to now – past, present and future – so we'd expect many languages which have tenses to have exactly three tenses. In fact, it is rare to find languages with exactly these three tenses. Modern Hebrew is one – but that's interesting, because Modern Hebrew is largely an invented language, designed to be uncomplicated. Similarly Esperanto, a simple invented language, has three:

present	mi kaptas	I catch
past	mi kaptis	I caught
future	mi kaptos	I will catch

(Hana 1998)

(Some grammars also include *mi kaptus*, "I would catch", as a fourth tense.) For English, the number of tenses that you propose depends on whether you consider *will* + bare infinitive to be a future tense (see section 2.1) and whether you consider *have* + past participle (the present perfect) to be a tense (see section 2.2). The three main positions are these:

(1) Both *will* and *have* can be used to form tenses. This yields the eight tenses below, a position held by some major scholars in the field such as Declerck et al. (2006) and Hornstein (1990).

1	Present	*I talk*
2	Past	*I talked*
3	Future	*I will talk*
4	Future in past	*I would talk*
5	Present perfect	*I have talked*
6	Past perfect	*I had talked*
7	Future perfect	*I will have talked*
8	Future perfect in past	*I would have talked*

(2) Neither *will* nor *have* can be part of a tense, so the present and the past are the only two English tenses. This position has been adopted by some of the most distinguished grammarians of English, including Otto Jespersen (1933: 231), Randolph Quirk (cf. Quirk et al. 1985) and Geoffrey Leech (most recently, Biber et al. (1999), which includes in its bibliography a list of previous grammars in this tradition).

(3) *Will* is not a tense marker, but *have* is. This allows four tenses: the present, the past, the present perfect and the past perfect, the position of Huddleston and Pullum et al. (2002), arguably the most sophisticated grammar of English.

The issue here is the best criteria for the identification of "tenses". Jespersen and Quirk assume that tenses (a) are verbal inflections which (b) mostly express time location. The first of these criteria keeps matters simple: English can have two tenses (assuming that the absence of an inflection can count – cf. section 1.3), and no more. If, on the contrary, we include other things than verbal inflections, then we have to decide whether we also count as tenses not only *will* and *have* but also *be going to* and *be to*, and ways of talking about the recent past such as Spanish *acabar de*, and French v*enir de*. (*Barack Obama acaba de llegar a Kabul, Afganistán, en un viaje sorpresa.* = B.O. has just arrived in Kabul for a surprise visit [*El País*] / *Elle vient de recevoir un appel d'une personne qu'elle ne connaît pas et qui me cherche.* = She has just received a call from someone who she does not know and who is looking for me [*Le Monde*]). The majority of grammarians of English choose the simple option; most studies of tense in a wide range of languages (e.g. Comrie (1986), Dahl and Velupillai (2011)) choose the more complex one.

The second criterion is about meaning and frequency. Here the crucial problems are first, whether frequency can be part of the definition of a grammatical category, and second, how frequently the item has to express (that particular) time location. As we have seen, the English "present tense" has uses where it does not refer to present time, and English *will* has modal uses (cf. section 2.1). One of the arguments against treating German *werden* as a future tense marker (cf. again section 2.1) is that German very often uses the present tense to refer to the future where English (for example) probably would not: for example, in the famous last line of Lessing's play *Minna von Barnhelm*, Sergeant Werner says to his bride-to-be Franziska "Über zehn Jahr' ist Sie Frau Generalin oder Witwe" (literally, "In ten years you are a general's wife or a widow"). It would be more natural in English to say "you'll be".

Depending on the criteria and how they are applied, the picture that emerges may thus be quite different.

2 Some controversial issues

2.1 Future tense

Consider a sentence like (4):

(4) It will rain tomorrow.

This sentence doubtless refers to future time, but the majority of grammarians treat *will* as a modal, not a future tense (see Chapter 21). The main reasons are:

a   Unlike the past tense in English, which is an inflection of a verb, *will* is a separate word. It is clear that the past tense ending is part of grammar: it is less clear for a separate word.
b   From a grammatical point of view, *will* is a modal verb like *can*, *may* and *must*. And in some cases, it seems to have a modal meaning: If I say "Oil will float on water" or "John will be at work now", I am not talking about the future but stating a general truth or speculating about the present time.
c   There are many other ways of referring to future time in English: *shall*, *be going to*, the present tense, modals like *may* (cf. *It may rain tomorrow*), etc. Is there a reason to single out one of these as the future tense?
d   The future is uncertain, unlike the present or the past: so it is similar to statements using modals like *may*.
e   If you remove the time adverb *tomorrow* and just say "It will rain", the sentence sounds incomplete and a little strange. Compare "It is going to rain", which sounds complete. So there is something fishy about *will*.

A minority of people disagree. They respond to these five points as follows:

a   Scholars who study tense in a range of languages accept that auxiliary verbs like *will* are less grammaticalised than inflections, but still treat them as tense markers when they are mainly used to express time relations. In French, for example, the normal way to express past time is to use the *passé composé* (compound past) with an auxiliary verb (*J'ai fini hier* "I finished yesterday") but an inflection for the future (*Je finirai demain* "I will finish tomorrow"). If we only allow inflections to be tenses, then we would have to say that French has a future tense but no past tense – a conclusion that few would accept.

b   It remains to be proved that the grammar of *will* is relevant to its meaning: the auxiliary verbs *have* and *be* share many of the grammatical properties of modals but it does not follow that they have modal meanings. What's more, the vast majority of instances of *will* in English refer to future time (Salkie 2010: 191–4); and examples with the future tense stating general truths or speculating about the present are found in languages like French and Italian which have future tense inflections.

c   French and Italian also have many ways of referring to future time.

d   It is a fact about time that the future is uncertain, but not necessarily a fact about language. We normally treat "It will rain tomorrow" as a confident assertion, especially if it is said by a meteorologist.

e   Bare future statements sound strange out of context in other languages too. What's more, bare past statements often look odd: If I say "It rained", is that any less strange than "It will rain"?

More sophisticated arguments against treating *will* as a future tense are given by Huddleston (1995), and summarised in Huddleston and Pullum et al. (2002: 209–10). The case for treating *will* as a future tense is presented in Salkie (2010). A similar controversy about the status of the *werden* + infinitive construction in German divides grammarians, with Vater (1997) claiming that it is modal, while Welke (2005: 365–448) argues that it is a future tense.

2.2 Present perfect

A first question that has been addressed is whether the present perfect (e.g. *I have talked*) is a tense or whether it should be classified as an aspectual marker. There are advocates of both positions, and some have argued that it has a sort of special status (Huddleston and Pullum et al. (2002) use "secondary tense"). Comrie writes that

> given the traditional terminology in which the perfect is listed as an aspect, it seems most convenient to deal with the perfect in a book on aspect, while bearing in mind that it is an aspect in a rather different sense from the other aspects treated so far.
>
> (1976: 52)

In aspectual analyses, the present perfect is said to communicate a perfect (sometimes also called a "consequent" or "result" or "present") state. This means that when the speaker produces a sentence with a present perfect, (s)he makes it clear that there is a result state that holds at present time. For instance, "Sarah has broken her leg" definitely communicates "Her leg is broken", a present result that is entailed by the lexical semantics, but the utterance is likely to communicate a pragmatically inferred present result as well, such as "She won't go skiing next week" or "That's why she looks a bit depressed". Those who argue against an aspectual approach tend to maintain that "current relevance" is a consequence of the temporal structure of the perfect; and they argue that the present perfect is a deictic category and therefore not concerned with aspect. Ritz (2012) is a useful summary of this debate.

The question of determining the number of perfects, or rather, uses of the perfect, is another one on which there is no consensus in the literature. McCawley (1971) is often cited in this context; he distinguishes between the following "uses" (1971: 263), which he argues are different "senses" (in other words, the present perfect is ambiguous): the universal perfect (5), the existential perfect (6), the stative perfect (7) and the hot news perfect (8):

(5) I've known Max since 1960.
(6) I have read the *Principia Mathematica* five times.
(7) I can't come to your party tonight. – I've caught the flu.
(8) Malcolm X has just been assassinated.

Even though there is disagreement on the number of uses of the perfect, most other researchers seem to agree that these are not different senses. Declerck et al. (2006) distinguish three "readings" of the perfect, depending on the type of situation expressed: the indefinite reading, in which the situation comes to an end before now, as (6); the continuative reading, where the terminal point of the situation includes now, as in (5); and the "up-to-now" reading, in which case the terminal point of the situation is adjacent to now, as in (7) and (8). Note that this is different from Declerck (1991), in which a distinction is made between the indefinite perfect, the continuative perfect and the repetitive perfect.

The present perfect in English has a feature that it does not share with languages like French, Dutch or German: it is not normally compatible with adverbials that explicitly locate the situation at a time that is completely over:

(9) *I have seen her yesterday.
(10) Je l'ai vue hier.
(11) I heb haar gisteren gezien.
(12) Ich habe sie gestern gesehen.

Various proposals have been made to explain this constraint, which appears to be weakening in some varieties of English. For Reichenbach (1947), the English present perfect has a reference time in the present, and its meaning therefore always involves the past and some connection with now (cf. section 3.1 below). This would explain why an adverb like *yesterday*, which does not have this connection, is not possible: if instead we say *I have seen her since yesterday*, where the time period expressed by *since yesterday* extends from the past up to now, then the sentence is fine. Declerck (1991) argues that the present perfect establishes a pre-present domain which extends up to now (as opposed to a past domain, wholly in the past, with the past tense – cf. section 3.2); here again, the meaning of the present perfect is said to be incompatible with time expressions like *yesterday*.

In a more recent paper, Schaden (2009) offers a critical analysis of these and other analyses and proposes instead that the cross-linguistic variation of the present perfect should be explained in terms of pragmatic competition between forms that refer to a situation located before now: both the present perfect and the past tense denote past time. In Schaden's words, they are "one-step past-referring tenses". On top of that, the present perfect communicates a perfect state. In English and Spanish, the default form to refer to past time is the simple past and the marked (unusual, special) form is the present perfect: one is almost always able to use the past tense, and occasionally one has to use it (when there is a past time adverbial, cf. (9)).

In French and German it is the other way round: one is almost always able to use the present perfect, and occasionally one has to use it (when there is reference to a present result state, for instance when pointing to a painting: *?Meine Tochter malte das (My daughter painted this)* [past] */Meine Tochter hat das gemalt* [present perfect]). The present perfect is the default form and the past tense is the marked form. The choice of a marked form triggers a pragmatic inference process: the hearer will infer that there is current relevance when the (marked) present perfect is used in English (as a "perfect state" is part of the semantics of the present perfect), while in German, (s)he will infer that there is no current relevance when the (marked) simple past is used.

While the past tense in English does not exclude the possibility of "current relevance", the form on its own does not trigger the search for a result. The presence of a past time adverbial makes it clear that the localisation of the event is crucial, and, the argument goes, the speaker is unlikely to be overinformative by using a form that also refers to a perfect state when the only requirement is to locate a situation in the past.

Sometimes the present perfect does combine with a past time adverbial. Schaden quotes the following example from the British National Corpus: "Thank you, the point that Mr *has made yesterday*, I think will continue to make [sic]"; in these cases, he argues, the speaker provides two pieces of information in a very explicit way: the localisation of the event is important (as is shown by the adverbial), but so are the consequences of the event.

Summing up, the perfect constitutes very fertile ground for the analysis of questions relating to the semantics-pragmatics interface. First, we have the question of the polysemy or monosemy of the perfect: are the different readings of the perfect the result of different semantics associated with each of them, or, rather, is there one common semantic profile with different contextually determined realisations? Second, there is the question of the nature and status of the results communicated by the perfect.

2.3 Tense in reported speech

Consider again example (1), repeated here:

(1) Ruby and Joe admitted that they enjoyed eating Marmite.

This is an example of Indirect reported speech (IRS). What were Ruby and Joe's original words? Most likely they said "We enjoy eating Marmite", but it's possible that they said "We enjoyed eating Marmite", especially if the sentence continues "... when we were little". Let's call the first of these the *simultaneous* interpretation of the past tense *liked*, and the second one the *anterior* interpretation. Although it is less salient, the anterior interpretation is straightforward: the past tense seems to be used with its normal meaning. It's the simultaneous interpretation which is problematic: the past tense seems to mean "simultaneous with the time of *admitted*". How can we explain this?

Grammarians disagree. There are three main analyses.

a   Sequence of tense (backshifting)

The traditional approach to the simultaneous interpretation of examples like (1) was to say that English has a rule called *Sequence of Tense* or *Backshifting*, which starts with the original words and changes *We enjoy eating Marmite* to *They enjoyed eating Marmite*. (The pronoun *we* changes to *they*, but that is thought to be automatic and doesn't vary from language to language; but not all languages change the tense in the way that English does.) Here is one version:

> If the tense of the verb of reporting is past, then the tense of the original utterance is backshifted into the past:

Direct speech (Not backshifted)	Indirect speech (Backshifted form)
(1) Present	Simple past
(2) Simple past	Past perfect
(3) Present perfect	Past perfect
(4) Future	Future in the past

(adapted from Thomson and Martinet (1986)).

A more sophisticated version of this analysis can be found in Comrie (1986: 104–17).

b   Two different past tenses

Declerck (1991) and Declerck et al. (2006) propose that the English past tense is ambiguous: normally it means "past in relation to now", but in special cases like IRS, the past tense is a relative tense which means "simultaneous to another past time in the context". Huddleston and Pullum et al. (2002: 151–8) give arguments in favour of this analysis, and a more complete defence can be found in Declerck et al. (2006: 383–426). For more on Declerck's framework see section 3.2 below.

c   Pragmatics

Salkie and Reed (1997) propose that the past tense in the simultaneous interpretation of (1) has its normal sense, and that the simultaneity comes from aspectual considerations and pragmatic factors. For criticisms see Declerck (1999).

3 Theories of tense

3.1 Reichenbach

In his 1947 book *Elements of symbolic logic*, the philosopher Hans Reichenbach devoted twelve influential pages to what he called "the tenses of verbs". Reichenbach noted that the pluperfect (past perfect) tense in a sentence like *Peter had gone* involves not two times (speech time and the time of Peter's going) but three. The third time, which he called *Reference Time*, is another time which is mentioned or implied in the context. In the case of the pluperfect, the Reference Time has to be past (in relation to speech time), and the pluperfect locates the time of the event (Peter's going) as past in relation to that Reference Time: in other words, the pluperfect means "past in the past". He quotes a passage from Somerset Maugham's great 1915 novel *Of Human Bondage*:

> But Philip ceased to think of her a moment after he had settled down in his carriage. He thought only of the future. He had written to Mrs. Otter, the *massière* to whom Hayward had given him an introduction, and had in his pocket an invitation to tea on the following day.

Reichenbach comments:

> The series of events recounted here in the simple past determine the point of reference as lying before the point of speech. Some individual events, like the settling down in the carriage, the writing of the letter, and the giving of the introduction, precede the point of reference and are therefore related in the past perfect.

(1947: 287)

For the present perfect (*Peter has gone*), the Reference Time is present, so this tense would mean "past in the present" (cf. section 2.2 above). Reichenbach went on to claim that every English tense involves a Reference Time: so the present tense would not mean "speech time simultaneous with the time of the event" but "speech time simultaneous with Reference Time which is simultaneous with the time of the event". Many grammarians now agree that this was a mistake, though Hornstein (1990) sets out a carefully argued neo-Reichenbachian model of tense which proposes a reference time in every tense. A comprehensive critique of Reichenbach is Declerck (1991: 225–32); for a discussion that retains his useful insights see Bennett (2002: 82–7).

3.2 Declerck

Declerck (1991) and Declerck et al. (2006) have developed a very systematic conceptual framework for the interpretation of tense and time in English. For Declerck, the present perfect and *will* + infinitive are tenses, rather than markers of aspect or modality (cf. sections 2.1 and 2.2 for more about these controversial issues). The past tense, the present perfect, the present tense, and the future tense are *absolute* tenses because they express a link between a situation and the time of speech, which Declerck calls the temporal zero-point (t_0). Whereas the absolute past tense refers to a period of time that is wholly in the past, the present perfect refers to a period that includes now, which Declerck calls the "pre-present". Compare:

(13)   a   I *visited* China (last year).
       b   I *have visited* China (during my lifetime).

As we noted in section 1.2, *relative* tenses are used to express time relations between situations where none of them is t_0. Declerck uses the term "situation time of orientation" (STO) to capture the fact that any situation that is represented in a clause may act as the known time or starting point for locating another situation (or another STO, for that matter). For example, in (1) above the time of admitting (past) is the STO for the time of enjoying.

Declerck says that the time of admitting in (1) "establishes a domain", a domain being a set of STOs that are temporally linked to each other by means of relative tenses. If the absolute tense that establishes the domain is past, as in (1), then the past tense is used to express simultaneity within the domain, as with *enjoyed* in (1). The past perfect (pluperfect) expresses anteriority within the domain (cf. (14)), and the future in the past expresses posteriority within the domain (cf. (15)):

(14)   Some 20 per cent of staff working in schools said they *had been attacked* by pupils or parents during the 2010/11 academic year, figures show. (www)
(15)   Mr. Whiskers knew that sooner or later the dog *would be* back to steal from his dish again. He also knew this would be the last time! (www)

If the tense that establishes the domain is future, then Declerck says that the future STO is reinterpreted as if it were present: he calls this a *shift of temporal perspective.* The relative tenses used within the domain are the ones that are also used to express temporal relations in the present: present for simultaneity (16), past or present perfect for anteriority (17) and (18), future for posteriority (19).

(16) It is anticipated that during the course of the strategic planning process, significant issues will emerge that *do* not fit neatly into the other themes. (www)
(17) In a few years you will realise that I *was* right.
(18) [If a magician constantly creates new effects,] then the audience will not realize that the tricks they *have seen* revealed are indeed the same method used in the new tricks. (www)
(19) Make it fun for people to talk to you, so they will realize that they *will enjoy* working with you as well. (www)

Declerck explains that speakers may choose not to grammaticalise time relations within the domain, and opt instead to express the link between the time of the situation and t_o directly, using absolute tenses as in (20–22). Here, the first choice (e.g. *had witnessed* in (20)) uses a relative tense, while the second option (*witnessed* in (20)) uses an absolute tense:

(20) John said that Mary *had witnessed/witnessed* the accident. (Declerck 1991: 46)
(21) I have never denied that I *had used/used* that money. (Declerck 1991: 29)
(22) The newspapers will print everything that *is/will be said*. (Declerck 1991: 155)

However, the choice is not always free. There are constraints, both on the use of relative tenses and on the use of absolute tenses. For instance, in the case of temporal clauses, it is not possible to say **I will do it when I **will have** time:* the relative present tense must be used (*I will do it when I **have** time*). In a similar way, when the domain is past, the relative past perfect cannot always be replaced by an absolute past tense (*He admitted that he was a fool* does not mean the same as *He admitted that he had been a fool*) – cf. (21), where it is possible.

When the tenses on their own do not provide information about the relationship between times, the "Principle of unmarked temporal interpretation (PUTI)" applies: this principle roughly corresponds to the rules that determine the progression of R in other frameworks such as Discourse Representation Theory (see section 3.5, and Chapters 3, 4 and 10). The PUTI basically says that an STO that is a State or an Activity will tend to overlap with other STOs whereas a sequence of Accomplishments or Achievements usually indicate a temporal sequence (see Chapter 19 for these terms) (Declerck 1991: 119, 138–9).

Declerck et al. (2006) is a more elaborate and updated version of the theory presented in Declerck (1991); it also includes a detailed discussion of aspectual categories, and a very systematic analysis of tense in discourse.

3.3 Computational linguistics

A great deal of interesting research on tense has been done by people working on language and computers, an area also known as Natural Language Processing (NLP) or Language Engineering. Programming computers to handle tense meanings and the use of tense in discourse is a complex task: much of the best work is collected in Mani et al. (2005). One key paper is Moens and Steedman (1988), which proposes that time relations in language are not fundamental but derive from causal relations. They compare:

(23) When they built the 39th Street bridge, a local architect drew up the plans.
(24) ??When my car broke down, the sun set.

They argue that (24) is odd because there is no obvious connection between the car breaking down and the sun setting, and they go on to propose a semantic analysis which starts from a causal or "enabling" relationship between the *when*-clause and the main clause. Nowadays most analysts would treat the time relations as semantic and the causal ones as pragmatic, but Moens and Steedman's alternative is worth considering. Steedman (2005) is a more developed version of this approach to tense.

Another key problem for computational linguists is how to model the way humans understand time sequences in discourse; other approaches to tense tend to concentrate mostly on individual sentences. Several papers in Mani et al. (2005) deal with this problem, including some that use Discourse Representation Theory (see section 3.4).

3.4 Discourse representation theory (DRT)

Discourse representation theory takes a formal approach to tense and time relations, and combines semantic and pragmatic information (see Chapters 3, 4 and 10). One of the starting points in this framework is the observation that tenses behave in similar ways to pronouns. Look at this example:

(25)   Jennifer entered. She smiled at John.

Here the interpretation of the past tense of *smiled* in the second sentence depends on the time referred to in the previous sentence, in the same way as the interpretation of the pronoun *she* in the second sentence depends on the NP *Jennifer* in the previous sentence. A distinction is made between events (e) like smiling and states (s) like being happy. In (25) both sentences introduce an event into the discourse structure, and a sequence is established between e_1 and e_2. If the discourse were to continue as follows . . . *She was happy*, introducing a state, the temporal relation between e_2 and s would be one of overlap.

Instances where events do not express temporal progression – *Mary fell. John pushed her* – or states do not overlap – *She opened the door. He was smiling* – have led researchers working in Segmented Discourse Representation Theory (SDRT) to assign a more important role to world knowledge and to discourse relations such as narration, result, exploration, background and explanation (Lascarides and Asher 1993). These are said to play a part in determining the hierarchical structure of the discourse. For a simple introduction to DRT see Mani et al. (2005: 321–3); for more details and for SDRT, try van Eijck and Kamp (2011).

3.5 Generative grammar

Within generative work on tense we can distinguish three main lines of research. The first is summarised in the claim that "many central aspects of the semantics of tense are determined by independently motivated principles of syntactic theory" (Stowell 2007: 437). The second strand can be traced back to an important paper by Pollock (1989), which proposed for a variety of reasons that every clause had a "Tense Phrase" in its underlying structure. This idea was further developed by Cinque (1999), who argued that the underlying structure of sentences contains a rich series of "functional heads", of which tense is one (cf. 1.4). Third, we should note some sophisticated work on tense in reported speech by Giorgi, most recently her (2010) book, and related work by Hatav (2012) and Ogihara and Sharvit (2012). Much of this work is discussed in Guéron and Lecarme (2004, 2008).

3.6 Philosophy of language

Philosophers who think about time distinguish two theories following a classic paper by McTaggart (1908): the A-theory which treats time as something objective and real which flows past us, and the B-theory, which regards time as part of our subjective experience. For A-theorists, the present moment is real and can be used to define tenses. For B-theorists, the present moment is something that people construct and has no objective reality. The B-theory holds that tenses are not semantically basic – it is relations such as "earlier than" or "simultaneous with" that are the only legitimate starting point. The A-theory says that tenses are semantically basic – deictic or "absolute" notions such as "earlier than now" and "simultaneous with now" are where we should begin. For an A-theorist, a statement about the future such as (4), repeated here, is not true or false at the time it is uttered but only when the event referred to actually happens or not: the real world has to flow in time before we can judge.

(4) It will rain in Lille tomorrow.

For a B-theorist, predictions about the future are true or false at the time they are uttered (in fact, they are always either true or false, because there is no objectively real flow of time on which our judgement depends). For useful discussion see Dowden (2013).

A related issue in the philosophical literature is whether tenses are referring expressions which are part of propositions (consistent with the A-theory) or operators that are external to propositions (in line with the B-theory). Formal work on the semantics of tense focuses on whether tenses quantify over times (see Chapter 18). Kuhn and Portner (2002) is an excellent summary of these issues. More recently, King (2007) uses tense to address the status of propositions from another direction. He considers the possibility that what is asserted by an utterance of a sentence is not the same thing that tense (and modal) operators operate on. This leaves the nature of propositions in need of reassessment. King argues that tenses are not sentence operators, and that propositions are structured entities consisting of properties, entities and relations. He rejects previous accounts of what holds these parts together, and puts forward the view that speakers of natural languages endow propositions with their truth conditions. This is a radical departure from traditional semantics.

4 Future directions: tense, semantics and pragmatics

In this chapter, we have highlighted some of the key issues in research on tense. Many of the issues depend on one's view of the relationship between semantics and pragmatics.

It is one thing to describe the specific time information conveyed in specific contexts (e.g. the possibly different uses of the past tense in section 1.3, or the different readings of the present perfect in section 2.2); it is another to decide whether each of these different interpretations have their own semantics or whether they share one core meaning, a kind of common denominator that underlies all the different uses. Issues like these relate to the interface between semantics and pragmatics, and researchers have tried to find evidence or tests that will tip the scales in one direction or another. Tenses in reported speech (section 2.3) raise similar issues: the prominent view that the past tense has two different meanings (absolute versus relative) tries to explain the facts using semantics, whereas other analyses stress pragmatic factors.

It is not only the meaning of the tenses themselves that brings up the question of where to draw the line between semantics and pragmatics. As we saw in sections 3.2 and 3.4, our knowledge of the world very often overrides any "rules" of temporal progression formulated in terms of situation types: what we know about causation and consequence often seems to drive the "temporal interpretation", as in examples such as *Today I signed a contract with a publisher and had tea with an old friend* (no specific ordering imposed) versus *The glass broke. John dropped it* (reversed order) (Wilson and Sperber 2012: 174). Here again, there is tension and interaction between semantic and pragmatic knowledge and the relation has to be spelt out to arrive at an analysis that can explain the facts.

The analysis of tense thus crucially connects with wider questions about semantics and pragmatics. We expect this to be a central research issue in the future.

Further reading

Leech, G. N. 2004. *Meaning and the English Verb*, 3rd edition. London: Longman and Depraetere, I. and C. Langford 2012. *Advanced English Grammar: A Linguistic Approach*. London: Continuum, 136–93 supply basic information about tense in English.

Bennett, P. 2002. *Semantics: An Introduction to Non-Lexical Aspects of Meaning*. (Lincom Coursebooks in Linguistics, 12). Munich: Lincom Europa, 78–101, and Fabricius-Hansen, C. 2006. Tense. In K. Brown (ed.), *The Encyclopedia of Language and Linguistics*, Vol. 12, (Oxford, Elsevier), 566–73 are overviews of theoretical issues in time and tense.

Comrie, B. 1986. *Tense*. (Cambridge Textbooks in Linguistics). Cambridge: Cambridge University Press, and Binnick, R. (ed.) 2012. *The Oxford Handbook of Tense and Aspect*. Oxford: Oxford University Press are in-depth analyses of tense in linguistics.

Dahl, Ö. 1985. *Tense and Aspect Systems*. Oxford: Blackwell, and Dahl, Ö. and V. Velupillai. 2011. Supplement: tense and aspect. In M.S. Dryer and M. Haspelmath (eds), *The World Atlas of Language Structures Online*. Munich: Max Planck Digital Library. Online: http://wals.info/supplement/7 sketch tenses around the world.

Borg, E. 2012. *Pursuing Meaning*. Oxford: Oxford University Press, is a polemical but clear contribution to current debates in semantics and pragmatics.

References

Bennett, P. 2002. *Semantics: An Introduction to Non-Lexical Aspects of Meaning*. (Lincom Coursebooks in Linguistics, 12). Munich: Lincom Europa.

Biber, D., S. Johansson, G. Leech, S. Conrad and E. Finegan. 1999. *Longman Grammar of Spoken and Written English*. London: Longman.

Binnick, R. (ed.). 2012. *The Oxford Handbook of Tense and Aspect*. Oxford: Oxford University Press.

Bittner, M. 2005. Future discourse in a tenseless language. *Journal of Semantics* 22: 339–87.

Borg, E. 2012. *Pursuing Meaning*. Oxford: Oxford University Press.

Cinque, G. 1999. *Adverbs and Functional Heads: A Cross-Linguistic perspective*. Oxford: Oxford University Press.

Comrie, B. 1976. *Aspect*. (Cambridge Textbooks in Linguistics). Cambridge: Cambridge University Press.

Comrie, B. 1986. *Tense*. (Cambridge Textbooks in Linguistics). Cambridge: Cambridge University Press.

Dahl, Ö. 1985. *Tense and Aspect Systems*. Oxford: Blackwell.

Dahl, Ö. and V. Velupillai. 2011. Supplement: tense and aspect. In M.S. Dryer and M. Haspelmath (eds), *The World Atlas of Language Structures Online*. Munich: Max Planck Digital Library. http://wals.info/supplement/7

Declerck, R. 1991. *Tense in English: Its Structure and Use in Discourse*. London: Routledge.

Declerck, R. 1999. Remarks on Salkie and Reed's (1997) 'pragmatic hypothesis' of tense in reported speech. *English Language and Linguistics* 3: 83–116.

Declerck, R., B. Cappelle and S. Reed. 2006. *The Grammar of the English Verb Phrase. Volume 1: The Grammar of the English Tense System. A Comprehensive Analysis*. Berlin: Mouton de Gruyter.
Depraetere, I. and C. Langford. 2012. *Advanced English Grammar: A Linguistic Approach*. London: Bloomsbury.
Dowden, B. 2013. Time. In J. Fieser (ed.), *Internet Encyclopedia of Philosophy*. http://www.iep.utm.edu/time
Dryer, M. 2011a. Feature 69A: position of tense-aspect affixes. In M.S. Dryer and M. Haspelmath (eds), *The World Atlas of Language Structures Online*. Munich: Max Planck Digital Library. http://wals.info/feature/69A
Dryer, M. 2011b. Feature 26A: prefixing vs. suffixing in inflectional morphology. In M.S. Dryer and M. Haspelmath (eds), *The World Atlas of Language Structures Online*. Munich: Max Planck Digital Library. http://wals.info/feature/26A
Dummett, M. 2004. *Truth and the Past*. New York, NY: Columbia University Press.
Evans, V. 2003. *The Structure of Time: Language, Meaning and Temporal Cognition*. Amsterdam: John Benjamins.
Fabricius-Hansen, C. 2006. Tense. In K. Brown (ed.), *The Encyclopedia of Language and Linguistics*. Vol. 12. Oxford: Elsevier, 566–73.
Giorgi, A. 2010. *About the Speaker: Towards a Syntax of Indexicality*. Oxford: Oxford University Press.
Guéron, J. and J. Lecarme (eds). 2004. *The Syntax of Time*. Cambridge, MA: MIT Press.
Guéron, J. and J. Lecarme (eds). 2008. *Time and Modality*. Dordrecht: Springer.
Hana, J. 1998. *Esperanto Grammar*. http://esperanto.50webs.com_
Hatav, G. 2012. Bound tenses. In R. Binnick (ed.), 2012. *The Oxford Handbook of Tense and Aspect*. Oxford: Oxford University Press, 611–37.
Hawking, S. 1988. *A Brief History of Time: From Big Bang to Black Holes*. New York, NY: Bantam.
Hornstein, Norbert. 1990. *As Time Goes By: Tense and Universal Grammar*. Cambridge, MA: MIT Press.
Huddleston, R. 1995. The case against a future tense in English. *Studies in Language* 19: 399–446.
Huddleston, R., G. Pullum et al. 2002. *The Cambridge Grammar of the English Language*. Cambridge: Cambridge University Press.
Jespersen, O. 1933. *Essentials of English Grammar*. London: Allen and Unwin.
King, J.C. 2007. *The Nature and Structure of Content*. Oxford: Clarendon Press.
Kuhn, S. and P. Portner. 2002. Tense and time. In D. Gabbay and F. Guenthner (eds), *Handbook of Philosophical Logic, Vol. 7*. Amsterdam: Kluwer, 277–346.
Lascarides, A. and N. Asher. 1993. Temporal interpretation, discourse relations and commonsense entailment. *Linguistics and Philosophy* 16: 437–93.
Leech, G.N. 2004. *Meaning and the English Verb*, 3rd edition. London: Longman.
Lin, J.-W. 2006. Time in a language without tense: the case of Chinese. *Journal of Semantics* 23: 1–53.
Lin, J.-W. 2012. Tenselessness. In R. Binnick (ed.), 2012. *The Oxford Handbook of Tense and Aspect*. Oxford: Oxford University Press, 669–95.
Lin, T.-H. J. 2007. Is there TP in Mandarin Chinese? *USTWPL* 3: 35–42. http://ling.nthu.edu.tw/USTWPL/vol3/4_Is%20there%20TP%20in%20Mandarin%20Chinese_T.-H.%20Jonah%20Lin.pdf
Mani, I., J. Pustejovsky and R. Gaizauskas (eds). 2005. *The Language of Time: A Reader*. Oxford: Oxford University Press.
Matthewson, L. 2006. Temporal semantics in a superficially tenseless language. *Linguistics and Philosophy*: 673–713.
McCawley, J.D. 1971. Tense and time reference in English. In T. Langendoen and C. Fillmore (eds), *Studies in Linguistic Semantics*. New York: Holt, Rinehart and Winston, 97–113. Reprinted in J.D. McCawley 1973. *Grammar and Meaning*. Tokyo: Taishukan: 257–76.
McTaggart, J.M.E. 1908. The unreality of time. *Mind* 17: 457–73.
Moens, M. and M. Steedman. 1988. Temporal ontology and temporal reference. *Computational Linguistics* 14.2: 15–28. Reprinted in I. Mani, J. Pustejovsky and R. Gaizauskas (eds), 2005. *The Language of Time: A Reader*. Oxford: Oxford University Press, 93–114.
Ogihara, T. and Y. Sharvit. 2012. Embedded tenses. In R. Binnick (ed.), 2012. *The Oxford Handbook of Tense and Aspect*. Oxford: Oxford University Press, 638–68.

Pollock, J.-Y. 1989. Verb movement, universal grammar, and the structure of IP. *Linguistic Inquiry* 20: 365–424.

Quirk, R., S. Greenbaum, G. Leech and J. Svartvik. 1985. A *Comprehensive Grammar of the English Language*. London: Longman.

Reichenbach, H. 1947. *Elements of Symbolic Logic*. London: Macmillan. (The section 'The tenses of verbs' is reprinted in I. Mani, J. Pustejovsky and R. Gaizauskas (eds) 2005. *The Language of Time: A Reader*. Oxford: Oxford University Press, 71.

Ritz, E.-M. 2012. Perfect tense and aspect. In R. Binnick (ed.), 2012. *The Oxford Handbook of Tense and Aspect*. Oxford: Oxford University Press, 881–907.

Salkie, R. 2010. *Will*: tense or modal or both? *English Language and Linguistics* 14: 187–215.

Salkie, R. and S. Reed. 1997. Time reference in reported speech. *English Language and Linguistics* 1: 319–48.

Schaden, G. 2009. Present perfects compete. *Linguistics and Philosophy* 32: 115–41.

Shaer, B. 2003. Toward the tenseless analysis of a tenseless language. In J. Anderssen, P. Menendez Benito and A. Werle (eds), *Proceedings of SULA 2, GLSA, University of Massachusetts at Amherst* (Amherst, MA: Umass), 139–56. http://www.umass.edu/linguist/events/SULA/SULA_2003_cd/files/shaer.pdf

Smith, C. and M. Erbaugh. 2005. Temporal interpretation in Mandarin Chinese. *Linguistics* 43: 713–56.

Steedman, M. 2005. The productions of time. http://homepages.inf.ed.ac.uk/steedman/papers/temporality/temporality2.pdf

Stowell, T. 2007. The syntactic expression of tense. *Lingua* 117: 437–63.

Thomson, A. and A. Martinet. 1986. *A Practical English Grammar*. Oxford: Oxford University Press.

van Eijck, J. and H. Kamp 2011. Discourse representation in context. In J. van Benthem and A. ter Meulen (eds), *Handbook of Logic and Language*. 2nd Edition. Amsterdam: Elsevier, 181–252.

Vater. H. 1997. Hat das Deutsche Futurtempora? In H. Vater (ed.), *Zu Tempus und Modus im Deutschen*. Trier: Wissenschaftlicher Verlag, 53–69.

Vendler, Z. 1957. Verbs and times. *The Philosophical Review* 66: 143–60.

Welke, K. 2005. *Tempus im Deutschen: Rekonstruktion eines semantischen Systems* (Linguistik – Impulse and Tendenzen 13). Berlin: Walter de Gruyter.

Wilson, D. and D. Sperber. 2012. *Meaning and Relevance*. Cambridge: Cambridge University Press.

Related topics

Chapter 19, Lexical and grammatical aspect; Chapter 21, Modality.

21
Modality

Ilse Depraetere

1 Introduction

Modality is among the most widely studied topics in linguistics. It is a concept that is used to designate a wide array of language facts. In his overview of the field, Portner (2009: 2–8) mentions the following examples that involve modality and groups them in three classes:

- modal phenomena at sentence level (modal auxiliaries such as *may, must, can, will, should*; modal adverbs like *possibly, probably*; generics, habituals; tense and aspect (the future, the use of the past to express unreality, as in *Even if you stayed until tomorrow, I'd be sad*, the progressive, the perfect); conditionals; covert modality (e.g. *Tim knows how to solve a problem* contains an implicit expression of ability, as is clear from the paraphrase *Tim knows how he can solve a problem*).
- modal phenomena at sub-sentential level (modal adjectives and nouns, propositional attitude verbs (e.g. *believe, hope*) and adjectives (e.g. *certain, pleased*), verbal mood (e.g. the subjunctive), dependent modals, as in *I'd be surprised if David should win*, negative polarity items).
- discourse modality (evidentiality (cf. section 2.2), specific functions of clause types).

The diverse range of potentially modal phenomena is also clear from research on modality from a cross-linguistic perspective (e.g. Bybee et al. (1994), Palmer (2001), de Haan (2005)).

It is not only the breadth of the field that is striking: modality is a phenomenon that has inspired research in widely divergent theoretical frameworks, and in neighbouring disciplines such as logic and philosophy. Modality has been studied extensively in:

- Formal semantics (Kratzer 1991, 2012)
- Cognitive linguistics and force dynamics (Talmy 1988; Langacker 2003)
- Pragmatic theory (Papafragou 2000)
- Corpus linguistics (modal verbs: Coates (1983), Palmer (1990), Westney (1995), Collins (2009); modal adverbs: Hoye (1997), Aijmer and Simon-Vandenbergen (2007); modal adjectives: Van Linden (2012))
- Diachronic linguistics (Goossens 1987, 1992, 2000; Traugott and Dasher 2002; Hart 2004; Bybee 2006; Narrog 2012)

In other words, both the phenomena that are examined under the heading of "modality" and the theories that have served as a framework for analysis are multiple and varied. Given the breadth of the field, a functional or semantic definition of modality encompassing all its potential formal realizations is not easy to achieve (cf. e.g. Narrog (2005), Nuyts (2005), and Declerck (2011) for useful discussion). A common characterization of modal verbs, which are fairly uncontroversial expressions of modality, is that these are forms the meanings of which hinge on the notions of possibility or necessity. However, even when restricted to the core set of English modals, the definition is already problematic: the meanings of *shall* and *will* cannot be captured, in a straightforward way, in terms of possibility or necessity (see Chapter 20). A broader definition is that modality refers to forms that represent situations as non-factual. Here again, even when restricting oneself to the core modals in English, a definition along these lines is not without problems: some (e.g. Salkie (2014)) have argued that *can* communicates enablement and does not express non-factuality at all.

Mood refers to the grammatical marking of specific meanings through affixes attached to the verb: certain affixes express the meaning of non-factuality; others express the meaning of factuality. In the traditional view, there are three moods in English: the indicative mood (e.g. *She **got** her PhD in 1993*), the imperative mood (*Leave me alone!*) and the subjunctive mood (*Parliament decreed no more soldiers **be** sent to the war zone*). The mandative subjunctive, illustrated in the example, is more frequent in American English than in British English (cf. Leech et al. (2009)). From a synchronic point of view, there seems little formal justification to recognize an inflectional subjunctive mood in present-day English as the form of the present subjunctive corresponds to the bare infinitive. *Be* is the only verb that has a so-called past subjunctive, and its form corresponds to the past indicative form *were*, as in *I wish you/ she were here*. Some have argued that it is more accurate to speak of a subjunctive clause type (Aarts 2012) or subjunctive constructions (Huddleston et al. 2002: 51, 993) rather than subjunctive mood. (The same line of meaning could be developed for the imperative (mood) in English.) Other languages have a wider range of moods, such as the optative in Turkish, to express a wish, a hope or a command. Nenets, a language spoken in Northern Russia, has as many as sixteen moods. Rothstein and Thieroff (2010) offers an overview of morphological mood in 36 European languages. Not all moods express modal meaning. The indicative, for instance, is typically used to represent a situation as a fact, which is clearly not modal. In sentences like *If I **got** the grant, I would be absolutely thrilled* though, *got* loses its unmarked temporal meaning: it no longer refers to the past, but to the future, and it no longer presents a situation as a fact, but as hypothetical. For these reasons, this form is labelled as a "modal indicative", at first sight a contradiction in terms. While "modal" captures the semantics, "indicative" refers to the morphological make-up – it is standard (but not universal) practice for "mood" to refer to a verbal inflection. (cf. Thieroff (2010)) A similar form-function tension is observed in the chapter on tense: not all instantiations of a particular tense, for instance, the present tense, refer to present time, but that does not stop one from referring to the verb in *The performance starts at eight* as a present tense form.

The conceptual pair "mood and modality" is similar to "tense and time", in that in both cases, the first item refers to a formal inflection and the second captures a specific function or meaning: that of expressing time (in the case of tense) and that of expressing (non-)modal meaning (in the case of mood). As will be clear from the overview at the beginning of this section, mood does not exhaust the list of forms that express modal meaning, in the same way as tense is not the only formal means to express time or a temporal relation (cf. Chapter 20).

"Modality/mood" is one of the components in the commonly used acronym TAM, the association with tense and aspect pointing to the interaction between three phenomena that pertain to the verb (phrase) (cf. e.g. Hogeweg et al. (2009)), even though one must bear in mind that tense and mood are formal categories while aspect and modality are notional categories. The discussion so far has already touched upon a link between tense/time and modality: specific tenses can be used in contexts that express non-factual meaning. The present tense, like the past tense (cf. example above), can express hypothetical meaning (*He behaves as though he **knows** everything about it* – hypothetical). The past tense and the past perfect can communicate counterfactual meaning (*If I **knew** how to replace a flat tyre, I wouldn't be stuck here.* – *I wish you **had told** her.*). The debate about whether English has a future tense (see Chapter 20) illustrates another link: here the question is whether, in the absence of an inflection that signals future time in English (or any language that does not have an inflectional morpheme for future time reference), and given the fact that a future situation is by definition not factual, *will* should be considered as a marker of modality rather than as a tense marker. Because non-present tenses are removed from the present and/or from reality, they have sometimes not been defined in terms of temporal relations, but in terms of detachment. In cognitive linguistics, the present tense has been analysed in terms of epistemic immediacy (cf. e.g. Langacker (2011) for discussion).

As for the link between aspect and modality (see Chapter 19), among the relations that have been studied is that between mood and modality and the imperfective/perfective (cf. e.g. Abraham and Leiss (2008)); the progressive in English has been analysed as a kind of modal operator as well (Dowty 1977).

In this chapter, the focus will be on verbs that express modal meaning in English. (Hansen and de Haan (2009) offer a description of the system of modals and modal constructions in languages spoken in the European area.) Despite extensive research in this subfield of modality, there are still a number of outstanding problematic areas:

- The more theoretically oriented work tends to be tested on a relatively small data sample, and it is not very clear if it can cope with a richer data set.
- Even meticulous empirical studies at times uncritically incorporate concepts such as subjectivity, source of modality or strength of modality into the analysis. While there seems to be unanimity that these concepts are crucial, there is still a need for careful clarification and operationalization for empirical (corpus) analysis.
- A key question in the characterization of modal expressions is the extent to which their meaning is determined by the independent lexical semantics of the verbs and to what extent it is contextually determined. In other words, do modal verbs have one core meaning that is contextually enriched (monosemy) or are the different meanings sufficiently differentiated semantically to consider modal expressions polysemous (see Chapter 13)? Answering this question means taking a theoretical stance towards the semantics-pragmatics interface (see Chapter 10).

The outline of the chapter is as follows. After a brief overview of the formal characteristics of modal verbs, I will present a few of the controversies in research on modal verbs in more detail; that is, questions of taxonomy, the polysemy/monosemy debate and the notions of subjectivity and strength. Section 4 draws a sketch of the historical development of modal meanings and grammaticalization. The conclusion touches upon the question of the semantics/pragmatics interface and gives an indication of possible routes for future research.

2 The meaning of modals: some controversial issues

2.1 A note on the formal behaviour of modals in English

Before examining the semantics of modal verbs, it is useful to sketch their formal profile. The core modals (*can, could, may, might, must, will, would, shall, should*) do not require *do*-support in four specific contexts: in negative sentences (*I can't help it*), in contexts in which there is subject-verb inversion (*Can you come?*), in contexts in which the main verb is unexpressed (*Can you come? – Yes, I can*), and in contexts in which a contrast is established (*You can't uncork a bottle with a fork. – Now watch this. See? I **can** uncork a bottle with a fork*). This is a feature they share with the auxiliaries *be* and *have*. They exhibit a further number of formal features:

- they do not inflect for person and number (*She can/*cans sing well*);
- they cannot be stacked (except in some varieties of English) (**She must can be available tomorrow*);
- they do not have non-finite forms (**to can*; **She is canning*);
- they are followed by a bare infinitive (*She can sing/* to sing*).

Ought to, need and *dare* are sometimes said to be peripheral modals, for different reasons: *ought* does not have all of the prototypical formal features; it is followed by a *to*-infinitive. The constraint on the latter two auxiliaries is that they only feature in non-assertive contexts; that is, sentences that are negative and/or interrogative (*Need(n't) I explain? – You needn't explain. – *You need explain.*). There is a further group of expressions with even fewer of the features of the core modals: modal expressions with *be*, including *be to, be supposed to, be able to, be permitted to, be liable to* are sometimes labelled quasi-modals or semi-modals. *Have to* and *need to* are lexical verbs that express the modal meaning of necessity; they are sometimes also included in the category of semi-modals. This brief overview does not provide an exhaustive list of verbal expressions that communicate modal meaning, the list including further verbs like *want to, have got to*, etc. (cf. section 3).

2.2 Taxonomies of modal meaning

Some classifications of modal meaning (e.g. Coates (1983)) make a binary distinction between epistemic modality and non-epistemic or root modality. The label "root" modality reflects the historical fact that non-epistemic meaning is the more basic one, epistemic meanings usually having developed out of non-epistemic ones (cf. section 3). Inspired by Palmer (1990), other authors advocate a three-fold classification and distinguish epistemic modality, deontic modality and dynamic modality (cf. e.g. Nuyts (2000), Verstraete (2001), Huddleston et al. (2002), Collins (2009)). An approach along these lines implies that the distinction between deontic and dynamic modality is considered to be as important as that between epistemic and deontic meaning or that between epistemic and dynamic meaning.

Table 21.1 Classifications of modal meaning

epistemic possibility/necessity	non-epistemic or root possibility/necessity	
epistemic possibility/necessity	deontic possibility/necessity	dynamic possibility/necessity

Modality is said to be *epistemic* if it communicates how likely or unlikely it is, according to the speaker, that a situation is the case. In other words, the scope of the modality is wide: the proposition is said to be necessarily (*He must be older than 50* – It is necessarily the case that he is older than 50), possibly (*He may be older than 50* – It is possibly the case that he is older than 50) or impossibly (*He can't be older than 50* – It is impossible that he is older than 50) the case in the speaker's opinion. In some definitions, the notion of truth is foregrounded: "Epistemics are clausal-scope indicators of a speaker's commitment to the truth of a proposition" (Bybee and Fleischman 1995: 6). While the delineation of epistemic modality with respect to the non-epistemic meanings of dynamic modality and deontic modality is relatively unproblematic, there is no unanimity on whether so-called evidential modality is a subclass of epistemic meaning or whether it is on a par with it. Nuyts (2000) defines this category of modal meaning as follows:

> Evidentiality concerns the speaker's indication of the nature (the type and quality) of the evidence invoked for (assuming the existence of) the state of affairs expressed in the utterance. This does not involve any explicit evaluation in terms of the state of affairs being true or not.
>
> (2000: 27)

Note that in English, evidentiality is not expressed through modal verbs, unlike in German, for instance (*Er soll krank sein.* – "He is said to be ill.") but through other markers, as in *Two hundred people are **alleged** to have died in the plane crash* or *I **hear** that you've been promoted*. In other languages, evidentiality is expressed morphologically (cf. e.g. Willett (1988) for a cross-linguistic survey of markers of evidentiality and Boye (2012) for an in-depth discussion).

Deontic modality encompasses permission (on the possibility side) and obligation (on the necessity side). The definitions that have been given of this type of modality often involve reference to speech acts, such as that of giving permission (deontic possibility), or that of giving an order or prohibiting an action (deontic necessity). In other words, for some people, the concept of deontic modality hinges on the pragmatic notion of (indirect) performativity, witness the fact that the meanings can be adequately glossed with a performative verb, *You must be back by twelve* corresponding to *I oblige/require/demand you to be back by twelve* and *You can park your car in front of my garage* corresponding to *I authorize you to park my car in front of my garage* or still *You can't have more cake* corresponding to *I forbid you to have more cake*.

If it is the pragmatic feature of "directive speech act" that is constitutive of "deontic necessity" and which sets it apart from dynamic necessity (cf. below), then one might wonder if Coates's (1983) view is not appropriate: she argues that the modal logic term "deontic", used by von Wright (1951) to analyse the logical relations between obligation, permission or prohibition, is inappropriate to discuss the semantics of (what she calls) root (that is, non-epistemic) modality. As she sees it, cutting up root necessity meanings, for instance, obscures the essential unity of root necessity utterances, which share a common, basic meaning; that is, "it is necessary for". Moreover, the cut-off points between the subclasses are bound to be arbitrary. A point to be borne in mind is that in some classifications of modal meaning, deontic necessity (or, for that matter, deontic possibility) is a subclass of root necessity (root possibility), while in other taxonomies, it is a cover term that encompasses both "performative" and "non-performative" instances of necessity (possibility). Verstraete (2001) offers a very illuminating discussion, whereby a distinction is drawn between "modal performativity" and "interactive performativity" (relating to the speech act value) and the role they have to play in the definition of modal meaning (cf. section 2.4).

Dynamic modality is concerned with "properties and dispositions of persons, etc. referred to in the clause, especially by the subject NP" (Huddleston et al. 2002: 178). Ability (*She can play the flute*) and volition (*She will help me with the BBQ*) illustrate the "clearest cases" on the possibility side, but dynamic possibility also includes "what is reasonable" (*You can always say you're too busy*), "what is circumstantially possible" (*Water can still get in*) and "what is sometimes the case: the 'existential' use" (*These animals can be dangerous*). A "clear" example of dynamic necessity is *Ed's a guy who must always be poking his nose into other people's business*; this category also includes "circumstantial necessity" (*Now that she's lost her job she must live extremely frugally*) (Huddleston et al. 2002: 184–5). All authors who distinguish between dynamic and deontic modality point out that the boundaries are somewhat fuzzy. Gisborne (2007) brings up some fundamental problems with the notion of dynamic modality and Depraetere and Reed (2011) are likewise critical of this category and try to offer a more explicit definition of modal non-epistemic possibility meaning that is "not ability" and "not permission". To do so, they use three criteria (scope, source, potential barrier), which enable them to pin down five subclasses of root possibility meaning: ability, opportunity, permission, general situation possibility (GSP) and permissibility. The scope is wide or narrow depending on whether the possibility bears on the entire proposition (as in *Cracks can appear overnight*) or on the VP (as in *This printer can also scan documents*). "Source" refers to the origin of the possibility, which may be subject-internal, in which case the possibility originates in innate capacities or acquired skills of the subject referent. Subject-external sources may be of different types: an external authority, rules and regulations or circumstances may be at the origin of the possibility. If the source has source status because it can potentially impose a barrier on actualization, it carries the feature [+ potential barrier]. For instance, in *All vehicles rented in Ireland may only be driven in Northern Ireland and the Republic of Ireland* (situation permissibility), the rental policy regulations owe their status of source to the fact they determine whether there can be actualization or not of the situation. The combination of features that define the different subtypes of non-epistemic meaning are summarized in Table 21.2:

While the triad "epistemic – dynamic – deontic" is a standard classification of modal meaning as expressed by modals, alternative proposals have been put forward. Bybee and Fleischman (1995) and Bybee et al. (1994) distinguish between *speaker-oriented* modality, which is expressed by forms that mark directives, such as the imperative form in English, *epistemic* modality and *agent-oriented* modality, a cover term encompassing what Huddleston et al. (2002) call dynamic modality and deontic modality. There is a further class of "subordinating moods", which they reserve for forms expressing the speaker-oriented and epistemic modalities used in subordinate clauses, such as complement clauses, concessives

Table 21.2 Classification of root possibility meanings based on Depraetere and Reed (2011)

	situation permissibility	*GSP*	*permission*	*opportunity*	*ability*
source	external	external	external	external	internal
scope	wide	wide	narrow	narrow	narrow
potential barrier	+ potential barrier	– potential barrier	+ potential barrier	– potential barrier	– potential barrier

and purpose clauses. Narrog (2012) identifies nine different subclasses of modal meaning (epistemic, deontic, teleological, preferential, boulomaic, participant-internal, circumstantial, existential and evidential), and they are characterized in terms of two dimensions: that of volitivity and that of speech act orientation.

Observations to the effect that the borderlines between categories are fuzzy, irrespective of the taxonomic approach taken, abound and this brings up a general taxonomic question, whether, ultimately, the gradience is of the "subsective" or "intersective" type (cf. Aarts (2007)): that is, does it relate to degree of typicality (within a class) or to degree of membership? Applied to modal meanings, the question is whether the indeterminate examples constitute less prototypical examples of a specific meaning or whether they are indicative of the existence of an intermediate class.

2.3 Polysemy/monosemy

The examples with *can* mentioned in section 2.2 show that one modal can communicate a variety of meanings. Many of the English modals are "multi-functional" and this is a phenomenon that has been observed cross-linguistically, but it is not universal and it is not spread evenly. In a typological study of 241 languages, Van der Auwera et al. (2005) have found that 49 languages have forms (including but not restricted to verbs) that are polyfunctional; that is, they can express epistemic as well as non-epistemic meaning, both for possibility and necessity. There are 30 languages that have forms that can express both types of necessity (for four of them the evidence is not conclusive yet as to whether the polyfunctionality is partial or also extends to possibility) and another 39 that have forms that express both types of possibility (for 11 of them the evidence is not conclusive yet as to whether the polyfunctionality is partial or also extends to necessity). One hundred and twenty-three languages do not have polyfunctional forms. It is interesting to observe that in certain languages, one form may be used both for possibility and necessity: for instance, in Danish, *må* can express both obligation and permission. The following examples from the British National Corpus (BNC) illustrate some of the meaning distinctions communicated by *must*:

(1) "What an unusual boy he *must* be," my mother remarked, "if he has the sense to see beneath the exterior to the person inside." (BNC) (epistemic)
(2) State House already houses a recruiting office for the Royal Navy and Marines, and visitors *must* apply for a temporary pass at the security ground floor entrance. (BNC) (non-epistemic)
(3) I feel I *must* write and thank my fellow citizens for the magnificent turnout at the main Battle of the Atlantic march-past. (BNC) (non-epistemic)
(4) "You *must* come out of the sun, Mr Gray," said Lord Henry. (BNC) (non-epistemic)
(5) Whatever the risk, she *must* go to him and tell him to go back. (BNC) (non-epistemic)
(6) Then she took a quick look at Vern and said to me, "You *must* come and see my photos, Bina." (BNC) (non-epistemic)

While *must* communicates non-epistemic necessity in a straightforward manner in (2) to (5), it is likely that Bina, in example (6), will take the sentence as an invitation rather than an order. In (2), there is reference to a general regulation which is represented as unlimited in time; in (3) the necessity is self-imposed and in (4) and (5) the source of the necessity is external to the "obligee". If it is true that the borderlines between modal categories are fuzzy (cf. section 2.2), then it will logically follow that the meaning of modals is fuzzy. Can we say that all modals have one meaning, the instantiations of which are just contextual realizations of the basic semantic core? Or should one argue anyway that modals are polysemous, and that the different meanings which they communicate (at least the distinction between epistemic and non-epistemic meaning) are sufficiently distinct to justify the conclusion that they are autonomous, semantic classes of their own (see Chapter 13)? Here again, opinions differ. The following are among the arguments used by "polysemists":

(a) Ambiguous examples exist:

(7) *The second part **must** contain the item name.* ((a) epistemic reading: "if it's not in the first part, then the only possible conclusion is that it can be found in the second, as the instructions say that the item name must be mentioned in the description"; (b) non-epistemic reading: "this is the requirement")

(8) *You know there is a tendency for malignant change anyway, and one of the reasons for removing a benign parotid tumour is that it **may** go malignant, in twenty years' time or so.* (British English component of the International Corpus of English (ICE-GB): S1B-010) ((a) epistemic reading: "(on the basis of information that is the speaker's disposal, (s)he concludes that) it is possible that a (specific) benign parotid tumor will go malignant", (b) non-epistemic reading: "the situation of a benign parotid tumor going malignant is conceivable/theoretically possible")

(b) Scope of negation testifies to the difference in meaning between epistemic and non-epistemic meaning in the following examples:

(9) *7.1 The Agreement shall be binding upon all the parties and **may** not be assigned without the prior written consent of the other party.* (BNC) (non-epistemic: the negation bears on the modal meaning, cf. "it is not permitted/possible")

(10) *These **may** not be recognized as symptoms of stress – that is, until the stress is reduced and the symptoms disappear.* (BNC) (epistemic: the negation bears on the proposition, cf. "it is possible that they won't be recognized as symptoms of stress")

Note that this test does not yield the same result with all modals. In both the epistemic and the non-epistemic example with *must* below, negation bears on the proposition/VP:

(11) *She had hinted darkly that Wilson herself must be to blame, that she **must** have been weak, must not have written plain enough and as she had been instructed* (BNC) (epistemic, "it is necessarily the case that she did not write plain enough")

(12) *He would be lost in the city on his own and besides he **must** not forget about his grandparents—they would die if he did not look after them.* (BNC) (non-epistemic, "it is necessary for him not to forget")

(c) Epistemic and non-epistemic meanings have different paraphrases, which shows that they are semantically distinct (cf. e.g. Coates (1983)). Epistemic meanings are brought out by a paraphrase with a *that*-clause: *it is necessarily/possibly the case that X*; the meaning of non-epistemic readings is adequately captured by a *for*-clause: *it is necessary/possible for X to Y*.

Polysemists often point out that there are fuzzy borderlines between the modal categories (deontic/dynamic, dynamic/epistemic) (cf. e.g. Huddleston et al. (2002): 179; Collins (2009): 23) and even though they do not always explicitly say so, the care with which they do seems to suggest that fuzziness as such may somewhat jeopardize the position taken. Monosemists (cf. e.g. Groefsema (1995: 55–7)) indeed use indeterminacy of meaning as an argument in favour of monosemy, but they also tend to qualify their approach. Papafragou, for instance, writes:

> My aim in this chapter has been to strike a middle way between polysemy-based and radical monosemy accounts of English modals. I have tried to offer a semantics rich enough to allow for difference in content in various modals, and yet underspecified to the extent of drawing on extensive pragmatic inferencing until it yields a complete truth-evaluable representation.
>
> (Papafragou 2000: 84)

To formulate a clear answer to the question, a number of issues need to be resolved: first, it is necessary to pin down criteria that will define, in an unambiguous way, the modal meanings involved. As will be clear from the discussion in section 2.2, this is not necessarily an item that can be ticked off the list. Second, it is necessary to turn to lexical semantics and look for adequate tests that can identify whether the different meanings taken stock of are indicative of polysemy or vagueness (see the discussion in Chapter 13). For instance, to what extent can identity-of-sense tests (cf. e.g. Riemer (2005): 140–1) be used to identify the status of the meaning distinctions? Third, one needs to settle on the impact of potentially indeterminate examples: do they fade away once the defining criteria have been fine-tuned and made fully operational for empirical analysis? If so, this may well pave the way for a polysemy account. If not, while fuzziness may, at first sight, be less of a problem for a monosemous approach, if the framework is to be explanatorily adequate, one does need to account for the meaning distinctions that arise in context anyway, which means that, eventually, monosemists basically face the same challenge as the polysemists. Fuzziness may well point to historical change, whereby indeterminate examples illustrate "bridging contexts" (Enfield 2003: 28); that is, they point to intermediate stages in the historical development of meanings.

2.4 Subjectivity

While *subjectivity* is a linguistic feature that is pervasive, occurring when a speaker "in making an utterance, simultaneously comments upon that utterance and expresses his attitude to what he is saying" (Lyons 1977: 739), it plays a major role in the characterization of modal meaning.

It is very closely associated with epistemic modality, since epistemic meaning reflects the speaker's subjective assessment of whether the proposition expressed is the case. The paraphrases of epistemic sentences bring out the subjective component relatively straightforwardly: *That must be Jennifer* can be glossed as *I confidently conclude* (on the basis of situational and world knowledge to which I have access) *that the person entering the house is Jennifer*, a paraphrase of *You may be right* being *I conclude* (on the basis of situational and world knowledge that is at my disposal) *that it is possible that your opinion is correct*. The subjectivity resides in the fact that the conclusion formulated is based on a personal assessment of evidence that is thought to be sufficient by the speaker to warrant the conclusion drawn. Even though subjectivity is characteristic of most epistemic sentences, examples of objective epistemic modality have also been signalled, even though they are rare (Coates 1983: 20, 55):

(13) The simple truth is that if you're going to boil eggs communally, they *must* be hard. (Coates 1983: 18)

In this sentence, it is not the speaker's subjective assessment of a situation that is communicated, but rather what the speaker regards as an empirically verifiable objective fact. (Others have called this intersubjectivity: cf. e.g. Nuyts (2012).) While it is still the speaker who makes an inference, and explicitly presents it like an inference, given the state of the world, this is in fact the only conclusion that can be drawn. Lyons uses the following example to explain objective epistemic modality (1977: 791, 798):

(14) Alfred *must* be unmarried.

This sentence may be uttered in a context in which this conclusion is the only one that is logically possible. For instance, if Alfred wears no wedding ring and if he is a member of a community in which married people wear wedding rings, then the epistemic judgement is objective. Examples of this type should still be distinguished from *alethic* modality (cf. e.g. Lyons (1977: 797ff), Hoye (1997: 48–53)), a term used by logicians to refer to the modality of the necessary truth of propositions of the type given in (15) and (16):

(15) If x is a prime number between 90 and 100 it *must* be 97. (Huddleston et al. 2002: 173)
(16) Alfred is a bachelor, so he *must* be unmarried. (Hoye 1997: 49)

Subjectivity is not restricted to epistemic modality. On the non-epistemic side, subjectivity is most commonly associated with deontic meanings. When the source of the obligation or the permission is "internal", in the sense that the obligation imposed or the permission granted or refused reflects an autonomous decision by the speaker, the obligation (*You must be back by 10*) and permission (*You may come in*) is subjective. When obligation or permission is seen as coming from some source external to the speaker, it is said to be objective (*You have to be back by 11* (these are the house rules) – (pointing to a traffic sign) *You can park your car on this side of the street*).

The criterion of subjectivity/objectivity is often appealed to in order to differentiate the semantic profile of modal verbs that communicate the same meaning. For instance, *have to* is said to typically express objective necessity while *must* is typically used to express subjective necessity; *ought to* is said to be more objective than *should*:

(17) You even *have to* pay extra if you want to have bread with your meal. (ICE-GB, W1B-002) (objective)
(18) You *must* believe me. (ICE-GB, W2F-008) (subjective)
(19) Appeals Procedure: Appellants *ought to* have adequate time in which to prepare their appeals, and an effective opportunity to present a counter-argument to the reasons for refusal. (BNC, CFH 166) (objective)
(20) You *should* stop whingeing and start trying to make things work. (BNC) (subjective)

Similarly, *can* is associated with "objective permission" examples, with permission *may* being (usually) subjective:

(21) You *can* only have showers on week-days after supper, and you have to pay 5 Francs each time. (ICE, W1B-002)
(22) *May* I sit down for a minute? (ICE, W2F-018)

Such basically introspective intuitions are widespread while clear definitions or indications as to how to operationalize the parameter of subjectivity are often lacking. Verstraete (2001) offers a very insightful discussion and puts forward a test to determine whether a sentence communicates subjective rather than objective modality (2001: 1521–2). When the sentence is turned into a question, in the case of subjective modality, it is the addressee's commitment to the necessity that is at stake (cf. *She must leave the room immediately* (subjective) – *Must she leave the room immediately?* – "Do you want her to leave?"), whereas in the case of objective modality, it is his commitment to the truth of the proposition (cf. *Seasnakes must surface to breathe* (objective) – *Must seasnakes surface to breathe?* – "Do you think it is true that it is necessary for seasnakes to surface to breathe?"). Depraetere and Verhulst (2008) and Verhulst et al. (2013) are further initiatives to pin down more explicitly the nature of "objective" and "subjective" modality to arrive at an empirically justified semantic profiling of modal verbs such as *ought to, should, be supposed to, have to* and *must*. Narrog (2012: 23–45) also provides very useful discussion of subjectivity in modality. Note that in cognitive grammar "subjectivity" is viewed differently: like tense inflections or person inflections, all modals relate the complement to the "ground" – that is, the speech situation – and are therefore said to be subjective (cf. e.g. Langacker 2003).

2.5 Strength

Strength is also often brought up as a defining criterion in discussions about modal meaning, in two different ways: in the field of modal necessity, some modals are said to be inherently "stronger" than others. No one would disagree with the fact that *You should do it* is not as forceful or "strong" as *You must do it*. In other words, there seems to be a scale of strength, and as in the case of subjectivity/objectivity, this feature helps to pin down the semantic profile of the different verbs that express necessity. Identifying the difference in strength between, for instance, *must* and *should*, is relatively straightforward and unproblematic. However, the judgement is a lot harder when one draws into the discussion the whole range of verbs that communicate non-epistemic necessity; that is, when we also try to position *have to, need to, ought to, be to, be supposed to* on the scale of modal strength. In Verhulst et al. (2013: 218), an overview is given of the opposing views on the matter concerning the inherent strength of *be supposed to, should* and *ought to*. The authors (2013: 219–21) argue for a definition of strength in terms of the inescapability (or not) of the necessity and the relative gravity of non-compliance. In other words, while it is beyond doubt that necessity modals differ in strength, the route of intuitive appreciation of "strength" is not convincing if this parameter is to function as a reliable and objective criterion to determine meaning distinctions between modals.

Strength also enters the discussion at the level of pragmatic effects: in this case, possibility modals can be strengthened to communicate necessity. For instance, in the context of an oral exam, an instructor saying *You can leave now* to a student will be understood to be expressing an order (*Please leave the room*). Likewise, *You must come and see my photos, Bina* (example (6)), is unlikely to be perceived as expressing a necessity or an order; it will rather be understood as a friendly but firm invitation. In this case, the necessity modal is pragmatically weakened. Note that the status of the strengthened or weakened meaning, while highly conventionalized, is truly pragmatic, in the sense that it constitutes implicated meaning, which, strictly speaking, can be cancelled (even though this is likely to happen in jocular contexts (*Can you leave the room? – Yes I can, but I won't*), with the interlocutor (mistakenly) responding to the literal (semantic) meaning.)

3 The diachronic development of modal meaning

With the exception of *willan* ("intend, want"), the Old English forms corresponding to the core modals *can* (*cunnan*, "know" and "have the mental ability, know how to"), *may* (*magan*, "have the physical ability to"), *must* (*motan*, participant-external "ability" and permission) and *shall* (*sculan*, "obligation, necessity, compulsion") were all preterite-present (lexical) verbs in Old English; that is, they all had a present tense like the past tense of a strong form and a past tense formed on an irregular stem with the endings of the weak past.

(23)
	present	*can*	*may*	*must*	*shall*	*will*
	1st/3rd ps sg	can(n)	mæg	mōt	sceal	wille/wile (wille)
	2nd ps sg	canst	meaht	mōst	scealt	wilt
	plural	cunnon	magon	mōton	sculon (sceo-)	willað
	past					
	1st/3rd ps sg	cūðe	meahte or mihte	mōste	sceolde	wolde
	2nd ps sg	cūðest	meahtest or mihtest	mōstest	sceoldest	woldest
	plural	cūðon	meahton or mihton	mōston	sceoldon	woldon

(Quirk and Wrenn 1989: 55–8)

In the late Middle English period the inflection in the second person singular was lost and the historically past form of *must* came to be used for present time reference.

It is interesting to observe the so-called *drag chain* effect in the development of modal meaning in Middle English, summarized as follows by Goossens:

> *shulen* (Modern English *shall*) gets partially grammaticalized for the future and the conditional, so that *moten* (the forerunner of *must*) is taking over the expression of obligation from *shulen* and clears the way for the use of *mowen* [ancestor of *may*] in the field of extra-subjective possibility (including the expression of permission). (...) *mowen* also retains (and has even expanded) its position in the area of intra-subjective possibility, so that there *conne(n)* and *mowen* are largely interchangeable.
>
> (1992: 383)

In other words, during the ME period, the permission uses of *must* became increasingly restricted and were slowly replaced by *may/magan* (have the physical ability) and *can/cunnan* (have the mental ability). *Must* developed from permission to necessity meaning in the context of negative (denied) permission: there was an inference from "you may not" to "you are obliged not to". "Invited inferencing", in the form of quantity implicatures arising from Grice's second Maxim of Quantity ("Do not make your contribution more informative than is required") that are conventionalized, have therefore been argued to play a major role in the shift of modal meaning. For instance, if one has permission to do something, this may implicate expectation: "So if I say *You may go*, I may, in the right circumstances, implicate that I want you to go, and in this sense you have some obligation to go" (Traugott 1989: 51). The frequent collocation of *motan* with *nedes* (*necessarily*) contributed to the development of epistemic necessity meaning and this collocation also led the past form to become used with present time reference. Another factor that influenced the latter shift is that non-epistemic necessity was understood as "coming to be obliged" and epistemic necessity as "coming to believe or conclude" (cf. e.g. Goossens (1982), Traugott (1999), Traugott and Dasher (2002)).

In Old English, *magan* functioned most extensively to communicate ability (internal possibility); that is, physical, perceptual and intellectual capacity, and only marginally expressed permission, some examples combining "internal" and "external" sources (such as circumstances) (Goossens 1987). The "internal possibility" core gradually shrank and the external possibility meaning was extended more and more to include permission (as *motan* was shifting its territory from permission to obligation). As the epistemic function became more important, *may* also developed epistemic meaning.

Cunnan only marginally expressed internal possibility (ability, intellectual capacity), its core meaning being "know (a person, a language)", but it invaded, little by little, the territory of *magan* and came to express possibility that not only depends on certain capacities of the subject, but also on external factors.

Even though it has been pointed out that examples can be found with *magan*, *sculan* and *willan* that show the first "traces of epistemic use" in Old English, there seems to be a consensus that epistemic meaning develops out of non-epistemic meanings in the fifteenth century, in a process of "subjectification", which "involves increase in coding of speaker attitude, whether of belief, assessment of the truth, or personal commitment to the assertion" (Traugott 1989: 49). Nordlinger and Traugott (1997) argue that "general participant-external wide-scope root/deontic necessity" should not be overlooked as a phase in the evolution from narrow scope root/deontic meaning to epistemic meaning. In line with this observation, Depraetere and Reed (2011) (cf. section 2.2) distinguish between "wide-scope" non-epistemic possibility, which they label "general situation possibility" and "narrow scope" non-epistemic possibility, which they label "opportunity". In other words, wide-scope modality should not be solely associated with epistemic modality in the classification of modal meaning as it can be observed in present-day English.

An important contribution to the study of the recent development in the English auxiliary domain has been made by Krug (2000). He offers an analysis of so-called emerging modals and shows how lexical structures are changing their categorial status and are developing features typical of the core modals in a process of grammaticalization. The following are the processes discussed and analysed by Krug:

want to	> wanta	> wanna
is/am/are going to	> 's/'m/'re going to	> gonna
have got to	> 've got to	> gotta

Ziegeler (2011) offers a more general overview of grammaticalization in the field of modality. Starting from the cross-linguistic evidence presented in Bybee et al. (1994), Van der Auwera and Plungian (1998) use semantic maps (see Chapter 25) both to capture polysemy from a synchronic point of view and to represent the semantic paths along which modal meanings have evolved; the paths are similar in languages from different families.

4 Conclusion and future directions

The domain of study of modality is such that any survey is unavoidably limited: morphological and syntactic realizations of modality (cf. section 1) and lexical realizations of modality other than modal verbs, and their impact on the concept of modality as such, have not been discussed. The question of how modal meaning as expressed by modals is approached in formal semantics (cf. e.g. Kaufmann et al. (2005), Portner (2009: chapter 3) for an overview; see also Chapter 4), in cognitive and force dynamic approaches (cf. e.g. Mortelmans (2012) for an overview; see also Chapter 5) or in Construction Grammar (Bybee 2010) has not been addressed.

The scope of the chapter notwithstanding, it has become clear that the semantics-pragmatics interface is relevant to the topic in more than one way: it was pointed out in the brief historical sketch that in some cases implicated meanings conventionalized and have in this way come to constitute the semantic core of specific modal verbs. It is important to distinguish between this development and the foregrounded pragmatic meanings that take the form of an indirect speech act value in specific contexts (cf. e.g. *You may want to put the table over there* (modal meaning: epistemic possibility; indirect speech act: mild order)). Even though these illustrate conventional(ized) uses, the foregrounded speech act value still has pragmatic status; that is, it is implicated, and it does not, as such, supersede or replace the semantic core of the modal in question (cf. Stefanowitsch (2003) for a different point of view).

Features such as strength of the modality or source of the modality obviously impact on the semantic profile of modals, but these features are not distinctive in the sense that they result in mutually exclusive meaning classes. Determining the status of these parameters is by no means a straightforward matter.

Finally, the discussion of the monosemy/polysemy question brings up the question of the extent to which context contributes to truth-conditional content, an issue at the heart of the debate between so-called minimalists (cf. e.g. Borg (2012)) and contextualists (cf. e.g. Recanati (2010)).

As well as the need to clarify theoretical issues, one of the major challenges in this field remains that of specifying fine-grained meaning distinctions and connecting them coherently with theoretical models. Much still needs to be done.

Further reading

Depraetere, Ilse and Chad Langford 2012. *Advanced English Grammar: A Linguistic Approach*. London: Continuum. Gives basic information about mood and modality in English (194–238).

Facchinetti, Roberta, Manfred Krug and Frank R. Palmer (eds) 2003. *Modality in Contemporary English*. Berlin: Mouton de Gruyter. Salkie, Raphael, Pierre Busuttil, and Johan Van der Auwera (eds) (2009). *Modality in English Theory and Description*. Berlin: Mouton de Gruyter. Both collections of papers address theoretical questions and present empirical studies on modality in English.

Kiefer, Ferenc 2009. Modality. In Frank Brisard, Jan-Ola Östman and Jef Verschueren (eds) *Grammar, Meaning and Pragmatics*. Amsterdam/Philadelphia: John Benjamins Publishing Company. A good overview of theoretical issues in the field of modality with special attention to the semantics/pragmatics divide.

Portner, Paul 2009. *Modality*. Oxford: Oxford University Press. Portner's book discusses possible worlds semantics developed in modal logic, as well as cognitive and functional linguistic approaches to modality.

Frawley, William (ed.) 2006. *The Expression of Modality*. Berlin: Mouton de Gruyter. Contains chapters on typological approaches, formal approaches and diachronic approaches to mood and modality.

References

Aarts, Bas 2007. *Syntactic Gradience*. Oxford: Oxford University Press.
Aarts, Bas 2012. The Subjunctive conundrum. *Folia Linguistica* 46: 1–20.
Abraham, Werner and Elisabeth Leiss (eds) 2008. *Modality-Aspect Interfaces: Implications and Typological Solutions*. Amsterdam: John Benjamins.

Aijmer, Karin and Anne-Marie Simon-Vandenbergen 2007. *The Semantic Field of Modal Certainty. A Corpus-Based Study of English Adverbs*. Berlin: Mouton de Gruyter.

Borg, Emma 2012. *Pursuing Meaning*. Oxford: Oxford University Press.

Boye, Kasper 2012. *Epistemic Meaning. A Cross-Linguistic and Functional-Cognitive Study*. Berlin: Mouton de Gruyter.

Bybee, Joan 2006. Mechanisms of change in grammaticization: the role of frequency. In Joan L. Bybee, *Frequency of Use and the Organization of Language*. Oxford: Oxford University Press, 336–57.

Bybee, Joan 2010. *Language, Usage and Cognition*. Cambridge: Cambridge University Press.

Bybee, Joan and Suzanne Fleischman (eds) 1995. *Modality in Grammar and Discourse*. Amsterdam: John Benjamins.

Bybee, Joan, Revere Perkins and William Pagliuca 1994. *The Evolution of Grammar: Tense, Aspect, and Modality in the Languages of the World*. Chicago: University of Chicago Press.

Coates, Jennifer 1983. *The Semantics of the Modal Auxiliaries*. London and Canberra: Croom Helm.

Collins, Peter 2009. *Modals and Quasi-Modals in English*. Amsterdam and New York: Rodopi.

De Haan, Ferdinand 2005. Typological approaches to modality. In William Frawley (ed.) *The Expression of Modality*. Berlin: Mouton de Gruyter, 27–69.

Declerck, Renaat 2011. The definition of modality. In Adeline Patard and Frank Brisard (eds) *Cognitive Approaches to Tense, Aspect and Epistemic Modality*. Amsterdam: John Benjamins, 21–44.

Depraetere, Ilse and Susan Reed 2011. Towards a more explicit taxonomy of root possibility in English. *English Language and Linguistics* 15: 1–29.

Depraetere, Ilse and An Verhulst 2008. Source of modality: a reassessment. *English Language and Linguistics* 12: 1–25.

Dowty, David R. 1977. Toward a semantic analysis of verb aspect and the English "imperfective" progressive. *Linguistics and Philosophy* 1: 45–77.

Enfield, Nicholas James 2003. *Linguistic Epidemiology: Semantics and Grammar of Language Contact in Mainland Southeast Asia*. London: Routledge.

Gisborne, Nikolas 2007. Dynamic modality. *SKASE Journal of Theoretical Linguistics* 4: 44–61. http://www.skase.sk/Volumes/JTL09/pdf_doc/4.pdf.

Goossens, Louis 1982. The development of the modals and of the epistemic function in English. In Anders Ahlqvist (ed.) *Papers from the 5th International Conference on Historical Linguistics*. Amsterdam: John Benjamins, 74–84.

Goossens, Louis 1987. Modal tracks: the case of *magan* and *motan*. In Anne-Marie Simon-Vandenbergen (ed.) *Studies in Honour of René Derolez*. Ghent: Seminarie voor Engelse en Oud-Germaanse taalkunde, 216–36.

Goossens, Louis 1992. *Cunnan, conne(n), can*: The development of a radical category. In Günter Kellermann and Michael D. Morrissey (eds) *Diachrony within Synchrony: Language History and Cognition. Papers from the International Symposium at the University of Duisburg, 26–28 March 1990*. Frankfurt-am-Main: Peter Lang, 377–94.

Goossens, Louis 2000. Patterns of meaning extenstion, "parallel chaining," subjectification and modal shifts. In Antonio Barcelona (ed.) *Metaphor and Metonymy at the Crossroads: A Cognitive Perspective*. Berlin: Mouton de Gruyter, 1–28.

Groefsema, Marjolein 1995. *Can, may, must* and *should:* a relevance theoretic account. *Journal of Linguistics* 31: 53–79.

Hansen, Björn and Ferdinand de Haan 2009. *Modals in the Languages of Europe*. Berlin: Mouton de Gruyter.

Hart, David (ed.) 2004. *English Modality in Context. Diachronic Perspectives*. Bern: Peter Lang.

Hogeweg, Lotte, Helen de Hoop and Andrej Malchukov (eds) 2009. *Cross-Linguistic Semantics of Tense, Aspect and Modality*. Amsterdam: John Benjamins Publishing Company.

Hoye, Leo 1997. *Adverbs and Modality in English*. London: Longman.

Huddleston, Rodney, Geoffrey K. Pullum et al. 2002. *Cambridge Grammar of the English Language*. Cambridge: Cambridge University Press.

Kaufmann, Stefan, Cleo Condoravdi and Valentina Harizanov 2005. Formal approaches to modality. In William Frawley (ed.) *The Expression of Modality*. Berlin: Mouton de Gruyter, 72–106.

Kratzer, Angelika 1991. Modality. In Arnim Von Stechow and Dieter Wunderlich (eds) *Semantics: An International Handbook of Contemporary Research*. Berlin: de Gruyter, 639–50.
Kratzer, Angelika 2012. *Modals and Conditionals: New and Revised Perspectives*. Oxford: Oxford University Press.
Krug, Manfred 2000. *Emerging Modals: A Corpus-Based Approach to Grammaticalization*. Berlin: Mouton de Gruyter.
Langacker, Ronald W. 2003. Extreme subjectification: English tense and modals. In Hubert Cuyckens, Thomas Berg, René Driven and Klaus-Uwe Panther (eds) *Motivation in Language: Studies in Honor of Günter Radden*. Amsterdam: Benjamins, 3–26.
Langacker, Ronald W. 2011. The English present: temporal coincidence vs. epistemic immediacy. In Adeline Patard and Frank Brisard (eds) *Cognitive Approaches to Tense, Aspect, and Epistemic Modality*. Amsterdam: Benjamins, 45–86.
Leech, Geoffrey, Marianne Hundt, Christian Mair and Nicholas Smith 2009. *Change in Contemporary English*. Cambridge: Cambridge University Press.
Lyons, John 1977. *Semantics*. Cambridge: Cambridge University Press.
Mindt, Dieter 1995. *An Empirical Grammar of the English Verb. Modal Verbs*. Berlin: Cornelsen.
Mortelmans, Tanja 2012. Modality in cognitive linguistics. In Dirk Geeraerts and Hubert Cuyckens (eds) *The Oxford Handbook of Cognitive Linguistics*. Oxford: Oxford University Press, 869–89.
Narrog, Heiko 2005. On defining modality again. *Language Sciences* 27: 165–92.
Narrog, Heiko 2012. *Modality, Subjectivity and Semantic Change: A Cross-Linguistic Perspective*. Oxford: Oxford University Press.
Nordlinger, Rachel and Closs Traugott, Elizabeth 1997. Scope and the development of epistemic modality: evidence from *ought to*. *English Language and Linguistics* 1: 295–317.
Nuyts, Jan 2000. *Epistemic Modality, Language, and Conceptualization: A Cognitive-Pragmatic Perspective*. Amsterdam: John Benjamins.
Nuyts, Jan 2005. The modal confusion. On terminology and the concepts behind it. In Alex Klinge and Hendrik Høeg Müller (eds) *Modality: Studies in Form and Function*. London: Equinox, 5–38.
Nuyts, Jan 2012. Notions of (inter)subjectivity. *English Text Construction* 5: 53–76.
Palmer, Frank R. 1990. *Modality and the English Modals*. 2nd edition. London: Longman.
Palmer, Frank R. 2001. *Mood and Modality*. 2nd edition. Cambridge: Cambridge University Press.
Papafragou, Anna 2000. *Modality and the Semantics-Pragmatics Interface*. Oxford: Elsevier Science.
Portner, Paul 2009. *Modality*. Oxford: Oxford University Press.
Quirk, Randoph and Christopher L. Wrenn 1989. *An Old English Grammar*. 2nd edition. London: Routledge.
Recanati, François 2010. *Truth-Conditional-Pragmatics*. Oxford: Oxford University Press.
Riemer, Nick 2005. *The Semantics of Polysemy. Reading Meaning in English and Warlpiri*. Berlin: Mouton.
Rothstein, Björn and Rolf Thieroff (eds) 2010. *Mood in the Languages of Europe*. Amsterdam: John Benjamins.
Salkie, Raphael 2014. Enablement and possibility. In Werner Abraham and Elisabeth Leiss (eds) *Modes of Modality*. Amsterdam: John Benjamins, 319–352.
Stefanowitsch, Anatol 2003. A construction-based approach to indirect speech acts. In Klaus-Uwe Panther and Linda Thornburg (eds) *Metonymy and Pragmatic Inferencing*. Amsterdam: John Benjamins, 105–26.
Talmy, Leonard 1988. Force dynamics in language and cognition. *Cognitive Science* 12: 49–100.
Thieroff, Rolf 2010. Moods, moods, moods. In Björn Rothstein and Rolf Thieroff (eds) *Mood in the Languages of Europe*. Amsterdam: John Benjamins, 1–29.
Traugott, Elizabeth Closs 1989. On the rise of epistemic meaning in English: an example of subjectification in semantic change. *Language* 65: 31–55.
Traugott, Elizabeth Closs 1999. Why *must* is not *moot*. Paper Presented at the Fourteenth International Conference on Historical Linguistics, Vancouver, Canada, August 1999.
Traugott, Elizabeth Closs and Richard B. Dasher 2002. *Regularity in Semantic Change*. Cambridge: Cambridge University Press.

Van Linden, An 2012. *Modal Adjectives. English Deontic and Evaluative Constructions in a Synchronic and Diachronic Perspective*. Berlin: Mouton de Gruyter.
Van der Auwera, Johan and Vladimir A. Plungian 1998. Modality's semantic map. *Linguistic Typology* 2: 79–124.
Van der Auwera, Johan, Cornelia Hamann and Saskia Kindt 2005. Modal polyfunctionality and Standard Average European. In Alex Klinge and Henrik Høeg Müller (eds) *Modality. Studies in Form and Function*. London: Equinox, 247–72.
Verhulst, An, Ilse Depraetere and Liesbet Heyvaert 2013. Source and strength of modality: an empirical study of root *should*, *ought to* and *be supposed to* in present-day British English. *Journal of Pragmatics* 55: 210–25.
Verstraete, Jean-Christophe 2001. Subjectivity and objectivity: interpersonal and ideational functions in the English modal auxiliary system. *Journal of Pragmatics* 33: 1505–528.
Westney, Paul 1995. *Modals and Periphrastics in English*. Tübingen: Niemeyer.
Willett, Thomas 1988. A cross-linguistic survey of the grammaticization of evidentiality. *Studies in Language* 12: 51–97.
Von Wright, Georg Hendrik 1951. *A Handbook of English Grammar*. 2nd edition. Amsterdam: North Holland.
Ziegeler, Debra P. 2011. The grammaticalisation of modality. In Bernd Heine and Heiko Narrog (eds) *Oxford Handbook of Grammaticalisation*. Oxford: Oxford University Press, 595–604.

Related topics

Chapter 13, Sense individuation; Chapter 19, Lexical and grammatical aspect; Chapter 20, Tense.

22
Event semantics

Jean-Pierre Koenig

The point of talking is to describe the way the world is, the way it changes or stays the same. Verbs play a critical role in that endeavour. Intuitively, verbs (or, more precisely, verb senses) describe categories of situations or events. One sense of *eat* describes a category of situations in which one entity ingests another one; one sense of *believe* describes a kind of state humans can be in with respect to a representation (or proposition). Discussing the semantics of verbs amounts to trying to answer several questions, some pertaining to the relation between our cognitive categories and our lexicons, some pertaining to the relation between verb meanings and the morphosyntax of clauses. Here is a list of some of these questions:

(1) Do categories of situations named by verb stems or described by sentences fall into natural classes?
(2) Can the meaning of verbs be decomposed into smaller components or primitives?
(3) How complex can the categories of situations described by a verb stem be?
(4) How should we compose the meaning of verbs and their dependents to derive natural classes of situations?
(5) Are there constraints on the kind of situation properties that morphosyntax can be sensitive to?

1 The nature of events

Clearly, this chapter cannot answer all of these questions, or even one completely. Its goal is more modest: to articulate the way in which attempts to answer these questions have shaped research in event semantics. I begin with two general issues about the notion of event. The first issue pertains to what an event is. We can go with Aristotle's definition of verbs: "A verb is that which, in addition to its proper meaning, carries with it the notion of time" (*De Interpretatione*, 3). Or, we can define events in a way less dependent on Greek morphology as processes (or, rather, classifications of processes) that are less stable than those constituting individuals (Link 1997). Whatever the metaphysical underpinnings of the distinction between entities (individuals) and situations, the difference is typically reflected in the arity of the predicates that name entity and situation categories. Since Davidson (1967), it is widely agreed that predicates of situations include an additional event argument position compared to predicates of entities: Whereas *dog* is a one-place predicate that categorizes entities, *walk* is a relation between an event and an animate entity. Whether names of stative events (e.g.

believe) also describe situations (and therefore include an event argument position) is a matter of debate. But, at the very least, they include an additional time argument (Galton 1984), something not true of categories of entities.

The second issue pertains to the structure of events and predicates that describe them. Kenny (1963) presents us with a challenge that takes the following form. If we define an event of eating as a relation between an eater and some food, how can we account for the entailment between the proposition expressed by (6) and that expressed by (7) or between the proposition expressed by (6) and that expressed by (8)? Whatever device we propose, Kenny fears, we will end up saying that predicates of actions are of variable polyadicity, or worse, infinite polyadicity. Now, we would not have to worry about this second issue *if* there was a principled way of distinguishing between how (6) relates to (7), and how (6) relates to (8) or (9). The traditional answer within linguistics is to distinguish between arguments and adjuncts of the predicate associated with the meaning of the verb. The relation described by the verb only involves arguments. But, of course, it begs the question of what constitutes arguments of a predicate.

(6) John ate.
(7) John ate something.
(8) John ate somewhere.
(9) John eats sushi with something.
(10) Bill tried to cut his meat with a butter knife.
(11) Marie hid her pearl earrings in the drawer.

One proposal (Koenig et al. 2003) is that arguments are those participants in an event that are required by the event category and are specific to a small range of event categories. The difference between sentences (6) and (7) and sentences (6) and (8) or between sentences (6) and (7) and (6) and (9) is explained as follows. Eating always requires food, so even when there is no syntactic expression that realizes the food argument, as in (6), it is understood. In contrast, you do not need an instrument to eat. You can just crash your mouth onto the plate (although with some cultural consequences). As a result, one can infer from the truth of (6) the truth of (7), but one cannot infer from the truth of (6) the truth of (9). Now, if obligatoriness was all there was to argumenthood, the location expressed by *somewhere* in (8) would constitute an argument and Kenny's concern would be back in full force. However, that an event took place somewhere and that it took place at some time does not tell us much about what kind of event occurred because almost all events take place somewhere and at some time (an exception, if they describe stative events, are sentences like *Two plus two equals four*). So in contrast to the eater and food arguments of *eat*, which tell us something about the event because they bear distinctive properties (e.g. causality in the case of the eater and changing state in the case of the food), there are no location and time properties that characterize events of eating (i.e. that serve as criterial properties for us to categorize an event as an event of eating). To see the relevance of obligatoriness and specificity to defining argumenthood for event-types, it is useful to compare the instrument of *eat* in sentence (9) and the instrument of *cut* in sentence (10). Events of cutting like those described in (10) require some kind of instrument (see Koenig et al. (2003) for qualifications). So in contrast to events of eating meat, events of cutting meat entail using something to cut the meat. Similarly, the location expressed by *in the drawer* in (11) differs from the location where eating occurs in (8). This is because almost all events take place somewhere, but not all verbs are like *hide* in describing situations where some entity is moved and ends up in a location as a result.

That kind of location is specific to a restricted set of situation categories and as such helps characterize the situation as an event of hiding.

2 Classifying events on the basis of time schemata

Having briefly addressed issues that pertain to the nature of events, I now turn to ways in which semanticists have tried to answer the questions I raised in the introductory paragraph. I will start with the issue of what *kinds* of categories of situations one can recognize. One very prominent classification of events distinguishes between four distinct kinds of categories of situations (Vendler 1957): states, activities, achievements, and accomplishments (see Chapter 19). The literature has often been unclear about whether these categories are categories of verb meanings, categories of sentence or clause meanings, or categories of predicate meanings, an issue that started with Vendler himself. I assume that these categories are categories associated with the meaning of sentences or clauses. Vendler distinguished kinds of situation categories on the basis of what he called time schemata; that is, states, activities, achievements and accomplishments are distinct kinds of situation categories because each relates differently to the time during which it occurs or holds. *Loving* is an example of states, *running* is an example of activities, *drawing a circle* is an example of accomplishments, and *spotting* is an example of achievements. Many "tests" of whether a clause or sentence describes a state, an activity, an achievement, or an accomplishment have been proposed starting with Vendler's own. We present here a subset of the tests (for English) provided in Dowty (1979).

(12) Bill loves/*?*is loving soccer.
(13) Bill spots a stallion a mile away/*?*is spotting a stallion.
(14) Bill ran (for an hour).
(15) Bill drew a circle (in an hour).

State descriptions are not welcome in the progressive, as (12) shows. Intuitively, the progressive indicates that a dynamic situation is ongoing, and static situations are therefore incompatible with it. Achievements are also not particularly welcome (without a change in meaning) in the progressive. This is because achievements are "punctual" and being ongoing makes little sense if the event occurs in an instant. Achievements, though, differ from states in that achievement verb constellations receive a habitual reading when combining with the English simple present. Thus the simple present in (13) describes a habit or habitual ability of Bill's, whereas in (12) it describes Bill's ongoing affection for soccer. Activities unfold through time homogeneously, as sentence (14) shows: any part of an event of running is an event of running. So, if Bill ran for an hour, he ran at all times during the hour (excluding intervals of time that are too small and irrelevant interruptions, e.g. bathroom breaks). In contrast, accomplishments do not unfold through time homogenously. If Bill drew a circle in an hour, it took him an hour to draw the circle and the same description – "drawing a circle" – is not true of any interval that is strictly smaller than the hour he took. The fact that activities are true at all times during an interval is often called the subinterval property; the fact that accomplishments (and achievements) are not can be called the anti-subinterval property. Bach (1986), Herweg (1991), Talmy (2000), and others have noted the parallel between activities and mass nouns on the one hand and accomplishments and count nouns on the other. Any subpart (that is not too small) of a mass of butter is butter, but any subpart of a horse is not a horse.

Further distinctions among Vendler-style classes can be made. Bach (1986), for example, distinguishes between happenings and culminations. The change for the former (*The balloon popped*; *John noticed the open jar of peanut butter*) occurs "instantaneously" without a preparatory phase. The change for the latter (*John reached the summit*) may be instantaneous, but there must be a phase leading to the change. You cannot reach the summit without some prior motion (e.g. prior walking). So, for most speakers, if Scottie (in Star Trek) were to beam John up onto the summit of the Everest, the description *John reached the summit* would be inappropriate, because standing on top of mount Everest after not standing there is not enough for an event to be described as a reaching event. One has had to first walk up (or otherwise move up) the mountain.

Similarly, one can distinguish among states. Some states are permanent (e.g. *Mont Blanc is high*, *whales are mammals*). Whales will always be mammals; mountains do not change height within the confines of our lifetimes. But other states are more temporary. Bach (1986) cites *John was drunk last night*; one hopes John will sober up. Grammatical formatives can be sensitive to distinctions among states. To take a well-known example, Spanish uses distinct copulas for permanent and temporary states. The copula *ser* is used in (16a) because individual traits do not change easily whereas the copula *estar* is used in (16b) because a house's dirtiness is more temporary.

(16) a Soy impaciente
"I am impatient"
 b La casa está sucia
"The house is dirty"

As it is hard to think of statements such as *I am impatient* as goings-on (and even harder for statements like *Mont Blanc is high*), the existence of permanent states suggests that we may not be able to reduce all situations to processes or to goings-on no matter how abstract they are, contrary to what Link (1997) claims.

One can distinguish even further among states: Those that follow some dynamic change that is permanent once reached (*The theorem is proven*; once proven the theorem remains proven indefinitely) and those that can be reset (*The keys are hidden*; the keys can later on be in plain view). Only with the latter (which Kratzer (2000) calls target states in contrast to the former, which she calls result states) are adverbs such as *still* appropriate, since only the latter can be reset. Note that result or target states are what perfect markers, according to some theories, entail to hold at reference time for their so-called resultative interpretations (*I have strained my knee so I cannot run*).

3 The ins and outs of predicate decomposition

The second question that has occupied semanticists interested in categories of situations is whether verb meanings can be decomposed into smaller components or primitives (see Chapter 12). This issue is not unrelated to the first question, as the components into which verb meanings can be decomposed constitute an implicit categorization of verb meanings and are often inspired by or related to Vendler-style categories. For example, if accomplishments are analyzed as situations that include changes that take time, the fact that they do not obey the subinterval property is easily accounted for: a change takes a certain amount of time and the change will not have occurred before that time. The decomposition of the meaning of verbs into smaller components goes back to the 60s and

Generative Semantics (see Lakoff (1970)). In its original incarnation and many of its offshoots, the decomposition of verb meaning was not only an analysis of event categories into subparts, but also a decomposition of *representations* of the meaning of verbs into subparts, which is why it is often known as predicate decomposition. The original impetus for decomposition was partly based on morphological relations (*hard/harden*) and partly on ambiguities, particularly that of *almost* or *again* (see Dowty (1979) for details). The first motivation for predicate decomposition ran as follows: The morphological rule deriving *redden* from *red* is easier to state if we can recognize in the meaning of *redden* the meaning of *red*. So, if we analyze informally the meaning of *red* as describing a particular category of state, we can state that the semantic effect of *-en* suffixation is to derive a meaning that describes situations that cause an entity to become red when it was not before. If we represent the meaning of a base adjective as P (Y), the meaning of a derived verb can be represented as CAUSE (X, P (Y)).

The second motivation for predicate decomposition is that the presence of some adverbs leads to ambiguities that are best explained by assuming the meaning of verbs is complex rather than atomic; the ambiguities can then be analyzed on a par with ambiguities of scope.

(17) Joan opened the door again.
(18) Joan almost freed the mouse from the trap.

Consider sentence (17). It can be used to describe situations in which Joan, who has a compulsion to try to open doors, performs the act of opening a door yet another time. But it can also be used to describe situations in which the door was previously open, the wind shut it, and Joan makes sure it is open again. Consider sentence (18). It can be used to describe situations where Joan was about to free the mouse because she is ambivalent about traps, but then thought better of it given her revulsion at the sight of mice. It can also be used to describe situations where Joan fiddles with the trap and manages to loosen its grip on the mouse, but cannot quite get the mouse free. In both cases, the ambiguity is easily explained if we recognize two parts to the meaning of *open* and *free*, an action on Joan's part and a possible result of that action, namely the door being open or the mouse being free. On the assumption that each adverb, *again* and *almost*, takes as argument a situation, the presence of two situations in the meaning of *open* and *free* explains the ambiguity of (17) and (18), as each of these two subparts (or the whole situation versus the result part in some analyses) can serve as argument of the meaning of the adverbs.

Note that this explanation of the ambiguity of (17) and (18) does not per se require that the *representation* of the meaning of the verbs in (17) and (18) be decomposed into two parts. My explanation was couched in terms of the complexity of the denoted categories of situations, not in terms of the complexity of the representations themselves. But many linguists since the early days of Generative Semantics have taken, off and on, the view that such ambiguities suggest that the representation of the meaning of the verbs in (17) and (18) should be decomposed into component parts, as shown in (19) ((19) is but one way of decomposing the representation of the meaning contributed by *open*.) The fact that this meaning includes two predicates over which the meaning of *again* can have scope (or which it can take as arguments) easily explains the ambiguity of (19), as shown in (20).

(19) CAUSE (e', x, BE-OPEN (e'', y))
(20) a AGAIN (CAUSE (e', x, BE-OPEN (e'', y)))
     b CAUSE (e', x, AGAIN (BE-OPEN (e'', y)))

This representational model of the ambiguity of (17) and (18) does not speak directly to the source of the ambiguity represented in (20). The source could be lexical, as in the approach proposed in Dowty (1979). Under that view, the ambiguity lies in the systematic complexity exhibited by the meaning of certain verbal stems, and the scopal potential of adverbs such as *again* and *almost* simply attest to the complexity of these lexical meanings. The source could also be syntactic. This is the tack proponents of Generative Semantics took when first discussing this ambiguity. Under that view, the complexity of the meaning of *open* in sentence (17) comes from the complexity of the *syntactic* structure associated with formulas like (19). In other words, decomposition amounts to treating the meaning contributed by verbs as molecular rather than atomic (i.e. treating it as composed of recognizable parts) and the original approach to decomposition was that the semantic parts should be associated with distinct syntactic parts. The re-composition of the parts of the decomposed meaning into a single verb meaning was the result of a syntactic operation called predicate raising. This view maintained a one-syntactic-atom one-semantic-atom assumption, but at the cost of multiplying structure. This view was attacked vehemently at the time (see Fodor (1970)), but has seen a resurgence in the 1990s and in the last decade, even to the point that it has become "evident" in some syntactic circles. Consider Ramchand (2008) (see also Borer (2005) for a more articulated, similar approach). Ramchand's first phase syntax amounts to reifying predicates used since Dowty (1979) into abstract (most often phonologically null) heads that roots merge with. The relevant heads correspond to the very same operators Generative Semantics introduced as null heads, RESult, PROcess, and INITiation. Underlying these more syntactic approaches to decomposition is, implicitly, something like Jackendoff's (1983) *Grammatical Constraint* which says that semantic representations that make interface with morphosyntax easier should be preferred.

A second impetus for analyzing the meaning of verbs into component parts was the long-standing desire to find primitives – primitives of thought in philosophical or Artificial Intelligence circles (see Shank (1973)), primitives of meaning in more linguistic circles. The strongest proponent of the analysis of verb meanings (in fact, all meanings) into a set of primitives is *Natural Semantic Metalanguage* (see Goddard and Wierzbicka (1994) for an overview), which since the early 70s has proposed to decompose *all* lexical meanings of *all* languages into a very small set of primitives (see Chapters 12 and 25). Aside from the obvious motivations behind finding primitives of meaning, a less obvious one, which has played a role in both Shank's and Jackendoff's (1983) proposals, is that decomposition would make it easier to model inference patterns. I call this motivation for decomposition the *Reasoning Constraint*. By assuming that the meaning of transitive uses of verbs like *open* or *free* can be decomposed as in (21) (where PRED is a variable over state meaning representations), we can posit a single inference rule that accounts for the fact that from knowing that (22) and (23) are true, speakers know that the door was open or that mouse was free from the trap.

(21) CAUSE (e', x, PRED (e'', y))
(22) Joan opened the door.
(23) Joan freed the mouse from the trap.

A third impetus for analyzing the meaning of verbs into component parts (whether the meanings of verbs are already present in the lexicon as is or are the result of a syntactic operation of predicate raising) comes from differences in what gets expressed in single verb stems versus in dependents of verbs across languages. A simple example from English and French will illustrate the problem.

(24) Bill entered the room.
(25) Bill came into the room.
(26) Bill est entré *(dans) la pièce.
    Bill is entered into the room

Aside from possible register differences, sentences (24) and (25) have very similar meanings. But in one case, the fact that the described event is one of change of location that results in Bill being inside a room is encoded by a single verb stem *enter* whereas the same information is contributed by two words in (25), namely *come* and *into*. Since that information is contributed by *two* words in (25) each contributing to the description of a distinct situation (a change of location and a static location, respectively), there must be *two components* to the meaning of *enter* in (24). Note that the argument affects studies of cross-linguistic differences in lexicalization patterns (such as those of Talmy (2000)), but also yet again studies of inferencing. One of the motivations for Conceptual Dependency, Shank's metalanguage for representing both our knowledge of the world and the content of texts and discourses (Shank 1973) was the need to develop a single *interlingual* semantic representation that one could define inference patterns over. And this makes sense, as it would seem odd to assume inference patterns depend on language-specific facts such as whether a language has words like *enter* or not. French sentence (26) adds an interesting twist to the story. The source of *enter*, French *entrer*, requires its complement to be a prepositional phrase that is headed by *dans*. *Dans* redundantly encodes the spatial configuration of Bill and the room at the end of the event. Without recognizing two components to the meaning of *enter* and *entrer* it is hard to explain the similarities and differences between these two cognate verbs.

I illustrate semantic decomposition and its challenges with the currently most prevalent decomposition scheme, the one proposed over the years by Jackendoff. A subpart of this scheme is provided (in a somewhat simplified form) in (21).

(27) a [EVENT] → [$_{Event}$ GO ([THING], [PATH])]
     b [EVENT] → [$_{Event}$ CAUSE ([EVENT/THING], [EVENT])]
     c [PATH]   → [$_{Path}$ TO/FROM/TOWARD/AWAY-FROM/VIA ([THING/PLACE])]
     d [STATE] → [$_{State}$ BE ([THING], [PLACE])]

Each of the semantic rules in (27) decomposes conceptual entities belonging to the categories within the square brackets on the left-hand side of the rules into the components on the right-hand side of the rules. So, (27a) says that a conceptual object that is an EVENT can consist of a GO relation between a conceptual object that is a THING and a conceptual object that is a PATH. Similarly, (27b) says that a conceptual object that is an EVENT can consist of a relation between a conceptual object that is either an EVENT or THING and a conceptual object that is an EVENT. Rules (27c–d) receive similar interpretations. Several aspects of this (as well as other) decomposition scheme deserves comment. First, the decomposition scheme defines categories of situations: there are states, there are events of change and there are causal events (because the primitive GO can be understood metaphorically, it is best to think of GO as denoting events of change, be they changes of location or changes of states). Second, the rule in (27b) leads to semantic recursion, as arguments of the relation CAUSE can themselves be events. Third, the "bottom" of conceptual structures (those conceptual objects that can be arguments of relations, but are not themselves relations), i.e. the set of basic predicates are categories of THING and PLACE (which, again, stands for both locations and what would intuitively be states). These last two aspects of (27) are the source of two of the objections to decomposition, (i) the difficulty of determining when to stop decomposing and (ii) the prediction of more complex root meanings than seem attested.

Consider the decomposition of the meaning of the verb *eat* in Jackendoff (1990).

(28)   CAUSE [α_{thing}, GO[$_{thing}$, [TO[IN[MOUTH-OF[α]]]]]]

Whether this is the right decomposition or not is not what is at issue; rather, the question is that with only THING and PLACE categories as open classes of semantic primitives, decomposition is required and it is difficult to know *which* decomposition to prefer. Thus, what evidence is there that *this* decomposition is how speakers understand *eat* rather than as CAUSE(X, INGESTED(Y)) (or even INGEST as in Shank (1973)). Various authors have proposed criteria for deciding among possible decompositions (cf. the *Grammatical* and *Reasoning Constraints* above), but there is still no consensus on many aspects of predicate decomposition, although all agree that CAUSE and BECOME (or an equivalent operator encoding change) must be part of any realistic predicate decomposition scheme.

The recursivity that arises out of (27b) has also been criticized. Since the relata of CAUSE are themselves conceptual objects that belong to the category EVENT, they can be decomposed, leading to ever more complex possible meanings. But Carter (1976) points out that there is little if any evidence that the meaning of simple stems can ever involve two CAUSE relations (i.e. CAUSE (CAUSE (X, Y), Z) or CAUSE (X, CAUSE (Y, Z)), and so forth). That is, whereas sentence (29) is grammatical (if complex), there is no word *scooked* in English that would mean something like CAUSE (x, CAUSE (y, COOKED (z))) and this absence does not appear to be a lexical accident, as it would have to be under the recursive decomposition scheme illustrated in (27).

(29)   Martha made Bill make his son clean his room.
(30)   Marc cooked the stew.

More generally, the difference between the semantic effects of syntactic composition, which freely lead to recursive semantic representations of the kind (CAUSE (x, CAUSE . . .)) and the maximum complexity of verb meanings disappears under a scheme such as (27). Note that having CAUSE in one's decomposition scheme only leads to this issue if one recognizes events in one's ontology and arguments of CAUSE can be categories of events (see Dowty (1979) for an approach to decomposition that eschews this problem).

4 Are there limits on the complexity of verb meaning?

The apparent systematic absence of embedded CAUSE predicates is part of a larger issue, namely what the limits are on lexical semantic complexity or, put in more general terms, what kinds of constraints on categories of situations can verb roots impose (the third question I listed at the beginning of this chapter). I illustrate this question with a few examples. Consider first the French verbs *chambrer*, *limoger* and *mander*. The first verb is transitive and means something like "let [red wine] sit in a tepid room so that it slowly warms up to the appropriate temperature for consumption." The second, also transitive, means something like "to relieve from his post a commanding officer." The third has two meanings, either "tell something to someone through a letter or message" or "have somebody tell somebody to do something." First, we should note that whether these verbs violate the two-CAUSE constraint is not certain, as it depends on one's particular analysis of these lexicographic paraphrases.

The description of the meaning I gave for *chambrer* seems to suggest two causal relations, as the *letting sit in a room* (or *putting in a room*) is typically analyzed as a causal event, and of course there is the causal relation between that event and the wine's change of temperature. But we can analyze the meaning differently, i.e. *chambrer* may mean that someone acts in such a way that the wine warmed up to room temperature and have the method for achieving this goal be a matter of world knowledge that is not part of the meaning of the verb. Similarly, the definition of *mander* seems to involve a sequence of two causal relations: A cause B to tell C (= cause to know in many analyses) to do D. But we need not analyze *tell* as involving CAUSE. We can, as Shank would assume, have an "MTRANS" predicate that more narrowly, as a primitive, encodes transmission of information. Or we can assume that we need to add to our list of primitives USE to model obligatory instruments, where instruments include possibly human intermediaries carrying out orders, as seems required to model sentences such as (31). If we take this route, then *mander* would "decompose" as USE (x, $y_{messenger}$, DO (z, ...)) where DO is a variable for actions. As we can see, whether root meanings violate the two-CAUSE constraint depends on one's analysis of what is part of the meaning proper and what is part of additional, typical information, as well as what one countenances as conceptual primitives.

(31)   The US liberated Grenada with only 2,000 men.

Second, *chambrer* and *limoger* require the inclusion of rather arbitrary restrictions on the arguments of predicates that are part of the decomposed meaning (something McCawley (1968) already mentioned, citing verbs such as *devein* that can only take shrimps or similar crustaceans as patients): the verb *chambrer* requires the patient be wine (or possibly a few other kinds of nutrients) and *limoger* requires the patient to be a commanding officer (or, at least, a high-ranking official).

A third potential wrinkle for the attempt to limit how complex stem meanings can be is illustrated by the meaning of the Wakashan root √*tek* that means "reluctant to go out (of harbour etc.) because of the weather" (I thank Emmon Bach, p.c., for this example). We can certainly analyze this meaning as CAUSE (STATE(weather), RELUCTANT (x, GO(x, OUT(HOME)))) (where STATE is a variable over names of states). But the lexicographic paraphrase suggests that the stem denotes a state of mind, not a causal event, i.e. that somebody is reluctant to go out *because* of the bad weather rather than the state of the weather causing somebody to be reluctant to go out. To express through decomposition the lexicographic paraphrase, conjunction is required (e.g. RELUCTANT (e, x, GO (e', x, OUT(HOME))) AND CAUSE (BAD(e'', WEATHER), e)). But introducing conjunctions in the lexical meaning of roots is opening Pandora's box, as it is hard to see how to limit arbitrary conjunctions.

Until now I have discussed limits on the complexity of situation categories encoded in mono-morphemic stems in terms of how many sub-events *can* be necessary parts of the situation categories associated with the meaning of verbs. But other limits on event complexity have received attention as well. Rappaport and Levin (2010) have argued that verb meanings can restrict the manner in which a result is obtained or the result that is obtained, but not both. So, there are verbs like *jog* and *wipe* that constrain the nature of the agent's activity and there are verbs like *shatter* or *dim* that constrain the nature of the result of the agent's activity, but no words like *brattier* that would mean something like *shatter using a hammer-like object and apply it forcefully*. That most verb stems are specific about either the manner in which an activity is performed or its result is indeed true. But there are reasons to doubt it is an absolute requirement on verb meaning. As Beavers and Koontz-Garboden (2012) have noted, verbs of manner of killing (*crucify*, *guillotine*, *electrocute*) seem to constitute systematic exceptions as they certainly put constraints on the result (death or a state that will lead to death) as well as constraints on how this result is induced.

The decomposition of verb meanings into a small set of primitive operators and a base (state or activity) predicate suggests verb meanings within and across languages could vary in their lists of base predicate constants, meaning complexity (is there a cause, is there an instrument . . . ?), and in properties of the participants in the events (selectional restrictions). Consider our example of *limoger*. What is specific to the meaning of that verb is the final state (not be in a commanding post) and the kind of entity undergoing that change (higher officer). But some variation in the meaning of verb stems across languages goes beyond this model of semantic variation. Mandarin sentences (32) and (33) illustrate the phenomenon (see Bar-El et al. (2005) for similar data from Salish, Paramasivam (1977) for data on Tamil, and Koenig and Chief (2008) for data on Mandarin, as well as reported data from Hindi and Thai). As the English translations of these sentences suggest, we would expect the relevant change to be reached at the end of the event. In Parsons' (1990) terms, we would expect the event to have culminated. This is why the phenomenon illustrated in (32) and (33) has come to be referred to as non-culminating accomplishments: contradicting the occurrence of the change (the event's culmination) is infelicitous in English, but not in these other languages. Note that the source of the difference does not seem to lie in differences in the meaning of the direct object or aspect marking. Even when the proto-patient argument is bounded (quantized) and the aspect is perfective (or perfect), the difference in entailments remains: one can still deny the accomplishment culminated, as shown in (33).

(32) Xu Mei he Sun Mazi ba Lao Luo sha le mei sha-si
Xu Mei and Sun Mazi BA Lao Luo kill PERF not kill-die
"Xu Mei and Sun Mazi killed Lao Luo but didn't make him die. (lit.)" (Google)

(33) wo (. . .) chi le liang chuan dakao, dan mei chi-wan
I (. . .) eat PERF two CL kabob, but not eat-finish
"I ate two kabobs, but didn't finish eating them. (lit.)" (Google)

Various models of the phenomenon have been proposed (see Koenig and Chief (2008) for an explanation that relies on a scalar analysis of change), but what is interesting here is that whatever the explanation is, it is not easily accounted for in a model of the meaning of verbs of the kind proposed in many models of decomposition, as these models limit the range of meaning differences to kinds of states or activities and properties of arguments of predicates and functors. (One possibility worth exploring would be to distinguish between various kinds of BECOME and have the BECOME operator relevant to languages in which non-culminating accomplishments are pervasive have a slightly different meaning than the BECOME operator in English.)

5 Deriving categories of situations

In sections 2 and 3 I discussed two classifications of situation categories, Vendler's (often called Aktionsart classes) and the categories that decomposition schemes induce. As I mentioned, the two categorizations are not unrelated and Dowty (1979) can be seen as a way of combining the two perspectives, i.e. as a lexical decomposition scheme whose goal is to model Vendler-style classes. But these two perspectives have different goals, as mentioned above, and much of the research on Vendler-style classes has focused on how to *compose* meanings to derive situation descriptions that belong to these classes rather than *decompose* the meaning of verbs. The reason it is difficult to explain *why* a particular sentence type belongs to one Vendler-style class or another is that various parts of the sentence can contribute to assigning the meaning of the sentence to one class or another. Not only does the verb play a role, but so do properties of its arguments, as do aspect markers.

(34) a   Mary ate a pound of cheese in an hour.
      b   Mary ate cheese for an hour.
      c   %Mary was eating a pound of cheese for an hour.

(35) a   Mary ran for 15 minutes.
      b   Mary ran a mile in 15 minutes.
      c   %Mary was running a mile for 15 minutes.

(36) John carried his brother for 15 minutes.

The contrast between (34a) and (34b) shows that the denotation of the direct object makes a difference in the Vendler-style class of the sentence (from now on, we will label the argument that the direct object corresponds to, the proto-patient argument, borrowing liberally from Dowty (1991)). Basically, if the proto-patient is bounded (quantized in Krifka's (1989) terminology) and the verb is "the right kind of verb" (see below for more on this issue), the sentence describes an accomplishment, but if the proto-patient is not bounded (not quantized), the sentence describes an activity. The contrast between (35a) and (35b) can be described along the same lines if we assume that when the amount of ground covered in an act of running is left unexpressed, it is per force unbounded. Of course, the boundedness of the proto-patient is not enough. You need to start with the right kind of verb, the crucial insight of Vendler's original proposal. Thus, events of carrying will never be accomplishments, even when the proto-patient is bounded, as sentence (36) shows. But, even if the proto-patient is bounded and we have "the right kind of verb," the sentence can still describe an activity if the aspect marker selects an unbounded portion of the overall event, as the progressive does in (34c) and (35c) (%indicates speaker variation: some speakers find these sentences hard to contextualize).

A lot of ink has been spilled in the last forty years (since at least Verkuyl (1972); see Rothstein (2004) for a recent approach) on how to best model the respective effects of verb meaning, proto-patient (as well as other argument) properties, and aspect on the assignment of a sentence's meaning to a Vendler-style class. Following the work of Hay et al. (1999), it is common to distinguish between non-scalar changes (what underlies activities) and scalar changes (what underlies achievements and accomplishments). Telic events are analyzed as bounded (quantized) scalar changes. Sentences (37)–(42) illustrate what is meant by scalar changes.

(37) Marc shortened his pants.
(38) Sue sharpened her knives (in an hour/for an hour).
(39) Marc cooked the fish (in an hour/for an hour).
(40) Martha went home.
(41) Marc died.
(42) Jack noticed the car.

Sentences (37)–(39) describe changes in the properties of the pants, the knives, and the fish respectively. The changes undergone by the pants and knives in (37) and (38) are changes in degree on a relevant dimension (length, sharpness) (see Kennedy and Levin (2008)). The scalar nature of the change described in (37) and (38) is easily explained by the scalarity of the verb's adjectival base, *short* and *sharp*. But sentence (39) shows that the presence of an adjectival base is not needed for a verb to describe a change in degree (of rawness in the case of *cook*). Sentence (40) also describes a scalar change, as long as we analyze the path Martha took to go home as a scale (where locations on the path serve as the degrees ordered by the direction of the movement), something relatively plausible. The scales involved in (37)–(40) are complex in that they consist of more than two degrees. But this is not the case for sentences (41) and (42). These sentences can be analyzed as describing scalar changes, but only provided we allow scales to be binary, i.e. to involve only two degrees (being alive/not alive for sentence (41); being aware/not aware for (42)), as Beavers (2008) suggests. Finally, descriptions of complex scalar changes need not be bounded, as the ability of both *for* and *in* phrases to combine with the verb and its dependents in (38) and (39) shows. The fact that one can sharpen a knife or cook fish indefinitely explains the possibility of *for* phrases (which characteristically pair with activities: see the discussion below), but the fact that there is also a contextually salient standard or norm for both kinds of situations explains the possibility of *in* phrases (which characteristically pair with accomplishments).

As I just mentioned, in contrast to accomplishments and achievements, activities do not involve a change that can be analyzed as scalar (i.e. as a change of degree of a property on a scale). Sentence (43), in its most salient interpretation, describes a sequence of minimal changes of location, a sequence of steps, say. But, there is no necessary order in this sequence of changes. Sam could have walked back and forth. This is why sentence (43) does not entail that there is change in location on a path (which, as mentioned above, can be analyzed as a scale, i.e. as an ordered set of degrees, the ordered set of locations on the (directed) path).

(43)   Sam walked.

Although the notion of non-scalar change appropriately characterizes many activities (particularly, manner-of-motion events), it is unclear whether all activities involve *change*. In some cases, the change, if present at all, would seem rather abstract. Consider verbs like *work* predicated of guards standing still outside Buckingham palace. What changes make up their work? Hard to say. The guards' work certainly involves internal activities (e.g., a heightened level of responsiveness), but whether those are continuous changes, as is the case for manner-of-motion verbs like *run*, is unclear. Worse, there seems to be no change at all involved in some basic human activities, such as holding a cup in your hand. This description does not pass classical tests of stativity (see Lakoff (1966); for example, the progressive is required for a non-habitual interpretation in the present for all these activities). But this activity only requires an expense of energy on the part of the person holding a cup. This is confirmed by the fact that for these activities, the subinterval property is true "all the way down." So, whereas a subevent of running is only still running as long as it is long enough, no matter how small the event or interval of time, you still hold the cup.

As we just have just seen, *in* and *for* temporal phrases are sensitive to the boundedness of event descriptions. But why? I follow Moltmann (1991) (expanding on Dowty (1979)) and analyze *for* phrases as quantifying over parts (either parts of time intervals or parts of events). So, if the *for*-version of a sentence like (44) is true, it entails that John ran for any relevant subinterval of ten minutes. ((45) shows that the domain of quantification does not necessarily include all intervals of time, but only the relevant ones given the event description: in this case, intervals of time that are a day long.)

(44) John ran for 10 minutes/#in ten minutes
(45) My dad shaved a pipe twice a day for 30 years
(46) John ran a mile %for 10 minutes/in 10 minutes

Following Dowty (1979), I analyze *in* temporal phrases (often called frame adverbials) as (uniquely) existentially quantifying over the event described by the verb constellation. Thus, sentence (46) says that there is a unique interval of time included in ten minutes during which the event described by *John ran a mile* unfolded.

Given these meanings for *in* and *for* phrases, we can easily explain their sensitivity to whether the described event is bounded. If an event description requires the described event to include an event's boundaries, then *the same description* will not be true of a proper sub-part of that event. If the description requires the event to be one of John running ten miles, that description will not be true of a smaller running event (where less than ten miles were run). Since *for* phrases require the description they have scope over to be true of all (relevant) subparts of the event, a *for* phrase will be incompatible with such an event description, *except* if the event description is understood as describing the *process* of a running a mile (the interpretation required by the % in sentence (46)). Conversely, for an event *as described by the verb and its dependents* to be included *in* an interval of time of 10 minutes, there must be a unique interval lasting at most 10 minutes during which the event described by the verb constellation unfolded. So, sentence (44) is incompatible with *in 10 minutes* because John running is true of many intervals of time since it is an homogenous event.

6 Which event properties matter to syntax?

The last question mentioned in the introductory paragraph pertains to potential limits on the range of distinctions among categories of situations that morphosyntactic processes are sensitive to. Pinker (1989) and Grimshaw (2005) suggest that there are strict a priori limitations in the aspects of event semantics morphosyntax cares about. Glossing over differences here, these authors view the categorization of event-types of the kind I described as part of linguistic semantics as distinct from conceptual structure or world knowledge (see also Van Valin and LaPolla (1997)). The idea here is that out of all potential categorizations of events, only some are relevant to the interface between syntax and semantics. It is those that form the basis of decomposition (which is only part of the lexical semantics of verbs). They then point out that syntactic constructions, morphological derivation, and other closed class expressions have a limited range of meanings they can contribute and those are similar to the kinds of meaning that appear in predicate decomposition (see Pinker (1989); Talmy (2000)). The explanation for this "fact" is then sought in a special semantic system that differs from world knowledge.

There is no doubt that grammars seem sensitive to only a small subset of properties of situation categories and that language use, in contrast, is sensitive to many more properties. Thus, when it comes to predicting the realization of arguments, grammars are sensitive almost exclusively to entailed properties of lexical items. So, what matters for determining the subject of a transitive verb like *sweeten* is that its proto-agent argument causes a change of state. Only properties *entailed* of the argument position seem relevant (see Dowty (1991) for details and some circumscribed exceptions). But, *typical* properties of fillers of argument position are very relevant to sentence processing, a point made forcefully by psycholinguists over the last twenty years. But while it may be tempting to reify the difference in the kinds of event properties relevant to grammar and processing and therefore assume two distinct cognitive subsystems responsible for those two distinct classes of situation properties, there are reasons for caution. First, even if limited, we do not yet know the exact limits of the situation properties relevant to grammar. The specification of the "subject" and "object" of kin verbs, for example, is sensitive to the property "being generationally older" and, possibly, sometimes, being older (see Evans (2000)). Second, the notion of closed class is itself difficult to maintain. Are prepositions a closed class as Talmy claims? Maybe, but what evidence do we have except that the meaning of prepositions is of the kind we associate with closed class expressions? And, as we know, adjectives can be closed class in some languages too (see Dixon (1982)). Third, and more importantly, the fact that there is a subsystem of meanings for closed class expressions does not necessarily mean that grammar should be sensitive only to those aspects of meaning *unless* one stipulates, like Pinker or Grimshaw, that only those event properties are "visible" to grammatical constraints. This is a strong claim whose truth would depend on the existence of a built-in architectural constraint, something we have little evidence for as of now. Another possibility explored in Koenig et al. (2015) is that the reason for the difference between the range of event properties relevant to grammar and processing has to do with the differences in the task the two cognitive systems are engaged in. In other words, the difference would arise out of boundary conditions (what the point of processing and grammar is) rather than built-in architectural differences.

Further reading

Dowty, D. 1979. *Word Meaning and Montague Grammar*. Dordrecht: Reidel. A classic with an incredible amount of insights that have shaped the research on event semantics since its publication.
Jackendoff, R. 1990. *Semantic Structures*. Cambridge, MA: MIT Press. The most detailed decompositional analysis of the meaning of verbs. It also shows how those proposed meanings interface with syntax.
Rothstein, S. 2004. *Structuring Events: A Study in the Semantics of Lexical Aspect*. Oxford: Blackwell. A good overview of various approaches to lexical aspect and presents a well-argued new proposal.
de Almeida, R. and C. Manouilidou 2015. *Cognitive Science Perspectives on Verb Representation and Processing*. Dordrecht: Springer. Provides a broader perspective on verb meaning and event categories. It includes papers by linguists, philosophers, psycholinguists, and neurolinguists.

References

de Almeida, R. and C. Manouilidou 2015. *Cognitive Science Perspectives on Verb Representation and Processing*. Dordrecht: Springer.
Bach, E. 1986. The algebra of events. *Linguistics and Philosophy 9*: 5–16.
Bar-El, L., H. Davis, and L. Matthewson 2005. On non-culminating accomplishments. In Leah Bateman and Cherlon Ussery (eds), *NELS 35*. Department of Linguistics, University of Massachusetts: GLSA, 87–102.
Beavers, J. 2008. Scalar complexity and the structure of events. In J. Dölling, T. Heyde-Zybatow and M. Schäfer (eds), *Event Structures in Linguistic Form and Interpretation*. Berlin: Mouton de Gruyter, 245–265.
Beavers, J. and A. Koontz-Garboden 2012. Manner and result in the roots of verbal meaning. *Linguistic Inquiry* 43: 331–369.
Borer, H. 2005. *The Normal Course of Events*. Oxford: Oxford University Press.
Carter, R. 1976. Some constraints on possible words. *Semantikos* 1: 27–66.
Davidson, D. 1967. The logical form of action sentences. In N. Resch (ed.), *The Logic of Decision and Action*, 81–95. Pittsburgh: University of Pittsburgh Press.

Dixon, R. M. W. 1982. *Where Have All the Adjectives Gone? And Other Essays in Semantics and Syntax.* Berlin: Mouton de Gruyter.

Dowty, D. 1979. *Word Meaning and Montague Grammar.* Dordrecht: Reidel.

Dowty, D. 1991. Thematic proto-roles and argument selection. *Language* 67: 547–619.

Evans, N. 2000. Kinship verbs. In P. Vogel and B. Comrie (eds), *Approaches to the Typology of Word Classes.* Berlin: Mouton de Gruyter, 1073–1089.

Fodor, J. A. 1970. Three reasons for not deriving *kill* from *cause to die*. *Language* 46: 429–438.

Galton, A. 1984. *The Logic of Aspect.* Oxford: Clarendon Press.

Goddard, C. and A. Wierzbicka (eds), 1994. *Semantic and Lexical Universals: Theory and Empirical Findings.* Amsterdam: John Benjamins.

Grimshaw, J. 2005. *Words and Structure.* Stanford, CA: CSLI Publications.

Hay, J., C. Kennedy and B. Levin 1999. Scalar structure underlies telicity in degree achievements. In T. Mathews and D. Strolovitch (eds), *SALT IX*. Ithaca, NY: CLC Publications, 127–144.

Herweg, M. 1991. A critical examination of two classical approaches to aspect. *Journal of Semantics* 8: 363–402.

Jackendoff, R. 1983. *Semantics and Cognition.* Cambridge, MA: MIT Press.

Jackendoff, R. 1990. *Semantic Structures.* Cambridge, MA: MIT Press.

Kennedy, C., and B. Levin 2008. Measure of change: the adjectival core of degree achievements. In L. McNally and C. Kennedy (eds), *Adjectives and Adverbs: Syntax, Semantics and Discourse.* Oxford: Oxford University Press, 156–182.

Kenny, A. 1963. *Action, Emotion, and Will.* London: Routledge and Kegan Paul.

Koenig, J.-P., and L.-C. Chief 2008. Scalarity and state-changes in Mandarin and other languages. In O. Bonami and P. Cabredo-Hofherr (eds), *Empirical Issues in Syntax and Semantics 7*. Paris: CNRS, 241–262.

Koenig, J.-P., G. Mauner, and B. Bienvenue 2003. Arguments for adjuncts. *Cognition*, 89: 67–103.

Koenig, J.-P., D. Roland, H. Yun, and G. Mauner 2015. Which event properties matter for which cognitive task? In R. de Almeida and C. Manouilidou (eds), *Cognitive Science Perspectives on Verb Representation and Processing.* Dordrecht: Springer, 211–232.

Kratzer, A. 2000. Building statives. In L. Conathan (ed.), *Proceedings of the 26th Annual Meeting of the Berkeley Linguistics Society.* Berkeley: Berkeley Linguistics Society, 385–399.

Krifka, M. 1989. Nominal reference, temporal constitution, and quantification in event semantics. In R. Bartsch, J. van Benthem and P. van Emde Boas (eds), *Semantics and Contextual Expressions.* Dordrecht: Foris, 75–115.

Lakoff, G. 1966. Stative adjectives and verbs in English. In A. G. Oettinger (ed.), *Mathematical Linguistics and Automatic Translation Report NSF*-17. The Computation Laboratory, Harvard, MA: Harvard University, 1–16.

Lakoff, G. 1970. *Irregularity in Syntax.* New York: Holt, Rinehart, and Winston.

Link, G. 1997. *Algebraic Semantics in Linguistics and Philosophy.* Stanford, CA: CSLI Publications.

McCawley, J. 1968. Concerning the base component of a transformational grammar. *Foundations of Language* 4: 243–269.

Moltmann, F. 1991. Measure adverbials. *Linguistics and Philosophy* 14: 629–660.

Paramasivam, K. P. 1977. *Effectivity and Causativity in Tamil.* Unpublished doctoral dissertation, University of Chicago.

Parsons, T. 1990. *Events in the Semantics of English.* Cambridge, MA: MIT Press.

Pinker, S. 1989. *Learnability and Cognition: The Acquisition of Argument Structure.* Cambridge, MA: MIT Press.

Ramchand, G. 2008. *Verb Meaning and the Lexicon: A First Phase Syntax.* Cambridge: Cambridge University Press.

Rappaport Hovav, M., and B. Levin 2010. Reflections on manner/result complementarity. In E. Doron, M. Rappaport Hovav, and I. Sichel (eds) *Syntax, Lexical Semantics, and Event Structure*. Oxford: Oxford University Press, 21–38.

Rothstein, S. 2004. *Structuring Events: A Study in the Semantics of Lexical Aspect.* Oxford: Blackwell.

Shank, R. 1973. *Identification of Conceptualizations Underlying Natural Languages.* San Francisco: W. H. Freeman and Co.
Talmy, L. 2000. *Toward a Cognitive Semantics.* Cambridge, MA: MIT Press.
Van Valin, R., and R. Lapolla 1997. *Syntax: Form, Meaning, and Function.* Cambridge: Cambridge University Press.
Vendler, Z. 1957. Verbs and times. *The Philosophical Review* 66: 143–160.
Verkuyl, H. 1972. *On the Compositional Nature of the Aspects.* Dordrecht: Reidel.

Related topics

Chapter 12, Lexical decomposition; Chapter 19, Lexical and grammatical aspect; Chapter 23, Participant roles

23
Participant roles

Beatrice Primus

1 Overview of participant roles and of role-related notions

Participant roles capture certain generalizations about the participation of entities in eventualities denoted by linguistic expressions regarding such issues as who did it, who it happened to and what got changed. Participant roles are found under a number of different names in the linguistic literature including thematic relations or roles (e.g. Jackendoff (1990); Parsons (1995); Davis (2011)), deep cases (e.g. Fillmore (1968)), theta-roles (e.g. Chomsky (1981); Reinhart (2002); Everaert (2012)) and semantic roles. Here we will refer to "participant roles" or "semantic roles". Among the linguistic expressions describing eventualities verbs play an important part as they select the widest range of participant roles. Thus, for example, *work*, as in *John is working*, has one participant role, which may be characterized as the agent, while *love* in *John loves his wife* selects two roles, an "experiencer" and a "theme" (these categories will be explained below). However, nouns, adjectives and adpositions (pre- and postpositions) also select participant roles. For ease of exposition, we will focus on verbs, although many statements also hold for other role-selecting categories.

The following overview of the most widely used participant roles and of the notions characterizing them serves as an introduction to the next sections of this chapter. Agent is the role of the participant that initiates and executes, possibly deliberately, the eventuality denoted by the verb, such as in *John is working* and *John baked a cake*. Related to the agent is instrument, which is also a causal factor in the eventuality denoted by the verb, such as *the key* in *the key opened the door*. Patient is the role of the participant that is causally affected, moved or otherwise changed in the eventuality denoted by the verb. The objects of the verbs *bake* and *open* in the examples above bear this role. So far, notions related to causation, intentionality (or control of action), execution of the eventuality described by the verb, on the one side, and causal affectedness and change, including locational or existential change, on the other side, have been used to characterize participant roles.

Other pertinent general notions that help us to identify participant roles are mental states, which are often used under the cover term sentience. They characterize the experiencer, which is the role of the participant that has the mental state denoted by the verb, such as *John* in *John knows the answer*. Mental states also characterize roles such as the addressee for verbs of communication in the broad sense, including *tell John a story*, *show John a picture* and *teach John English*. With these verbs, the mental state of John, e.g. his knowledge or attentional focus, is changed in the eventuality described by the verb.

Possession is another general concept that is relevant for participant roles, including the possessor and the object of possession (possessum) as in *John owns three cars* and the recipient of verbs denoting transfer of possession, e.g. *give John money*.

The location, orientation and movement of participants in space is important for roles such as locative (e.g. *lying on the floor*), source, path and goal, e.g. *driving from home* (source) *through the forest* (path) *to the railway station* (locational goal). In many instances, locational notions co-occur with non-locational ones. Thus, for example, if *Mary sold her car to the church* is true, the car changes its possessor and location in the normal course of events. Space roles are intimately connected to time roles, e.g. *driving from six in the morning* (the temporal beginning) *the whole day through* (the temporal "path" or duration) *to midnight* (the temporal end).

Some participant roles are more difficult to pin down, since none of the general notions mentioned above seem to be applicable to them, e.g. the role of the subject in *the stone is falling* and of the object in *know the answer*. Therefore, most researchers include an underspecified role in their inventory such as theme (as opposed to patient, which is usually used for participants undergoing a change, as mentioned above).

As this role overview shows, a participant role is usually realized as a syntactic argument (i.e. subject or object) of a verb or of another role-selecting category. This chapter focuses on this type of realization for semantic roles. However, semantic roles, such as locative and time, for instance, may also be adverbial modifiers, such as in *working in the garden at noon*. In this case, they fall into an area of linguistic research specialized in adverbial modification.

Participant roles are involved in a multitude of grammatical phenomena. Besides, they also play a crucial role in language acquisition and in the way language is processed in the brain. Section 2 will present phenomena that form the main topics of research in role semantics. Whether these phenomena are adequately captured by a list of atomic participant roles or, alternatively, by some other role-related theoretical means will be discussed in section 3. The chapter ends with an overview of the latest developments and of future directions in role semantics (section 4).

2 Main topics

2.1 Lexical semantics and language acquisition

Participant roles are intimately connected to the meaning of argument-selecting words. This is most evident in language acquisition:

> Thus, for example, when children learn the word *give*, there is really no learning of the word apart from the participant roles that invariably accompany acts of giving: the giver, the thing given, and the person given to; in fact, we cannot even conceive of an act of giving in the absence of these participant roles.
>
> (Tomasello 2000: 134)

Well in advance of using verbs, infants show considerable insight into the general concepts that characterize participant roles, including change of location, movement, causation and the difference between accidental and intentional results of events (see Hirsch-Pasek and Golinkoff (2006); see also Chapter 26). Evolutionary psychologists (see Spelke and Kinzler

(2007)) assume that both human neonates and non-human animals are endowed with evolutionarily ancient core knowledge about objects (e.g. cohesion, i.e. objects move as connected and bounded wholes) and agentivity (e.g. goal directedness). Such general concepts are needed to discern what is the basic distinction between a giver, i.e. the initiator and executor of the act of giving, and the thing given, i.e. the causally affected, passive entity. This knowledge helps children to learn novel verbs that exhibit an analogous distinction and to form more general role concepts such as agent and patient.

However, there is more to the meaning of a verb than the characterization of the types of participant roles it selects. Each verb includes additional, lexeme-specific role information. Thus, for example, there is more in the concept of a seller than the information that the seller is the agent of the event in question. Hence, a giver and a seller bear the same general agent role but different verb-specific roles.

These remarks lead us to the general problem of granularity in semantic-role research: some phenomena, including lexical semantics, need a fine-grained analysis of the individual roles a lexeme selects; yet other phenomena – notably the mapping of the multitude of lexeme-specific roles onto a small number of syntactic functions (i.e. subject and object) – are best explained by a small number of more abstract, generalized participant roles.

2.2 Mapping participant roles onto syntactic functions

Both within and across languages, there are principles guiding the mapping of participant roles onto syntactic functions such as subject and object. This kind of mapping is also named *linking*, *alignment*, *argument realization* or *argument selection*. It is the main area of application of role notions and the principal testing ground for semantic-role theories.

A basic assumption of several semantic-role theories is role uniqueness. This means that only one representative of a given participant role may appear in a sentence that denotes a simple event (e.g. Fillmore (1968); Carlson (1998)). Many researchers go one step further and hypothesize bi-uniqueness of mapping between syntactic arguments and participant roles, as stated in Chomsky's Theta-Criterion (1981: 36):

(1) The Theta-Criterion: Each argument bears one and only one theta-role, and each theta-role is assigned to one and only one argument.

A similar principle is Function-Argument-Biuniqueness in Lexical Functional Grammar (Bresnan 2001).

The Theta-Criterion and similar principles are confronted with serious problems (for a critique, see e.g. Jackendoff (1990); Dowty (1991)). First, there are expletive arguments with no corresponding role, such as *it* in *it rains*. Second, some participant roles cannot be expressed syntactically, cf. particle verbs in German such as *zuschlagen* "beat, punch" and *losschreiben* "to start writing": *Peter schlug (*jemanden) zu* "Peter punched somebody"; *Peter schrieb (*etwas/*einen Brief) los* "Peter started writing something/a letter".

A third, more subtle problem is role accumulation, i.e. one syntactic argument bearing two roles in one event or subevent (see Jackendoff (1990)): in *Mary sold her car to the church*, Mary is the causer of the selling event and the initial possessor of the car. A possible solution is to assume that a participant may be involved in different relations, in this example causation and possession (see Dowty (1991) and section 3.3 below, Carlson (1998) and Koenig and Davis (2006) for other cases). Another solution is to dissociate two levels of role representation: a level where arguments may bear several thematic (or semantic) roles, and a theta-structure, where these roles are bundled into a small set of theta-roles (see Carnie (2007: chapter 8.2), Wunderlich (1997) and section 3.2 below).

The fourth problem is role dispersion, i.e. two syntactic arguments bearing the same role. Symmetric predicates such as *Fred resembles Bob* are a case in point. *Fred resembles Bob* is truth-functionally equivalent to *Bob resembles Fred*, i.e. one cannot accept the truth of one sentence while denying that of the other. This does not hold for *Fred is slapping Bob* and *Bob is slapping Fred*. Fillmore (1970: 262), among others, proposes a solution to this problem in terms of reference-related notions: the argument in subject position must be a referring expression, the one in object position can have a non-referring (de dicto) reading, cf. the irreversibility of *Fred resembles a horse*.

This solution raises one of the biggest, still open questions in role semantics: What counts as a semantic-role notion? According to Dowty (1991: 562):

> no semantic distinction will count as relevant data for our theory of roles unless it can be shown to be relevant to argument selection somewhere in some language, no matter how traditional a role it characterizes; and any semantic distinction that can definitely be shown to be relevant to argument selection can count toward defining a role type, no matter whether it relates to a traditional role or not.

Surprisingly, in view of this statement, Dowty (1991) hesitates to include reference-related notions in his role entailments since they may be tied to subjecthood in a direct way (see (22e) and (23e) in section 3 below). As to perspective-related roles such as figure and ground (see Talmy (2000: chapter 5)), he bans them from his inventory. However, they determine subject selection, as do the reference-related properties mentioned above. Thus, for example, a bicycle is smaller and normally more variable in its position than a house. So in the normal course of events, the former may act as a figure in relation to the latter, which is the perceptual ground, but not the other way round. In copular locative constructions in English and other languages, the figure is selected as subject, e.g. *The bicycle is near the house* vs. #*The house is near the bicycle*. ("#" stands henceforth for a semantic anomaly in the reading under discussion.)

The question of delimiting the range of semantic-role notions is tackled in two ways in pertinent research. One solution is to consider all semantic distinctions that are relevant to argument selection to be role notions, as stated by Dowty above and as pursued by Fillmore (1970) for *resemble* (see above). Another way is to allow argument realization to be determined by semantic information that is distinct from role semantics. This solution is favoured, for example, by Dowty (1991) for figure and ground and, tentatively, also for reference-related distinctions. How difficult the decision is can be shown for figure and ground. This distinction combines perspective and information-packaging notions (the figure is in the centre of attention) with role-related notions (the figure is more movable and the ground more stationary). So finding the divide between semantic-role notions and other types of concepts that determine argument realization is not a trivial enterprise.

General mapping principles such as the Theta-Criterion do not restrict the semantic-role content assigned to a particular type of syntactic function. Therefore, it has to be supplemented by principles that restrict the mapping between certain roles and certain syntactic functions. Among the multitude of proposals that have been put forward in the literature, the following (or a similar) principle for the basic transitive construction has gained wide acceptance (e.g. Dowty (1991: 576); Levin and Rappaport Hovav (2005: 24); Lasnik and Uriagereka (2005: 6) in different frameworks):

(2) Basic mapping of agent^S and patient^S in accusative languages:
If the verbal predicate selects an agent^S and a patient^S, the agent^S is mapped onto the subject and the patient^S onto the direct object.

In (2), we have made some qualifications that are adopted implicitly or explicitly in many publications. First, the principle makes the best prediction for strongly specified agents and patients as used in the standard definition given in section 1 above (abbreviated as agent^S and patient^S). Recall that the agent – now marked agent^S – was defined as the role of the participant that initiates and executes, possibly deliberately, the eventuality denoted by the verb. Patient^S is the role of the participant that is causally affected, that is moved or otherwise changed.

Second, the mapping of agent^S and patient^S has to accommodate the distinction between accusative and ergative languages, which is the centrepiece of alignment typology. This typological parameter separates accusative languages, where (2) holds for syntactic functions interpreted as structural positions and morphosyntactic cases (e.g. English, German, French, Japanese and Korean) from ergative languages (e.g. Basque, Avar, Hindi and Dyirbal), that exhibit a different basic mapping, at least in terms of morphosyntactic cases. In the ergative construction, the patient^S is in the absolutive, the morphosyntactic case that corresponds to the nominative, while the agent^S is in the ergative, a case that is formally more marked than the absolutive (see e.g. Dixon (1994); Primus (1999) for an overview). Besides ergative mapping, there are several other alignment types (see e.g. Bickel (2011)). In this chapter, we will focus on the better-known accusative languages.

Third, the principle (2) only holds for the basic transitive construction of accusative languages, which is illustrated by an English example in (3a):

(3) a *John* (agent^S, subject) *opened the door* (patient^S, direct object).
    b **The door* (patient^S, subject) *opened John* (agent^S, direct object).
    c *The door* (patient^S, subject) *was opened by John* (agent^S, oblique).

Example (3b) shows that an inverse basic transitive construction in which the patient^S is linked to the subject and the agent^S to the direct object is ungrammatical in accusative languages. The patient^S may surface as the subject of semantically poly-valenced verbs only if the agent^S is barred from becoming a subject, for instance, by the passive morphology of the verb, as shown in (3c).

Pairs of verbs like *borrow–lend*, *buy–sell* and *get–give* pose a problem for bi-uniqueness of mapping (see (1) above) as well as for the basic mapping principle (2). Cf. (4a, b):

(4) a *Jill borrowed a pen from Sandy.*
    b *Sandy lent a pen to Jill.*

The mapping problem is that such verbs imply both a transfer and a counter-transfer of possession, an obtaining and a giving event with their own agent and recipient. The problem for the mapping principle (2) is that one needs a criterion to decide which of the agents (the taker or the giver) becomes the subject. One solution to this problem is to assume that argument mapping is not solely determined by role semantics but also by perspective- or salience-related notions (see Fillmore (1970); Koenig and Davis (2006)). The verbs *borrow*, *buy* and *get* highlight the obtaining relation, i.e. they lexicalize the transfer of possession from the perspective of the obtainer of goods. The verbs *lend*, *sell* and *give* emphasize the giving relation. Another solution is to claim that the verb pairs under discussion have different semantic representations (see Jackendoff (1990)). This solution is corroborated by the fact that although some situation tokens involving these pairs of verbs are truth-functionally equivalent, i.e. mutually entail each other, this does not hold for all situations. Cf. (5a, b):

(5) a *Jill readily borrowed a pen from Sandy.*
    b *Sandy readily lent a pen to Jill.*

Alternatively, the proponents of the perspective-based solution have to acknowledge that perspectivization may have truth-functional effects.

In sum, despite the fact that they have to be parameterized and further specified in different ways, mapping principles, including the mapping principle for the basic transitive construction presented in this section, are strong evidence for the viability of role notions that are more abstract than verb-specific roles. They also have a bearing on language acquisition and language parsing. Young children are more successful in the acquisition of basic (also: *canonical*) mapping and show a strong tendency to overgeneralize it (e.g. Chan et al. (2009)). Many psycholinguistic experiments also reveal that basic mapping is preferred in language parsing (see Bornkessel-Schlesewsky and Schlesewsky (2009: chapter 9)). Despite the appeal of the basic mapping principle, we have to bear in mind that its scope is very limited typologically and semantically. If one takes other alignment types (e.g. ergative languages), roles, semantic factors or syntactic functions into consideration, the picture becomes more diffuse. One challenging case has been illustrated above by *borrow* and *lend*; other cases will be discussed in the context of mapping alternations in the next section.

2.3 Mapping alternations

Mapping alternations, i.e. different argument realizations for one verb, are a tantalizing problem for role semantics. For English, Levin (1993) distinguishes almost 60 verb classes, most of them with a number of subclasses, that show distinct syntactic behaviour (see also Riemer (2010: 352–359) for an overview). The different syntactic realizations are determined by fine-grained role differences that interact with other semantic or pragmatic phenomena tied to animacy, aspect, definiteness, givenness and perspectivization (e.g. figure and ground). Additional challenges arise from performance-based factors such as constituent weight and a strong frequency bias in favour of one variant. A well-studied alternation that has been considered to be determined by several interacting factors is the dative alternation in English.

The dative alternation concerns the following syntactic patterns, called the Direct Object (DO)-construction and the Prepositional Object (PO)-construction. Cf. the examples and the rudimentary argument structures in (6a, b):

(6) a *Ann gave Beth the car.*   x gave y z   DO-construction
    b *Ann gave the car to Beth.* x gave z to y   PO-construction

Many authors assume that the different syntactic patterns can be explained by the following semantic difference between them (e.g. Krifka (2004); see Bresnan and Nikitina (2003) for further references): the DO-construction entails that y is the possessor of z after the event denoted by the verb, whereas the PO-frame implies that z is at some local region of y after the event denoted by the verb. (Henceforth, this assumption will be referred to as the possessor-locative assumption.) Krifka (2004) uses this semantic difference to explain the oddity of the examples (7b)–(9b):

(7) a *Beth sent a package to London.*
    b #*Beth sent London a package.*
(8) a *Ann lowered the parcel to Beth.*
    b #*Ann lowered Beth the parcel.*
(9) a *Ann threw the ball halfway to Beth.*
    b #*Ann threw Beth the ball halfway.*

Krifka explains the asymmetries in (7)–(9) as follows: (7b) is semantically anomalous in the literal reading of *London* since the participant y must satisfy the selectional restrictions for possession in the DO-construction: if Beth sent a package to London, we cannot say that London possesses the package, except if *London* is a metonym for an organization, like Scotland Yard. In the PO-construction, the participant z must undergo movement, while movement is assumed to be lacking in the pure change-of-possession reading of the DO-construction. The DO-construction in (8b) is odd because verbs such as *lower*, *haul*, *push* and *pull* denote a continuous imparting of force of the agent upon the patient all the way along a path. This means that motion and change of possession are homomorphic. Since the DO-construction involves no movement event according to the view under discussion, it is odd with these verbs. This is also the explanation offered by Krifka for the fact that the adverb *halfway*, which modifies a path, is semantically uninterpretable in the DO-construction (9b).

A problem for the possessor-locative assumption arises when it is extended to verbs of communication, cf. (10a, b):

(10) a *Ann showed the car to Beth.*
     b *Ann showed Beth the car.*

According to Krifka (2004: 3), "[v]erbs like *show*, *read*, *tell*, *quote* do not express transfer of possession in the literal sense, but they do indicate that the recipient gets hold of some information". The problem is that the notion of possession is metaphorically extended and thereby diluted to include the addressee of verbs of communication (see Chapter 15).

Even more intriguing is the notion of possession for the role of the DO in idiomatic uses such as illustrated in (11) and (12):

(11) a *The explosion gave Beth a headache.*
     b #*The explosion gave a headache to Beth.*
(12) a *His behaviour gave Beth an idea.*
     b #*His behaviour gave an idea to Beth.*

Krifka (2004), among others, explains the oddity of the PO-construction in (11b) and (12b) by the fact that ideas and headaches cannot move literally. However, the possessive analysis of the DO-construction is as strained as the locative reading of the PO-construction for such idiomatic uses, since ideas and headaches cannot be a possessum if one takes possession literally.

Another problem is that metaphorical meaning extension is also used to explain why all verbs of transfer of possession (with the morpho-phonologically motivated exception of latinate verbs such as *donate*) allow for the PO-frame with no truth-conditional difference. According to Krifka (2004: 11), among others:

the reason for this is that every transfer of possession can be conceptualized as an abstract movement event in the dimension of possession spaces: When Ann gives Beth a car, then the car is moved from the possession of Ann into the possession of Beth.

Under closer scrutiny, one is not obliged to resort to "possession spaces" to explain that many verbs occur in both constructions. As mentioned in section 1 above, verbs of transfer of possession often imply two simultaneous events, a change of possession and a change of location. The DO-construction highlights the change of possession, the PO-construction the locational change (see Koenig and Davis (2006) where verbs are represented by a set of elementary predicates, one of them being highlighted as the KEY). A change of possession is conceptualized as instantaneous, so the DO-construction is odd when a path is presupposed (see Jackendoff (1990)). This nicely explains the oddity of *halfway* in (9b).

A general problem for Krifka's semantic distinction between the possessive and the locative reading and his strict mapping assumption is that they only hold as a tendency. In their corpus-based analysis, Bresnan and Nikitina (2003) showed that the examples assumed to be ungrammatical in the pertinent literature do occur, though admittedly only in the much larger corpus of web documents. They appear not to be grammatically impossible, but just improbable. Here we only show two counterexamples to Krifka's assumptions. Cf. (13) and (14):

(13) *As Player A pushed him the chips, all hell broke loose at the table.* www.cardplayer.com/?sec=afeature&art id=165 (from Bresnan and Nikitina (2003: 6))

(14) *She found it hard to look at the Sage's form for long. The spells that protected her identity also gave a headache to anyone trying to determine even her size, the constant bulging and rippling of her form gave Sarah vertigo.* http://lair.echidnoyle.org/rpg/log/27.html (from Bresnan and Nikitina (2003: 9))

(13) challenges the assumption that verbs like *lower* and *push*, which denote a continuous imparting of force of the agent upon the patient, cannot be used in the DO-construction (see (8b) above)). (14) casts a doubt on the claims that the PO-construction is ungrammatical for idiomatic uses of *give* and that the anomaly arises from the fact that headaches cannot move literally (see (11b) and (12b) above)).

As Bresnan and Nikitina, among others, show, the dative alternation in English is determined by several soft constraints that may compete with each other. One constraint is to avoid overt (i.e. PO) marking for recipient-possessors. This is proposed as a hard constraint by the proponents of the possessor-locative-assumption, who additionally assume that PO-marking is obligatory for locative goals. Bresnan and Nikitina's soft constraint against overt marking of recipient-possessors is able to explain the strong statistical bias in favour of the DO-construction for verbs of change of possession (87% DO vs. 13% PO for *give*, see Bresnan and Nikitina (2003: 13)) as well as the fact that such verbs occur in both constructions with no palpable semantic-role difference.

If the DO-construction is basic (the default) for *give*, then the preference asymmetry shown in (11) and (12) above for idiomatic uses can be explained without resorting to the questionable assumption that *give somebody an idea* and *give somebody a headache* have a possessive reading. It would suffice to claim that the default construction, the DO-construction in this case, is used if a verb, e.g. *give*, is used idiomatically.

Another soft constraint used by Bresnan and Nikitina is to place shorter constituents before longer ones. This is a solution to (14), where *to anyone* is supplemented by a gerundive modifier. In addition, information packaging, reference-related notions, and animacy also play a role in this framework. When both are objects, the recipient, i.e. ultimate possessor, tends to dominate the possessum on hierarchies of informational prominence (given > accessible > new), definiteness (definite > indefinite) and animacy (animate > inanimate). The animacy, givenness and lightness of *him* in (13) is a plausible explanation for its use in DO-position.

A multi-dimensional approach to the dative alternation in English captures the data more appropriately than one-dimensional semantic-role assumptions (see Levin (1993); Aissen (2003); Levin and Rappaport Hovav (2005) for other mapping alternations). The appeal of a multi-dimensional approach sheds light on the general issue of mapping participant roles onto syntactic functions. Role-based mapping principles including the principle for the basic transitive construction (see (2) above) can be overridden in many cases by various grammatical factors and in some cases also by performance constraints. If one takes a typologically broader vista, additional factors that determine not only non-basic constructions but also the basic transitive construction come into play. These include clause type (subordinate vs. main clause), polarity (negative vs. affirmative) as well as verbal time, aspect and mood (see Dixon (1994) for ergative-accusative mapping alternations).

Let us sum up and compare the possessor-locative-assumption as an example of a strict role-based analysis with a multi-dimensional approach to mapping alternations from a broader perspective. When the same verb appears in two (or more) constructions, proponents of strict role-based assumptions claim that the role-related meaning of the constructions differs. Either the verbs are lexically polysemous, or polysemy is imposed by the differing constructional contexts they appear in, depending on the specific grammatical frameworks (lexical or constructional; see Chapter 13). In a multi-dimensional view, by contrast, the two constructions differ in use but not necessarily in their role-related meaning. This view presupposes that the selection of syntactic constructions is determined by several factors, one of them, undoubtedly an important one, being role semantics.

This leads us back to the fundamental question of what counts as a semantic-role notion. As evident from our brief survey of argument realization in the last two sections, argument selection in both basic and non-basic constructions is determined by a wide range of factors that cannot be subsumed under semantic roles without diluting their content and thereby dramatically weakening their explanatory value. This casts a serious doubt on the viability of Dowty's (1991: 562) above-quoted assumption that any semantic distinction that can be shown to be relevant to argument selection can count toward defining a role type.

3 Theoretical approaches

In section 2 we presented main topics and fundamental questions in role semantics. This section offers an overview of the most influential theoretical solutions to these issues. Theoretical approaches to participant roles can be broadly classified into two types. In one type of framework (see section 3.1 below), roles are basic, unanalyzable entities that are listed in the lexical representation of a predicate (role-list approaches, following Levin and Rappaport Hovav (2005)). In the other view, roles are derived from basic notions such as causation, change, motion or sentience by different means (see sections 3.2–3.3 below).

3.1 Role lists

Fillmore's Case Grammar (1968: 24–25) uses a list of roles that are characterized by more basic terms such as volitional instigation (agent), causal involvement (instrument), affectedness (dative) and existential change (factitive). However, these basic notions do not play a role in his theory. Instead, the lexical entries of verbs and the subject selection principle proposed by him resort to roles taken as atoms. The lexical entries of the verbs *open*, *show* and *give* are illustrated in (15). Parentheses indicate optional roles (1968: 27, 35):

(15) *open*:   [__ objective (instrumental) (agentive)]
      show, *give*: [__ objective + dative + agentive]

His list of six deep cases, which also includes objective as an underspecified role and locative, is considered preliminary, but Fillmore is confident that they form a small set (1968: 5). A small inventory of roles is needed to guarantee that participant roles are mapped onto a small number of syntactic functions in a uniform way. The following rule captures the unmarked subject choice (1968: 35):

(16) If there is an agentive, it becomes the subject (see (18a, b));
      otherwise, if there is an instrumental, it becomes the subject (see (18c));
      otherwise, the subject is the objective (see (18d)).

The role hierarchy that motivates Fillmore's subject selection rule is (17):

(17) agent > instrumental > objective

In accordance with the subject selection rule, the verb *open* can be used in the following surface structures:

(18) a *John opened the door with a key.*
      b *John opened the door.*
      c *The key opened the door.*
      d *The door opened.*

Fillmore's main assumptions characterize many subsequent role-list approaches even if they use different roles and different hierarchies.

Neo-Davidsonian approaches following Parsons (1995) also use role lists. The representation in (19) is meant to capture the fact that a sentence like *Brutus stabbed Caesar in the agora* entails the following: *There was a stabbing; The stabbing was by Brutus; The stabbing was of Caesar; The stabbing was in the agora* (see Parsons (1995: 636)):

(19) $(\exists e)[Stabbing(e)$ & $Agent(e, Brutus)$ & $Theme(e, Caesar)$ & $In_{Location}(e, the\ agora)]$

As Parsons admits (1995: 639–640), his treatment does not offer any substantive information on semantic roles and argument realization. Nevertheless, Neo-Davidsonian representations are still used (e.g. Krifka (2004)).

Role lists are a convenient tool for preliminary role analyses and mapping hypotheses. However, they have serious weaknesses (see Levin and Rappaport Hovav (2005); Primus (2009) for a critical survey). First, the number of individual roles exceeds by far the number of core syntactic functions. As soon as one takes other roles than agent[s] and patient[s] into consideration, the number of alternative roles for one syntactic function expands considerably. Role-list approaches are forced to claim that many alternative roles, e.g. agent and instrument, as shown in (18b, c), belong together in some way that is left unexplained. This shortcoming and the necessity to keep the number of roles as small as possible lead to a serious problem when roles have to be split up into similar yet distinct specimens. Let us show this briefly for instruments, which are more varied than traditionally assumed (see Schlesinger (1989); Kamp and Rossdeutscher (1994); Koenig et al. (2008)). Cf. (20):

(20) a *John cleaned the dishes with the dishwasher/soap/rag.*
     b *The dishwasher/#soap/##rag cleaned the dishes.*

To capture the asymmetries in (20b), one has to differentiate between agent-causers which, once the agent has applied them, can be conceived of as acting on their own, and pure instruments, which lack this capacity. The first interpretation is most easily obtainable for machines like dishwashers, more difficult for cleaning "agents" such as soaps and hardly possible for rags. This cline matches the ease of becoming the subject in (20b), as suggested by the increasing number of anomaly marks. Note that Fillmore's example (18c) implies that the key has some property that is the crucial causal factor for the opening of the door.

A second problem for role-list approaches is that the roles are not hierarchically organized in the lexical entry of role-selecting words. As a consequence of this, argument selection has to resort to role hierarchization by additional means (hierarchies or role embedding, see Grimshaw (1990)). A third problem is that (typically but not necessarily) proponents of the list view adhere to bi-uniqueness of mapping between syntactic functions and roles. As shown above for verbs such as *sell* and *give*, many problems for bi-uniqueness can be solved if one admits that verbs entail several elementary predicates (or events) with their own roles. Unfortunately, most role-list approaches only take one event into consideration.

3.2 Structured lexical decomposition

An alternative approach that copes with some of the problems of role-listing is to derive and thereby eliminate participant roles by postulating a decompositional structure for verb meanings (see for a more extensive discussion Levin and Rappaport Hovav (2005: 68f.); Engelberg (2011)). Decompositional structures have been developed in Generative Semantics, where they were posited at syntactic deep structure. Later theories employed them as representations on a lexical-semantic level (e.g. Dowty 1979) or on a conceptual level in Jackendoff's Conceptual Semantics (see also Chapters 12 and 22). Parallel to these developments, syntactic approaches to structured decomposition emerged (see Hale and Keyser (1992); Harley (2012); Levin and Rappaport Hovav (2005: 131f.); Engelberg (2011: 385f.)). We will illustrate this kind of approach by Wunderlich's (1997: 38, 44) treatment of ditransitive verbs such as *give* and *show* in (21):

(21) a $\lambda z \lambda y \lambda x$ [CAUSE (x, BECOME (POSS(y, z)))]
     b $\lambda z \lambda y \lambda x$ [CAUSE (x, (SEE (y, z)))]

Wunderlich splits the lexical representation of a predicate into two levels. The first level is theta-structure; it contains the lambda-bound variables which are associated with theta-roles (lambda operators are a formal means to represent the free arguments of a predicate). The second, more elaborate level (in square brackets in (21) for convenience) contains semantic roles and their characterization in terms of primitive predicates such as CAUSE, BECOME (for change) and POSS (for possession). The relative embedding of the argument variables in the semantic form is mapped onto theta-structure. Leaving details aside, the relative rank of the argument variables determines linking to syntactic functions: the role that is highest (i.e. has lower but no higher co-arguments) is mapped onto the subject, the role that is lowest (i.e. has higher but no lower co-arguments) is linked to the second object position, and the role that has both lower and higher co-arguments is mapped onto the first object position. This mapping device captures the DO-construction discussed in section 2.3 above (see for a more detailed discussion Primus (2009); Engelberg (2011)).

Wunderlich's structure-based linking principles correctly predict the basic patterns for accusative languages. Mappings that do not conform to structure-determined principles are assumed to be lexical, i.e. idiosyncratic cases. Traditional roles such as agent, patient, recipient (for *give*) and addressee (for *show*) and a role hierarchy are not needed in this kind of approach. The fact that both verbs of communication and verbs of transfer of possession favour the DO-construction (see section 2.3 above) is explicable as follows: a recipient and an addressee share the same structural position in the lexical representation of the respective verb type. In contrast, approaches using role lists (e.g. Krifka (2004)) cannot offer a common denominator for these roles. Despite their merits, decompositional approaches that use only one event structure cannot capture the fact that some verbs, including those denoting a transfer of possession, incorporate more than one event in their meaning and a wider array of basic predicates besides CAUSE, BECOME and POSS (see section 2.3 above).

3.3 Proto-roles

Another view that eliminates some of the weaknesses of role-listing is to derive the traditional roles from basic notions such as causation, sentience and change and to cluster these notions into a few superordinate (i.e. generalized) roles. The basic notions are treated as entailments (e.g. (Dowty 1991); Ackerman and Moore (2001)), as role features (e.g. Reinhart (2002); Haiden (2012)) or as a set of elementary, possibly internally structured predicates that are entailed by verb meanings (Primus (1999); Koenig and Davis (2006)). A related proposal that combines structured lexical decompositions with generalized roles is Role and Reference Grammar (see Van Valin and LaPolla (1997)). Here we will discuss Dowty's influential work (1991). Dowty defines two superordinate proto-roles by bundles of entailments generated by the verb's meaning with respect to one of its arguments. The agent proto-role is characterized as follows (1991: 571):

(22) Agent proto-role:
    a   x does a volitional act: *John refrains from smoking.*
    b   x is sentient of or perceives another participant: *John knows/sees/fears Mary.*
    c   x causes an event or change of state in another participant: *His loneliness causes his unhappiness.*
    d   x is moving: *Water filled the boat.*
    [e   x exists independently of the event named by the predicate: *John needs a car.*]

Although most verbs select more than one proto-agent property for their subject argument (e.g. *murder*, *nominate* and *give*), each of these properties can occur in isolation as shown by the subject argument in the examples in (22a)–(22e). The patient proto-role is defined and illustrated by the object argument of the examples in (23):

(23) Patient proto-role (Dowty 1991: 572):
- a   x undergoes a change of state: *John moved the rock.*
- b   x is an incremental theme: *John filled the glass with water* (also stationary relative to other participants).
- c   x is causally affected by another participant: *Smoking causes cancer.*
- d   x is stationary relative to another participant: *The bullet entered the target.*
- [e   x does not exist independently of the event, or not at all: *John needs a car/seeks a unicorn.*]

Incremental theme is introduced for a participant whose degree of affectedness parallels the degree of completeness of the event, e.g. *read a book* and *memorize a poem*. The other basic notions mentioned in (22) and (23) are straightforward. Reference-related properties including the referential reading of the subject and the non-referential reading of the object in *John needs a car* and *John seeks a unicorn* are tentatively included by Dowty, as suggested by the brackets (see also section 2.2 above). The list in (22) and (23) is preliminary for Dowty. Properties have been deleted or added in subsequent research without changing the logic of his approach (see telic entity as a new property in Ackerman and Moore (2001) and possession in Primus (1999)).

The specific roles of role-list approaches can be defined in terms of proto-role entailments: agents by volition and possibly more proto-agent properties; instruments and causers by causation without volition; experiencers by sentience without other properties. But proto-role approaches are also able to subsume a high number of specific roles under a small set of general roles.

Syntactic argument selection is assumed to be sensitive to the higher or lower number of entailments accumulated by an argument (Dowty 1991: 576):

(24) In predicates with grammatical subject and object, the argument for which the predicate entails the greatest number of proto-agent properties will be lexicalized as the subject of the predicate; the argument having the greatest number of proto-patient entailments will be lexicalized as the direct object.

The principle is meant to capture lexical default mappings for arguments with a high number of consistent properties such as those selected by the verbs *break* and *hit*. Underspecified roles that accumulate a low number of consistent proto-role properties or none at all may have a variable realization. If two arguments accumulate the same number of proto-agent properties, either of them may be selected as a subject. This explains the reversibility of symmetric predicates such as *Fred resembles Bill/Bill resembles Fred*, if information packaging, reference-related properties and perspectivization do not interfere (see section 2.2 above). Both role dispersion as in this case as well as role accumulation can be handled straightforwardly. If one includes possession, recipient and similar roles can be treated uniformly since roles that combine proto-agent and proto-patient entailment pose no problem. Recipients are causally affected possessors, addressees are causally affected sentient roles (cf. the derived concept of Proto-Recipient in Primus (1999)). This explains why Proto-Recipients are mapped onto the same syntactic function in many languages: the first object in the DO-construction as a default, the oblique object in the PO-construction as a marked option in English (cf. section 2.3 above) and the dative object in German and other languages with dative case.

Despite its merits, the predictions of Dowty's argument selection principle are limited to transitive predicates with grammatical subject and object in accusative languages and to predicates with a high number of consistent proto-role entailments. The limitation to syntactically transitive predicates is unwarranted (cf. Primus (1999); Ackerman and Moore (2001) for an extension to intransitive predicates). Another shortcoming is that Dowty offers no principled explanation for the semantic coherence of a proto-role and no principled way of capturing structure-based meaning components that lie in the focus of approaches using decompositional structures (see above). To remedy these problems, subsequent approaches incorporate the proto-role defining properties into predicate structures (see Primus (1999); Koenig and Davis (2006)).

4 Future directions

As discussed in the previous sections, semantic-role notions play an important part in grammar, language acquisition and language processing. Arguably, notions related to agentivity and objecthood belong to evolutionarily ancient core knowledge of our species. Starting with a small list of participant roles in the late 1960s, modern linguistics has rapidly gained many new insights pertaining to participant roles. New impulses and future directions of research emerge from developmental studies, neurolinguistics, corpus-linguistics and linguistic typology, each of these fields producing a considerable amount of qualitatively new data.

As a reaction, there is an ongoing trend to depart from simple role-listing. Instead, as shown in sections 3.2 and 3.3 above, new approaches use basic notions such as causation, change, sentience or possession in decompositional structures or in the definition of superordinate roles. Some approaches introduce two levels of role representation (see the distinction between thematic or semantic roles and theta-roles in Carnie (2007: chapter 8.2) and Wunderlich (1997) and the distinction between macro- and microroles in Van Valin and LaPolla (1997)). Using concepts such as causation, change, sentience or possession has shifted the burden of future work toward explaining these intriguingly elusive notions: are they cognitive primitives or derived cluster categories? (See e.g. Haiden (2012) for causation and volition as cluster concepts.) The departure from simple role-listing will also lead to a proliferation of more fine-grained role notions (e.g. Koenig et al. (2008) for several role notions that substitute the traditional instrument role).

Recent research has shown that role notions interact with a wide array of other semantic or pragmatic concepts in determining mapping alternations and basic mapping if one takes other roles than strongly specified agents and patients and a typologically broader data base into consideration. As a consequence of these findings and of the above-mentioned proliferation of more fine-grained role notions, an open question of increasing importance is what counts as a semantic-role notion.

An issue that has received comparatively little attention in previous research is the context-dependence of role assignment and argument realization. So another issue for future research is how verb meaning, inter- or intrasentential contextual information and world knowledge interact in role assignment and argument mapping (e.g. Klein (2012) for the influence of world knowledge on argument realization).

Further reading

Levin, B. and M. Rappaport Hovav 2005. *Argument Realization*. Cambridge: Cambridge University Press. A comprehensive account of participant roles and their syntactic realization in different approaches.

Primus, B. 2009. Case, grammatical relations, and semantic roles. In: A. Malchukov and A. Spencer (eds.) *The Handbook of Case*. Oxford: Oxford University Press, 261–275; Riemer, N. 2010. *Introducing Semantics*. Cambridge: Cambridge University Press and Davis, A.R. 2011. Thematic roles. In: C. Maienborn, K. von Heusinger and P. Portner (eds.) *Semantics. An International Handbook of Natural Language Meaning*. Vol. 1, Berlin: de Gruyter, 399–419 are compact overviews.

References

Ackerman, F. and J. Moore 2001. *Proto-Properties and Grammatical Encoding: A Correspondence Theory of Argument Selection*. Stanford: CSLI Publications.

Aissen, J. 2003. Differential object marking: iconicity vs. economy. *Natural Language and Linguistic Theory* 21: 435–483.

Bickel, B. 2011. Grammatical relations typology. In J.J. Song (ed.) *The Handbook of Linguistic Typology*. Oxford: Oxford University Press, 399–444.

Bornkessel-Schlesewsksy, I. and M. Schlesewsky 2009. *Processing Syntax and Morphology. A Neurocognitive Perspective*. Oxford: Oxford University Press.

Bresnan, J. and T. Nikitina 2003. *On the Gradience of the Dative Alternation*. http://www-lfg.stanford.edu/bresnan/download.html.

Bresnan, J. 2001. *Lexical-Functional Syntax*. Oxford: Blackwell.

Carlson, G.N. 1998. Thematic roles and the individuation of events. In: S. Rothstein (ed.) *Events and Grammar*. Dordrecht: Kluwer, 35–51.

Carnie, A. 2007. *Syntax: A Generative Introduction*. 2nd ed. Malden, MA: Blackwell.

Chan, A., E. Lieven and M. Tomasello 2009. Children's understanding of the agent-patient relations in the transitive construction: cross-linguistic comparisons between Cantonese, German, and English. *Cognitive Linguistics* 20: 267–300.

Chomsky, N. 1981. *Lectures on Government and Binding*. Dordrecht: Foris.

Davis, A.R. 2011. Thematic roles. In: C. Maienborn, K. von Heusinger and P. Portner (eds) *Semantics. An International Handbook of Natural Language Meaning*. Vol. 1. Berlin: de Gruyter, 399–419.

Dixon, R.M.W. 1994. *Ergativity*. Cambridge: Cambridge University Press.

Dowty, D.R. 1979. *Word Meaning and Montague Grammar*. Dordrecht: Kluwer.

Dowty, D.R. 1991. Thematic proto-roles and argument selection. *Language* 67: 547–619.

Engelberg, S. 2011. Frameworks of lexical decomposition of verbs. In: C. Maienborn, K. von Heusinger and P. Portner (eds) *Semantics. An International Handbook of Natural Language Meaning*. Vol. 1. Berlin: de Gruyter, 358–399.

Everaert, M., M. Marelj and A.T. Siloni (eds) 2012. *The Theta System. Argument Structure at the Interface*. Oxford: Oxford University Press.

Fillmore, C.J. 1968. The case for case. In: E. Bach and R. Harms (eds) *Universals in Linguistic Theory*. New York: Holt, Rinehart & Winston, 1–90.

Fillmore, C.J. 1970. Subjects, speakers, and roles. *Synthese* 21: 251–274.

Grimshaw, J.B. 1990. *Argument Structure*. Cambridge, MA: MIT Press.

Haiden, M. 2012. The content of semantic roles: predicate-argument structure in language and cognition. In: M. Everaert, M. Marelj and A.T. Siloni (eds) *The Theta System. Argument Structure at the Interface*. Oxford: Oxford University Press, 52–77.

Hale, K. and S.J. Keyser 1992. The syntactic character of thematic structure. In: I.M. Roca (ed.) *Thematic Structure. Its Role in Grammar*. Berlin: Foris, 107–144.

Harley, H. 2012. Lexical decomposition in modern syntactic theory. In: M. Werning, W. Hinzen and E. Machery (eds) *The Oxford Handbook of Compositionality*. Oxford: University Press, 328–350.

Hirsch-Pasek, K. and R. Golinkoff (eds) 2006. *Action Meets Word: How Children Learn Verbs*. Oxford: Oxford University Press.

Jackendoff, R. 1990. *Semantic Structures*. Cambridge, MA: MIT Press.

Kamp, H. and A. Rossdeutscher 1994. Remarks on lexical structure and DRS construction. *Theoretical Linguistics* 20: 97–164.

Klein, U. 2012. Contextually enriched argument linking. In: R. Finkbeiner, J. Meibauer and P.B. Schumacher (eds) *What is a Context?* Amsterdam, Philadelphia: John Benjamins: 199–228.
Koenig, J.-P. and A. Davis 2006. The KEY to lexical semantic representations. *Journal of Linguistics* 42: 71–108.
Koenig, J.-P., G. Mauner, B. Bienvenue and K. Conklin 2008. What with? The anatomy of a proto-role. *Journal of Semantics* 25: 175–220.
Krifka, M. 2004. Semantic and pragmatic conditions for the dative alternation. *Korean Journal of English Language and Linguistics* 4: 1–32.
Lasnik, H. and J. Uriagereka 2005. *A Course in Minimalist Syntax*. Oxford: Blackwell.
Levin, B. and M. Rappaport Hovav 2005. *Argument Realization*. Cambridge: Cambridge University Press.
Levin, B. 1993. *English Verb Classes and Alternations*. Chicago: University of Chicago Press.
Parsons, T. 1995. Thematic relations and arguments. *Linguistic Inquiry* 26: 635–662.
Primus, B. 1999. *Cases and Thematic Roles–Ergative, Accusative and Active*. Tübingen: Niemeyer.
Primus, B. 2009. Case, grammatical relations, and semantic roles. In: A. Malchukov and A. Spencer (eds) *The Handbook of Case*. Oxford: Oxford University Press, 261–275.
Reinhart, T. 2002. The theta system – an overview. *Theoretical Linguistics* 28: 229–290.
Riemer, N. 2010. *Introducing Semantics*. Cambridge: Cambridge University Press.
Schlesinger, I.M. 1989. Instruments as agents: on the nature of semantic relations. *Journal of Linguistics* 25: 189–210.
Talmy, L. 2000. *Toward a Cognitive Semantics. Vol. I: Concept Structuring Systems*. Cambridge, MA: MIT Press.
Spelke, E.S. and K.D. Kinzler 2007. Core knowledge. *Developmental Science* 10: 89–96.
Tomasello, M. 2000. *The Cultural Origins of Human Cognition*. Cambridge, MA: Harvard University Press.
Van Valin, R.D. and R. LaPolla 1997. *Syntax. Structure, Meaning and Function*. Cambridge: Cambridge University Press.
Wunderlich, D. 1997. Cause and the structure of verbs. *Linguistic Inquiry* 28: 27–68.

Related topics

Chapter 12, Lexical decomposition; Chapter 22, Event semantics; Chapter 24, Compositionality; Chapter 26, Acquisition of meaning.

24
Compositionality

Adele E. Goldberg

1 Introduction

How do people glean meaning from language? A principle of compositionality is generally understood to entail that the meaning of every expression in a language must be a function of the meaning of its immediate constituents and the syntactic rules used to combine them. Frege (1892) is often credited with the principle that natural languages are compositional, although no explicit statement has been found in his writings (and it is not entirely clear that he even embraced the idea) (Pelletier 2001: section 3). Partee (1984: 153) states the principle of compositionality thus: "The meaning of an expression is a function of the meanings of its parts and of the way they are syntactically combined" (cf. also Dowty (2006: 3)). Likewise, Cann (1993: 4) notes, "The meaning of an expression is a monotonic function of the meaning of its parts and the way they are put together."

Montague (1970) stated the condition that there must be a homomorphism—a structure preserving mapping—from syntax to semantics. That is, the meaning of the whole is taken to result from applying the meanings of the immediate constituents via a semantic operation that corresponds directly to the relevant syntactic operation (Dowty 1979; 2006). We can represent the claim as follows in (1), where σ is understood as a function that maps expressions to meaning.

(1) $\sigma(x +_{\text{syntactic-composition}} y) = \sigma(x) +_{\text{semantic-composition}} \sigma(y)$ (Goldberg 1995: 13)

Dowty provides the following example for the phrase, *Fido barks* (2006: 11):

(2)   meaning-of (Syntactic-Combination-of(Fido, barks)) = Semantic-Function-of (meaning-of (Fido), meaning-of (barks))

Although what is intended by "meaning" and "syntactic combination" are not universally agreed upon, it is clear that the principle of compositionality espouses a bottom-up, or building block model of meaning: the meaning of the whole is built from the meanings of the parts. The principle is typically assumed to further imply that the syntactic composition ("$+_{\text{syntactic-composition}}$") must be straightforwardly related to semantic composition ("$+_{\text{semantic-composition}}$") (although see section 2 for more complicated ways in which syntax and semantics can be related). Because the principles of semantic combination are so widely assumed to be transparent, it is easy to overlook the fact that there are any substantive principles at all. Carter (1988) observed, "In a strictly compositional language, all analytic content comes from the lexicon, and no semantic rules . . . are needed to account . . . [for] adding meaning to the sentence which is not directly contributed by some lexeme of the sentence." Even Jackendoff (1992) who has recently explicitly challenged the principle of compositionality (Culicover and Jackendoff 2006) had said "[i]t is widely assumed, and I will take for granted, that the basic units out of which a sentential concept is constructed are the concepts expressed by the words in the sentence, that is, lexical concepts" (Jackendoff 1992: 9). Compositionality implies that words are the key conveyers of meaning, and there is much to be said in favour of this idea. *Hypochondria*, *football*, *exam*, *bodice*, *lemonade*, *anaconda*, *wedding* and *death* certainly evoke particular meanings, however we are to construe the notion of "meaning."

Before discussing various problematic issues that compositionality faces, we first motivate why the principle has been so compelling to so many. The reason seems to be that compositionality is widely assumed to follow from the fact that we can assign meanings to new (i.e. productively created) sentences (Dowty 2006: 3; Groenendijk and Stokhof 2004). That is, it is assumed that people would be unable to glean meaning from new combinations of familiar words unless there exist predictable ways in which meaning is derived from the words and the way those words are combined. Paraphrasing the reasoning of Dowty (2006: 3–4) for example:

Standard argument in favour of compositionality (based on Dowty 2006: 3–4)

a   Speakers produce and listeners parse sentences that they have never spoken or heard before.
b   Speakers and listeners generally agree upon the meanings of sentences.
c   Since there exists an infinite number of sentences, they cannot all be memorized.
d   There must be some procedure for determining meaning.
e   Sentences are generated by some grammar of the language.
f   The procedure for interpreting sentences must be determined, in some way or other, by the syntactic structures generated by the grammar together with the words.

The principle of compositionality is widely acknowledged to be a foundational claim in formal semantics (Groenendijk and Stokhof 2004; Partee et al. 1990), which is compositional by design. Insofar as natural languages lend themselves to description within a formal language, they too should be compositional. And yet, there are many ways in which natural languages depart from formal languages. Several of these divergences present challenges to strict claims of compositionality.

2 Challenges to compositionality: critical issues and topics

2.1 Idioms

If we define idioms to be phrasal patterns in which the meaning of the whole is more than a simple combination of the meanings of the parts, then idioms are, by definition, noncompositional. Expressions such as those in (3), for example, convey something above and beyond what the words mean:

(3) a *Get hitched* (≈ "become married")
   b *Keep a straight face* (≈ "prevent oneself from laughing")
   c *Stay the course* (≈ "continue doing what has been done despite difficulties")

To preserve compositionality, one could deny that such idioms have internal constituent structure, and instead assign the meaning directly to the whole (Hodges 2012), but in fact there is ample evidence that idioms do have constituent structure. For example, the verbs involved can typically be inflected for tense and agreement, and in many cases idioms are *deformable* in that they allow, for example, modification, passivization or conjunction. It has been observed that deformable idioms are typically "compositional" in the sense that the constituents that are semantically modified or appear in non-canonical positions are interpretable (Nunberg et al. 1994; but cf. Fellbaum (2011)). *To pull strings* is an example of a deformable idiom, since it can passivize and *strings* may be modified as in (4):

(4) A lot of strings were pulled to get him the part in the movie.

The quantification of *strings* indicates that *strings* is interpreted to mean roughly "connections," so that the meaning of the idiom in this case can be assigned at least in part to the interpretation of the words that make it up. To preserve compositionality, then, we might adopt the position that each of the words of a deformable idiom is assigned a part of the meaning of the whole. But of course *strings* only means "connections" when it is pluralized and is the theme argument of *pull* (and *pull* means "make use of" but only in the context of *strings)*. The reliance on context for determining the intended senses of words within idioms appears to violate compositionality; e.g., the meaning of *strings* depends on its linguistic context, not simply on the constituent immediately dominating it (*a lot of strings*).

As noted above, the primary argument in favour of compositionality relies on the existence of linguistic creativity: since we can produce and understand sentences we have never heard before, meanings must be arrived at compositionally. Although the principle of compositionality, as generally understood and as stated at the outset, is a statement about *all* of language, the possibility of creativity does not demand that all of language be strictly compositional. If we weaken compositionality to the claim that *some* of language is compositional, idioms need not present a problem. We can allow idioms to be noncompositional, and recognize that they may not be interpreted correctly if heard for the first time. However, there are other, potentially more serious challenges to compositionality.

2.2 Discontinuous semantic units

The principle of compositionality does not specify whether it applies to the surface structure or the "underlying" structure of sentences. Pelletier (1994) points out certain cases of non-lexical ambiguity, e.g. *Every linguist knows two languages* could be viewed as preserving compositionality if two distinct underlying structures are posited. In fact, the existence of semantic units that appear discontinuously in the surface string requires that Compositionality must hold of some level other than surface structure. For example, free word order languages allow meaningful semantic units to correspond to discontinuous syntactic phrases (e.g. "the woman's dog" in (5)); and even fixed word order languages like English occasionally allow discontinuous semantic units (6):

(5) Walpiri (Austin and Bresnan 1996):
   Kupuju-lu   *kaparla-nha*   yanga-lkin   *warirra-ku-nha*
   Child-erg   dog-acc   chase-pres   woman-dat-acc
   "The child chased the woman's dog."

(6) *The man* walked across the tightrope *with a monkey on his shoulders.*

The need for compositionality to apply to some sort of underlying structure raises the issue of just how complex and distinct from surface structure the underlying structure is allowed to be. Without limits, just about any meaning could be attributed to any overt linguistic string (Janssen 1986). Moreover, there is a risk of circularity if we assume that speakers know the meanings of new sentences because of the way those sentences are put together, and yet we also assume that the way sentences are put together depends on the meanings of the sentences.

(7) Circularity in appealing to underlying structure to retain compositionality:
   a   The agreed-upon meaning of a sentence is determined by the meanings of the words and the way those words are put together underlyingly.
   b   The way the words of a sentence are put together underlyingly is determined by the agreed-upon meaning of the sentence.

What would be needed to escape the circularity is a further assumption that speakers are able to "read off" the underlying structure(s) of a sentence on the basis of the sentence's surface structure. But as we will see in section 3, a sentence's surface structure is generally quite underdetermined and/or ambiguous.

2.3 Aspects of morphology

It is unclear whether the principle of compositionality is intended to apply within the word level, but the same "Standard argument in favour of compositionality" outlined in section 1 above would seem to apply equally well to productive morphology. If speakers can create new words they have not witnessed before, and the meanings of those words is agreed upon by other speakers, the meanings of new words would seem to need to be derivable from the component parts and the way those parts are put together. However, Gurevich (2006: section 3.2) provides a compelling case of productive yet noncompositional morphology in Georgian, a language notorious for its complex morphology. Consider Table 24.1 below.

Notice that based on the interpretations in 1 and 2 of Table 24.1, it would seem that *–av* is a second-person subject agreement marker, and that *da-* is a future tense marker. However, we find the same form, *–av*, followed by *–di* used in a sentence with third-person subject agreement in 3. One might hypothesize that *–avdi* is interpreted as third person, but in 4 we see the same suffix interpreted with a second-person subject. Moreover, in 5, we see a second-person interpretation assigned to a combination of a preverb *–da* together with a new suffix *–e*. Gurevich (2006) ultimately makes sense of this complex Georgian morphology by appealing to morphological templates that provide top-down interpretations. There simply is no compositional way to assign consistent meanings to the individual morphemes in Table 24.1. The interpretation of individual morphemes relies on the appearance of other morphemes in a non-monotonic (non-additive) way. Thus we see that morphemes do not necessarily combine in a compositional way, even in a highly agglutinating language like Georgian.

Table 24.1 Georgian morphological paradigm based on Gurevich (2006: section 3.2)

		Pre-verb	Agreement	Version	ROOT	Thematic suffix	Screeve	Agreement
1	you draw				xat'	av		
2	you will draw	da			xat'	av		
3	he was drawing				xat'	av	di	
4	if you would draw	da			xat'	av	di	
5	you drew	da			xat'		e	
6	you should draw	da			xat'		o	
7	you have drawn	da	g	i	xat'	av		s
8	you should have drawn	da	g	e	xat'		a	

The issue in morphology is a general one with the majority of morphologists arguing in favour of a templatic or *realization-based* approach, as opposed to a compositional item and arrangement view (e.g. Ackerman and Nikolaeva (2004); Blevins (2001); Aronoff (1983); Booij (2010)). But if compositionality does not apply at the word level, it is not clear why it must apply at the sentence level. In both cases, new forms can be created and are readily interpreted.

2.4 Argument structure constructions

Recall that the semantics associated with syntactic combination is widely assumed to be straightforward and direct. That is, the syntax should directly determine which argument is where in the sentence (e.g. an agent is subject in an active sentence, but in an adjunct *by*-phrase in a passive), but it is typically assumed that the contentful relational meaning comes from the specifications of the main verb. It is the main verb, for example, that determines that there is an agent; more generally, the main verb is assumed to determine who did what to whom. Almost any traditional grammar book, or beginning logic or linguistics class will likely begin a discussion of sentence types with a classification of verbs according to how many arguments they "take." It is generally taken for granted, for example, that *sneeze* is intransitive, *kick* is transitive, and *give* requires an agent, a theme, and recipient arguments. In this way, basic sentence patterns of a language are believed to be determined by syntactic and semantic information specified by the main verb. For example, the sentence pattern in (8) appears to be due to the specifications of *put*:

(8) Pat put the ball on the table.

That is, *put* is a verb that requires an agent, a theme and a location, and it is *put*'s meaning that determines that the agent "puts" the theme on or in a location (see Chapter 23).
 But if argument structure were *always* projected exclusively from the main verb's semantics, we would need special verb senses for each of the verbs in the expressions in (9) (e.g. Goldberg (1995, 2006), Jackendoff (2002)):

(9) a "he was drinking the heart right out of a fine spring afternoon." (James Crumley, The Last Good Kiss [1978])
   b "The people of this small town [. . .] have been unable to pray Mrs. Smith's two little boys home again." (Mark Turner, personal communication)
   c "his thousands of travelling fans [. . .] had roared him into the Thomas and Mack Center ring." (www.topix.net/wire/world-soccer/manchester-united)
   d "She tried to avoid blinking the tears onto her cheeks." (Anne Tyler, *Dinner at the Homesick Restaurant* [1992])
   e "Demi Moore thinks this will Halle Berry her back to the B List." (personal communication 2007)
   g "I actually had a moth go up my nose once. I [. . .] coughed him out of my mouth." (bikeforums.net/archive/index.php/t-292132)

That is, we would need a sense of *drink* that meant roughly "to spend time by drinking"; a special sense of *pray* "to cause to move by praying," a special sense of *roar* that entails motion and so on. These senses are implausible in that one doesn't find languages that devote unique stems to these meanings. For example, it is unlikely that one would find a word *kamo*, meaning "to cause to move by coughing," because this is not a situation that is likely to occur regularly enough to warrant a lexical meaning (Goldberg 2010).

To avoid such implausible verb senses, it has been proposed that argument structure patterns are associated with abstract meanings independently of the verbs that appear in them. On this view, verbs can occasionally combine with argument structure constructions on the fly to create novel sentences like those in (9). Examples of such *argument structure constructions* are given in Table 24.2.

There exists theoretical and experimental evidence in support of argument structure constructions. Theoretical arguments have typically emphasized the ad hoc and implausible nature of certain verb senses that would otherwise be required, as just mentioned (see Goldberg (1995, 2006, 2013) for further details. Other work has noted that learners use the semantics associated with syntactic patterns to figure out what new verbs mean (Fisher 1996; Gillette et al. 1998; Landau and Gleitman 1985); this "syntactic bootstrapping" process presupposes the idea that the syntactic patterns are associated with meanings independently of the main verb. More recent work based on a sorting paradigm (Bencini and Goldberg 2000), off-line comprehension (Kaschak and Glenberg 2000; Goldwater and Markman 2009; Kako 2006), on-line priming (Johnson and Goldberg 2013), and neural representations (Allen et al. 2012) provides further evidence that argument structure patterns are associated with contentful semantics. It is possible to posit multiple senses for each verb, but to determine which sense is involved, the comprehender must attend to the phrasal array of grammatical relations. That is, even if one did wish to posit a special sense of *drink*, for example, that meant

Table 24.2 English argument structure constructions (Goldberg 1995)

Ditransitive: (Subj) V Obj1 Obj2	X CAUSES Y to RECEIVE Z
Caused-Motion: (Subj) V Obj Oblique$_{path}$	X CAUSES Y to MOVE Z
Resultative: (Subj) V Obj Pred	X CAUSES Y to BECOME Z
Transitive: (Subj) V Obj	X ACTS on Y; X EXPERIENCES Y
Removal: (Subj) V Obj Oblique$_{source}$	X CAUSES Y to MOVE from Z
Way construction: (Subj$_i$) V [poss$_i$ *way*] Oblique$_{path}$	X CREATES PATH and MOVES Z$_{path}$

"to spend time drinking" to account for (9a), it is clear that that sense could only be identified by the comprehender by observing the complement array. Therefore, at least from a comprehension point of view, the pairing of argument structure patterns with meanings must be primary. As Goldberg (1995) points out, it is possible to preserve compositionality for these cases by recognizing that the syntactic means of combination can be paired with richer semantics such as the meanings suggested in Table 24.2. Nothing rules this out, other than an assumption that the rules of composition must be trivial. Montague (1970), Gazdar et al. (1985), and Jacobson (2002) allow for multiple rules of composition that could in principle be richer than is often assumed.

2.5 Intonation

Intonation would seem to provide part of what we generally think of as the "meaning" of an utterance. The meaning of a sentence with default intonation in (10) is not the same as the same sentence with question intonation (11), sarcastic intonation (12), or sentence focus intonation (13) as these are all felicitous in distinct contexts.

(10) Sam CALLED again.
(11) Sam called again?   (question intonation)
(12) Sure, the President called for you. (sarcastic intonation)
(13) SAM called again. (sentence focus, possible answer to "what happened?")

If intonation is incorporated into what is intended by "syntax" in claims about compositionality, these sorts of distinctions could be accounted for. Alternatively, intonation could be included as part of "context," which clearly plays a role in the determination of interpretations (see Chapter 10).

3 Context

Oddly enough, given that he is often credited for the principle of compositionality, Frege is the author of a distinct principle of contextuality. The principle of contextuality requires that the meaning of each part relies on the meaning of the whole: "[o]nly in the context of a sentence does a word stand for anything" (Frege 1884: xxii; cf. also Wittgenstein (1961 [1921])). Insofar as compositionality requires that word meanings exist in isolation, and contextuality asserts that they do not, the two principles appear to contradict one another (Janssen 1986, 1997; Pelletier 2001; Filip 2012). The principle of contextuality argues that context is used in the full interpretation of utterances, and there are many ways in which this clearly holds true.

3.1 Quantifiers

As is widely recognized, the interpretation of quantifiers often relies on context (Westerstahl 1985). For example, the quantifiers in the following examples do not refer to *all* entities, but instead refer to some contextually determined set of entities:

(14) a   They fixed all the roads. (= all the roads that need to be fixed)
      b   When it snows in Aspen, everyone is happy. (= everyone in Aspen)
      c   No one is here. (= no one other than the speaker; or no one who the speaker wished to see)

That is, the sentence in (14b) implies that the city fixed all the roads that needed fixing, not all the roads in the universe or even all the roads within city limits. More specifically, *all the roads* is not interpreted compositionally, but requires appeal specifically to the verb, *fixed*, which is a part of the sentence, but not part of the constituent *all the roads*. The sentence in (14b) is likely to mean that everyone *in Aspen* is happy, although, depending on the context, it could mean everyone who is looking forward to the X-games (which are held in Aspen) is happy, or that everyone in a particular family who is planning a ski trip is happy. While the meaning is generally agreed upon in context, the quantifiers themselves do not determine their universe of discourse.

To allow for facts such as these, the compositional meaning of a sentence must be viewed as partially underspecified. For example, quantifiers may contain an open variable for the domain of discourse. This variable must be fixed before a sentence can be fully interpreted, but it may depend on context. This then requires a distinction between "meaning" and "interpretation." Similarly, the existence of ellipsis and deixis also require that the meaning that is determined compositionally must be underspecified allowing certain aspects of interpretation to be filled in by context (see Chapter 11).

3.2 Ellipsis, deixis

Fodor (2001) argues that language is not compositional on the basis of definite descriptions that are typically interpreted in context-sensitive ways (cf. also Janssen (1983)). For example, *He saw the dog* does not entail that he saw the one and only one dog existing in the universe, but rather that he saw the particular dog that is assumed to be identifiable to the listener in a given context. Likewise, (15) can refer to Queen Beatrix or Queen Wilhelmina, depending on when the sentence was uttered:

(15) The Queen of Holland is married to Prince Claus. (Janssen 1983: 3)

One could conceivably stipulate that the time of utterance is somehow syntactically represented in each utterance, but we would have to also include the place being discussed or the place of speaking (e.g. *of Holland* goes unmentioned in 16), and potentially all of the speaker's and listener's common ground (e.g. if an epithet is used as in 17).

(16) The Queen is married to Prince Claus.
(17) You-know-who is in jail.

This would seem to lead to a *reductio ad absurdum*, as language is rife with ellipsis and deictic references.

> Either the content of the thought is different from the content of the sentence that expresses it, or the sentence isn't compositional. I take it that the first disjunct is preposterous; so I take it that the second disjunct must be true.
>
> (Fodor 2001: 12)

Those who *do* grant a distinction between "meaning" and "interpretation" (the latter equivalent to Fodor's "thought"), not finding the distinction "preposterous," may instead allow an underspecified level of compositional meaning (Partee 1995); interpretation or "thought" then would require the combination of meaning and context, including the background knowledge of speaker and listener. We return to examine this proposal more fully in section 4.

3.3 Polysemy

Words that are used frequently tend to have more than one related sense because old words often get extended for use in new contexts (see Chapter 15). Initially, these extended senses are created on the fly, but they often become conventionalized senses over time. Polysemous senses often center around a rich, prototypical (or stereotypical) sense, with extensions being based on some attribute of the prototypical sense (Lakoff 1987; see Chapter 7). For example, prototypically, *home* evokes a house where a family unit lives and sleeps, where children grow into adulthood, where one feels comfortable and a sense of belonging. Yet it can be used for many of these aspects in isolation from the others (Fillmore 1992):

(18) HOME

a 138 Main Street is Aliza's and Zach's home.	a House, where one grows up, lives with one's family, feels comfortable and belongs
b She owns 14 homes.	b House
c She went home to her dorm room.	c Place where one lives and sleeps
d She travelled home to see her family.	d Place where one grows up
e She's at home in the mountains.	e Place where one feels a sense of belonging

Which sense of a word is intended typically depends on the linguistic and non-linguistic context (Piantadosi et al. 2012). That is, the meanings of words often cannot be determined in isolation and then combined as one would combine building blocks to arrive at the meaning of a whole. Information beyond the immediate constituent is used to arrive at the meanings of words, and there are not always any linguistic cues about the required interpretation. In addition, we often use a word or phrase to appeal to a conceptually related but distinct meaning via a process of *metonymy* (Nunberg 1994). For example,

(19) The tummy tuck in 3A is asking for some chocolate.
(20) Nunberg's on the top shelf.
(21) We have guests, so please set another couple of plates.

The tummy tuck in (19) refers to the person who received a tummy tuck, *Nunberg* refers to a book by Nunberg in (20), and the perhaps more familiar case of *plates* in (21) refers to additional place settings. The meanings of the sentences do not make sense without the meanings supplied by these metonymies and yet it is not obvious that the meanings are "in" the words of the sentence. Instead, the metonymic interpretation is supplied by context via semantic and pragmatic inferences (Culicover and Jackendoff 2006).

Combining one polysemous word with n senses, and another polysemous word with m senses would require $n \times m$ possible meanings. If there are several polysemous words in a sentence, the computation becomes unwieldy extremely quickly. Even if our minds were able to perform this computation, it is clear that we have no conscious access to this large set of meanings. For us to arrive at the agreed-upon meaning (that *is* consciously accessible), we narrow down the result of a possibly huge computation to at most one or two meanings. To do this we have to rely on contextual cues.

4 Attempting to reconcile context and compositionality

From the discussion of quantifiers, ellipsis, deixis, and polysemy, it is clear that the way words combine into constituents does not deterministically convey the entirety of the *interpretation* or thought that is conveyed by utterances. Inferences that are drawn in particular contexts contribute importantly to the relevant range of a given quantifier, the intended referents of definite noun phrases, pronouns and all deictic terms, the intended interpretation of unexpressed or polysemous arguments, and all conversational inferences. As Gilles Fauconnier has described it, if the interpretation of a sentence is an iceberg, the sentence itself provides only the above-the-water-line peaks of the iceberg. People supply the rest of the meaning on the basis of shared context and world knowledge.

This recognition has led different researchers to differing conclusions about the fate of compositionality. Groenendijk and Stokhof argue that thoughts or intended interpretations of sentences are not what is expressed by sentences (2004: 11). They thus draw a distinction between "thoughts," and the "meanings" of sentences, the latter being vague or underspecified. Sentential "meaning" is assumed to be context-free and compositionally determined. On the other hand, interpretation or thought is not conveyed directly by the "meaning" of an utterance and is not compositional. If "meaning" is not equivalent to interpretation or thought, then meaning would seem to be a formal construct created by theorists. In this way, compositionality is not a claim that is open to empirical verification or falsification.

Returning to the deductive argument put forward in the "Standard argument in favour of compositionality" outlined in section 1, however, it seems necessary that whatever "meaning" is, it must be accessible to ordinary speakers, since that is an important assumption in the argument (see "Standard argument" (b): "Speakers and listeners generally agree upon the meanings of sentences"). That is, what speakers recognize and agree on (more or less, most of the time) is the *intended interpretation of utterances in contexts*. Thus it would seem that "Standard argument" (b) actually presupposes access to contextual cues to meaning, since it is a combination of an utterance *and a context* that results in the agreed-upon interpretation. This motivates Fodor's (2001) conclusion that meaning and thought are one and the same and are simply not compositional, since "language is strikingly elliptical and inexplicit about the thoughts that it expresses and as a simple matter of fact, in the general case, sentences are remarkably inexplicit with respect to how the thoughts they express are put together."

To see just how powerful context can be in the determination of intended meaning, consider the fact that a simple pointing gesture is typically readily understood in a given context.

4.1 Pointing is understood, but the meaning does not reside in the point

The reasoning in favour of compositionality in the "Standard argument" seems to assume that the meaning of an expression must reside in the expression itself for the expression's meaning to be shared across people. And yet, humans are remarkably good at gleaning others' intended meanings even when language is not used. For example, we generally share an understanding of what is meant when someone points at something. If two boys are walking down the street and point to a hoagie restaurant, it could mean "let's get something to eat," "that place is still there!," or "let's cross the street because the school bully hangs out there." Oftentimes, no words need to accompany a pointing gesture as the intended interpretation is often recognized as obvious in context; and yet clearly, the meaning is not in the point itself (Tomasello 2009). Instead, the shared common ground provided by the context and background knowledge helps to determine what is intended. Language can be viewed as not entirely unlike pointing in that the language itself typically only offers incomplete clues to the overall interpretation of sentence.

5 Current contributions and research

Piantadosi et al. (2012) point out that the underspecification inherent in language is advantageous. They note that utterances routinely underspecify meaning, relying on context for full interpretation due to the need for efficiency. It would be needlessly long-winded to spell out every aspect of intended meaning, or the intended sense of every potentially ambiguous word. Instead, context supplements the cues provided by utterances. This allows interlocutors to arrive at a shared interpretation while minimizing the redundancy that would occur if language were to spell out all of the information that is already accessible in context.

Although the principle of compositionality is generally interpreted as entailing that the meaning of each constituent be determined only with reference to its immediate daughters, the "Standard argument" does not entail that this is the only way for meaning to be determined. Instead, language could involve a network of formal patterns, which may contain open slots. Some of these slots may be defined recursively, and this in itself would allow for infinite creative potential. The argument structure constructions in Table 24.2 are examples of formal patterns with open slots. Another example is the English *The Xer, the Yer* construction exemplified in (22) (see Fillmore et al. (1988)):

(22) The larger the audience, the easier the show. (COCA corpus, Davies 2008)

The construction requires that the comprehender construct a relationship between two variables, one independent (determined by the first comparative phrase), and the other dependent (determined by the second comparative phrase). The rule of composition is thus nontrivial, in that syntax itself is quite unusual—it is not even clear what type of phrase *the larger the audience* is—and the linked variable interpretation does not come from any particular word, at least in any obvious way. Still, the construction licenses an open-ended set of sentences.

The original argument suggested in favour of compositionality does not require that the rules of combination are trivial, that world knowledge and context are irrelevant, or that meaning is determined in a strictly bottom-up way on the basis of the words and their immediate constituents. Shared interpretation can be arrived at by recognizing the existence of constructions that can contribute nontrivial aspects of semantics, and by recognizing that people come to the task of interpretation with a vast amount of shared world knowledge and context. This allows for interpretation to involve a top-down component, moving us away from the building block metaphor of meaning.

Kirby (2000) has investigated *why* languages tend to involve component pieces that can be reconstituted in new ways (or why languages involve templates with open slots that can be combined). He creates simulations of computer "agents" that aim to maximize expressive power while minimizing the number of rules. The simulations begin by generating random forms that correspond to intended meanings, but over time, as multiple agents interact and aim to express new meanings, a type of compositionality emerges. Namely, the simulations eventually settle into a system that involves component pieces that can be reassembled in new ways. Intuitively, it is clear that learning a completely noncompositional language—wherein each distinct meaning would correspond to a wholly unique form—would not only be extremely cumbersome but would fail to allow agents any way to express or comprehend any new meanings.

The issues involved in any approach to meaning are complex and quite daunting. A measure of the difficulty involved is evident in the fact that the field of machine understanding has made little progress over the past half century. Both Piantadosi et al. (2012) and Kirby (2000) provide computational models that aim to motivate how and why new utterances are interpretable, and this promises to be a rich arena for additional research.

6 Conclusion

It is often debated whether the principle of compositionality is an empirical claim (Fodor 2001; Pelletier 1994) or a methodological assumption (Barker and Jacobson 2007; Dowty 2006; Groenendijk and Stokhof 2004; Janssen 1983; Partee 1995). The present overview tends toward the position that there exist empirical questions that need to be addressed for the principle of compositionality to be upheld.

An understanding of how humans interpret language has been a goal of philosophy, literature, and linguistics for hundreds of years. The present chapter does not pretend to solve the problem in any way, but only to present evidence that the issues involved are complex. The apparently noncompositional meaning evident in idioms, discontinuous semantic units, and complex words must be addressed, and the contribution of argument structure constructions, intonation, and non-linguistic context to our shared interpretation of sentences must be taken into account.

Acknowledgments

I'd like to thank Christiane Fellbaum, Hana Filip, Sam Glucksberg, Clarice Robenalt, Nick Riemer, and Edwin Williams for helpful discussion and references on this topic. Any errors are solely my own responsibility.

Further reading

Dowty, David 2006. *Compositionality as an Empirical Problem*, 1–62. http://www.ling.ohio-state.edu/~dowty/context-free-semantics.pdf. Outlines the basic argument in favour of the idea that language must be compositional.

Fodor, Jerry A. 2001. Language, thought and compositionality. *Mind and Language*, 161: 1–15. Argues that language is not compositional.

Partee, B. 1995. Quantificational structures and compositionality. In E. Bach, E. Jelinek, A. Kratzer, and B.H. Partee (eds) *Quantification in Natural Languages*. Dordrecht: Kluwer Academic Publishers, 541–601. Offers a nuanced intermediate perspective.

Janssen, Theo 1997. Compositionality. In Johan F.A.K. van Benthem and Alice ter Meulen (eds) *Handbook of Logic and Linguistics*. Elsevier/MIT Press, 495–541. Discusses Frege's controversial role in the debate about compositionally.

Kirby, S. 2000. Syntax without natural selection: how compositionality emerges from vocabulary in a population of learners. In C. Knight (ed.) *The Evolutionary Emergence of Language: Social Function and the Origins of Linguistic Form*. Cambridge University Press, 1–19. Provides a demonstration that a certain degree of compositionally serves the function of reducing ambiguity.

References

Ackerman, F. and Irina Nikolaeva 2004. *Comparative Grammar and Grammatical Theory: A Construction-Based Study of Morphosyntax*. Stanford: Center for the Study of Language and Information.

Allen, K., F. Pereira, M. Botvinick and A.E. Goldberg 2012. Distinguishing grammatical constructions with fMRI pattern analysis. *Brain and Language* 123: 174–82.

Aronoff, M. 1983. Potential words, actual words, productivity and frequency. In Shirō Hattori and Kazuko Inoue (eds) *Proceedings of the 13th International Congress of Linguists*. Tokyo: The Committee, 163–71.

Austin, Peter, and Joan Bresnan 1996. Non-configurationality in Australian Aboriginal languages. *Natural Language & Linguistic Theory* 14.2: 215–68.

Barker, C. and P.I. Jacobson (eds) 2007. *Direct Compositionality*. Oxford University Press.

Bencini, Giulia M.L. and Adele E. Goldberg 2000. The contribution of argument structure constructions to sentence meaning. *Journal of Memory and Language* 43: 640–51.

Blevins, J.P. 2001. Realisation-based lexicalism. *Journal of Linguistics* 37: 355–65.

Booij, G. 2010. *Construction Morphology*. Oxford: Oxford University Press.

Cann, Ronnie. 1993. *Formal Semantics: An Introduction*. Cambridge: Cambridge University Press.

Carter, R. 1988. Compositionality and polysemy. In Beth Levin and Carol Tenny (eds) *On Linking: Papers by Richard Carter*. Cambridge, MA: Lexicon Project, Center for Cognitive Science, MIT, 167–204.

Culicover, P.W. and R. Jackendoff 2006. The simpler syntax hypothesis. *Trends in Cognitive Sciences*, 10: 413–18.

Davies, Mark 2008. *The Corpus of Contemporary American English: 450 million words, 1990–present*. http://corpus.byu.edu/coca.

Dowty, David 1979. *Word Meaning and Montague Grammar: The Semantics of Verbs and Times in Generative Semantics and in Montague's PTQ*. Dordrecht: Springer.

Dowty, David 2006. *Compositionality as an Empirical Problem*, 1–62. http://www.ling.ohio-state.edu/~dowty/context-free-semantics.pdf.

Fellbaum, C. 2011. Idioms and collocations. In C. Maienborn, K. von Heusinger, and P. Portner (eds) *Handbook of Semantics*. Berlin: de Gruyter, 441–56.

Filip, Hana 2012. Lecture 1: Compositionality and Model Theory. LOT winter school handout. Tilburg, the Netherlands.

Fillmore, Charles J. 1992. 'Corpus Linguistics' or 'Computer-Aided Armchair linguistics'. In Jan Svartvik (ed.) *Directions in Corpus Linguistics: Proceedings of Nobel Symposium* 82. Berlin: Mouton de Gruyter, 35–62.

Fillmore, Charles J., Paul Kay, and Mary Catherine O'Connor. Regularity and idiomaticity in grammatical constructions: the case of let alone. *Language*: 501–38.

Fisher, Cynthia 1996. Structural limits on verb mapping: the role of analogy in children's interpretations of sentences. *Cognitive Psychology* 31: 41–81.

Fodor, Jerry A. 2001. Language, thought and compositionality. *Mind and Language*, 161: 1–15.

Frege, Gottlob 1980. *The Foundations of Arithmetic*: *A Logico-mathematical Enquiry into the Concept of Number*. JL Austin (trans). Evanston, IL: Northwestern University Press.

Frege, Gottlob 1892. Über Sinn und Bedeutung. *Zeitschrift für Philosophie und philosophische Kritik* 100: 25–50. Translated as On sense and reference, in P.T. Geach and M.Black (eds) *Translations form the Philosophical Writings of Gottlob Frege*. Oxford: Blackwell 1952, 56–78.

Gazdar, Gerald, Ewan Klein, Geoffrey K. Pullum, and Ivan A. Sag. 1985. *Generalized Phrase Structure Grammar*. Oxford: Basil Blackwell and Cambridge, MA: Harvard University Press.

Gillette, Jane, Henry Gleitman, Lila R. Gleitman, and Anna Lederer 1998. *Human Simulations of Vocabulary Learning*. Philadelphia: University of Pennsylvania Press.

Goldberg, Adele E. 1995. *Constructions: A Construction Grammar Approach to Argument Structure*. Chicago: Chicago University Press.

Goldberg, Adele E. 2002. Surface generalizations. An alternative to alternations. *Cognitive Linguistics* 13: 327–56

Goldberg, Adele E. 2006. *Constructions at Work: The Nature of Generalization in Language*. Oxford: Oxford University Press.

Goldberg, Adele E. 2010. Verbs, constructions, and semantic frames. In Malka Rappaport Hovav, Edit Doron and Ivy Sichel (eds) *Syntax, Lexical Semantics and Event Structure*. Oxford: Oxford University Press, 39–58.

Goldberg, Adele E. 2013. Argument structure constructions vs. lexical rules or derivational verb templates. *Mind and Language* 28: 435–50

Goldwater, Micah B. and Arthur B. Markman 2009. Constructional sources of implicit agents in sentence comprehension. *Cognitive Linguistics* 20: 675–702.

Groenendijk, J. and Stokhof, M. 2004. Why compositionality? In G. Carlson and F. Pelletier (eds) *The Partee Effect*. Stanford: CSLI Publications, 1–20.

Gurevich, Olga J. 2006. *Constructional Morphology: The Georgian Version*. PhD thesis, University of California, Berkeley.

Hodges, W. 2012. Formal features of compositionality. *Journal of Logic, Language and Information* 10: 7–28.

Jackendoff, Ray 1992. *Semantic Structures*. Cambridge, MA: MIT Press.

Jackendoff, Ray 2002. *Foundations of Language: Brain, Meaning, Grammar, Evolution*. Oxford: Oxford University Press.

Jacobson, Pauline 2002. The disorganization of the grammar. *Linguistics and Philosophy* 25: 601–25.

Janssen, Theo 1983. *Foundations and Applications of Montague Grammar*. PhD thesis, Department of Mathematics, University of Amsterdam.

Janssen, Theo 1986. *Foundations and Applications of Montague Grammar, Part I: Philosophy, Framework, Computer Science*. CWI tract 19, Center of Mathematics and Computer Science, Amsterdam.

Janssen, Theo 1997. Compositionality. In Johan F.A.K. van Benthem and Alice ter Meulen (eds) *Handbook of Logic and Linguistics*. Elsevier/MIT Press, 495–541.

Johnson, Matt A. and Adele E. Goldberg 2013. Evidence for automatic accessing of constructional meaning: Jabberwocky sentences prime associated verbs. *Language and Cognitive Processes* 28: 1439–52.

Kako, Edward 2006. The semantics of syntactic frames. *Language and Cognitive Processes* 21: 562–75.

Kaschak, Michael and Arthur Glenberg 2000. Constructing meaning: the role of affordances and grammatical constructions in sentence comprehension. *Journal of Memory and Language* 43: 508–29.

Kirby, S. 2000. Syntax without natural selection: how compositionality emerges from vocabulary in a population of learners. In C. Knight (ed.) *The Evolutionary Emergence of Language: Social Function and the Origins of Linguistic Form*. Cambridge: Cambridge University Press, 1–19.

Lakoff, George 1987. *Women, Fire, and Dangerous Things: What Categories Reveal about the Mind*. Chicago: University of Chicago Press.

Landau, Barbara and Lila R. Gleitman 1985. *Language and Experience: Evidence from a Blind Child*. Cambridge, MA: Harvard University Press.

Montague, Richard 1970. English as a formal language. In Bruno Visentini et al. (eds) *Linguaggi nella Società e nella Tecnica*. Milan: Edizioni di Comunità, 189–224.

Murphy, Gregory L. and Edward J. Wisniewski 1989. Categorizing objects in isolation and in scenes: what a superordinate is good for. *Journal of Experimental Psychology: Learning, Memory, and Cognition* 15: 572.

Nunberg, Geoffrey 1995. Transfers of meaning. *Journal of Semantics* 12: 109–32.

Nunberg, Geoffrey, Ivan A. Sag, and Thomas Wasow 1994. Idioms. *Language* 70: 491–538.

Partee, Barbara 1984. Compositionality. In Frank Landman and Frank Veltman (eds) *Varieties of Formal Semantics*. Dordrecht: Foris, 281–312.

Partee, Barbara 1995. Lexical semantics and compositionality. In D. Osherson (ed.) *An Invitation to Cognitive Science*. Cambridge, MA: MIT Press, 311–60.

Partee, Barbara, ter Meulen, Alice, and Robert E. Wall 1990. *Mathematical Methods in Linguistics.* Dordrecht: Kluwer Academic Publishers.
Pelletier, F.J. 1994. The principle of semantic compositionality. *Topoi* 13: 11–24.
Pelletier, F.J. 2001. Did Frege believe Frege's Principle? *Journal of Logic, Language and Information* 10: 87–114.
Piantadosi, S.T., H. Tily, and E. Gibson 2012. The communicative function of ambiguity in language. *Cognition* 122: 280–91.
Tomasello, M. 2009. *Why We Cooperate.* Cambridge, MA: MIT Press.
Westerstahl, Dag 1985. Determiners and context sets. *Generalized Quantifiers In Natural Language* 1: 45–71.
Wittgenstein, Ludwig. 1961 [1921]. *Tractatus Logico-Philosophicus.* (D.F. Pears and B.F. McGuinness, trans.). London: Routledge and Kegan Paul.

Related topics

Chapter 5, Cognitive semantics; Chapter 15, Semantic shift; Chapter 23, Participant roles.

25
The semantics of lexical typology

Maria Koptjevskaja-Tamm, Ekaterina Rakhilina and Martine Vanhove

1 Introduction

Generally speaking, lexical typology is the systematic study of cross-linguistic variation in words and vocabularies (cf. Koptjevskaja-Tamm (2008)). Opinions differ, however, on what exactly can be meant by this relatively recent term. Many linguists will probably agree with Lehrer's (1992: 249) widely quoted definition that lexical typology is concerned with the "characteristic ways in which language [...] packages semantic material into words" (cf. Koch (2001); Brown (2001)). It is lexical typology in this understanding that will be our main interest here. Until recently lexical typology was both limited and marginal compared to the cross-linguistic research on grammar and on phonetics/phonology, apart from a few classical studies (e.g. Andersen (1978); Berlin and Kay (1969); Greenberg (1980); Talmy (1985); Viberg (1984)). The past two decades have, however, seen an increased interest in lexical-typological issues, both in the number and diversity of relevant studies and publications stemming from them, as well as in several publications suggesting various definitions of lexical typology, situating it within a broader research field and providing overviews over the field (e.g. Behrens and Sasse (1997); Brown (2001); Evans (2011); Goddard (2001); Koch (2001); Koptjevskaja-Tamm (2008); Lehmann (1990)).

The core concern of lexical typology, i.e. how languages express meanings by words, can be approached from slightly different perspectives. We can start from the *meanings*, or *concepts*, and ask how these are expressed in different languages – among other things, how semantic domains are distributed among the lexical items across languages. A simple example of this is given in Table 25.1, which shows how the inventories of body-part terms in six languages differ in the extent to which they distinguish between hand vs. arm, foot vs. leg, and finger vs. toe by conventionalized, lexicalized expressions.

Lexical-typological research in this understanding typically asks questions such as how languages categorize particular domains (human body, kinship relations, colour, motion, perception, etc.) by means of lexical items, what parameters underlie categorization, whether languages are completely free to "carve up" the domains at an infinite and arbitrary number of places or whether there are limits on this, and whether any categories are universal (e.g. "relative", "body", or "red"). For many people lexical typology par excellence would primarily

Table 25.1 Hand vs. arm, foot vs. leg, finger vs. toe in English, Italian, Romanian, Estonian, Japanese and Khalkha Mongolian

English	Turkish	Romanian	Estonian	Japanese	Khalkha Mongolian
hand	el	mină	käsi	te	gar
arm	kol	brat,	käsi (vars)	ude	
foot	ayak	picior	jalg	ashi	höl
leg	bacak				
finger	parmak	deget	sõrm	yubi	huruu
toe			varvas		

be associated with these kinds of issues, but lexical typology is broader than that, as will be shown immediately below.

Lexico-typological research can also start from the *expressions (lexemes)* and ask what different meanings can be expressed by them or by lexemes that are related to them synchronically and/or diachronically. The main focus here is on cross-linguistically recurrent patterns in the relations among the words and lexical items in the lexicon, e.g. semantic motivation (polysemy, semantic associations/semantic shifts; see Chapter 15) and morphological motivation (derivational patterns, including compounding).

For some researchers, the main interest of lexical typology is different again. For instance, Lehmann (1990: 163) defines lexical typology as research that focuses on "typologically relevant features in the grammatical structure of the lexicon", rather than on "the semantics of individual lexical items, their configurations in lexical field or individual processes of word formation" (Lehmann 1990: 165). This view of lexical typology is also promoted in Behrens and Sasse (1997), in Nichols et al. (2004) and in the rich research on motion verbs stemming from Talmy's seminal chapter (1985).

In this chapter we will mainly focus on lexical typology understood as cross-linguistic research on domain categorization. We start by introducing some of the critical issues inherent in such research (section 2), and then turn to the presentation and discussion of four different approaches to lexical typology in sections 3–6. Section 7 is devoted to semantic maps as representations of meanings and generalizations in lexical typology, while section 8 suggests a few future directions for lexical typology.

2 Critical issues

Lexical typology has to find its own way for balancing the methodological and theoretical ambitions of theoretical semantics, lexicography and general typology.

Typological research takes linguistic diversity as its point of departure, assumes that the variation across languages is restricted and aims at discovering systematicity behind it. Its central theoretical issues include the following: What are the parameters/dimensions along which a specific phenomenon varies across languages? In what patterns do these parameters (co-)occur? What generalizations can be made about attested vs. possible patterns? What is universal vs. language-particular in a given phenomenon? While cross-linguistic generalizations constitute a major result, many typological studies want to go further and find explanations for them. Possible explanations for the typological patterns and the generalizations over them may be environmental (rooted in the properties of the real world), biological (shaped by human perceptual and cognitive predispositions or simply innate), socio-historical or cultural. But also the distribution of the patterns across the languages, i.e. why language X has a certain pattern, calls for explanation. These are big and exciting questions, which all presuppose meticulous work, methodological awareness and, ideally, firm theoretical foundations, to which we now turn.

Typological research in general is dependent on comparable data coming from (many) different languages. Cross-linguistic identification of studied phenomena presupposes a procedure which ensures we compare like with like. For data collection and cross-linguistic identification of phenomena, grammatical typology has historically been largely dependent on secondary data sources (such as reference grammars), with first-hand data sources gradually gaining more and more importance. However, for lexical typology first-hand sources of data are crucial, since the lexicon for most languages of the world is relatively poorly described. Although some lexico-typological studies use dictionaries as their main source (e.g. Andersen (1978); Brown (2005a, 2005b)), most of the cross-linguistic research on the lexicon is based on elicited data – either by extra-linguistic stimuli (cf. sections 5, 7) or by means of questionnaires, ranging from simple translational questionnaires to much more sophisticated "frame-based" questionnaires, which elicit verbal descriptions of various situations (cf. section 6). These are frequently complemented by corpus studies, with comparison of parallel texts (translations of one and the same text) as a relatively new but promising method for data collection (cf. section 7). One particularly prominent feature of the lexicon as compared to grammar is its vastness and diversity, which creates additional challenges for both data collection and analysis (compare such culturally specific and subjective notions as emotions with the much more "visible" events of cutting and breaking). A lexico-typological study is typically restricted to one cognitive domain, often (although not necessarily) with additional constraints on the part of speech of the studied words (e.g. verbs of perception); it typically requires a serious involvement of language experts, capable of discerning and discussing intricate meaning nuances, and usually operates with a much more limited language sample (normally between 10 and 50 languages) than what is the norm in grammatical and phonetic typology. There are notable exceptions here, such as Brown (2005a, 2005b) on body-part terminologies, Kay and Maffi (2005) on colour terms, Nerlove and Romney (1967) on sibling terminologies, and Wälchli and Cysouw (2012) on motion verbs, which all include between 100 and 500 languages.

A further issue is how the data may be analyzed and how the results of the analysis may be represented. The problem of a consistent metalanguage for describing meaning, and in particular lexical meaning, cannot be overestimated. This is, in turn, related to the general enormous gap between theoretical semantics and theoretical lexicology, on the one hand, and actual lexicographic practices on the other. Two of the major stumbling blocks are the problem of what can be meant by meaning – *denotation/extension* vs. *sense/descriptive meaning/intension* (see Chapters 1 and 2) – and the problem of *polysemy/semantic generality/vagueness* (see Chapter 13). Although for many serious semanticists, lexicographers and lexicologists semantic analysis stands for understanding descriptive meanings, or senses, the enterprise gets easily insurmountable, especially when several languages are involved. As a consequence, much of cross-linguistic comparison is based on meanings defined as the denotational ranges of the expressions involved (cf. sections 5, 7). Similarly, there are many different opinions on what counts as polysemy (see Riemer (2005) for a recent overview of the problem), but distinguishing between several meanings of one and the same lexeme or one more general meaning typically requires sophisticated analyses and tests that are too difficult to carry out in cross-linguistic studies. As a rule of thumb, polysemy is acknowledged whenever a word may be used to denote entities, properties or situations that are assumed to belong to very different cognitive domains (e.g. "foot of a person" vs. "foot of a mountain", or "to see a picture" vs. "to see what somebody means"). Things become much more complicated when the two uses appear to belong to the same domain. Are the Khalkha Mongolian *gar* and the Russian *ruka* simply vague in not distinguishing between "hand" and "arm", or are they polysemous between the two meanings? How can we describe the fact that Russians can "hear" smells, i.e. that the verb *slyšat'* "hear" can combine with "smell" for talking about smell perception (*slyšat' zapax* "feel (lit. hear) a smell")? Different researchers choose different strategies for dealing with such cases, stretching between explicit agnosticism (as François's (2008) notion of "colexification" or Wälchli and Cysouw's (2012) view on situational contextually embedded meanings as analytic primitives, cf. section 7) to pragmatic and partly ad hoc solutions, to insistence on a strict demarcation between semantic generality and polysemy (as typical for Natural Semantic Metalanguage, cf. section 4).

A further question is whether meanings should be analyzed and represented in terms of classical Aristotelian categories with necessary and sufficient meaning components or in terms of prototype categories (see Chapter 7). Related to this is the issue of compositionality, i.e. whether meanings can be decomposed and if so, to what extent, what the basic building blocks are (e.g. whether there are universal or language-specific concepts, or a mixture of both, cf. sections 3 and 4), and how the "composition" is carried out and represented (see Chapter 12). Logical formulas, explications (section 4), semantic maps and diagrams (section 7), and pictures and tables (section 3) have all been used for representing meaning, with relatively little communication among the different schools of semantics and lexicology and lexicographic practices.

3 Componential analysis

A once-influential trend in semantics, componential analysis was prevalent in the 1950s–70s as a part of the structuralist paradigm. It was essentially an attempt to apply to the lexicon the concept of oppositions and binary features with roots in phonological and morphological analysis (see Chapters 12 and 15).

The main principle is to define each term in a domain by a set of distinctive semantic features, e.g. *horse* [+adult, ±female] vs. *colt* [-adult, -female] vs. *mare* [+adult, +female] etc., and ultimately to use such oppositions to define the whole meaning of a term, e.g. *horse* [+animate, +quadruped, +mammal, +equine, +adult, ±female . . .].

The chief contribution of componential analysis to lexical typology concerns kinship terminologies, which have for a long time been a favourite semantic domain among anthropologists and anthropologically oriented linguists. Detailed and systematic descriptions of the domain are normally structured by a few relevant parameters, are available for many hundreds of languages, and there is a long tradition of classifying the resulting systems into a small number of types. As a rule, such classifications concentrate only on subparts of the kinship systems: Nerlove and Romney's (1967) study, for example, probably the most cross-linguistically systematic, focuses on sibling (i.e. children of the same biological parents) terminologies in 245 languages. These are based on eight logical KIN types as defined by three parameters (sex of ego, sex of relative, relative age) – e.g. whether one and the same term is used for all siblings, whether there are two separate terms for "brother" and "sister", whether there are four different terms ("younger brother", "elder brother", "younger sister", "elder sister"). A simple example of this is given in Table 25.2, which shows the inventories of sibling terms in six languages – Russian (Indo-European: Slavic), Palula (Indo-European: Dardic), Turkish (Altaic: Turkic), Ewe (Niger-Kongo: Kwa), Jakarta Indonesian (Austronesian: Malayic), and Nukuoro (Austronesian: Polynesian).

Maria Koptjevskaja-Tamm et al.

Table 25.2 Sibling terms in six languages

Language	male sibling	female sibling	relative age
Russian	*brat*	*sestra*	age difference irrelevant
Palula	*bhróo*	*bheén*	age difference irrelevant
	káaku	*kéeki*	elder
	kúuču	*kúuči*	younger
Turkish	*aga*	*aba*	elder
	kardaş		younger
Ewe	*efo*	*eda*	elder
	etse	*efoe*	younger
		nɔvi	age difference irrelevant
	abang		elder
Jakarta Indonesian	*kakak*		elder
	adik		younger
	saudara		age difference irrelevant
Nukuoro	*teina*		age difference irrelevant

Restricting ourselves to sibling terms that are not hyperonyms of any others (e.g. excluding "sibling" in languages distinguishing "brother" and "sister"), there are 4,140 logically possible types, but only 12 of those are attested in more than one language from the 245 languages. The absolutely most dominant type (in its pure version attested in 78 languages) has four terms – elder brother, elder sister, younger brother, and younger sister (cf. Palula and Ewe in Table 25.2); the next most frequent type (in its pure version attested in 38 languages) has three terms – elder brother, elder sister, and younger brother/sister (see Turkish in Table 25.2). The two next types occur in 21 languages each (i.e., in less than 10% of the sample) and include the average European type with a distinction between brother and sister, and another two-term type, with a distinction between elder and younger siblings (with Indonesian in Table 25.2 approaching it).

Importantly, not only do Nerlove and Romney present their classification and statistics, but they also suggest that the paucity of the attested systems may be explained by universal restrictions, such as the cognitive restriction on avoidance of disjunctive categories (Bruner et al. 1956: 41–43). For instance, a category comprising male younger and elder siblings, i.e. "brother", is conjunctive, since it contains the same component [male relative] combined with the two values of the component [relative age], as opposed to the disjunctive category comprising, say, male siblings and siblings of a male. Another universal constraint, this time of a more social character, is avoidance of categories in which sex of ego is a primary distinction. Nerlove and Romney go even further and try to link cross-linguistic variation to social variables, for example connecting the existence of sibling categories based on the relative sex of ego and relative in a language with brother-sister avoidance in the group speaking it.

Componential analysis of different denominations has been subject to massive criticism from various quarters, primarily for its categorical view of meaning (see Chapter 12). Its main appeal for lexical typology lies, however, in the promise of bringing out the structure behind a semantic domain and in this way facilitating systematic cross-linguistic comparison. Consider the above-mentioned kinship asymmetry. It is an example of *linguistic universals*, i.e. generalizations on what is generally preferred/dispreferred (or even possible/impossible) in human languages. Componential analysis, with its formalized and simplified metalanguage, offers a seemingly smooth method for discovering and formulating generalizations based on combinations of co-occurring features. This is true in particular if the features are "easily" recognizable, not only within one language but also across languages, and if their values are clearly distinct from each other. However, even for these purposes componential analysis is of limited value, in that it may impose "artificial" structuring on a domain and obscure some of the important generalizations on the factors behind its categorization, as will be discussed below.

Apart from kinship terminology, there have hardly been any serious attempts to apply full-fledged componential analysis to cross-linguistic research on the lexicon whereby all the words in a domain will be decomposed into matrices of (binary) features, ideally independent of each other and relevant for the whole domain (a possible exception, although on a much smaller scale, is spatial dimension terms, cf. Lang (2001)). Very few domains are in fact organized as paradigms. In practice, many features are dependent on each other, with many of them only applicable to a subset of the terms, often leading to taxonomies of various kinds. Lehrer, in her comparison of cooking terms across several languages, which she couches in terms of components such as "the use of water: [±water]", "source of heat: radiated vs. conducted vs. hot surface", "cooking time: long vs. short", "cooking action: gentle vs. vigorous", etc., wrote the following:

> A cursory examination of cooking words shows why many components are not combined into a single word: when cooking with water, it does not matter what the heat source is so long as it is sufficient to keep the water at a high enough temperature; when something cooked in liquid is cooked a long time, a gentle action is preferred so the liquid does not boil out.
>
> (Lehrer 1974: 101)

The moral here is that the semantic properties of kinship terms, of cooking verbs and in fact of many (or perhaps even most?) other lexical systems are not randomly combined with each other, but form meaningful clusters that often lack symmetry. Even pairs of words that are generally considered to be antonyms and therefore only differ in the value of one component are normally asymmetrical – they differ in the scope of their meaning and in patterns of polysemy, so that one and the same word often has different antonyms in its different uses (cf. Paradis and Willners (2011); see Chapter 14).

Lexical systems, with the lexical meanings and oppositions forming them, emerge from human experience of recurrent situations, including interaction with other people and various objects, and in this sense their asymmetries are inherent. Domains are often structured around several distinct prototypical situations or prototypical entities, and it may be more reasonable to take those as the main unit of description/analysis in a lexico-typological study rather than decomposing them into their particular distinctive features, the status of which is often quite questionable. Coming back to kinship terminologies, Wierzbicka (1987) points out the hidden circularity in defining "mother" and "father" via the component "ascending generation", which can itself only be understood via parenthood. "Mother", as "birth-giver", is, on the other hand, a highly important and universally lexicalized concept. Therefore, as Wierzbicka argues, it may be more fruitful to use the concept of "mother" in the semantic analysis of kinship than to resort to such abstract components as "ascending generation" and "linearity".

4 Natural semantic metalanguage

Anna Wierzbicka, cited immediately above, and Cliff Goddard are the portal figures for *Natural Semantic Metalanguage* (*NSM*), which shares the idea of meaning decomposition with componential analysis, but has a different philosophical foundation and embodies a completely different ideology. This approach is consistently anthropocentric, i.e. taking man as the measure of all things (cf. the notions of embodiment and perspectivization in Cognitive Linguistics; see Chapters 5 and 15). For instance, the seemingly random clusters of features that make up lexical meanings are described and explained as stemming from the functions of their referents in human life. Thus, the definition of "cup" does not only mention a "handle" as one of its components (as might be done in componential analysis), but also explicitly describes cups as meant for hot liquids "to be drunk from while sitting at a table, lifting them to the mouth to drink a little and putting them down again" (Wierzbicka 1984: 215). Definitions of colour terms explicitly refer to prototypical natural objects such as the sun for "yellow" or living vegetation for "green" (Wierzbicka 2005), while temperature terms are described via fire (Goddard and Wierzbicka 2007).

At the heart of this method lies the hypothesis that there is a small lexical-conceptual core shared by all languages, "semantic primes", i.e., basic and universal meanings, which can be expressed by words or other linguistic expressions in all languages. The current list contains 64 items. Due to their universal "translatability", these can further be used as the *tertium comparationis* in the systematic investigation of lexical phenomena across languages, as the main building blocks in reductive paraphrases that aim at providing precise definitions, or "explications", of their meanings (e.g. Goddard and Wierzbicka (2007); Goddard (2001); Wierzbicka (2007)).

According to the NSM homepage, NSM "can lay claim to being the most well-developed, comprehensive and practical approach to cross-linguistic and cross-cultural semantics on the contemporary scene" (http://www.griffith.edu.au/humanities-languages/school-languages-linguistics/research/natural-semantic-metalanguage-homepage), with a track record of 35 years in empirical research and a wealth of publications. NSM has been applied to such traditionally central domains for lexical typology as kinship, colour and body (Wierzbicka 1987; 2005; 2007). However, the area where this method has led to particularly interesting results is cross-linguistic semantic comparison of complex, culturally relevant emotional and mental phenomena, where cross-linguistic diversity often arises from cultural stereotypes that profile different aspects of reality and speakers' attitudes (Wierzbicka 1999; Harkins and Wierzbicka 2001). A very fruitful idea for semantic comparison is to use a common structural pattern for words semantically related to each other (a "semantic template"). Similar ambitions are, of course, present in other semantic approaches, at least for the words belonging to one and the same language. However, NSM remains unrivalled in the extent to which this has been employed for cross-linguistic comparison, where semantic templates offer effective tools for analyzing, comparing and representing meanings across languages, in a way that enables capturing both similarities and fine-grained distinctions among them. To take an example, one of the semantic templates for emotion words builds on the idea that being happy, sad, pleased etc. means being in a particular state of mind (for instance, thinking that something good has happened) and because of that experiencing a particular kind of feeling (e.g. feeling good), which, in turn, is viewed as normally linked to this mental state. By a consistent application of such patterns, NSM researchers claim to demonstrate how words for seemingly similar emotions (say, "anger" or "happiness") differ across languages and in pinpointing what makes certain emotion terms (e.g. *amae* in Japanese) extremely culture-specific and seemingly untranslatable into other languages (see the contributions in Harkins and Wierzbicka (2001)).

Much of the recent work within NSM has been directed towards elaborating and testing semantic templates and other analytical constructs (primarily semantic molecules) for further semantic domains across languages, such as various subclasses of physical activity verbs (cf. Goddard (2012)).

The theory has both positive and negative sides and its strong basic assumption on the existence of universally lexicalized semantic primes and on their manifestations in concrete languages is particularly debatable (cf. e.g. the discussion in Krifka (2003); Riemer (2006); Evans (2011)). To give just one example, it is far from clear whether any of the two Russian near-synonyms *xotet'* and *želat'* is a good candidate for the prime WANT, because both of them are influenced by being opposed to each other and develop connotations beyond the meaning of pure intent that the prime should signify (example from Apresjan (2000)).

5 Denotation-based or etic-grid semantics

The denotation-based approach to cross-linguistic semantics was first launched in the second half of the 1960s by Brent Berlin and Paul Kay, who equipped their students with Munsell colour charts and sent them to see how these were mapped to the colour terms in the different languages spoken in the San Francisco Bay area. This was the birth of the groundbreaking systematic cross-linguistic research on colour often called "the Berlin-Kay paradigm". The Munsell colour charts provide a number of extra-linguistic contexts, or an "etic grid" for capturing possible distinctions within the colour domain (organized according to the three dimensions of hue, value/lightness, and chroma/colour purity), which enables comparison of denotational ranges of colour terms both within one and the same language and across languages. The various tasks that informants perform with the colour chips allow comparison with further cognitive findings. In the Berlin-Kay view, although languages are very different as to how many colour names they distinguish in their lexicon, as well as to exactly which portions of the colour spectrum each of them covers, this variation is severely restricted, primarily by the neurophysiology of vision (Berlin and Kay 1969; Kay and McDaniel 1978; Kay and Maffi 2005). Colour remains the cross-linguistically most widely studied lexical domain in terms of the languages systematically covered by means of comparable and elaborated methodology (Kay and Maffi (2005), lists 119 languages), and the intensity, diversity and depth of theoretical discussions (cf. e.g. Robertson and Hanley (2010) for a recent overview; MacLaury et al. (2007), and the references there; and http://www.icsi.berkeley.edu/wcs/ for the World Color Survey Site).

In addition to colour, the denotation-based approach to cross-linguistic comparison has been actively promoted in the rich research at the Department of Language and Cognition at the Max-Planck Institute for Psycholinguistics in Nijmegen. The major results of this research have so far been achieved for "body" (Majid et al. 2006), "cut/break" (Majid and Bowerman 2007), "put/take" (Narasimhan and Kopecka 2012), "location" (Ameka and Levinson 2007) and "space" in general (Levinson and Wilkins 2006) (http://www.mpi.nl/research/research-projects/categories). The "Nijmegen method" uses standardized stimuli, such as sets of pictures, videoclips and films for collecting data on a number of cognitive domains directly in the field (cf. http://fieldmanuals.mpi.nl/). Each set covers a shared denotational grid allowing systematic comparisons of semantic distinctions potentially relevant for the domain and may be used under different elicitation conditions, including games. To give a couple of examples, the data for the 24 languages in the "cut/break" domain and for 19 languages in the "put/take" project were collected by means of videoclips, such as "X is tearing cloth into two pieces by hand", "X is slicing a carrot across into multiple pieces with a knife", "X is cutting hair with scissors", "X is smashing a plate with a single blow of a hammer", etc. (Majid and Bowerman 2007), or "X is putting a cup on the table/taking a cup off the table", "X is pouring liquid into a container/pouring water out of a tin can", "X is putting on a coat/taking off a coat" (Narasimhan and Kopecka 2012). The data on the "body" for the ten languages in Majid et al. (2006) involve, among others, drawing outlines of the various body-part terms on a picture of a human body.

A huge appeal of this approach is its objectivity. With a standard set of stimuli, the researcher's influence on the results is minimal, and it is easy to compare data from different speakers and different languages, no matter when or where it has been gathered. This makes the method particularly suited for studies of underdescribed languages.

However, it is not free from problems. Some domains do not lend themselves to representations by stimuli sets – complex mental and social phenomena such as emotions, unpleasant physical sensations such as pain, or abstract notions, such as possession, are obvious examples. These require other methods of data collection and analysis, for instance, verbal descriptions. A deeper problem lies within the stimuli themselves: the set needs to be complete and cover the domain exhaustively, since anything not featured in the experiment is likely to be overlooked. However, there may also be various interesting and unexpected sides of the phenomena that the researcher has not been aware of while preparing the stimuli and that may turn out to be important for their understanding – these may be disclosed by non-elicited data. Also the fact that the stimuli are artificial and largely divorced from the context may affect the results, as debated by people such as Levinson (2000) and Wierzbicka (2005), who have questioned the validity of the decontextualized denotation-based methodology underlying the lion's share of the studies in the Berlin-Kay paradigm.

For example, colour terms are often chosen depending on the type of the object. *Red* as a hair colour is very different from the prototypical red and is, in fact, close to orange, but calling hair *orange* strongly implies that it is dyed. Colours related to humans and animals tend to have very specific terms, such as *blond* (only human hair) or *bay* (only horses). When new colour terms emerge, often inspired by new objects, old terms shift their meanings to accommodate the change and gradually fall out of use. For instance, the old word for brown in Russian, *buryj*, has been almost completely displaced by *koričnevyj*, which is derived from the word for the exotic spice cinnamon. Among the last objects for which *buryj* is still used are dirt and animal fur. The rule behind this process is that new and exotic terms are used to describe artificial colours, while old terms stick with natural objects. This means that by disregarding the names of natural colours, with their limited scope and declining usage, the researcher might miss what once used to be the core colour vocabulary of the language and will not be able to fully understand its evolution, which has been one of the major goals in the Berlin and Kay enterprise.

To be fair to the denotation-based approach, the degree of decontextualization varies significantly between different techniques and studies. Both retelling a film for someone who has not seen it or exchanging verbal instructions during a game come closer to language in normal use than describing a series of disconnected videoclips or naming colour chips. And in fact, most of the data acquired by stimuli-based elicitation in the research at the Max-Planck institute are complemented by data coming from other sources (e.g. texts in the relevant languages). A successful study in lexical typology obviously benefits from a combination of different types of data.

6 Combinatorial lexical typology

Combinatorial lexical typology, primarily developed by the Moscow Lexico-Typological group (directed by Ekaterina Rakhilina), is the most recent contribution to cross-linguistic semantic comparison in lexicon (e.g. Rakhilina (2010); Reznikova et al. (2012); Koptjevskaja-Tamm et al. (2010)). This method can be traced back to the early claim of the Moscow school of semantics (with Apresjan as the main figure, e.g. Apresjan (2000)) that even the closest synonyms have different collocations, and that every word should be described with particular attention to its surroundings. The idea, also shared by Wierzbicka and Firth and strongly argued for by cognitive linguistics, assumes that the combinability of a lexeme in different contexts, its "linguistic behaviour" (Wierzbicka) or "semantic range" (Firth 1957), is normally motivated by its semantic properties and can provide cues for the understanding of its meaning, where the meaning of a word is its intension, rather than denotation, or extension. The semantic properties of every single lexeme are therefore to be studied individually, by a systematic analysis of its combinability. A semantic description of a lexeme includes both a description of its linguistic behaviour and a suggestion as to what semantic properties might motivate it. In Russia, this idea gave rise to a rich lexicographic tradition (e.g. NOS (2004)) whereas the development of corpus linguistics has enabled its serious application to lexical typology. Corpora, available for an increasing number of languages, give a relatively full and reliable picture of words in context, and, most importantly, of the contexts preferred by a given lexeme (see Chapter 6).

A key notion in the combinatorial approach is a "frame", which is understood somewhat differently than in the mainstream cognitive linguistics (e.g. Fillmore (1982); FrameNet https://framenet.icsi.berkeley.edu/fndrupal/home). Whereas for Fillmore a frame is defined as a set of participants with their assigned syntactic roles, combinatorial lexical typology views a frame as a group of prototypical situations (and contexts that represent these situations in texts) which have functional similarity and are relevant for lexicalization. Similarly to NSM, this approach is anthropocentric and assumes that words partition semantic domains by breaking up reality into cognitively relevant fragments, rather than randomly. In particular, the prototypical situations are so closely related to the predicate's argument types that a description of its arguments can serve as a sufficient representation of a situation. For example, "oldness" is a small domain that consists of four main frames that can roughly be described as "worn" (*old shoes, rags . . .*), "aged" (*old people, horses, trees . . .*), "former" (*old address, government, procedure . . .*) and "ancient" (*old myths, music, grammatical construction . . .*) (cf. Taylor 1992). The English adjective *old* covers all of them, even though it can have specific antonyms corresponding to some of the frames – *new*, *young*, *current* and *modern* respectively. Other languages divide the domain between two or more lexemes, and the richest systems (found in Nanai, Yakut, Komi, Kurdish, Malagasy, Quechua and Ossetic) have separate adjectives for all four situations.

Combinatorial lexical typology is similar to the denotation-based approach in working with "etic grids" of contexts, enabling systematic comparison of how languages group these contexts within their own concepts. However, whereas in the denotation-based approach the grid consists of extra-linguistic stimuli, the lexical-combinatorial method uses a list of frames, or rather a list of diagnostic contexts that represent them. For instance, for "old" it would be "shoes", "people" etc., for the verbs of rotation such contexts as "the Earth around the Sun", "barrel on the ground" and "hawk over its prey" and some others (Rakhilina 2010), for the verbs of oscillation "trees in the wind", "a broken chair", "a long skirt when walking" etc. Searches for the key words and their collocations are made in dictionaries and corpora, and the list is also used as a questionnaire for native speakers. The core of the method consists in finding contexts in which a word cannot be replaced by a particular near-synonym, and determining which of their properties determine such restrictions.

In this approach each domain presents a landscape of frames that languages carve up by their lexemes. Lexemes can both overlap in their ranges and leave parts of the landscape unlabelled. Frames are believed to constitute the analytic primitives in a lexico-typological comparison. They have been extensively discussed for several domains such as aquamotion, swaying and shaking, rotation, sharpness and bluntness, pain, etc. (for details see Rakhilina and Reznikova (2014)).

7 Semantic maps

As noted at the end of the preceding section, much of the cross-linguistic research on the lexicon (e.g. both combinatorial lexical typology and denotation-based semantic typology) departs from "etic grids" of contexts and asks the question of how languages group these contexts within their own concepts. In sections 3 and 4 we showed how two different decompositional approaches to semantics (componential analysis and Natural Semantic Metalanguage) formulate the results of cross-linguistic semantic comparison in terms of their specific metalanguages. This section deals with a family of representational techniques that are particularly suitable for "etic-based" semantic comparison, namely semantic maps.

A semantic map is a tool for visualizing (representing) cross-linguistic commonalities in the multifunctionality patterns manifested by semantically/functionally "comparable" linguistic expressions (e.g. morphemes, words, constructions) of particular languages. The idea is that one and the same linguistic expression normally has a range of functions (uses, meanings, contexts), and these ranges usually show considerable overlaps across languages, without necessarily being completely identical. The main guiding principle for constructing a semantic map may be called the "contiguity/connectivity requirement". That is, functions (uses, meanings, contexts) that are often associated with one and the same linguistic expression are represented as nodes adjacent to each other, or as a contiguous region in a semantic map (cf. Haspelmath (2003) for an illuminating presentation of the semantic map methodology). However, and importantly, the fact that one and the same linguistic expression is represented as associated with several nodes does not necessarily mean that it is analyzed as polysemic. In other words, "multifunctionality", inherent in the method, "does not imply a commitment to a particular choice among monosemic and polysemic analyses" (Haspelmath 2003: 213).

Semantic maps have become a popular method in grammatical typology of the last two decades, where they have been used for capturing both synchronic facts and patterns of development (cf. Cysouw et al. (2010) for a recent contribution). Most attempts to apply semantic maps to lexical typology are more recent and date back to the second half of the 2000s. These can be grouped into two main types – semantic maps per se, or implicational semantic maps (see section 7.1), and probabilistic semantic maps (section 7.2).

The explicit non-commitment of semantic maps methodology to the issues of monosemy/polysemy makes it particularly suitable for lexical typology, where it has been applied both to the uses of one and the same lexeme within one domain (i.e. to the issues of domain categorization), as well as to the uses of one and the same lexeme or of lexemes related to it in different domains (normally seen as patterns of polysemy and semantic shifts). In particular the latter applications share certain similarities with conceptual/semantic networks as these are practised in Cognitive Linguistics (cf. Chapters 5 and 15), but are theoretically much less sophisticated. Keeping in line with the main interest of this chapter, we will predominantly focus on the use of semantic maps in the research on domain categorization; however, we will start with two examples of semantic maps that aim at capturing patterns of polysemy and semantic shifts.

7.1 Implicational semantic maps in lexical typology

The generalization (prediction) inherent in a semantic map is that if a linguistic expression is associated with two non-adjacent nodes *a* and *c*, it will also be associated with the node *b* connecting the two. The "contiguity/connectivity requirement" underlying the methodology of semantic maps is therefore reminiscent of – but also simultaneously weaker than – the traditional typological tool of implicational generalizations (if *a* then *b*). Early examples of graphical representations of implicational lexico-typological generalizations are found in Viberg's (1984) influential paper on perception verbs in about 50 languages. As Viberg demonstrates, "[o]ne of the most striking characteristics of the lexicalization patterns of the verbs of perception is the large amount of polysemy with respect to the sense modalities" (Viberg 1984: 136). He shows that lexicalization of perception by verbs across languages and the patterns of sense conflation ("patterns of polysemy") follow the sense-modality hierarchy, from sight followed by hearing, as the highest sense modalities, to smell, taste and touch as the lowest ones. To give an example, if a language has a dedicated verb for touching, tasting or smelling, it will distinguish between hearing and seeing verbs.

One of the first attempts to fully elaborate the methodology of implicational semantic maps for lexical typology is found in François (2008). François' semantic maps target cross-linguistically recurrent patterns of semantic shifts as manifested by polysemous words and words related to them by derivation and compounding and illustrate the methodology by means of the pivot concept "breath" (cf. Chapter 15 for details on François' methods and an illustration).

Semantic maps are currently widely used by the Moscow Lexico-Typological Group (cf. section 6 and Rakhilina and Reznikova (2014)), where the nodes correspond to "frames", i.e. the typologically relevant situations. Figure 25.1 shows the semantic map for the domain of EMPTINESS and its lexicalization in Chinese and Serbian, where the cross-linguistically relevant frames are defined as "hollow shape" (e.g. "a hollow cylinder") "empty container" (e.g. "an empty bottle"), "location empty of people" (e.g. "an empty house"), "large space without objects in it" (e.g. "an empty field"), "small flat surface without things on it" (e.g. "an empty table"), and "empty hanger".

7.2 Probabilistic semantic maps

Probabilistic semantic maps make use of statistical methods based on correspondence analysis of similarity matrices, where matrices contain occurrences of particular linguistic expressions (e.g. lexemes) in a number of different contexts across languages. Although also anchored in the notions of semantic spaces and semantic maps, the resulting representations differ significantly from those considered in section 7.1. The data themselves may come from very different sources – e.g. informants' replies to a particular set of stimuli, or particular sentences in parallel texts, i.e. translations of one and the same text into different languages. Below we will illustrate both approaches.

The earliest example of a cross-linguistic probabilistic semantic map comes from the denotation-based Nijmegen project on "cutting" and "breaking" events (Majid and Bowerman 2007), where the data consist of descriptions of events represented in videoclips by speakers of 24 languages (cf. section 5 for the details). These are arranged, for each of the languages separately, in a similarity matrix which is built on the assumption that clips that are often described with the same predicate are more similar semantically than clips described with different predicates. Correspondence analysis was then jointly

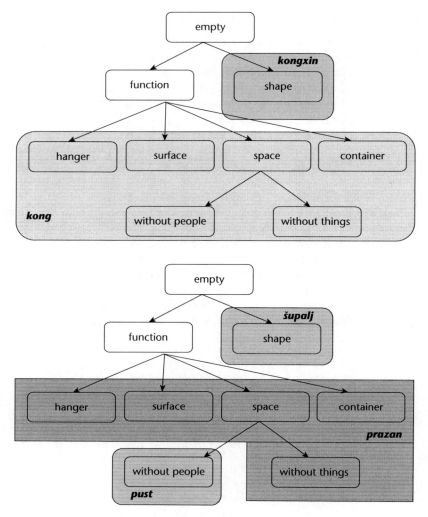

Figure 25.1 Semantic maps of EMPTINESS in Mandarin and Serbian (adapted from Rakhilina and Reznikova (2014))

applied to these matrices to extract the main dimensions along which the languages (or rather the informants) grouped or differentiated events. All in all, four dimensions suffice to categorize the replies cross-linguistically, with the main dimension being the relative predictability of the locus of separation in the affected object: cf. high predictability for slicing carrots with a small knife, poor predictability for smashing a plate with a hammer, and in-between predictability for chopping off a branch with an axe. Within events with a poorly predictable locus of separation some languages make a further distinction between smashing a rigid object like a plate, pot, or carrot with a sharp blow and snapping a long object like a stick or a carrot into two pieces between the hands or over the knee. Finally, tearing events (e.g. a hand action on a two-dimensional flexible object) are very often endowed with a verb of their own. The resulting semantic space and the first three dimensions underlying it are shown in Figure 25.2.

The semantics of lexical typology

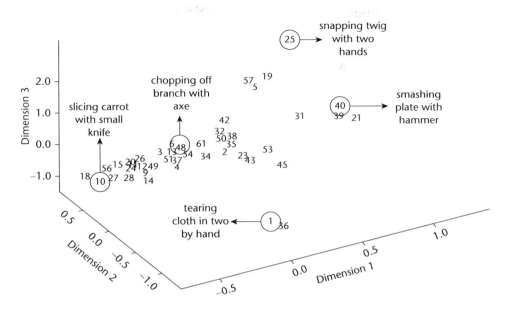

Figure 25.2 A three-dimensional plot of cutting and breaking events (Majid and Bowerman 2007: 143)

The most recent example of a cross-linguistic probabilistic semantic map comes from Wälchli and Cysouw's (2012) study of motion events in parallel texts, i.e. in translations of the Gospel according to Mark into 100 languages from all continents. The method uses Multidimensional Scaling (MDS) for visualization and the Hamming distance (here the fraction of languages for which the relevant predicates are lexicalized differently) for the statistics, and the idea is that:

> [t]he closer two contextually embedded situations are represented in a semantic map the more likely it is that they are represented by the same category in any language in the database. A probability space is accurate to the extent that it predicts crosslinguistically recurrent tendencies in the categorization of form classes.
>
> (Wälchli and Cysouw 2012: 679)

The domain of motion verbs turns out to require ten to twenty dimensions for capturing the cross-linguistically most frequent lexicalization patterns (cf. the four dimensions for breaking and cutting events), with several cross-linguistically recurrent lexicalization clusters for which the authors use descriptive labels such as "go", "come" or "arrive". These three serve as the main illustration in the paper and are represented below by the semantic maps for two unrelated languages – Classical Greek and Sora (Austroasiatic: Munda).

Semantic maps are particularly useful when the arrangement of the nodes and/or their general geometry receives a further explanation and/or can be used for various predictions. For instance, due to the intermediate level of predictability of the locus of separation for chopping off a branch with an axe, some languages group this event together with "precise control" events (such as slicing carrots with a small knife), while others group it with "imprecise control" events (such as smashing a plate with a hammer; Majid and Bowerman (2007)). Another example concerns the temperature domain (Koptjevskaja-Tamm 2015), where one of the main

447

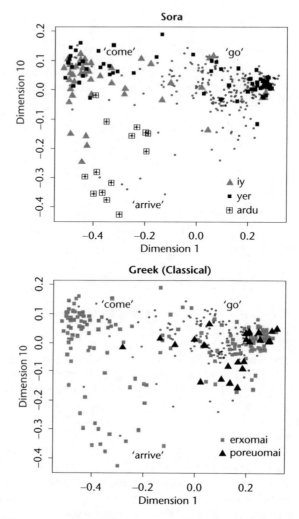

Figure 25.3 Probabilistic semantic maps of the "go", "come" and "arrive" domain in Sora and Classical Greek in the Gospel according to Mark (adapted from Wälchli and Cysouw 2012: 701)

dimensions underlying the cross-linguistic variation concerns the distinctions among three frames of temperature evaluation – tactile temperature (*The stones are cold*), ambient temperature (*It is cold here*), and personal-feeling temperature (*He feels cold*). While English "cold" can be used for all the three frames (competing with *freeze* for personal-feeling temperatures), other languages may require several different lexemes here. Armenian distinguishes between the "tactile cold" adjective *sařn*, the "ambient cold" adjective *c"urt*, and the "personal-feeling be cold" verb *mrsel*; Kamang (Timor-Alor-Pantar) distinguishes between the "non-personal cold" (i.e., tactile + ambient) *kamal* and the "personal-feeling cold" *faatei*, while Palula (Indo-European: Dardic), finally, distinguishes between the "tactile cold" *taátu* and the "non-tactile cold" (i.e., ambient + personal-feeling) *húluk*. The recurrent pattern, visualized in the semantic maps in Figure 25.4, is that personal-feeling temperatures are often singled out by languages

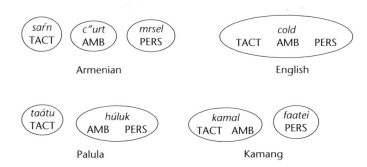

Figure 25.4 "Cold" in Armenian, English, Palula and Kamang

in various ways, whereas the linguistic encoding of ambient temperature may share properties with those of either tactile or personal-feeling temperature.

The motivation for this lies in the conceptual and perceptual affinities of ambient temperature with both other frames of temperature evaluation. On the one hand, ambient and personal-feeling temperatures are rooted in the same type of experience, thermal comfort, whereas tactile temperature relates to evaluation of the temperature of other entities based on perception received by the skin. On the other hand, tactile and ambient temperatures are about temperatures that can be verified from "outside", whereas personal-feeling temperature is about a subjective "inner" experience of a living being (for details cf. Kopjevskaja-Tamm 2015).

Now, while semantic maps in general offer a practical method for representing cross-linguistic generalizations, they do not embody any stance on the relation between an "etic" concept (i.e. the range of the uses of a particular linguistic expression) and the corresponding "emic" concept (i.e. its descriptive meaning/sense/intension). And in fact most of the researchers do not even touch upon this issue. The question that is, however, sometimes discussed is whether semantic maps necessarily correspond to a speaker's mental representations, with some voices arguing for, or at least assuming this position (e.g. Haspelmath (2003)) and some against (Wälchli and Cysouw 2012).

An interesting and so far unexploited aspect of semantic maps is their potential applicability for combining cross-linguistic generalizations on domain categorization with those on cross-domain semantic shifts. First of all, semantic extensions normally originate not from the lexeme as a whole, but from its particular use, or "frame", and the same frame, or the same use, may lead to similar semantic shifts across languages. For instance, adjectives denoting functional sharpness (as in *sharp knife*) frequently evolve into intensifiers (as in *sharp contrast*). This shift, however, is not observed for a similar class of adjectives denoting pointed shape (as in *pointed shoes*). Specialized adjectives like *pointed* are not likely to develop intensifier meaning, although both types of "sharpness" are semantically very close, and are typically expressed by one and the same polysemous lexical item cross-linguistically.

In addition, there may be interesting regularities in mapping across whole domains. As an example, take the extensive research on the semantic extensions from perception to cognition, cf. "to see" as "understand" in *Do you see what I mean* (Sweetser 1990; Evans and Wilkins 2000), further enriched with prehension predicates, such as "seize", in Vanhove (2008). Vanhove proposes an implicational hierarchy to describe the predicates' potential for semantic extension into cognition: hearing > vision > prehension. In other words, if a language has a prehension word which maps onto the domain of mental perception, it also has another lexical item with a similar semantic association for vision and the auditory sense, but the reverse is not true.

A possible solution for capturing such generalizations might be three-dimensional semantic maps, with maps of the source and target domains aligned as layers and shifts connecting the nodes on one layer to the nodes on the other.

8 Future prospects

Systematic research in lexical typology has so far been carried out on rather limited language samples. These samples are often quite sufficient for falsifying some assumptions about the universality of a particular phenomenon and for unveiling major patterns in its cross-linguistic variation, but are hardly adequate for drawing safe conclusions on the interplay among the various factors behind it or for clearly distinguishing between universal determinants and those due to historical relations among the languages. Systematic research in lexical typology needs therefore to be extended to more linguistic phenomena and to more languages. In particular, sign languages have been largely missing in most lexico-typological studies.

An important task facing lexical typology is to focus more on historical processes, and especially on cross-domain semantic shifts, i.e. on the emergence and functioning of metaphoric and metonymical word-senses (see also Chapters 5 and 15). While Cognitive Linguistics emphasizes the universality of many cognitive metaphors, the research on regular semantic shifts across languages is so far very limited. There is, however, ample evidence of cross-linguistically recurrent patterns here. A few examples, in addition to the development of cognitive verbs mentioned in section 7.2, include the research on the sources of body-part terms (e.g. Wilkins (1996); Koch (2008)), Urban's (2012) large-scale study of motivational patterns underlying many different kinds of referring expressions, and Reznikova et al.'s (2012) study of metaphorical sources of pain expressions. Of the approaches discussed above, the classic structuralist method is inherently static, psycholinguistic experiments lack the tools to capture lexical metaphors, and the NSM school with its interest in abstract domains and culture-specific concepts is less concerned with the typology of shifts from physical domains. But even for the purposes of domain-categorization research, semantic shifts are worthy of special attention in providing additional clues for understanding the structure of their source domain. Just as a word having several antonyms is usually an indication of polysemy, with antonyms corresponding to distinct word-senses that can be represented by separate lexemes in some other language, the source of a semantic shift may also point out a word-sense, even though this does not necessarily hold in all cases (cf. the example of "sharp contrast" mentioned in section 7.2).

A related issue concerns syntactic and morphosyntactic properties of words. It is well established in lexicology and lexicography that collocation, valency, case marking and other patterns of argument realization, as well as many morphological characteristics such as countability of nouns or verbal aspectual classes, can be motivated by semantics. However, there is a long tradition of distinguishing between grammatical typology, focusing on the grammatical behaviour of words and on morphosyntactic patterns as encoding meanings, and lexical typology, that has to a large extent been restricted to domain categorization by lexical means, without further considering their grammatical behaviour. Fortunately, the recent developments within the cross-linguistic research on domain categorization are witness of an ambition to reconcile lexical and grammatical interests and to engage in a dialogue with linguistic grammatical theory. For instance, one of the leading issues in the project on cutting and breaking events (Majid and Bowerman 2007) has been the interface between syntax and lexical semantics, i.e. to what extent and how the argument structure properties of a verb are predictable from its meaning. Construction Grammar is gaining popularity as an appropriate framework for lexico-typological research, e.g. on PAIN predicates (Reznikova et al. 2012), TEMPERATURE (Koptjevskaja-Tamm 2008), and LOCATION–EXISTENCE–POSSESSION (Koch 2012). Construction Grammar-inspired schemas are capable of covering linguistic phenomena on different levels (lexicon and grammar) and their interaction.

An in-depth study of lexical items that would take into account polysemy and formal properties requires exponentially more time and labour than simply identifying the core vocabulary in a domain. To make it feasible lexical typology needs to look for methods that would automate the collection and preliminary analysis of data as much as possible. Computational linguistics, in particular machine translation, has made significant progress in word-sense disambiguation, identifying and grouping contexts, aligning parallel texts and other related tasks. Implementing computational methods in a lexico-typological study would alleviate some of the manual work involved, and increased use of statistics, in particular, would give more weight to typological generalizations.

Of course, only a handful of languages at present have corpora of sufficient size and representativeness to make them fully useful to lexical typology, but as corpus linguistics continues growing, more corpora in more languages become available, with new tools developing for extracting a wealth of relevant information from them.

Further reading

Koptjevskaja-Tamm, M. and Vanhove, M. (eds) 2012. *New Directions in Lexical Typology*. [special issue] *Linguistics* 50 (3). This volume is the most recent update, representing a whole range of approaches to lexical typology.

Majid, A. and Bowerman, M. (eds) 2007. "Cutting and breaking" events: a crosslinguistic perspective. [special issue] *Cognitive Linguistics*, 18 (2). A detailed research on cross-linguistic similarities and differences in semantic categorization, applying statistical modeling to the descriptions of cutting and breaking events.

Narasimhan, B. and Kopecka, A. (eds) 2012. *Events of "Putting" and "Taking": a Crosslinguistic Perspective*. Amsterdam, Philadelphia: John Benjamins. An in-depth cross-linguistic study of placement and removal event descriptions describing their lexical and grammatical means, syntax-semantics mappings, lexical semantics, and asymmetries in the encoding of the two domains.

Wierzbicka, A. 1999. *Emotions Across Languages and Cultures: Diversity and Universals*. Cambridge: Cambridge University Press. A classic of the Natural Semantic Metalanguage approach: an introduction to the theory as a tool for cross-cultural analysis and the discovery of semantic primes and universals, clearly illustrated by the domain of emotions.

References

Ameka, F.K. and S.C. Levinson (eds) 2007. *The Typology and Semantics of Locative Predication: Posturals, Positionals and Other Beasts*. [special issue] *Linguistics* 45 (5).

Andersen, E. 1978. Lexical universals of body-part terminology. In Joseph H. Greenberg (ed.) *Universals of Human Language*. Stanford: Stanford University Press, 335–368.

Apresjan, J.D. 2000. *Systematic Lexicography*. Translated from Russian by K. Windle. Oxford: Oxford University Press.

Behrens, L. and H.-J. Sasse, 1997. *Lexical Typology: A Programmatic Sketch. Arbeitspapier* Nr. 30 (Neue Folge). Cologne: University of Cologne, Department of Linguistics.

Berlin, B. and P. Kay 1969. *Basic Color Terms: Their Universality and Evolution*. Berkeley, CA: University of California Press.

Brown, C.H. 2001. Lexical typology from an anthropological point of view. In M. Haspelmath et al. (eds) 2001. *Language Typology and Language Universals*, v.1–2. Berlin: Walter de Gruyter, 1178–1190.

Brown, C.H. 2005a. Hand and arm. In M. Haspelmath et al. (eds) 2001. *Language Typology and Language Universals*, v.1–2. Berlin: Walter de Gruyter, 522–525.

Brown, C.H. 2005b. Finger and hand. In M. Haspelmath et al. (eds) 2001. *Language Typology and Language Universals*, v.1–2. Berlin: Walter de Gruyter, 526–529.

Bruner, J.S., J.J. Goodnow and G.A. Austin (eds) 1956. *A Study of Thinking*. New York: John Wiley.

Cysouw, M., M. Haspelmath and A. Malchukov (eds) 2010. Semantic maps: methods and application. *Linguistic Discovery* 8 (1). http://journals.dartmouth.edu/cgi-bin/WebObjects/Journals.woa/1/xmlpage/1/issue/34.

Evans, N. 2011. Semantic typology. In Jae Jung Song (ed.) 2011. *The Oxford Handbook of Typology*. Oxford: Oxford University Press, 504–533.

Evans, N. and D.P. Wilkins 2000. In the mind's ear: the semantic extensions of perception verbs in Australian languages. *Language* 76: 546–592.

Fillmore, C.J. 1982. *Frame Semantics. Linguistics in the Morning Calm*. Seoul, South Korea: Hanshin Publishing Co, 111–137.

Firth, J.R. 1957. *Studies in Linguistic Analysis*. Oxford: Blackwell.

François, A. 2008. Semantic maps and the typology of colexification: intertwining polysemous networks across languages. In M. Vanhove (ed.) *From Polysemy to Semantic Change*. Amsterdam, Philadelphia: John Benjamins, 163–215.

Goddard, C. and A. Wierzbicka 2007. NSM analyses of the semantics of physical qualities: Sweet, hot, hard, heavy, rough, sharp in cross-linguistic perspective. *Studies in Language* 31: 765–800.

Goddard, C. 2001. Lexico-semantic universals: a critical overview. *Linguistic Typology* 5: 1–65.

Goddard, C. 2012. Semantic primes, semantic molecules, semantic templates: key concepts in the NSM approach to lexical typology. In M. Koptjevskaja-Tamm and M. Vanhove (eds). *New Directions in Lexical Typology*. [special issue] *Linguistics* 50: 711–743.

Greenberg, J.H. 1980. Universals of kinship terminology: their nature and the problem of their explanation. In J. Maquet (ed.) *On Linguistic Anthropology: Essays in Honor of Harry Hoijer*. Malibu: Undena Publications, 9–32. [Reprinted in Keith Denning and Suzanne Kemmer (eds) 1990. *Selected Writings: Selected Writings of Joseph H. Greenberg*. Stanford: Stanford University Press, 310–327.]

Harkins, J. and A. Wierzbicka (eds) 2001. *Emotions in Cross-Linguistic Perspective*. Berlin: Mouton de Gruyter.

Haspelmath, M. 2003. The geometry of grammatical meaning: semantic maps and cross-linguistic comparison. In M. Tomasello (ed.) 2003. *The New Psychology of Language* 2, Mahwah, NJ: Lawrence Erlbaum, 211–242.

Haspelmath, M., M. Dryer, D. Gil and B. Comrie (eds) 2005. *The World Atlas of Language Structures (WALS)*. Oxford: Oxford University Press.

Haspelmath, M., E. König, W. Oesterreicher and W. Raible (eds) 2001. *Language Typology and Language Universals*, v.1–2. Berlin: Walter de Gruyter.

Kay, P. and McDaniel, C. K. 1978. The linguistic significance of the meanings of basic color terms. *Language* 54: 610–646.

Kay, P. and L. Maffi 2005. Colour terms. In M. Haspelmath et al. (eds) *The World Atlas of Language Structures (WALS)*. Oxford: Oxford University Press, 534–545.

Koch, P. 2001. Lexical typology from a cognitive and linguistic point of view. In M. Haspelmath et al. (eds) *Language Typology and Language Universals*, v.1–2. Berlin: Walter de Gruyter, 1142–1178.

Koch, P. 2008. Cognitive onomasiology and lexical change: around the eye. In M. Vanhove (ed.) *From Polysemy to Semantic Change*. Amsterdam, Philadelphia: John Benjamins, 107–137.

Koch, P. 2012. Location, existence, and possession: a constructional-typological exploration. In M. Koptjevskaja-Tamm and M. Vanhove (eds). *New Directions in Lexical Typology*. [special issue] *Linguistics* 50: 533–604.

Koptjevskaja-Tamm, M. 2008. Approaching lexical typology. In M. Vanhove (ed.) *From Polysemy to Semantic Change*. Amsterdam, Philadelphia: John Benjamins, 3–52.

Koptjevskaja-Tamm, M. (ed.) 2015. *The Linguistics of Temperature*. Amsterdam, Philadelphia: John Benjamins.

Koptjevskaja-Tamm, M., D. Divjak and E. Rakhilina 2010. Aquamotion verbs in Slavic and Germanic: a case study in lexical typology. In V. Driagina-Hasko and R. Perelmutter (eds) 2010. *New Approaches to Slavic Verbs of Motion*. Amsterdam, Philadelphia: John Benjamins, 315–341.

Koptjevskaja-Tamm, M. and Vanhove, M. (eds) 2012. *New Directions in Lexical Typology*. [special issue] *Linguistics* 50 (3).

Koptjevskaja-Tamm 2015 should come before Koptjevskaja-Tamm and collaborators.

Krifka, Manfred (ed.) 2003. Natural semantic metalanguage. *Theoretical Linguistics* 29 (3).

Lang, Ewald. 2001. Spatial dimension terms. In Haspelmath et al. (eds) 2001. *Language Typology and Language Universals*, v-2. Berlin: Walter de Gruyter, 1251–1275.

Lehmann, C. 1990. Towards lexical typology. In W. Croft, K. Denning and S. Kemmer (eds) 1990. *Studies in Typology and Diachrony: Papers Presented to Joseph H. Greenberg on his 75th Birthday*. Amsterdam, Philadelphia: John Benjamins, 161–185.

Lehrer, A. 1992. A theory of vocabulary structure: retrospectives and prospectives. In M. Pütz (ed.). *Thirty Years of Linguistic Evolution. Studies in Honour of René Dirven on The Occasion of His Sixtieth Birthday*. Amsterdam, Philadelphia: John Benjamins, 243–256.

Lehrer, A. 1974. *Semantic Fields and Lexical Structure*. Amsterdam, London: North-Holland Publishing Company.

Levinson, Steven 2000. Yélî Dnye and the theory of basic color terms. *Journal of Linguistic Anthropology*, 10: 3–55.

Levinson, S. and D. Wilkins 2006. *Grammars of Space*. Cambridge: Cambridge University Press.

MacLaury, R.E., G.V. Paramei and D. Dedrick (eds) 2007. *Anthropology of Color: Interdisciplinary Multilevel Modeling*. Amsterdam, Philadelphia: John Benjamins.

Majid, A. and M. Bowerman (eds) 2007. "Cutting and breaking" events: a crosslinguistic perspective. [special issue] *Cognitive Linguistics* 18 (2).

Majid, A. M., Bowerman, M., van Staden and J.S. Boster 2007. The semantic categories of cutting and breaking events: a crosslinguistic perspective. *Cognitive Linguistics* 18: 133–152.

Majid, A., N.J. Enfield and M. van Staden (eds) 2006. *Parts of the Body: Cross-Linguistic Categorisation*. [special issue]. *Language Sciences* 28 (2–3).

Narasimhan, B. and A. Kopecka (eds) 2012. *Events of "Putting" and "Taking": A Crosslinguistic Perspective*. Amsterdam, Philadelphia: John Benjamins.

Nerlove, S. and A.K. Romney 1967. Sibling terminology and cross-sex behavior. *American Anthropologist* 74: 1249–1253.

Nichols, J., D. A. Peterson and J. Barnes 2004. Transitivizing and detransitivizing languages. *Linguistic Typology* 8: 149–211.

NOS = *Novyj Objasnitel'nyj Slovar' Sinonimov Russkogo Jazyka* [A new explanatory dictionary of synonyms in the Russian language] 2004. Moskva; Vena: Jazyki slavjanskoj kul'tury: Venskij slavističeskij al'manax.

Paradis, C. and C. Willners 2011. Antonymy: from conventionalization to meaning-making. *Review of Cognitive Linguistics* 9: 367–391.

Rakhilina, E. 2010. Verbs of rotation in Russian and Polish. In V. Hasko and R. Perelmutter (eds) *New Approaches to Slavic Verbs of Motion*. Amsterdam, Philadelphia: John Benjamins, 291–314.

Rakhilina, E. and T. Reznikova 2014. Doing lexical typology with frames and semantic maps. *Higher School of Economics Working Papers in Linguistics* (WP BRP 10/LNG/2014).

Reznikova, T., E. Rakhilina and A. Bonch-Osmolovskaya. 2012. Towards a typology of pain predicates. In M. Koptjevskaja-Tamm and M. Vanhove (eds) *New Directions in Lexical Typology*. [special issue] *Linguistics* 50: 421–466.

Riemer, N. 2005. *The Semantics of Polysemy*. Berlin, New York: Mouton de Gruyter.

Riemer, N. 2006. Reductive paraphrase and meaning: a critique of Wierzbickian semantics. *Linguistics and Philosophy* 29: 347–379.
Robertson, D. and J.R. Hanley 2010. Relatively speaking: an account of the relationship between language and thought in the color domain. In B.C. Malt and P. Wolff (eds) *Words and the Mind. How Words Capture Human Experience*. Oxford: Oxford University Press, 183–198.
Sweetser, E. 1990. *From Etymology to Pragmatics. Metaphorical and Cultural Aspects of Semantic Structure*. Cambridge: Cambridge University Press.
Talmy, L. 1985. Lexicalization patterns. In Timothy Shopen (ed.) *Language Typology and Synchronic Description*. Vol. 3. Cambridge: Cambridge University Press, 57–149.
Taylor, J.R. 1992. Old problems: adjectives in Cognitive Grammar. *Cognitive Linguistics* 3: 1–35.
Urban, M. 2012. *Analyzibility and Semantic Associations in Referring Expressions. A Study in Comparative Lexicology*. PhD diss., Leiden University.
Vanhove, M. 2008. Semantic associations between sensory modalities, prehension and mental perceptions: a crosslinguistic perspective. In M. Vanhove (ed.) *From Polysemy to Semantic Change*. Amsterdam, Philadelphia: John Benjamins, 342–370.
Vanhove, M. (ed.) 2008. *From Polysemy to Semantic Change*. Amsterdam, Philadelphia: John Benjamins.
Viberg, Å. 1984. The verbs of perception: a typological study. In B. Butterworth, B. Comrie and Ö. Dahl (eds) *Explanations for Language Universals*. Berlin, New York, Amsterdam: Mouton, 123–162.
Wälchli, B. and M. Cysouw. 2012. Lexical typology through similarity semantics: toward a semantic map of motion verbs. In M. Koptjevskaja-Tamm and M. Vanhove (eds) *New Directions in Lexical Typology*. [special issue] *Linguistics* 50: 671–710.
Wierzbicka, A. 1984. Cups and mugs: lexicography and conceptual analysis. *Australian Journal of Linguistics* 4: 205–255.
Wierzbicka, A. 1987. Kinship semantics: lexical universals as a key to psychological reality. *Anthropological Linguistics* 29: 131–156.
Wierzbicka, A. 1999. *Emotions Across Languages and Cultures: Diversity and Universals*. Cambridge: Cambridge University Press.
Wierzbicka, A. 2005. There are no "color universals". But there are universals of visual semantics. *Anthropological Linguistics* 47: 217–244.
Wierzbicka, A. 2007. Bodies and their parts: an NSM approach to semantic typology. *Language Sciences* 29: 14–65.
Wilkins, David P. 1996. Natural tendencies of semantic change and the search for cognates. In Mark Durie and Malcolm Ross (eds) *The Comparative Method Reviewed. Regularity and Irregularity in Language Change*. New York/Oxford: Oxford University Press, 264–304.

Related topics

Chapter 5, Cognitive semantics; Chapter 7, Categories, prototypes and exemplars; Chapter 12, Lexical decomposition; Chapter 13, Sense individuation; Chapter 14, Sense relations; Chapter 15, Semantic shift.

Part VII
Extensions

26
Acquisition of meaning

Soonja Choi

1 Introduction

Acquiring the meaning of a word requires integration of a number of skills, linguistic, cognitive, and socio-pragmatic. Consider a situation of an 18-month-old child learning a novel noun ("novel" for the child), such as "rabbit." The child hears his/her mother say, "There's a rabbit!" in a park where there are trees, benches, dogs, squirrels, and rabbits. First, the child needs linguistic ability to segment the speech stream and identify word boundaries and extract the word "rabbit." Second, he needs to identify the referent of the word "rabbit" among many possible ones in the environment. This may require some socio-pragmatic skills, e.g., use of the mother's eye-gaze or pointing as cue for identification. Third, even when the child has identified the referent, he needs to figure out which aspects/properties of the rabbit the word expresses (e.g., the whole entity, its tail, its furriness). This requires some cognitive ability to narrow down the possibilities: For example, the child may have an a priori assumption that the word "rabbit" refers to the whole entity and thus he may not need to entertain a large number of other possibilities.

Acquiring meanings of non-nominal words, such as verbs, may be even more challenging than nouns: a verb refers to an action/event or a state that may occur only briefly with no clear boundaries about when it begins and ends. Furthermore, verbs are relational in that their meanings inherently include some information about participants of the event/state. For example, a transitive verb "push" requires two participants (an agent who pushes and a patient who is pushed) as in "The man pushes the cart." As such information is encoded in the syntactic frame (i.e. clause), attention to the linguistic structure would be necessary to get the full meaning of the verb.

During the first few months of language production (until they acquire about 50 words), children typically produce one-word utterances, for example saying *mommy* when they need Mommy's help or *allgone* when they finish a meal. From this single-word period, children learn various types of word: Nouns, verbs and other relational words (e.g., particles), attributes, and social words. Intriguingly, children are remarkably good at honing in on the correct word meaning from the beginning. (Although at the beginning, children may overextend word meaning, they are in the right track to acquire the full meaning.) From 2 to 6 years children acquire at a fast pace, about nine or ten words a day (Clark 2009: 75). This ability is often labeled "fast mapping."

Given the challenges facing semantic acquisition as illustrated above, children's fast-mapping ability suggests that they have a sophisticated and efficient system for learning word meaning. Such a system should include not only children's cognitive ability (as acquisition of meaning must be based on some understanding about how entities/events can be categorized) but also their socio-pragmatic skills and their sensitivity to language-specific input as children acquire meaning through interaction with caregivers.

1.1 Issues in earlier periods

Over the past four decades, different theories and research programmes have explored the nature of semantic acquisition.

From the 70s through the mid-80s, predominant theories took a universalist approach, in line with the general trend of linguistic theories of that period (i.e. dominance of Chomskyan theory of universal grammar). In particular, in the 70s, in the semantic domain (as well as other domains such as phonology), a feature theory was widely explored. According to the Semantic Feature theory, a word meaning in our mental lexicon is made up of a set of conceptually primitive features that together represent the essence of word meaning (H. Clark 1973; E. Clark 1973). Note that a word (e.g. *dog*, *run*) labels a concept/category that denotes a class of individuals. Thus, the set of features would represent those that all members of the category share (e.g., [+four-legged, +domestic, +barks, etc.] for *dog*). In this framework, children learn word meaning by building up the relevant features for the category over time. That is, children would start with an incomplete list of features (e.g. only [+ four legs] for *dog* or only [+ round] for *ball*) and complete it as they learn more about the category. The Semantic Feature theory could explain overextension errors that young children sometimes make (e.g. referring to all four-legged animals as *dog* or all round things as *ball*).

In large part, early theories of semantic acquisition also followed the Piagetian tradition, namely the view that language acquisition follows and stems from general cognitive development. This view was also concerned about discovering universal and general cognitive underpinnings of semantic acquisition (e.g., Bates (1976); E. Clark (1973)).

According to this view, universal cognitive concepts are the major driving force for early semantic acquisition. In particular, during the first 18 months of life, infants develop concepts that are foundational for understanding how the world operates and is organized. For example, during the first year of life, infants develop concepts related to object permanence, causality, and space. These concepts are prerequisites for early semantic acquisition as children can map them directly onto words at an early stage. For example, in the spatial domain, infants develop conceptual categories of "containment" and "support" (Piaget and Inhelder 1967). Thus, when 18-month-olds acquire a word, say, *in* (in English) they can get its meaning directly from the already established concept of "containment." In this theory, then, the direction between cognition and language is unidirectional, from cognition to language development.

This theoretical framework was adopted by a number of important studies in the 70s, such as studies on acquisition of early words (Bates 1976), grammatical morphemes (Slobin 1973), and spatial terms (Johnston and Slobin 1979; Clark 1973). As semantic development should progress based on conceptual development, the general order in which words/morphemes appear in children's speech (within and across languages) in these studies was explained by the order in which relevant cognitive concepts developed. For example, infants develop spatial concepts (e.g. containment) before temporal concepts (e.g. past) (Piaget and Inhelder 1967). Reflecting this order, children produce or comprehend spatial words/morphemes (e.g. *in/on*) earlier than temporal words/morphemes (e.g. *today*, Verb-*ed*) (Brown 1973).

Johnston and Slobin's work (1979) is important in this regard: they examined the development of "locative" terms in four languages, English, Turkish, Serbo-Croatian, and Italian. The locative terms express various types of spatial relationship between two entities (Figure and Ground objects), e.g. containment (*in* in English), support (*on*), front (*in front of*), and back (*in back of*). Johnson and Slobin (1979) found that the order of acquisition was remarkably similar across languages: regardless of target language, children acquire terms for containment/support before those for front/back. Interestingly, however, the pace of acquisition depended on the language. For example, children acquiring Serbo-Croatian took more time to acquire their locative terms than Turkish children did. Johnston and Slobin explain that while the order of acquisition followed universal cognitive development, the timing of acquisition depends on the degree of formal complexity in a specific language. For example, the locative terms in Turkish are suffixed to the Ground noun with a clear morpheme boundary and carry only spatial meaning. But in Serbo-Croatian, locative terms not only express spatial meaning, but they also inflect in case (e.g. instrumental, genitive). Thus, children learning Serbo-Croatian need to acquire case inflections to produce correct locative terms. Johnston and Slobin (1979) conclude that while cognitive concepts are established around the same time for all children, linguistic complexity could delay acquisition of words.

In summary, early studies (early 1970s through mid-1980s) were concerned with finding universal cognitive bases for semantic acquisition. In this approach, findings of a particular language (e.g. English) were assumed to be the same in other languages. In crosslinguistic studies, similarities across languages were highlighted more than differences, as the goal was to find common cognitive prerequisites for semantic acquisition.

1.2 Current issues

In the last two decades or so (from the late 1980s to the present), a new set of questions emerged, as researchers recognized that semantic acquisition involved more than matching preverbal cognitive concepts with word forms and that it requires integration of a number of factors (cognitive, linguistic, and social) and learning mechanisms. Recent research addresses the two major issues discussed in the next sections.

1.2.1 Language-specific semantics and its interaction with cognitive development

Recent studies examining typologically very different languages discovered that words that appear similar in meaning are actually quite different, particularly in the domain of non-nominal words (Bowerman et al. 1995; Choi and Bowerman 1991). For example, Choi and Bowerman (1991) showed that languages divide up spatial relations (e.g. containment, support) significantly differently (see section 2.2 below). Moreover, children acquire language-specific meanings from very early on. These findings implicated that semantic learning involved more than a direct matching of preverbal cognitive concept onto word.

Search for the basis for early acquisition of language-specific semantics motivated developmental psycholinguists to examine preverbal concepts in infancy that may be relevant to early semantics. In fact, with new experimental methods (e.g. preferential looking paradigm, habituation paradigm, see section 2.2), research in recent years on preverbal infant cognition has given new insight into understanding language-specific semantic development in early years. For example, in the domain of spatial development recent findings suggest that preverbal infants are sensitive to a large number of spatial features, larger than what the target language requires. As they attend to language-specific input, they pick out (or combine) relevant ones from the large repertoire to learn the semantic system of the target language.

Recent studies suggest that to acquire word meaning, early cognitive development interacts with language-specific input. These findings lead to a number of questions: How early does language-specific input begin to shape semantic categories? Does language-specific semantics influence conceptual categories? If yes, then to what extent? Do the degrees to which language influences cognition differ across different semantic domains?

1.2.2 Word-learning mechanisms and constraints

Another major issue in semantic acquisition is discovering cognitive mechanisms and environmental factors that come into play during the acquisition process: exactly what cognitive assumptions and operating mechanisms do young children use to acquire word meaning? Given that there are many possible candidates for referent and meaning, *how* does the child know which ones are the right ones, and know them fast when there is a potentially infinite number of possible candidates (e.g. part of object, shape, material, event)? In terms of environmental factors: how much and how early do children use socio-pragmatic aspects in caregiver-child interactions (e.g. joint attention, intentionality)? Also, how much and how early do they attend to structural aspects of language (e.g. morphological cues for nouns and verbs)?

Semantics is a complex system that denotes many different types of concept (e.g. object, action/event, space, time). So far, in the field of developmental psycholinguistics, no single mechanism has been proposed to account for the acquisition of all types of meaning. Rather, researchers assume that semantic acquisition involves multiple resources from which children draw appropriate ones to acquire a given meaning. Depending on the type of meaning, the degrees to which those mechanisms and factors are used may differ. Thus, it is also important to discover how much the child relies on each factor and mechanism in a given task. For example, for referent identification, socio-pragmatic skills are important. Such skills include ability to follow the speaker's eye-gaze to understand the speaker's intention. Conversely, once the referent is identified, some cognitive mechanisms must be at play for children to hypothesize about which aspects/properties of the referent the word encodes.

While earlier studies focused on learning mechanisms for object names, more recent studies have explored mechanisms for verb learning. Action verbs are more abstract than object nouns. As mentioned earlier, actions do not have clear boundaries. In fact, a series of actions (each being labeled with a unique verb) may flow without pause. Consider, for example, a situation where a child watches her mother *wash a dish* and *dry it* without any pause in between. To acquire the verb "wash" in this context, the child needs to segment the "washing" part from the "drying" part. In addition, as verb meaning includes its argument structure (e.g. X (agent) washes Y (patient)), the child needs to attend to the syntactic frame when learning verb meaning.

In this chapter, I review recent findings on these issues in three semantic areas: In section 2.1, I review acquisition of object nouns and action verbs particularly focusing on recent proposals on word-learning mechanisms. Then, in section 2.2, I focus on acquisition of spatial words (verbs and spatial prepositions), reviewing the relationship between spatial cognition and language-specific spatial semantics. Finally, in section 2.3, I review acquisition of modality, particularly epistemic modality, a grammatical category that expresses abstract concepts.

2 Current contributions and research

2.1 Acquisition of object nouns and action verbs: learning mechanisms

Among the various types of words that children acquire during the single-word period (e.g. nouns, adjectives, particles, verbs and social words), nouns occupy a significant proportion: studies on lexical composition of the first 50 words in language acquisition show that in English, nouns occupy about 60% of the first 50 words (Choi and Gopnik 1995). Even in verb-prominent languages like Korean, nouns still occupy 44% (Choi and Gopnik 1995). Nouns that children learn early, for the most part, label concrete objects and entities, such as *dog*, *ball*, *water*, and *milk*, as well as some proper names, e.g. *mommy*, *daddy*.

Children also learn relational words and verbs from early on. However, growth of verbs varies across languages, i.e., it is slower and more protracted in some languages than others. As is well documented (Gopnik 1982), children learning English produce words such as *no*, *up/down* and *gone* from the one-word stage. With these words children express various types of relational notions: rejection/prohibition of propositions (*no*), spatial relations (*up/down*), success of intended action (*there!*) and presence or absence of object (*gone*). Interestingly, although smaller in number of types, in token frequency, children produce these words more frequently than nouns. Gopnik (1982; Gopnik and Choi 1990) interprets this to mean that children are cognitively interested in relational concepts from the one-word stage. She also suggests that early production of these words in turn enhances further development of those concepts, and thus cognitive and linguistic development interact in a dynamic way.

In Korean, many relational concepts are encoded by verbs. Based on spontaneous speech data of eight children, Choi and Gopnik (1995) report that a substantial proportion (31%) of the first 50 words in Korean acquisition are verbs. These data challenge the universal "Noun-bias" theory (Gentner 1982) that object names are cognitively easier to access than relational words are during the single-word period.

As mentioned earlier, children are excellent word learners: from the start they home in on the correct meanings. And even when they make overextension errors (e.g. saying *dog* to both cats and dogs, *run* to both running and jumping), they are in the right direction. Moreover, their "errors" may not mean that they misinterpret the meaning, but rather that they have difficulty in lexical retrieval or they may not know the right word (Bloom 2000). This remarkable ability leads us to assume that children possess a set of a priori assumptions and word-learning mechanisms that help them narrow down possibilities to just the right ones.

Over the last two and a half decades (since the mid-1980s), a number of proposals have been made. Below, I summarize a few major ones. (A full review of all the proposals would be beyond the scope of this chapter.) I should note, however, that we are far from understanding the full process of learning word meaning. Moreover, each of the proposed assumptions or mechanisms addresses different aspect of the process. At a given moment, several of these mechanisms must work together in the child's mind to support the learning of word meaning.

(a) Sensitivity to speaker's intention and non-verbal cues

There are two essential aspects about language that young children understand as they embark on semantic acquisition. First, language is a system of convention in which form-meaning relations have already been established by fluent speakers (Clark 1993; 2009). To learn meaning, then, children need to rely on caregivers' use of word forms and extract necessary information about meaning, taking into account the context. Second, speakers convey specific intentions when they use language. That is, speakers use language as a tool to communicate a particular message that they have in mind at the time of speech. Thus, a critical skill for children in learning a language is the ability to detect speakers' intended meaning.

In conversational interaction, the speaker provides a number of non-verbal cues to indicate his/her intention, such as providing eye-gaze and pointing to the referential object/event. Caregivers provide these cues prominently to young children to facilitate communication. In return, children pay attention to these cues (understanding that the cues are highly relevant for detecting intended meaning) and they connect the new label to the entity or activity that the caregiver is focusing on during her speech. Children have this ability from early on. In addition, 16 to 19-month-olds know that the speaker's eye-gaze is more important than their own to identify the reference of a novel word (Baldwin 1991).

Children are also sensitive to presence or absence of intentionality of the speaker. They can distinguish between intentional and accidental (i.e. erroneous) speech and learn a novel word only when they judge it to be intentional. Two-year-old children do *not* learn a label for what they think is an accidental action (e.g. when the speaker says "oh no," or "uh-oh", signalling an error) or what they think is a rejected object (Tomasello and Barton 1994).

Children can also detect caregivers' intended meaning using other means. For example, temporal contiguity is an important cue for verb meaning. When a caregiver labels an action, children consider the label to refer to an immediately anticipated/impending action (rather than an action that was already completed) (Tomasello 1995). For example, when the caregiver requests an action from the child (e.g. *drink milk*), the child considers the label to refer to the anticipated action.

(b) Principle of contrast

Children assume that "different words express different meanings" (Clark 1990). This narrows down possible meanings of a novel word. For example, in a classic study, Carey and Bartlett (1978) introduced a novel word "chromium" to 4- and 5-year-olds, juxtaposing it with a color word they already knew e.g. "red." Later, when the children were asked to pick out the object with "chromium" color, between a red object and one for which they did not have a name yet (e.g. an object with olive-like color), they chose the latter.

Note, however, that an entity can have several names. For example, a "dog" can also been called an "animal" or a "puppy" depending on which aspect of the entity the speaker wants to focus on. "Principle of contrast" still explains this phenomenon as it simply states that "different words express different meanings." Thus, even when a novel word clearly refers to an entity for which children already have a label, children accept the novel word and consider it to encode a different aspect of the entity. For example, when the caregiver says "that's an animal" pointing to a dog, children (who already possess the word "dog" in their mental lexicon) would consider it to refer to another aspect of the dog and make some corresponding hypothesis.

(c) Boundary detection for object and action: "whole object" constraint and segmentation of action sequences

In identifying the referent of a noun or a verb, children need to know the boundary of an entity or an action. For an object label, children consider the whole object to be the unit of reference. Saliency of the "whole object" is probably related to a principle of object perception in infancy. Five-month-olds consider an object to be a single entity when it moves as a unit (Spelke 1990). (Note that, at a later stage, children need to abandon this assumption since parts of an object/entity (e.g. *tail*) also have labels.)

As noted earlier, boundaries of events/actions are not obvious. Nevertheless, from 10 to 11 months of age, infants have the ability to segment a series of actions into discrete units that relate to the actor's goals/intentions (Baldwin et al. 2001; Saylor et al. 2007). Baldwin et al. (2001) familiarized infants with a video sequence in which a person carried out a series of activities smoothly without pause. For example, a person moved toward an ice-cream container on the kitchen counter, took the container, turned toward the freezer, and opened the freezer door. Infants watched the video multiple times during the familiarization phase. In the *test* phase, they saw the same action sequence, but this time the flow of action was interrupted by still-frame pauses. In one test video, a pause was inserted at the completion/initiation of each intended act. In the second test video, a pause was inserted in the middle of an intentional act (e.g. in the middle of the opening action). Of the two test videos, infants looked longer at the second one in which action units were disrupted. The results revealed infants' ability to parse continuous action into "intention-relevant" units (Baldwin et al. 2001: 710). Notice that in the above example, each intentional act is expressed by a unique verb (e.g. *move*, *take*, *turn*). With the ability to identify units of action, young children can associate a novel verb with the correct action boundaries.

(d) Non-perceptual essence of semantic category

One major limitation of the early Semantic Feature Theory is that it only addresses perceptual features for possible semantic content for a category (e.g. [+ four-legged] for *dog*, [+round] for *ball*). But many semantic categories are abstract, e.g. *justice*. Even what we call concrete words may form categories based on some abstract, non-visual properties (Murphy and Medin 1985). For example, a skunk is an animal that has a specific visual feature, i.e. white horizontal stripes. But if a skunk is merely painted like a raccoon, does the skunk then become a raccoon? Most adults would answer "no," because people believe the essence of a natural category lies in non-perceptual biological features. Children gradually learn about abstract essences of categories through education and experience. However, the extent to which non-perceptual components determine the category membership may differ from one semantic domain (e.g. natural kinds) to another (e.g. artifacts) (cf. Medin et al. 2000).

(e) Morphological and syntactic bootstrapping for word meaning

Children pay attention to morphology and syntax, using them as bootstrapping tools for semantic acquisition. For example, morphology can play an important role in distinguishing across nouns, adjectives and verbs. In English, a noun is often preceded by a determiner (e.g. *a*, *the*, *some*) while a verb is not. Many adjectives have an *-y*, *-ful* or *-ish* ending. Children narrow down possible reference of a novel word based on these morphological cues (e.g. Soja et al. (1991); Waxman (1990)).

As mentioned in section 1.2.2, verb meaning is in part realized in syntax. Naigles (1990) showed that 22-month-olds attend to the syntactic frame of a novel verb (i.e. syntactic bootstrapping) to understand whether it has causative meaning. When they hear the verb in a transitive syntactic frame (i.e. SVO), children assign a causative meaning to it. But they do not do so when they hear the verb in an intransitive syntactic frame. Naigles' study, together with other more recent studies on children's sensitivity to syntax (e.g. Arunachalam and Waxman 2012), suggests that 2-year-olds consider syntax to be an important source for acquiring verb meaning. In fact, Nappa et al. (2009) have recently reported that 3- to 5-year-olds pay attention to syntax (clauses introduced with full NPs) more so than speaker's eye-gaze when it comes to learning verb meaning. This suggests that children understand the abstract nature of verbs and look for cues in the language itself more than non-linguistic context.

2.2 Acquisition of spatial semantics

From the single-word stage, children talk about going *up* and *down*, and putting something *in* a container or *on* a surface. While in English these spatial relations are expressed by spatial prepositions, in Korean they are expressed by verbs such as *kkita* ("fit tightly"), *nehta* ("put loosely in container"), and *nohta* ("put loosely on surface").

Spatial words (regardless of the morphological form, e.g. particles, verbs) occupy a good portion of early relational words (Choi and Bowerman 1991; Choi and Gopnik 1995). English learners produce spatial prepositions, *in* and *on*, and Korean children produce spatial verbs *kkita*, *nehta*, and *nohta*. Thus, children are cognitively ready to learn spatial semantics from early on. There is good reason to assume so: space is a fundamental and universal aspect of human experience and infants begin to explore it virtually from the beginning of their life.

For example, 2.5-month-old infants can already recognize that a container must have an opening for an object to go in (i.e. one cannot put an object in a "container" that has no opening) and that the object contained moves with the container (Hespos and Baillargeon 2001). At 6 months, infants develop a conceptual category of containment, generalizing the relation to novel objects and novel containers (Casasola et al. 2003). As for the support relation (e.g. cup *on* table), 4-month-olds can also distinguish between situations in which an object will fall or be supported (Needham and Baillargeon 1993). And 8-month-olds can calculate how much support is needed for an object to be adequately supported by another (Baillargeon and Hanko-Summers 1990).

As mentioned in section 1.1, spatial notions were traditionally considered to be a domain where one could demonstrate pre-established cognitive concepts determining the order of acquisition of spatial words. In this framework, early-acquired semantic notions are universal across languages, and language-specific meanings are acquired gradually later on.

Spatial meanings are significantly different across languages, however. Choi and Bowerman (1991) demonstrated this comparing English and Korean. First, the two languages encode spatial relations in differential morphological classes (i.e. prepositions in English and verbs in Korean). Second, they also differ significantly in the way they semantically categorize spatial relations. The spatial preposition *in* in English and the spatial verb *kkita* are cases in point, as the two categories cross-cut each other. While *in* in English refers to "containment" regardless of whether it involves tight fit (e.g. putting a jigsaw puzzle piece tightly *in* its slot) or loose fit (e.g. putting an apple *in* a bowl), *kkita* in Korean refers to "tight fit" regardless of whether it involves containment (e.g. *kkita* is used for "putting a jigsaw puzzle piece tightly in its slot") or support (e.g. *kkita* is also used for "putting a ring tightly on the finger"). The two terms also differ in their syntactic function. In English, *in* is a particle that can be used for both spontaneous (intransitive) and caused (transitive) motions (e.g. *go in(to)* the room; *put* a piece *in* its slot), but in Korean *kkita* is used only for caused motion.

When and how do children acquire language-specific meanings of spatial words? The "cognitive prerequisite" view would predict that regardless of the target language, children would initially apply the same "pre-established" concepts to spatial words, and then later acquire the language-specific meaning. Contrary to this assumption, Choi and Bowerman (1991) found that English- and Korean-learning children used spatial terms in language-specific ways from the beginning, 14–19 months of age. Their database was longitudinal recordings or diary notes of children's spontaneous speech from 14 to 24 months. English learners used *in* to express a containment relation regardless of whether it involved tight or loose fit (e.g. apple *in* bowl, puzzle piece *in* slot) but did not use *in* for a support relation (e.g. cup *on* table; Lego piece *on* another). In contrast, Korean children used *kkita* to express tight fit regardless of containment or support but not for the loose-fit relation. And while English learners used *in* in both intransitive and transitive constructions (*go in*; *put in*), Korean children used *kkita* only in transitive constructions.

To confirm early acquisition of language-specific semantics, Choi et al. (1999) conducted an experiment testing comprehension of *in* in English learners and *kkita* in Korean learners (between 14 and 24 months) using a "Preferential Looking" method: As the child hears the target word (*in* or *kkita*), he/she sees two videos side by side on the screen. The child's eye-gaze to each video is measured with the assumption that the child will look longer at the video that matches the target word meaning. The results showed that from at least 17 months, children comprehend spatial terms in a language-specific way.

To understand the possible mechanisms that would allow such early acquisition of language-specific semantics, McDonough et al. (2003) conducted *non-verbal* experiments with pre-verbal infants (aged 9–14 months) being exposed to English or to Korean. In one condition, infants first saw multiple pairs of tight containment events with a variety of objects (e.g. putting a book tightly into its matching cover, putting a puzzle piece tightly into its slot) one after another until they were familiarized with the relation. (In the other condition, infants were familiarized with a variety of events that depicted loose containment, e.g. putting an apple in a bowl, putting a pencil loosely in a cup. Each infant was assigned to one of the two conditions.) Then, during test trials infants saw both a tight containment event and a loose containment event side by side on the screen. If infants conceptually distinguish between tight and loose containment relations, their looking pattern to the two relations (one would be the familiar relation whereas the other would be a novel relation) would be significantly different. Note that in English the two types of containment are *not* distinguished in the spatial prepositional system. The result was interesting: preverbal infants distinguished the two relations by consistently looking longer at the familiar relation than the novel relation. That is, infants in *both* language groups distinguished tight containment from loose containment, and vice versa, demonstrating that they could attend to tightness or looseness of containment relation in a categorical manner.

More recent studies showed that detection of the tight- or loose-fit feature can start as early as five months. Hespos and her colleagues (Hespos and Piccin 2009; Hespos and Spelke 2004), using the "Habituation" paradigm," showed that 5-month-olds can distinguish the two types of containment relation, as well as the tight covering and loose covering relation. (The "Habituation" paradigm is similar to the "Preferential Looking" paradigm except that in the "Habituation" paradigm, infants are shown the same relation repeatedly until they are no longer interested (i.e. look away out of boredom), before test trials begin.) Infants also consider different types of tight-fit relation as distinct categories: They consider tight attachment (e.g. putting a Lego piece tightly on another) to be distinct from tight encirclement (e.g. putting a ring tightly onto pole) (Choi and Casasola 2005).

These findings suggest that infants start with an ability to make fine distinctions, finer than their target language may require. During the preverbal period infants seem to develop sensitivity to a large repertoire of spatial features. Such sensitivity would essentially allow them to learn the spatial semantic categories of any language. As infants attend to language-specific input, they can pick out the relevant spatial features from their large repertoire. If this is the case, then linguistic input guides semantic acquisition from its onset. In fact, recent studies have shown evidence that linguistic input is critical for the development of certain semantic categories. Casasola (2005; Casasola and Bhagwat 2007) demonstrated that it is language that unites different types of support into a single semantic category of *on*.

Eighteen-month-olds could form a category of support that includes loose horizontal support (e.g. put a cup *on* a table), attachment (e.g. put a Lego piece *on* another), and encirclement (e.g. put a ring *on* a pole) when they heard the word "on" during the habituation phase (i.e. training phase), but they could not form the category when they viewed them in silence (i.e. no word during the training phase). Similarly, 18-month-olds (learning English as a first language) could form an abstract category of tight-fit relation with linguistic training (i.e. hearing a novel word during the habituation of all types of "tight fit") but could *not* do so just by viewing tight-fit events in silence. The study suggests that development of a tight-fit category needs linguistic guidance as well.

If language guides semantic categorization from an early age, does it in turn influence conceptual (i.e., non-linguistic) categories of space? There is evidence that over time, language-specific semantics does affect, at least partially, our conceptual categorization. Recall that preverbal infants (regardless of language environment) can distinguish between tight and loose containment (McDonough et al. 2003). A follow-up study by Choi (2006) with older children found that from 29 months of age, English learners, overall, significantly lost their ability to distinguish between tight and loose containment. (But Korean learners continued to distinguish between the two types.) Intriguingly, however, a detailed analysis of the data revealed an asymmetry of perceptual/conceptual sensitivity for tightness vs. looseness in English learners. English learners were actually still quite good at detecting the tight-fit feature in a tight containment event. The difficulty they had was detecting the loose-fit feature when they saw a loose containment event. The results suggest then that language-specific semantics influence non-verbal spatial categorization only partially and that certain features (e.g. tight-fit feature of containment) continue to be salient at a perceptual/conceptual level. Choi and Hattrup (2012) recently confirmed this partial influence of language-specific semantics on spatial cognition in adult speakers as well.

2.3 Acquisition of modal meanings

So far, I have discussed acquisition of meaning that relates to objects and spatial actions. In this section, I discuss how young children acquire an abstract domain of semantics, that of modality, particularly focusing on epistemic modality and evidentials. Modality can be divided into two types, deontic and epistemic (see Chapter 21). Deontic modality expresses some condition on the agent with regard to the main predicate. The "conditions" include ability, obligation, and permission (e.g. *Mary can/must do her homework.*). Deontic modality also includes the agent's desire and intention toward an action (e.g. *Mary wants to study linguistics*). In contrast, epistemic modality expresses degree of certainty on the part of the speaker about the truth of proposition. The speaker may estimate that the event or state expressed in the main proposition is possible, probable, or certain (see example (1)). This category may include "evidentials," expressions that mark the particular type of source of information. This is because, by specifying whether the information comes from hearsay or direct evidence, the speaker conveys varying degrees of certainty of the proposition.

(1)   *Mary may be home by now.* (= It is possible that Mary is home at this time.)

Languages differ in selecting a morphological class that systematically expresses modality (e.g. auxiliary verb, verbal suffix). They also differ in the kinds of modal meaning expressed in the grammar. In English, both deontic and epistemic modality are grammaticized in modal auxiliary verbs (e.g. *can*, *will*, *must*, *should*).

Korean uses two types of morphological class to express modality: auxiliary verbs and sentence-ending (SE) suffixes/particles. While deontic modality is expressed by an auxiliary verb preceded by a specific connective (example (2) below), epistemic modality is grammaticized either in auxiliary verbs or in SE suffixes. SE suffixes constitute an obligatory class, i.e., a sentence must end with a SE suffix. As shown in example (3), SE suffixes can specify whether the information in the propositions is old, new to the speaker, shared between speaker and listener, or indirectly obtained (i.e. hearsay) (Choi 1991, 1995). These forms occur only in informal spoken interaction, indicating that they have rich discourse-pragmatic meaning. At the same time, these modal meanings are quite abstract, as they specify the differential status of information in the speaker's mind.

(2) *Mary-nun swukcey-lul hae-ya tway(-e)*.
Mary-TOP homework-OBJ do-**CONN BECOME**(-SE)
"Mary must do homework."
(Note: To express a given modal meaning, a specific auxiliary verb must be preceded by a specific connective. Thus, in (2), the connective *–ya* and the auxiliary verb *–tway* together express "obligation.")

(3) *Mary-ka cikum cip-ey iss-e/-ta/-ci/-tay*.
Mary-SUBJ now home-LOC be.located-**SE (old/new/shared (=certain)/hearsay)**
"Mary is home now (old/new/shared (certain) knowledge/hearsay)."

A number of verb-final languages, e.g. Japanese and Turkish, also express epistemic modality and evidentials with SE suffixes, expressing interactionally rich meanings like those in Korean. Impressively, children start acquiring these from well before 2;0. Korean children acquire the SE epistemic modals, *-ta*, *-e*, *-ci*, and *-tay*, (see (3) above) in that order, between 1;8 and 2;6 (even before they start acquiring deontic modals). Children learning Japanese and Turkish also acquire SE forms during this age period, starting as early as 1;6 (Clancy (1985) for Japanese; Aksu-Koç and Slobin (1986) for Turkish). This is notably earlier compared to children learning languages such as English. English learners acquire epistemic modals after age 2;6 and after they have acquired some deontic modals (e.g. ability/inability) (Shatz and Wilcox 1991).

SE forms in Korean, Japanese, and Turkish have the following features in common: (1) SE forms are perceptually salient as they are mono-syllabic and occur in sentence-final position. The forms may also be highlighted in speech. In fact, Lee and Davis (2001) report that Korean mothers exaggerate high pitch for SE suffixes in their speech to 1-year-olds. (2) SE forms are highly frequent in the input, as they belong to an obligatory grammatical class. (3) SE forms have rich discourse-interactional functions. They indicate how much speaker vs. listener knows about an event or state of affairs. Using SE suffixes appropriately, the caregiver and child can co-construct coherent information and build up shared knowledge, creating an affective bond between them (Choi 1995). These factors undoubtedly enhance acquisition of SE forms and their meanings.

Within the commonality across the three languages, however, the meanings of SE forms are remarkably fine-tuned and language-specific. Acquisition data show that children acquire language-specific meanings from the onset of their acquisition of these SE forms. Let's compare Korean and Turkish. In Turkish, two types of verbal suffixes are acquired early, *-dI* and *-mIş*. These two forms carry tense information, namely past tense, as well as evidential meaning (Aksu-Koç and Slobin 1986): *-dI* expresses past events that the speaker has directly witnessed whereas *-mIş* expresses non-witnessed past events (inferred from the present) that are new to the speaker. Turkish children first acquire *-dI* to express information that they have assimilated through direct experience. They then acquire *-mIş* to refer to new information (that the child has not realized before) and use it in storytelling and pretend plays.

The *-dI* and *-mIş* distinction can be likened to the *-ta* and *-e* distinction in Korean. However, their functions also differ in significant ways: whereas in Korean the two forms express purely modal meanings, in Turkish modal markers are fused with tense/aspectual information. The two systems also differ in the kinds of epistemic/evidential meanings each form expresses. For example, while both *-dI* and *-ta* express direct experience, *-dI* refers to information that is assimilated into the speaker's mind whereas *-ta* does not. *-Ta* actually expresses a newly perceived event/state.

Choi and Aksu-Koç (1999) compared acquisition of SE verbal suffixes in Korean- and Turkish-learning children between 1;6 and 3;0. What is similar between the two languages is the kinds of notions the two groups of children encode with modal markers and the general developmental trajectory of modal meanings. In both Korean and Turkish, direct experience is expressed early (*-dI* in Turkish and *-ta* in Korean). Both groups also distinguish between new and old information from early on. At around 2;6, both groups begin to express hearsay (*-mIs* in Turkish and *-tay* in Korean). Within this common developmental pattern, however, children in each language are remarkably sensitive to the language-specific meanings of the modal forms. In congruence with the adult grammar, Turkish children use *-dI* for past events but Korean children use *-ta* for both past and present events. Turkish children use *-mIs* in reference to past processes that were inferred from the present state (i.e. non-witnessed) and to signal novelty of information. In contrast, Korean children use *-ta* for novelty of information but not for inferential function.

Looking at Korean and Turkish (as well as Japanese) data, it is remarkable that children acquire language-specific modal meanings from the onset. How do we explain this? On the one hand, children must be cognitively sensitive, at some level, to notions that relate to new/old, shared/non-shared, directly/indirectly obtained knowledge. At the same time, children must also attend to caregivers' speech and extract appropriate meaning components of a given modal form taking into account discourse-pragmatic aspects of the context. Such interaction between cognitive readiness and linguistic input seems similar to the one I suggested for acquisition of spatial terms. That is, during the preverbal stage, infants develop sensitivity to the differential information status of speaker and hearer and to different types of information source. (A recent study (Song and Baillargeon 2008) suggests that at 15 months of age, infants may understand that another person may not know what they know.) As children get linguistic input, they can then pick out (or combine) relevant features to acquire the modal meanings of the target language.

What is the precise relationship between language and cognition in the domain of modality? Studies have reported influence in both directions. On the one hand, there is evidence that cognitive abilities are foundational to particular linguistic abilities. Gonsalves and Falmagne (1999) conducted both linguistic and nonlinguistic tests relevant to deontic and epistemic modality to children aged between 2;6 and 5;0. Concerning epistemic modality, only those children who passed the nonlinguistic tests could also pass language comprehension tests. The result suggests that cognitive ability is foundational to understanding epistemic modality.

(For deontic modality, however, there was no particular direction that was significant.) The order of acquisition of epistemic modal verbs in English and French also suggests that it is based on general cognitive development: children express "certainty" before they express probability/possibility (Bassano 1996; Moore et al. 1990). Other studies have reported children's linguistic ability to be precursor to development of the knowledge structure called "theory of mind"; namely, the ability to differentiate between one's own beliefs and others'. For example, the speaker (but *not* the hearer) may know that an object is actually a candle, although it looks like an apple. In Farrar and Maag (2002), general language development (development of vocabulary, syntax, verbal memory) predicted later performance on "theory of mind" tests. In de Villiers and Pyers (1997), acquisition of sentential complements (*I think/ know that . . .*), which provide the representational structure, is a critical prerequisite for development of false belief reasoning. Clearly, more research is needed to understand the relationship between linguistic development of modality and cognition.

3 Conclusion and future directions

Acquisition of semantics in young children is a complex process involving cognitive, linguistic, and socio-pragmatic factors. During the last two decades, developmental psycholinguists have proposed a number of learning mechanisms to explain the "fast-mapping" ability in first language acquisition. These mechanisms have revealed sophistication in children's detection of multiple types of cue at all levels of language that would enhance their semantic acquisition. However, they explain only the early stages of the acquisition process and do so only partially. More research is needed to identify the processes at later stages and to understand how those mechanisms interact with one another in a given semantic domain.

Recent studies have also demonstrated that children acquire language-specific semantics (particularly in the domain of relational words) from early on and that linguistic input and children's cognitive ability interact in a dynamic way from the beginning of semantic acquisition. Studies in spatial development have further shown that during the preverbal period infants build up sensitivity to a large number of spatial features, which would essentially allow them to learn the spatial semantic categorizations of any language. Further research should explore whether such is also the case in other semantic domains.

Early interaction between linguistic input and cognitive development has raised questions about the extent to which one influences the other. While early theories focused predominantly on the influence of cognition on language, recent studies have shown that semantic acquisition in early years can influence nonlinguistic cognitive categorization. Studies in different domains of semantics should pursue this area of research to identify the precise nature of the interaction between semantic and cognitive development.

Further reading

Bloom, P. 2000. *How Children Learn the Meanings of Words (Learning, Development, and Conceptual Change)*. Cambridge, MA: MIT Press. Bloom lays out and explains with examples the details of the complex mechanisms (linguistic, cognitive, and socio-pragmatic) by which children learn concepts underlying concrete and abstract words.

Choi, S. 2006. Acquisition of modality. In W. Frawley (ed.). *Modality*. Amsterdam: Mouton de Gruyter. The chapter reviews recent research on development of deontic and epistemic modality as well as of theory of mind in children learning different languages.

Clark, E. 2009. *First Language Acquisition*. 2nd (ed.) Cambridge: Cambridge University Press. Clark traces developmental stages of children's language acquisition in all aspects of grammar phonology, morphology, syntax, pragmatics, and discourse, focusing on how children use language as they learn them and integrating actual data with current relevant theories and debates on language acquisition.

Gentner, D. and S. Goldin-Meadow 2003. *Language in Mind: Mapping the Nature of Change in Spatial Cognitive Development.* Oxford: Oxford University Press. The chapters in this edited book present current research studies on possible influence of language-specific semantics on cognition in children and adults in a variety of domains, e.g. space, motion, number, gender, theory of mind, object, and actions.

Medin, D., B. Lynch and K. Solomon 2000. Are there kinds of concepts? *Annual Review of Psychology* 51: 121–147. This article proposes distinguishing object and non-object concepts based on three criteria – structure, process, and content – and reviews possible and plausible categories of events, objects, and properties in support of such criteria.

References

Aksu-Koç, A. and D. I. Slobin 1986. A psychological account of the development and use of Evidential in Turkish. In: W. Chafe and J. Nichols (eds) *Evidentiality: The Linguistic Coding of Epistemology.* Norwood, NJ: Ablex Publishing, 159–167.

Arunachalam, S. and S. Waxman 2012. Meaning from syntax. *Cognition* 114: 442–446.

Baillargeon, R. and S. Hanko-Summers 1990. Is the top object adequately supported by the bottom object? Young infants' understanding of support relations. *Cognitive Development* 5: 29–53.

Baldwin, D. 1991. Infants' contribution to the achievement of joint reference. *Child Development* 65: 875–890.

Baldwin, D. A., J. A. Baird, M. M. Saylor and M. A. Clark 2001. Infants parse dynamic action. *Child Development* 72: 708–717.

Bassano, D. 1996. Functional and formal constraints on the emergence of epistemic modality: a longitudinal study on French. *First Language* 16: 77–113.

Bates, E. 1976. *Language and Context: Acquisition of Pragmatics.* New York: Academic Press.

Bloom, P. 2000. *How Children Learn the Meanings of Words.* Cambridge, MA: MIT Press.

Bowerman, M., L. de Leon and S. Choi 1995. Verbs, particles and spatial semantics: learning to talk about spatial actions in typologically different languages. In: E. Clark (ed.) *The Proceedings of the 27th Annual Child Language Research Forum.* Stanford, CA: CSLI, 101–110.

Brown, R. 1973. *A First Language: The Early Stages.* Cambridge, MA: Harvard University Press.

Carey, S. and E. Bartlett 1978. Acquiring a single new word. *Papers and Reports on Child Language Development* [Stanford University] 15: 17–29.

Casasola, M. 2005. Can language do the driving? The effect of linguistic input on infants' categorization of support spatial relations. *Developmental Psychology* 41: 183–192.

Casasola, M. and Bhagwat, J. 2007. Do novel words facilitate 18-month-olds' spatial categorisation? *Child Development* 78: 1818–1829.

Casasola, M., L. B. Cohen and E. Chiarello 2003. Six-month-old infants' categorization of containment spatial relations. *Child Development* 74: 1–15.

Choi, S. 1991. Early acquisition of epistemic meanings in Korean: a study of sentence-ending suffixes in the spontaneous speech of three children. *First Language* 11: 93–119.

Choi, S. 1995. The development of epistemic sentence-ending modal forms and functions in Korean children. In: J. Bybee and S. Fleischman (eds) *Modality in Grammar and Discourse.* Amsterdam: John Benjamins, 165–204.

Choi, S. 2006. Influence of language-specific input on spatial cognition: categories of containment. *First Language* 26: 207–232.

Choi, S. and B. Aksu-Koç 1999. Development of modality in Korean and Turkish: a crosslinguistic comparison. In: E. Erguvanli-Taylan, A. Ozsoy and A. Kuntay (eds) *Selected Papers from the VIIth International Congress for the Study of Child Language.* Istanbul: Bogaziçi University Press.

Choi, S. and M. Bowerman 1991. Learning to express motion events in English and Korean: the influence of language-specific lexicalization patterns. *Cognition* 41: 83–121.

Choi, S. and M. Casasola 2005. Preverbal categorization of support relations. *Society for Research in Child Development* Atlanta, Georgia, USA, 7–10 April 2005.

Choi, S. and A. Gopnik 1995. Early acquisition of verbs in Korean: a crosslinguistic study. *Journal of Child Language* 22: 497–530.

Choi, S. and K. Hattrup 2012. Relative contribution of cognition/perception and language on spatial categorization. *Cognitive Science* 36: 102–129.

Choi, S. et al. 1999. Early sensitivity to language-specific spatial terms in English and Korean. *Cognitive Development* 14: 241–268.

Clancy, P. 1985. The acquisition of Japanese. In: Slobin, D.I. (ed.). *Crosslinguistic Study of Language Acquisition*, Vol. 1. Hillsdale, NJ: Lawrence Erlbaum Associates, 135–144.

Clark, E. V. 1973. What's in a word? On the child's acquisition of semantics in his first language. In: T. E. Moore (ed.) *Cognitive Development and the Acquisition of Language*. New York: Academic Press, 65–110.

Clark, E. V. 1990. The pragmatics of contrast. *Journal of Child Language* 17: 417–431.

Clark, E. V. 1993. *The Lexicon in Acquisition*. Cambridge: Cambridge University Press.

Clark, E. V. 2009. *First Language Acquisition*. 2nd ed. Cambridge: Cambridge University Press.

Clark, H. 1973. Space, time, semantics, and the child. In: Moore, T. E. (ed.) *Cognitive Development and the Acquisition of Language*. New York: Academic Press.

De Villiers, J. and J. Pyers 1997 Complementing cognition: the relationship between language and theory of mind. *Boston University Conference on Language Development* 21: 136–147.

Farrar, J. and L. Maag 2002. Early language development and the emergence of a theory of mind. *First Language* 22: 197–213.

Gentner, D. 1982. Why nouns are learned before verbs: linguistic relativity versus natural partitioning. In S. A. Kuczaj (ed.) *Language Development Vol. 2: Language, Thought and Culture*. Hillsdale, NJ: Erlbaum, 301–334.

Gonsalves, J. and R. J. Falmagne 1999. Cognitive prerequisites for modal verb acquisition. *Boston University Conference on Language Development* 23: 204–215.

Gopnik, A. 1982. Words and plans: early language and the development of intelligent action. *Journal of Child Language* 9: 303–318.

Gopnik, A. and S. Choi 1990. Does cognitive development lead to linguistic development? A crosslinguistic study. *First Language* 10: 199–215.

Hespos, S. and R. Baillargeon 2001. Reasoning about containment events in very young infants. *Cognition* 78: 207–245.

Hespos, S. and T. Piccin 2009. To generalize or not to generalize: spatial categories are influenced by physical attributes and language. *Developmental Science* 12: 88–95.

Hespos, S. and E. Spelke 2004. Conceptual precursors to language. *Nature* 430: 453–456.

Johnston, J. and D. I. Slobin 1979. The development of locative expressions in English, Italian, Serbo-Croatian and Turkish. *Journal of Child Language* 6: 529–545.

Lee, S. and B. Davis 2001. Salience of nouns and verbs in Korean: infant-directed speech. *Proceedings of the 25th Annual Boston University Conference on Language Development*: 436–445.

McDonough, L., S. Choi and J. Mandler 2003. Understanding spatial relations: flexible infants, lexical adults. *Cognitive Psychology*: 229–259.

Medin, D., B. Lynch and K. Solomon 2000. Are there kinds of concepts? *Annual Review of Psychology* 51: 121–147.

Moore, C., K. Pure and D. Furrow 1990. Children's understanding of the modal expression of speaker certainty and uncertainty and its relation to the development of a representational theory of mind. *Child Development* 61: 722–730.

Murphy, G. and D. Medin 1985. The role of theories in conceptual coherence. *Psychological Review* 92: 289–316.

Naigles, L. 1990. Children use syntax to learn verb meanings. *Journal of Child Language* 17: 357–374.

Nappa, R. et al. 2009. Use of speaker's gaze and syntax in verb learning. *Language Learning and Development* 5: 203–234.

Needham, A. and R. Baillargeon 1993. Intuitions about support in 4.5-month-old infants. *Cognition* 47: 121–148.

Piaget, J. and B. Inhelder 1967. *The Child's Conception of Space*. New York: Norton.

Saylor, M. et al. 2007. Infants' on-line segmentation of dynamic human action. *Journal of Cognition and Development* 8: 113–128.

Shatz, M. and S. Wilcox 1991. Constraints on the acquisition of English modals. In S. Gelman and J. Byrnes (eds) *Perspectives on Language and Thought: Interrelations in Development*. Cambridge, MA: Cambridge University Press, 319–353.

Slobin, D. I. 1973. Cognitive prerequisites for the development of grammar. In C.A. Ferguson and D. I. Slobin (eds) *Studies of Child Language Development*. New York: Holt, Rinehart & Winston, 175–208.

Soja, N. N., S. Carey and E. Spelke 1991. Ontological categories guide young children's inductions of word meaning: object terms and substance terms. *Cognition* 38: 179–211.

Song, H. and R. Baillargeon 2008. Infants' reasoning about others' false perceptions. *Developmental Psychology* 44: 1789–1795.

Spelke, E. 1990. Principles of object perception. *Cognitive Science* 14: 29–56.

Tomasello, M. 1995. Pragmatic contexts for early verb learning. In M. Tomasello and W. Merriman (eds) *Beyond Names for Things: Young Children's Acquisition of Verbs*. Hillsdale, NJ: Lawrence Erlbaum, 115–146.

Tomasello, M. and M. Barton 1994. Learning words in non-ostensive contexts. *Developmental Psychology* 30: 639–650.

Waxman, S. 1990. Linguistic biases and the establishment of conceptual hierarchies: evidence from preschool children. *Cognitive Development* 5: 123–150.

Related topics

Chapter 9, Linguistic relativity; Chapter 12, Lexical decomposition; Chapter 21, Modality.

27
Expressives

Ad Foolen

1 The expressive function of language

After having read the other chapters in this volume, the reader might exclaim: How fine an instrument language is to talk about the world! Indeed it is. No wonder that this "world-relatedness" is widely accepted as a core function of language (Bühler 1934).

Twentieth-century linguistic research has shown that language is an even finer instrument, in that it provides means to indicate *why* something is said (illocutionary function), how it relates to the assumed background knowledge of the hearer (information structure), what the source of the conveyed information is (evidentiality), and how certain the speaker is about a specific claim (modality). Linguistic means for these functions "customize" the talking about the world to the actual speech situation.

There is, however, another dimension of communication that is still missing in the picture just sketched. Human beings often have feelings about what they say, about what others say, or about what happens in the here-and-now environment. These feelings are typically expressed in non-verbal ways (facial expression, gesture, posture, etc.), but, as it turns out, language itself also provides means for expressing such feelings. Language not only has a referential, but also an expressive function. In recent literature, the verbal means that fulfill this latter function are called expressives. We will use this term here too.

As we will see in section 2, the expression of feelings has not been at the centre of attention of twentieth-century linguistics. Linguists have developed models which are primarily meant for the informative, referential function of language, with the natural consequence that other aspects, like expressivity, do not naturally fit in. However, the recent interest in expressives has shown that the expressive component of language takes a bigger place in the language system than these earlier models suggested. In this sense, the study of expressives is relevant for, and will have an impact upon general linguistic theorizing.

Like many other linguistic topics, the expressive function of language involves all kinds of terminological problems. First, in the psychological literature on emotions, feelings are sometimes distinguished from emotions, and attitude, stance, and mood are distinguished as well. In the context of the present chapter, we will not go into these finer distinctions and their relevance for a linguistic theory of expressives. When we talk here about feelings or emotions, attitudes etc. are meant as well.

Second, the referential and expressive function are labeled differently, often related to specific theoretical frameworks. The referential function is also known as the propositional, denotational, informational, conceptual, descriptive, truth-conditional, denotative, objective, and *mode pur* function of language. For the expressive function, labels like affective, emotive, connotative, involved, subjective, and *mode vécu* are used. Again, we will not be able to go into the question of how far these labels imply different theoretical views.

Third, some of the terms are used in different contexts as well. For example, in formal logic, the term connotation is sometimes used as equivalent to intension, the definition of a concept, in contrast to extension, the referents of the concept. And in research on sound symbolism, the term "expressives" is sometimes used as an equivalent for ideophones and mimetics (see Dingemanse (2012)).

Misunderstandings can not only arise through such terminological matters; different perspectives can also cause confusion. It is important to realize from the beginning that emotions are relevant for language and linguistics in two ways. The first one, which will be the focus of this chapter, regards the question of how emotions are expressed in language, or the other way around, which linguistic elements have expressive meaning. The second way in which emotions are relevant for linguistics has to do with the way emotions are conceptualized in languages. This is not the main concern of this chapter, so we will restrict ourselves here to a few remarks on this topic of research. In the perspective of conceptualization of emotions in grammar and lexicon, emotions are not different in principle from colors, body parts, time, space, etc. They are all specific fields of experience, conceptualized in partly universal, partly language-specific ways. Linguistic research on the conceptualization of emotions in different languages takes place, or should take place, in interdisciplinary cooperation with psychological research on emotions. This research raises questions like the following: Which emotions should be distinguished; do "basic emotions" exist; what exactly is the difference between emotions, moods, and attitudes; how should we model the strength of emotions and their valence (their positive or negative orientation)? The Whorfian question of how far lexical and structural differences between languages have an impact on the experiencing of emotions is also intriguing (cf. Lindquist and Gendron (2013)). For some recent overviews of research on the conceptualization of emotions see Majid (2012) and Fontaine et al. (2013). However interesting such questions regarding the conceptualization of emotions are, in the rest of this chapter we will focus on emotions as they are expressed in language.

2 The expressive function in early twentieth-century linguistics

As we pointed out in the first section, linguistics has traditionally focused on the referential aspect of language. Linguistic historiographers have attributed this focus to the fact that linguistics has a traditional link with philosophy (interested in the relation between language, thinking, and the world), and with philology (focusing on written, informative, language data) (see Chapter 3). The unequal importance of the referential and emotive aspect of language was worded succinctly by Sapir (1921: 38) when he stated that "[on] the whole, it must be admitted that ideation reigns supreme in language, that volition and emotion come in as distinctly secondary factors". However, there have always been defenders of the importance of the expressive aspect for a complete theory of language, as we will illustrate in this section with a few examples, restricting ourselves to the twentieth century.

Although in the first half of the twentieth century linguistics turned to a primarily synchronic perspective on its object of study, nineteenth-century diachronic research did not disappear immediately. In semantics, a diachronic line of research was continued in which the emotive factor stayed on the agenda, for example in the work of Sperber (1914), Stern (1931), and Ullmann (1977 [1962]). In this research, it has often been observed that the emotional loading of a word can change through time. Due to social changes, the loading can change from positive to negative (pejorization, cf. Schreuder (1970), also called pejoration, see Hom (2010)), or the other way around (amelioration, for example *nice*, which meant 'silly' in Middle English). Sometimes, speakers want to get rid of a word with strong negative emotional loading (taboo word), introducing a euphemism (Casas Gómez 2009). The replacement is typically cyclical, as the connotation of the old taboo word will, after a while, re-connect to the new word (cf. Horn (2011)). Replacement can also be motivated by the loss of emotive meaning through frequent use, as can be observed with intensifiers; see section 5.2.

The twentieth-century turn to synchronic linguistics is emblematically linked to Ferdinand de Saussure's *Cours de linguistique générale*, published in 1916. As a colleague of Saussure in Geneva, Charles Bally (1865–1947) supported the synchronic turn in linguistics. But even before his co-editorship of the *Cours*, Bally developed his own research program (cf. Curea (2010)), which he called somewhat misleadingly "stylistique", cf. his *Précis de stylistique* (1905). The central focus of his program was the expressive value of linguistic forms and their use in discourse. As such, Bally can be considered as the father of modern synchronic linguistic research on expressive language. He already sensed that this type of meaning has a certain preference for holistic ways of expression: intonation contours, constructions and fixed expressions (phraseologisms). Like in Geneva, expressivity has been on the research agenda of the Prague School branch of European structuralism, cf. the *Thèses* (1929), Pos (1933/34), Jakobson (1960), and Daneš (1994).

Modern French and German researchers on expressive language regularly refer back to the inspirational work of Bally and other structuralists, cf. Legallois (2012), Legallois and François (2012), Hübler (1987, 1998), and Drescher (2003). This shows that Bally's insight that the expressive part of coded meaning is bigger than most linguists assumed in the past century, has gained increasing interest in the past years, cf. also the overviews in Foolen (1997, 2012) and Schwarz-Friesel (2007, 2008). In the next section, we will consider two frameworks in which this growing interest can be observed.

3 Expressives in cognitive and formal semantics

Cognitive semantics, as part of Cognitive Linguistics (see Chapter 5), has focused, from its beginnings in the 1980s, on the conceptualizing function of language, cf. Maynard (2002: 48), who notes that "Cognitive semantics most frequently analyzes language *about* emotion, and only limited numbers of studies analyze language *as* emotion. Thus, the *mode vécu* of language remains largely untouched." Langacker (2012: 100) confirms this perception, at the same time conceding that there is more to language than descriptive content:

> To some extent, every instance of language use (and every linguistic unit) has conceptual import involving four dimensions: descriptive, expressive/emotive, interactive, and discursive. (...) Expressive/emotive import is internal to the interlocutors, being conveyed but not described. (...) An example would be the expression of pain, e.g. *Ouch* or *Ow!*, differing in intensity of the pain experienced. These are conventional units of English which express an experience, rather than putting it onstage as a focused object of description.

Despite this acknowledgement of the importance of the expressive function of language by one of the founding fathers of Cognitive Linguistics, the number of cognitive linguistic publications on this topic is still restricted. However, in Construction Grammar, as part of Cognitive Linguistics, the expressive aspect of certain constructions has been increasingly noticed (see section 5.5).

In Cognitive Linguistics, metaphor and metonymy are central topics of study. In this framework, they are studied primarily from the perspective of conceptualization. But earlier and modern stylistics has stressed their expressive value as well; see, for example, Ullmann (1977: 136), who stated that "simile and metaphor are among the most effective devices available for the expression of emotive meaning" (cf. also the discussion in Foolen (2012: section 4)). For the expressive value of metonymy, see Feyaerts and Brône (2005).

The primary goal of Formal Semantics has been and still is providing a formal logical treatment of those aspects of meaning that have to do with reference to the world (see Chapters 1 and 4). Truth conditions, compositionality, and possible worlds are the main ingredients of this enterprise. In recent years, in particular since the unpublished paper by David Kaplan (1997), formal semanticists (Potts 2005, with revisions by McCready (2010) and Gutzmann (2012)) have developed multidimensional formalisms for the "conventional implicatures that provide content which supplements the main, at-issue content of the sentence in which they are used" (McCready 2010: 1). These formalisms will not be discussed here, but their availability has strongly stimulated research into meaning aspects that do not belong to the at-issue propositional content, also called conventional implicature, a label that covers a diversity of meaning aspects, one of them being expressive aspects (see Chapter 10). A special issue of the journal *Theoretical Linguistics* (33: 2, 2007) was devoted to this "expressive dimension". The target paper by Christopher Potts and the subsequent discussing contributions have played a catalyzing role in this line of research. Potts (2007a: 166–167) proposed six properties of expressive items: independence (from descriptive content), non-displaceability (expressives need to relate to the utterance situation), perspective dependence (typically the speaker's), descriptive ineffability (descriptive paraphrase doesn't fully catch the meaning or impact of the expressive original), immediacy (the performative character of expressives), and repeatability (repeating expressive items generally strengthens the emotive impact). These properties are the target of discussion in the commenting papers in the same issue of the journal and the discussion has been continued since then; see, among others, Blakemore (2011), Croom (2013), Hedger (2012, 2013), and the contributions in Gutzmann and Gärtner (2013).

One of the many points in the discussion pertains to the question whether items can have descriptive and expressive content at the same time, so called *mixed expressives*. Potts (2007b: 267) admits that in terms of his formalism "it is difficult . . . to analyze expressions that seem to have both descriptive and expressive content: *Redskins* and *Commie*, for instance". Gutzmann and Turgay (2013: 152) analyze expressive intensifiers (EIs) and comment that:

> [s]emantically, EIs are . . . two-dimensional expressions that contribute to both dimensions of meaning (. . .). Hence, EIs add further evidence against Potts' (2007: 7) claim that no lexical item contributes both descriptive and expressive meaning. Using McCready's (2010) terminology, EIs are *mixed expressives*.

This fits the traditional position that items often have a denotational and connotational meaning at the same time, cf. also Croom's (2014) argumentation against considering slurs as "pure expressives" (as defended in Hedger (2012, 2013)).

4 The demarcation of expressives and descriptives

The expressive-descriptive distinction, introduced in the first section without further argumentation, has a strong intuitive appeal. But how exactly is the expressive aspect of language and language use "special", what makes it different from the conceptual function (see Chapter 2)? It is not exclusively the fact that the expressive function has to do with the (actual) feelings and attitudes of the speaker. The speaker can refer to his feelings and tell the hearer how he feels at the moment of speaking (*I feel happy*), the same way he can report what he sees or thinks in the here and now. What is special, in the view of many researchers, is the way the linguistic item relates to these feelings and attitudes. This special way of relating has been characterized in semiotic terms as direct, indexical, or procedural (Wharton 2009).

Different authors capture this distinction between the conceptual and direct way in their own theoretical vocabulary, for example Volek (1987: 26), who states that:

> [t]he emotive components are based . . . on a reflection of the emotive experiences that are not notionalized.(. . .) There is thus a direct connection between the sign containing such a component and the object expressed (rather than referred to). It is this directness between the sign and its object that is recognized in the term "expressive".

Kaplan (1997) contrasts *oops* and *I just observed a minor mishap* and comments (p. 12) that they are informationally equivalent, "but they convey it through different modes of expression". Potts (2007b) points out that language users feel that a descriptive rendering of an expressive utterance misses something (he calls this property of expressives their "ineffability"). Horn (2013) proposes to call conventional implicatures with expressive value "F-implicatures", as a tribute to Frege, who already pointed out that words often have a subjective "tone", in addition to their truth-conditionally relevant referential meaning.

The difference in status shows itself in contexts like negation and quotation, which thus can be used as tests, when a researcher is uncertain about the status (conceptual or expressive) of a semantic aspect of a given linguistic form. Expressive aspects are typically ascribed to the speaker, even if they occur in indirect quotation. And they cannot occur in the scope of negation (unless it is metalinguistic negation).

In the literature, besides the Kaplan-Potts position just sketched, another view exists, which draws the distinction between referential and expressive meaning along different lines. An early representative of this position can be found in Ogden and Richards (1923: 125), cf. their discussion on the ethical use of *good*:

> This peculiar ethical use of "good" is, we suggest, a purely emotive use. When so used the word stands for nothing whatever, and has no symbolic function. Thus, when we so use it in the sentence, "This is good" (. . .) it serves only as an emotive sign expressing our attitude to *this*, and perhaps evoking similar attitudes in other persons, or inciting them to actions of one kind or another.

Stevenson (1937) is a classic statement of this view, and Morris (1946: 60ff.) reformulates it in behaviouristic terms, thus keeping

> the distinction which Ogden and Richards wish to make between referential and emotive modes of signifying and yet anchoring these distinctions in objectively determinable

criteria. In so doing we but move further in the direction which they themselves have seen to be desirable.

(p. 72)

A more recent and influential argument along similar lines has been made by Lasersohn (2005). He calls predicates like *tasty*, as used in *those tomatoes are tasty* predicates of personal taste. Statements with such predicates are not really open for discussion in terms of truth conditions. We have to acknowledge that, despite the fact that the subject NP of these statements refers to something in the world, the utterance is in fact a statement of the speaker's appreciation of that referent, so that no real debate about the truth is possible ("faultless disagreement", as it is called).

Riemer (2013) concedes that it looks surprising that, in the Ogden and Richards line of thinking, statements with predicates of personal taste end up in the expressive group, but in his view, this conclusion is unavoidable:

[M]any expressions relate to the inner experience of the speaker: we can classify these expressions as either *outbursts* (*yuck*, *damn*, etc.) or *evaluations* (*good*, *bad*, *sad*, *happy* etc.). While outbursts are standardly recognized as expressive, evaluations are not. I will argue, however, that both categories are expressive, and that both are, as a result, implausible candidates for conceptual explanation.

(p. 11)

Riemer's main argument is that "assertions involving evaluative predicates like *good* cannot be assigned truth-values in an objective, speaker-independent manner" (p. 11).

The clustering of *statements* about private states and *expressions* of private states doesn't mean that we can't distinguish between them on a finer level, as the following test shows. In conversations, it makes sense to react to a statement on a private state with a statement about one's own state, which can be the opposite of the state of the previous speaker (*That cake is tasty – That cake isn't tasty*). In contrast, a continuation of *ouch* with *not ouch* would be strange.

Both positions, the one represented by Kaplan and the Ogden and Richards position, are needed to fully understand the discussion in Liu (2012), who analyzed evaluative adverbs like *sadly*, *fortunately*, and *unbelievably*. These adverbs don't contribute at-issue content, they cannot be used in the scope of negation or conditionals and they are typically attributed to the speaker. They are, thus, candidates for being considered as expressives in the sense of Kaplan. Consequently, Liu uses and further develops the formal framework of multidimensional semantics as proposed in Potts (2005). At the same time, she discusses these adverbs in relation to predicates of personal taste. As she points out, *sadly* etc. typically express an evaluation from the side of the speaker, like predicates of personal taste do, and they also share the property of faultless disagreement. The hearer can accept a proposition without sharing the *sadly* etc. evaluation of the speaker.

We have to end this section with the conclusion that the demarcation of expressives in relation to predicates of personal taste (and other linguistics elements with a "subjective" meaning aspect) still needs further empirical research and theoretical discussion. In the rest of this chapter, we will follow a "conservative" strategy and restrict the category of expressives to linguistic items with a direct, indexical link to their emotional referent, at the same time conceding that more theoretical work has to be done to fully understand this specific type of meaning.

5 Expressive forms on different linguistic levels

Expressivity can be found everywhere in language, in the lexicon, in phonology, morphology and syntax. In this section, we will illustrate this with a few examples. We will start with the lexicon, thereby distinguishing between content and function words.

5.1 Content words

In psychology, there exists an interest in emotion-laden words, which is rather independent from linguistics. To illustrate this line of research, let's consider the word *lion*. It is linked to our mental concept "lion", which relates to a certain type of animal. However, the word is not only associated with the concept and the referents, it also evokes feelings. It is a rather fruitless discussion whether these emotive aspects of words are considered as part of the meaning of the word or not. Words have connotations, and these are not purely private associations. For most words, the emotional associations of different people tend to go in the same direction, so there is an intersubjective (thus, in a sense, "objective") side to it.

Osgood et al. (1957) developed a method for measuring word valence. Valence is the strength of the emotion that the word evokes, from strongly negative to strongly positive. Osgood et al. asked subjects to score words on different scales, among them valence. In recent years this method has been applied to word lists in different languages, for example to English by Bradley and Lang (2010). More than 1000 English words were scored on valence, from 1 to 9, where 1 is very negative and 9 very positive. This led to their ANEW list: "Affective Norms for English Words". Since then, other lists have been produced for English (Warriner et al. 2013) and for other languages, for example Kanske and Kotz (2010) for German, Ferré et al. (2012) for Spanish, Ric et al. (2013) for French, and Moors et al. (2013) for Dutch. Such lists are interesting for linguists but also for experimental psychologists, as valenced words behave differently in language processing.

In the linguistic and philosophical literature, strongly negative valenced words have attracted special attention. There are studies on "swear words" (Pinker 2008), slurs (Croom 2013; Hedger 2012, 2013) like *nigger* and *kraut* and religious or sexual taboo words. These words typically have a "mixed meaning"; they are partially expressive, partially conceptual. The study of such words is not only relevant for theorizing on expressive meaning but also in relation to the effects of their use in society and the question of how far regulation is possible (cf. Meibauer (2013)). Allan (2006a) and Nunberg (2013) stress that the expressive value and impact of this kind of word strongly depends on who uses them in which context.

5.2 Function words

Emotional interjections are the prototype of expressive function words. Even if they are derived from content words, like *damn*, their original meaning doesn't really play a role in their actual expressive functioning, in other words, they are not of a mixed type. Some recent studies on emotional interjections are Goddard (2014), Golato's (2012) analysis of German *oh*, which marks an emotional change of state (in contrast to English *oh*, which can also mark an epistemic change of state) and Reber's (2012) study on the conversational use of *oh*, *ooh*, *ah*, and other affect-laden "sound objects". For an overview of research on interjections, see Norrick (2011).

Pos (1933/34) showed that words like French *mais* "but", *enfin* "finally", *donc* "thus", which typically have what Pos called a "logical" use, can also function in a primarily emotive way: *Mais Monsieur!, Enfin! (But sir, really!)*. Koo and Rhee (2013) analyzed Korean sentence-final particles which express "discontent", cf. the sentence-final use of *what* or *or what* in certain varieties of English (see Koo and Rhee (2012: 82) for references).

Intensifiers like *very* indicate that a certain property holds to a high degree (*very nice*, etc.). Some intensifiers, however, have the additional meaning that the high degree has an impact on the speaker, cf. Waksler (2012). Gutzmann and Turgay (2012: 150) call intensifiers of this type expressive intensifiers (EIs):

> Semantically, the difference between EIs and standard degree elements is that beside their intensifying function, EIs convey an additional expressive speaker attitude, which is not part of the descriptive content of the sentence they occur in. That is, besides raising the degree to which the party was cool in (2) [*Du hast gestern eine sau coole Party verpasst* "yesterday, you missed a EI cool party"], *sau* expressively displays that the speaker is emotional about the degree to which the party was cool.

Foolen et al. (2013) collected new emotional intensifiers in Dutch and found that many of them are recruited from emotive content words, in particular from negatively laden content words, like *akelig* "scary", *gruwelijk* "horribly", etc. The preference for negative words as a source for intensifiers can be explained on the basis of two principles, or biases, see Jing-Schmidt (2007): the negativity bias and the positivity bias, also known as the Pollyanna hypothesis, as Boucher and Osgood (1969) called it. According to the negativity bias, negative feelings are stronger than positive feelings. This has an evolutionary explanation: it is more important to react to negative things which might harm you than to enjoy positive things. Enjoyment is a bonus, but need not be very strong to be adaptive. So negatively laden words are stronger and therefore better candidates for strong intensification. When they are grammaticalized into intensifiers, their literal meaning is backgrounded and their strong emotional meaning becomes the salient part of the meaning. The positivity bias claims that the baseline of everyday discourse is not neutral but positive. Recently, this idea has been tested empirically by Garcia et al. (2012). First, they analyzed English, German, and Spanish lexica and found that averaging the emotional content over all the words in each of them leads to a neutral result. Next, they looked at language use and found that "the everyday usage frequency of these words . . . is strongly biased towards positive values, because words associated with a positive emotion are more frequently used than those associated with negative emotion" (p. 1). Like the negativity bias, the positivity bias can be explained from an evolutionary point of view: it motivates us to see the world in a sunny perspective, we like to be with people who ascribe to such a perspective, etc. When used against such a positive background, the negativity based intensifiers stand out even more strongly. Together, the negativity and positivity biases strengthen the impact of negative words when used as intensifiers.

5.3 Phonology

Non-segmental, prosodic aspects of sound structure provide many opportunities for coding expressive meaning; cf., among many others, Hancil (2009). But expressive phenomena on the segmental phonological level have also been observed, as will be briefly illustrated.

Myers-Schulz et al. (2013) show that phonemes are not emotionally neutral, they have an emotional connotation, for example depending on the rising and falling formants in consonants. In *bupaba*, the F2's in all three labial consonants rise, in *dugada*, a word with non-labial consonants they fall. Myers-Schulz et al. asked subjects to pair these words with pictures of aggressive and cute dogs. It turned out that the subjects associate *bupaba* with the cute dog and *dugada* with the aggressive one. The authors conclude (p. 6) "that certain strings of

English phonemes have a non-arbitrary emotional quality, and, moreover, that the emotional quality can be predicted on the basis of specific acoustic features." And they also claim (p. 7) "that our data suggest that *Darth Vader* (...) is an acoustically more appropriate name for an intergalactic miscreant than *Barth Faber*, by virtue of the downward frequency shifts and thus inherently negative emotional connotation."

Phonetic variation in the articulation of phonemes, for example lengthening (cf. Mischler (2008)), can convey expressive meaning. Kochetov and Alderete (2011: 346) observe a type of palatalization

> that is not phonologically conditioned, but has a specific iconic function, being associated with "smallness", "childishness", or "affection" (...). Expressive palatalization of this kind is used cross-linguistically in sound symbolism, diminutive morphology, hypocoristics, and in "babytalk" – conventionalized adults' speech directed to small children.

In her research on American preadolescents, Eckert (2010: 97) found that "the fronting and backing of low vowels correlated with the expression of positive and negative emotional states, respectively". Eckert's general point is that sociolinguistic variation often has the function of affective display.

5.4 Morphology

In morphology, both derivation and compounding can involve expressive meaning. Among the derivational affixes, diminutive suffixes have been found to easily develop expressive meanings, cf. Volek (1987), Steriopolo (2008), and Fortin (2011); cf. also Schnoebelen (2012), who did experimental-pragmatic and corpus linguistic research on emotive aspects of *little*. Rossi (2011) found that lexical reduplication (*It's a little little house, I want coffee coffee*) can activate positive or negative affective evaluations.

Meibauer (2013) showed that in German compounds the expressive part can be put in the first or in the second position, cf. *Arschgesicht* "arse face" (first non-head part is pejorative) and *Politikerarsch* "politician arse" (with a final pejorative head). Hampe (2002) studied verb-particle constructions like *cover up*, *tighten up*, *sketch out*, etc., in which the particle is often considered redundant. According to Hampe (2002: 101), "a semantically redundant verb-particle construction can function as an index of an emotional involvement of the speaker, since it is the marked member of a formal opposition between two elements: a simple verb and a verb-particle construction". When we consider surprise as an emotion, mirative evidentials can be considered as expressives as well, cf. Rett and Murray (2013). Mirative evidentials (often coded by affixes, like in Turkish) indicate "that a particular proposition has violated the speaker's expectations" (p. 3). A condition on the use of mirative evidentials is that the content of the proposition must have been discovered by the speaker just before the utterance (*Wow, Bill has a new car!*). Rett and Murray (2013: 4) call this the "recency restriction" on mirativity. This is in line with the indexical property of expressives, as discussed in section 4.

5.5 Syntax

Lambrecht (1990) analyzed the incredulity response construction in English (*What, me worry?*). Potts and Roeper (2006) included this construction in their study on expressive small clauses (*You idiot!*), see also Arsenijević (2007) for discussion of Potts and Roeper's paper. Günthner (2011) analyzed similar "dense constructions" (utterances without a finite verb, like *ich in die Bahnhofshalle* "I went into the station concourse"), in German.

Hübler (1998) studied grammatical devices in different periods of English, like possessive dative, ethic dative, the present perfect, periphrastic *do*, the *get*-passive, "which function, at one time or another within the course of roughly a thousand years, as primary means of indexically expressing emotional attitudes toward propositional states of affairs" (p. 187).

Foolen (2004) made a comparative study of the *hell of a job* construction in Germanic and Romance languages. In Dutch, this construction is rather productive. The first N is typically occupied by a valenced word like *schat* "treasure" or *duivel* "devil", but more neutral words like *wolk* "cloud", *kast* "cupboard", *boom* "tree" or *dijk* "dike" occur as well. When such words are used, the construction forces foregrounding of the emotive associations we possibly have with this word; in *boom* "tree", for example, the size and the associated impressiveness will be typically foregrounded. In certain contexts, this impressiveness can be further interpreted as threatening impressiveness: *een boom van een kerel kwam op me af* "a tree of a guy approached me" (suggesting that the speaker was emotionally affected in some way, for example being impressed or frightened). Another construction that often involves expressive meaning is provided by dependent sentences used independently (insubordinate constructions, as Evans (2007) called them), like *that you dare to do that!*

Hoeksema and Napoli (2008) studied constructions like *Let's get the hell out of here* and *I beat the hell out of him*, which typically contain a taboo term (like *hell* in these examples). Corver (2014) investigated the internal syntax of complex curse expressions in Dutch. Legallois (2012) analyzed a French construction containing the phrase *histoire de* + *infinitive*, like in *On va leur téléphoner, histoire de voir s'ils sont là* "Let's ring them up, just to see if they're there". As Legallois points out (p. 269), "the attitude [expressed by the construction] is very difficult to describe: it consists in a kind of detachment from the speaker, with regard to the motivation of the process X". Whereas expressive constructions typically convey a strong attitude, this construction seems to indicate that "it is not a big deal if X is not the case". Amaral (2013) studied the *vivir*+V [Gerund] construction in the Spanish of Bogotá and found (p. 196) that "[b]y using this construction, the speaker conveys the implication that the event occurs more frequently than it [sic] *should* be the case (given the speaker's expectations)".

Horn (2013) studied certain uses of dative first and second person pronouns, which are known in the literature as non-argument, free, ethical, or personal datives. This use of the dative is normal in spoken standard German, but also occurs in certain varieties of English, like in *I need me a Coke*. According to Horn (2013: 167) such pronouns contribute "subject affect": "the speaker assumes that the action expressed has or would have a positive effect on the subject, typically satisfying the subject's perceived intention or goals." Note that the affect is attributed to the subject of the sentence, who is, however, in utterances with this type of dative, typically identical to the speaker.

6 Speech acts and discourse

In Searle's (1976) classification of illocutionary acts, expressive speech acts constitute one of the five classes (the others are representatives, directives, commissives, and declarations). According to Searle's definition (1976: 12):

> the illocutionary point of this class is to express the psychological state specified in the sincerity condition about a state of affairs specified in the propositional content. The paradigms of expressive verbs are 'thank', 'congratulate', 'apologize', 'condole', 'deplore', and 'welcome'.

In the past, speech act research has not focused on expressive speech acts, but this might change, now that expressivity is gaining more attention in general, cf. King and van Roojen (2013) on praising and blaming, Oishi (2013) on apologies, Vingerhoets et al. (2013) on swearing, and Alfonzetti (2013) on compliments.

There has been quite a lot of discussion about the relation between exclamative sentence types (and whether such sentence types can be distinguished at all) and the class of expressive speech acts, cf. Villalba (2008) and the contributions in Krause and Ruge (eds) (2004). Rett (2011) provides a formal-semantic analysis of exclamation as a speech act, claiming that it makes a difference whether the speech act is realized as what she calls a sentence exclamation, formed with a declarative sentence (*Wow, John bakes delicious desserts!*) or "with something other than a declarative sentence" (Rett 2011: 412), called exclamatives. Rett distinguishes three types of exclamatives: wh-exclamative (*My, what delicious desserts John bakes!*), inversion exclamatives (*Boy, does John bake delicious desserts!*) and nominal exclamatives (*My, the delicious desserts John bakes!*). Interestingly, exclamatives have a falling intonation pattern, whereas declarative exclamations are rising (Rett 2011: 413).

Expressive language use "happens" in real discourse (cf. Baider and Cislaru eds. 2014). The expressive aspect of discourse has gained attention in different frameworks. In the context of conversation analysis, Du Bois and Kärkkäinen (2012: 435) point out that affect is seen here primarily "as crucially involving public display to others within the context of social interaction". They discuss expressive meaning as an important aspect of "stance". See for further conversational work on emotion in interaction the contributions in Peräkylä and Sorjonen (2012).

Maynard (2002) studied linguistic emotivity from the perspective of what she calls "Place of Negotiation" theory. Stylistic shift is one of the devices she analyzes, for example how the use of unexpected verb morphology (Japanese informal *da* instead of formal *desu/masu*) contributes to expressivity. Another framework is Systemic Functional Grammar, in which expressive meaning is considered as one aspect of the broader functional category "interpersonal meaning", cf. Thompson (2008: 171): "All acts of appraisal are in essence expressions of the appraiser's positive or negative feelings about something". Appraisal, evaluation and affect are the main labels used in this framework, cf. Bednarek (2008) and Thompson and Alba-Juez (2014).

A different line of research focuses on what is called "semantic prosody" (see Chapter 6), the phenomenon that in a text different words and constructions are on the same emotive wavelength, cf. Ebeling (2013: 1): "Semantic prosody can be defined as the evaluative meaning of extended lexical units." An example is English *cause*, both as a verb and a noun, which typically co-occurs with negatively evaluated items. Ebeling (2013) studies this item and its translations into Norwegian. For a critical discussion of the assumptions of the semantic prosody approach see Steward (2010).

An important text type for the study of "emotional language" is narrative. As Labov (2013: 227) points out, the main aim of narrative is "the residual emotional impact on the reader." Labov (1972: 378–380) already observed expressive phonology, quantifiers (*I knocked him* all *out in the street*), repetition and gesture as means for intensifying the narrative (cf. also Romano, Porto and Molina (2013)). The affective impact of literary narratives is strengthened by "the use of metaphors, sound play and repetition of words" (Sandford and Emmott (2012: 195)). See also Burke (2011) for research on the affective dimension of literary reading. In his (2006) study, Burke showed that the choice for indirect, direct or free indirect discourse makes a difference with respect to the expressive quality of spoken and written discourse. An increasingly important genre is computer-mediated language. Research on the emotive aspect of this type of texts is expanding, cf. Vandergriff (2013), who analyzed emoticons, non-standard and multiple punctuation (". . .," "!!!"), and lexical surrogates ("hmmm").

With the availability of big corpora, searching and analyzing expressive content gets a new methodological turn, cf. Potts and Schwarz (2008) and Constant et al. (2009). The computer linguistic enterprise to automatize the search for emotive cues in big corpora is known as "sentiment analysis", cf. Ahmad (2011). A central methodological question is in what way expressive elements in texts can be identified: are there any formal diagnostics to distinguish them from elements with non-expressive meaning? A challenge for the future will be to program computers in such a way that they can automatically produce and process expressive aspects of language use, cf. Ovesdotter Alm (2012).

7 Conclusion

It is the fine detail in which we can talk about the world (the outside as well as our private inside world) which makes language such a powerful communicative tool. The dominant traditional view is that we have our bodies (face, voice, posture) to indicate how we feel about what we are telling the other about the world. But what the present chapter has intended to show is that the distinction between descriptive language and expressive body is not absolute. Language isn't a purely rational tool. Meanings are partly emotive, and language takes its share in expressing our feelings and attitudes towards what we are talking about. In reverse, our body and senses participate in conceptualization and expression, as research on gesture (cf. Müller et al. (2013)) has made increasingly clear in recent years.

Looking at the linguistic landscape of the early 2010s, we can conclude that the marginal role that has been traditionally attributed to the expressive function of language is not that marginal anymore. But questions like the following are still central on the research agenda: Which feelings can be or are typically expressed via expressives? Do languages differ in how big a part expressives take in the totality of the language system and do they differ in their structural preferences for coding expressive meaning? Is there a principled difference between verbal and non-verbal expression of feelings, for example between a painful face and screaming *ouch*? To answer this last question, the semantic study of expressives has to be embedded in a framework of multi-modal communication studies. The increased availability of video-recorded and transcribed verbal interaction data is the best antidote to the written language bias and this will certainly lead to more descriptive research on expressive language. This research will, hopefully, also contribute to a better theoretical understanding of the descriptive-expressive contrast and the relation between expressivity and such notions as "commitment (cf. De Brabanter and Dendale (2008)) and "subjectivity" (cf. Baumgarten et al. (2012)). Integrating these different approaches to the scientific study of "self-expression" of the speaker (cf. Lyons 1981: 240) and the role of emotion in human communication is one of the challenges of future semantic research.

Further reading

Foolen, Ad 2012. The relevance of emotion for language and linguistics. In A. Foolen, U.M. Lüdtke, T.P. Racine and J. Zlatev (eds) *Moving Ourselves, Moving Others. Motion and Emotion in Intersubjectivity, Consciousness and Language*. Amsterdam: Benjamins, 349–368, Majid, Asifa. Current emotion research in the language sciences, *Emotion Review* 4: 432–443, and Schwarz-Friesel, Monika 2007. *Sprache und Emotion*. Tübingen & Basel: A. Francke Verlag. Provide general overviews of research on expressives.

Lasersohn, Peter 2005. Context dependence, disagreement, and predicates of personal taste, *Linguistics and Philosophy* 28: 643–686 and Potts, Christopher 2007a. The expressive dimension. *Theoretical Linguistics* 33: 165–198 inspired a recent discussion on the demarcation of expressives.

Bally, Charles 1905. *Précis de stylistique*. Genève: A. Eggimann and Cie and Stern, Gustaf (1965) [1931]. *Meaning and Meaning Change. With Special Reference to the English Language*. Bloomington: Indiana University Press are still inspiring classics.

References

Ahmad, Khurshid (ed.) 2011. *Affective Computing and Sentiment Analysis. Emotion, Metaphor and Terminology*. Dordrecht: Springer.

Alfonzetti, Giovanna 2013. Compliments, in Marina Sbisà and Ken Turner (eds) *Pragmatics of speech actions*. [Handbook of Pragmatics 2]. Berlin: de Gruyter, 555–586.

Allan, Keith 2006a. Connotation. In K. Brown (ed.) *Encyclopedia of Language and Linguistics*. Second edition. Amsterdam: Elsevier, 41–44.

Allan, Keith 2006b. The pragmatics of connotation. *Journal of Pragmatics* 39: 1047–1057.

Amaral, Patricia 2013. The pragmatics of number: the evaluative properties of *vivir* + V[Gerund], *Journal of Pragmatics* 51: 105–121.

Arsenijević, Boban 2007. Disapprobation expressions are vocative epithets, *ACLC Working Papers* 2: 87–98.

Baider, Fabienne and Georgeta Cislaru (eds) 2014. *Linguistic Approaches to Emotions in Context*. [Pragmatics & Beyond New Series, 241]. Amsterdam: Benjamins.

Bally, Charles 1905. *Précis de stylistique*. Genève: A. Eggimann & Cie.

Bally, Charles 1926 [1931]. Mécanisme de l'expressivité linguistique, in Ch. Bally, *Le langage et la vie*. Paris: Payot, 139–181.

Baumgarten, Nicole, Inke Du Bois and Juliane House (eds) 2012. *Subjectivity in Language and Discourse*. [= *Studies in Pragmatics* 10]. Bingley: Emerald Group.

Bednarek, Monika 2008. *Emotion Talk across Corpora*. New York: Palgrave Macmillan.

Blakemore, Diane 2011. On the descriptive ineffability of expressive meaning. *Journal of Pragmatics* 43: 3537–3550.

Boucher, Jerry and Charles E. Osgood 1969. The Pollyanna hypothesis. *Journal of Verbal Learning and Verbal Behavior* 8: 1–8.

Bradley, M.M. and P.J. Lang 2010. *Affective Norms for English Words (ANEW): Stimuli, Instruction Manual and Affective Ratings*. Technical Report C-2, Gainesville, FL. The Center for Research in Psychophysiology, University of Florida.

Bühler, Karl 1934. *Sprachtheorie. Die Darstellungsfunktion der Sprache*. Leipzig: Fischer Verlag.

Burke, Michael 2006. Emotion: stylistic approaches. In K. Brown (ed.) *Encyclopedia of Language and Linguistics*. Second edition. Amsterdam: Elsevier, 127–129.

Burke, Michael 2011. *Literary Reading, Cognition and Emotion. An Exploration of the Oceanic Mind*. New York/London: Routledge.

Curea, Anamaria 2010. Y a-t-il une *linguistique de l'expression* chez Charles Bally et Charles-Albert Sechehaye?. *Cahiers Ferdinand de Saussure* 63: 115–133.

Casas Gómez, Miguel 2009. Towards a new approach to the linguistic definition of euphemism. *Language Sciences* 31: 725–739.

Constant, Noah, Christopher Davis, Christopher Potts and Florian Schwarz 2009. The pragmatics of expressive content: evidence from large corpora. *Sprache und Datenverarbeitung* 33: 5–21.

Corver, Norbert 2014. Recursing in Dutch. *Natural Language and Linguistic Theory* 32: 423–457.

Croom, Adam M. 2011. Slurs. *Language Sciences* 33: 343–358.

Croom, Adam M. 2013. How to do things with slurs: studies in the way of derogatory words, *Language & Communication* 33: 177–204.

Croom, Adam M. 2014. The semantics of slurs: a refutation of pure expressivism. *Language Sciences* 41: 227–242.

Daneš, František 1994. Involvement with language and in language. *Journal of Pragmatics* 22: 251–264.

De Brabanter, Philippe and Patrick Dendale (eds) 2008. *Commitment* [= Belgian Journal of Linguistics 22]. Amsterdam: Benjamins.

Dingemanse, Mark 2012. Advances in the cross-linguistic study of ideophones. *Language and Linguistics Compass* 6: 654–672.

Drescher, Martina 2003. *Sprachliche Affektivität. Darstellung emotionaler Beteiligung am Beispiel von Gesprächen aus dem Französischen.* Tübingen: Max Niemeyer Verlag.

Du Bois, John W. and Elise Kärkkäinen 2012. Taking a stance on emotion: affect, sequence, and intersubjectivity in dialogic interaction, *Text and Talk* 32: 433–451.

Ebeling, Signe Oksefjell 2013. Semantic prosody in a cross-linguistic perspective. *Studies in Variation, Contacts and Change in English* 13: 1–14. http://www.helsinki.fi/varieng/series/volumes/13/ebeling/

Eckert, Penelope 2010. Affect, sound symbolism, and variation, *University of Pennsylvania Working Papers in Linguistics* 15: 70–100.

Evans, Nicholas 2007. Insubordination and its uses. In I. Nikolaeva (ed.) *Finiteness. Theoretical and Empirical Approaches.* Oxford: Oxford University Press, 366–431.

Ferré, Pilar, Marc Guasch, Cornelia Moldovan and Rosa Sánchez-Casas 2012. Affective norms for 380 Spanish words belonging to three different semantic categories. *Behavior Research Methods* 44: 395–403.

Fontaine, Johnny R.J., Klaus R. Scherer and Christina Soriano (eds) 2013. *Components of Emotional Meaning. A Sourcebook.* Oxford: Oxford University Press.

Foolen, Ad 1997. The expressive function of language: towards a cognitive semantic approach. In Susanne Niemeier and René Dirven (eds) *The Language of Emotions.* Amsterdam: Benjamins, 15–31.

Foolen, Ad 2004. Expressive binominal NPs in Germanic and Romance languages, in G. Radden and K.-U. Panther (eds) *Studies in Linguistic Motivation.* Berlin: Mouton de Gruyter, 75–100.

Foolen, Ad 2012. The relevance of emotion for language and linguistics. In A. Foolen, U.M. Lüdtke, T.P. Racine and J. Zlatev (eds) *Moving Ourselves, Moving Others. Motion and Emotion in Intersubjectivity, Consciousness and Language.* Amsterdam: Benjamins, 349–368.

Foolen, Ad, Verena Wottrich and Martine Zwets 2013. *Gruwelijk interessant. Emotieve intensiveerders in het Nederlands.* [Horribly interesting. Emotive intensifiers in Dutch]. Unpublished paper.

Fortin, Antonio 2011. *The Morphology and Semantics of Expressive Affixes.* PhD thesis, Oxford.

Feyaerts, Kurt and Brône, Geert 2005. Expressivity and metonymic inferencing: stylistic variation in nonliterary language use, *Style* 39: 12–36.

Garcia, David, Antonios Garas and Frank Schweitzer 2012. Positive words carry less information than negative words. *EPJ Data Science* 1: 1–12.

Goddard, Cliff 2014. Interjections and emotion (with special reference to "surprise" and "disgust"). *Emotion Review* 6: 53–63.

Golato, Andrea 2012. German *oh*: Marking an emotional change of state. *Research on Language and Social Interaction* 45: 245–268.

Günthner, Susanne 2011. The construction of emotional involvement in everyday German narratives: interactive uses of 'dense constructions'. *Pragmatics* 21: 573–592.

Gutzmann, Daniel 2012. *Use-Conditional Meaning. Studies in Multidimensional Semantics.* Doctoral dissertation. Institute of Linguistics, University of Frankfurt.

Gutzmann, Daniel 2013. Expressives and beyond. An introduction to varieties of use-conditional meaning. In Daniel Gutzmann and Hans-Martin Gärtner (eds) *Beyond Expressives: Explorations in Use-Conditional Meaning.* Leiden: Brill, 1–58.

Gutzmann, Daniel and Katharina Turgay 2012. Expressive intensifiers in German: syntax-semantics mismatches. In Christopher Piñón (ed.) *Empirical Issues in Syntax and Semantics* 9: 149–166. http://www.cssp.cnrs.fr/eiss9

Gutzmann, Daniel and Hans-Martin Gärtner (eds) 2013. *Beyond Expressives: Explorations in Use-Conditional Meaning*. Leiden: Brill.

Hampe, Beate 2002. *Superlative Verbs. A Corpus-Based Study of Semantic Redundancy in English Verb-Particle Constructions*. Tübingen: Gunter Narr Verlag.

Hancil, Sylvie (ed.) 2009. *The Role of Prosody in Affective Speech*. Bern: Peter Lang.

Hedger, Joseph A. 2012. The semantics of racial slurs: using Kaplan's framework to provide a theory of the meaning of derogatory epithets. *Linguistic and Philosophical Investigations* 11: 74–84.

Hedger, Joseph A. 2013. Meaning and racial slurs: derogatory epithets and the semantics/pragmatics interface. *Language & Communication* 33: 205–213.

Hoeksema, Jack and Donna Jo Napoli 2008. Just for the hell of it: a comparison of two taboo-term constructions. *Journal of Linguistics* 44: 347–378.

Hom, Christopher K. 2010. Pejoratives. *Philosophy Compass* 5: 164–185.

Horn, Laurence R. 2011. Etymythology and taboo. Talk presented at ISLE2 (International Society for the Linguistics of English). http://ling.yale.edu/sites/default/files/files/horn/EtymythologyTabooISLE.pdf.

Horn, Laurence R. 2013. I love me some datives: expressive meaning, free datives, and F-implicature. In Daniel Gutzmann and Hans-Martin Gärtner (eds) *Beyond Expressives: Explorations in Use-Conditional Meaning*. Leiden: Brill, 143–189.

Hübler, Axel 1987. Communication and expressivity. In R. Dirven and V. Fried (eds) *Functionalism in Linguistics*. Amsterdam: Benjamins, 357–380.

Hübler, Axel 1998. *The Expressivity of Grammar. Grammatical Devices Expressing Emotion across Time*. Berlin: Mouton de Gruyter.

Jakobson, Roman 1960. Linguistics and poetics. In T.A. Sebeok (ed.) *Style in language*. Cambridge, Mass.: The MIT Press, 350–377.

Jing-Schmidt, Zhuo 2007. Negativity bias in language: a cognitive-affective model of emotive intensifiers. *Cognitive Linguistics* 18: 417–443.

Kanske, Philipp and Sonja A. Kotz 2010. Leipzig affective norms for German: a reliability study. *Behavior Research Methods* 42: 987–991.

Kaplan, David 1997. *The Meaning of 'Ouch' and 'Oops': Explorations in The Theory of Meaning as Use*. Unpublished ms.

King, Matt and Mark van Roojen 2013. Praising and blaming. In Marina Sbisà and Ken Turner (eds) *Pragmatics of speech actions*. [Handbook of Pragmatics 2]. Berlin: de Gruyter, 467–500.

Koo, Hyun Jung and Seongha Rhee 2012. On an emerging paradigm of sentence-final particles of discontent: a grammaticalization perspective. *Language Sciences* 37: 70–89.

Kochetov, Alexei and John Alderete 2011. Patterns and scales of expressive palatalization: experimental evidence from Japanese. *Canadian Journal of Linguistics* 56: 345–376.

Krause, Maxi and Nikolaus Ruge (eds) 2004. *Das war echt spitze! Zur Exklamation im heutigen Deutsch*. Tübingen: Stauffenburg Verlag.

Labov, Willliam 1972. *Language in the Inner City*. Philadelphia: University of Pennsylvania Press.

Labov, William 2013. *The Language of Life and Death. The Transformation of Experience in Oral Narrative*. Cambridge: Cambridge University Press.

Lambrecht, Knud 1990. "What, me worry?" – "Mad Magazine Sentences" revisited. *Proceedings of the Berkeley Linguistics Society* 16: 215–228.

Langacker, Ron 2012. Interactive cognition: toward a unified account of structures, processing, and discourse. *International Journal of Cognitive Linguistics* 3: 95–124.

Lasersohn, Peter 2005. Context dependence, disagreement, and predicates of personal taste. *Linguistics and Philosophy* 28: 643–686.

Legallois, Dominique 2012. From grammaticalization to expressive constructions: the case of *histoire de* + inf. In Myriam Bouveret and Dominique Legallois (eds) *Constructions in French*. Amsterdam: Benjamins, 257–282.

Legallois, Dominique and Jacques François 2012. Définition et illustration de la notion d'expressivité en linguistique. In Nicole Le Querler, Frank Neveu and Emmanuelle Roussel (eds) *Relations, connexions, dépendances. Hommage au professeur Claude Guimier.* Rennes: Presses Universitaires de Rennes, 197–222.

Lindquist, Kristen A. and Maria Gendron 2013. What's in a word? Language constructs emotion perception. *Emotion Review* 5: 66–71.

Liu, Mingya 2012. *Multidimensional Semantics of Evaluative Adverbs.* Leiden and Boston: Brill.

Lyons, John 1981. *Language, meaning & context.* Bungay: Fontana Paperbacks.

Majid, Asifa 2012. Current emotion research in the language sciences, *Emotion Review* 4: 432–443.

Maynard, Senko K. 2002. *Linguistic Emotivity.* Amsterdam: Benjamins.

McCready, Eric 2010. Varieties of conventional implicature, *Semantics and Pragmatics* 3: 1–57.

Meibauer, Jörg 2013. Expressive compounds in German. *Word Structure* 6: 21–42.

Meibauer, Jörg (ed.) 2013. *Hassrede/Hate speech. Interdisziplinäre Beiträge zu einer aktuellen Diskussion.* Giessener Elektronische Bibliothek. http://geb.uni-giessen.de/geb/volltexte/2013/9251/.

Mischler, James J. 2008. Expressive phonology as evaluative comment in personal oral narrative: the play frame and language learning. *System* 36: 241–252.

Moors, Agnes et al. 2013. Norms of valence, arousal, dominance, and age of acquisition for 4300 Dutch words. *Behavior Research Methods* 45: 169–177.

Morris, Charles 1955 [1946]. *Signs, Language and Behavior.* New York: George Braziller.

Müller, C., A. Cienki, E. Fricke, S.H. Ladewig, D. McNeill and S. Tessendorf (eds) 2013. *Body – Language – Communication: An International Handbook on Multimodality in Human Interaction* [Handbooks of Linguistics and Communication Science, 38.1]. Berlin, New York: De Gruyter Mouton.

Myers-Schulz, Blake, Maia Pujara, Richard C. Wolf and Michael Koenigs 2013. Inherent emotional quality of human speech sounds. *Cognition and Emotion* 27 (6): 1105–1113.

Norrick, Neal R. 2011. Interjections. In Gisle Andersen and Karin Aijmer (eds) *Pragmatics of Society.* [Handbook of Pragmatics 5]. Berlin: De Gruyter Mouton, 243–291.

Nunberg, Geoff 2013. *Slurs aren't special.* MS.

Ogden, C.K. and I.A. Richards 1923. *The Meaning of Meaning.* New York: Harcourt, Brace and World, Inc.

Oishi, Etsuko 2013. Apologies. In Marina Sbisà and Ken Turner (eds) *Pragmatics of Speech Actions.* [Handbook of Pragmatics 2]. Berlin: de Gruyter, 523–554.

Osgood, Charles E., George J. Suci and Percy H Tannenbaum 1957. *The Measurement of Meaning.* Urbana: University of Illinois Press.

Ovesdotter Alm, Cecilia 2012. The role of affect in the computational modeling of *natural* language. *Language and Linguistics Compass* 6: 416–430.

Peräkylä, Anssi and Marja-Leena Sorjonen (eds) 2012. *Emotion in Interaction.* New York: Oxford University Press.

Pinker, Steven 2008. *The Seven Words You Can't Say on Television.* London: Penguin Books. [Also as chapter 7 in Pinker 2007. *The Stuff of Thought.* London: Allen Lane, 323–372].

Pos, H.-J 1933/34. Les particules, leurs functions logiques et affectives. *Recherches Philosophiques* 3: 321–333.

Potts, Christopher 2005. *The Logic of Conventional Implicatures.* Oxford: Oxford University Press.

Potts, Christopher 2007a. The expressive dimension. *Theoretical Linguistics* 33: 165–198.

Potts, Christopher 2007b. The centrality of expressive indices. *Theoretical Linguistics* 33: 255–268.

Potts, Christopher 2012. Conventional implicature and expressive content. In Claudia Maienborn, Klaus von Heusinger and Paul Portner (eds) *Semantics: An international Handbook of Natural Language Meaning*, Volume 3. Berlin: Mouton de Gruyter, 2516–2536.

Potts, Christopher and Tom Roeper 2006. The narrowing acquisition path: from expressive small clauses to declaratives. In L. Progovac, K. Paesani, E. Casielles and E. Barton (eds) *The syntax of Nonsententials.* Amsterdam: Benjamins, 183–201.

Potts, Christopher and Florian Schwarz 2008. Exclamatives and heightened emotion: extracting pragmatic generalizations from large corpora. http://semanticsarchive.net/Archive/jFjNGNjZ/potts-schwarz-exclamatives08.pdf

Reber, Elisabeth 2012. *Affectivity in Interaction: Sound Objects in English*. Amsterdam: Benjamins.

Rett, Jessica 2011. Exclamatives, degrees and speech acts. *Linguistics and Philosophy* 34: 411–442.

Rett, Jessica and Sarah E. Murray 2013. A semantic account of mirative evidentials. *Proceedings of SALT* 23: 1–20.

Ric, François, Theodore Alexopoulos, Dominique Muller and Benoîte Aubé 2013. Emotional norms for 524 French personality trait words. *Behavior Research Methods* 45: 414–421.

Riemer, Nick 2013. Conceptualist semantics: explanatory power, scope and uniqueness. *Language Sciences* 35: 1–19.

Romano, Manuela, Maria Dolores Porto and Clara Molina 2013. The structure of emotion discourse: From Labovian to socio-cognitive models. *Text & Talk* 33: 71–93.

Rossi, Daniela 2011. Lexical reduplication and affective contents. A pragmatic and experimental perspective. *Belgian Journal of Linguistics* 25: 148–175.

Sandford, Anthony J. and Catherine Emmott 2012. *Mind, Brain and Narrative*. Cambridge: Cambridge University Press.

Sapir, Edward 1921. *Language. An Introduction to the Study of Speech*. New York: Harcourt Brace Jovanovich.

Saussure, Ferdinand de 1916. *Cours de linguistique générale*. Paris: Payot.

Sbisà, Marina and Ken Turner (eds) *Pragmatics of speech actions*. [Handbook of Pragmatics 2]. Berlin: de Gruyter.

Schnoebelen, Tyler Joseph 2012. *Emotions are Relational: Positioning and Linguistic Use of Affective Linguistic Resources*. PhD dissertation, Stanford University.

Schreuder, Hindrik 1970. *Pejorative Sense Development in English*. College Park, MD: McGrath Publishing Company.

Schwarz-Friesel, Monika 2007. *Sprache und Emotion*. Tübingen & Basel: A. Francke Verlag.

Schwarz-Friesel, Monika 2008. Sprache, Kognition und Emotion: Neue Wege in der Kognitionswissenschaft. In Heidrun Kämper and Ludwig M. Eichinger (eds) *Sprache-Kognition-Kultur: Sprache zwischen mentaler Struktur und kultureller Prägung*. Berlin: Walter de Gruyter, 277–301.

Searle, John R. 1976. A classification of illocutionary acts. *Language in Society* 5: 1–23.

Sperber, Hans 1914. *Über den Affekt als Ursache der Sprachveränderung. Versuch einer dynamologischen Betrachtung des Sprachlebens*. Halle. a.S.: Verlag von Max Niemeyer.

Stern, Gustaf 1965 [1931]. *Meaning and Meaning Change. With Special Reference to the English Language*. Bloomington: Indiana University Press.

Steriopolo, Olga 2008. *Form and Function of Expressive Morphology: A Case Study of Russian*. PhD thesis, The University of British Columbia.

Stevenson, Charles Leslie 1937. The emotive meaning of ethical terms. *Mind* 46: 14–31.

Steward, Dominic 2010. *Semantic Prosody. A Critical Evaluation*. New York: Routledge.

'Thèses' (1929). *Travaux du Cercle Linguistique de Prague* 1, 7–29. [Nendeln/Lichtenstein: Kraus Reprint, 1968].

Thompson, Geoff 2008. Appraising glances: evaluating Martin's model of appraisal. *Word* 59: 169–187.

Thompson, Geoff and Laura Alba-Juez (eds) 2014. *Evaluation in Context*. [Pragmatics and Beyond New Series, 242]. Amsterdam: Benjamins.

Ullmann, Stephen 1977 [1962]. *Semantics. An Introduction to the Science of Meaning*. Oxford: Basil Blackwell.

Vandergriff, Ilona 2013. Emotive communication online: a contextual analysis of computer-mediated communication (CMC) cues. *Journal of Pragmatics* 51: 1–12.

Villalba, Xavier 2008. Exclamatives: a thematic guide with many questions and few answers. *Catalan Journal of Linguistics* 7: 9–40.

Vingerhoets, Ad J.J.M., Laura M. Bylsma and Cornelis de Vlam 2013. Swearing: a biopsychosocial perspective. *Psychological Topics* 22: 287–304.
Volek, Bronislava 1987. *Emotive Signs in Language and Semantic Functioning of Derived Nouns in Russian*. Amsterdam: Benjamins.
Waksler, Rachelle 2012. *Super, uber, so*, and *totally*: over-the-top intensification to mark subjectivity in colloquial discourse. In Nicole Baumgarten, Inke Du Bois and Juliane House (eds) *Subjectivity in Language and Discourse*. [= *Studies in Pragmatics* 10]. Bingley: Emerald Group, 17–31.
Warriner, Amy Beth, Victor Kuperman and Marc Brysbaert 2013. Norms of valence, arousal, and dominance for 13,915 English lemmas. *Behavior Research Methods* 45: 1191–1207.
Wharton, Tim 2009. *Pragmatics and Non-Verbal Communication*. Cambridge: Cambridge University Press.

Related topics

Chapter 2, Internalist semantics; Chapter 3, History of semantics; Chapter 5, Cognitive semantics; Chapter 6, Corpus semantics; Chapter 8, Embodiment, simulation and meaning.

28
Interpretative semantics

François Rastier (translated by Nick Riemer)

1 Some context

Interpretative semantics (henceforth IS) first appeared as a research programme in France in the middle of the 1980s. As part of the Saussurean tradition, it rests in particular on a synthesis of European structural semantics as developed by such authors as Louis Hjelsmlev, Eugenio Coseriu, Émile Benveniste, Klaus Heger, Kurt Baldinger, Horst Geckeler, Bernard Pottier, and Algirdas-Julien Greimas (see Rastier (1987) for an initial presentation of the theory).

In the 1970s the generative perspective was dominant in both linguistics (in the form of the Chomskyan paradigm) and semiotics (in the form of the Greimasian paradigm). This perspective inherited the legacy of the philosophical grammars that predate linguistics' constitution as a science: at issue was the explanation of "surface" linguistic phenomena through cognitive operations of a logical nature applying to deep structures, a process that received an axiomatic presentation (see Chapter 3). The interpretative problematic represents a break with this traditional dualistic approach.

Since languages' expression and content are inseparable, semantics cannot be an autonomous discipline: it only describes a methodologically determined *perspective* on signs and therefore must be complemented by a *perspective* on expression: syntax (in part), morphology, phonology and graphemics describe a complementary perspective on the same signs. Linguistics is thus defined as the semiotics of languages – quite independent of the semiotics found in logical positivism and the syntax/semantics/pragmatics division (see Chapters 10 and 11), which cannot be applied to natural languages.

Relative to the dominant paradigms in competition on the international scale, cognitive (see Chapter 5) and logical semantics (see Chapter 4), IS opens up a third way. Indeed, it rejects both the cognitive and logical forms of dualism, expressed through the separation between ideas and signs, or between signs – or names – and referents. IS does not advance hypotheses about either the theory of knowledge or ontology, and does not deal with either representations or entities in the world. Indeed, it describes linguistic meaning and the meaning of oral texts without any appeal to conceptual or wordly realities, but as the product of *differences* between signs and other units, whether in context or within texts and corpora.

If linguistic meaning does not consist in representations, it still imposes constraints on their formation; thus, within texts, semantic structures promote various referential impressions.

In this difference-based problematic, value is the fundamental concept. (i) Value is the true reality of linguistic units. (ii) It is determined by the position of units in the system (and hence by differences: see Saussure, *Course in General Linguistics*, Part II, chapter 4). (iii) Nothing preexists the determination of value by the system. Value therefore is not a sign, but a relation between signifieds. It excludes an atomistic definition of the sign, which would provide it with a priori signification – for a signification is a result, not a pregiven fact. It proscribes the compositional definition of meaning, since it establishes the determination of the local by the global as a structural principle. As a result, a sign must be acknowledged not to be a universal concept, but a signified which is relative to a language, or, in fact, to a text and a corpus.

The logical and ontological tradition which has prevailed in grammar and subsequently in the language sciences has isolated the word from its connection with its referent, the phrase from its connection with a situation, and the text from its relation with a world, whether fictional or not. For this paradigm of *signification*, the basis of which is, at the end of the day, metaphysical, I think it useful to substitute that of *meaning* [*sens*], a term originally from the rhetorical and hermeneutic tradition. This allows us to break the triple isolation of sign, phrase and text: the word takes on meaning in the syntagm, the syntagm in the period, the period in the text, the text in the social practice in which it is produced, relative to other texts. As a result, since languages are not denotationally or psychologically "transparent", their content and their expression jointly constitute an autonomous domain of objectification.

2 General principles

2.1 The semiotic environment

Furthermore, to avoid isolating signs and reifying meaning, it seems useful to recall the following principles:

i   Since the characterization of signs depends on interpretative processes which vary according to context, the "same" sign can function as an interpretative "clue", an index, a symbol, etc. The study of signs is therefore dependent on that of interpretative practices.
ii The object of semiotics is not made up of signs, but of complex performances such as opera, rituals, and so on. The complex precedes the simple, and since oral or written texts are the empirical object of linguistics, methodological procedures of a non-trivial kind are needed to delimit signs.
iii The differential characterization of texts and other semiotic performances presupposes the constitution and critical analysis of corpora.
iv By their nature, signs are neither instruments of thought nor the expression of perceptual impressions. The semiotic realm, which consists of complex performances, is what constitutes the human milieu: this milieu is not an instrument, but the world in which we live and to which we have to adapt ourselves. The interpretative problematic is therefore no longer that of representation, but that of *coupling* in the biological sense, extended to *cultural coupling* with the semiotized environment.
v   Although pragmatics privileges the here and now, the human environment contains masses of objects which are absent, or which, at least, lack any immediate perceptual substrate: they populate the *distal zone* of the semiotic environment, which is the intended object of sciences as much as religions. Since signs are not referential, they allow worlds to be created.

2.2 Meaning

Briefly: (i) Meaning is a level of objectivity which is reducible neither to reference nor to mental representations. It can be analysed into *semantic features* (or *semes*), which are moments of stability in the interpretative process. (ii) The typology of signs depends on the typology of the interpretative processes which have them as their objects. (iii) Since it is made up of differences that are perceived and characterized in actual practices, meaning is a property of texts and not of isolated signs – which have no empirical existence. (iv) The meaning of a unit is determined by its context. Since the context is the entire text, *microsemantics* depends on *macrosemantics*. (v) The elementary textual units are not words but *passages*. A passage's expression will be referred to as an *extract*; its content as a *fragment*. (vi) On the semantic level, relevant semantic features are organized in such a way as to constitute *semantic forms*, such as themes, which emerge against the *semantic background*, consisting especially in isotopies (recurring identical semes). For example, in the phrase *The admiral ordered the furling of the sails*, the generic feature /navigation/ is recurrent in "admiral", "furling", and "sails" and therefore constitutes an isotopy (see section 3.2 below). Semantic forms are moments of stability within series of transformations, both within a single text, and between different ones. A form is a cluster of semantic features: for example, in *Dawn lights the source* (Eluard) the cluster /inchoative/+/flow/+/clear/ is recurrent in "dawn", "lights", and "source".

2.3 Signs

i   If the *morpheme* is the elementary linguistic unit, the *text* is the minimum unit of analysis, since the global determines the local.
ii Every text is derived from a genre which determines, without completely constraining, its genetic, mimetic, and hermeneutic modes. The genetic mode is what regulates the text's production, the mimetic mode is what regulates the referential impression the text produces and the hermeneutic mode is what regulates its interpretation.
iii Every genre belongs to a discourse-type. Through its genre every text is therefore connected to a discourse-type.
iv Every text depends on a corpus and must be related to it to be interpreted.
v   A text's preferred corpus is composed of texts of the same genre. The genetic and interpretative procedures within the text are inseparable from the interpretative procedures in the intertextual structure of the corpus.

2.4 Languages

A language is made up of a corpus of oral or written texts and a system (cf. Chapter 6). The system as linguists reconstruct it is a rational hypothesis formulated on the basis of regularities observed in the corpus. Between the corpus and the system, *norms* play a mediating role: anchored in social practices, norms of discourse, genre, and style testify to the influence of social practices on the texts which depend on them. To avoid the spurious opposition between a language as a system of forms and as the product of a culture, the system should be considered as possessing (compulsory) *rules* and (non-compulsory) *norms* of varying regulative force; for example, the norms of the French ballad differ from those of the English one.

Rules and norms presumably only differ in the regularities of their diachronic evolution. As is well known, words (lexemes, then morphemes) develop from the crystallization and erosion of syntagmatic strings; what is true of these linguistic units is no doubt also true of the rules which regulate their relations and thereby constitute them as units: rules are probably frozen norms of discourse.

In synchrony, every rule is contiguous with the norms that accompany – or, in fact, condition – its application: without them, for instance, indefinitely recursive, though grammatically correct, embeddings could not be prevented. The grammaticality of a phrase can therefore only be assessed if the discourse, the genre and the text from which it is extracted are known – in addition, obviously, to the dating and the geographical origin of the text in question. Elementary though this observation is, it reveals the inanity of the discussions of ungrammaticality and asemanticity which cannot fail to arise as soon as we agree to discuss unattested or out of context phrases. Thus, in contrast to that of a formal language, the system of a *natural* language is in fact plural, unfolding in different structural regimes according to the levels and scales of analysis. Its local or regional arenas of organization are not unified in any hierarchy which attests to the existence of a unique and homogeneous system – as is confirmed by the continuous evolution of languages, whose systemic heterogeneity constitutes the internal driver of their unending alteration through a process of disturbance and readjustment.

Natural language is thus never the only normative system at work; a text (oral or written) is the point of junction, in the context of an actual practice, between a language, a discourse, a genre, and a style.

3 Scales of description

IS recognizes four scales of complexity, starting with the morpheme and extending to the period, the text and the corpus. Working backwards, the corpus determines the meaning of the text, and the text determines the meaning of its parts, down to the period and the morpheme.

3.1 Lexical semantics ("microsemantics")

3.1.1 Semes

There are two principal levels of lexical complexity:

a   The *morpheme* is the minimal linguistic sign. For instance, the word *rétropropulseurs* ["back thrusters"] contains five morphemes: *rétro-*, *pro-*, *puls-*, *-eur*, *-s*. A word is composed of one or more morphemes. They are divided into a signifier (whether overt or not: e.g. in French, *substantif*, the singular of *substantifs* "substantives" has a zero signifier) and a signified, the *sememe*.

b   The *lexeme* is the integrated group of morphemes which constitutes the unit of signification. A lexeme may be composed of only a single morpheme (e.g. the preposition *to*).

A sememe is a structured whole of relevant features or *semes*. They are defined as relations of opposition or of equivalence within classes of sememes: for instance, "*bistouri*" is opposed to "*scalpel*" by the seme /for the living/; the opposition /animal/ or /vegetable/ distinguishes "venomous" from "poisonous"; "mausoleum" is opposed to "memorial" in virtue of the seme /presence of the body/ but is equivalent to it in virtue of the seme /funerary monument/. (We use the following conventions: cited expressions are italicized, contents – here, sememes – are

Interpretative semantics

in quotation marks, semes are enclosed in slashes, and semantic classes by double slashes.) Since semes are units particular to specific languages, we do not make any universalist hypothesis about them.

Two types of seme can be distinguished: (a) *Generic* semes index the sememe in semantic classes of higher orders of generality. (b) S*pecific* semes distinguish sememes in the context of lexemes belonging to the same minimal class, e.g. "poir"- and "pomm"- in the context of "poire" [pear] and "pomme" [apple] or of "poirier" [pear tree] and "pommier" [apple tree] (but not "poireau" [leek] or "pommeau" [pommel]).

Semes can assume two different statuses according to their mode of actualization, understood as the instantiation of a type by a token.

a *Inherent* semes are inherited by default from type to token, unless contradicted by the context. Each of the semes in a type is an attribute with a typical value. For instance, in "crow", the attribute (or semantic axis) <colour> has /black/ as its typical value. /Black/ is therefore said to be an inherent seme for "crow". But a contextual determination could very well prevent this inheritance taking place and impose an atypical <colour> value (e.g. *I see a white crow*). No inherent seme therefore appears in every context.
b *Afferent* semes are divided into two classes. The first designate the relations that apply a minimal class of sememes (a *taxeme*) to another. For instance, in French the members of the taxeme //"man", "woman"// are the targets of an application relation whose source is the members of the taxeme //"strength", "weakness"//. This kind of application explains so-called connotational phenomena, as well as certain prototypicality ones.

The distinction between actualization and virtualization has to be specified in degrees of relevance. Four of these can be distinguished, according to whether the seme is neutralized (excluded) or virtualized (but able to be reactualized), actualized, or salient. For instance, in "Guillaume was the woman in the household" (Zola), the seme /feminine sex/ is neutralized in "woman". Furthermore, the seme /human/ is actualized, but not made salient; by contrast, /weakness/, though afferent, is salient.

3.1.2 Lexical classes

Since the definition of semes depends on the structurally and contextually established semantic classes in a language, these classes need to be characterized.

(1) The minimal class is the *taxeme*. The sememe's specific semes are defined within its scope, just like its least generic (taxemic) seme, e.g. /funerary monument/ for "mausoleum" and "memorial". Taxemes reflect situations of choice; for example, "bus" belongs to the same taxeme as "underground", unlike "coach" (which belongs to the same class as "train"). Within a taxeme, different kinds of relation can be found: oppositions between contraries (*male, female*), between contradictories (*possible, impossible*), graded oppositions (*burning, hot, warm, cold, freezing*), implications (*demobilized* presupposes *mobilized*), complementarity (*husband, wife; theory, practice; hunger, thirst; sell, buy*).
(2) The *field* is a structured set of taxemes; for instance, the field //forms of transport// includes taxemes like //"bus", "underground"// and //"coach", "train"//. In texts, sememes belonging to different hierarchical levels within the field can be juxtaposed (e.g. "Wine or Perrier?" "Beaujolais or water?").

(3) The class of highest generality is the *domain*. Each domain is linked to a type of specific social practice. Lexicographical indicators like *chem.* (chemistry) or *mar.* (marine) are domain indicators. In the written languages of developed countries, 300–400 domains can be counted. Their number, nature and content differ from culture to culture.
(4) Last, *dimensions* are classes of high generality, but not superordinate to the preceding ones. Small in number, they divide the semantic universe into broad oppositions like /vegetable/ vs. /animal/ or /human/ vs. /animal/. They are often lexicalized (cf. "poisonous" vs. "venomous" for the first opposition, "bouche" [human mouth] vs. "gueule" [animal mouth] for the second).

3.1.3 Interpretative operations

In context, lexemes' meanings are determined by three operations which transform the significations available in language: semes' activation or inhibition, and the propagation of activated semes from one sememe to another. These three operations observe laws of dissimilation or assimilation, which increase or reduce semantic contrasts. Without in any way claiming exhaustivity, we will now exemplify these three operations.

a   *Inhibition* prevents the activation of inherent semes, which are therefore virtualized. Phraseological uses provide excellent examples of this process. "Step up" includes the inherent seme /spatiality/, "battlement" includes the inherent semes /architecture/ and /verticality/. Both are activated in *Sir Bayard, noble knight, steps up to the battlement* (*créneau*) but virtualized in *Sarkozy steps up into the breach* (*créneau*). If these semes are not fully suppressed, their perceptual salience is still reduced. The content "Sarkozy", indexed in the domain //politics//, prompts a generic allotopy (domain discrepancy) with "battlement", indexed in the domain //war//. Governed in this case by the principle of assimilation, interpretation inhibits certain semes which index the sememe in the //war// domain, throwing into relief those compatible with //politics//.

The law of dissimilation can also prevent semes' activation. For instance, in the menu formula *fromage ou fromage blanc* ["cheese or fromage blanc" (a yoghurt like soft creamy cheese, literally "white cheese")] the first occurrence of *fromage* receives a restricted sense relative to the one it takes on in *fromage ou dessert* ["cheese or dessert"]: all the inherent semes in *fromage* which are specific to *fromage blanc* are inhibited. Contrastively, it signifies "fermented cheese", and the seme /fermented/ is salient.

b   *Activation* allows afferent semes to be activated—these are present in the core meaning in the form of categories rather than of specified features (or, in terms of frame theory, that of attributes of unknown value). For example, the seme /standing upright/ does not belong to the meaning of "shepherdess": it is simply one of the virtual features which can be inferred from the inherent seme /human/. Nevertheless, in the context *Bergère ô tour Eiffel* ["Shepherdess, O Eiffel Tower"] (Apollinaire, *Zone*), /standing upright/ is actualized by the presence of the inherent seme /verticality/ belonging to "tower". (When readers represent the shepherdess to themselves, they imagine her standing upright.) The law of assimilation thus applies in an equative syntactic construction.

Interpretative operations are not put into effect without any conditions. In each case, to trigger the interpretative process, it is necessary to distinguish: (i) the *problem* whose solution it results in; (ii) the *interpretant* which selects the inference to be made; (iii) the *reception condition* which lowers the activation threshold and allows or facilitates the process.

3.2 The semantics of the period, or mesosemantics

Mesosemantics explains the intermediate level between the lexeme and the text and thus covers the phrase or, more precisely, the region extending from the syntactically functioning syntagm up to the complex phrase and its immediate connections.

A   *Case theory* distinguishes *agency zones* (Pottier 1974; 1992: 124–127; Rastier 1997): an event zone of *primary agency*, two zones of *secondary agency*, one anterior to the event, the other subsequent to it; and last, a zone of *dependence* where the event's *circumstantial complements* are located. We suggest distinguishing two forms of primary agency, which we will refer to as *intrazone* or *interzone agency*, depending on whether the content which they articulate is located within a single zone or between two different ones. Interzone agency is distributed across three pairs: identity-proximal, proximal-distal, or identity-distal.

   The primary agents are the nominative and the attributive cases, the ergative and the accusative, the sender, and the receiver. Secondary agency includes the agents which are not engaged in the process underway in the primary agency, such as the initial agents – the final and the causal – and the peripheral ones – the benefactive and the resultative. In *Mary lends a book to Paul for Tom*, Mary and Paul are the primary agents, and Tom is a secondary one, located in a distal zone.

   i   *Attribution.* The distinction between the three anthropic zones allows us to specify various forms of attribution, distinguishing the situation where two zones are put in relation to each other from that in which two contents of a single zone are. Intrazone attributive predications correspond to so-called analytic propositions, and interzone attributive predications to synthetic propositions.
   ii *Non-attributive predications.* If transitivity in the strong sense is defined – respecting its etymolocgy – as the crossing of a boundary, three kinds of transitivity can be distinguished: identity-proximal, proximal-distal and identity-distal, each of them open to two perspectives depending on whether the source of the action is located in one zone or in another.
   iii *The circumstantial complements.* Circumstantial complements situate the utterance and its agents with respect to the zones (on the axes of time, space, mode and evaluation).

B   IS privileges agreement relations – so much so, in fact, that it describes dependence relations in terms of agreement, since agreement relations bind successive syntagms without any a priori limit and thus do not break up the syntagmatic order of the text. It defines morphosyntax as a system regulating the spreading of semantic features: their reiteration in bundles establishes semantic backgrounds; their combination in structures establishes semantic forms which develop throughout the text. Semantic analysis consists in describing the mechanisms which regulate the spreading of semantic features. Certain syntactic structures on the level of the syntagm encourage the spreading of semantic features, while others inhibit it. Beyond the period, other syntagmatic structures take over. Starting from the level of the syntagm, they are superimposed over syntactic structures, but have not yet been described by linguistics, since they are a matter of norms rather than of rules.

   The concept of isotopy can now be invoked – a notion in principle independent of syntactic structures and putative phrase boundaries. An isotopy can extend over two morphemes, two words, a paragraph, or a whole text. It is possible to distinguish between isotopies triggered by the recurrence of a specific feature (e.g. /inchoative/ in *The dawn lights up the spring* (Éluard), where this feature is recurrent in "dawn", "light up", and "spring"; or by that of a generic feature (like /navigation/ in *the admiral ordered the sails to be furled*). It is also necessary to distinguish isotopies prescribed by the functional system of language, as well as those that are optional because they belong to other systems of norms. The problem of the connections between syntax and semantics therefore concerns the relations between the isotopies prescribed by the functional system of language and those governed by other norm systems. Five noteworthy cases can be highlighted.

   i   Absence of both optional isotopy and isosemy, e.g. *That uselessly to the but I Bianca cardinal the* (a sequence obtained by random excerpting from *The lovers of Venice*, by Michel Zévaco). This sequence is neither a phrase nor an utterance.
   ii Isosemies without any optional isotopy, e.g. *the vertebral silence indisposes the licit veil* (Tesnière) ou *a paved pupil paraded presbyterally* (Martin). Such utterances, which are syntactically correct, refer to no semantically identifiable domain; a logician could therefore call them absurd.
   iii Two interlaced domain isotopies, e.g. *Shepherdess, O Eiffel Tower, the herd of bridges is bleating this morning* (Apollinaire). The utterance triggers a complex referential impression, and remains indeterminable. (According to several authors, cognitive *blending* theories take up the principles of the analysis of isotopies presented in Rastier (1987)).
   iv An optional isotopy, but with the violation of compulsory isotopies, e.g. *Once the train disappears, the station leaves laughing to look for the passenger* (René Char). This utterance triggers a referential impression by referring to the domain //forms of transport//: "train", "station", "passenger", "leaves" all include a generic seme which indexes them to this domain. As a result, the utterance appears to refer to a counterfactual world: it remains truth-functionally determinable, but logically false.
   v   An optional isotopy, accompanied by isosemies, e.g. *The green signal shows the track is clear* (Tesnière); *Every woman, even the ugliest, has made their lover suffer* (Apollinaire); *without tacking, and with the wind behind it, Eric Loiseau's catamaran won the race*. These utterances refer to the domains //forms of transport//, //love// and //navigation//, respectively. In this kind of utterance, several sememes or semies are indexed to a single domain; no other sememe stands in contradiction to this domain. The utterance triggers a referential impression, and is therefore determinable.

C   While what is described on the microsemantic level is the activation of semes, the mesosemantic level deals with the problem of how they are incorporated into semantic forms or backgrounds. Considered in isolation, syntagms and periods appear to be sites in which semantic forms or their components are constituted. Reinserted into the continuity of the text, however, they are sites in which backgrounds and forms are updated, a process which consists in their continuation, reiteration, or deformation. From this point of view, the syntactic structures in which they participate are means by which semantic features are channelled and semantic activity distributed: they mutually govern the course of semantic and expressive activity and constitute semiosis on their own scale of complexity. Formalisms with their origin in unification grammars allow this course of activity to be described without resort to the hierarchical and ontological categorizations bequeathed to linguistics by school grammars, first and foremost the traditional inventory of parts of speech, which is inadequate for most languages (cf. Vaillant (2014) on Caribbean creoles).

The articulation between the expression and the content occurs within the *passage*, a privileged site of local semiosis. In the interpretative perspective, this local unit can variously correspond, among other things, to a sign, a phrase or a paragraph. On the level of the signifier, the passage is an *excerpt*, placed between two blank spaces in the case of a minimal string of characters, or between two pauses or punctuation marks in the case of a period. On the level of the signified, the passage is a *fragment* which points to its immediate and remote left and right contexts. This is true for both the sememe and for the content of the syntagm or the period.

3.3 Textual semantics (macrosemantics)

A text is an attested empirical linguistic sequence, produced within a determinate social practice, and fixed on some kind of support. The production and interpretation of texts can be conceived of as a non-sequential interaction of various independent components – specifically, the thematic, dialectic, dialogic, and tactic ones.

i *Thematic.* IS describes the theme as a structured grouping of semes (a *semic molecule*). It is not necessarily dependent on any particular lexicalization; in technical texts, however, themes have a privileged, or even exclusive lexicalization.
ii *Dialectic.* As it deals with intervals of represented time and the developments which occur within it, dialectic particularly includes theories of narrative. It is defined on two levels. The first, called the *event level*, appears in all texts structured by a dialectic component. Its basic units are *actors*, *roles*, and *functions* – in the sense of types of action represented.

   Functions are typical interactions between actors: they are classes of process. Like actors, they are defined by a semic molecule and generic semes: thus, the *gift* is a pacifying function (a transmission function of ternary valency), the *challenge* is a polemical function (a confrontational function of binary valency). Functions correspond to actorial *valencies*. Functions can be grouped in functional syntagms; for instance, an *exchange* is made up of two transmissions, a *confrontation* of an attack and a counter-attack.

   The agonistic level, which is hierarchically superior to the event level, has *agonists* and *sequences* as its basic units. An *agonist* is a type which constitutes a class of actors, a sequence is a connection between analogous functional syntagms. In general, the dialectic component of practical texts only includes an event level, while fictional or mythical texts add an agonistic level to it.
iii *Dialogic.* Dialogic accounts for the modalization of semantic units at all the levels of complexity of the text. A *universe* is the set of textual units associated with an actor or an enunciatory focus: every modality is relative to a site (a universe) and a reference point (an actor). For instance, when the narrator of Balzac's *Cousin Betty* speaks of a "good bad deed", "good" refers to the universe of the two characters, and "bad" to his own universe.
iv *Tactic.* This final element accounts for the linear arrangement of semantic units on all levels.

   Each semantic unit, on the different levels of analysis, can therefore be characterized in virtue of the four components. Only a methodological decision can isolate these four components, which interact with each other simultaneously and non-hierarchically.

On the textual level as on others, units result from segmentations and categorizations over semantic forms and backgrounds, which can be given the general name *morphologies*. Their study is divided into three sections: links between backgrounds, for example in the case of genres which include several generic isotopies, like the parable; links between forms; and, above all, links between forms and backgrounds, crucial for the study of *semantic perception* (cf. Rastier (1993: 7)).

Depending on the components, semantic morphologies can be the objects of different descriptions. For example, in connection with the four components, a stable grouping of semantic features (a semic molecule) can be described as theme, actor, goal, or source of a modal point of view, and as a position in the linearity of the text. Further, different types of productive and interpretative operation correspond to each component.

Description must reproduce the dynamic aspect of the production and interpretation of texts. The first step consists in describing the dynamics of these backgrounds and forms: for example, the construction of semic molecules, their development, and their potential dissolution. These dynamics and their optimisations are parameterized in different ways according to genre and discourse, because the forms and backgrounds are constituted and recognized in them as a function of different norms: the perception of semantic backgrounds seems to be linked to rhythms, and that of forms to contours, in a way reminiscent of prosodic contours.

Accordingly, the meaning of a text is not something that is deduced from a series of propositions, but rather something that results from the perusal of macrosemantic forms, each with their own signifying capacity, and through the particular way they unfold and the valuations which are conferred on them. One thus encounters analogous problems in the understanding of texts to those posed by the *recognition* of incomplete forms.

The morphosemantic conception of the text can be modelled by dynamical systems theory, in which case the semantic backgrounds appear as series of regular points, and the semantic forms are individuated by their singular points (cf. Rastier (1999a)).

Accordingly, beyond a concatenation of symbols, the text can be conceived as a semiotic *course of action* (any text, as the semiotic part of a social practice, takes part in a codified set of actions). The genre codifies the way in which the action is conducted, but what could be called the *ductus* specifies an utterer, and allows the semantic style to be characterized by the particular rhythms and outlines of the forms' contours.

The generation of a text consists in a series of metamorphisms (transformation relations between forms) and transpositions (transformations of relations between forms and backgrounds), which can be revealed in speech by the study of reformulations and in writing by the study of drafts. Its interpretation consists in the main in the identification and evaluation of metamorphisms: for instance, the meaning of a narrative is articulated through thematic and dialectic transformations.

3.3 Corpus semantics (megasemantics)

An isolated text has no more existence than an isolated word or phrase: to be produced and understood, it must be related to a genre and a discourse, and, via them, to a type of social practice.

A corpus is a structured grouping of whole documented texts, potentially enriched through labelling and assembled (i) reflexively theoretically, taking discourses and genres into account; (ii) practically, with a view to a range of applications.

Several details need to be clarified at this point. (i) The *archive* brings together the entirety of documents available for a particular application or descriptive task. It is not a corpus because it is not put together for a particular investigation. (ii) The *reference corpus* is constituted by the entirety of the texts. It will stand in contrast to the study corpus. (iii) The *study corpus* is delimited by the needs of the application. (iv) Finally, the *working sub-corpora* vary from one stage of the research to the next and may only contain the relevant passages from the text or texts under study.

Corpora are thus not merely reservoirs of citations, or even collections of texts. As long as they are set up critically, taking into account genres and discourses, and protected by the necessary philological guarantees, they can become sites for the description of the three regimes of textuality – the genetic, the mimetic, and the hermeneutic. In point of fact, a text has its sources in a corpus, it is produced from this corpus and has to be maintained or reinserted in it to be correctly interpreted: the genetic and the hermeneutic regimes thus mutually adjust themselves to each other. As for the mimetic regime, which determines the referential impression, it also depends on the corpus and especially on the commonsense beliefs for which it gives evidence.

The well-confirmed correlation between global variables like discourse, generic field, or genre and local variables (e.g. morphosyntactic as much as graphic or phonological ones) leads us to raise the problem of *textual semiosis* (cf. Rastier (2000, 2010)). Semiosis is usually defined on the level of the sign, as a connection between signified and signifier; however, the effect of a genre is precisely in defining a normative connection between signifier and signified on the textual level: for instance, in the genre of the short story, the first paragraph is most often a description, not an introduction, as it is in a scientific article. The local and conditional semiosis that language structure provides on lower levels of complexity, from the morpheme to the lexeme, is only realized if it is compatible with the generic or even stylistic norms which make textual semiosis possible.

4 Methodology of an instrumental semantics

The essentially lexical character of currently available semantic theories and their adoption of mentalist postulates (cognitive semantics, prototype theory, etc.) make the methodological requirements of semantics even greater. Corpus semantics, however, may advance reflection on the methodological (practical) and epistemological (theoretical) levels alike. An instrumental semantics may render new data objectively observable and hypotheses of different kinds testable.

Since IS has the ambition of *applicability*, its methodology proposes to reconcile three requirements: the principles of corpus choice, the definition of hypotheses, and the choice of descriptive concepts (certain distinctions being able to be neutralized as a function of the application). It uses software programmes as experimental instruments, particularly since certain functions (in Hyperbase and Txt) have been developed in light of the problematic to which IS is addressed.

a   Since meaning consists of differences, the methodological incorporation of instrumental processes allows differences to be constructed – between words, passages, texts, authors, genres, and discourse. Relevance emerges not from quantitative data, but from the meeting of two horizons: "subjective" relevance as determined by the task itself, and "objective relevance" specific to the qualitative differences within and between texts.

b   On the epistemological level, the recourse to experiment allows objectivity to be attained (i) by undermining or confirming hypotheses and (ii) by allowing the object's structural regularities to emerge, when different instrumental procedures obtain congruent results despite differences in experimental material, scale, etc.

Corpus analysis allows polysemy to be relativized and reduced, and ambiguity to be checked for; it also allows the values of grammatical forms to be determined: for instance, the future does not have the same values in legal discourse as in novels.

A renewed relation to empirical data entails a new relation to theory: to articulate the connections between theory and practice more clearly, IS provides for simplifications as a function of different applications. Last, corpus semantics, from the moment it adopts a reflexive point of view with respect to its own procedures, allows us to make a break from candid objectivism: it does not practise the automatic analysis of *data*, in so far as this must first be taken *as* data, then interpreted after processing.

New facts that remained unnoticed until not long ago, and that have now been made objectively observable, take on scientific import, because they are inconceivable for the most widespread linguistic theories. Most of these theories are based on the entirely suspect tripartite division between semantics, syntax, and pragmatics, and can only consign the phenomena in question to rhetorical or stylistic research outside linguistics itself. Within this programme, corpus-based IS emphasizes two general complementarities: that of linguistic levels or planes of description (morphology, syntax, semantics) and that of the levels of organization and complexity (word, phrase, text, intertext).

5 Applications

Applications of IS concern disciplinary domains that deal with texts, just as much in the domain of the humanities (Latin and medieval corpora) as in contemporary corpora, whether literary, scientific, or journalistic.

i *Descriptive linguistics*. IS has been enlisted in work on Romance and Amerindian languages (see especially the work on Quechua agrarian vocabulary and on Chipaya by Enrique Ballón-Aguirre et al. (1992, 2002, 2011)).

ii *Textual semantics*. Since IS is originally a text-based semantics, it can be applied in multiple domains, for instance ancient and modern literary corpora (Amiri 2004; Ballón-Aguirre 2001; Canon-Roger and Chollier 2009; Choi 2006; Botchkarev 1999; Mézaille 2003; Gérard 2007), philosophical corpora (Loiseau and Rastier (2011) on Deleuze) and scientific ones (Valette (2003) on Guillaume; Djaoud et al. (2012) on Bourdieu (in Rastier and Valette forthcoming); Poudat (2006) on linguistics articles). Pedagogic developments privilege the use of digital corpora in the teaching of grammar and literature.

iii *Automated processing and corpus linguistics*. In its application to corpus linguistics, IS has the task of renewing the domains of information retrieval and knowledge representation (cf. Pincemin (1999); Tanguy (1997); Thlivitis (2000); Beust (1998); Perlerin (2004); Roy (2007)). In particular, IS can further applications which are increasingly the objects of social demand: recognizing a text type by its lexical or morphological characteristics; detecting a type of website; aiding in thematic analysis; achieving targeted dissemination by defining proximity between texts, etc. Most applications today presuppose tasks of characterization (identification through contrast): within a corpus, the aim is to single out the components relevant to the application. This reconnects linguistics, via a new path, with the problematic of the description of singularities specific to the sciences of culture; the description of laws, long deemed the necessary condition of scientificity, is subordinated to the systematic study of actually occurring uses. Corpus linguistics also participates in the programme of cross-linguistic language comparison;

but most of all, it allows this programme to be pursued within each language, by comparing discourses, genres and texts with each other (see Bourion (2001), Rastier (2011)).

iv *Non-linguistic semiotics and the semiotics of cultures.* The methodological principles governing the critical constitution of corpora are valid for all digital documents, for instance corpora of photos (Kanellos et al., 2000) or web sites (Beauvisage 2004; Trudel 2013). An overview on the languages of icons is presented in Vaillant (1999). Other domains, such as interactive virtual narratives, are also used (Cavazza and Pizzi 2006).

The fact that cultural objects depend on their conditions of creation and interpretation does not alter the fact that the values which they actualize can still be rendered objective in the form of facts. Everywhere now people are dealing with digital corpora, whether they are of music, images still or moving, dance, or polysemiotic performances like cinema, opera, rituals, etc. The scientific necessity of describing such corpora intersects here with social demand. With digital corpora, the sciences of culture discover new epistemological and methodological perspectives, and even a unifying project that could bring them together.

How to reconcile language and thought, content and expression, the supposed universality of the human mind and the diversity of cultures? How to describe the human environment in its massive semiotization? It is necessary to go beyond theories of the origin of language to better understand the emergence of the semiotic order, relying in particular on recent results of linguistics and anthropology (Rastier 2013). Since languages are human creations more than they are the providential products of evolution, summary oppositions between the innate and the acquired or nature and culture must be relativized. This task falls to the semiotics of cultures to avoid our species disappearing before it has been described.

Further reading

Signo (www.signosemio.com) is a bilingual semiotic theory website.
Texto! Textes et cultures (http://www.revue-texto.net) is an online journal.
Greimas, A. J. 1983. *Structural Semantics: An Attempt at a Method*, trans. Daniele McDowell, Ronald Schleifer and Alan Velie, Lincoln (Nebraska) University of Nebraska Press [1966]. Advances a semantic theory extending from the word (semic analysis) to the text (narrative and thematic analysis).
Pottier, Bernard 1974. *Linguistique générale. Théorie et description*, Paris, Klincksieck. Integrates semantics into general linguistics, particularly in lexicon and syntax.
Coseriu, Eugenio 2007. *Lingüística del texto. Introducción a la hermenéutica del sentido*. Edición, anotación y estudio previo de Òscar Loureda Lamas. Madrid: Arco/Libros. Problematizes a textual linguistics mainly based on semantics.
Albrecht, Jörn 2007. *Europäischer Strukturalismus. Ein forschungsgeschichtlicher Überblick*. 3., erweiterte Auflage. Tübingen, Narr. A clear presentation of an epistemological history of European structuralism.
Saussure, F. de 2006. *Writings in General Linguistics* (S. Bouquet, R. Engler, C. Sanders, M. Ires, eds). Oxford: Oxford University Press. Overturns the conventional conception of Saussureanism and of linguistics in its connections with semiotics.

References

Ablali, Driss, Sémir Badir and Dominique Ducart 2013. *Documents, textes, œuvres*, Rennes: Presses Universitaires de Rennes.
Choi, Yong Ho 2004. *Tekst Umiron Kwangei Course in Text Semantics*. Seoul: Ingan Sarang.
Hébert, Louis 2001. *Introduction à la sémantique des textes*. Paris: Honoré Champion.

Amiri, Bassir 2004. *Chaos dans l'imaginaire antique de Varron à l'époque augustinienne. Etude sémantique et herméneutique.* Nancy: ADRA; Paris: diff. de Boccard-Paris.

Belghanem, Ali 2012. Sémantique du discours scientifique de Pierre Bourdieu. Construction et classification d'un corpus de travail. *Texto!* 17. http://www.revue-texto.net/index.php?id=3068.

Beust, P. 1998. *Contribution à un modèle interactionniste du sens. Amorce d'une compétence interprétative pour les machines.* Computer science thesis, Université de Caen.

Botchkarev, Andréï 1999. *Le motif végétal dans "A la recherche du temps perdu".* Villeneuve d'Ascq: Presses universitaires du Septentrion.

Ballón-Aguirre, Enrique 2001. *Desconcierto barroco.* Mexico: Universidad Nacional Autónoma de México.

Ballón-Aguirre, Enrique 2003. De la semántica componencial a la semántica interpretativa (el léxico agrario andino). *Perfiles semióticos* 1: 17–41.

Ballón-Aguirre, Enrique 2006. *Tradición oral peruana – Literaturas ancestrales y populares.* 2 vol. Lima: Fondo Editorial de la PUC.

Ballón-Aguirre, Enrique and Rodolfo Cerrón-Palomino 1992. *Vocabulario razonado de la actividad agraria andina – Terminología quechua.* Cuzco: Centro de Estudios Regionales Andinos "Bartolomé de las Casas".

Ballón-Aguirre, Enrique and Rodolfo Cerrón-Palomino 2002. *Terminología agraria andina–Nombres quechumaras de la papa.* Lima: International Potato Center – Centro de Estudios Regionales Andinos "Bartolomé de las Casas".

Ballón-Aguirre, Enrique and Rodolfo Cerrón-Palomino 2011. *Chipaya. Léxico y etnotaxonomía.* Lima, Radboud Universiteit Nijmegen: Fondo Editorial de la PUC.

Beauvisage, Thomas 2004. *Sémantique des parcours des utilisateurs sur le Web.* Doctoral thesis, Université Paris X.

Beust, Pierre, Stéphane Ferrari and Vincent Perlerin 2003. NLP model and tools for detecting and interpreting metaphors. In D. Archer, P. Rayson, A. Wilson and T. McEnery (eds) *Domain-Specific Corpora, Corpus Linguistics. Proceedings of the Corpus Linguistics 2003 conference. University Centre for Computer Corpus Research on Language Technical Papers* 16, 114–123.

Bourion, E. 2001. *L'aide à l'interprétation des textes électroniques.* Thesis, Université de Nancy II. http://www.revue-texto.net/Corpus/Publications/Bourion/Bourion_Aide.html.

Cavazza, M. O. and D. Pizzi 2006. Narratology for interactive storytelling: a critical introduction. In S. Gobel, R. Malkewitz and I.A. Iurgel (eds) *Technologies for Interactive Digital Storytelling and Entertainment. Lecture Notes in Computer Science* 4326. Berlin, Heidelberg: Springer, 72–83.

Choi, Yong Ho 2002. Discursive space – an introduction to text semantics. *Semiotic Inquiry* 12: 286–310.

Choi, Yong Ho 2004. 'Text Semantics of François Rastier: a critical reading about the short story of Bernard Werber'. *French Studies* 30: 367–386.

Choi, Yong Ho 2006. *Umi wa Sulwhasung Meaning and narrativity,* Seoul. Ingan Sarang.

Canon-Roger, Françoise and Christine Chollier 2008. *Des genres aux textes. Essais de sémantique interprétative en littérature de langue anglaise.* Arras: Artois Presses Université.

Canon-Roger, Françoise and Christine Chollier 2009. A comparison of several interpretations of 'Snow' by Louis MacNeice. *Imaginaires* 13: 155–75. [*L'interprétation au pluriel*]

Canon-Roger, Françoise 2009. Traduction et réélaboration interprétative. *Revue Française de Linguistique Appliquée* 14: 25–38.

Chollier, Christine 2005. Essai d'interprétation des rythmes sémantiques dans The Heart Is A Lonely Hunter de Carson McCullers. *Imaginaires* 11: 255–272.

Chollier, Christine 2010. Rôles créateurs des contextes dans les parcours interprétatifs des passages. *Texto!* 15. http://www.revue-texto.net/index.php?id=2662.

Djaoud, Smaïl 2009. Quelques processus d'élaboration de concepts sur le Maghreb dans les sciences sociales (Julien, Bourdieu et Tillion) *Texto!* 14. http://www.revue-texto.net/index.php?id=2165.

Duteil-Mougel, Carine et al. 2012. Semiotics and semantic: tools for an effective appropriation of information, communication and health technologies. *Medetel 2012. The International eHealth,*

Telemedecine and Health ICT Forum For Education, Networking and Business, Luxembourg, 17–20 April 2012.

Gérard, Christophe 2007. Sémantique et linéarité du texte. La place du rythme en sémantique des textes. In M. Ballabriga (ed.) *Rythme et textualités*. Toulouse: Éditions Universitaires du Sud.

Kanellos, Ioannis 2012. Patrimonial traditions meet educational preoccupations: the interpretive shift of the accessibility requirement. In Olivier Bruneau, Pere Grapí, Peter Heering, Sylvain Laubé, Maria-Rossa Massa-Esteve and Thomas de Vittori (eds) *Innovative Methods for Science Education: History of Science, ICT and Inquiry Based Science Teaching*. Berlin: Frank & Timme, 203–222.

Kanellos, Ioannis, Théodore Thlivitis and Alain Léger 2000. Indexation anthropocentrée d'images au moyen de textes: arguments théoriques et directions applicatives du projet SEMINDEX. *Cognito* 17: 33–44.

Loiseau, Sylvain 2010. Investigating the interactions between different axes of variation in text typology. In P. Grzybek and E. Kelih (eds) *Text and Language: Structures, Functions. Interrelations*. Vienna: Praesens, 109–118.

Loiseau, Sylvain and François Rastier 2011. Linguistique de corpus philosophiques: l'exemple de Deleuze. In Patrice Maniglier (ed.) *Le moment philosophique des années 1960 en France*. Paris: PUF, 73–93.

Mézaille, Thierry 2000. Accès sémantique aux banques textuelles. L'exemple de Balzac. In *Champs du Signe* 10: 291–313.

Mézaille, Thierry 2003 *La blondeur, thème proustien*. Paris: L'Harmattan.

Missire, Régis 2010. Unités linguistiques à signifiant discontinu, du morphème au texte. Une approche néo-saussurienne. In J.-P. Bronckart, C. Bota and E. Bulea (eds) *Le projet de Ferdinand de Saussure*. Geneva: Droz, 289–312.

Missire, R. 2007. Rythmes sémantiques et temporalité des parcours interprétatifs. In M. Ballabriga and P. Mpondo-Dicka (eds) *Rythme, sens & textualité: hommage à G. Maurand*. Toulouse: Éd. universitaires du Sud, 75–115.

Missire, R. 2004. Normes linguistiques et afférence sémantique: une lecture de *Sémantique interprétative* à partir d'Eugenio Coseriu sistema, norma y habla. In *Texto!* 9: 1–28.

Missire, R. 2005. Une larme baudelairienne, essai de description morphosémantique de *Tristesses de la lune*. *Champs du signe* 20: 87–114.

Perlerin, Vincent 2004. *Sémantique légère pour le document*. Computer science thesis, Université de Caen.

Pincemin, Bénédicte 1999. *Diffusion cible automatique d'informations: conception et mise en œuvre d'une linguistique textuelle pour la caractérisation des destinataires et des documents*. Linguistics thesis, Université de Paris IV.

Pottier, Bernard 1992. *Sémantique générale*. Paris: PUF.

Poudat, Céline 2006. *Étude contrastive de l'article scientifique de revue linguistique dans une perspective d'analyse des genres*. Doctoral thesis, Université d'Orléans.

Rastier, François 1971. *Idéologie et théorie des signes*. The Hague: Mouton.

Rastier, François 1987. *Sémantique interprétative*, Paris: PUF 1987. 2nd revised and extended edition 1996; 3rd edition, 2009.

Rastier, François 1993. Problems of cognitive semantics. In Franson D. Manjali (ed.) *Language and Cognition*. New Dehli: Bahri Publications, 211–232.

Rastier, François 1997. *Meaning and Textuality*. Toronto: Toronto University Press. [English translation by Frank Collins and Paul Perron of *Sens et textualité*, Paris, Hachette, 1989. Text revised and extended.]

Rastier, François 1998. Sign and symbol. Semiotics and cognitive science. In Manjali, F. éd. *Cognitive Science*. New Delhi: Bahri Publications. Réédition en ouvrage de 1997 h.

Rastier, François 1998. Prédication, actance et zones anthropiques. In M. Forsgren, K. Jonasson, and H. Kronning (eds) *Prédication, assertion, information: actes du colloque d'Uppsala en linguistique française, 6–9 juin 1996*. Stockholm: Uppsala, 443–461.

Rastier, François 1999a. Representation or interpretation? In Linguistic Society of Korea (ed.) *Linguistics in the Morning Calm*, 4. Seoul: The Linguistic Society of Korea, 115–135.

Rastier, François 1999b. Cognitive semantics and diachrony. In Andreas Blank and Peter Koch (eds) *Historical Semantics and Cognition*. Berlin: Mouton de Gruyter, 109–144.
Rastier, François 1999c. Sign and symbol: semiotics and cognitive science. In H.S. Gill and G. Manetti (eds) *Signs and Signification II*. New Delhi: Bahri Publications, 199–208.
Rastier, François 2000. On signs and texts: cognitive science and interpretation. In P. Perron et al. (eds) *Semiotics as a Bridge between the Humanities and the Sciences*. New York, Toronto: Legas Press, 409–450.
Rastier, François 2005. On signs and texts. *Applied Semiotics/Sémiotique appliquée* 2: 195–244.
Rastier, François 2009a. Interview. In F. Stjernfeld and P. Bundgaard (eds.) *Signs and Meaning: Five Questions*. Automatic Press, 139–152.
Rastier, François 2009b. Passages and paths within the intertext. *Belgian Journal of Linguistics* 23: 7–29.
Rastier, François 2010. Web semantics vs. the semantic web: the problem of keyness. In Marina Bondi and Mike Scott (eds) *Keyness in Texts*. Amsterdam, Philadelphia: Benjamins, 93–112.
Rastier, François 2011. *La Mesure et le Grain. Sémantique de corpus*. Paris: Champion.
Rastier, François 2012. Text semiotics: between philology and hermeneutics – from the document to the work *Semiotica* 192: 99–122.
Rastier, François 2013. *L'Homme de signes*. Paris: Éditions du Cerf.
Rastier, François, Anne Abeille and Marc Cavazza 2002. *Semantics for Descriptions*. Chicago: CSLI Publications.
Rastier, François and Simon Bouquet (eds) 2002. *Une introduction aux sciences de la culture*. Paris: PUF.
Rastier, François and Kjersti Floettum (eds) 2003. *Academic Discourse, Multidisciplinary Approaches*. Oslo: Novus.
Rastier, François and Mathieu Valette (eds) forthcoming. *Concepts en contexte*. Paris: AFK.
Roy, Thibault 2007. *Visualisations interactives pour l'aide personnalisée à l'interprétation d'ensembles documentaires*. Computer science thesis, Université de Caen.
Tanguy, Ludovic 1997. *Traitement automatique de la langue naturelle et interprétation: contribution à l'élaboration d'un modèle informatique de la sémantique interprétative*. Thesis, Université de Rennes.
Thlivitis, Théodore 1998. *Sémantique interprétative intertextuelle: assistance anthropocentrée à la compréhension des textes*. Computer science thesis, Université de Rennes.
Trudel, Éric 2013. Sémantique des sites Web de restaurants: analyse de productions polysémiotiques. Doctoral thesis, Université du Québec à Trois-Rivières.
Vaillant, Pascal 1999. *Sémiotique des langages d'icônes*. Paris: Éditions Honoré Champion.
Vaillant, Pascal forthcoming. La syntaxe, c'est de la sémantique. In Ablali et al. (eds) *Documents, textes, œuvres*. Rennes: PUR.
Valette, M. 2003. Conceptualisation and evolution of concepts. The example of French linguist Gustave Guillaume. In K.J. Fløttum and F. Rastier (eds) *Academic Discourse: Multidisciplinary Approaches*. Oslo: Novus Press, 55–74.
Vaxelaire, Jean-Louis 2005. *Les noms propres. Une analyse lexicologique et historique*. Paris: Honoré Champion.

Related topics

Chapter 3, History of semantics; Chapter 6, Corpus semantics; Chapter 12, Lexical decomposition.

29
Semantic processing

Steven Frisson and Martin J. Pickering

1 Introduction

In contrast to the theorizing and model building in linguistic semantics, psycholinguistic research has not yet led to unified theories of how language users process words and larger chunks semantically. Rather, psycholinguists have concentrated on specific semantic phenomena, for example how ambiguous words are interpreted on-line, and have tended not to use their findings to support general theories of semantic processing. In addition, the cross-pollination between linguists and psycholinguists is still, regrettably, rather limited, with psycholinguists rarely relating their findings to contemporary theoretical semantics, and theoretical linguists paying little attention to relevant experimental results.

In this chapter, we discuss a range of psycholinguistic findings that should be interesting to linguists and could inform linguistic theories. These are, obviously, not the only topics that psycholinguists have studied, and readers can find much more information in, for example, the *Handbook of Psycholinguistics* (Traxler and Gernsbacher 2006, e.g., chapters 10, 11, 14, 15, 18, 20, 21, 23), the *Oxford Handbook of Psycholinguistics* (Gaskell 2007), and the *Cambridge Handbook of Psycholinguistics* (Spivey et al. 2012). The bulk of the present chapter will be devoted to studies of semantic comprehension, but we also make some reference to research on language production, a field that has been growing steadily over the last 20 years or so. One issue that needs addressing is to what extent language comprehension and production should be integrated. Most models keep production and comprehension quite separate, but sometimes assume that they share representations but involve inverse mappings between these representations.

2 Incrementality

One of the most important features of language processing is that it is incremental (e.g. Just and Carpenter (1980); Marslen-Wilson (1973)), with comprehenders starting to interpret each word as soon as it becomes available. Hence, language users do not wait until, for example, the end of a clause (see Fodor et al. (1974)) before they start interpreting the text. This can be seen, for example, in the processing of lexical ambiguities where it is commonly found that an immediate selection is made between the different meanings of a word like *bank* (Rayner and Duffy (1986); see detailed discussion below). For the initial interpretation of a word, language users can only use contextual (and possibly situational) information that has already been processed, together with the knowledge that has been stored about that word. In addition, more extensive semantic interpretation is extremely fast, given that people normally understand what they are reading at speeds of about 300 words per minute (Rayner et al. 2012). This suggests that the semantic system must be flexible to quickly deal with a large variety of input. However, this does not necessarily mean that all words are immediately interpreted fully. A classic counterexample comes from the Moses illusion (Erickson and Mattson 1981), in which participants are asked questions such as *How many animals of each kind did Moses take on the Ark?* A staggering 81% of the respondent incorrectly answered "two." Such mistakes are not due to participants not knowing the story. It was also not the case that the respondents failed to process the incorrect word or did not pay attention to it: in the original experiment by Erickson and Mattson, respondents read the questions aloud themselves; and Reder and Kusbit (1991), using self-paced reading, showed that respondents spent slightly *more* time processing the incorrect word than the correct version before answering incorrectly. If readers had immediately activated all relevant information about Moses, or about what it means to be a survivor in *Where should we bury the survivors?* (Barton and Sanford 1993), then such errors should not have occurred.

The same research also suggests that the depth of processing can be affected by linguistic factors. For example, when *Moses* is the topic of the sentence, error rates drop to 41% (Erickson and Matteson (1981), Experiment 2; see also Sturt et al. (2004) and Ward and Sturt (2007) for evidence of discourse focus on depth of processing). This indicates that the amount of lexical information that is activated, or at least used immediately, can vary, so that processing can be relatively shallow or more detailed, depending on syntactic structure and possibly the task at hand (see also Ferreira and Patson (2007)). This kind of flexibility in the extent that language users activate relevant information is not normally part of linguistic models, though any model that purports to be psychologically valid will need to be compatible with the idea of flexible incremental processing. Of course, this does not mean that linguistic theories have always ignored contextual effects. For example, in Relevance Theory (Sperber and Wilson 1995; Wilson and Sperber 2004; see also Carston 2013), it is assumed that comprehenders make use of contextual clues in order to determine the writer's or speaker's intent (see Chapters 10 and 11).

There is other evidence for partial, rather than full, incremental interpretation. For example, while one meaning of a noun-noun ambiguity is selected immediately (see below), readers seem to slightly delay this process in the case of noun-verb (*a/to duck*) and verb-verb (*pen letters/sheep*) ambiguities (Boland 1997; Frazier and Rayner 1987; Pickering and Frisson 2001; see also Folk and Morris (2003)). Second, quantifier resolution can also be delayed. In a study using event-related (brain) potentials, Urbach and Kutas (2010) first established that a sentence such as *Farmers grow worms* elicited a greater N400 amplitude compared to a sentence such as *Farmers grow crops*. This effect is associated with semantic anomaly and indicates an immediate problem with the interpretation of *worms*. They then constructed sentences with a quantifier so that the acceptability of the two sentences switched: *Few farmers grow worms* was more acceptable than *Few farmers grow crops*, and *Farmers rarely grow worms* was more acceptable than *Farmers rarely grow crops*. Hence, one would expect that *if* readers immediately used the contextual information to its fullest extent during on-line processing, the *Few farmers grow worms* sentence would not result in a processing cost (i.e. no N400 effect) but the *Few farmers grow crops* would. When they tested these modified sentences, the N400 effect was attenuated, indicating an early influence of context, but, crucially, the effect did not reverse: *worms* still elicited a larger N400 amplitude than *crops*. This result suggests that the fully specified contextual meaning of the sentence fragment, as exemplified by the acceptability results, had not yet been computed (see also Filik et al. (2005) for eye-tracking evidence). Third, the finding that readers spent longer processing the last word of a sentence (a so-called wrap-up effect) may reflect additional, higher-order integrative processing of the sentence as a whole (Just and Carpenter 1980). This suggests that interpretation of words in sentences, and how sentences relate to each other, is not always accomplished at the earliest possible moment (see Frazier (1999) for a similar argument).

3 Predictability

While it is clear that language users very quickly integrate incoming information into an unfolding interpretation (incremental processing), there is also good evidence suggesting that people don't just wait for information to come in but actively predict what might come next.

During reading, readers move their eyes to bring text into the fovea (2 degrees in the centre of vision, approximately 6–8 letters), as it has the highest acuity. However, although the acuity is less, they can also extract some information from the parafovea (about 5 degrees to the left and right from the centre of vision, approximately 15–20 letters on each side). It's a matter of (strong) debate in eye movement research as to exactly what type of information (letter shape, orthographic, phonologic, morphological, and/or semantic) can be extracted from outside the foveal region (see Rayner (2009) for an overview).

Eye movement research has shown that words that are predictable from the preceding context are fixated for a shorter time and/or are more likely to be skipped altogether (e.g. Balota et al. (1985); Drieghe et al. (2005); Ehrlich and Rayner (1981); Frisson et al. (2005); Gordon et al. (2012); Rayner and Well (1996)). This indicates that readers must have either predicted the upcoming word or processed it parafoveally (i.e. without looking directly at it) before fixating or skipping that word, and that when the target word corresponds to the predicted word, processing is facilitated. Exactly why predicted words are often skipped remains a matter of debate, with some researchers arguing for an "educated guess" strategy in which only coarse information about the upcoming word is processed (e.g. Brysbaert and Vitu (1998)) and others claiming that the upcoming word can be fully processed when the reader fixates towards the end of the preceding word (e.g. Reichle et al. (2003)).

While evidence suggests that words that often co-occur are processed faster than words that do not co-occur (Arnon and Snider 2010; McDonald and Shillcock 2003a, b), predictability effects are due to more than mere co-occurrence frequencies or lexical priming between words close in a sentence. For example, Fitzsimmons and Drieghe (2013) showed comparable predictability effects when the degree of predictability was determined by information directly preceding the target word (*hairy* preceding *spider* in 1) or information coming from a preceding sentence (2):

(1) Bill has always been a fearful person. He screamed when he saw the hairy spider in the bath.
(2) Bill is scared of eight-legged creatures. He screamed when he saw the spider in the bath.

Evidence from ERP experiments also indicates that language users can quickly predict upcoming words. DeLong et al. (2005) presented sentences one word at a time while measuring electrical brain activity. They used sentences such as:

(3) The day was breezy so the boy went outside to fly a kite/an airplane.

The noun *kite* is highly predictable, as determined by a cloze task (in which participants completed the sentence fragment up to the critical noun phrase with the first word(s) that came to their mind), while *airplane* is plausible but much less predictable. Previous work had shown that words that were less predictable elicited a larger N400 amplitude than words that were more predictable (Kutas and Hillyard 1984). What DeLong et al. (2005) found was that this N400 effect was already noticeable when participants read the indefinite determiner (*a* or *an*), before they had seen the noun. Thus, the presence of the determiner *an*, which does not fit with the phonology of the predicted word *kite*, resulted in a significantly larger N400 amplitude than was the case when the determiner *a* was presented (see also van Berkum et al. (2005)).

More evidence for the pre-activation of specific upcoming information comes from the so-called Visual World paradigm in which a (typically static) scene is presented on a computer screen (e.g. a scene with a boy sitting in a room, with a ball, a cake, a toy car, and a toy train set around him; cf. Altmann and Kamide (1999)) and a sentence is presented auditorily. Eye movements are recorded during the sentence presentation. Altmann and Kamide (1999) found that participants, when hearing the sentence *The boy will eat the cake*, already started fixating the target object *cake* by the offset of the verb and, thus, before the noun itself was presented. This indicates that the participants had used the verb's selectional restrictions (i.e. that one eats something edible) to winnow down the possible candidates in the visual scene.

Further experiments have shown that it is not (only) the lexical association between the verb *eat* and the noun *cake* that drives these anticipatory eye movements to the target. Kamide et al. (2003) found that world knowledge information related to the subject was quickly integrated as well. When a scene was presented with two possible agents (e.g. a girl and an adult man) and two possible candidates for the object slot (e.g. a beer and a candy), participants started fixating the most likely object upon hearing the verb. Concretely, more looks to the beer occurred when the sentence started with *The man will taste . . .* , whereas more looks to the candy occurred for *The girl will taste . . . .* In addition, real-world contingencies, e.g. that the use of a past tense might indicate that the nature of an object has changed (e.g. that a pile of feathers is a good representation for birds when hearing *The cat has killed all the . . .*; cf. Altmann and Kamide (2007); see also Knoeferle and Crocker (2007)), are integrated very quickly as well.

The evidence suggests that people employ a variety of sources to predict upcoming information quickly and process that information readily if it indeed appears. Importantly, this upcoming information is often semantic (though people also predict other aspects of language such as phonology). However, many questions remain (see Altmann and Mirković (2009) for discussion). For instance, do people predict continuously (i.e. in advance of every single word of a sentence)? Do people use all sources of information to make predictions and if so, which information takes precedence (e.g. visual vs. lexical vs. auditory input)? And what happens if an unpredicted word appears (is it more costly to process?) and does it matter how closely the word is related to the predicted word? In addition, we shall see below that evidence about the processing of words with multiple meanings suggests that there are limits to the influence of context on the selection of word meanings.

4 Lexical semantics

For a long time, psycholinguistic research in lexical semantics was largely restricted to the processing of semantically ambiguous or homonymous words – words that share orthography (or phonology) but have distinct meanings. (In the interest of clarity, we use homonymy to refer to a single word-form with separate, semantically non-overlapping meanings and polysemy to refer to a single word-form with semantically overlapping meanings, which we will call "senses". Some papers have, confusingly, used polysemy to include homonomy. See Chapter 13.) The central research question, which is related to the modularity debate (see Fodor (1983)), was whether comprehenders selectively accessed contextually appropriate meanings or whether they initially accessed all meanings and then used context to select among them (see Swinney (1979)).

Most evidence suggests that both bottom-up (the activation of all the word's meanings) and top-down (contextual influence) processes interact during the recognition of homonyms. Good evidence that bottom-up processes are involved comes from the observation that the frequency of the different meanings affects comprehension. For example, in (4) *coach* is a homonym, with the two meanings (*bus* and *trainer*) having roughly equal frequency (Rayner and Duffy 1986); in (5), the word *cabin* is unambiguous.

(4) He found the coach too hot to sleep in.
(5) He found the cabin too hot to sleep in.

Readers spent longer fixating *coach* than *cabin* before encountering the rest of the sentence. It therefore appears that they activated both meanings of *coach* and competition ensued.

When a neutral context precedes a biased homonym, which has one meaning that is of substantially higher frequency than the other, the dominant meaning becomes available first and no competition ensues. For example, *port* has a frequent meaning referring to a harbour and an infrequent meaning referring to wine, whereas *soup* is unambiguous (Rayner and Duffy 1986).

(6) Last night the port had a strange flavor.
(7) Last night the soup had a strange flavor.

Readers spent the same amount of time fixating *port* and *soup* before processing the rest of the sentence. This suggests that the two meanings of *port* did not compete. However, when the following information related to the less frequent meaning of *port*, as in *had a strange flavor* interpretation difficulties ensued, which suggests that readers had initially interpreted *port* as expressing the more frequent harbour meaning.

However, a preceding context affects ambiguity resolution in a different way (Duffy et al. 1988). When preceding context supports the disfavoured meaning of a biased ambiguous word such as *port*, immediate difficulty ensues. This suggests that the context provides support for the less frequent meaning so that this meaning becomes available at more or less the same time as the more frequent meaning (which is activated in a bottom-up manner). Since both meanings are now available, competition arises. In contrast, when the preceding context supports one meaning of a balanced homonym such as *coach*, this meaning receives a boost, making it available before the other meaning and the difficulty observed in neutral contexts disappears.

The so-called subordinate bias effect observed for biased homonyms, with extra processing when the subordinate meaning is intended, is very difficult to overcome, even in strongly biasing contexts (e.g. Kambe et al. (2001); Sheridan et al. (2009)), though selective access has been observed in special contexts (e.g. Wiley and Rayner (2000)). These findings about homonym resolution are compatible with the Reordered Access Model (Duffy et al. 1988). Such results pose a challenge to models that assume interpretation depends on lexical co-occurrence, for example as operationalized in Latent Semantic Analysis (LSA; Landauer and Dumais 1997), which have trouble dealing with the representation of multiple meanings

(McRae and Jones (2013); but see Griffiths et al. (2007)) and for models that posit that meaning is in effect an averaging over episodic traces a word has appeared in (e.g. Kwantes (2005)). In LSA, a word's meaning is thought of as a matrix containing information about all the contexts it appears (and does not appear) in. In practice, this workspace or dimensional representation is then reduced to calculate the similarity between texts a word appears in. This allows a calculation of the similarity of two words which do not often appear together in the same text (e.g. synonyms). However, given that matrices are constructed for specific word forms, homonyms are collapsed to a single point and the two meanings cannot be distinguished from each other.

While homonyms show clear and immediate effects of both context and frequency, the number of homonyms is in fact quite limited, at least in English and most related languages. In contrast, the vast majority of words are polysemous; for example, *book* can refer to the object or the content, *school* can refer to an edifice or an institution. Are these words processed in the same way as homonyms? Most evidence suggests that they are not.

First, the results of lexical decision experiments, in which participants have to respond as quickly as possible whether a letter string presented on a computer screen constitutes a real word or not, indicate that polysemous words are processed differently from homonyms. While older research suggested that ambiguous words are responded to faster than (polysemous and non-polysemous) control words (e.g. Hino and Lupker (1996); see Rodd et al. (2002) for a critical evaluation), newer research specifically contrasting ambiguous to polysemous words showed a processing advantage for the latter (Rodd et al. 2002; Klepousniotou and Baum 2007; see Rodd et al. (2004) for a simulation in an attractor network). Second, data from ERP experiments show different effects for the two types of words, with N400 effects reflecting an effect of dominance/frequency for homonyms, which is absent for polysemous words (Klepousniotou et al. 2012). This means that about 400 ms after word onset electrical brain response signals to homonyms show an influence of the frequency of the different meanings, but no such frequency modification is found for the different senses of a polyseme. Third, studies using magnetoencephalography (MEG) offer neurophysiological support for such meaning/sense distinctions (Beretta et al. 2005; see also Pylkkänen et al. (2006)). And fourth, eye movement experiments have shown distinct processing patterns for homonymous and polysemous words (see below).

In contrast, evidence from more off-line tasks, such as categorization of phrases and sensicality judgements, suggests that individual word senses might be processed and represented in the same way as the individual meanings of a homonym (Klein and Murphy 2001; 2002). For example, Klein and Murphy (2001) asked participants to indicate whether phrases such as *liberal paper* and *yellow lecture* made sense or not. The previous (prime) trial could contain the same polysemous noun, either in the same sense (*daily paper*) or a different sense (*wrapping paper*). They found faster reaction times when prime and target involved the same sense compared to when they did not, and this pattern was comparable to that found for homonyms when the same meaning was re-used (*commercial bank* followed by *savings bank*). However, Klein and Murphy did not test for relatedness of the senses and quite a few of their "polysemous" items might in fact be homonyms (i.e. have unrelated meanings) rather than polysemes (i.e. have related meanings). For example, they labelled *nail* (*gun* and *polish*), *navy* (*blue* and *recruit*), and *coat* (*winter* and *paint*) as polysemous even though the relatedness of the two interpretations is far from certain. In addition, it is unclear whether this task reflects early lexical activation or later integration processes (for a more in-depth discussion, see Frisson (2009)).

Several eye movement experiments have examined the processing of polysemous words during normal reading, though only two studies compared polysemy to homonymy directly.

Frazier and Rayner (1990) used words such as *book* in either their object or content sense and found that, in contrast to the pattern for homonyms, subsequent disambiguation towards the less frequent sense was no more difficult than disambiguation towards the dominant sense. Pickering and Frisson (2001), using ambiguous verbs, found earlier frequency effects for homonyms than polysemes as well as longer processing times for homonyms. In addition, a number of studies looked at the processing of different types of polysemous words by themselves. In a series of experiments (Frisson and Pickering 1999; 2007; McElree et al. 2006), we found that metonymic senses such as the institution sense of *school*, the event sense of *Vietnam*, or the product sense of *Dickens*, were processed as fast as their literal counterparts, at least when the metonymic senses were known by the reader. In addition, the frequency of the individual senses did not affect immediate processing (though later processing measures, arguably reflecting more in-depth processing, sometimes did show an influence of frequency). Recently, Foraker and Murphy (2012; Experiment 3) confirmed the lack of an early processing difficulty for polysemous words such as *cotton* (the fabric or the crop).

Results from studies about homonymy and polysemy are instructive as they relate to important distinctions in lexical processing and representation. Frazier and Rayner (1990) interpreted their results as reflecting a difference in semantic commitment when processing homonymous and polysemous words, with comprehenders committing immediately to a specific interpretation only when the alternative interpretations are semantically unrelated, as is the case for homonyms. Frisson and Pickering's (1999) results suggest that for polysemous words, a semantically underspecified meaning is initially activated, which can then be fleshed out or become more specified in later processing (see Frisson and Pickering (2001) for discussion). According to this view, the initial activation of lexical features is sense-neutral. In the case of homonyms, when the processor is faced with two separate meanings, a potentially costly selection process has to take place first before the ambiguity is resolved.

The idea of underspecification is compatible with the view that meaning assignment involves the initial activation of a lexical representation, followed by contextual specification and/or activation of more refined interpretations. This view is compatible with semantic accounts such as the Generative Lexicon approach (Pustejovsky 1995; see also Copestake and Briscoe (1995)), even though it is not clear what exactly is represented in an underspecified meaning. Arguments have been raised, however, against the idea of distinguishing between a semantic (sometimes called "core") and a pragmatic ("non-core") meaning (for an in-depth discussion, see e.g. Geeraerts (2010); cf. Chapter 11). To some degree, this discussion resembles current controversy over whether semantic memory is truly separate from general world knowledge (McRae and Jones 2013). At present we are unaware of conclusive experimental evidence favouring one account over the other and will therefore refrain from taking a position on this issue. It should also be noted that there might be gradations of polysemy. For example, Klepousniotou et al. (2008; see also Rabagliati and Snedeker 2013, discussed below) found differences in processing depending on how semantically overlapping the different senses of a polysemous word were. This issue clearly needs further research.

Finally, the decision to home in on a specific interpretation and the extent to which a language user homes in are likely to be affected by linguistic and extra-linguistic factors. For example, when a word is in focus position, it will attract more attention, possibly leading to a deeper level of interpretation (cf. the Moses illusion above). In addition, non-linguistic factors, such as the desire to critically evaluate information (e.g. as a reviewer), might also affect how quickly a more refined understanding will be achieved. On other occasions, the representation people build of a sentence may be much more superficial, though "good enough" for the task at hand (see Ferreira and Patson (2007)).

5 Combinatorial semantics

Semantic interpretation involves not only looking up word meanings but also combining them to arrive at the interpretation of a larger chunk of text. This follows from the principle of compositionality ("(t)he meaning of an expression is a function of the meanings of its parts and the way they're syntactically combined"; Pylkkänen and McElree (2006), after Frege (1892); see also Chapter 24). Pylkkänen and McElree identified three basic compositional rules or operations that they believe should be part of any psycholinguistic account of interpretation. First, functional application (and semantic types) describes how basic argument structures are set up and interpreted (with assignment of thematic roles to arguments; see also Chapter 23). Second, predicate modification is a compositional rule that allows the intersective interpretation of adjective-noun constructions such as *wise president*. Third, predicate abstraction allows, among other things, the interpretation of relative clauses.

These operations are compatible with a large amount of psycholinguistic work. For example, with respect to functional application, evidence suggests that language users project thematic roles without having to wait for the argument to be actually expressed. Mauner et al. (1995; see also Carlson and Tanenhaus 1988) found that when a verb such as *sink* was used in a construction that implied an agent (*The ship was sunk to collect a settlement from the insurance company*), readers projected an implicit agent and processed the infinitival clause as fast as when the agent was expressed (*The ship was sunk by the owners to collect...*) and faster than when an implicit agent was not expected (*The ship sank to collect...*). This result shows that language users construct inferences on-line on the basis of a verb's argument structure. Another example of functional application comes from the dissimilarity in the processing of arguments and adjuncts. People tend to read arguments faster than adjuncts (e.g. Clifton et al. (1991); Traxler (2008)) and have a preference for argument interpretation over adjunct interpretations of ambiguous phrases, indicating a preference to interpret new incoming information as being part of the evolving argument structure rather than being an optional sentential element (for in-depth discussions, see Frazier and Clifton (1996); Schütze and Gibson (1999); and Traxler and Tooley (2007)).

A challenge to strict compositionality comes from so-called coercive expressions, in which there is a semantic type mismatch blocking a straightforward application of basic compositional operations (see Jackendoff (2002); Pustejovsky (1995); Pylkkänen and McElree (2006)). One type of coercion, complement coercion, has attracted quite some interest from psycholinguists and has generated relatively consistent experimental results.

Complement coercion can occur when there is a semantic mismatch between the verb and its complement. For example, in (8), taken from McElree et al. (2001), the verb *starting* selects for an event complement. However, the complement *the book* denotes an entity and thus needs to be type-coerced into an event. In (9), the verb selects for an entity and this role is fulfilled by the complement *the book*.

(8) The author was starting the book in his house on the island.
(9) The author was writing the book in his house on the island.

Much evidence has revealed that interpreting complement coerced constructions such as (8) takes extra processing effort (and involves different brain processes) compared to a sentence such as (9), which has a straightforward, non-coerced interpretation (e.g. Kuperberg et al. (2010); Lapata et al. (2003); McElree et al. (2001); Pylkkänen and McElree (2007); Traxler et al. (2002); see also Frisson et al. (2011) for evidence from adjectival phrases such as *difficult mountain*).

To summarize the results from reading experiments, it has been shown that the coercion cost is unrelated to processing characteristics of the verb itself. For example, *start the fight*, in which the complement already refers to an event, does not generate a processing cost (Traxler et al. 2002), indicating that a verb such as *start* does not make processing of the complement more difficult by default, but only when paired with a non-eventive expression. It is also unrelated to differences in how acceptable language users judge these constructions (Traxler et al. 2005), in their plausibility (McElree et al. 2006), in cloze probability (Traxler et al. 2005), or in how often these types of verb co-occur with a specific complement in text (as measured by Latent Semantic Analysis co-occurrence frequencies; Traxler et al. (2002)). The cost also does not seem to be associated with having to generate or select an appropriate coerced event interpretation (Traxler et al. 2005), with having to select one interpretation among several possible ones or competition between different interpretations (Frisson and McElree 2008; Scheepers; Keller and Lapata 2008), nor with the relative frequency of a particular event interpretation (Frisson and McElree 2008). Rather, there is a fixed cost to coercion, which appears to reflect the time needed to set up a semantically enriched interpretation. In other words, to interpret a complement that does not have the required semantic type, extra semantic structure needs to be generated so that it can acquire the right type and this process is the locus of the cost.

A second type of coercion that has been investigated experimentally is aspectual coercion, which refers to the reinterpretation that occurs when the semantics of a punctual verb such as *jump* mismatches the semantics of an external modifier (e.g. *for hours*). However, since the psycho- and neuro-linguistic data on the processing of this type of coercion is less clear than for complement coercion, we will not discuss this construction further (see Brennan and Pylkkänen (2008); Pickering et al. (2006)).

6 (Im)plausibility

The idea of incrementality (see section 1 above) indicates that people are good at making sense of information as it unfolds. Results from homonym processing, which show immediate effects of relative meaning frequency, indicate that (at least some degree of) lexical processing occurs straight away. But when we process language, does the plausibility or likelihood of what we're interpreting play a role and if so, how quickly does it affect processing? Alternatively, how good and quick are language users at noticing when something becomes strange?

Using eye-tracking, Rayner et al. (2004) examined how readers processed sentences containing either an inappropriate theme (using a pump to chop carrots), an unlikely theme (using an axe to chop carrots), or an acceptable theme (using a knife to chop carrots). Both the inappropriate and the unlikely condition led to processing difficulty but in different ways. Whereas the inappropriate condition led to immediate disruption in the eye movement record, the unlikely condition only showed (temporally and spatially) later disruption. In other words, reading about someone using an axe to chop carrots does not immediately strike one as totally implausible. These and similar (see Warren and McConnell (2007)) results make a case for a distinction between semantic knowledge and world knowledge: violations of semantic knowledge (e.g. a clash with a word's selection restrictions) immediately disrupt processing, but mismatches with world knowledge, which express possible but very unlikely relationships, take somewhat longer to compute.

Warren et al. (2008; see also Ferguson and Sanford (2008)) hypothesized that if there were no distinction between the two types of memory and if the difference in processing merely reflects the degree with which the information clashes with real-world knowledge, then having a context which makes the implausible reading possible (e.g. a fairy-tale context) should eliminate the effect. However, the early processing cost was still observed, but the later processing cost, arguably reflecting higher-order, integrative and evaluative processing, was attenuated. Hence, these results suggest that some processing, such as managing selection restrictions, happens immediately and is impervious to higher-order information that could impact upon early interpretation. This view, however, is not accepted by all researchers and there is evidence more consistent with the view that processing at different levels – semantic and pragmatic – can occur at the same time. For example, Filik (2008; see also Matsuki et al. (2011)) found that implausibility effects (e.g. someone lifting up his car) could be overridden by an appropriate context (e.g. if that person is the Incredible Hulk).

More evidence in line with the unitary view comes from a series of brain imaging experiments, which point to a close link between semantic and encyclopaedic knowledge, with discourse violations eliciting comparable temporal and distributional effects to semantic violations (e.g. Hagoort et al. (2004); Nieuwland and van Berkum (2005); van Berkum et al. (1999); van Berkum et al. (2003)). For example, Nieuwland and van Berkum (2006) used sentences containing an animacy violation, such as (10) and (11):

(10) The girl comforted the clock.
(11) The peanut was in love.

In isolation, these sentences generated the expected N400 effect. However, when embedded in a larger context, this effect disappeared (e.g. a girl talking to a clock about its depression) or, even more strikingly, reversed the effect (e.g. in a story about an amorous peanut), such that the sentence containing the lexical-semantic violation became easier to process than one not containing the violation (*the peanut was salted*). (Note that this pattern is different from Urbach and Kutas's (2010) finding discussed above. It's not obvious why context can override an N400 effect in one case but not another.) Hagoort et al. (2004) compared sentences containing a semantic violation (12) or a pragmatic violation (13) (Dutch trains are uniquely yellow) to sentences containing no semantic or pragmatic violation (14).

(12) The Dutch trains are sour and very crowded.
(13) The Dutch trains are white and very crowded.
(14) The Dutch trains are yellow and very crowded.

They found that both types of violations resulted in an N400 effect, indicating that at the physiological level, there might not be a distinction between the integration of semantic and world knowledge information during sentence comprehension. It remains unclear, however, what an N400 effect exactly reflects in terms of on-line processing. In addition, Hagoort et al. did find a difference in oscillatory brain activity between the two types, though what exactly this implies is unclear. Clearly, the discussion about when exactly semantic and world knowledge comes into play has not been settled and it appears that experimentation using different methodologies, patient research (e.g. semantic dementia research: Graham et al. (2000)) and research in neighbouring fields (e.g. memory) may help resolve this issue.

7 Semantics in language production

As we have noted, the great majority of work on semantic processing relates to language comprehension rather than language production. Whereas researchers in the production of syntax appear to make use of similar linguistic models to those assumed by researchers in the comprehension of syntax, this does not appear to be the case in semantics. For example, Clark and his colleagues have conducted many investigations of how people select referring expressions. Language production involves many choices about whether to produce an utterance that makes all aspects of meaning explicit or whether to leave out certain components of content that can be inferred from some part of the context. Thus, responses to questions (e.g. *What time do you close?*) can be full (*We close at nine*) or elliptical (*At nine*; e.g. Clark (1979)). Similarly, referring expressions can be more or less detailed. For example, when speakers refer to an object that they have already successfully referred to, they can choose to produce a detailed referring expression (e.g. *looks like a person who's ice-skating, except they're sticking two arms out in front*), or – more often – choose a shorter but less detailed alternative (e.g. *the ice-skater*; Clark and Wilkes-Gibbs (1986); Krauss and Weinheimer (1964)). It turns out that people tend to produce shorter referring expressions as a conversation proceeds, so long as their interlocutors make it clear that they understand. In fact, many of these expressions can be seen as metonymic and the studies therefore provide evidence about how people may develop metonymy on the fly.

Research has also addressed the question of ambiguity avoidance. Thus, Ferreira et al. (2005) had participants name pictures of objects such as a baseball bat in the presence of a distractor ("foil") object with a homophonous name, in this case a flying bat. Surprisingly, participants often mistakenly produced an ambiguous name, sometimes followed by a self-correction (e.g. *bat . . . no, baseball bat*). But when the foil was another instance of the same category (here, another baseball bat), they almost always avoided the ambiguity. Ferreira et al. also found that speakers often corrected themselves after producing an ambiguous expression, indicating that they detected the ambiguity "after the fact," and that once corrected, they consistently avoided the ambiguity. This implies that ambiguity detection is much more effective after the expressions are produced compared to when they are about to be produced.

Rabagliati and Snedeker (2013) extended Ferreira et al.'s research and found that regular polysemes such as *chicken* (the animal and the meat) patterned with same-category descriptions (e.g. different instances of the baseball bat), while irregular polysemes such as *button* (shirt button and emergency button) patterned with true homonyms such as *bat*. This suggests that polysemes are represented and accessed differently from homophones and in fact are treated similarly to different exemplars of the same meaning of a homophone. For example, polysemes might access the same lemma, whereas homophones access different lemmas (Levelt et al. 1999). Moreover, people appear to represent regular polysemes together, but irregular polysemes separately (though the extent to which the different interpretations of the irregular polysemes were related to each other was not completely clear). These results suggest that speakers make use of fine-grained semantic distinctions during production (for supportive evidence from comprehension studies, see Klepousniotou et al. (2008)).

There are many other issues in language production that clearly relate to semantic processing. For example, many researchers have addressed the issue of the relationship between language and thought, such as in relation to space or time (e.g. see Casasanto (2008) and Chapter 9). Clearly the relevant aspects of language involve semantics. At the other extreme, a vast number of studies have used the picture-word interference paradigm, in which participants name a picture while ignoring a printed or spoken word. Naming is generally slower when the word and picture are semantically related than when they are unrelated (e.g. Schriefers et al. (1990)). Finally, semantic relationships affect syntax, with participants being more likely to repeat syntactic structure (e.g. saying *the sheep that's red*) after hearing an utterance with the same structure and a noun with related meaning (*the goat that's red*) than a noun with unrelated meaning (*the book that's red*; Cleland and Pickering (2003)). At this point, it appears that most of these studies are concerned with the relationship between semantic processing and other aspects of production rather than with the details of semantic representation itself.

8 Summary and conclusions

The study of semantic processing has for a long time played second fiddle to syntactic processing in psycholinguistic research. Over the last 10–15 years, this focus has shifted somewhat and more and more attention has gone to issues of lexical processing, semantic interpretation and their link with pragmatics. Lately, this focus has been extended into the field of language production and some researchers have started to look at how individual differences affect semantic processing (e.g. Hannon and Daneman (2004)).

When talking about semantic (and pragmatic) processing, the main focus is on what happens immediately: what information is used immediately and incrementally to build up a representation of what people are hearing or reading? How do comprehenders gain access to a word's meaning? How and when does other information impact on this activation? By using sensitive measurements, we might be able to address these questions and arrive at a model of how bottom-up and top-down processes work together to give the language user a sense of understanding.

One way of making incremental processing faster is by predicting what will come next in the text. While predictability effects are robust and ubiquitous, they in themselves do not equate to semantic processing. For example, most experiments investigating a specific aspect of semantic processing control for predictability and consequently these effects hold independently from predictability effects. In addition, it remains unclear whether language users at every single moment in time calculate the odds of the next word occurring.

Research on words with multiple meanings (homonyms) and words with multiple senses (polysemes) generally points to different processing profiles for the two types of words. Since the processor, in the vast majority of cases, does not know whether a homonym or polyseme will follow next, the difference in processing could potentially be linked to differences in lexical representation. Research on combinatorial semantics, and specifically coercion, indicates that when an expression cannot be interpreted in a straightforward compositional manner, extra processing is required, which suggests that in most cases simple semantic composition is the default for interpretation. Research on plausibility effects, and specifically whether (pragmatic) context can overwrite (lexical) implausibility, is still far from conclusive, with some impressive examples of immediate pragmatic effects but also of some stubborn lexical-first effects. Finally, research on language production addresses some questions about representation considered in the much more extensive literature on comprehension (e.g. the nature of polysemy), but the literature has not so far addressed the relationship between semantic theory and the mechanisms of production in great detail.

Obviously, our overview has only scratched the surface of psycholinguistic semantic research and several topics have been woefully ignored. For example, research on figurative language interpretation has been extensive and has recently shifted more into the neurological representation of literal and non-literal language (for overviews, see e.g. Coulson (2008); Gibbs and Colston (2006)). Similarly, work on perspective-taking during language processing, which can be related to Theory of Mind processing (e.g. Frisson and Wakefield (2012)) and on how individual (communicative) goals, situations and time constraints affect depth of processing (e.g. Ferreira and Patson (2007)) will need to be accommodated for in a psychologically realistic model of language comprehension.

Further reading

Rayner, K., A. Pollatsek, J. Ashby and C. Clifton, Jr. 2012. *The Psychology of Reading*. 2nd ed. New York: Psychology Press. This is the second and much updated edition of the seminal book on reading research, with a strong emphasis on eye movements and psycholinguistics.

Traxler, M. J. 2012. *Introduction to Psycholinguistics: Understanding Language Science*. Sussex, UK: John Wiley and Sons Ltd. A textbook offering an excellent introduction to psycholinguistic research aimed at a diverse audience of psychologists, linguists, philosophers, computer scientists, etc.

Gibbs, R. W. Jr. and H. L. Colston 2012. *Interpreting Figurative Meaning*. New York: Cambridge University Press. This textbook brings together psycholinguistic and neurolinguistic research on figurative language and critically evaluates models of figurative language interpretation from different fields such as psychology, linguistics, and philosophy.

Van Berkum, J. J. A. 2009. The neuropragmatics of 'simple' utterance comprehension: an ERP review. In U. Sauerland and K. Yatsushiro (eds) *Semantics and Pragmatics: From Experiment to Theory*. Basingstoke: Palgrave Macmillan, 276–316. This chapter provides an overview of neurophysiological research on how language users comprehend the pragmatics of a sentence.

McRae, K. and M. N. Jones 2012. Semantic memory. In D. Reisberg (ed.), *The Oxford Handbook of Cognitive Psychology*. Oxford: Oxford University Press, 206–219. An interesting overview of contemporary thinking about semantic and episodic knowledge and its representation in memory.

References

Altmann, G. T. M. and Y. Kamide 1999. Incremental interpretation at verbs: restricting the domain of subsequent reference. *Cognition* 73: 247–264.

Altmann, G. T. M. and Y. Kamide 2007. The real-time mediation of visual attention by language and world knowledge: linking anticipatory and other eye movements to linguistic processing. *Journal of Memory and Language* 57: 502–518.

Altmann, G. T. M. and J. Mirković 2009. Incrementality and prediction in human sentence processing. *Cognitive Science* 33: 583–609.

Arnon, I. and N. Snider 2010. More than words: frequency effects for multi-word phrases. *Journal of Memory and Language* 62: 67–82.

Balota, D. A., A. Pollatsek and K. Rayner 1985. The interaction of contextual constraints and parafoveal visual information in reading. *Cognitive Psychology* 17: 364–390.

Barton, S. B. and A. J. Sanford 1993. A case study of anomaly detection: shallow semantic processing and cohesion establishment. *Memory and Cognition* 21: 477–487.

Beretta, A., R. Fiorentino and D. Poeppel 2005. The effect of homonymy and polysemy on lexical access: an MEG study. *Cognitive Brain Research* 24: 57–65.

Boland, J. E. 1997. Resolving syntactic category ambiguities in discourse context: probabilistic and discourse constraints. *Journal of Memory and Language* 36: 588–615.

Brennan, J. and L. Pylkkänen 2008. Processing events: behavioral and neuromagnetic correlates of aspectual coercion. *Brain and Language* 106: 132–143.

Brysbaert, M. and F. Vitu 1998. Word skipping: implications for theories of eye movement control in reading. In G. Underwood (ed.) *Eye Guidance in Reading and Scene Perception*. Oxford: Elsevier, 125–147.

Carlson, G. and M. Tanenhaus 1988. Thematic roles and language comprehension. In W. Wilkins (ed.) *Thematic Relations*. New York: Academic Press, 263–300.

Carston, R. 2013. Word meaning, what is said and explicature. In C. Penko and F. Domaneschi (eds) *What is Said and What is Not*. Stanford: CSLI Publications, 175–204.

Casasanto, D. 2008. Who's afraid of the Big Bad Whorf? Cross-linguistic differences in temporal language and thought. *Language Learning* 58: 63–79.

Clark, H. H. and D. Wilkes-Gibbs 1986. Referring as a collaborative process. *Cognition* 22: 1–39.

Clark, H. H. 1979. Responding to indirect speech acts. *Cognitive Psychology* 11: 430–477.

Cleland, A. A. and M. J. Pickering 2003. The use of lexical and syntactic information in language production: evidence from the priming of noun-phrase structure. *Journal of Memory and Language* 49: 214–230.

Clifton, C., Jr., S. Speer and S. P. Abney 1991. Parsing arguments: phrase structure and argument structure as determinants of initial parsing decisions. *Journal of Memory and Language* 30: 251–271.

Copestake, A. and T. Briscoe 1995. Semi-productive polysemy and sense production. *Journal of Semantics* 12: 15–67.

Coulson, S. 2008. Metaphor comprehension and the brain. In R. W. Gibbs (ed.) *Metaphor and Thought*. 3rd edition. Cambridge and New York: Cambridge University Press.

DeLong, K. A., T. P. Urbach and M. Kutas 2005. Probabilistic word pre-activation during language comprehension inferred from electrical brain activity. *Nature Neuroscience* 8: 1117–1121.

Drieghe, D., K. Rayner and A. Pollatsek 2005. Eye movements and word skipping during reading revisit(ed.) *Journal of Experimental Psychology: Human Perception and Performance* 31: 954–969.

Duffy, S. A., R. K. Morris and K. Rayner 1988. Lexical ambiguity and fixation times in reading. *Journal of Memory and Language* 27: 429–446.

Ehrlich, S. F. and K. Rayner 1981. Contextual effects on word perception and eye movements during reading. *Journal of Verbal Learning and Verbal Behavior* 20: 641–655.

Erickson, T. A. and M. E. Matteson 1981. From words to meaning: a semantic illusion. *Journal of Verbal Learning and Verbal Behavior* 20: 540–552.

Ferguson, H. J. and A. J. Sanford 2008. Anomalies in real and counterfactual worlds: an eye movement investigation. *Journal of Memory and Language* 58: 609–626.

Ferreira, F. and N. D. Patson 2007. The 'good enough' approach to language comprehension. *Language and Linguistics Compass* 1: 71–83.

Ferreira, V. S., L. R. Slevc and E. S. Rogers 2005. How do speakers avoid ambiguous linguistic expressions? *Cognition* 96: 263–284.

Filik, R. 2008. Contextual override of pragmatic anomalies: evidence from eye movements. *Cognition* 106: 1038–1046.

Filik, R., K. B. Paterson and S. P. Liversedge 2005. Parsing with focus particles in context: Eye movements during the processing of relative clause ambiguities. *Journal of Memory and Language* 53: 473–495.

Fitzsimmons, G. and D. Drieghe 2013. How fast can predictability influence word skipping during reading? *Journal of Experimental Psychology: Learning Memory and Cognition* 39: 1054–1063.

Fodor, J. A. 1983. *The Modularity of Mind*. Cambridge, MA: MIT Press.

Fodor, J., T. Bever and M. Garrett 1974. *The Psychology of Language*. New York: McGraw-Hill.

Folk, J. R. and R. K. Morris 2003. Effects of syntactic category assignment on lexical ambiguity resolution in reading: an eye movement analysis. *Memory and Cognition* 31: 87–99.

Foraker, S. and G. L. Murphy 2012. Polysemy in sentence comprehension: effects of meaning dominance. *Journal of Memory and Language* 67: 407–425.

Frazier, L. 1999. *On Sentence Interpretation*. Dordrecht: Kluwer Academic Publishers.

Frazier, L. and C. Clifton Jr. 1996. *Construal*. Cambridge, MA: MIT Press.

Frazier, L. and K. Rayner 1987. Resolution of syntactic category ambiguities: eye movements in parsing lexically ambiguous sentences. *Journal of Memory and Language* 26: 505–526.

Frazier, L. and K. Rayner 1990. Taking on semantic commitments: processing multiple meanings vs. multiple senses. *Journal of Memory and Language* 29: 181–200.

Frege, G. 1952 (1892). On sense and reference. In P. Geach and M. Black (eds) *Translations from the Philosophical Writings of Gottlob Frege*. Oxford: Blackwell, 42–55.

Frisson, S. 2009. Semantic underspecification in language processing. *Language and Linguistics Compass* 3: 111–127.

Frisson, S. and B. McElree 2008. Complement coercion is not modulated by competition: evidence from eye movements. *Journal of Experimental Psychology: Learning, Memory and Cognition* 34: 1–11.

Frisson, S. and M. J. Pickering 1999. The processing of metonymy: evidence from eye movements. *Journal of Experimental Psychology: Learning, Memory and Cognition* 25: 1347–1365.

Frisson, S. and M. J. Pickering 2001. Figurative language processing in the underspecification model. *Metaphor and Symbol* 16: 149–171.

Frisson, S. and M. J. Pickering 2007. The processing of familiar and novel senses of a word: why reading Dickens is easy but reading Needham can be hard. *Language and Cognitive Processes* 22: 595–613.

Frisson, S., M. J. Pickering and B. McElree 2011. The difficult mountain: enriched composition in adjective-noun phrases. *Psychonomic Bulletin and Review* 6: 1172–1179.

Frisson, S., K. Rayner and M. J. Pickering 2005. Effects of contextual predictability and transitional probability on eye movements during reading. *Journal of Experimental Psychology: Learning, Memory and Cognition* 31: 862–877.

Frisson, S. and M. Wakefield 2012. Psychological essentialist reasoning and perspective taking during reading: a donkey is not a zebra, but a plate can be a clock. *Memory and Cognition* 40: 297–310.

Gaskell, M. G. 2007. *The Oxford Handbook of Psycholinguistics*. Oxford: Oxford University Press.

Geeraerts, D. 2010. *Theories of Lexical Semantics*. Oxford: Oxford University Press.

Gibbs, R. W. and H. L. Colston 2006. Figurative language. In M. Traxler and M. Gernsbacher (eds) *Handbook of Psycholinguistics*, 2nd ed. Oxford: Elsevier, 835–862.

Gordon, P. C., P. Plummer and W. Choi 2012. See before you jump: full recognition of parafoveal words precedes skips during reading. *Journal of Experimental Psychology: Learning, Memory and Cognition* 39: 633–641.

Graham, K. S., J. S. Simons, K. H. Pratt, K. Patterson and J. R. Hodges 2000. Insights from semantic dementia on the relationship between episodic and semantic memory. *Neuropsychologia* 38: 313–24.

Griffiths, T. L., M. Steyvers and J. B. Tenenbaum 2007. Topics in semantic representation. *Psychological Review* 114: 211–244.

Hagoort, P., L. Hald, M. Bastiaansen and K. M. Petersson 2004. Integration of word meaning and world knowledge in language comprehension. *Science* 304: 438–441.

Hannon, B. and M. Daneman 2004. Shallow semantic processing of text: an individual-differences account. *Discourse Processes* 37: 187–204.

Hino, Y. and S. J. Lupker 1996. Effects of polysemy in lexical decision and naming: an alternative to lexical access accounts. *Journal of Experimental Psychology: Human Perception and Performance* 22: 1331–1356.

Jackendoff, R. 2002. *Foundations of Language*. New York: Oxford University Press.

Just, M. A. and P. Carpenter 1980. A theory of reading: from eye fixations to comprehension. *Psychological Review* 85: 109–130.

Kambe, G., K. Rayner and S. A. Duffy 2001. Global context effects on processing lexically ambiguous words: evidence from eye fixations. *Memory and Cognition* 29: 363–372.

Kamide, Y., G. T. M. Altmann and S. L. Haywood 2003. The time-course of prediction in incremental sentence processing: evidence from anticipatory eye movements. *Journal of Memory and Language* 49: 133–159.

Klein, D. E. and G. L. Murphy 2001. The representation of polysemous words. *Journal of Memory and Language* 45: 259–282.

Klein, D. E. and G. L. Murphy 2002. Paper has been my ruin: conceptual relations of polysemous senses. *Journal of Memory and Language* 47: 548–570.

Klepousniotou, E. and S. Baum 2007. Disambiguating the ambiguity advantage effect in word recognition: an advantage for polysemous but not homonymous words. *Journal of Neurolinguistics* 20: 1–24.

Klepousniotou, E., G. B. Pike, K. Steinhauer and V. Gracco 2012. Not all ambiguous words are created equal: an EEG investigation of homonymy and polysemy. *Brain and Language* 123: 11–21.

Klepousniotou, E., D. Titone and C. Romero 2008. Making sense of word senses: the comprehension of polysemy depends on sense overlap. *Journal of Experimental Psychology: Learning, Memory and Cognition* 34: 1534–1543.

Knoeferle, P. and M. W. Crocker 2007. The influence of recent scene events on spoken comprehension: evidence from eye movements. *Journal of Memory and Language* 57: 519–543.

Krauss, R. M. and S. Weinheimer 1964. Changes in reference phases as a function of frequency of usage in social interaction: a preliminary study. *Psychonomic Science* 1: 113–114.

Kuperberg, G. R., A. Choi, N. Cohn, M. Paczynski and R. Jackendoff 2010. Electrophysical correlates of complement coercion. *Journal of Cognitive Neuroscience* 22: 2685–2701.

Kutas, M. and S. A. Hillyard 1984. Brain potentials during reading reflect word expectancy and semantic association. *Nature* 307: 161–163.

Kwantes, P. J. 2005. Using context to build semantics. *Psychonomic Bulletin and Review* 12: 703–710.

Landauer, T. K. and S. T. Dumais 1997. A solution to Plato's problem: the latent semantic analysis theory of acquisition, induction and representation of knowledge. *Psychological Review* 104: 211–240.

Lapata, M., F. Keller and C. Scheepers 2003. Intra-sentential context effects on the interpretation of logical metonymy. *Cognitive Science* 27: 649–668.

Levelt, W. J. M., A. Roelofs and A. S. Meyer 1999. A theory of lexical access in speech production. *Behavioral and Brain Sciences* 22: 1–75.

Marslen-Wilson, W. D. 1973. Linguistic structure and speech shadowing at very short latencies. *Nature* 244: 522–523.

Matsuki, K., T. Chow, M. Hare, J. L. Elman, C. Scheepers and K. McRae 2011. Event-based plausibility immediately influences on-line language comprehension. *Journal of Experimental Psychology: Learning, Memory and Cognition* 37: 913–934.

Mauner, G., M. K. Tanenhaus and G. N. Carlson 1995. Implicit arguments in sentence processing. *Journal of Memory and Language* 34: 357–382.

McDonald, S. A. and R. C. Shillcock 2003a. Eye movements reveal the on-line computation of lexical probabilities during reading. *Psychological Science* 14: 648–652.

McDonald, S. A. and R. C. Shillcock 2003b. Low-level predictive inference in reading: the influence of transitional probabilities on eye movements. *Vision Research* 43: 1735–1751.

McElree, B., S. Frisson and M. J. Pickering 2006. Deferred interpretations: why starting Dickens is taxing but reading Dickens isn't. *Cognitive Science* 30: 181–192.

McElree, B., L. Pylkkänen, M. J. Pickering and M. Traxler 2006. The time course of enriched composition. *Psychonomic Bulletin and Review* 13: 53–59.

McElree, B., M. Traxler, M. J. Pickering, R. Seely and R. Jackendoff 2001. Reading time evidence for enriched composition. *Cognition* 78: B17–25.

McRae, K. and M. N. Jones 2013. Semantic memory. In D. Reisberg (ed.) *The Oxford Handbook of Cognitive Psychology*. Oxford: Oxford University Press, 206–219.

Nieuwland, M. S., J. J. A. Van Berkum 2005. Testing the limits of the semantic illusion phenomenon: ERPs reveal temporary semantic change deafness in discourse comprehension. *Cognitive Brain Research* 24: 691–701.

Nieuwland, M. S. and J. J. A. Van Berkum 2006. When peanuts fall in love: N400 evidence for the power of discourse. *Journal of Cognitive Neuroscience* 18: 1098–1111.

Pickering, M. J. and S. Frisson 2001. Processing ambiguous verbs: evidence from eye movements. *Journal of Experimental Psychology: Learning, Memory and Cognition* 27: 556–573.

Pickering, M. J., B. McElree, S. Frisson, L. Chen and M. J. Traxler 2006. Underspecification and aspectual coercion. *Discourse Processes* 42: 131–155.

Pustejovsky, J. 1995. *The Generative Lexicon*. Cambridge, MA: MIT Press.

Pylkkänen, L. and B. McElree 2006. The syntax-semantics interface: on-line composition of sentence meaning. In M. Traxler and M. A. Gernsbacher (eds) *Handbook of Psycholinguistics*, 2nd ed. New York: Elsevier, 537–577.

Pylkkänen, L. and B. McElree, 2007. An MEG study of silent meaning. *Journal of Cognitive Neuroscience* 19: 126–149.

Pylkkänen, L., R. Llinas and G. L. Murphy 2006. The representation of polysemy: MEG evidence. *Journal of Cognitive Neuroscience* 18: 97–109.

Rabagliati, H. and J. Snedeker 2013. The truth about chickens and bats: ambiguity avoidance distinguishes types of polysemy. *Psychological Science* 24: 1354–1360.

Rayner, K. 2009. Eye movements and attention in reading, scene perception and visual search. *The Quarterly Journal of Experimental Psychology* 62: 1457–1506.

Rayner, K. and Duffy, S. A. 1986. Lexical complexity and fixation times in reading: effects of word frequency, verb complexity and lexical ambiguity. *Memory and Cognition* 14: 191–201.

Rayner, K., T. Warren, B. J. Juhasz, and S. P. Liversedge 2004. The effect of plausibility on eye movements in reading. *Journal of Experimental Psychology: Learning, Memory and Cognition* 30: 1290–1301.

Rayner, K., A. Pollatsek, J. Ashby and C. Clifton 2012. *The Psychology of Reading*. New York: Psychology Press.

Rayner, K. and A. D. Well 1996. Effects of contextual constraint on eye movements in reading: a further examination. *Psychonomic Bulletin and Review* 3: 504–509.

Reder, L. M. and G. W. Kusbit 1991. Locus of the Moses Illusion: imperfect encoding, retrieval, or match? *Journal of Memory and Language* 30: 385–406.

Reichle, E. D., K. Rayner and A. Pollatsek 2003. The E-Z Reader model of eye-movement control in reading: comparisons to other models. *Behavioral and Brain Sciences* 26: 445–476.

Rodd, J., G. Gaskell and W. Marslen-Wilson 2002. Making sense of semantic ambiguity: semantic competition in lexical access. *Journal of Memory and Language* 46: 245–266.

Rodd, J. M., M. G. Gaskell and W. D. Marslen-Wilson 2004. Modelling the effects of semantic ambiguity in word recognition. *Cognitive Science* 28: 89–104.

Scheepers, C., F. Keller and M. Lapata 2008. Evidence for serial coercion: a time course analysis using the visual-world paradigm. *Cognitive Psychology* 56: 1–29.

Schriefers, H., A. S. Meyer and W. J. M. Levelt 1990. Exploring the time course of lexical access in production: Picture–word interference studies. *Journal of Memory and Language* 29: 86–102.

Schütze, C. T. and E. Gibson 1999. Argumenthood and English prepositional phrase attachment. *Journal of Memory and Language* 40: 409–431.

Sheridan, H., E. M. Reingold and M. Daneman 2009. Using puns to study contextual influences on lexical ambiguity resolution: evidence from eye movements. *Psychonomic Bulletin and Review* 16: 875–881.

Sperber, D. and D. Wilson 1995. *Relevance: Communication and Cognition*, 2nd ed. Oxford: Blackwell.

Spivey, M., K. McRae and M. Joanisse 2012. *The Cambridge Handbook of Psycholinguistics*. Cambridge: Cambridge University Press.

Sturt, P., A. J. Sanford, A. Stewart and E. Dawydiak 2004. Linguistic focus and good-enough representations: an application of the change-detection paradigm. *Psychonomic Bulletin and Review* 11: 882–888.

Swinney, D. A. 1979. Lexical access during sentence comprehension: reconsideration of context effects. *Journal of Verbal Learning and Verbal Behavior* 18: 645–659.

Traxler, M. J. 2008. Structural priming among prepositional phrases: evidence from eye movements. *Memory and Cognition* 36: 659–674.

Traxler, M. J. and M. A. Gernsbacher 2006. *The Handbook of Psycholinguistics*. San Diego, CA: Elsevier.

Traxler, M., B. McElree, R. S. Williams and M. J. Pickering 2005. Context effects in coercion: evidence from eye movements. *Journal of Memory and Language* 53: 1–25.

Traxler, M. J. and K. M. Tooley 2007. Lexical mediation and context effects in sentence processing. *Brain Research* 1146: 59–74.

Traxler, M., M. J. Pickering and B. McElree 2002. Coercion in sentence processing: evidence from eye movements and self-paced reading. *Journal of Memory and Language* 4: 530–547.

Urbach, T. P. and M. Kutas 2010. Quantifiers more or less quantify on-line: ERP evidence for partial incremental interpretation. *Journal of Memory and Language* 63: 158–179.

Van Berkum, J. J. A., P. Hagoort and C. M. Brown 1999. Semantic integration in sentences and discourse: evidence from the N400. *Journal of Cognitive Neuroscience* 11: 657–671.

Van Berkum, J. J. A., C. M. Brown, P. Zwitserlood, V. Kooijman and P. Hagoort 2005. Anticipating upcoming words in discourse: evidence from ERPs and reading times. *Journal of Experimental Psychology: Learning, Memory and Cognition* 31: 443–467.

Van Berkum, J. J. A., P. Zwitserlood, P. Hagoort and C. M. Brown 2003. When and how do listeners relate a sentence to the wider discourse? Evidence from the N400 effect. *Cognitive Brain Research* 17: 701–718.

Ward, P. and P. Sturt 2007. Linguistic focus and memory: an eye movement study. *Memory and Cognition* 35: 73–86.

Warren, T. and K. McConnell 2007. Investigating effects of selectional restriction violations and plausibility violation severity on eye-movements in reading. *Psychonomic Bulletin and Review* 14: 770–775.

Warren, T., K. McConnell and K. Rayner 2008. Effects of context on eye movements when reading about possible and impossible events. *Journal of Experimental Psychology: Learning, Memory and Cognition* 34: 1001–1010.

Wiley, J. and K. Rayner 2000. Effects of titles on the processing of text and lexically ambiguous words: evidence from eye movements. *Memory and Cognition* 28: 1011–1021.

Wilson, D. and D. Sperber 2004. Relevance theory. In L. R. Horn and G. Ward (eds) *The Handbook of Pragmatics*. Oxford: Blackwell, 607–632.

Related topics

Chapter 2, Internalist semantics; Chapter 8, Embodiment, simulation and meaning; Chapter 9, Linguistic relativity; Chapter 10, Semantics and pragmatics; Chapter 11, Contextual adjustment of meaning; Chapter 13, Sense individuation.

Index

Abelard, P. 49
abstract concepts 151–2, 463
abstract stable system 268
accomplishments 339, 341, 350, 389, 397; non-culminating 396
accusative languages 407
achievements 339, 341, 350, 389
acquisition of meaning 457–69; nouns vs. verbs 457
action 143
action verbs 461–4
activation of semes 496
activities 339, 348, 389, 397, 398
actualization of semes 495
adaptation 148
addressee 403
adjunct 387–8
adjustment: lexical 195–208, 201; mutual parallel 203
affect *see* emotion
affectiveness 310
agency zones 497
agent 151, 395, 403, 407, 414
agonistic level 499
agreement relations 497
Aktionsionsart 341
ambiguity 75, 178, 234–5, 391–2, 507, 508, 510–13, 517; non-lexical 421
analogy 95–7
analyticity 222–3
anaphora 83, 237, 296; associative 291
anti-additivity 313
antonymy 219, 249–54, 258–60, 305; affinity 251, 257, 262; complementary 250; converse 250; gradable 250; reversive 250
aorist 342
approximate number system 167–9
Arabic 342

argument 387–8; mapping 405–11; mapping alternations 408–11; relational 285; structure constructions 423–5
Aristotle 39, 41; *On Interpretation* 39, 48
artifact concepts 130, 131
aspect 338–352, 372; grammatical 151, 340–8; lexical 339–40, 341, 348; present perfect 359–61; viewpoint 340–8, 349, 350, 351
atomicity of meaning 218
atoms (formal semantics) 82
attention 93, 226–7
attribute: of functional nouns 292; restrictive 291
attribution 497
autoexemplificationality 224

background 346, 349
backshifting 361–2
Bally, C. 475
basic transitive construction 406–7
Berkeley, George 41
Berlin and Kay paradigm 441–2
binding 76–8
biological kind terms 130
bootstrapping: morphological and syntactic 424, 463–4
Borg, E. 187–8
brain damage 147
brain imaging 145, 146, 147
breaking events *see* cutting events
Bréal, M. 51
British Empiricism 30
British National Corpus 106
Broca, P. 147
Burley (Burleigh), W. 50

cardinal numerals 293
Case Grammar 411–13
case theory 497

525

Index

categories: graded membership 130
categorization 32, 127, 128, 434, 437; individual differences 132; intransitivity 132; typicality 136
Chomsky, N. 15–16, 57
classifiers 286–7, 293; count 292–3; mass 293; sortal 292
clique 274
coercion 101, 102, 250–1, 295, 514–15; aspectual 340, 350, 352
cognitive prerequisite view 464
co-hyponymy *see* incompatibility
cognitive impairment 147
Cognitive Linguistics 90–103, 143, 190–1, 268–71, 475–6
Cognitive Principle of Relevance 185
cognitive styles 154
cohesion: textual 115
collective reading (plural indefinites) 326, 327
colligation 113–16; textual 118
collocation 106, 108, 111–16
collostruction 112
colour 7, 441
combinatorial lexical typology 442–4
communication 35, 37
Communicative Principle of Relevance 185
compatibility effects 146
componential analysis 51–4, 214, 216–18, 220, 437–9; critiques 438–9; *see also* decomposition
compositionality 73, 74, 90, 110, 112, 201, 214, 223; challenges 420–5; circularity 422; in quantifiers 333–4; morphology 422–3; principle of 419–20, 514; psycholinguistic research 514–15
computational implementation 149
computational linguistics 364–5
computational modeling 148–9
computational theory of mind 33
concepts 30–43, 206–7, 434; *ad hoc* 201–206; atomic 206, 207; contextual 207; evolution 144; experiential grounding 92; explanatory power 38–9; explanatory priority 39; features of 31–7; learning 144; regress problem 42–3; schema-based 134–5; static nature of 39–40; storage 144; strong sense 31, 39; weak sense 31
conceptual blending 271
Conceptual Dependency 393
conceptual development 458–60
conceptual networks 94–9
conceptual semantics 58, 219, 413

conceptual spaces 130
conceptualisation 91–103, 269
concgram 110, 111
concord: negative 307–8
concordance 108, 115
conjunction 133; fallacy 132
connotation 41, 107, 116, 227
consistency (formal semantics) 72
construal 93, 258–60
construction grammar 114, 257–8
constructional semantics 101–3
containment 464–6
content words 479
context 133, 150–1, 181–6, 226–8, 234, 239, 268, 425–9; in formal semantics 83–6
context-sensitivity 19–22, 238, 249
contextual modulation 98
contextualism 182–7, 197, 201, 208, 383
contiguity/connectivity requirement 444
continuative 345
Contradiction, Law of 305
contrast, principle of 462
convention 48
conventional meaning 238–40
conversational implicature: features 180–1; generalised 181; particularised 181; working out-schema 179; *see also* implicature
co-occurrence 112
Cooperative Principle 178–9
coordination 237–8
corpus 106–18, 242–3, 248, 253–7, 268, 273, 274–5, 443, 493, 494, 500–3
correspondence analysis 274
countability 284, 285–7
coupling 492
creativity 420, 421, 429
culminations 390
cultural practice 154
cutting events 445–7
Cummins, R. 228–9
cumulative reading (plural indefinites) 326, 327

dative alternation: English 408–9
Declerck, R. 363–4
decomposition, lexical 206, 213–229, 390–4, 413–4; *see also* componential analysis
defaults 184
defeasability 134
definite descriptions 60–1
definiteness 295–7; bare 297; marking 297; possessive chains 297; pragmatic 296–7; semantic 297

definition 213, 216, 222–227, 237, 249
deixis 187, 359, 426
demonstratives 296
denotation *see* reference
depth of processing 508
derelationalization 289, 291
descriptions 222
descriptive meaning 41, 475–7
descriptive semantics 14–15, 134, 502
designation, metalinguistic vs. referential 224–5
determination 288–99, 324
development, cognitive 163–4
dialectic 499
dialogic 499
dictionary/encyclopaedia distinction 35, 92, 94–5, 166, 191, 223; *see also* encyclopaedic knowledge
dictionaries 106, 107, 109, 118, 273–4
dimensions 496
direct object construction 408–11, 414
disambiguation 108, 109
discontinuous semantic units 421–2
discourse 226–8; conversational 347; narrative 347; type 493
Discourse Representation Structure *see* Discourse Representation Theory
Discourse Representation Theory 62, 188–90, 364, 365; Segmented 365
displacement: syntactic 78
dissociation 147, 148
disquotational lexicon 207
distal zone 492
distributional semantics 144
distributive numeral reduplication 332
distributive operator 326, 329
distributive universals 327–9, 330
distributivity 341
domains: conceptual/semantic 92, 99–100, 436–7; in formal semantics 73–4, 81; in interpretative semantics 496; quantificational 315; widening 315, 316
donkey sentences 328
dormitive virtue 38
Dowty, D. 414–6
durative 345
Dutch 163–4
dynamic construal *see* construal
dynamic semantics 61–2, 83–4, 188–90

E-language, 16
effector 145
ellipsis 426

Embodied Construction Grammar 149
Embodied Metaphor Hypothesis 152
embodied simulation 142, 143, 144
embodiment 143
emic/etic categories 449
emotion 31, 41–42, 227, 440, 473–84; and abstract concepts 42; conceptualization 474
empirical methods 4, 106, 113
encyclopaedic knowledge 150, 191, 202, 223, 515–16 *see also* dictionary/encyclopaedia distinction
English 160–1
entailment 72, 180, 220, 222, 223; cross-categorial 31; downward 310–11, 323; Strawson downward 311–12; upward 310
equivocation 272
ergative languages 407
ERP experiments 509–10
etic-grid semantics 441–2
etymology 51
event: boundaries 463; level 499; representation 160; semantics 387–400; and syntax 399–400
event-based semantics 61
Excluded Middle, Law of 305, 309
exemplars 135–8; critique 138
experiments 242, 273
explanation 6, 228–9; cognitive level of 35–7; shorthand concepts in 7
explicature 185–6, 196, 198, 202; higher-level 186
expressive-descriptive distinction 473–4, 477–8, 484
expressivity 41, 227, 473–484; in discourse 483–4; in lexicon 479–80; in morphology 481; in phonology 480–1; in speech acts 482–3; in syntax 481–2
extension 222, 273, *see also* reference
externalism 13–26, 30, 33; arguments for 22–5; internalist critiques of 16–22
eye-gaze 462
eye-movement research 145, 146, 509–10, 512, 515

Farsi 163–4
fast mapping ability 457, 469
features: characteristic 128; defining 128
feelings *see* emotion
figure-ground structure 93–4, 406
fMRI (functional magnetic resonance imaging) 147
focusing 191
folk psychology 30–1

for-phrases 398–9
foreground 346, 349
formal language 72
formal semantics 60, 71–86, 476
foundational semantics 14–15
fragment answer 307
frames 55–6, 443–4
François, A. 275
Frank, Michael 169–70
free choice item 316–17
free pragmatic process 201, 207
free word order languages 421–2
Frege, G. 49, 60, 74, 191, 419, 425
frequency 273, 358
function words 479
functions 499

Gadamer, H.-G. 5
Geach Rule 76
gender 167
generalized quantifier theory 22, 284, 320, 321–5, 333
generative linguistics 219, 365, 491
generative semantics 57, 391
genre 493
Georgian 422–3
German 250–1
Gestalt 225–6
gesture 153–4
Gordon, P. 168–70
gradability 305
grammatical typology 450
grammaticalization 118, 272
Greek 161–2, 342
Grice, H.P. 177–185
Gricean maxims: Manner 179; Quality 179; Quantity 179, 381; Relation (Relevance) 179, 309
Gries, S. 274–5

habituality 341, 344
Habituation paradigm 465
hand rotation 145
handshape 145
happenings 390
hermeneutics 3, 229
homesigning 170
homonymy 510–12, 517
homophony 517
Horn scale 182
hyperbole 203
hyponymy 237, 260–1

I-heuristic 183
I-language 15–16
ideal language philosophers 20
idealized cognitive models 92, 191
idioms 101–2, 109, 409, 410, 420–1
illocutionary acts 51, 114, 196, 482
illocutionary adverbs 186
imagery 144, 147; conceptual 93
image schemas 92, 191
imparfait 342
imperfect 342
imperfective 341
implicature 177–182, 184–7, 196, 198, 202, 306; conventional 180; conversational 178–181; scalar 85–6, 314, 315–17; *see also* conversational implicature
impliciture 181, 198
in-phrases 398–9
inceptive 345
incompatibility 261
incremental theme 340
incrementality 507–9
indefinites: free-choice 296; interrogative 296; negative 296; partitive 299; plain 325–7; plural 325–7; simple 296; special 296; unspecific 296
independent cue model 136
indeterminacy 234
indexicals 196; covert 199, 200, 205
indigenous languages 3
indirect reported speech 361
individual differences 154
induction 132
inference 153
inferential role 33–4
inhibition of semes 496
innateness 90
instantiation principle 138
instrument 403, 413
instrumental semantics 501–2
instrumentalist conception of language 5–6
integrativity 285–6, 292, 293, 298
intensifiers 480
intension *see* sense
intention, speaker's 5, 51, 114, 178, 201, 208, 461–2
intentional relations 13–29
Interface Transparency Thesis 331
interference effects 146, 161, 163
interjections 479
internalism 14, 30–43, 132, 134; critiques of 37–43

interpretation 428; function 74
interpretative semantics 491–503
intersubjectivity 6, 224, 225, 379, 479
intonation 425
introspection 235–6
intuitions 72, 236
invariance 34, 220
islands 82
isosemy 498
isotopy 497–8
iterativity 341

Jackendoff, R. 58, 219, 393

Katz, J. 56
Katz and Fodor 218–19
kinship terms 52, 437–8, 439
Korean 159
Koyukon, relational nouns 288–90
Kripke, Saul 48

Langacker, R. 269–70
language acquisition 352, 404–5, 408
language comprehension 507
Language of Thought 153
language production 507, 517–18
language use 23, 145; and concepts 42–3; causal explanation 23; justification 23; planned vs. free 226–7
Latent Semantic Analysis 511–12
lemma 106, 112
Levinson, S. 183–4
lexeme *see* lexical item
lexical classes 495–6
lexical item 109, 249, 112, 405, 435, 443–4, 493–4
lexical meaning 196, 201
lexical relations *see* sense relations
lexical semantics 213–300, 434–51, 494–6; early history 50–1; psycholinguistic research 510–13
lexical typology 275–7
lexicography 39, 51, 118
lexicon 74
Linear Discriminability 137
linguistic relativity 158–171
linguistic unit 106
literal: meaning 4, 7, 92, 101, 107, 177, 222; language 149
localization of function (brain) 146
locative 404, 459
Locke, J. 50
loose use continuum 203

M-heuristic 183, 184
macrosemantics 499–500
Mandarin Chinese 344–6, 356, 396, 446; mass-count distinction 286–7, 292–4
manner of motion 159
mapping principle 407
markedness 341
mass to count shifts 293
meaning *passim*; centrality 273; computational models 229; encoded 196, 207–7; entities 16; neural substrate; 142, 143; postulates 216, 222, 223; stored vs. derived 239–40; utterance 235–6
memory 159–60
mental metaphors 163–5
mental representation 30–3, 33, 165–7, 235, 239, 493
meronymy 261–2
mesosemantics 497–9
metaphor 99–101, 149, 152, 203–4; conceptual 99, 204
metarepresentationality 205
methodology 241–3
metonymy 99–101, 427
microsemantics 496
Middle English 381
Mill, J. S. 38
minimalism 187, 197, 208, 383
minority languages 3
mixed expressives 476
modality (cognitive) 42
modality (grammatical) 370–83; acquisition 466–9; deontic 372–6, 379; diachrony of 381–2; dynamic 373–6; epistemic 373–83; future 359; imperative 371; in English 373; indicative 371; root 373–6, 382; subjunctive 371
model 73, 81–2
modularity 90–1
modulation 191
monotonicity 81, 310, 311
Montague, R. 72, 320
morpheme 494
morphology 481
motor control 142, 145, 146, 147
mortor cortex 146, 148
Moses illusion 508
motion verbs 159, 340, 447
mouse-tracking 145
movement 78
MTRANS predicate 395
multi-word unit 107, 113
multiple realizability 37

529

N400 508, 510, 512, 516
n-gram 110
names 48
narrative 483
natural kinds 36
Natural Language Processing 364–5
Natural Semantic Metalanguage 53–4, 219–20, 392, 439–441
neg-raising 308–9
negation 262, 303–17, 349; constituent 304–5; contrary 305; covert 307; echoic 305–6; lexical 304, 305; logic 303; metalinguistic 305–6; sentential 304–5
negative asymmetry 184
negative polarity items 81, 306, 307, 309–14; strong 312–14; superstrong 313; weak 313
negativity bias 480
networks: radial 95, 97; schematic 96, 101–2
neural mechanisms 145
neuropsychology 147–8
Nicaragua 170
Nijmegen method 441–2
nominalism 49–50
nominals 283–299, 461–4: definiteness layer 284; ordering layer 284; quality layer 283; quantification layer 284; quantity layer; relation layer 283, 290–1; unit layer 283
nominal onion 283
non-compositional meaning 110, 112
non-literality 203–4
non-natural meaning 179
non-referring terms 18
nonveridicality 312
norms 493–4
noun 94, 150, 350–1; absolute 285; count 285, 350; functional 288; individual 288; mass 350; modification 291–2; relational 285, 288; sortal 288
Noun Phrase: core 284; partitive 299
nucleus of NP 283, 284–8; relationality 284
number conceptualization 167–71
numerals 293, 299; distributive 332–3; ordinal 294, 295

object nouns 461–4
objectivism 190
objectivity 2, 6, 21, 34, 50, 107, 114, 378–80; *see also* intersubjectivity
occasional meaning 238–40
Old English 381–2
open-class words 150

opposition: contrary 305
order specification 294–5
ordinary language philosophy 20
overgeneration 200

paradigmatic relations *see* sense relations
parallel individuation system 167
paraphrase 108, 213–14; partitive 298
participant roles 403–16: accumulation 405; dispersion 406; hierarchy 412; lists 411–13; Neo-Davidsonian approaches 412; psycholinguistic research 514; syntactic function 405–8; uniqueness 405; *see also* proto-roles
partonymy *see* meronymy
passage 499
passé composé 342, 358
path of motion 159
patient 403, 407, 415
Paul, H. 238
perception 32, 142, 143, 145, 146, 445
perfect 151, 342, 344, 346, 357, 359–61, 363
perfective 341
performative 343, 374–5, 476
period 497–9
personality ascriptions 130
perspective 191
phenomenology 43, 214
philosophy of language 178, 366
phonology 214, 480–1
phraseology 109
Piaget, J. 458
picture-word interference paradigm 517
Pirahã 168
pitch: musical 162–3
planned/free distinction 226–7
Plato 48
plausibility 515–16
pluractionality 332–3
plurality 286, 292
pointing 428–9
polarity 303–17; sensitivity 314–17
polysemy 220, 233–44, 235, 427; and modality 376–8; nouns 284; psycholinguistics 512–13, 517; tests 236–8, 378, 436–7; and vagueness (monosemy) 98, 150, 444;
PoS-gram 111
positive polarity item 306, 317
positivity bias 480
possession 283; contextual 291; determiner 297; existential 291; inalienable 289; relational 290; secondary 289

possessive chains 290
possessor 404; saturation 289; specification 290–1
possessor-locative assumption 409
potential barrier 375
Potts, C. 476
pragmatics 177–192, 366–7; lexical 186, 201–204; and modals 380; and past tense 362; and the perfect 360–1; and semantics 20, 234, 239, 491
pragmatic enrichment 185, 198–201 free 187, 196, 200
pragmatic intrusion 184
pragmaticism 208
predicates of personal taste 478
predication 74, 81–2, 114, 497; summative 286, 292, 298
predictability 509–10
Preferential Looking method 465
prefixation 347, 352, 289–91, 305
premotor cortex 146
prepositional object construction 408–11
presupposition 85, 177, 306, 311, 313–14
priming 145
principal components analysis 274
principle of contextuality 425–9
probabilistic inferences 131
pro-concept 206
productivity *see* creativity
progressive 341, 343–5, 372, 389
prominence 191
pronouns 75–7, 188–90, 196–7, 365, 482
proposition 177
proto-agent 399, 414
proto-patient 396–7, 415
proto-recipient 415
proto-roles 414–6
prototypes 54–5, 95–8, 128, 129–34, 241, 268, 273, 347, 437; context effects 133–4; critiques 134; validation 134
psychiatric categories 130
psycholinguistics 257, 352, 408
Putnam, H. 15, 55

Q-heuristic 183
Q-principle 182
quality 291–2
quantification 79–80, 298–9, 320–334, 425–6; adverbial 298; counting 330–1, 332; degree 331; diversity 325–33; domain 298; genuine 298–9; modified numeral 330–1; negative 306–8; universal 342

quantifiers *see* quantification
quantity: attribute 294; specification 293–4, 299
Quine, W.V.O. 222–3

R-principle 182
rationalism 218
reaction time 145, 146
realism 49–50
Reasoning Constraint 392
Recanati, F. 186–7
recipient-possessor 410
recurrence 109
reduction 35–7
reduplication 345
reference 48, 132, 178, 242–3, 436, 441–2, 473–4, 517 *see also* extension
Reference Time 362–3
Reichenbach, H. 216, 362–3
relational coding model 136
relationalization 289, 290
relative clause, 296
Relevance Theory 185–6, 198, 201–204
Reordered Access Model 511
repair 227
repeaters 293
reported speech 361–2
restrictor 324
result 348
resultative verb complements 345
Rosch, E. 54, 129
rule/list fallacy 91
rules 493–4
Russell, B. 60–1
Russian 347–8

saturation 187, 196, 199, 201; existential 291; possessor 295
Saussure, F. de 51, 90, 215, 267–8, 475
scales 182–3, 305, 397–8
schema 134, 268, 273
schematicity 207, 241
schematic network 268
scope 322–5, 327, 375, 377, 382; adverbs and 391–2; distributive 326; existential 326; split 308
semantic acquisition 457–69; Semantic Feature theory of 457
semantic background 492, 497, 498, 500
semantic decomposition 33–4, *see also* componential analysis
semantic determiners 324

semantic distinguishers 218–19
semantic extension 241
semantic features 493, 497
semantic fields 52–3, 215, 216, 218, 221
semantic forms 492, 497, 498, 500
semantic learning *see* semantic acquisition
semantic maps 275, 444–50; implicational 445; probabilistic 445–50
semantic markers 218–19
semantic memory: network models 125–7; feature models 127–8
semantic morphologies 500
semantic preference 113, 114, 115, 116
semantic primitives (primes) 53, 218, 224–5, 392
semantic processing 145, 507–519
semantic prosody 113, 114, 115, 116–17, 483
semantic roles *see* participant roles
semantic shift 266–78
semantic space 137
semantic storage 144
semantic template 440
semantic traits 221
semantic transparency 112
semantic values 73
semelfactives 339, 348, 350
sememe 494–5
semes 492, 494–5; activation 496; afferent 495; generic 495; inherent 495; inhibition 496; specific 495
semic molecules 500
semilattices 81–2
semiotic environment 492
sense 60, 132, 228, 436, 443, 474
sense individuation *see* polysemy
sense relations 215–16, 248–62; *see also* antonymy, hyponymy, meronymy, synonymy
sentence-ending (SE) suffixes/particles 467–8
sentence meaning 94–5
sentence-relations 71–2
sequence of tense 361–2
Shank, R. 392–3
signs 493
similarity: featural 127
simulation 39, 42, 142, 144, 145, 149–54
Sinclair, J. 113–16
single word period 457
singular 293
situation time of orientation 363–4
situation type 339, 348, 349, 350, 352
skip-gram 110
Slavic languages 347, 348–50
social construct 115

source (modality) 375
Spaepen, E. 170
spatial semantics: acquisition 464–6
speaker meaning 195–6, 198, 208; *see also* utterance meaning
specificity, levels of 94
special sciences 36
specificity 191
speech acts 114, 130
Spivey, M. 278
Standard Average European 3, 31
statistical methods 117
stativity 224, 339, 344, 348, 389, 390; change of state 340, 345; individual level 339; stage-level 339
stereotypes 55, 183, 202
Stern, G. 268, 272
strength (modality) 380
structuralism 52, 215–18, 235, 248–9, 437, 491
subinterval property 389
subjectification 382
subjectivity 41, 93, 349, 378–80
subordinate bias effect 511
suffixation 347
summativity *see* predication, summative
superlatives 294
symbol grounding 130, 143, 144
symmetric predicates 406, 415
syncategorematic meaning 150
synonymy 249, 251–2, 254–8, 274
syntagmatic relations 252
syntax 56–7, 73, 481–2
systemic meaning 235–6

tactic 499
taxonomy 71
telic situations 339, 340, 341, 348, 350
temperature 447–9
tense 354–67, 372; absolute 355, 363; and time 354–5; deictic 355; future 343–4, 358–60; past 342–4, 352; pluperfect 362; present 343, 352; present perfect 359–61; relative 355, 363; reported speech 361–2; typology 356–8
text 493, 499–500
text-type 113
textual semantics 499–500
textual semiosis 501
thematic roles *see* participant roles
theme 404, 499
theory evaluation 2, 44
Theta-Criterion 405–6
thinking for speaking 159–60

Thorne, S. and Lantolf, J. 277
time: A and B theories 365
time and space: representations 160–5
topicalization 78
Transcranial Magnetic Stimulation 148
transduction 32
transitivity (logical) 260
translational semantics 197
truth 72, 134
truth-conditions 13, 21, 24, 58–9, 72, 144, 196
two-CAUSE constraint 394–5
type-token distinction 37, 351, 495
type shift 289, 292, 295, 296, 297, 299
typology, lexical 434–451; data 436

unarticulated constituents 196, 199, 205
underdetermination: linguistic 196; of theories 217
underspecification 201, 207, 234, 426, 429, 513
uniqueness 296, 297; inherent 284, 287–8
unit 292–3; of meaning 107, 109, 110, 116
universe 499
use theory of meaning 108
utterance meaning 181, 235–6 *see also* speaker meaning

vagueness 98, 130, 131, 150, 178, 234–5, 236
value 492
variability 116, 117

variable assignment 75–6
Venant, F. 273
Vendler, Z. 339–41, 389–90
verbs 94, 150, 355, 387–400, 461; semantic complexity 394–6
vision 147
visual cortex 146
Visual World paradigm 510
voice 151

weight 216
Wells, R. 271–2
Wernicke, C. 142, 147
what is said 198
Whitney, W. 51
whole object constraint 462–3
Whorf, B. 158
Whorfian psychophysics paradigm 160–5
Wierzbicka, A. 4, 235, 439–441
Wilkins, D. 275
William of Ockham 49
Williams, J. 273
Wittgenstein, L. 43, 225
word 107
word: family 106, 111; form 106; learning 460
Wunderlich, D. 413–4

Z Rule 78
Zalizniak, A. 275, 277

eBooks
from Taylor & Francis

Helping you to choose the right eBooks for your Library

Add to your library's digital collection today with Taylor & Francis eBooks. We have over 50,000 eBooks in the Humanities, Social Sciences, Behavioural Sciences, Built Environment and Law, from leading imprints, including Routledge, Focal Press and Psychology Press.

Choose from a range of subject packages or create your own!

Benefits for you
- Free MARC records
- COUNTER-compliant usage statistics
- Flexible purchase and pricing options
- All titles DRM-free.

Benefits for your user
- Off-site, anytime access via Athens or referring URL
- Print or copy pages or chapters
- Full content search
- Bookmark, highlight and annotate text
- Access to thousands of pages of quality research at the click of a button.

Free Trials Available
We offer free trials to qualifying academic, corporate and government customers.

eCollections

Choose from over 30 subject eCollections, including:

Archaeology	Language Learning
Architecture	Law
Asian Studies	Literature
Business & Management	Media & Communication
Classical Studies	Middle East Studies
Construction	Music
Creative & Media Arts	Philosophy
Criminology & Criminal Justice	Planning
Economics	Politics
Education	Psychology & Mental Health
Energy	Religion
Engineering	Security
English Language & Linguistics	Social Work
Environment & Sustainability	Sociology
Geography	Sport
Health Studies	Theatre & Performance
History	Tourism, Hospitality & Events

For more information, pricing enquiries or to order a free trial, please contact your local sales team:
www.tandfebooks.com/page/sales

www.tandfebooks.com